LOCAL

BRIAN WOOD ★ RYAN KELLY

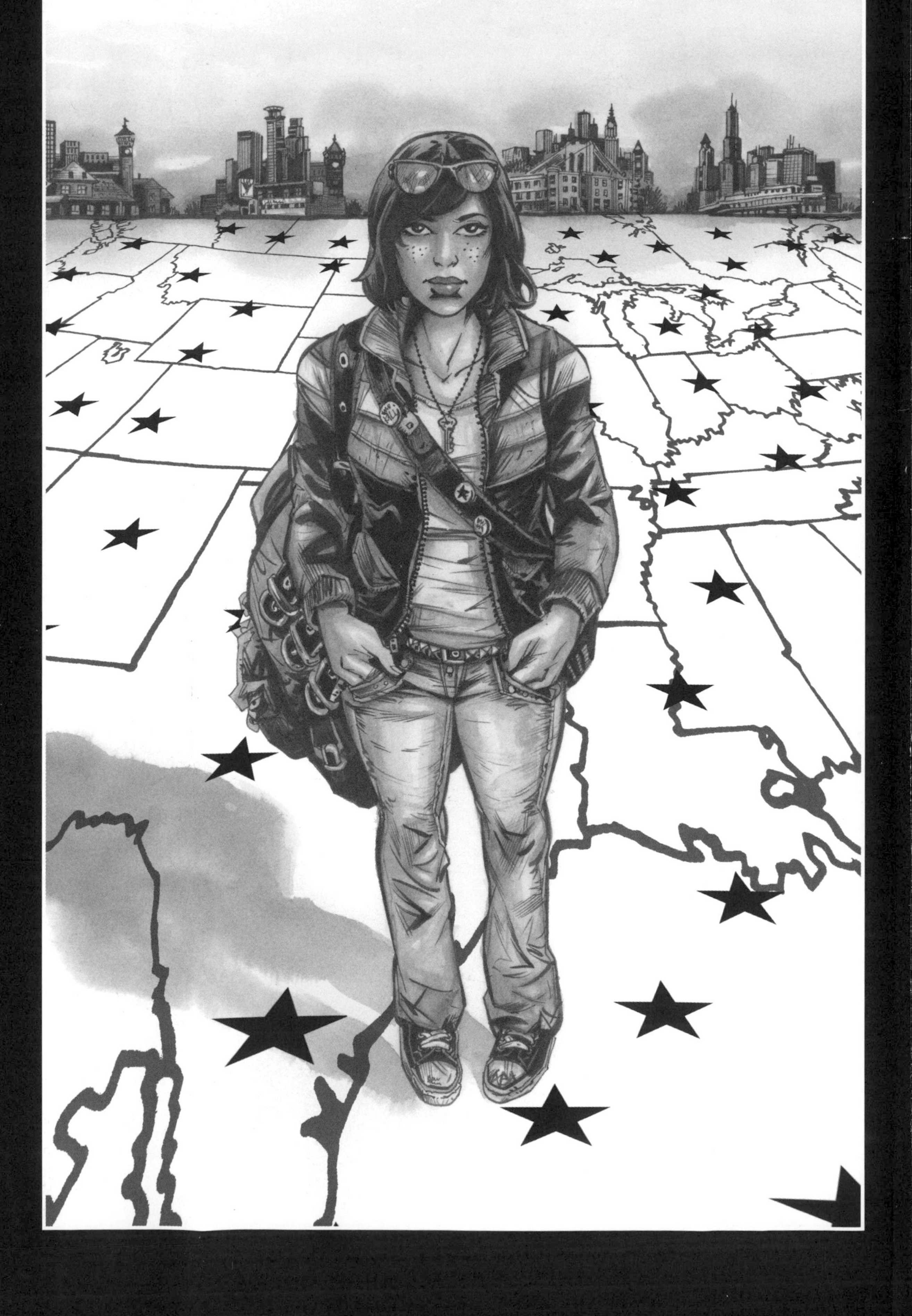

LOCAL ™

written by
BRIAN WOOD

illustrated by
RYAN KELLY

lettered by
HOPE LARSON,
BRYAN LEE O'MALLEY,
and
DOUGLAS E. SHERWOOD

cover by
RYAN KELLY

book design by
KEITH WOOD

logo and design elements by
BRIAN WOOD

edited by
JAMES LUCAS JONES
with
JILL BEATON

Published by Oni Press, Inc.
JOE NOZEMACK, publisher
JAMES LUCAS JONES, editor in chief
RANDAL C. JARRELL, managing editor
CORY CASONI, marketing director
JILL BEATON, assistant editor
DOUGLAS E. SHERWOOD, production assistant

This volume collects issues 1-12 of the Oni Press comics series *Local*.

ONI PRESS, INC.
1305 SE Martin Luther King Jr. Blvd.
Suite A
Portland, OR 97214
USA

www.onipress.com
www.brianwood.com
www.funrama.blogspot.com

First edition: September 2008
ISBN-13: 978-1-934964-00-2

1 3 5 7 9 10 8 6 4 2

Printed in China.

BRIAN WOOD:

Dedicated to Meredith and Audrey.

RYAN KELLY:

Dedicated to Katherine, for putting up with everything.
And I mean everything.

CHAPTER 1
"TEN THOUSAND THOUGHTS PER SECOND"
Portland, Oregon

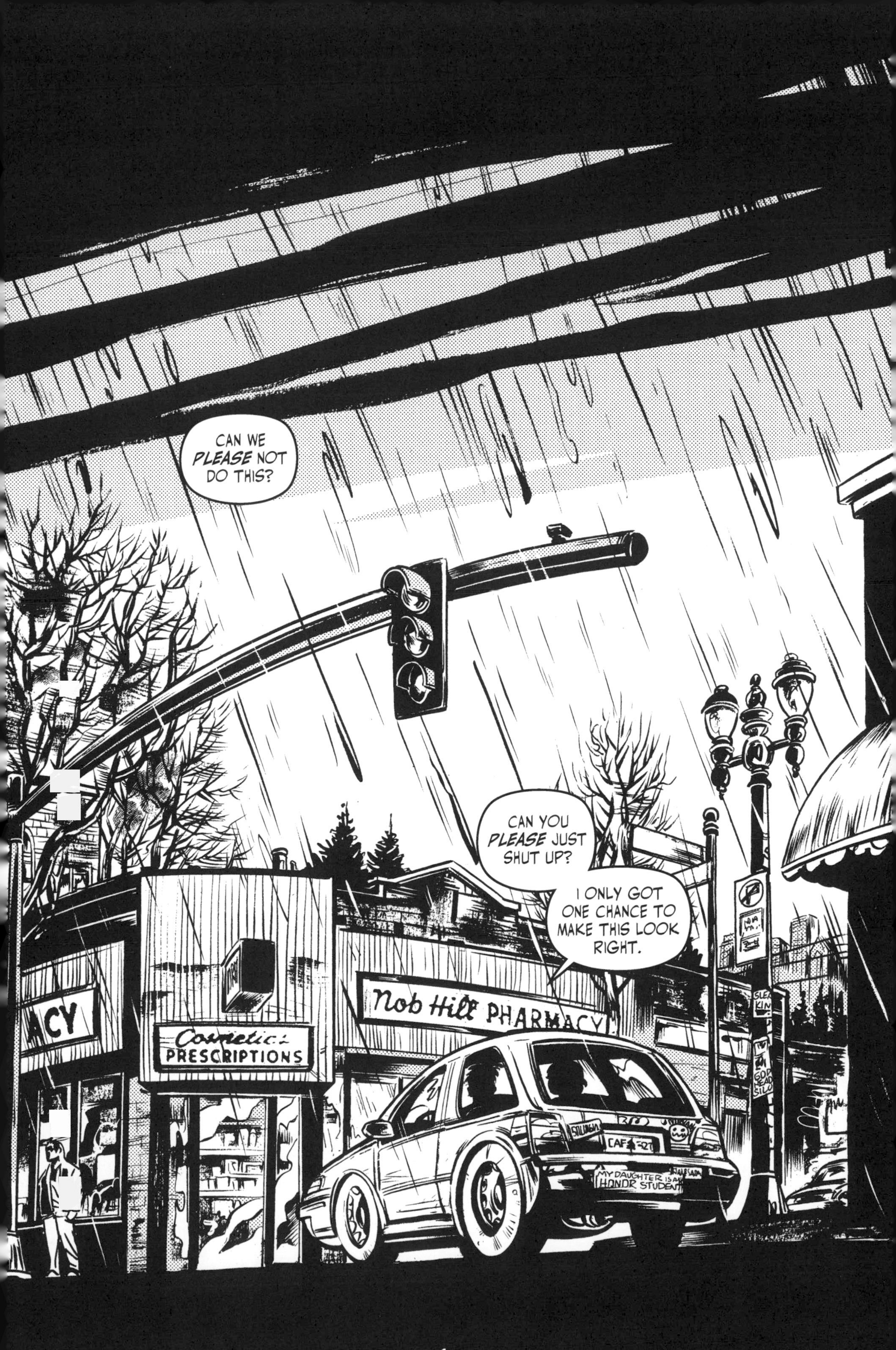
CAN WE *PLEASE* NOT DO THIS?
CAN YOU *PLEASE* JUST SHUT UP?
I ONLY GOT ONE CHANCE TO MAKE THIS LOOK RIGHT.
ACY
Cosmetics
PRESCRIPTIONS
Nob Hill PHARMACY
HONOR STUDENT

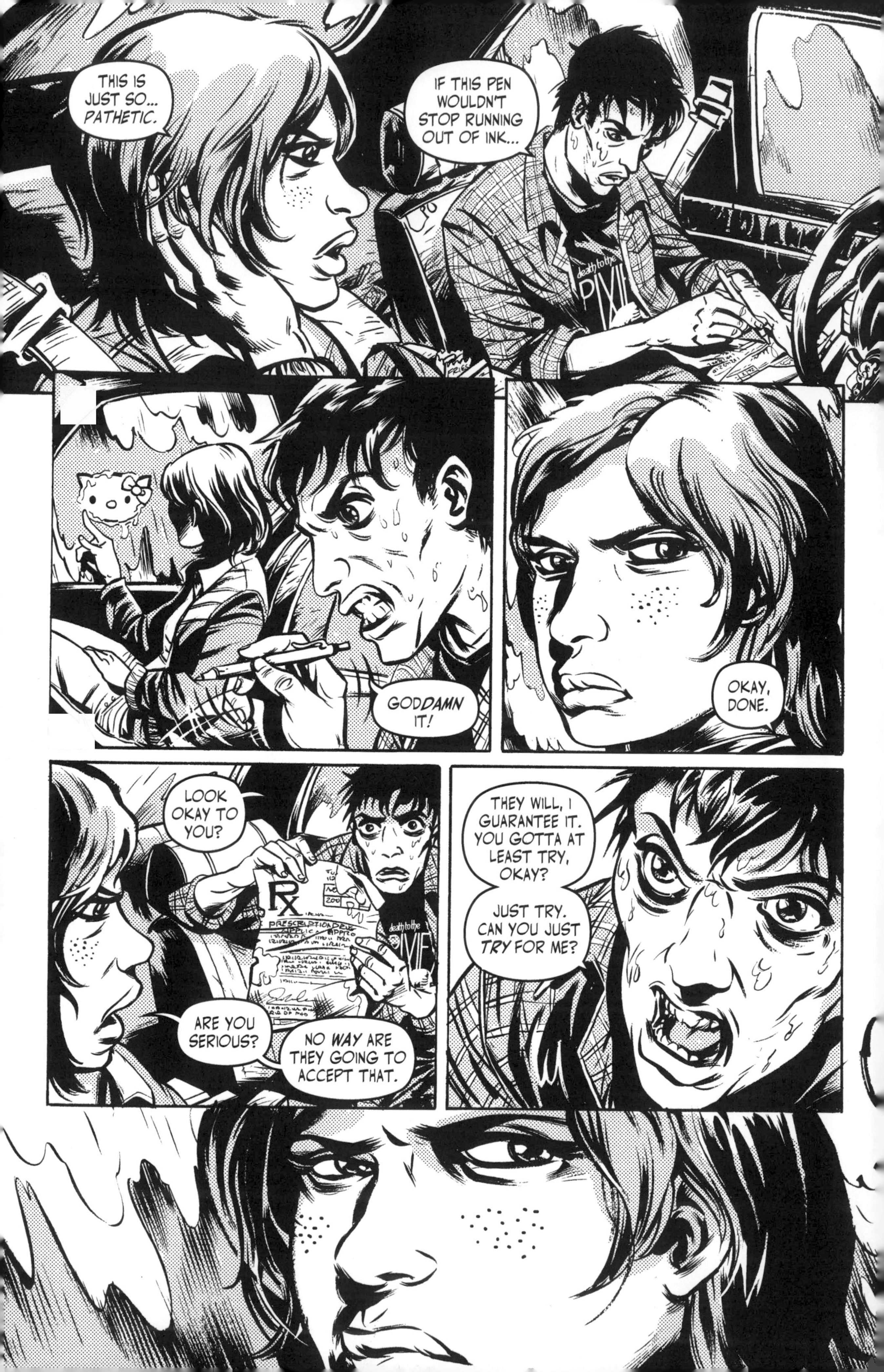
THIS IS JUST SO... PATHETIC.
IF THIS PEN WOULDN'T STOP RUNNING OUT OF INK...
GODDAMN IT!
OKAY, DONE.
LOOK OKAY TO YOU?
ARE YOU SERIOUS?
NO WAY ARE THEY GOING TO ACCEPT THAT.
THEY WILL, I GUARANTEE IT. YOU GOTTA AT LEAST TRY, OKAY?
JUST TRY. CAN YOU JUST TRY FOR ME?

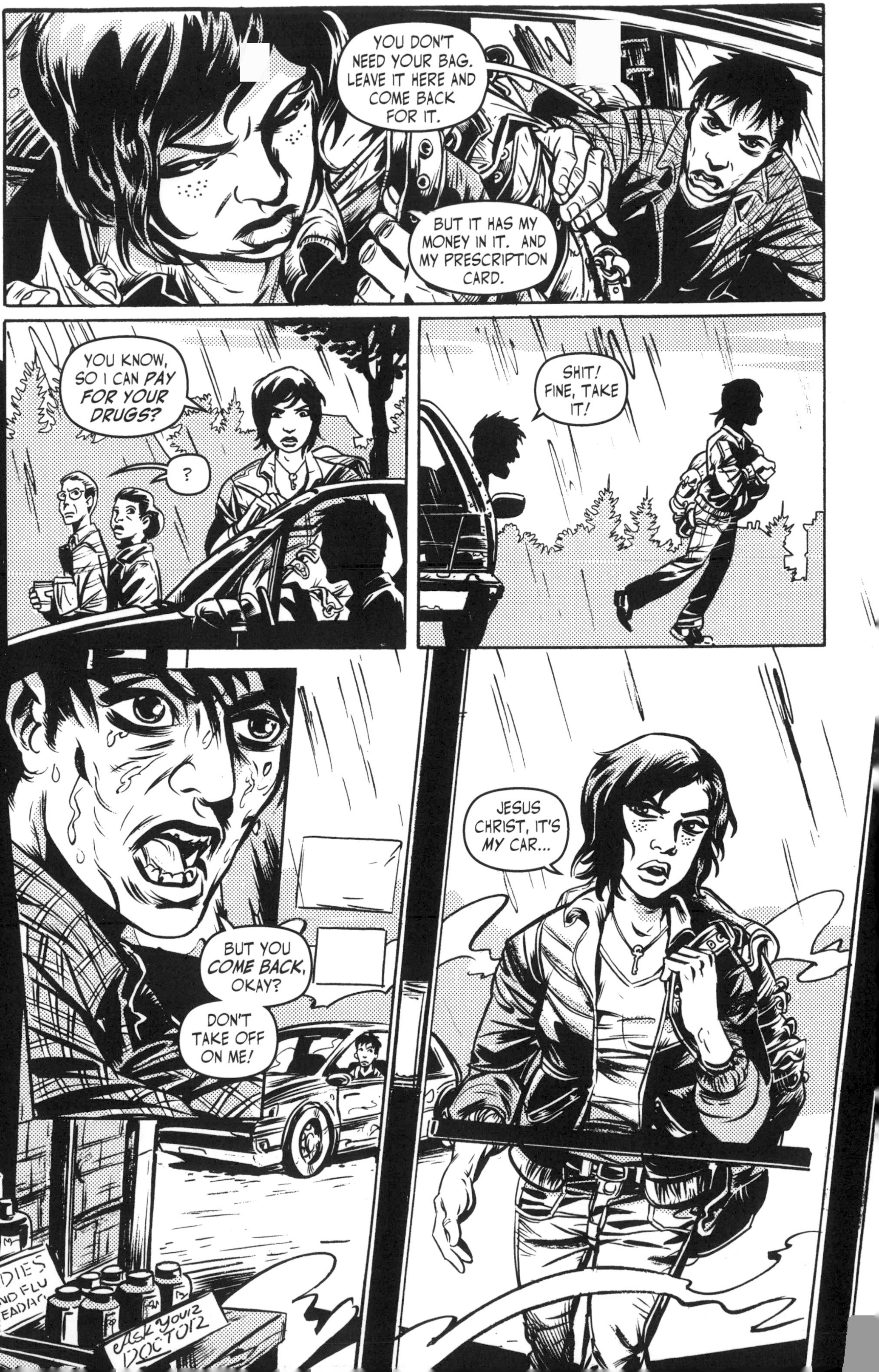
YOU DON'T NEED YOUR BAG. LEAVE IT HERE AND COME BACK FOR IT.
BUT IT HAS MY MONEY IN IT. AND MY PRESCRIPTION CARD.
YOU KNOW, SO I CAN *PAY FOR YOUR DRUGS?*
?
SHIT! FINE, TAKE IT!
BUT YOU *COME BACK,* OKAY?
DON'T TAKE OFF ON ME!
JESUS CHRIST, IT'S *MY* CAR...
ask your DOCTOR

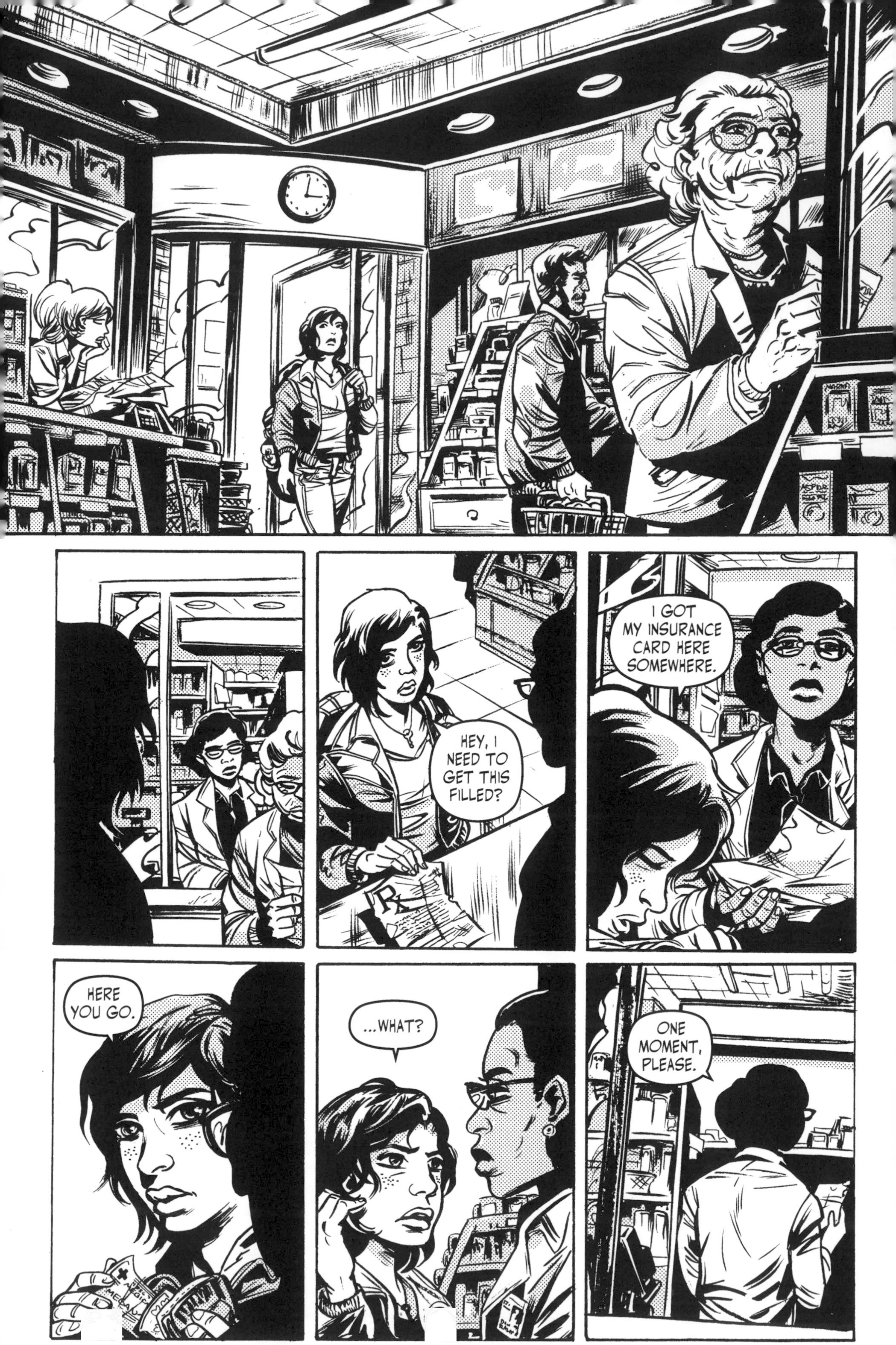
HEY, I NEED TO GET THIS FILLED?
I GOT MY INSURANCE CARD HERE SOMEWHERE.
HERE YOU GO.
...WHAT?
ONE MOMENT, PLEASE.

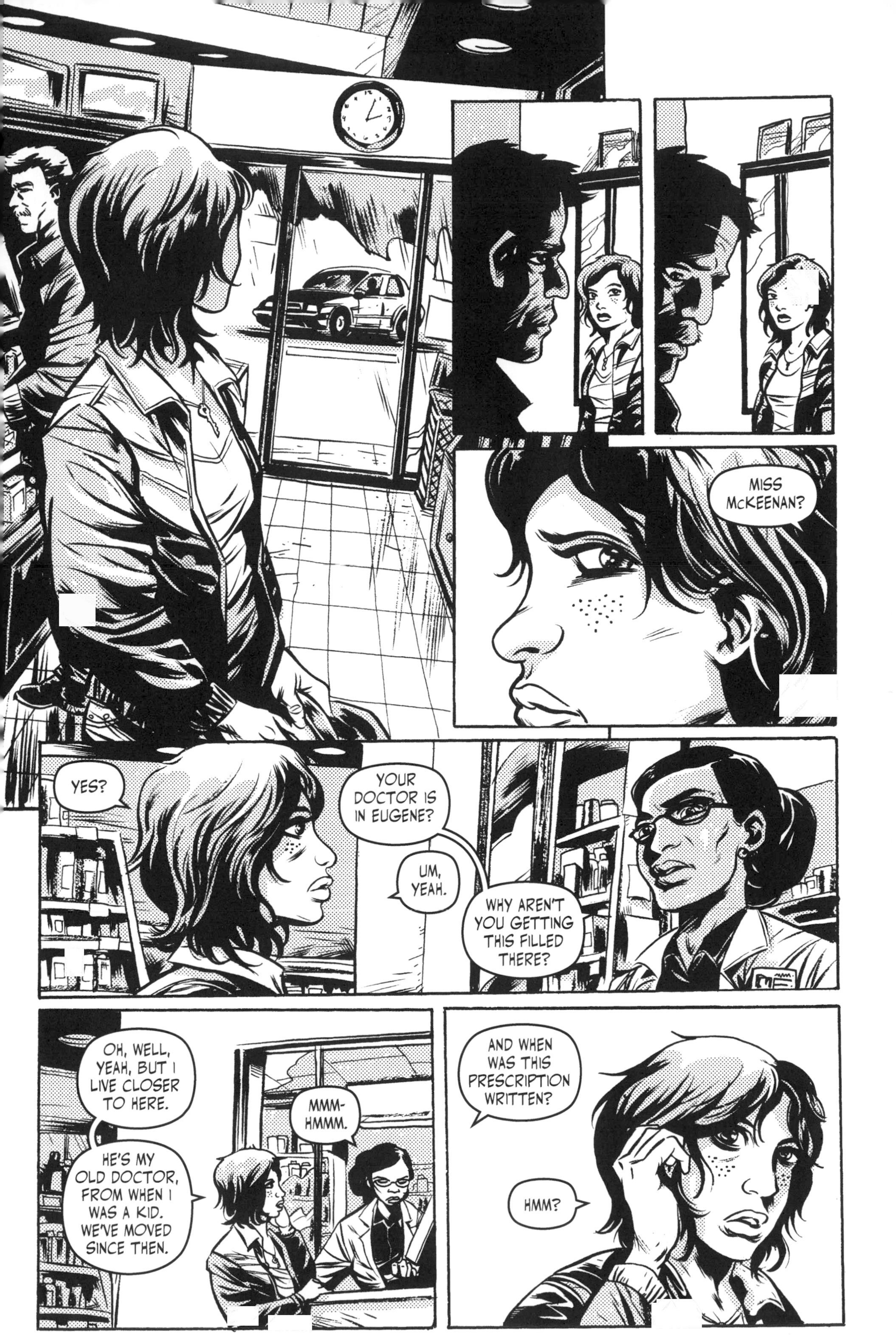
MISS McKEENAN?
YES?
YOUR DOCTOR IS IN EUGENE?
UM, YEAH.
WHY AREN'T YOU GETTING THIS FILLED THERE?
OH, WELL, YEAH, BUT I LIVE CLOSER TO HERE.
HE'S MY OLD DOCTOR, FROM WHEN I WAS A KID. WE'VE MOVED SINCE THEN.
MMM-HMMM.
AND WHEN WAS THIS PRESCRIPTION WRITTEN?
HMM?

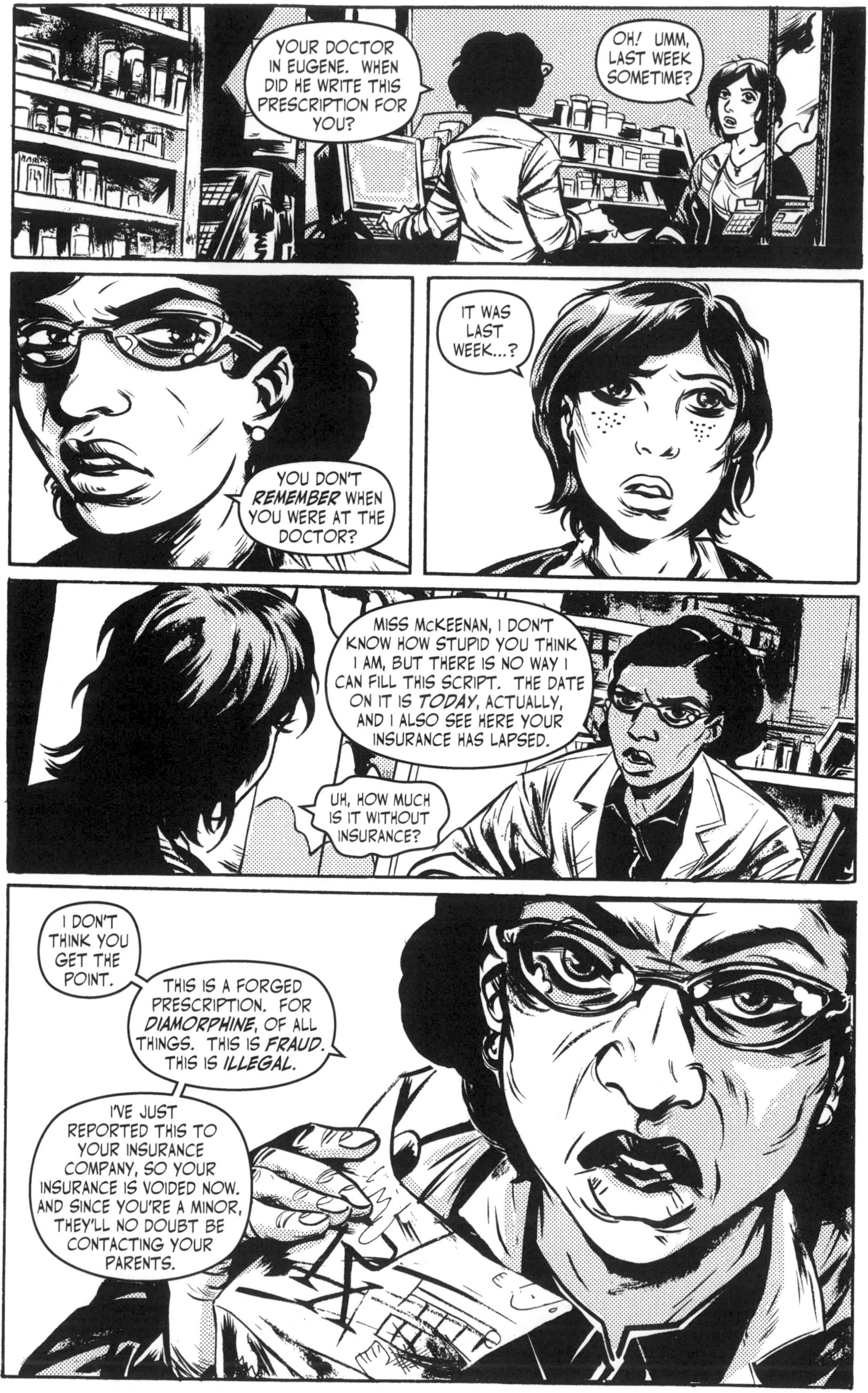
YOUR DOCTOR IN EUGENE. WHEN DID HE WRITE THIS PRESCRIPTION FOR YOU?
OH! UMM, LAST WEEK SOMETIME?
IT WAS LAST WEEK...?
YOU DON'T *REMEMBER* WHEN YOU WERE AT THE DOCTOR?
MISS McKEENAN, I DON'T KNOW HOW STUPID YOU THINK I AM, BUT THERE IS NO WAY I CAN FILL THIS SCRIPT. THE DATE ON IT IS *TODAY*, ACTUALLY, AND I ALSO SEE HERE YOUR INSURANCE HAS LAPSED.
UH, HOW MUCH IS IT WITHOUT INSURANCE?
I DON'T THINK YOU GET THE POINT.
THIS IS A FORGED PRESCRIPTION. FOR *DIAMORPHINE*, OF ALL THINGS. THIS IS *FRAUD*. THIS IS *ILLEGAL*.
I'VE JUST REPORTED THIS TO YOUR INSURANCE COMPANY, SO YOUR INSURANCE IS VOIDED NOW. AND SINCE YOU'RE A MINOR, THEY'LL NO DOUBT BE CONTACTING YOUR PARENTS.

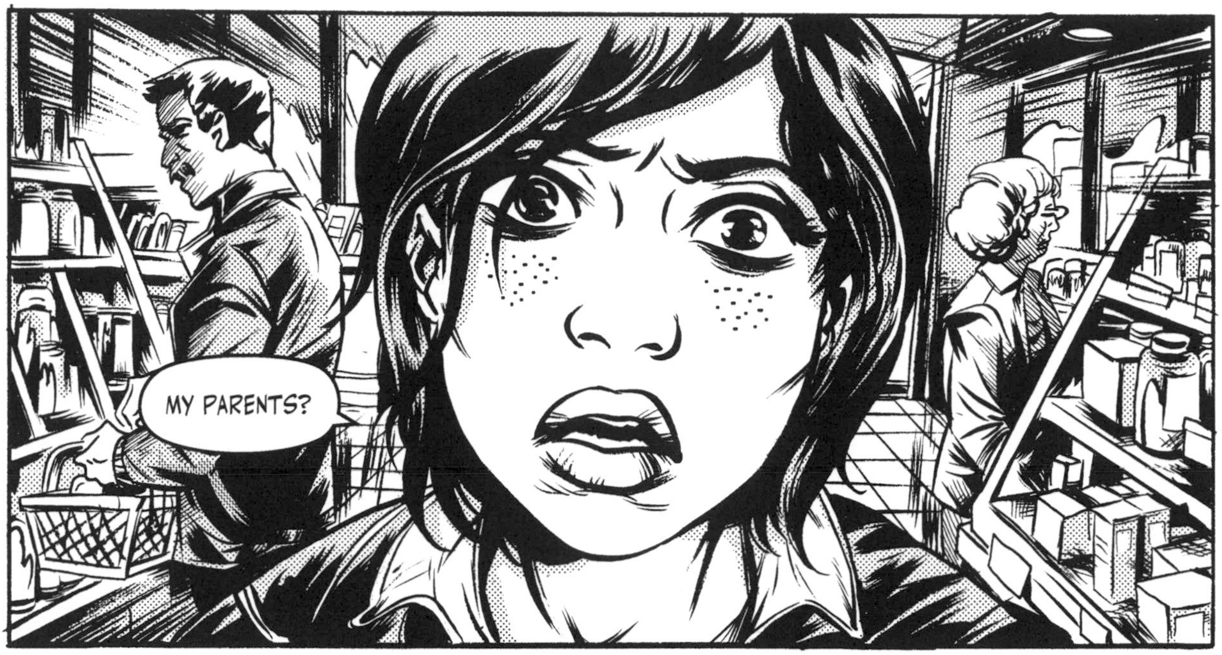
MY PARENTS?

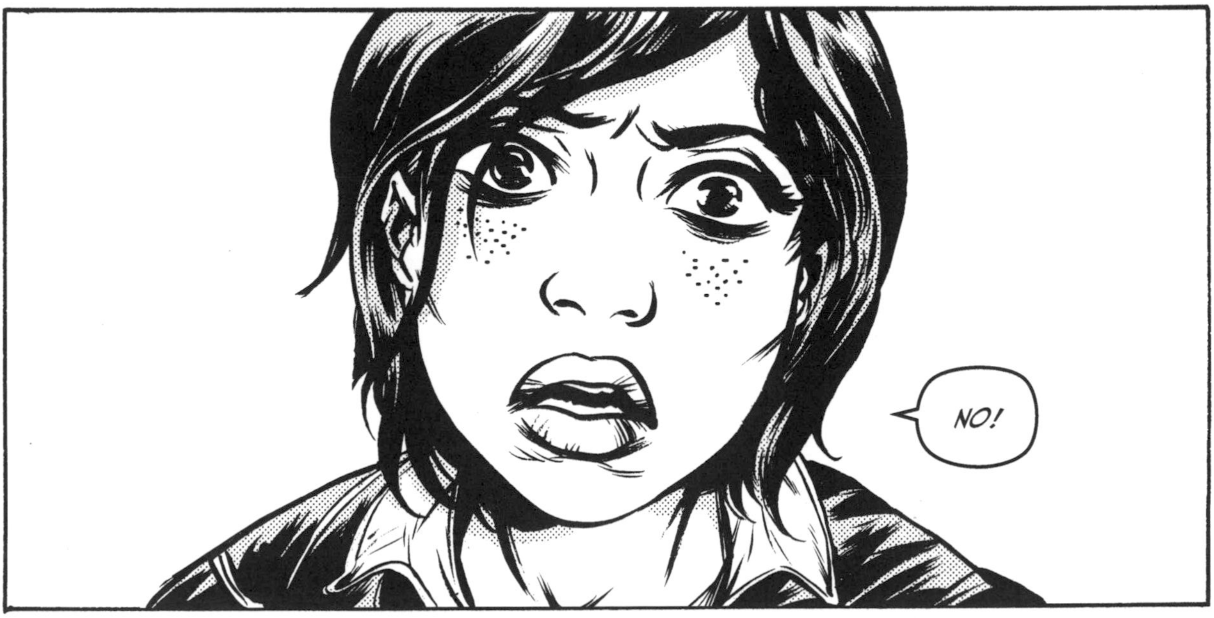
NO!

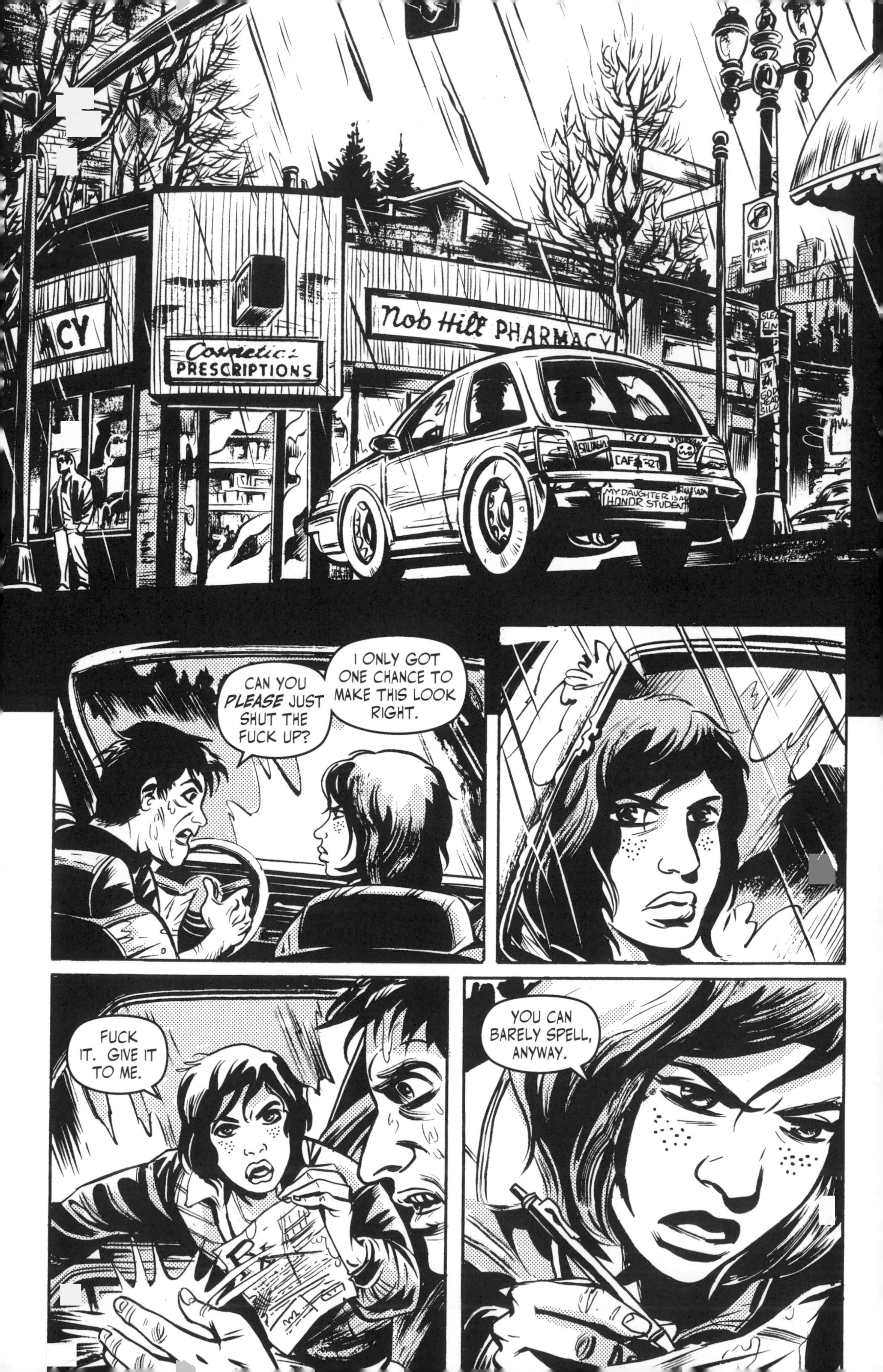
Nob Hill PHARMACY
PRESCRIPTIONS
MY DAUGHTER IS AN HONOR STUDENT
CAN YOU PLEASE JUST SHUT THE FUCK UP?
I ONLY GOT ONE CHANCE TO MAKE THIS LOOK RIGHT.
FUCK IT. GIVE IT TO ME.
YOU CAN BARELY SPELL, ANYWAY.

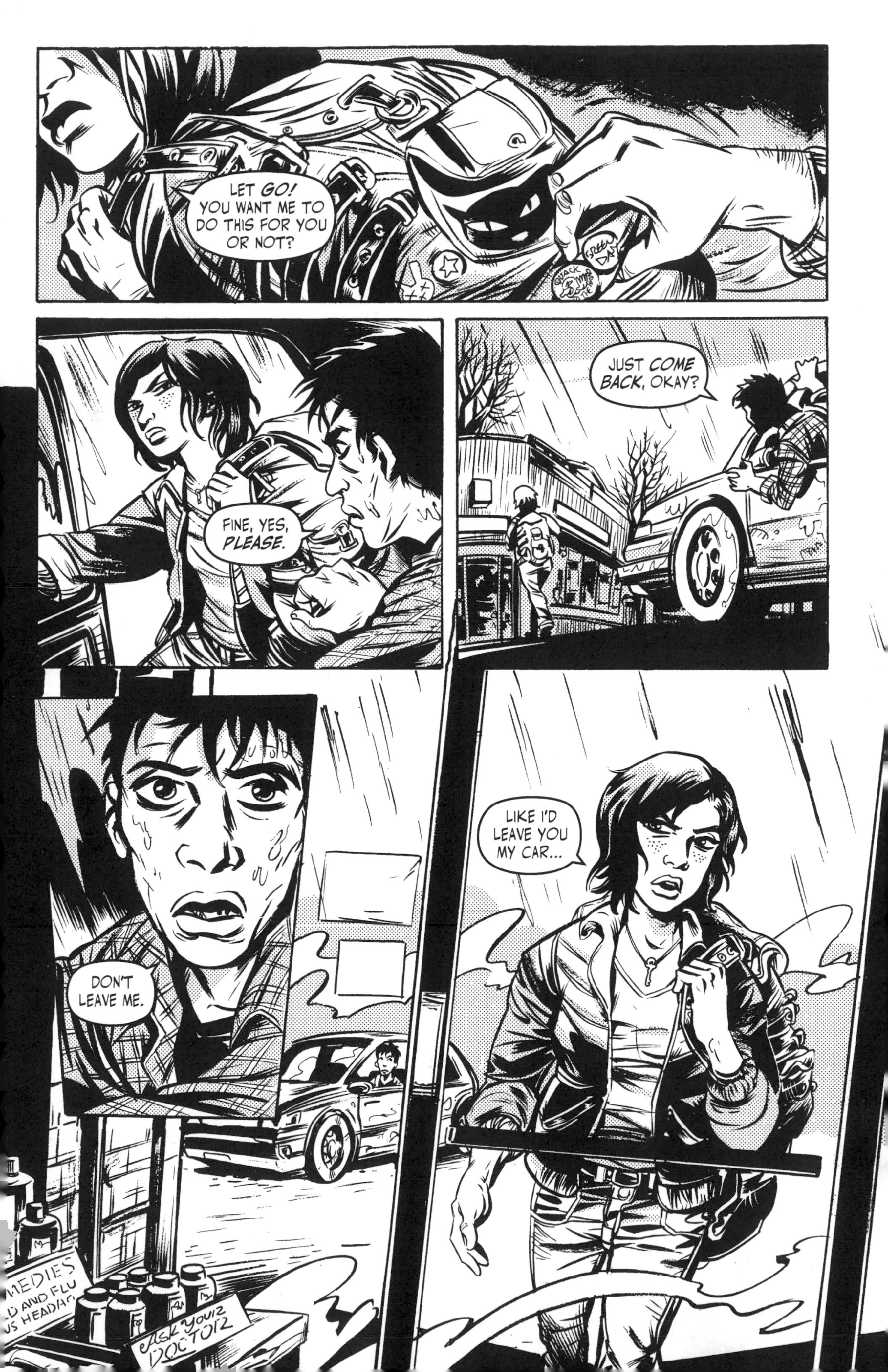
LET GO! YOU WANT ME TO DO THIS FOR YOU OR NOT?
FINE, YES, PLEASE.
JUST COME BACK, OKAY?
DON'T LEAVE ME.
LIKE I'D LEAVE YOU MY CAR...
ASK YOUR DOCTOR

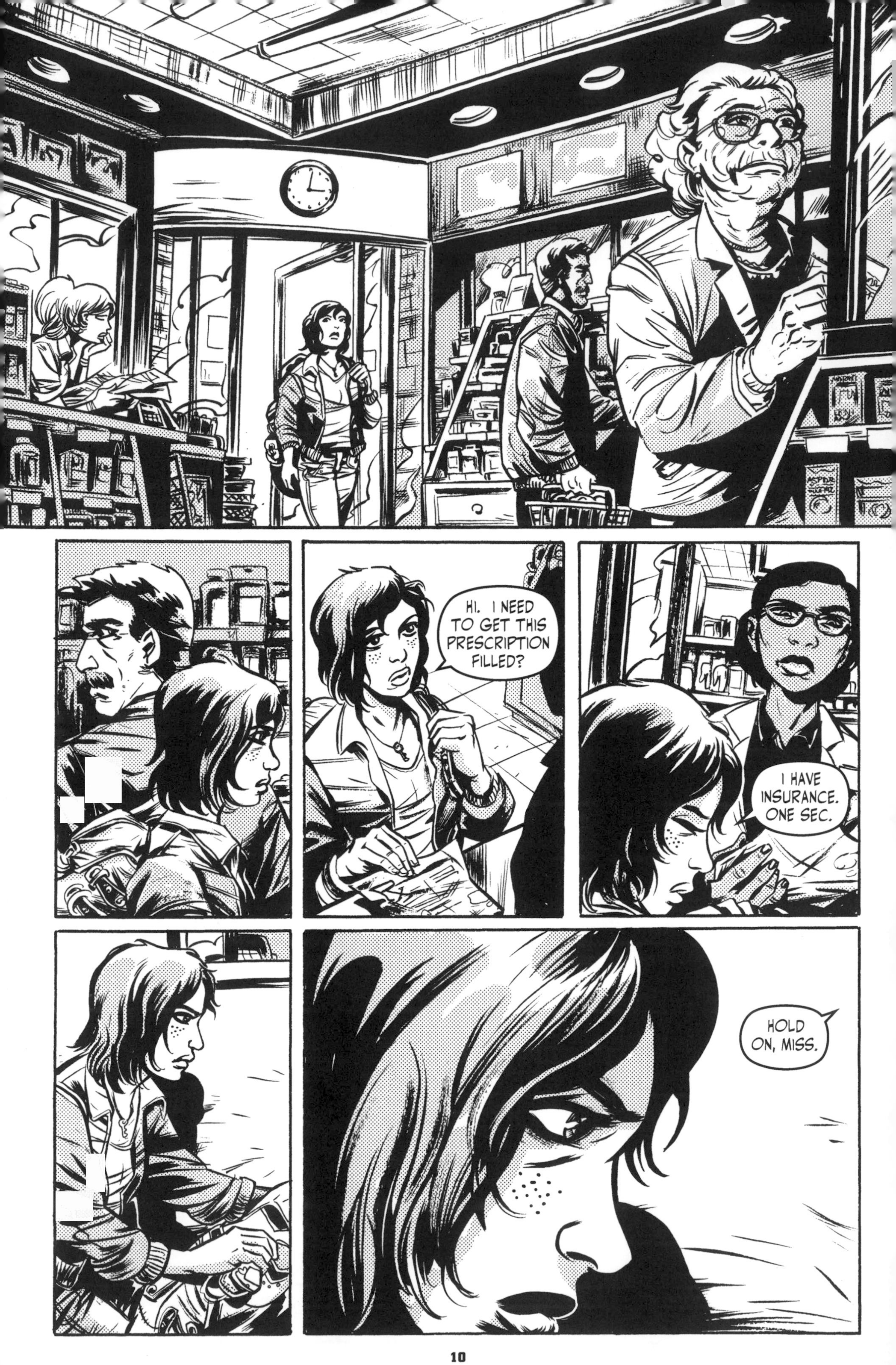
HI. I NEED TO GET THIS PRESCRIPTION FILLED?
I HAVE INSURANCE. ONE SEC.
HOLD ON, MISS.

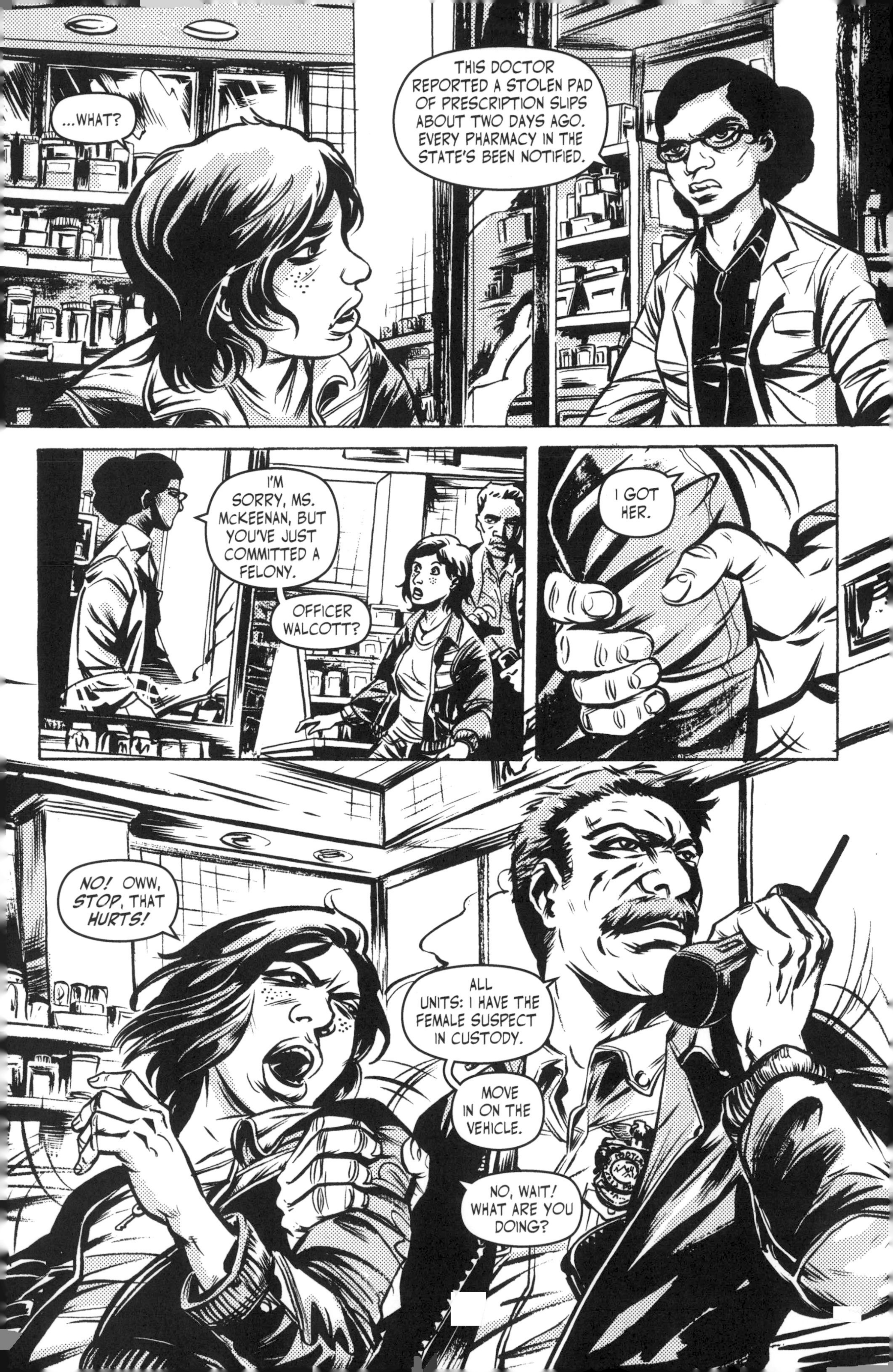
...WHAT?
THIS DOCTOR REPORTED A STOLEN PAD OF PRESCRIPTION SLIPS ABOUT TWO DAYS AGO. EVERY PHARMACY IN THE STATE'S BEEN NOTIFIED.
I'M SORRY, MS. McKEENAN, BUT YOU'VE JUST COMMITTED A FELONY.
OFFICER WALCOTT?
I GOT HER.
NO! OWW, STOP, THAT HURTS!
ALL UNITS: I HAVE THE FEMALE SUSPECT IN CUSTODY.
MOVE IN ON THE VEHICLE.
NO, WAIT! WHAT ARE YOU DOING?

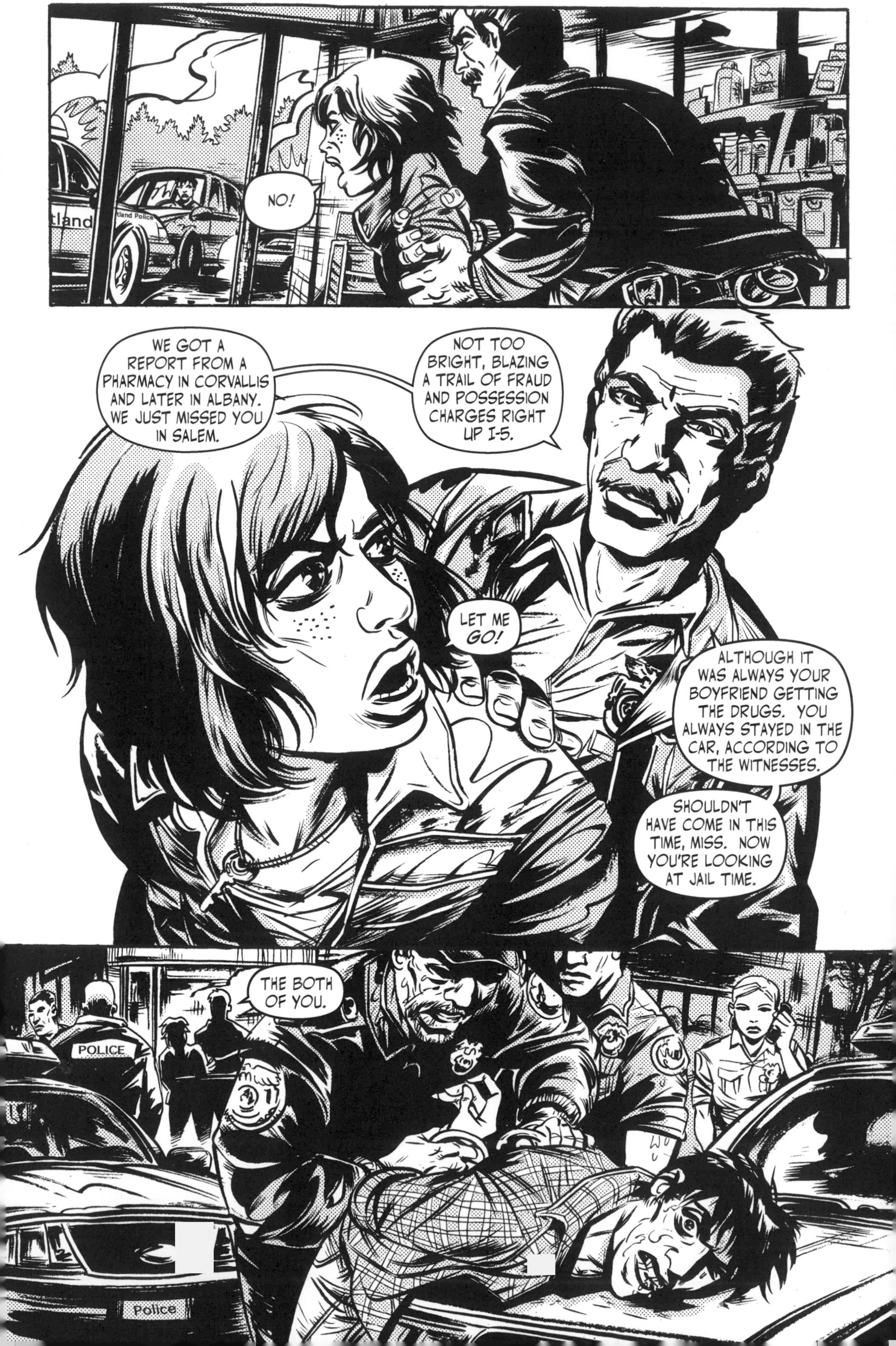
NO!
tland
tland Police
WE GOT A REPORT FROM A PHARMACY IN CORVALLIS AND LATER IN ALBANY. WE JUST MISSED YOU IN SALEM.
NOT TOO BRIGHT, BLAZING A TRAIL OF FRAUD AND POSSESSION CHARGES RIGHT UP I-5.
LET ME GO!
ALTHOUGH IT WAS ALWAYS YOUR BOYFRIEND GETTING THE DRUGS. YOU ALWAYS STAYED IN THE CAR, ACCORDING TO THE WITNESSES.
SHOULDN'T HAVE COME IN THIS TIME, MISS. NOW YOU'RE LOOKING AT JAIL TIME.
THE BOTH OF YOU.
POLICE
Police

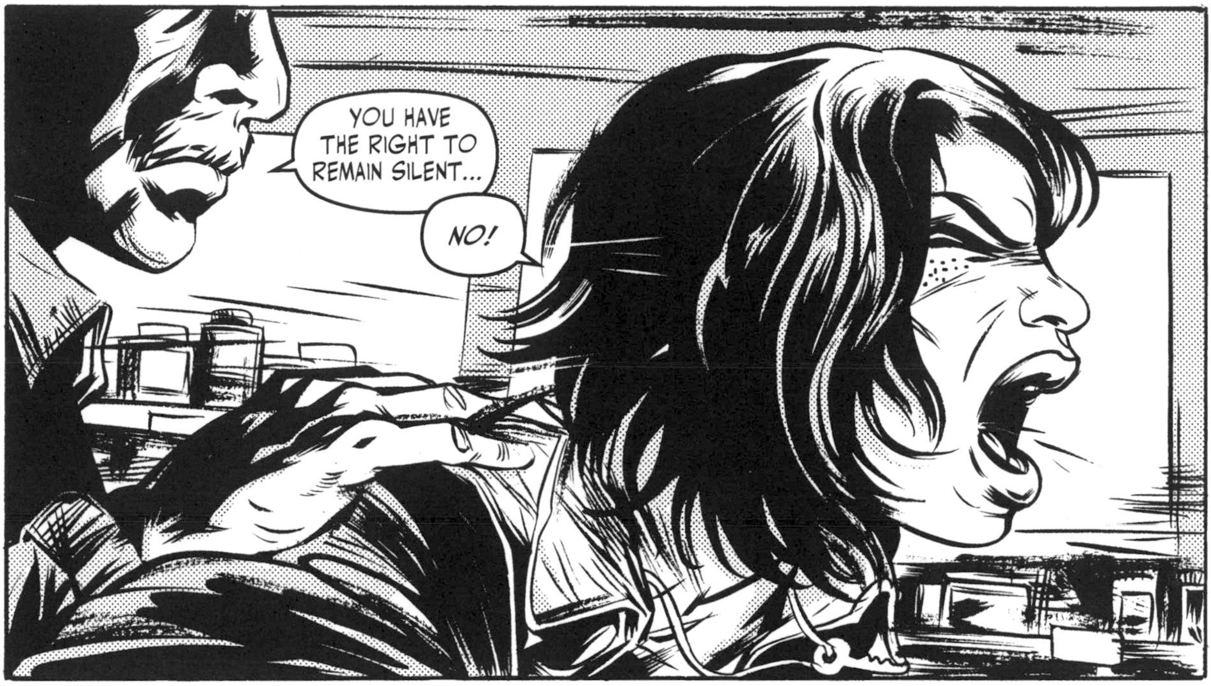
YOU HAVE THE RIGHT TO REMAIN SILENT...
NO!

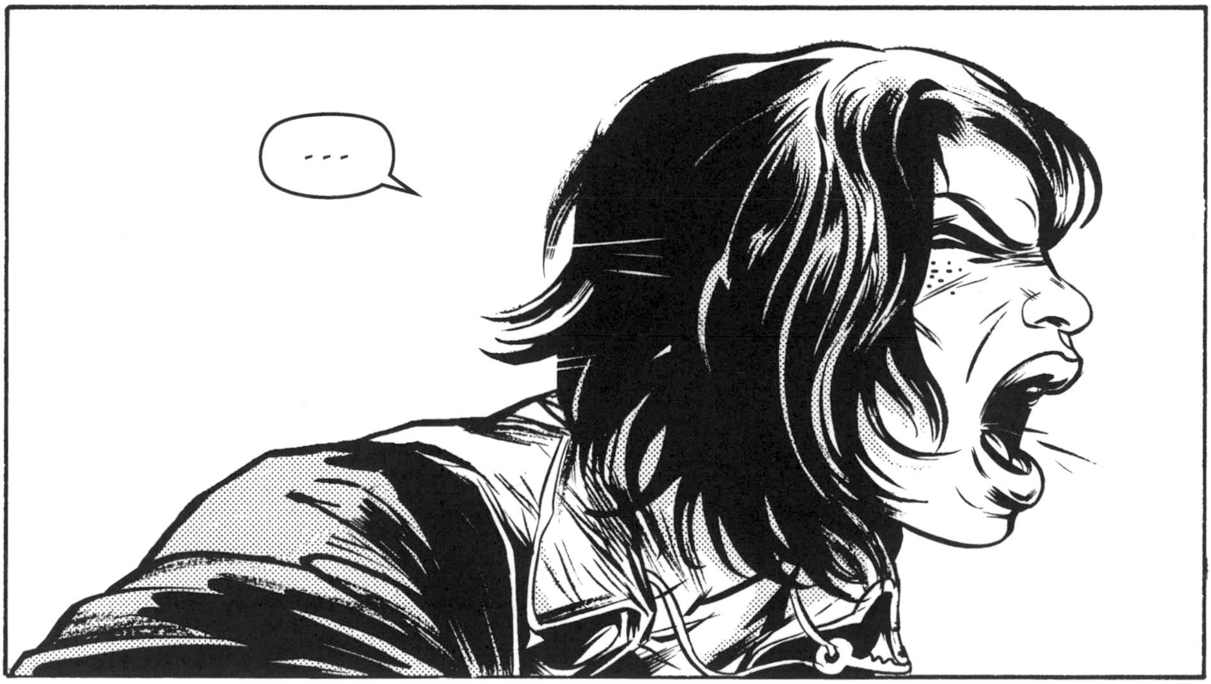
...

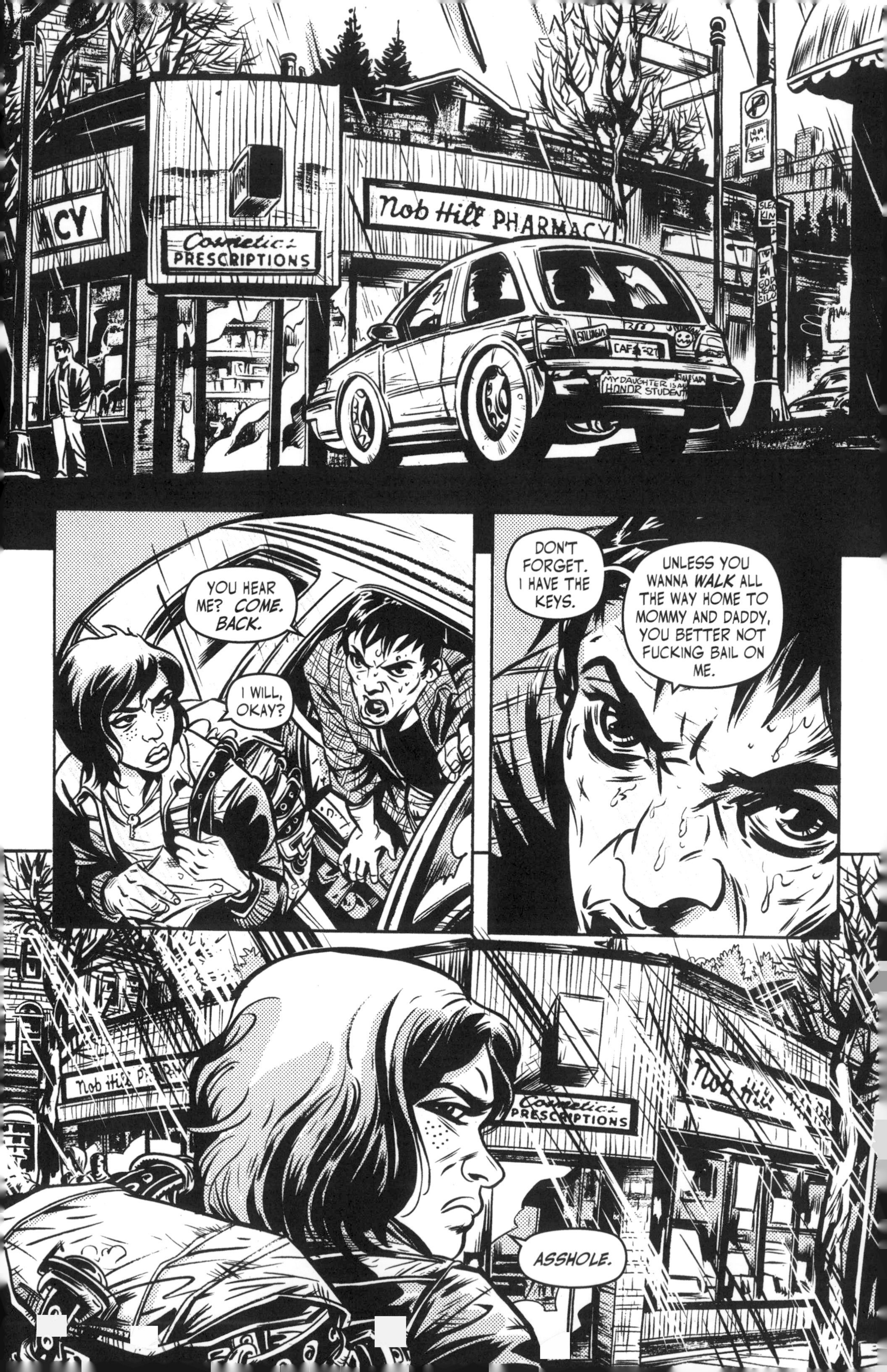

Nob Hill PHARMACY
Cosmetics
PRESCRIPTIONS
MY DAUGHTER IS AN HONOR STUDENT
YOU HEAR ME? COME. BACK.
I WILL, OKAY?
DON'T FORGET. I HAVE THE KEYS.
UNLESS YOU WANNA WALK ALL THE WAY HOME TO MOMMY AND DADDY, YOU BETTER NOT FUCKING BAIL ON ME.
Cosmetics
PRESCRIPTIONS
ASSHOLE.

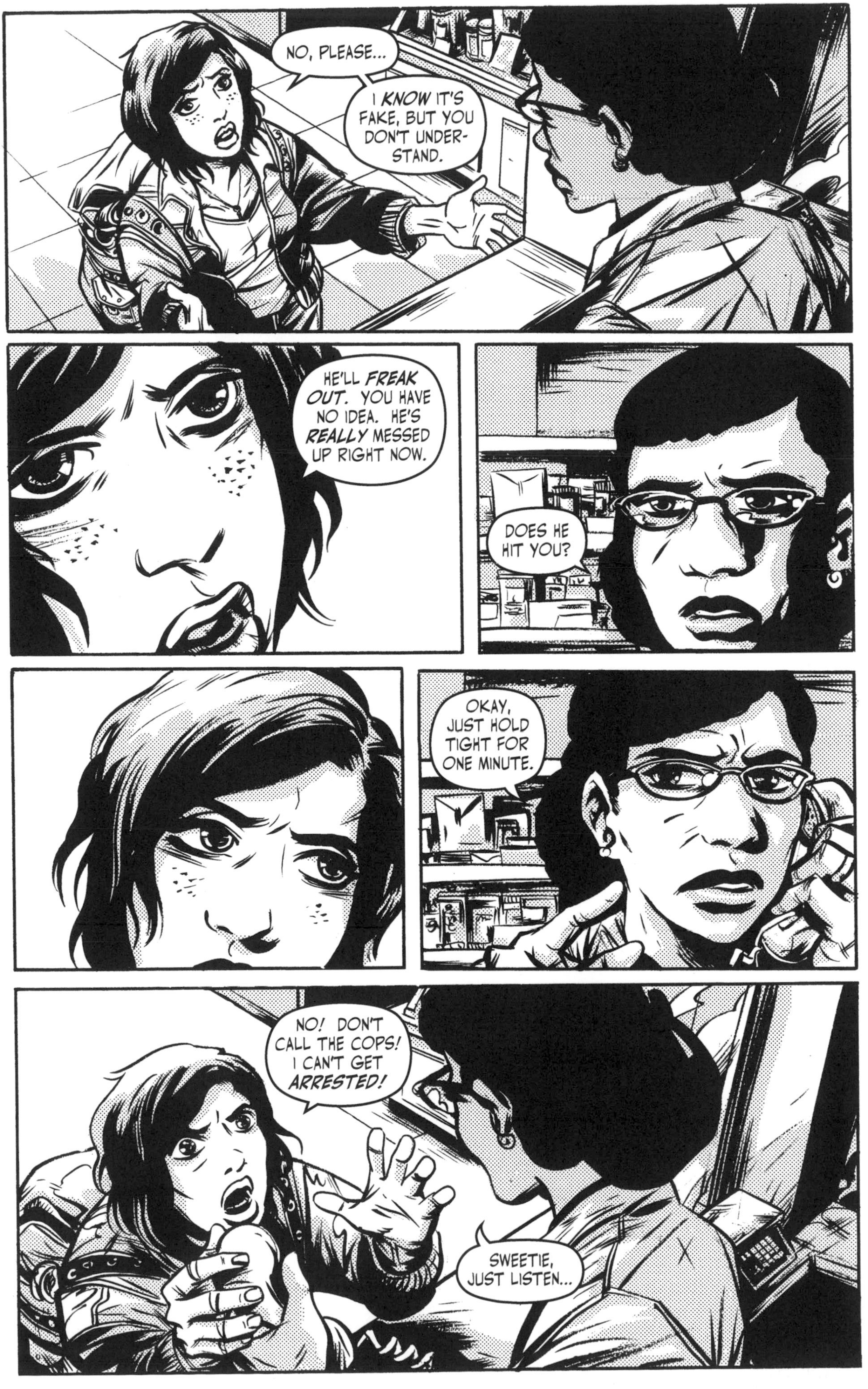
NO, PLEASE...
I KNOW IT'S FAKE, BUT YOU DON'T UNDER-STAND.
HE'LL FREAK OUT. YOU HAVE NO IDEA. HE'S REALLY MESSED UP RIGHT NOW.
DOES HE HIT YOU?
OKAY, JUST HOLD TIGHT FOR ONE MINUTE.
NO! DON'T CALL THE COPS! I CAN'T GET ARRESTED!
SWEETIE, JUST LISTEN...

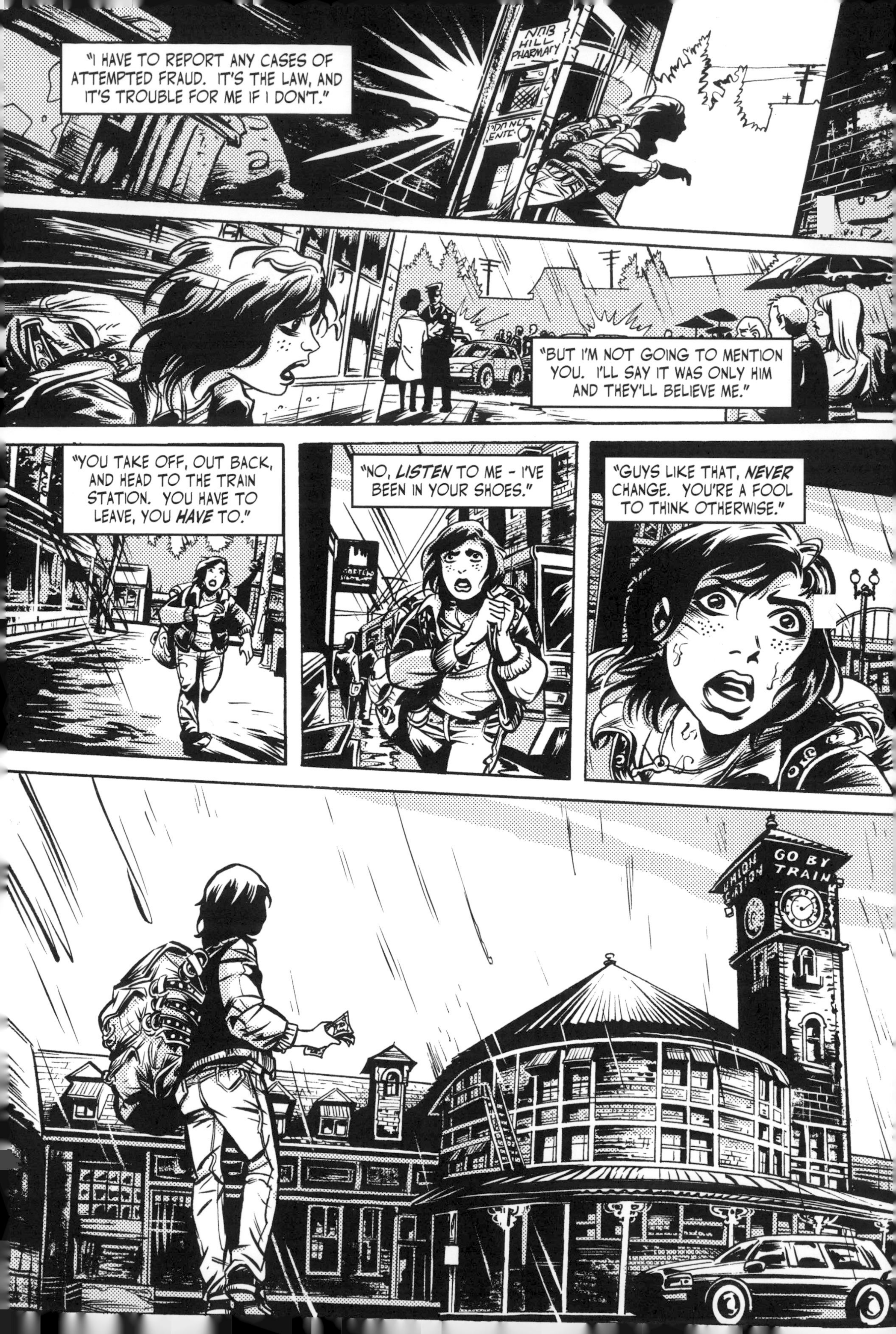
"I HAVE TO REPORT ANY CASES OF ATTEMPTED FRAUD. IT'S THE LAW, AND IT'S TROUBLE FOR ME IF I DON'T."
NOB HILL PHARMACY
"BUT I'M NOT GOING TO MENTION YOU. I'LL SAY IT WAS ONLY HIM AND THEY'LL BELIEVE ME."
"YOU TAKE OFF, OUT BACK, AND HEAD TO THE TRAIN STATION. YOU HAVE TO LEAVE, YOU HAVE TO."
"NO, LISTEN TO ME - I'VE BEEN IN YOUR SHOES."
"GUYS LIKE THAT, NEVER CHANGE. YOU'RE A FOOL TO THINK OTHERWISE."
UNION STATION
GO BY TRAIN

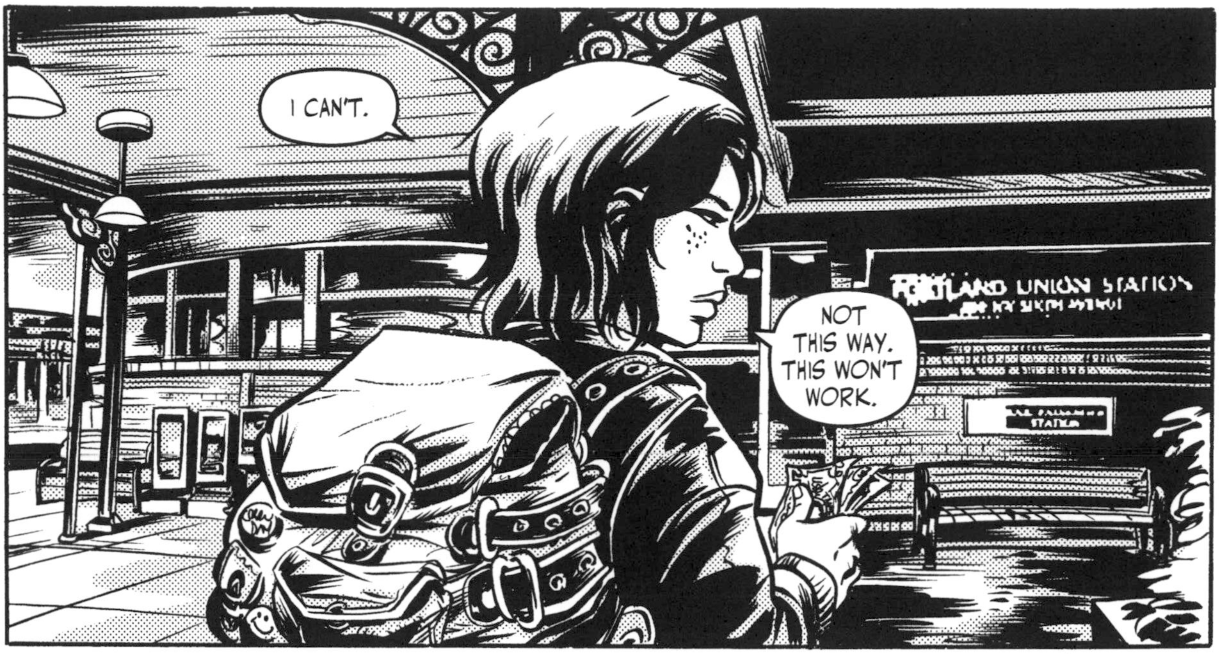
I CAN'T.
NOT THIS WAY. THIS WON'T WORK.

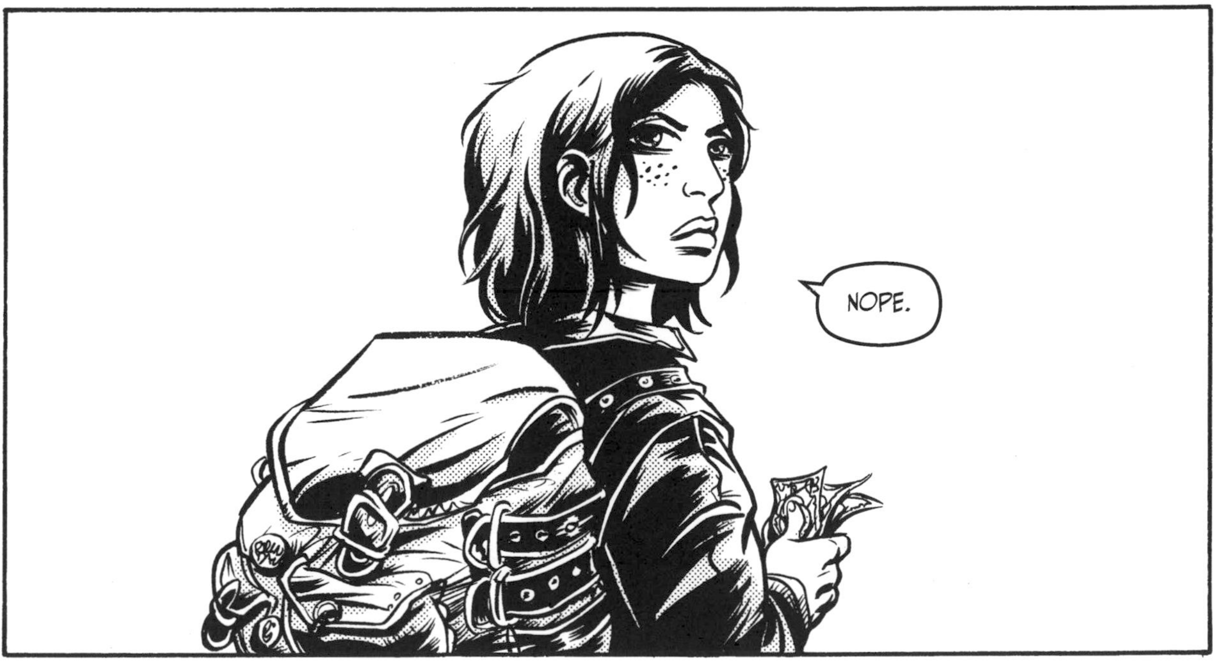
NOPE.

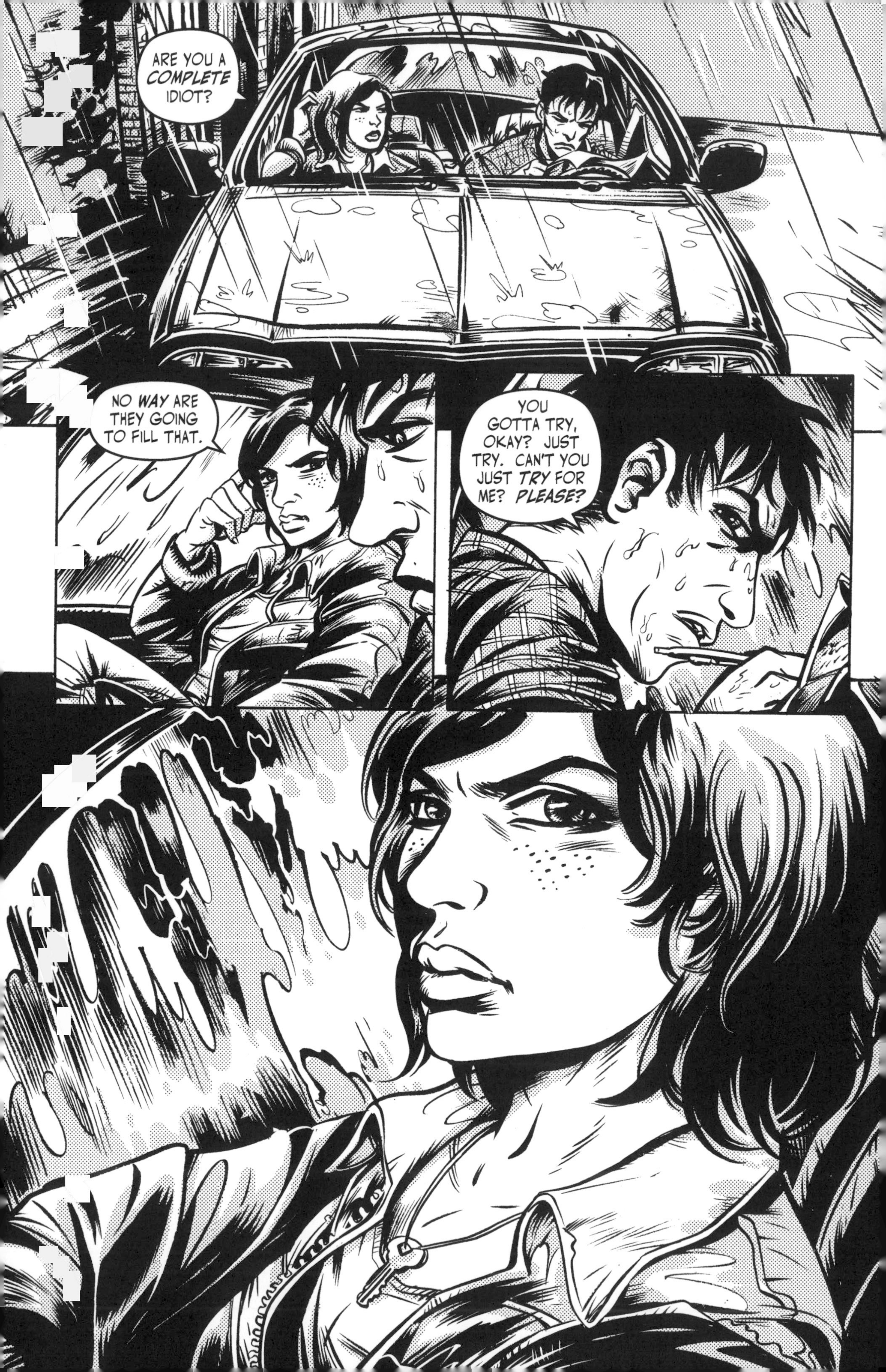
ARE YOU A COMPLETE IDIOT?
NO WAY ARE THEY GOING TO FILL THAT.
YOU GOTTA TRY, OKAY? JUST TRY. CAN'T YOU JUST TRY FOR ME? PLEASE?

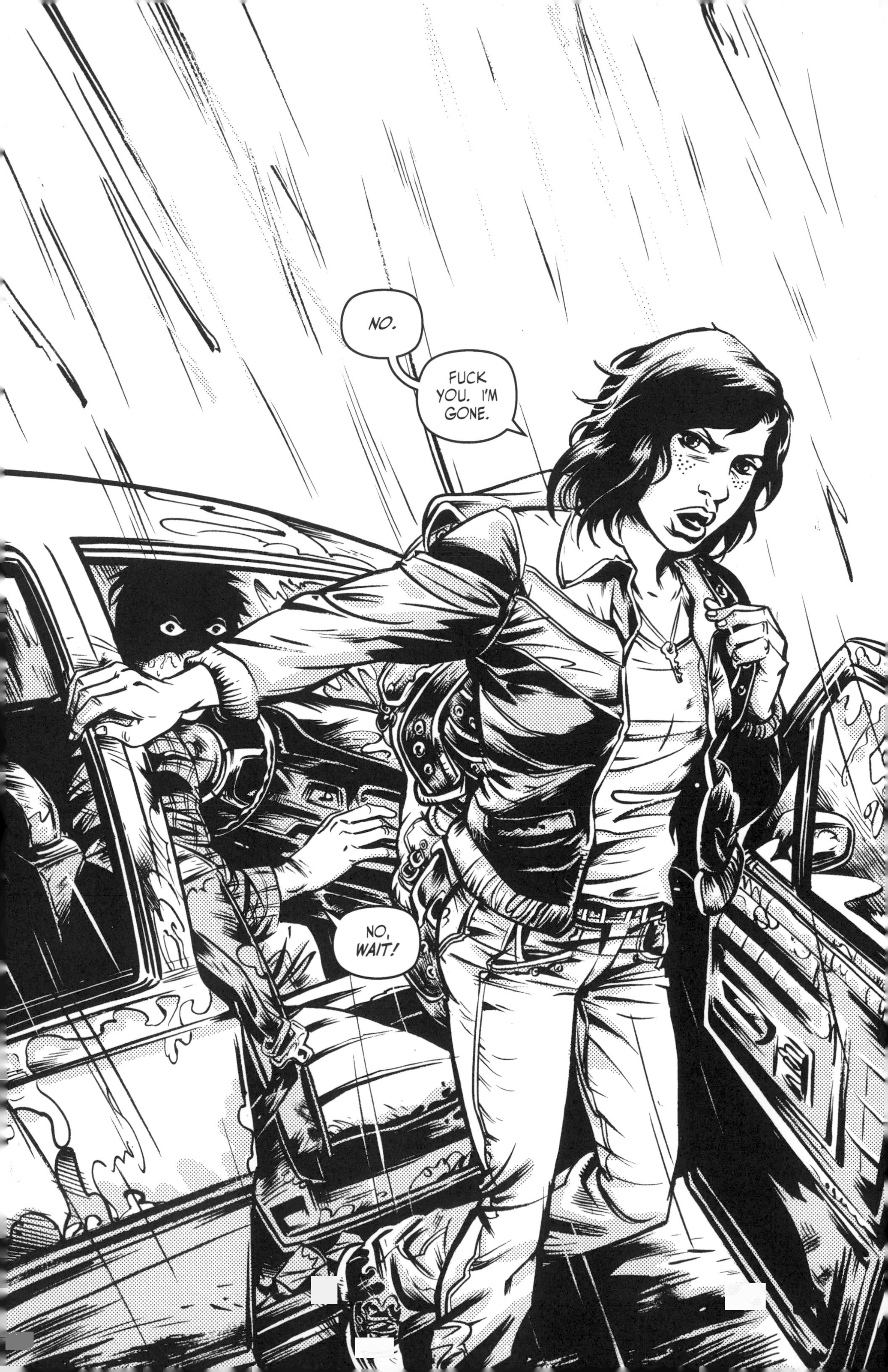
NO.
FUCK YOU. I'M GONE.
NO, WAIT!

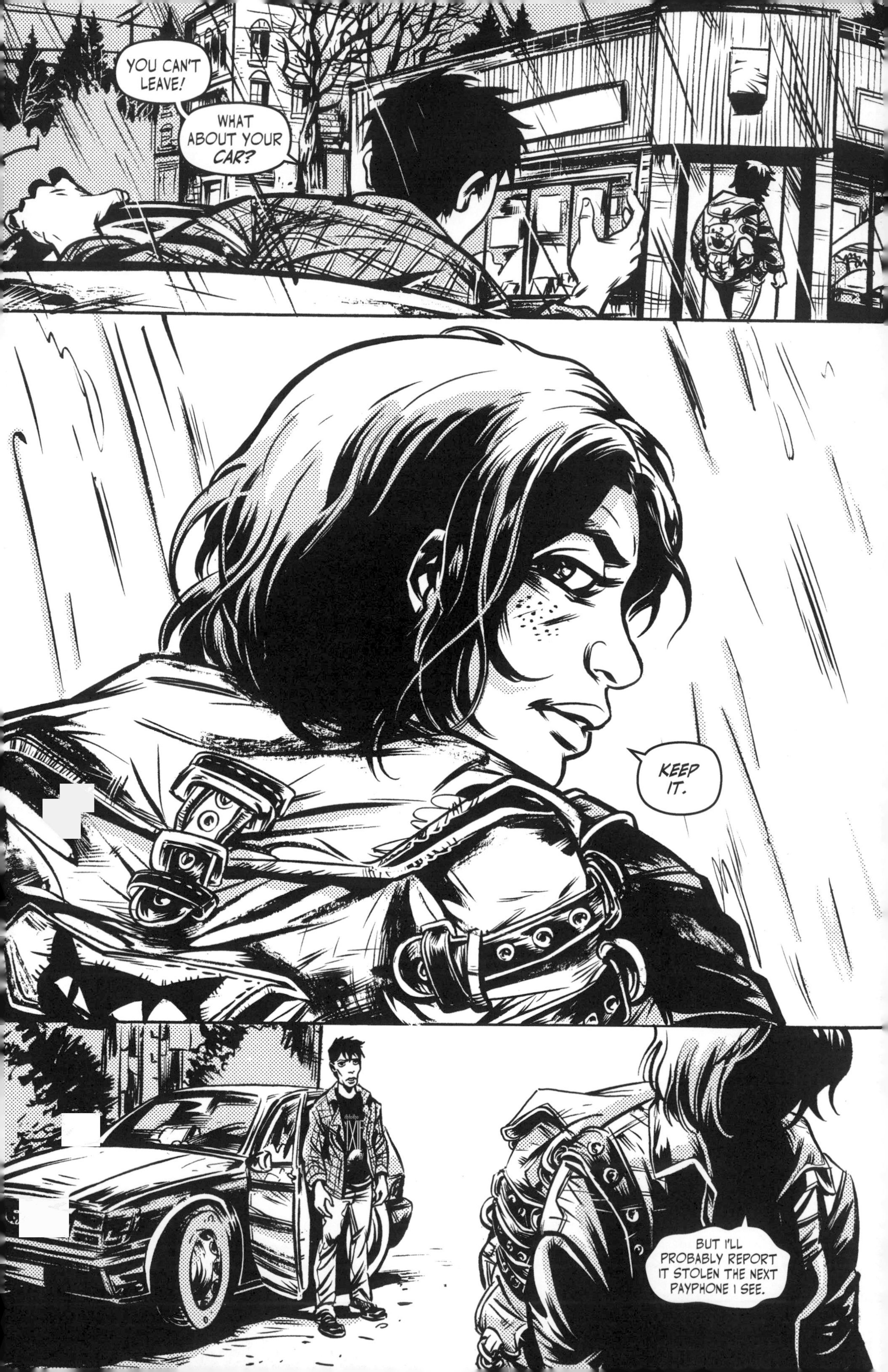
YOU CAN'T LEAVE!
WHAT ABOUT YOUR CAR?
KEEP IT.
BUT I'LL PROBABLY REPORT IT STOLEN THE NEXT PAYPHONE I SEE.

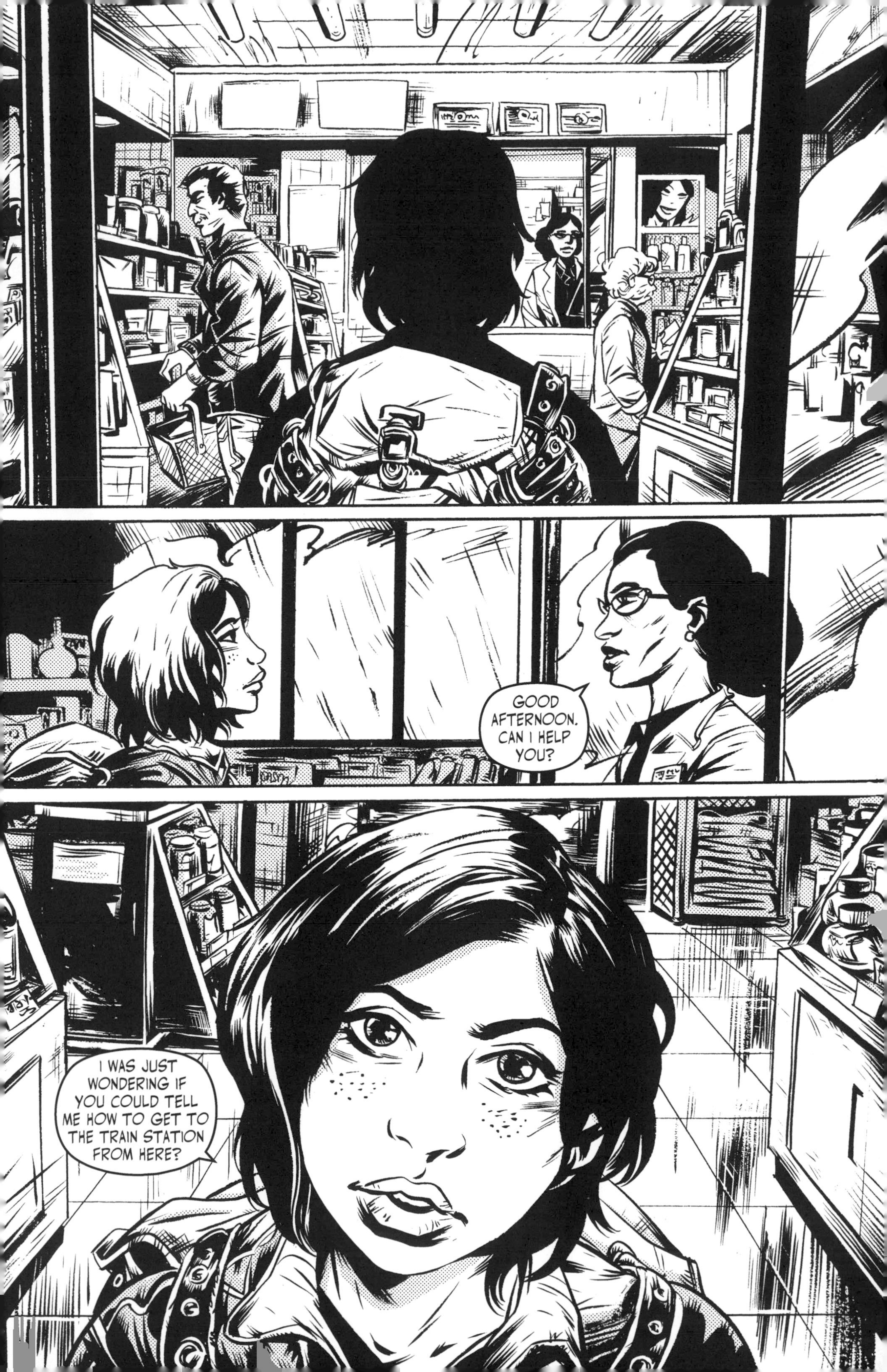
GOOD AFTERNOON. CAN I HELP YOU?
I WAS JUST WONDERING IF YOU COULD TELL ME HOW TO GET TO THE TRAIN STATION FROM HERE?

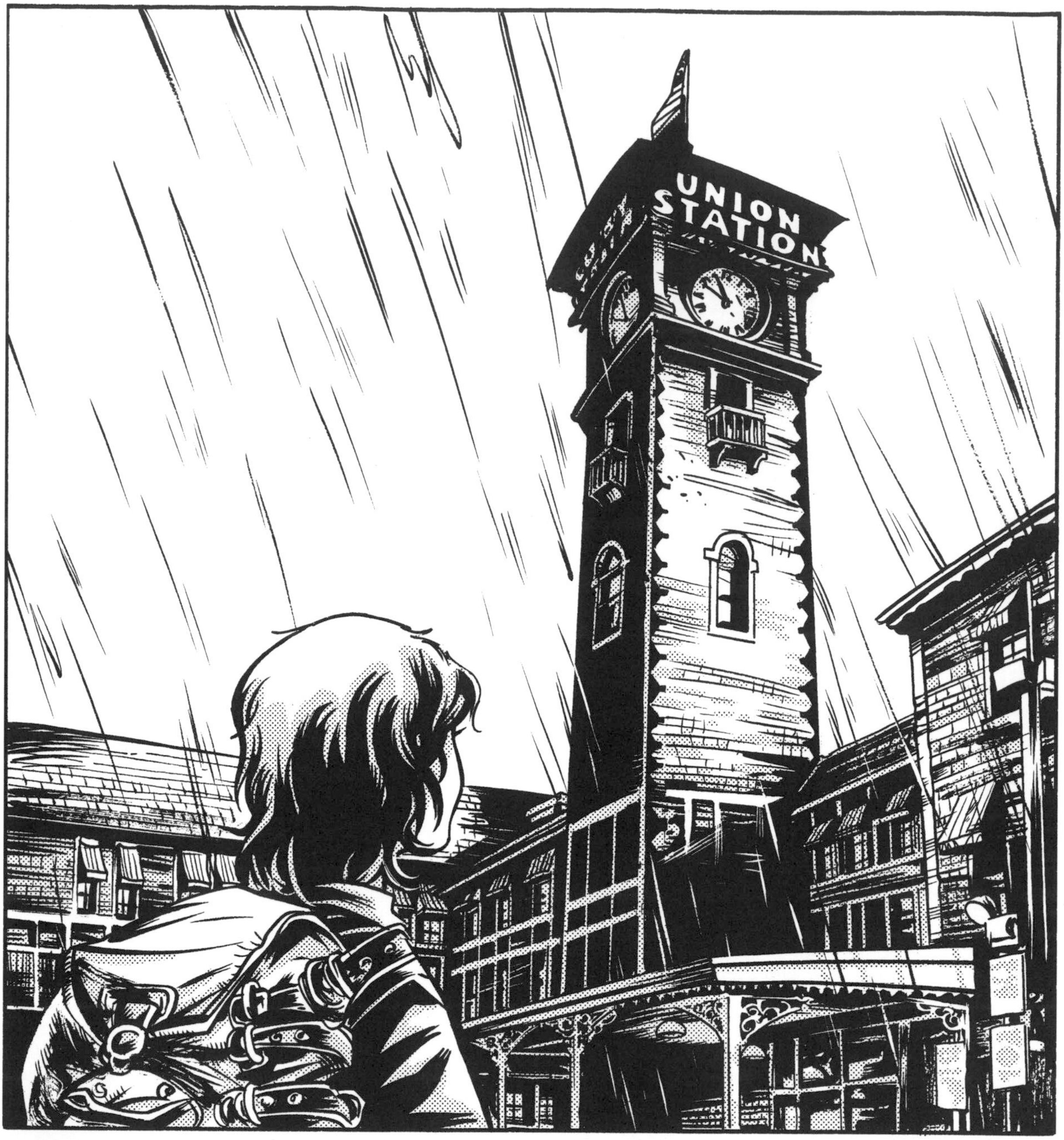
UNION STATION

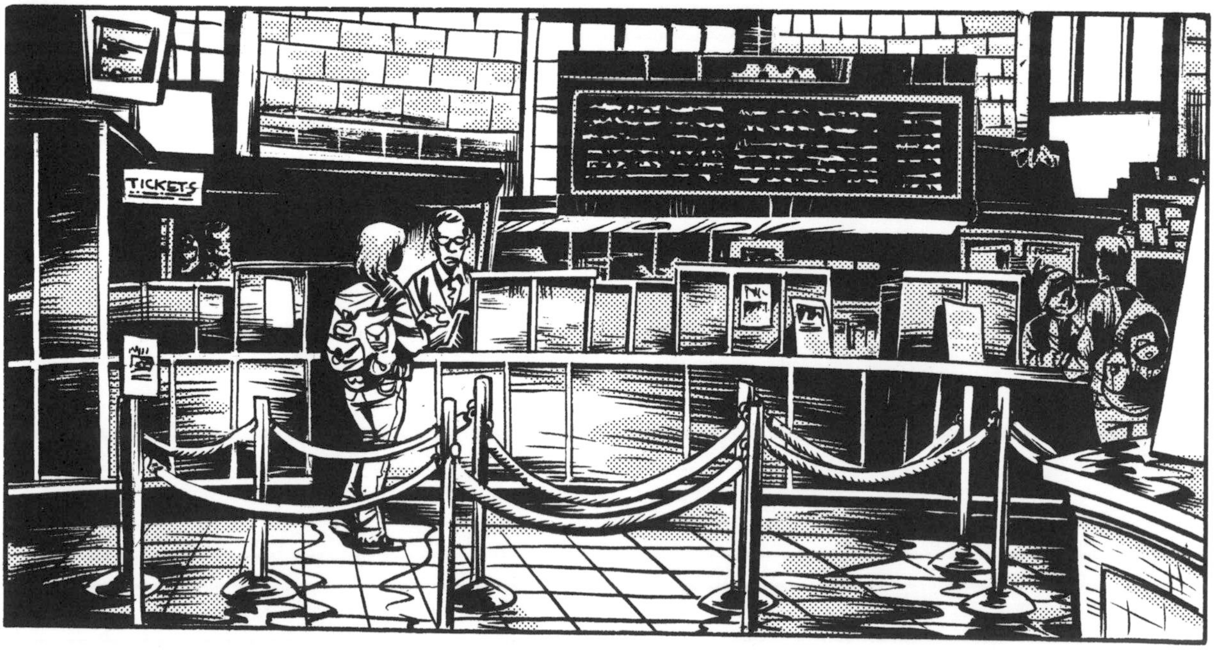
TICKETS

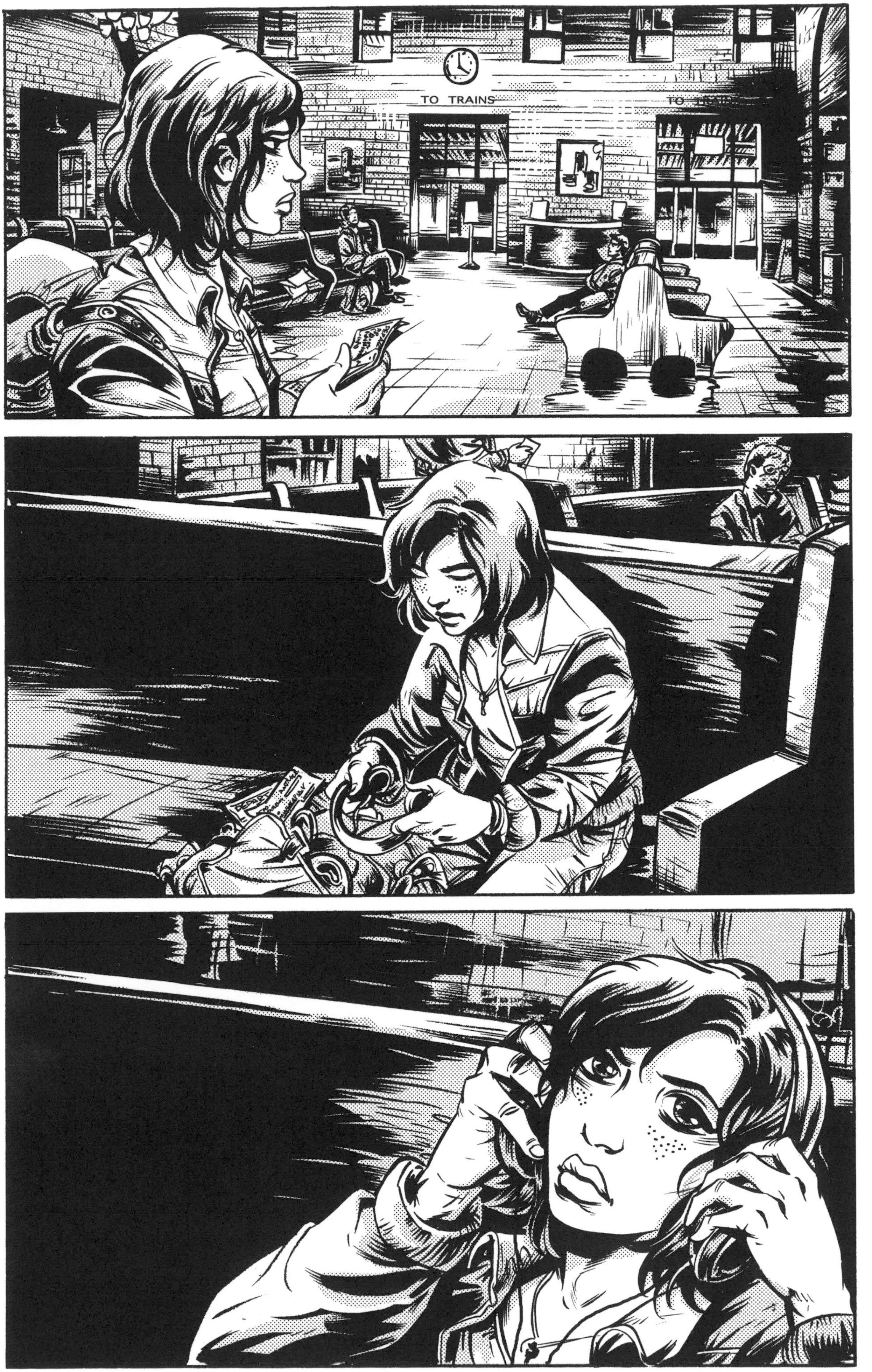
TO TRAINS

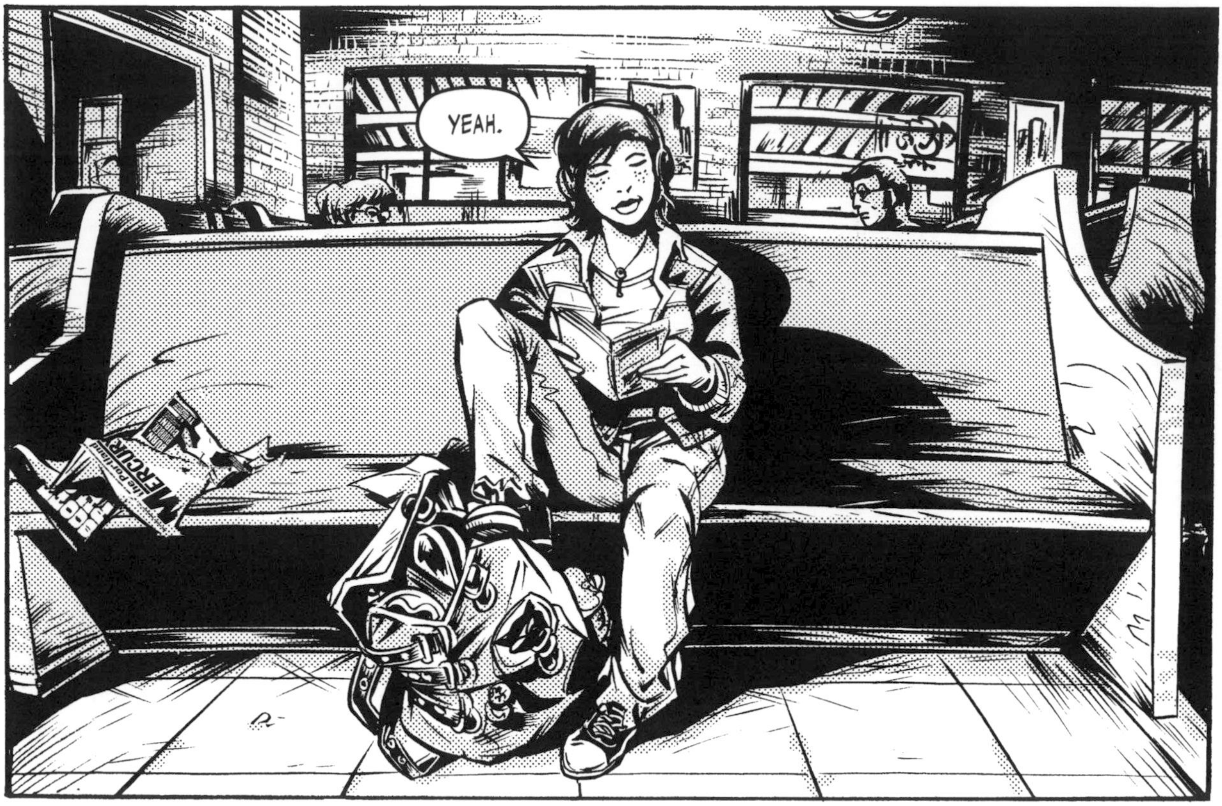
YEAH.
MERCURY

LOCAL #1

"ten thousand thoughts per second"

STORY: BRIAN WOOD / ART: RYAN KELLY
LETTERED BY HOPE LARSON AND BRYAN LEE O'MALLEY

CHAPTER 2
"POLAROID BOYFRIEND"
Minneapolis, Minnesota

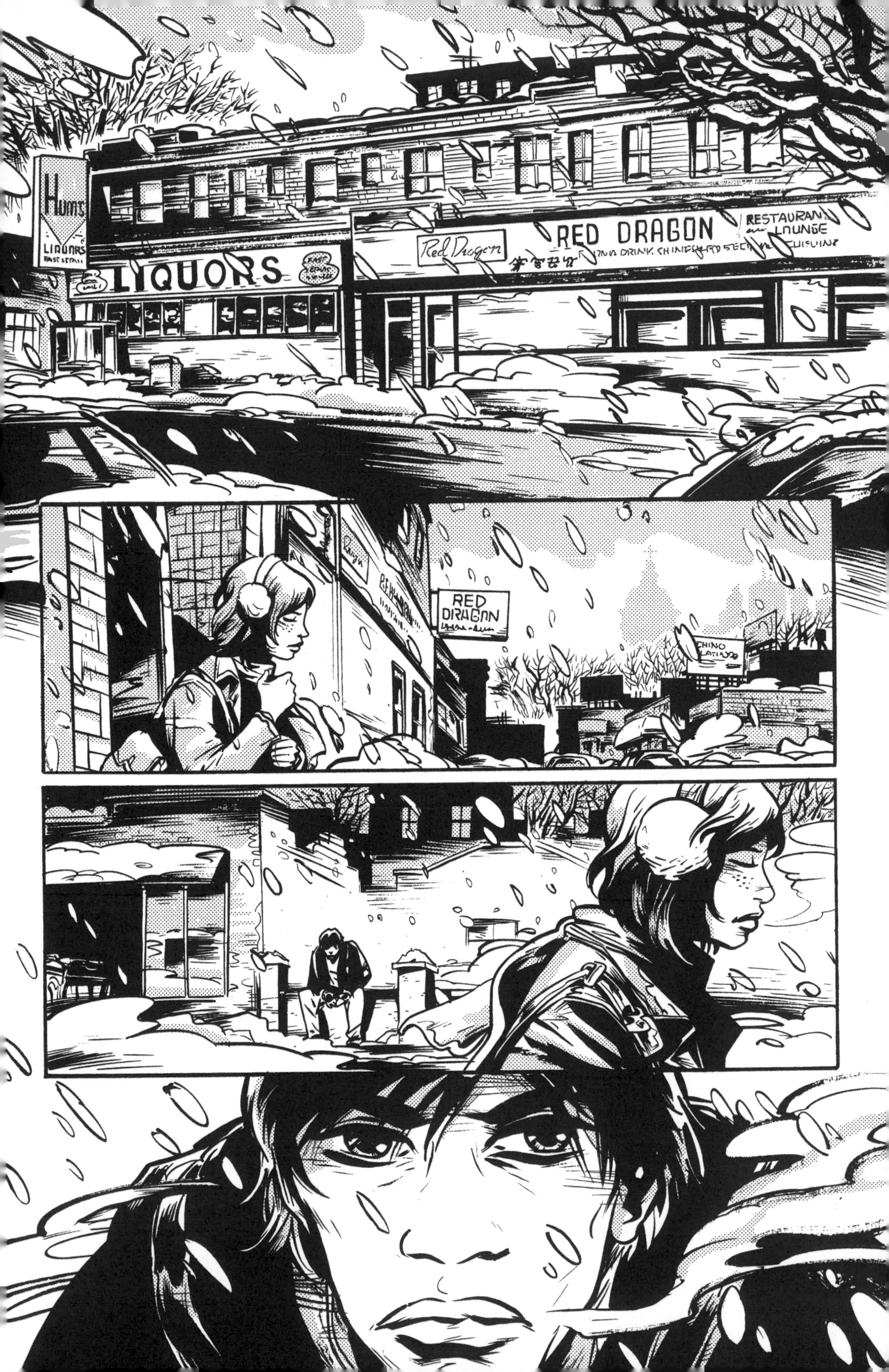
LIQUORS
Red Dragon
RED DRAGON
RESTAURAN
LOUNGE
RED DRAGON

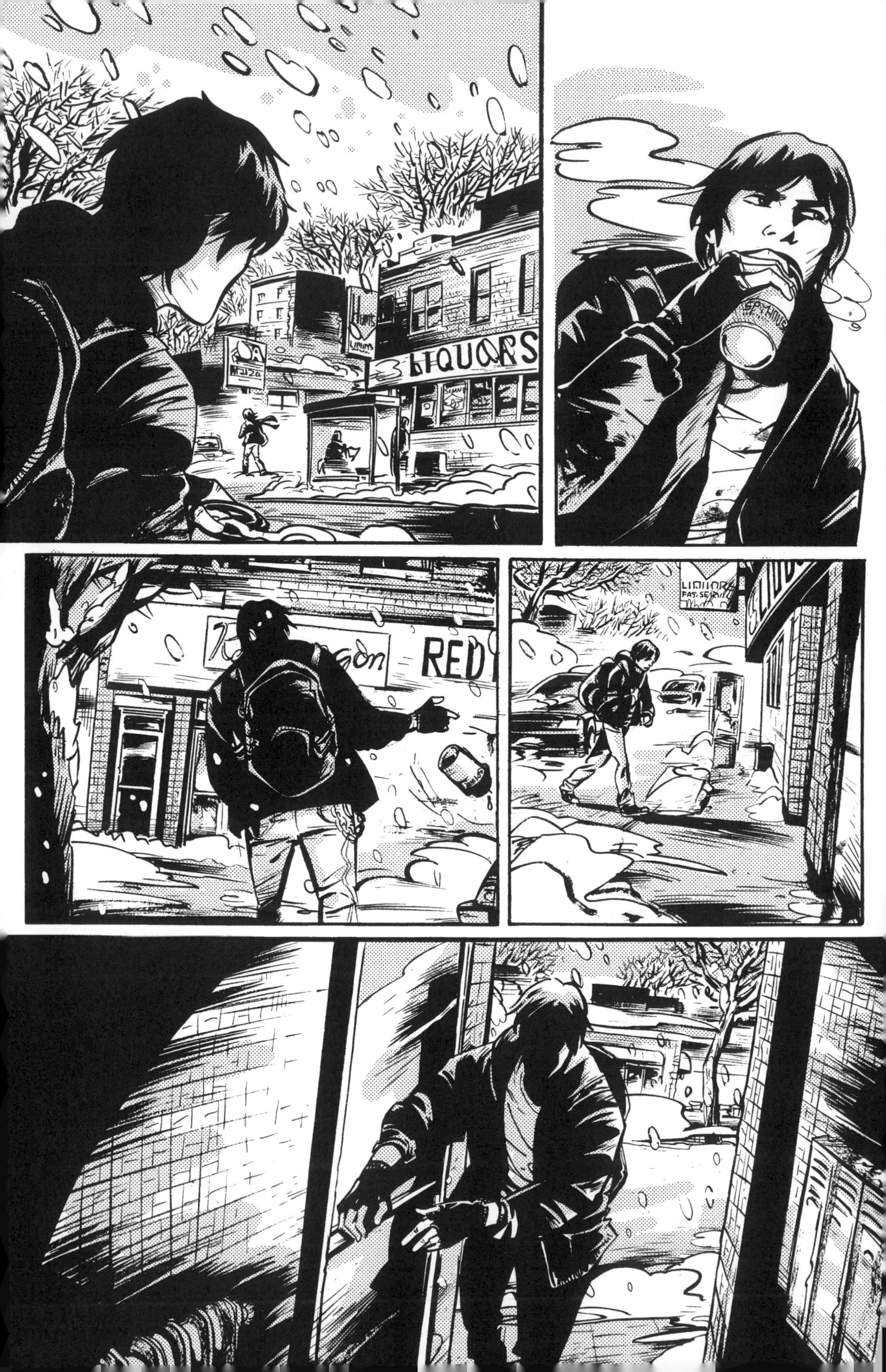

LIQUORS
RED

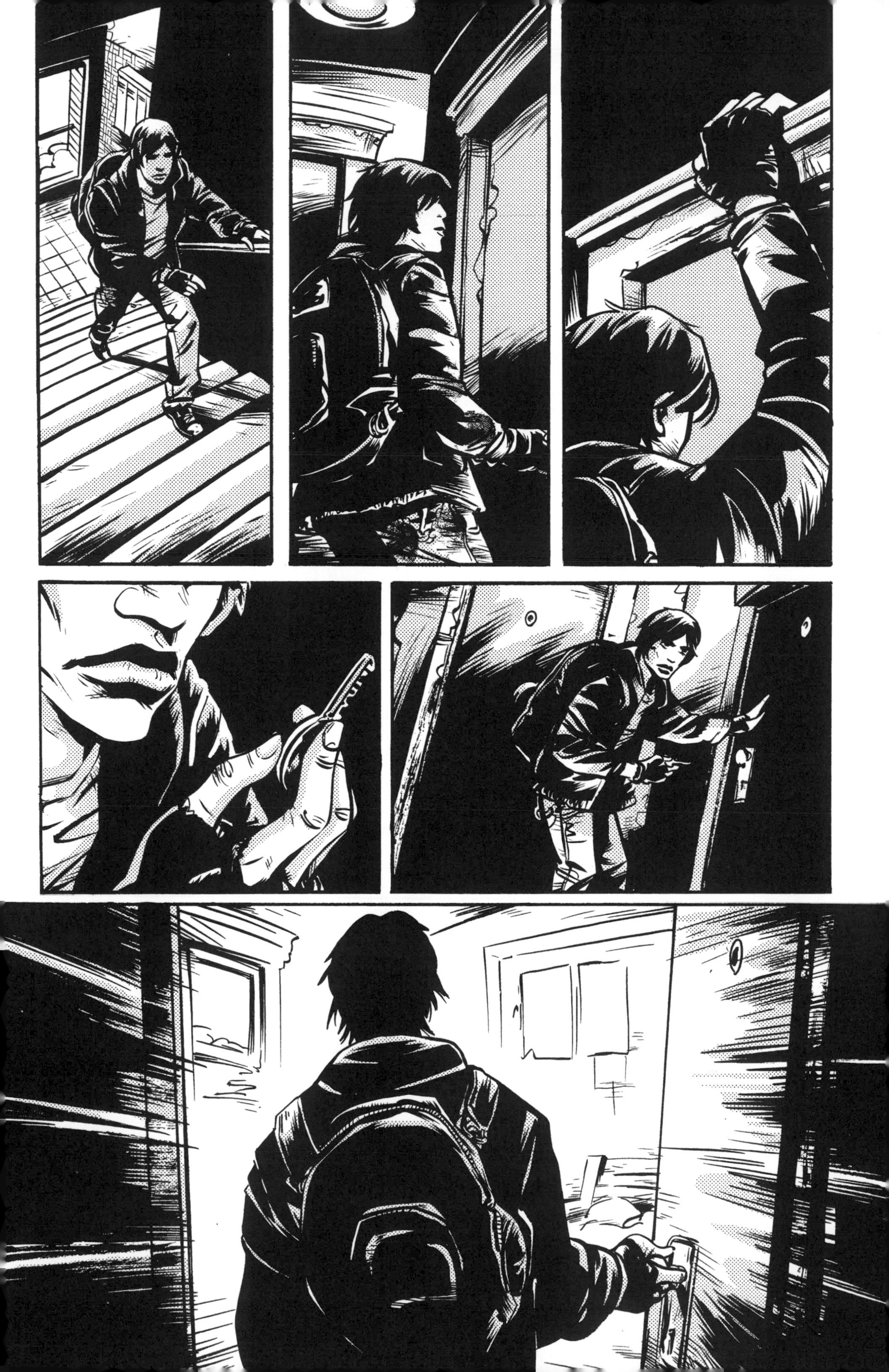

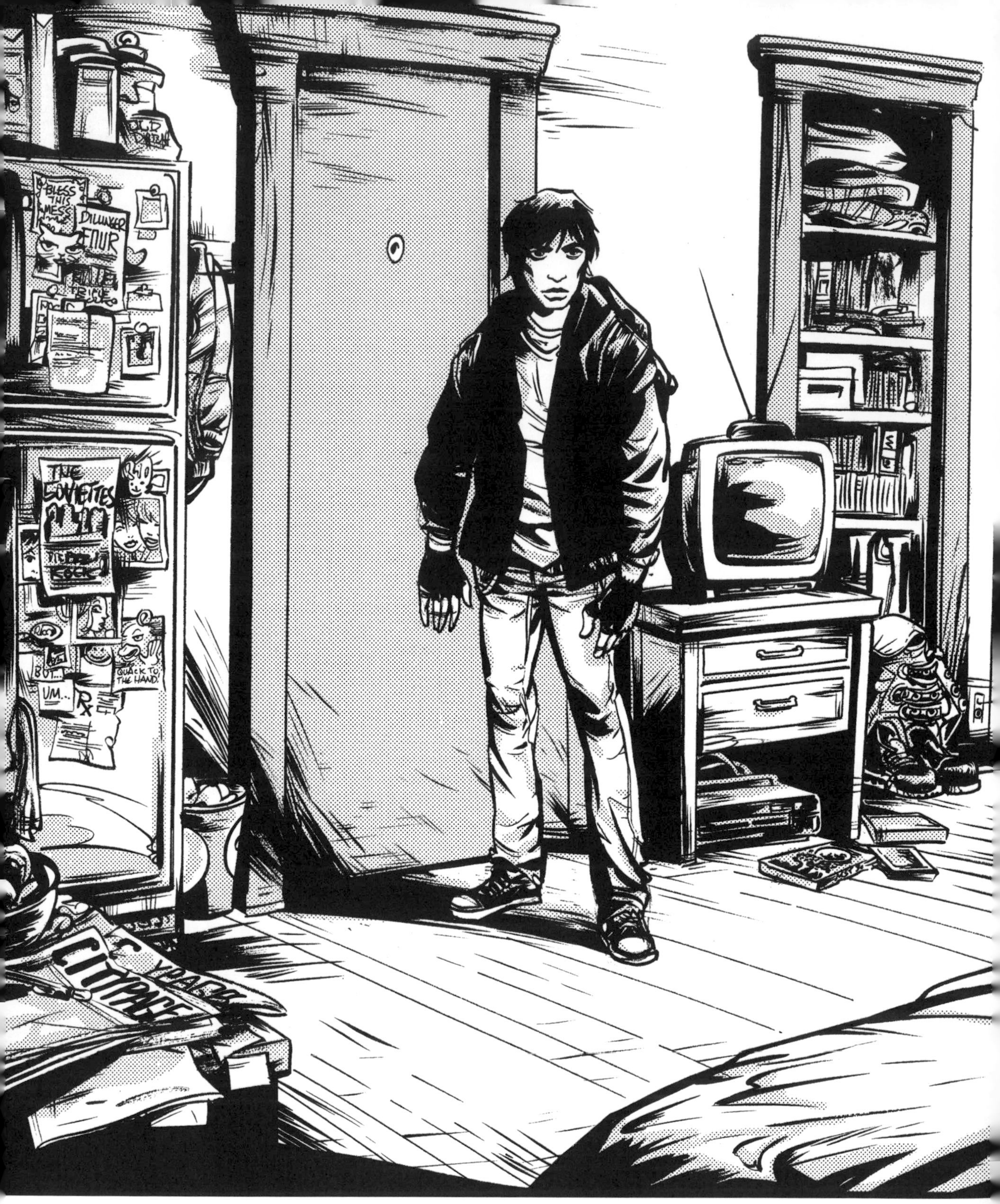
BLESS THIS MESS
DILLINGER FOUR
THE SOVIETTES
BUT...
QUACK TO THE HAND!
UM...
Rx

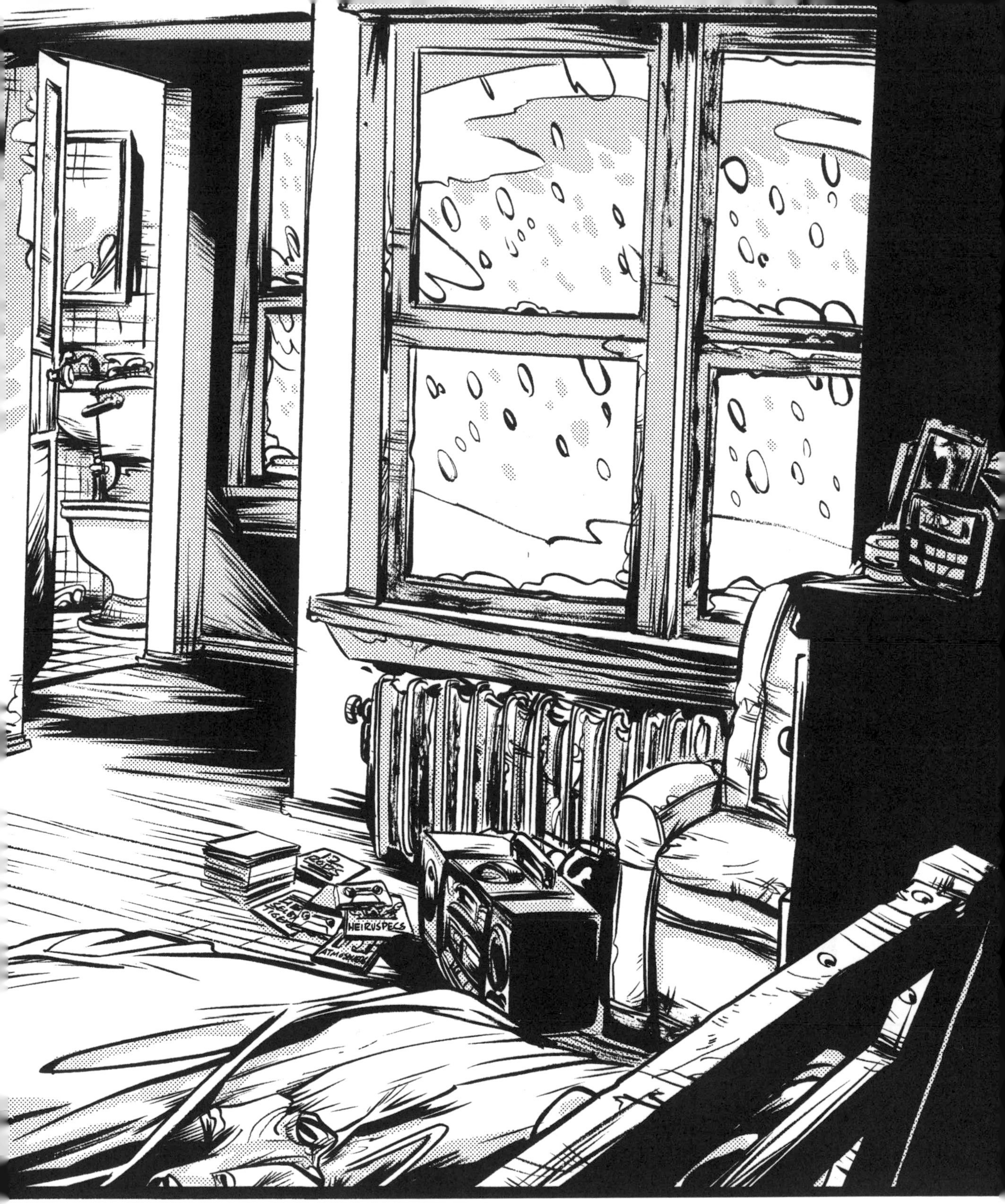
HEIRUSPECS

LOCAL #2

"polaroid boyfriend"

STORY: BRIAN WOOD / ART: RYAN KELLY

LETTERED BY HOPE LARSON AND BRYAN LEE O'MALLEY

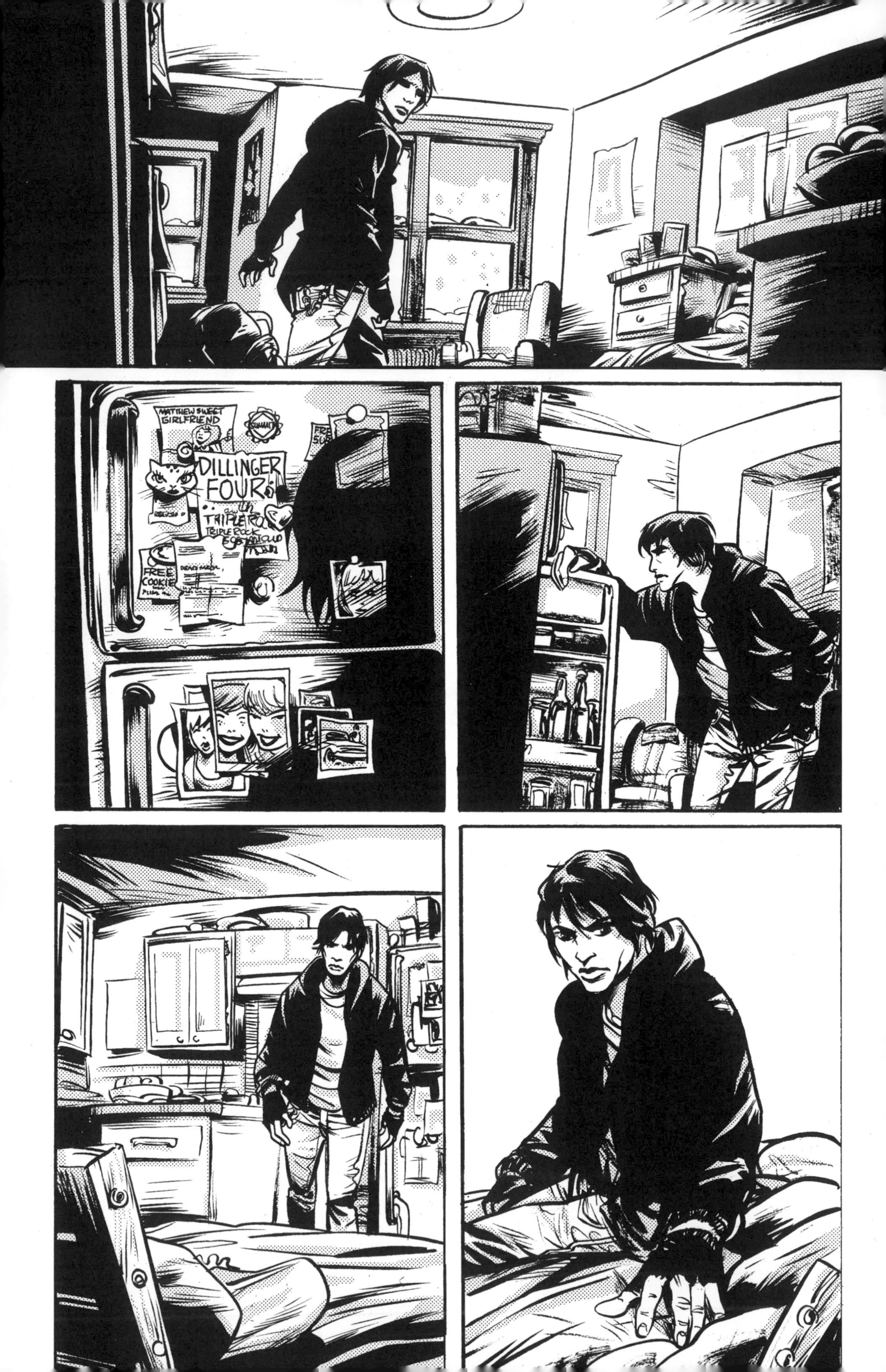
MATTHEW SWEET
GIRLFRIEND
DILLINGER
FOUR
TRIPLE ROCK
FREE
COOKIE

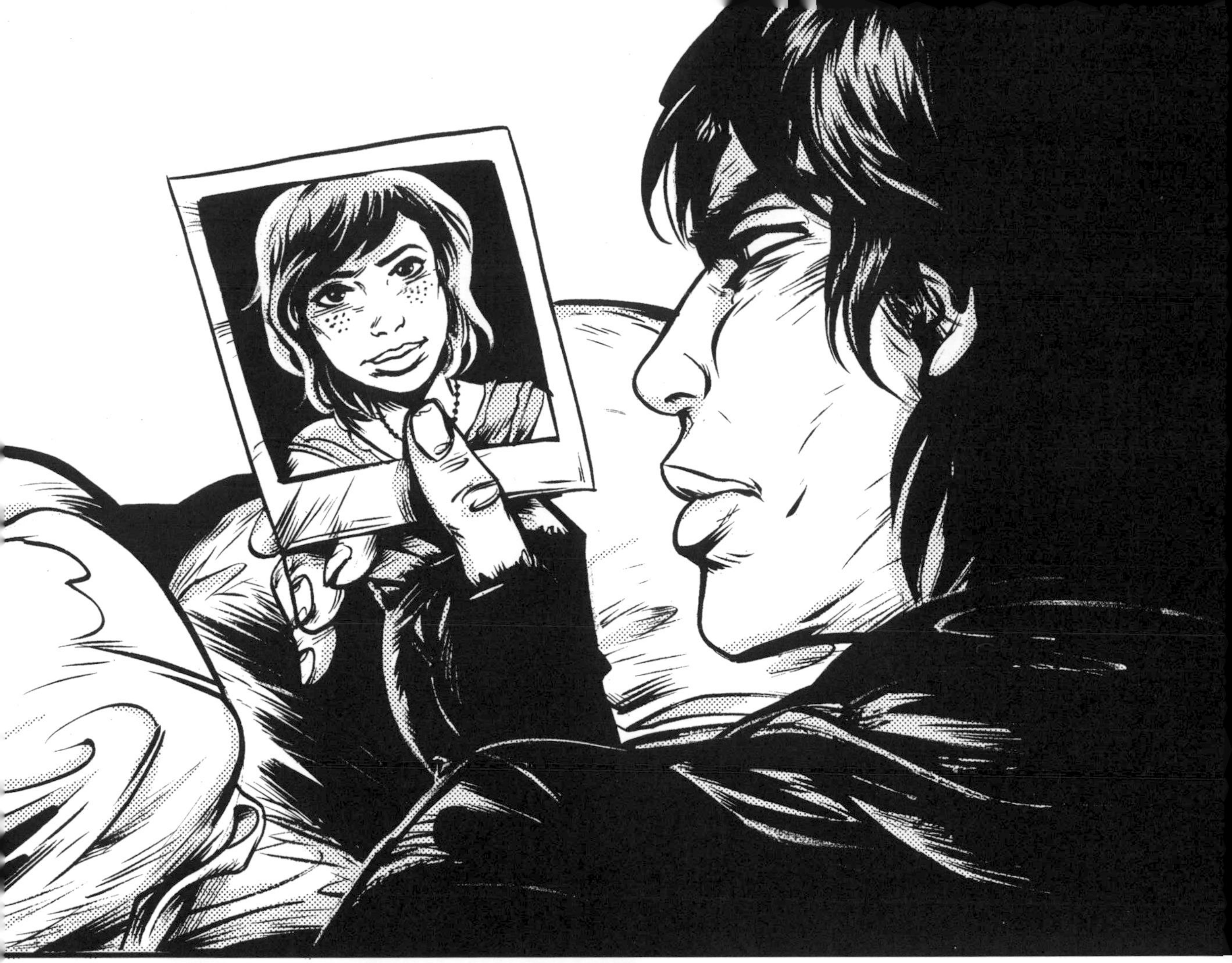

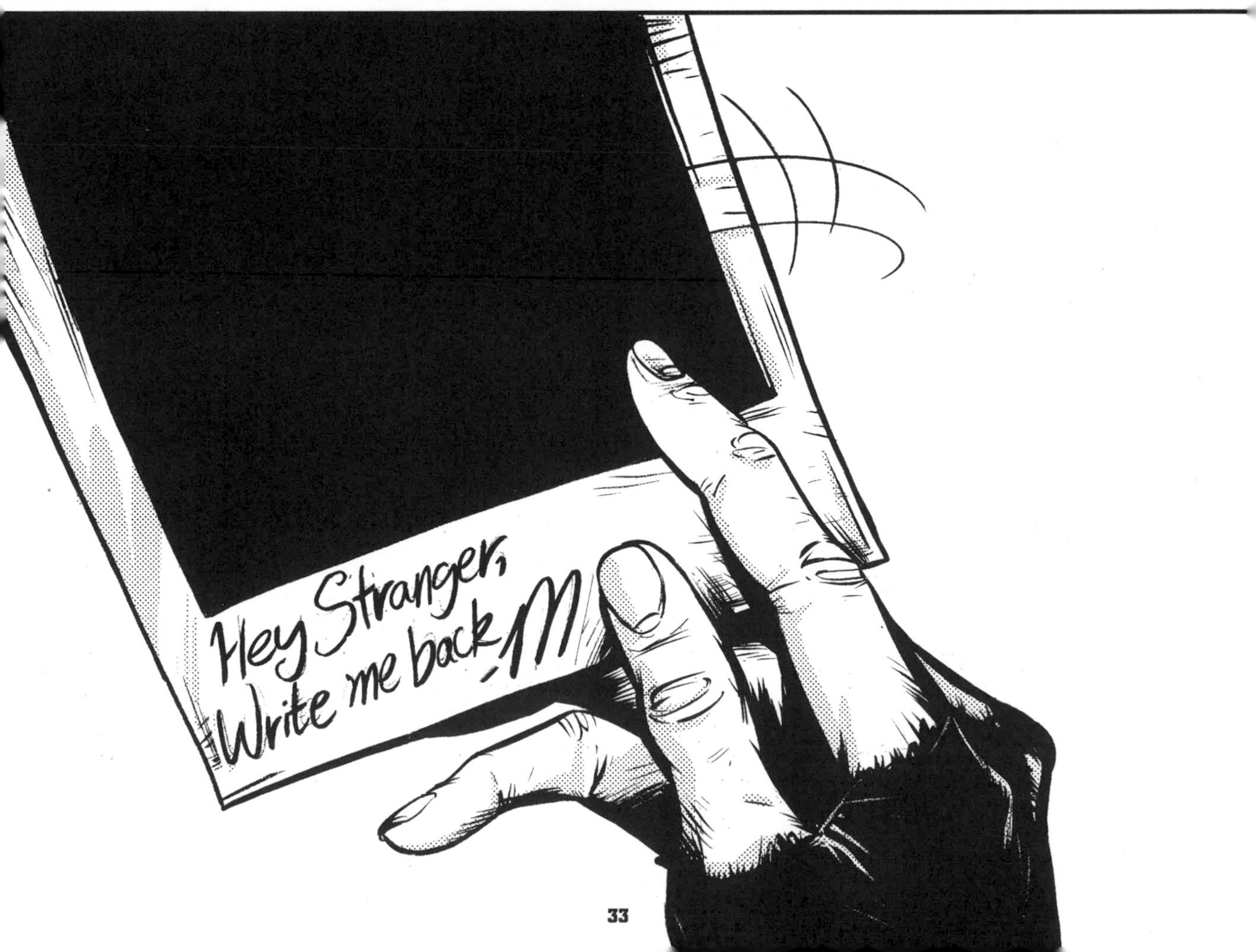
Hey Stranger,
Write me back -M

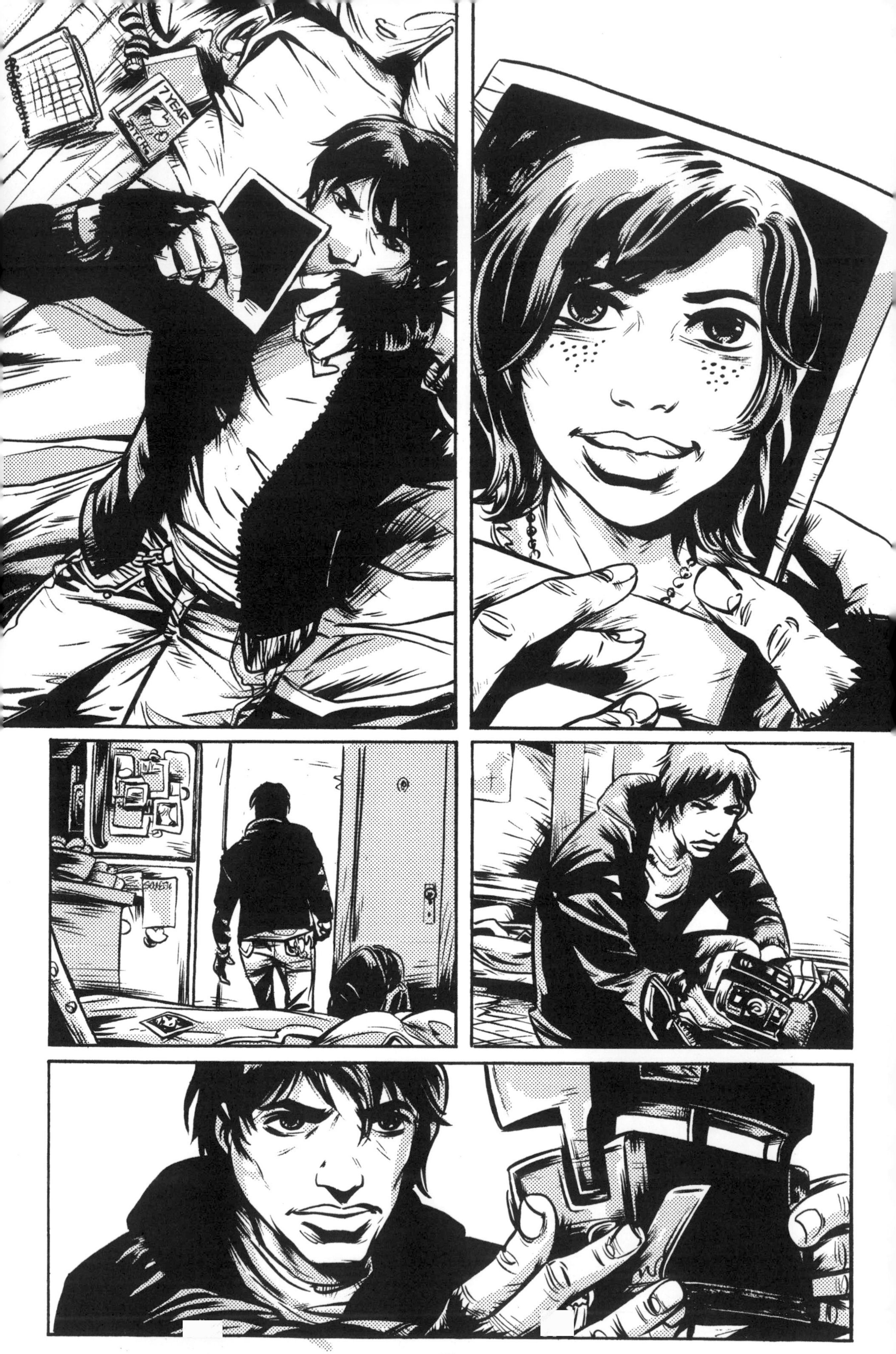
7 YEAR BITCH

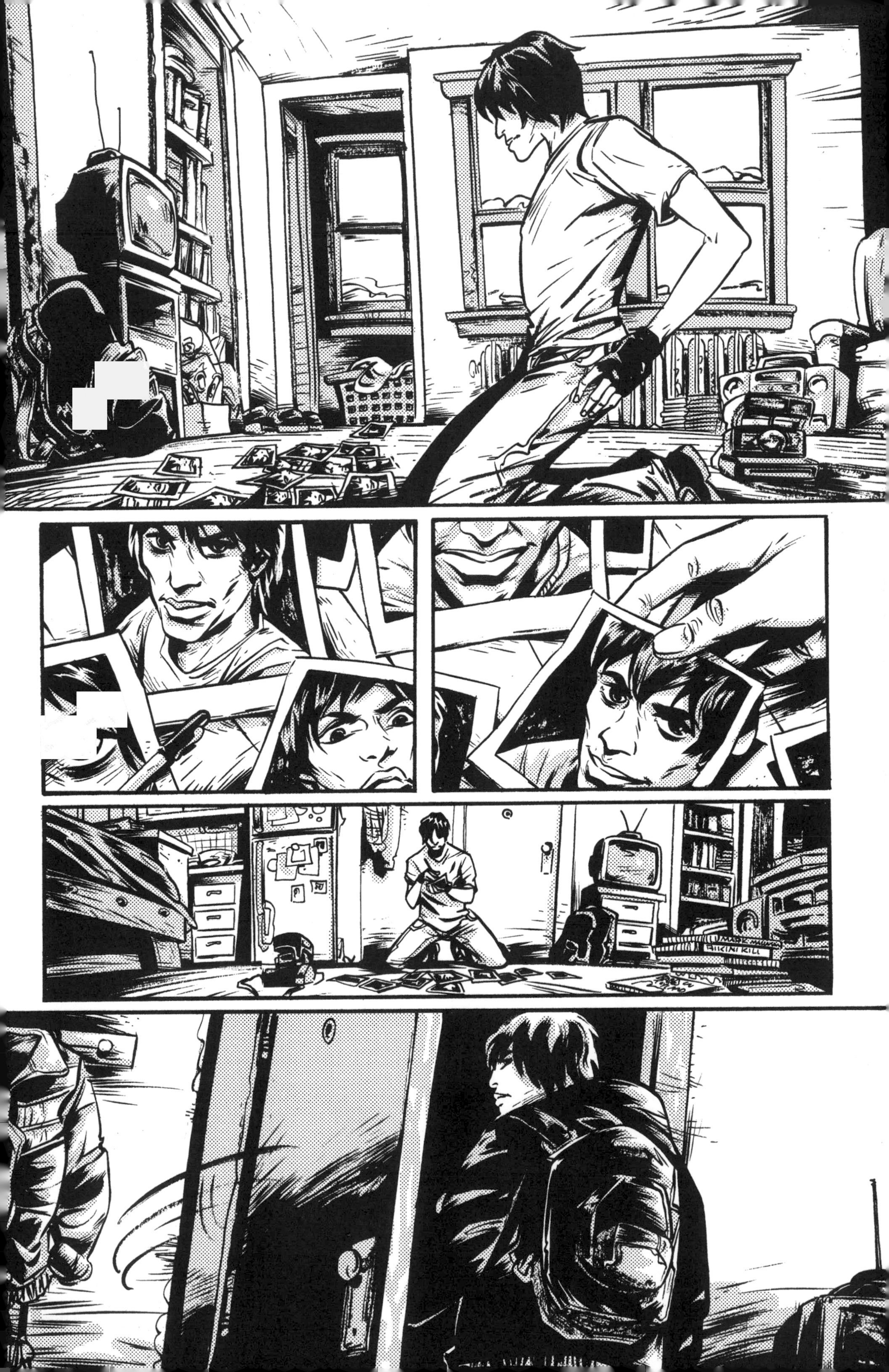
BIKINI KILL

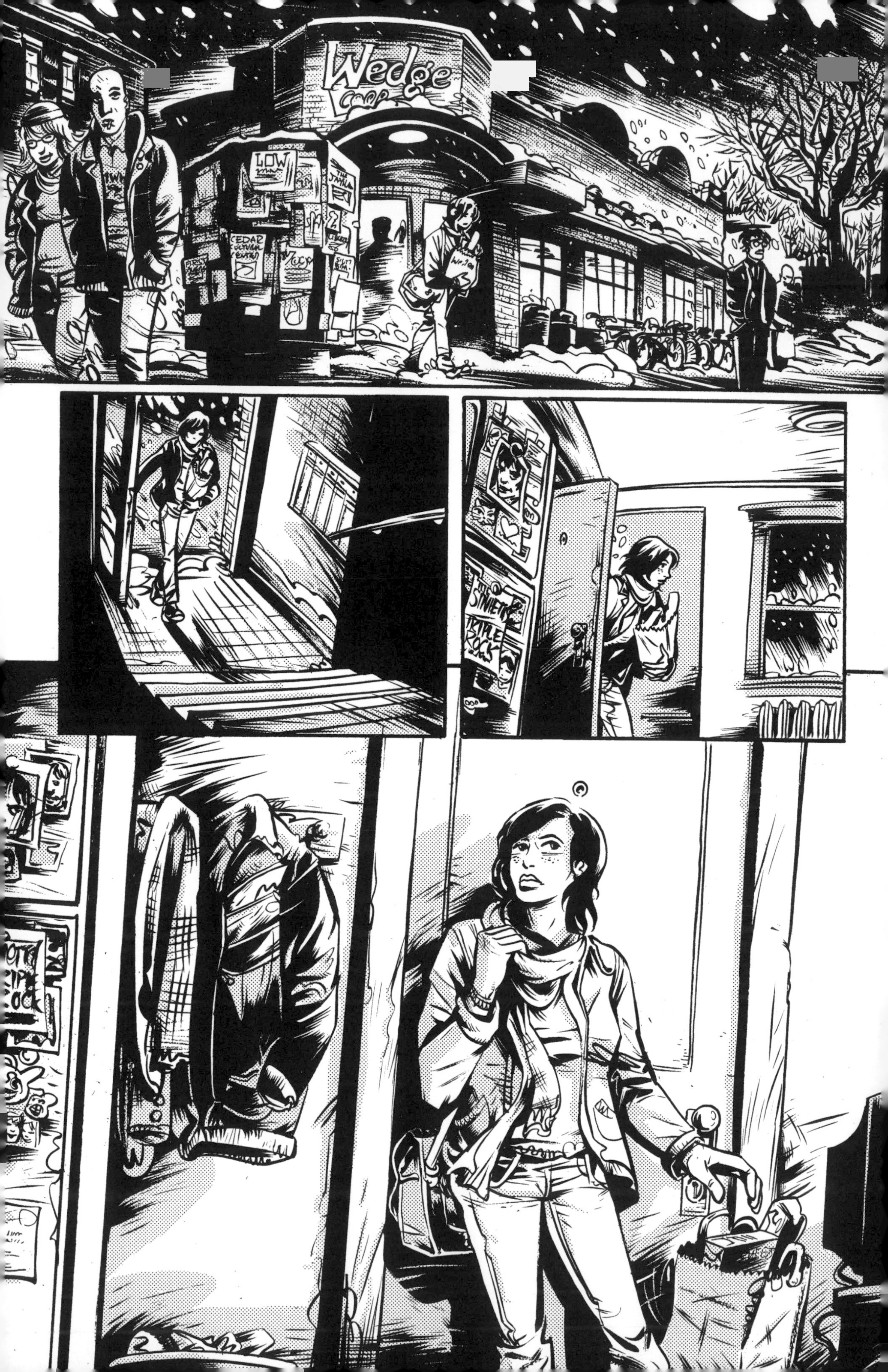

Wedge
LOW
TRIPLE ROCK

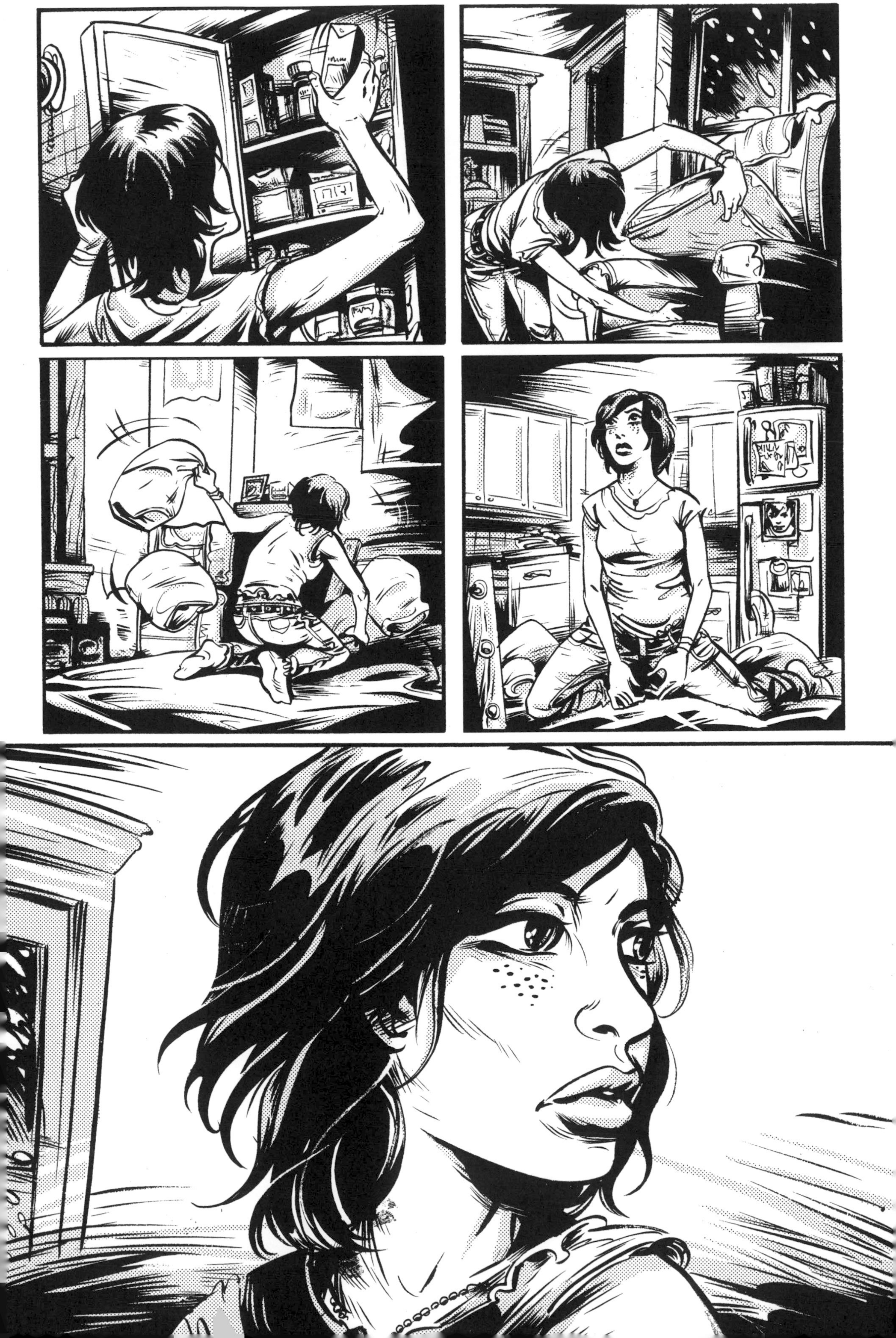

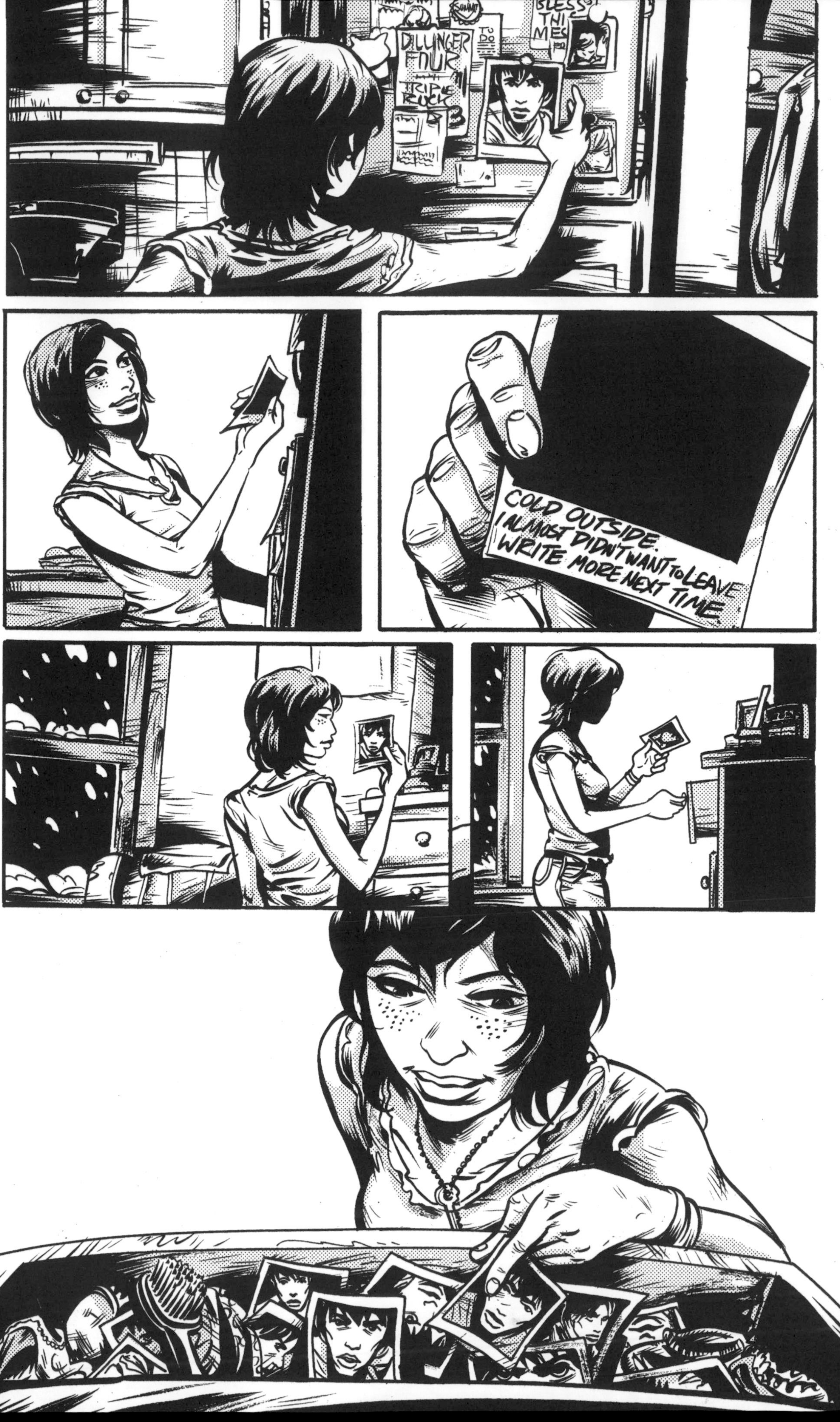
DILLINGER FOUR
COLD OUTSIDE.
I ALMOST DIDN'T WANT TO LEAVE
WRITE MORE NEXT TIME

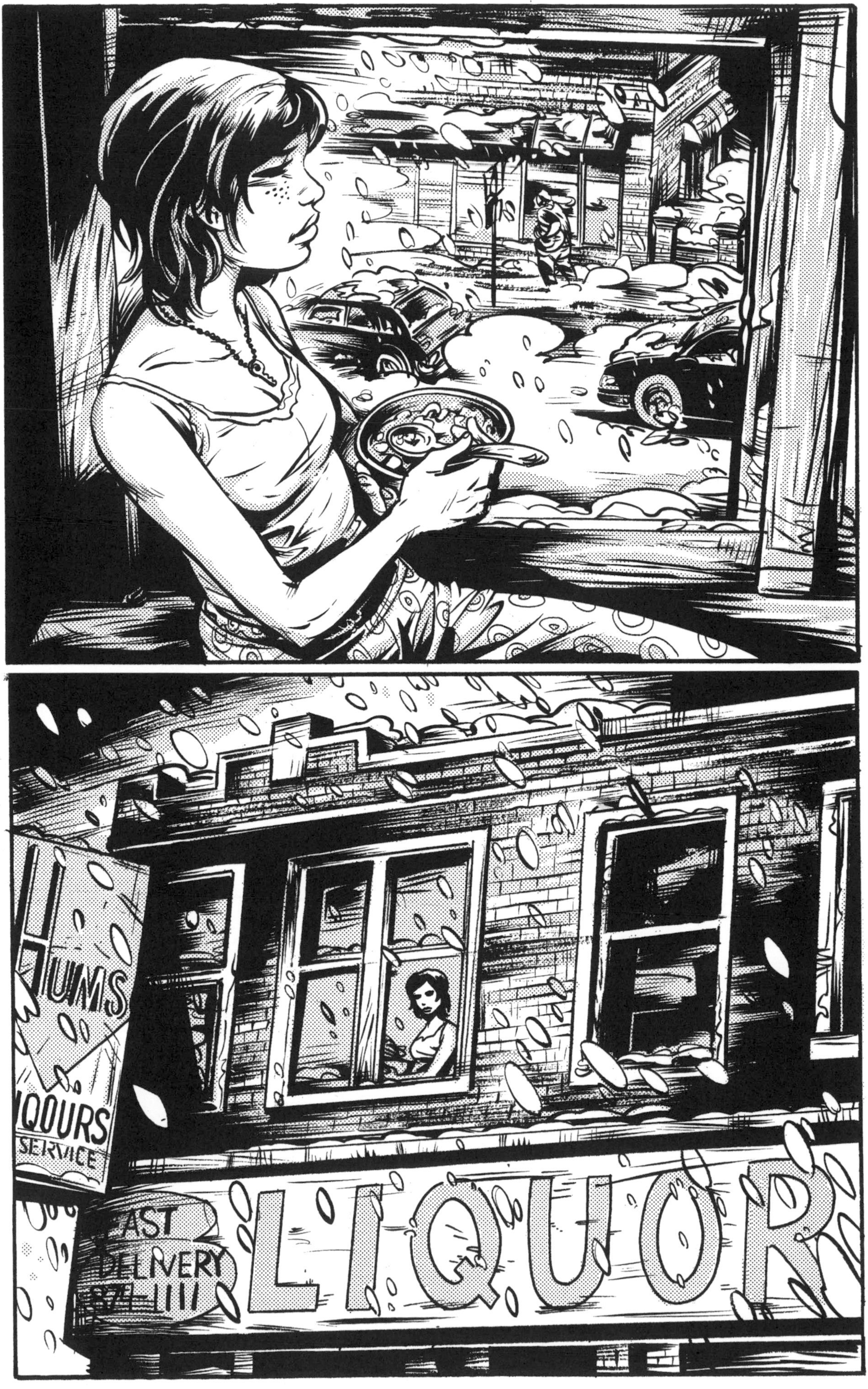
HUMS
IQOURS
SERVICE
AST
DELIVERY
LIQUOR

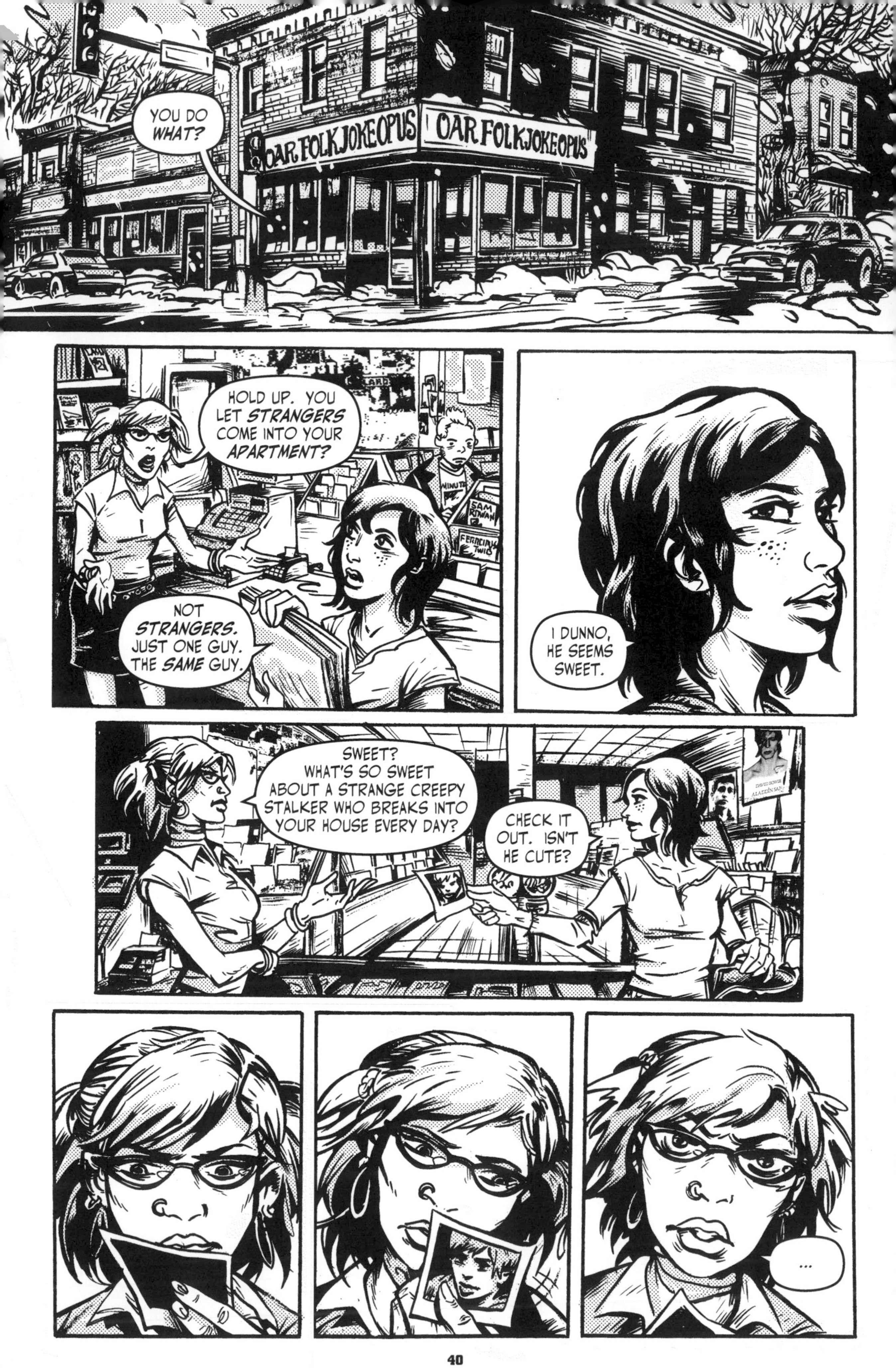

OAR FOLKJOKEOPUS
OAR FOLKJOKEOPUS
YOU DO WHAT?
HOLD UP. YOU LET STRANGERS COME INTO YOUR APARTMENT?
NOT STRANGERS. JUST ONE GUY. THE SAME GUY.
I DUNNO, HE SEEMS SWEET.
SWEET? WHAT'S SO SWEET ABOUT A STRANGE CREEPY STALKER WHO BREAKS INTO YOUR HOUSE EVERY DAY?
CHECK IT OUT. ISN'T HE CUTE?
DAVID BOWIE
ALADDIN SANE
...

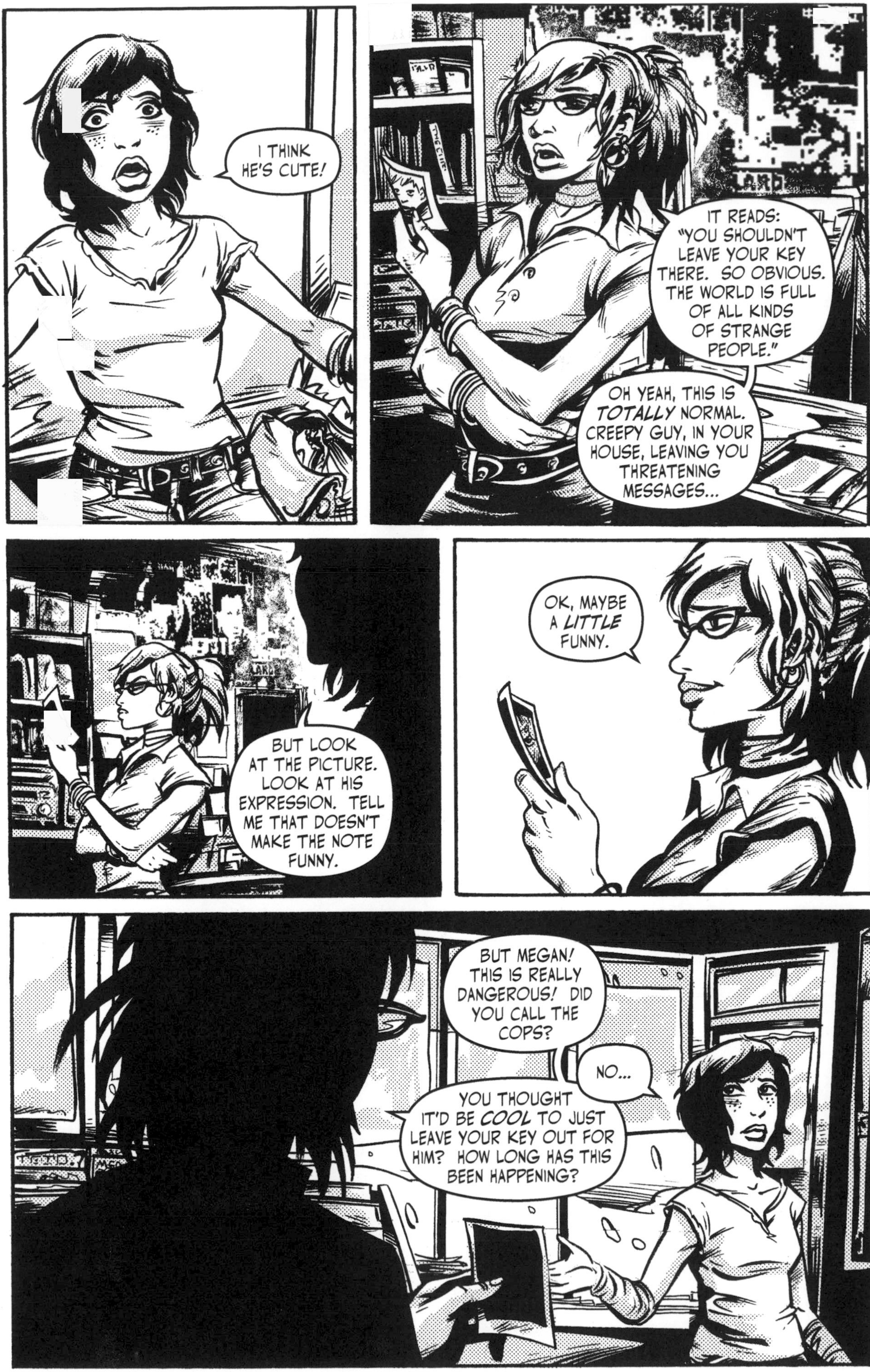
I THINK HE'S CUTE!
IT READS: "YOU SHOULDN'T LEAVE YOUR KEY THERE. SO OBVIOUS. THE WORLD IS FULL OF ALL KINDS OF STRANGE PEOPLE."
OH YEAH, THIS IS *TOTALLY* NORMAL. CREEPY GUY, IN YOUR HOUSE, LEAVING YOU THREATENING MESSAGES...
BUT LOOK AT THE PICTURE. LOOK AT HIS EXPRESSION. TELL ME THAT DOESN'T MAKE THE NOTE FUNNY.
OK, MAYBE A *LITTLE* FUNNY.
BUT MEGAN! THIS IS REALLY DANGEROUS! DID YOU CALL THE COPS?
NO...
YOU THOUGHT IT'D BE *COOL* TO JUST LEAVE YOUR KEY OUT FOR HIM? HOW LONG HAS THIS BEEN HAPPENING?

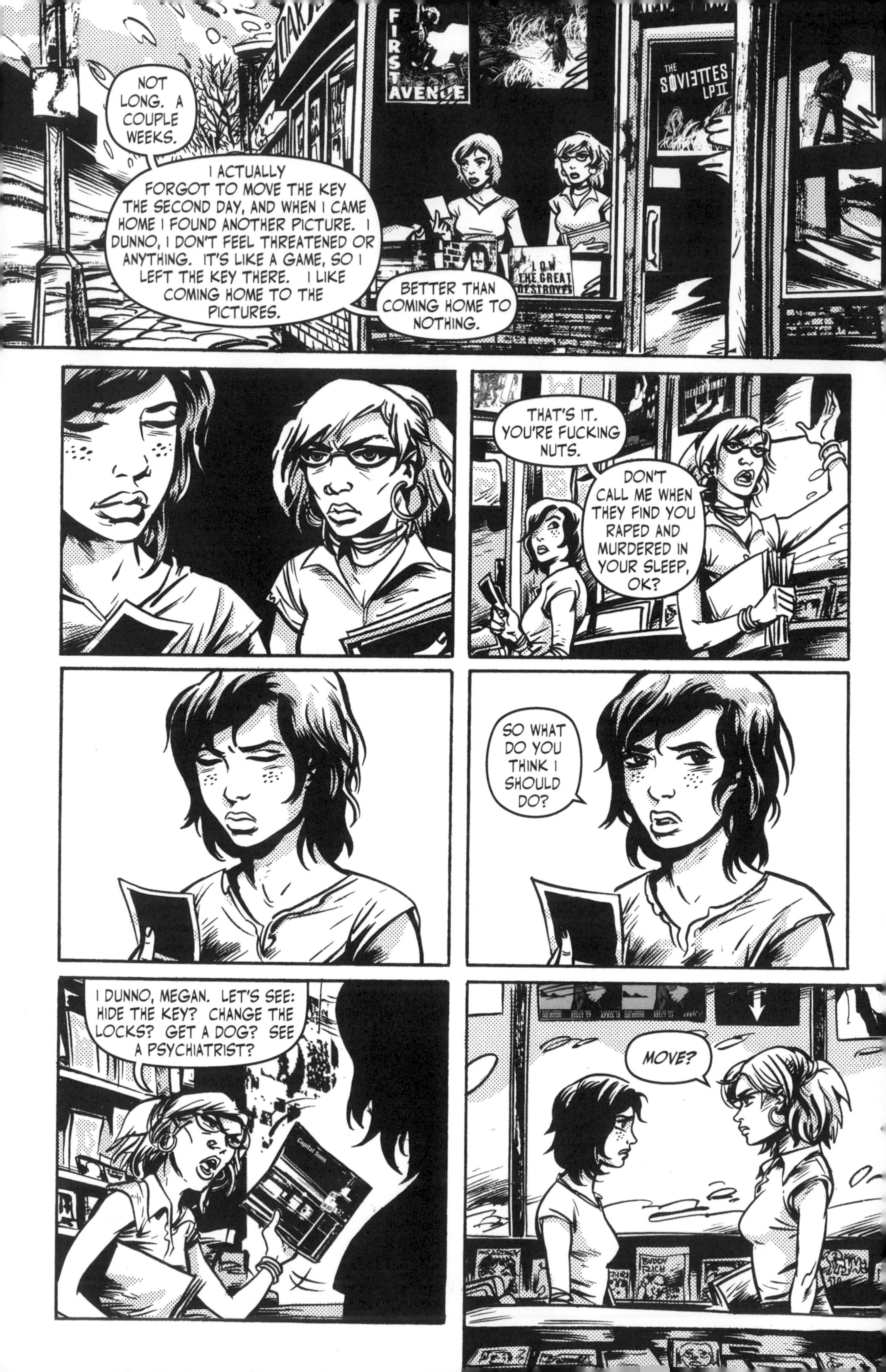
FIRST AVENUE
THE SOVIETTES LP II
NOT LONG. A COUPLE WEEKS.
I ACTUALLY FORGOT TO MOVE THE KEY THE SECOND DAY, AND WHEN I CAME HOME I FOUND ANOTHER PICTURE. I DUNNO, I DON'T FEEL THREATENED OR ANYTHING. IT'S LIKE A GAME, SO I LEFT THE KEY THERE. I LIKE COMING HOME TO THE PICTURES.
LOW THE GREAT DESTROYER
BETTER THAN COMING HOME TO NOTHING.
SLEATER-KINNEY
THAT'S IT. YOU'RE FUCKING NUTS.
DON'T CALL ME WHEN THEY FIND YOU RAPED AND MURDERED IN YOUR SLEEP, OK?
SO WHAT DO YOU THINK I SHOULD DO?
I DUNNO, MEGAN. LET'S SEE: HIDE THE KEY? CHANGE THE LOCKS? GET A DOG? SEE A PSYCHIATRIST?
Capital Sons
MOVE?

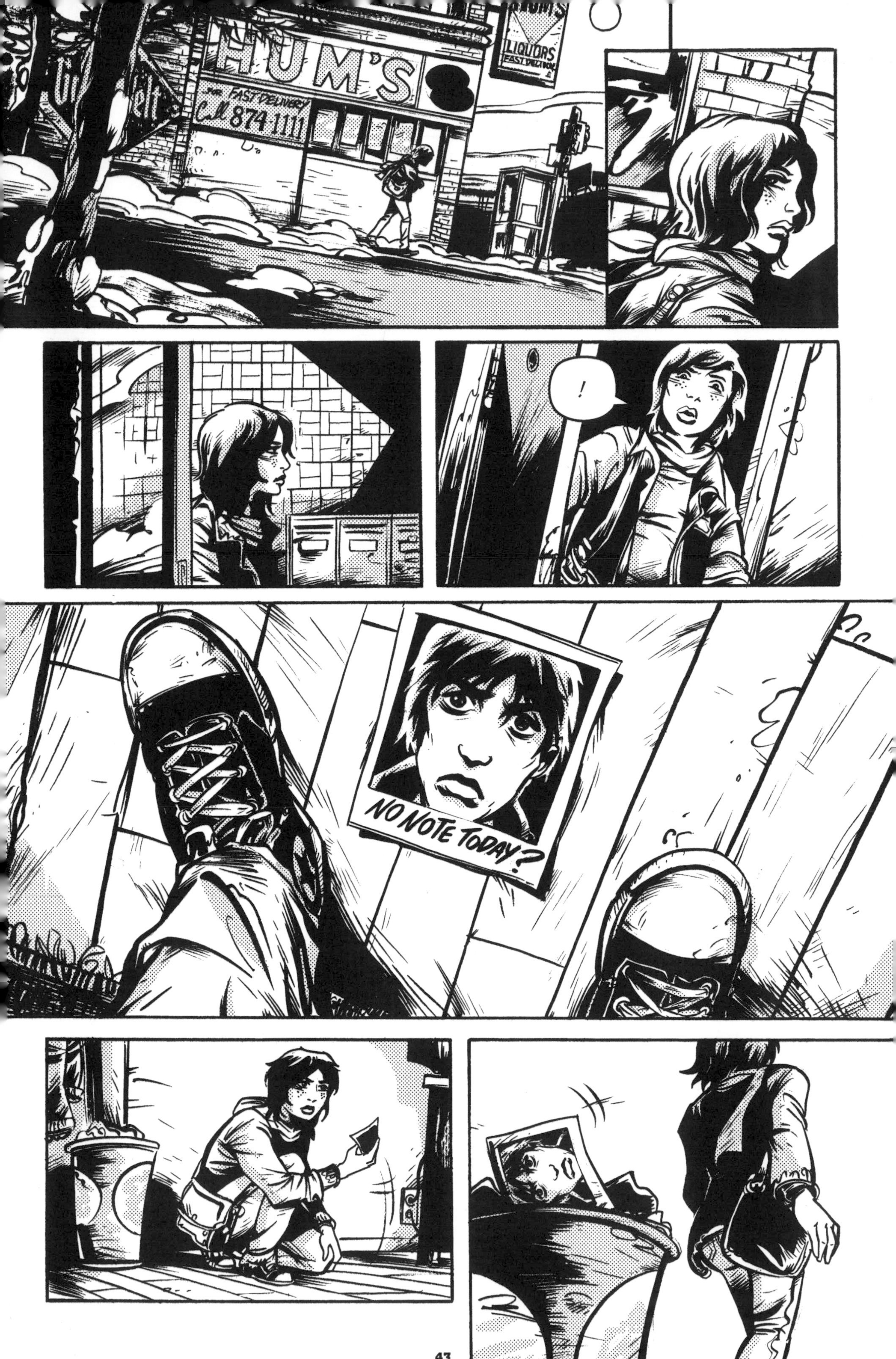
HUM'S
FAST DELIVERY
Call 874-1111
LIQUORS
!
NO NOTE TODAY?

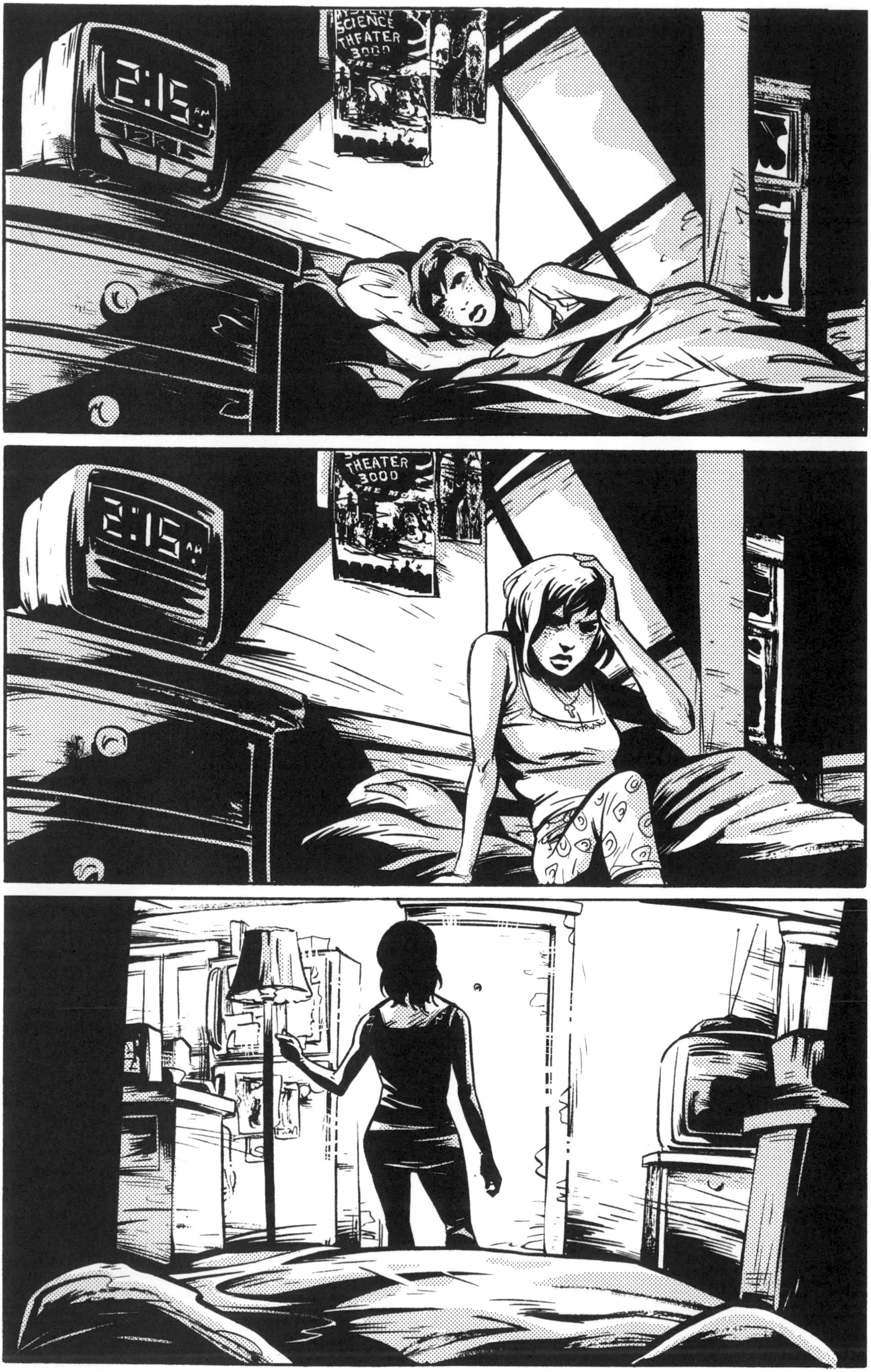
2:15 AM
SCIENCE
THEATER
3000
2:15 AM
THEATER
3000

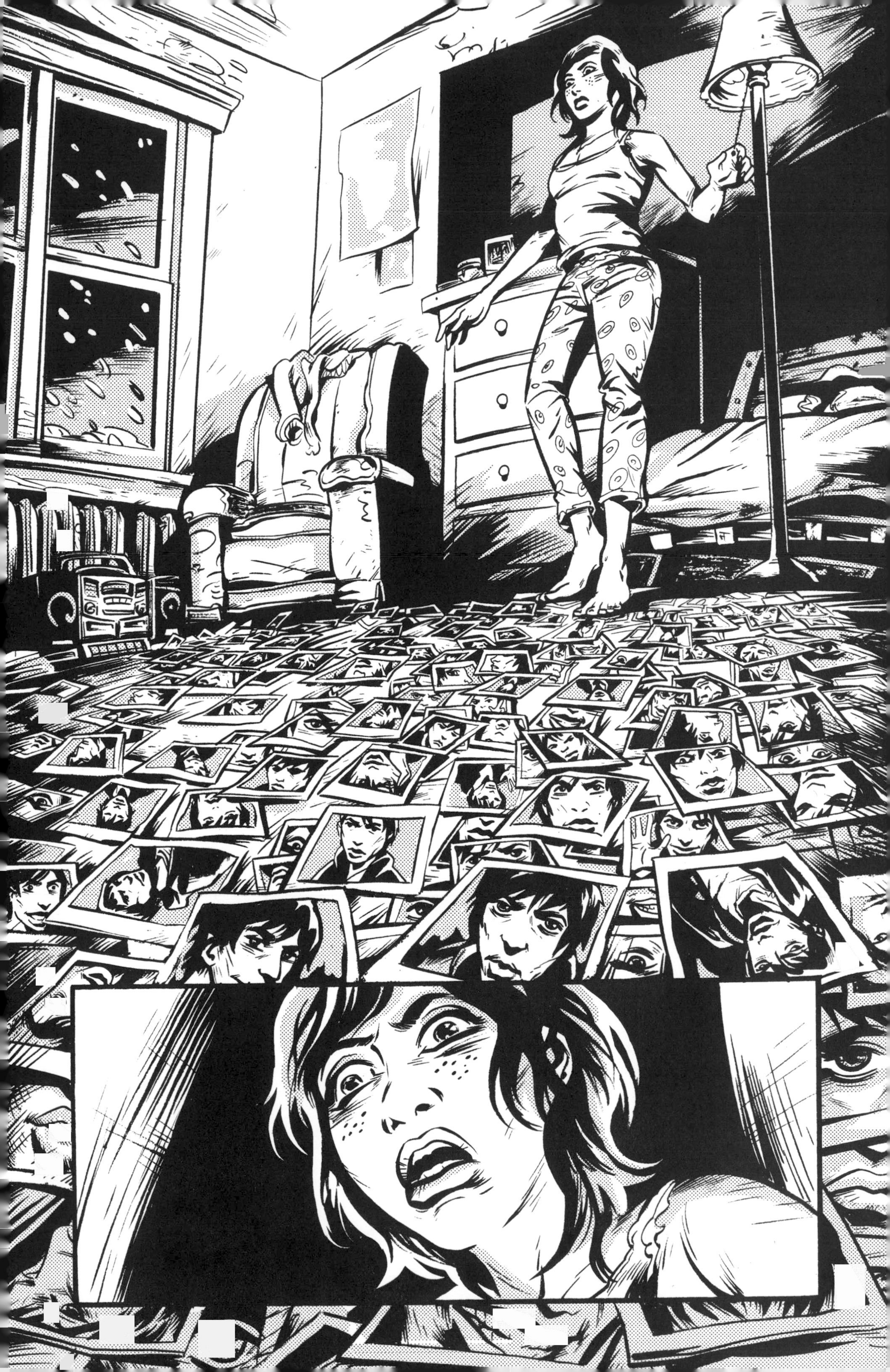

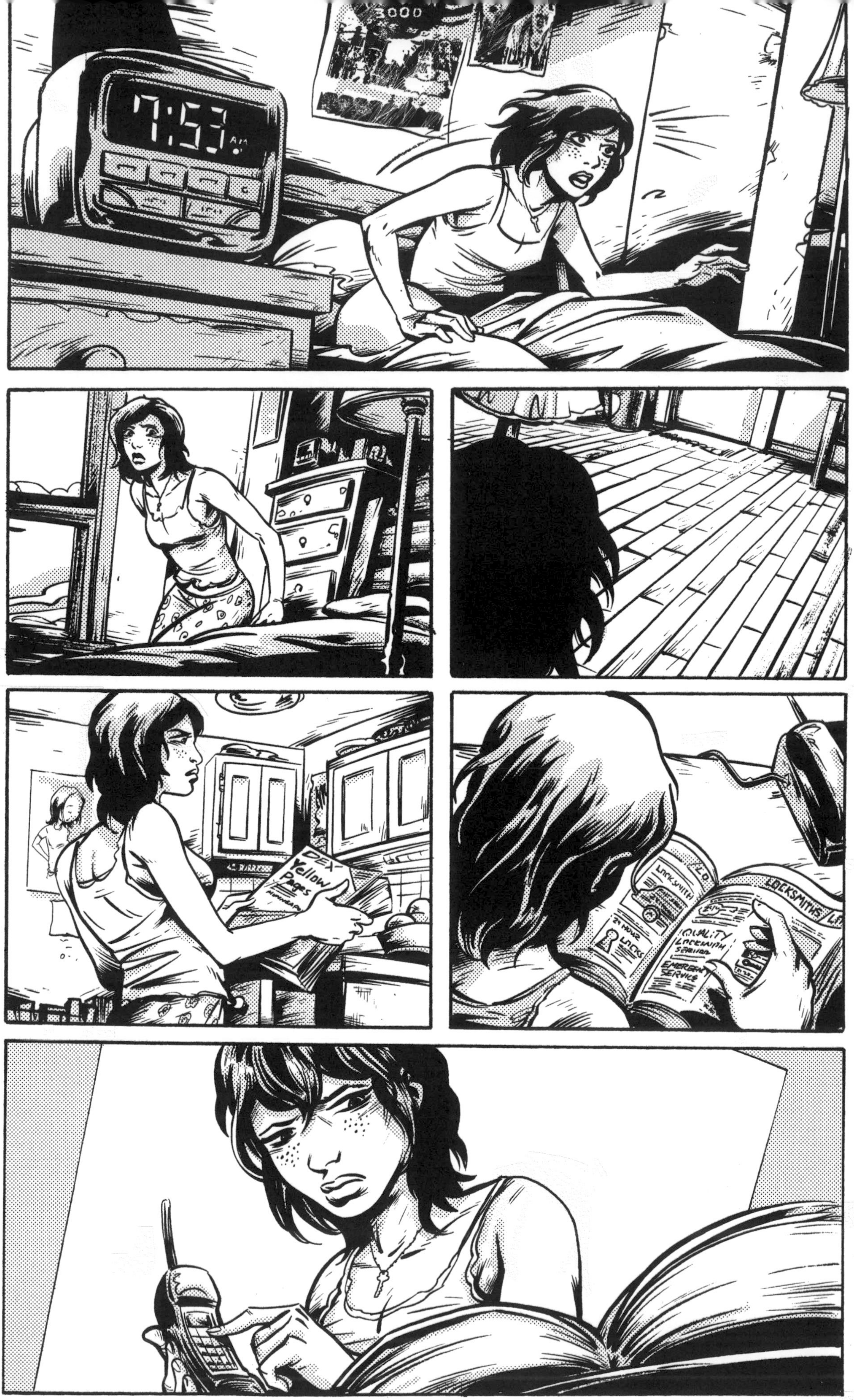
7:53 AM
DEX Yellow Pages
LOCKSMITHS
QUALITY LOCKSMITH SERVICE
EMERGENCY SERVICE

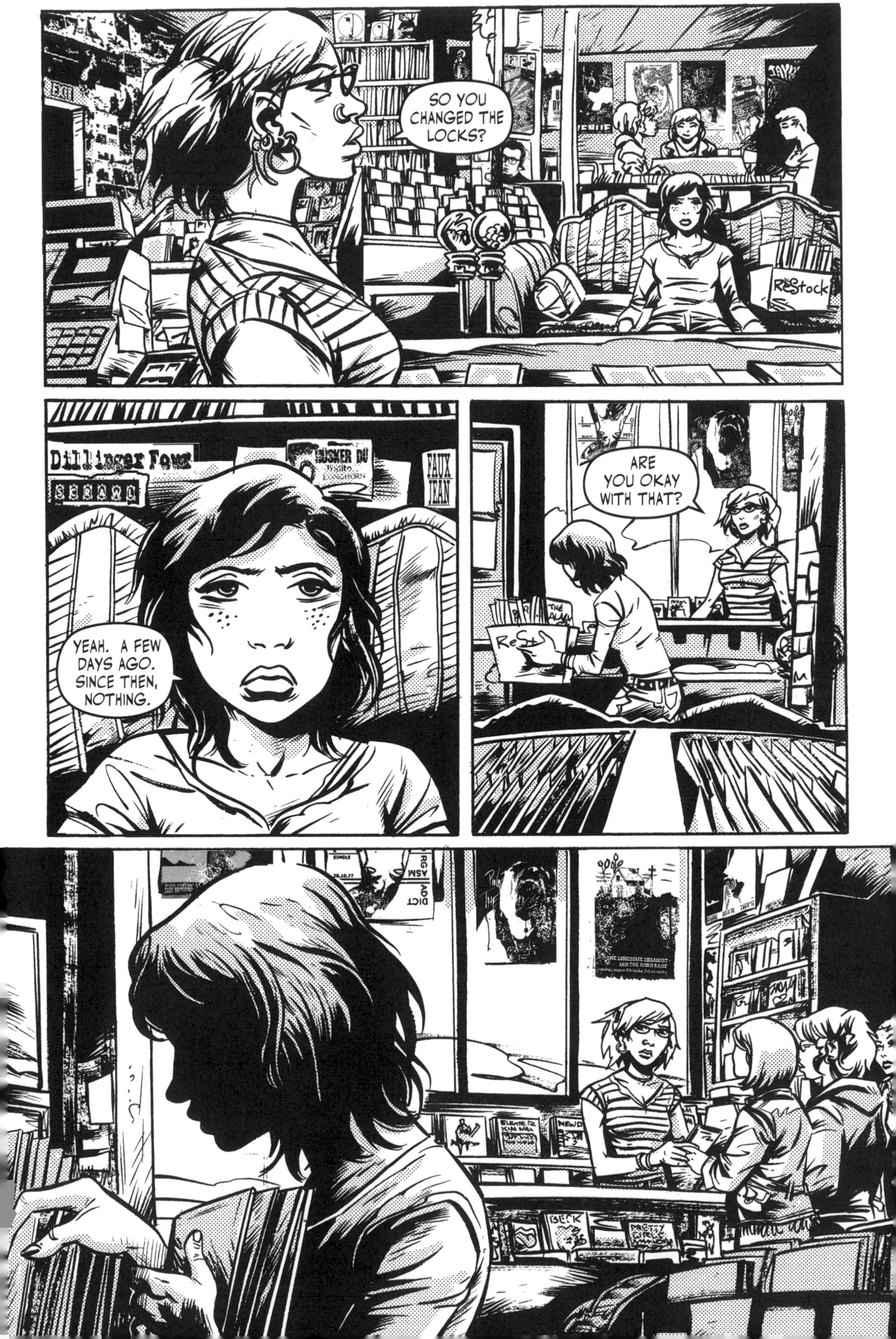
SO YOU CHANGED THE LOCKS?
ReStock
Dillinger Four
HUSKER DU
FAUX JEAN
YEAH. A FEW DAYS AGO. SINCE THEN, NOTHING.
ARE YOU OKAY WITH THAT?
THE LONESOME ORGANIST
BECK
PRETTY GIRLS

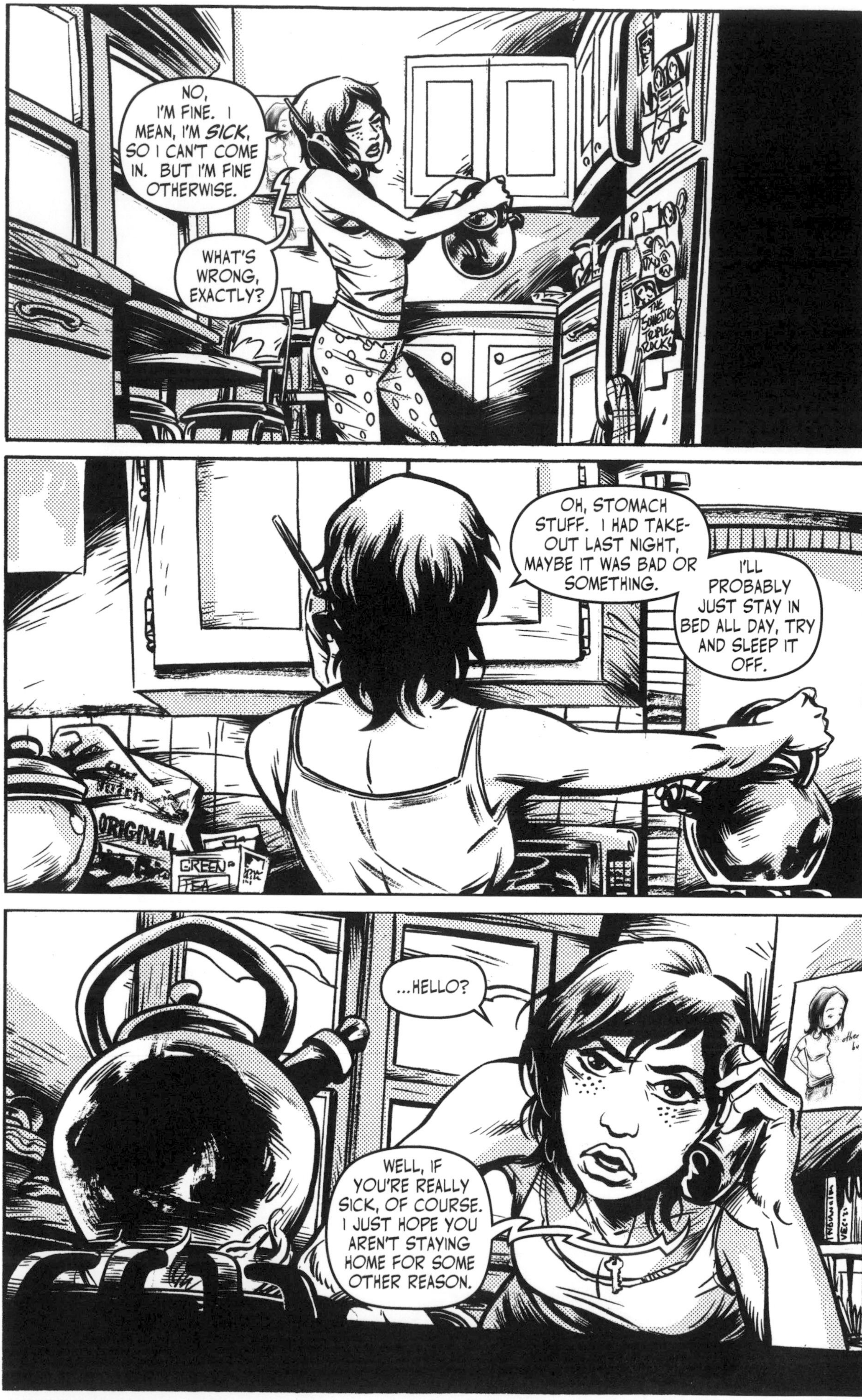
NO, I'M FINE. I MEAN, I'M *SICK*, SO I CAN'T COME IN. BUT I'M FINE OTHERWISE.
WHAT'S WRONG, EXACTLY?
OH, STOMACH STUFF. I HAD TAKE-OUT LAST NIGHT, MAYBE IT WAS BAD OR SOMETHING.
I'LL PROBABLY JUST STAY IN BED ALL DAY, TRY AND SLEEP IT OFF.
ORIGINAL
GREEN TEA
...HELLO?
WELL, IF YOU'RE REALLY SICK, OF COURSE. I JUST HOPE YOU AREN'T STAYING HOME FOR SOME OTHER REASON.

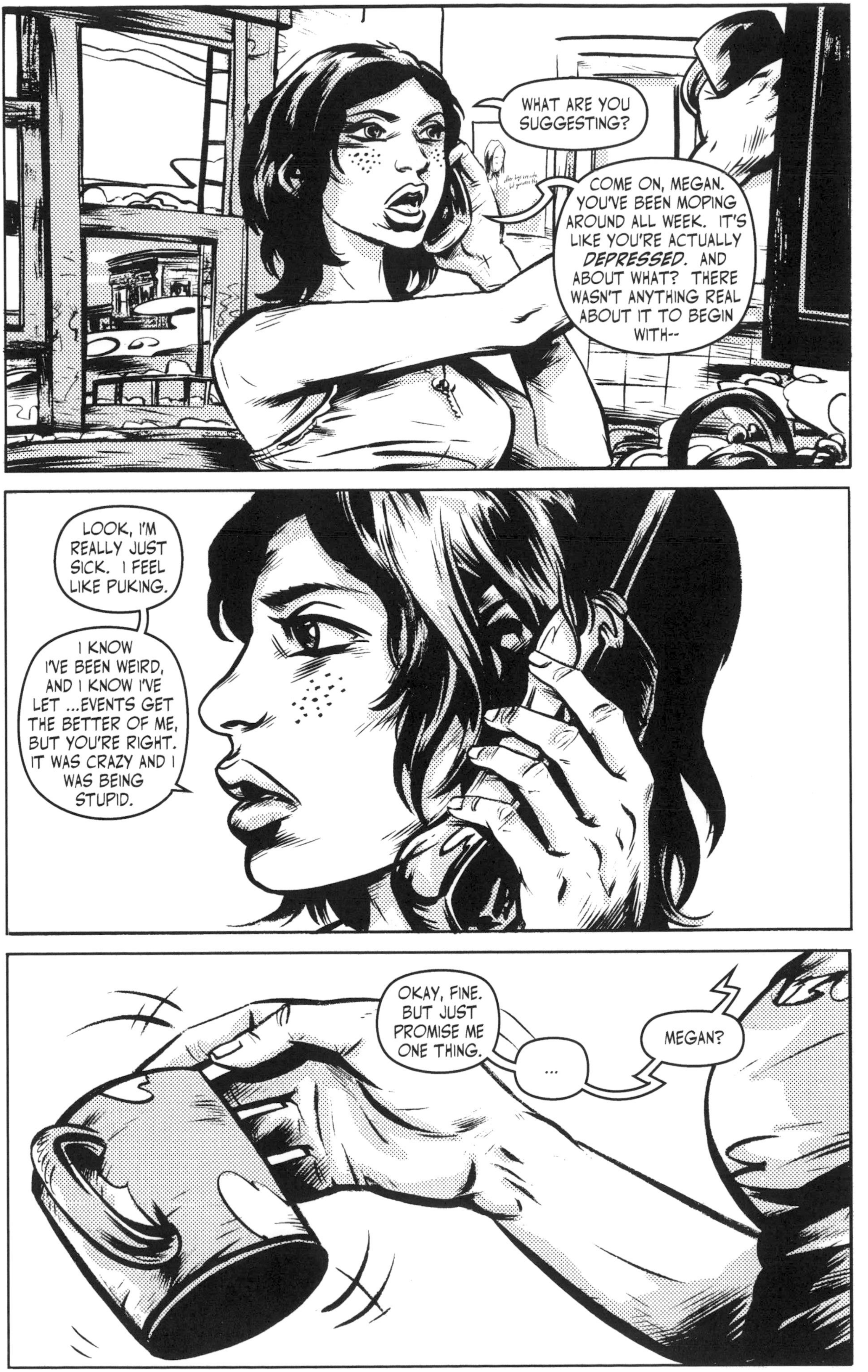
WHAT ARE YOU SUGGESTING?
COME ON, MEGAN. YOU'VE BEEN MOPING AROUND ALL WEEK. IT'S LIKE YOU'RE ACTUALLY *DEPRESSED.* AND ABOUT WHAT? THERE WASN'T ANYTHING REAL ABOUT IT TO BEGIN WITH--
LOOK, I'M REALLY JUST SICK. I FEEL LIKE PUKING.
I KNOW I'VE BEEN WEIRD, AND I KNOW I'VE LET ...EVENTS GET THE BETTER OF ME, BUT YOU'RE RIGHT. IT WAS CRAZY AND I WAS BEING STUPID.
OKAY, FINE. BUT JUST PROMISE ME ONE THING.
...
MEGAN?

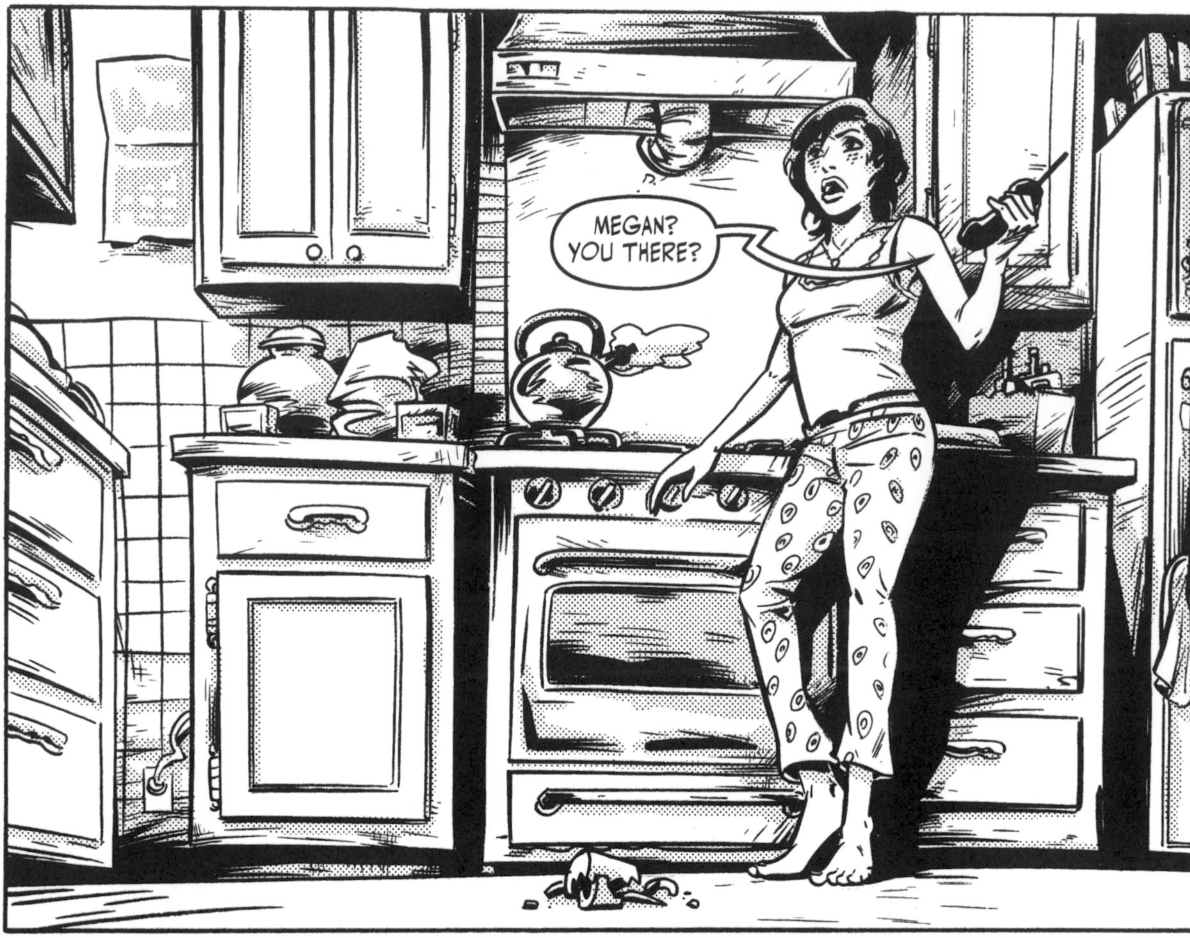
MEGAN? YOU THERE?

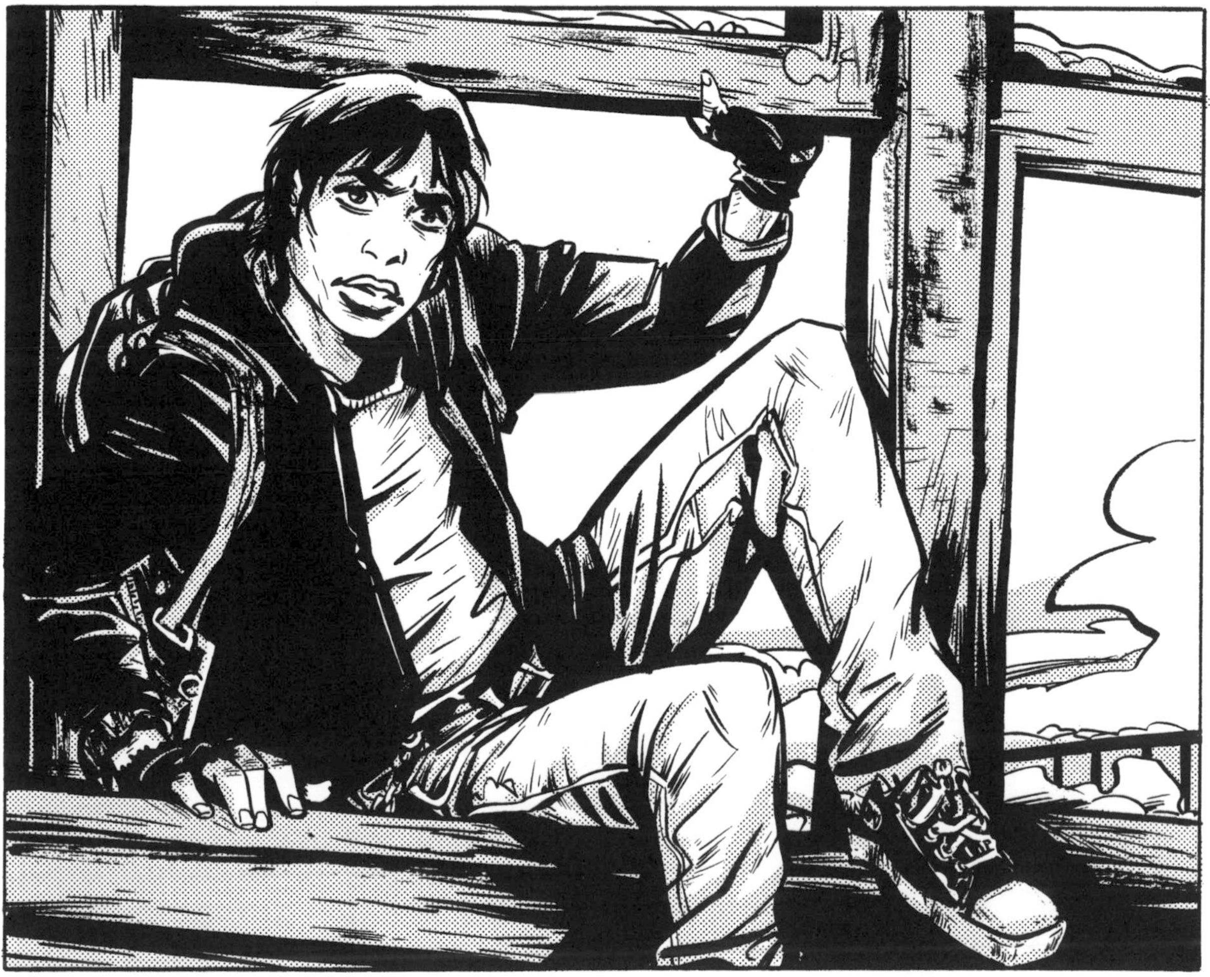

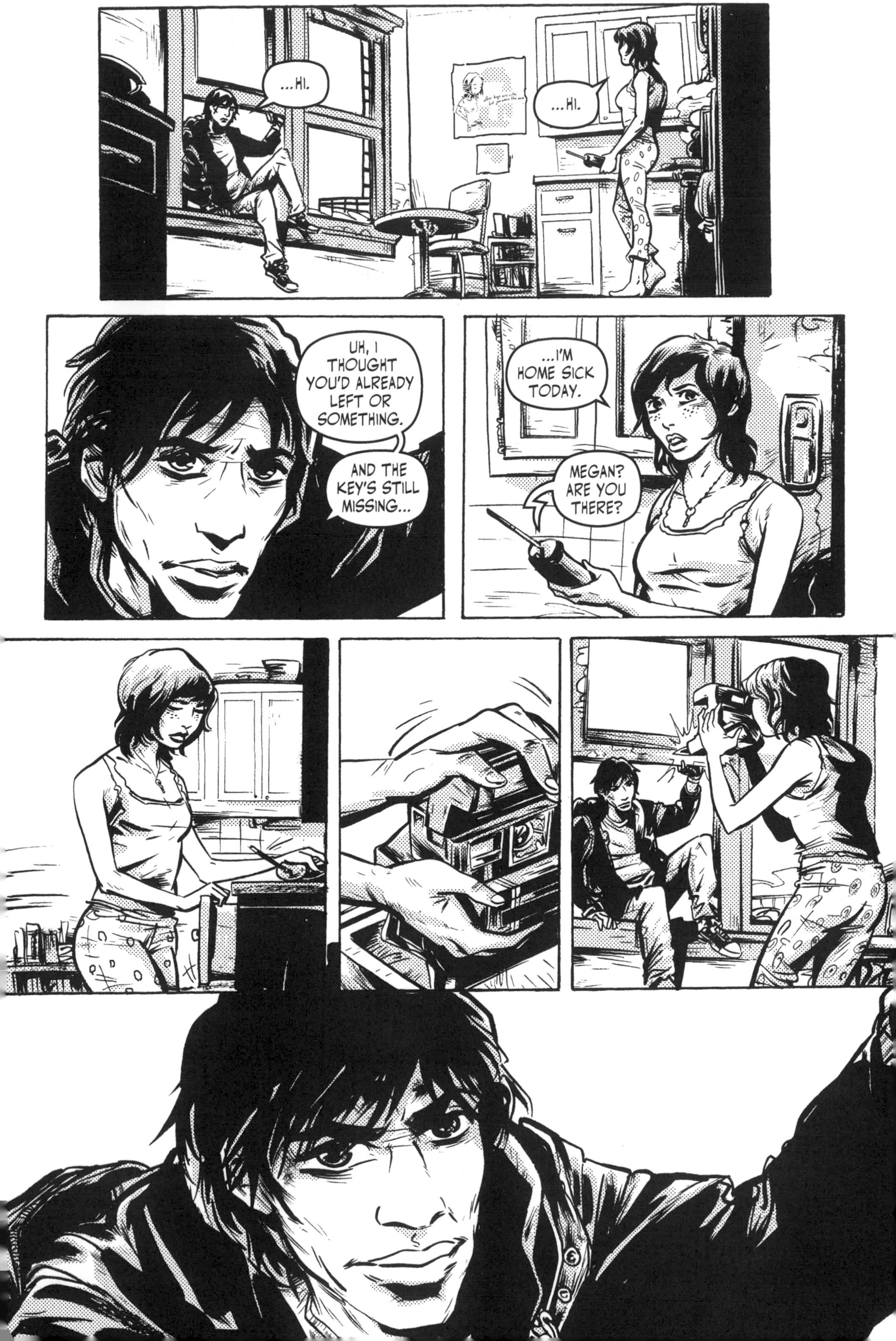
...HI.
...HI.
UH, I THOUGHT YOU'D ALREADY LEFT OR SOMETHING.
AND THE KEY'S STILL MISSING...
...I'M HOME SICK TODAY.
MEGAN? ARE YOU THERE?

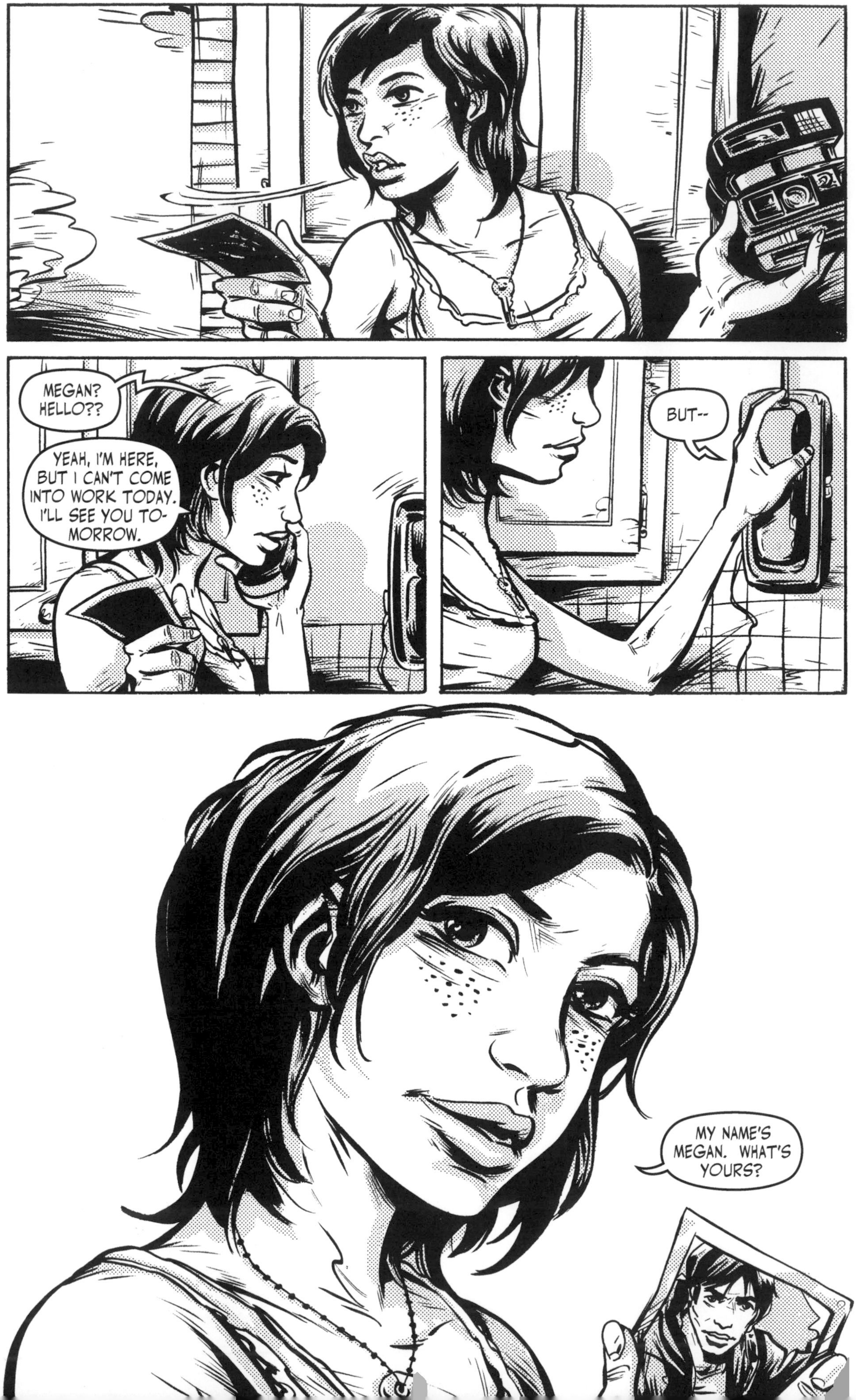
MEGAN? HELLO??
YEAH, I'M HERE, BUT I CAN'T COME INTO WORK TODAY. I'LL SEE YOU TO-MORROW.
BUT--
MY NAME'S MEGAN. WHAT'S YOURS?

CHAPTER 3
"THEORIES AND DEFENSES"
Richmond, Virginia

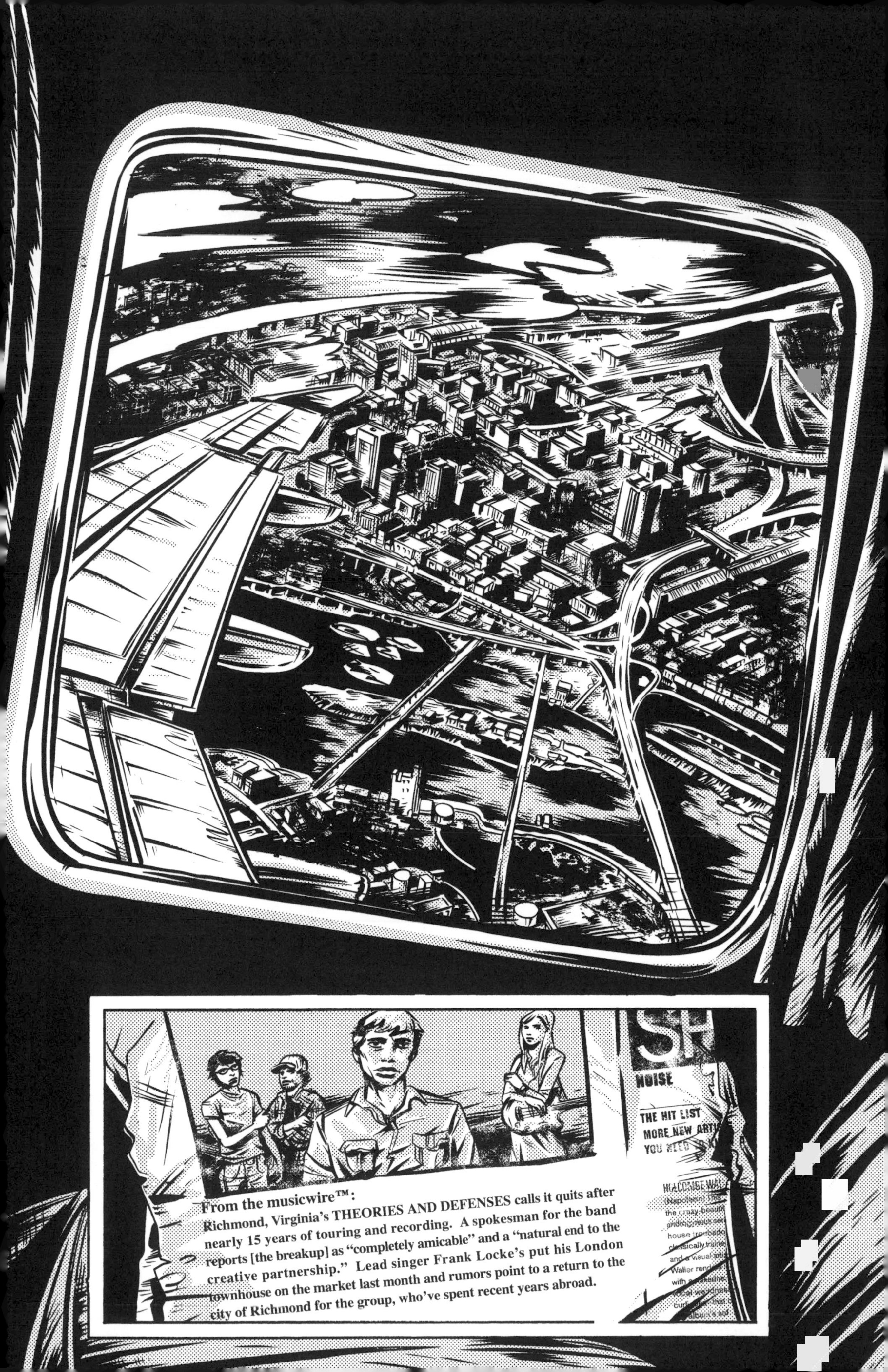
NOISE
THE HIT LIST
From the musicwire™:
Richmond, Virginia's THEORIES AND DEFENSES calls it quits after
nearly 15 years of touring and recording. A spokesman for the band
reports [the breakup] as "completely amicable" and a "natural end to the
creative partnership." Lead singer Frank Locke's put his London
townhouse on the market last month and rumors point to a return to the
city of Richmond for the group, who've spent recent years abroad.

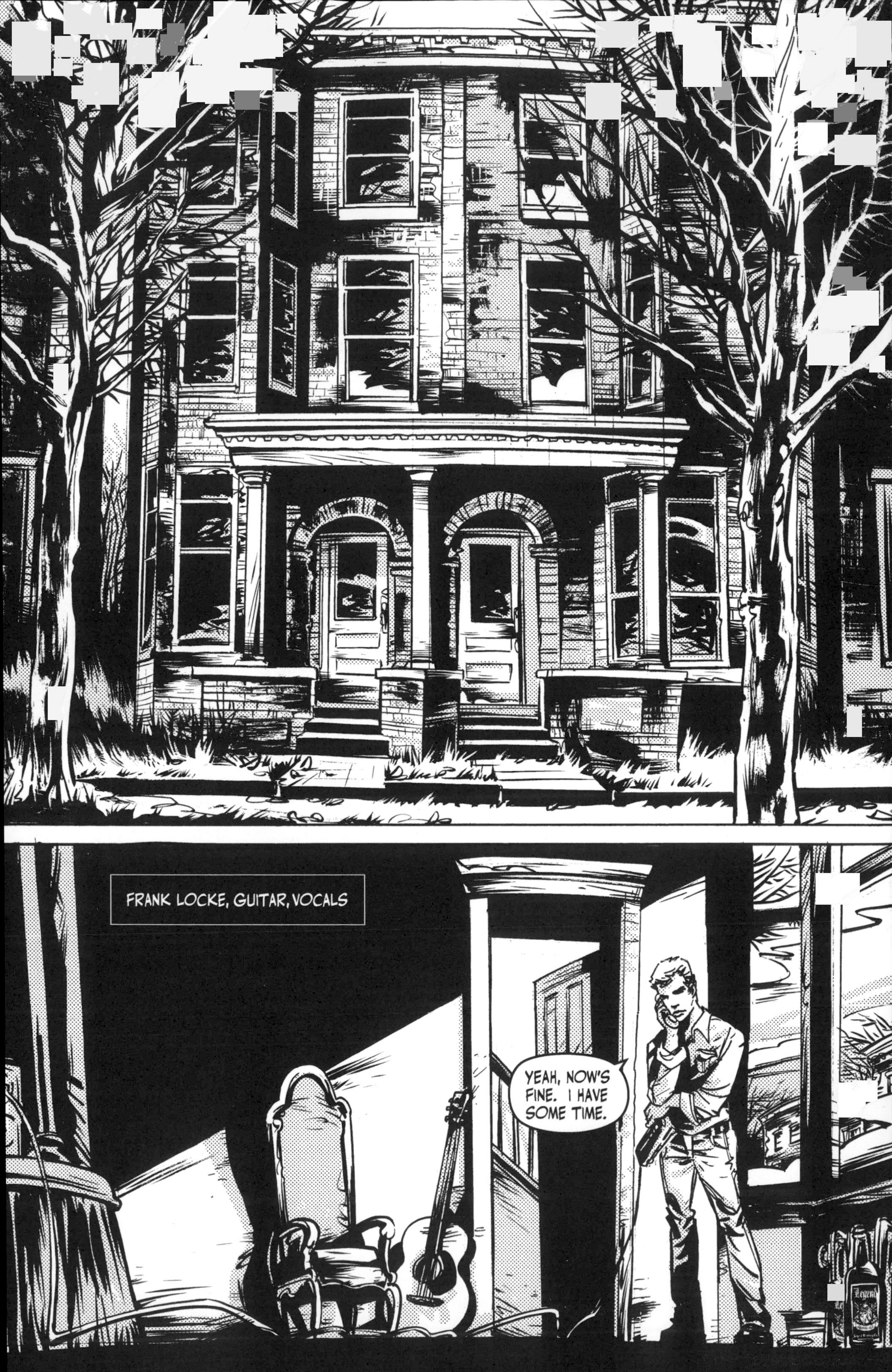
FRANK LOCKE, GUITAR, VOCALS
YEAH, NOW'S FINE. I HAVE SOME TIME.

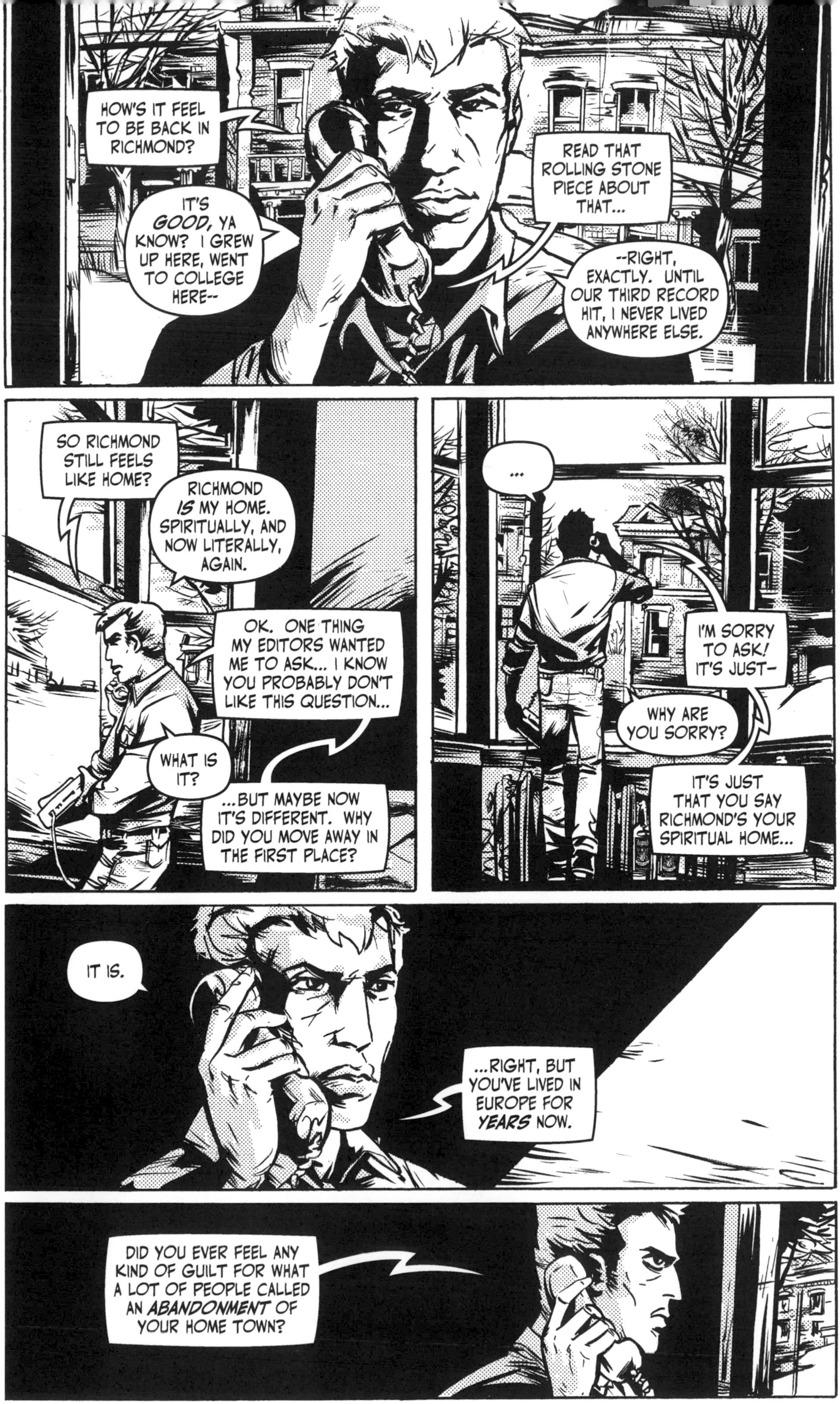
HOW'S IT FEEL TO BE BACK IN RICHMOND?
IT'S *GOOD*, YA KNOW? I GREW UP HERE, WENT TO COLLEGE HERE--
READ THAT ROLLING STONE PIECE ABOUT THAT...
--RIGHT, EXACTLY. UNTIL OUR THIRD RECORD HIT, I NEVER LIVED ANYWHERE ELSE.
SO RICHMOND STILL FEELS LIKE HOME?
RICHMOND *IS* MY HOME. SPIRITUALLY, AND NOW LITERALLY, AGAIN.
OK. ONE THING MY EDITORS WANTED ME TO ASK... I KNOW YOU PROBABLY DON'T LIKE THIS QUESTION...
WHAT IS IT?
...BUT MAYBE NOW IT'S DIFFERENT. WHY DID YOU MOVE AWAY IN THE FIRST PLACE?
...
I'M SORRY TO ASK! IT'S JUST-
WHY ARE YOU SORRY?
IT'S JUST THAT YOU SAY RICHMOND'S YOUR SPIRITUAL HOME...
IT IS.
...RIGHT, BUT YOU'VE LIVED IN EUROPE FOR *YEARS* NOW.
DID YOU EVER FEEL ANY KIND OF GUILT FOR WHAT A LOT OF PEOPLE CALLED AN *ABANDONMENT* OF YOUR HOME TOWN?

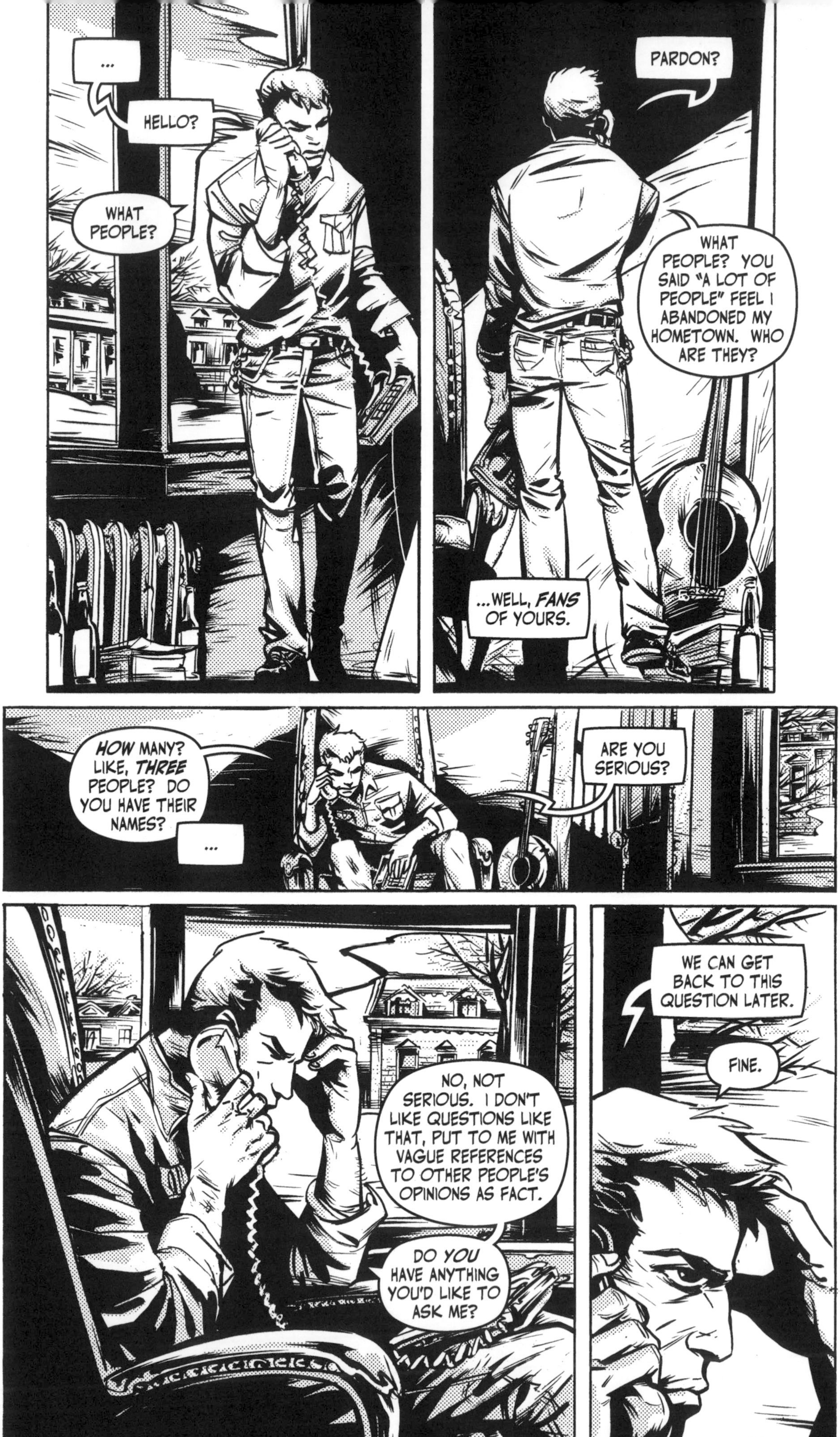
...
HELLO?
WHAT PEOPLE?
PARDON?
WHAT PEOPLE? YOU SAID "A LOT OF PEOPLE" FEEL I ABANDONED MY HOMETOWN. WHO ARE THEY?
...WELL, *FANS* OF YOURS.
HOW MANY? LIKE, *THREE* PEOPLE? DO YOU HAVE THEIR NAMES?
...
ARE YOU SERIOUS?
NO, NOT SERIOUS. I DON'T LIKE QUESTIONS LIKE THAT, PUT TO ME WITH VAGUE REFERENCES TO OTHER PEOPLE'S OPINIONS AS FACT.
DO *YOU* HAVE ANYTHING YOU'D LIKE TO ASK ME?
WE CAN GET BACK TO THIS QUESTION LATER.
FINE.

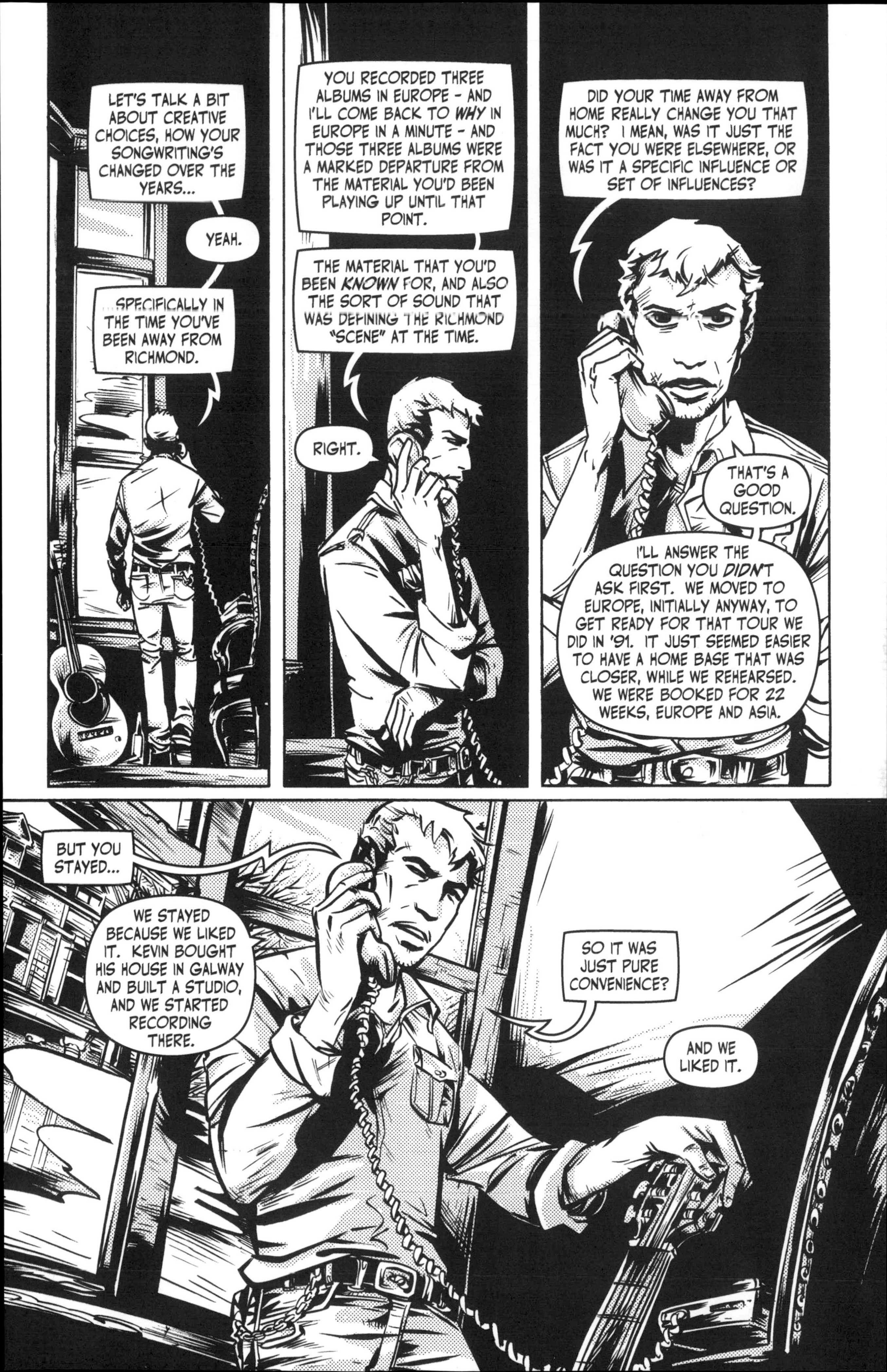
LET'S TALK A BIT ABOUT CREATIVE CHOICES, HOW YOUR SONGWRITING'S CHANGED OVER THE YEARS...
YEAH.
...SPECIFICALLY IN THE TIME YOU'VE BEEN AWAY FROM RICHMOND.
YOU RECORDED THREE ALBUMS IN EUROPE - AND I'LL COME BACK TO *WHY* IN EUROPE IN A MINUTE - AND THOSE THREE ALBUMS WERE A MARKED DEPARTURE FROM THE MATERIAL YOU'D BEEN PLAYING UP UNTIL THAT POINT.
THE MATERIAL THAT YOU'D BEEN *KNOWN* FOR, AND ALSO THE SORT OF SOUND THAT WAS DEFINING THE RICHMOND "SCENE" AT THE TIME.
RIGHT.
DID YOUR TIME AWAY FROM HOME REALLY CHANGE YOU THAT MUCH? I MEAN, WAS IT JUST THE FACT YOU WERE ELSEWHERE, OR WAS IT A SPECIFIC INFLUENCE OR SET OF INFLUENCES?
THAT'S A GOOD QUESTION.
I'LL ANSWER THE QUESTION YOU *DIDN'T* ASK FIRST. WE MOVED TO EUROPE, INITIALLY ANYWAY, TO GET READY FOR THAT TOUR WE DID IN '91. IT JUST SEEMED EASIER TO HAVE A HOME BASE THAT WAS CLOSER, WHILE WE REHEARSED. WE WERE BOOKED FOR 22 WEEKS, EUROPE AND ASIA.
BUT YOU STAYED...
WE STAYED BECAUSE WE LIKED IT. KEVIN BOUGHT HIS HOUSE IN GALWAY AND BUILT A STUDIO, AND WE STARTED RECORDING THERE.
SO IT WAS JUST PURE CONVENIENCE?
AND WE LIKED IT.

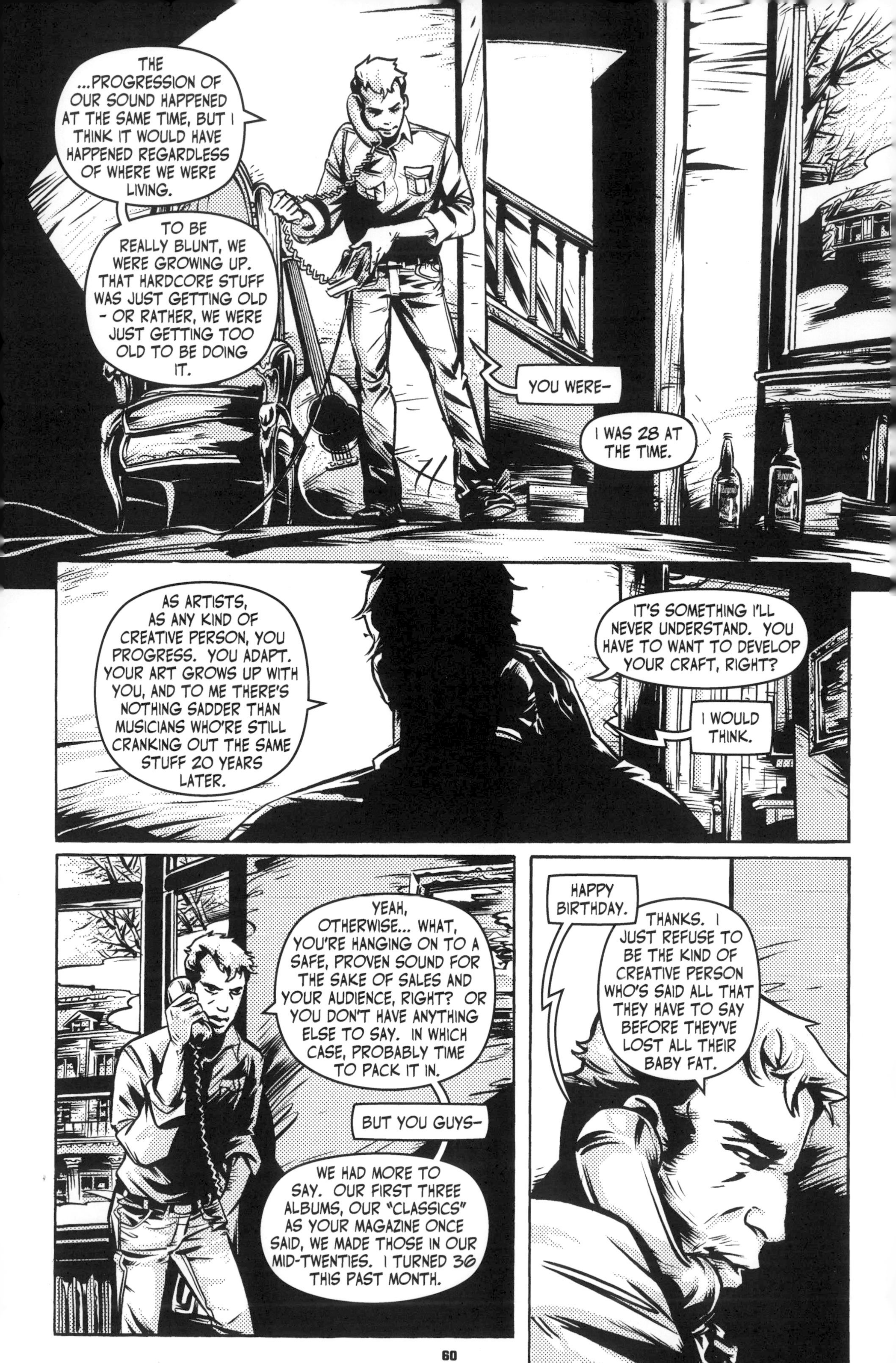

THE ...PROGRESSION OF OUR SOUND HAPPENED AT THE SAME TIME, BUT I THINK IT WOULD HAVE HAPPENED REGARDLESS OF WHERE WE WERE LIVING.
TO BE REALLY BLUNT, WE WERE GROWING UP. THAT HARDCORE STUFF WAS JUST GETTING OLD - OR RATHER, WE WERE JUST GETTING TOO OLD TO BE DOING IT.
YOU WERE-
I WAS 28 AT THE TIME.
AS ARTISTS, AS ANY KIND OF CREATIVE PERSON, YOU PROGRESS. YOU ADAPT. YOUR ART GROWS UP WITH YOU, AND TO ME THERE'S NOTHING SADDER THAN MUSICIANS WHO'RE STILL CRANKING OUT THE SAME STUFF 20 YEARS LATER.
IT'S SOMETHING I'LL NEVER UNDERSTAND. YOU HAVE TO WANT TO DEVELOP YOUR CRAFT, RIGHT?
I WOULD THINK.
YEAH, OTHERWISE... WHAT, YOU'RE HANGING ON TO A SAFE, PROVEN SOUND FOR THE SAKE OF SALES AND YOUR AUDIENCE, RIGHT? OR YOU DON'T HAVE ANYTHING ELSE TO SAY. IN WHICH CASE, PROBABLY TIME TO PACK IT IN.
BUT YOU GUYS-
WE HAD MORE TO SAY. OUR FIRST THREE ALBUMS, OUR "CLASSICS" AS YOUR MAGAZINE ONCE SAID, WE MADE THOSE IN OUR MID-TWENTIES. I TURNED 36 THIS PAST MONTH.
HAPPY BIRTHDAY.
THANKS. I JUST REFUSE TO BE THE KIND OF CREATIVE PERSON WHO'S SAID ALL THAT THEY HAVE TO SAY BEFORE THEY'VE LOST ALL THEIR BABY FAT.

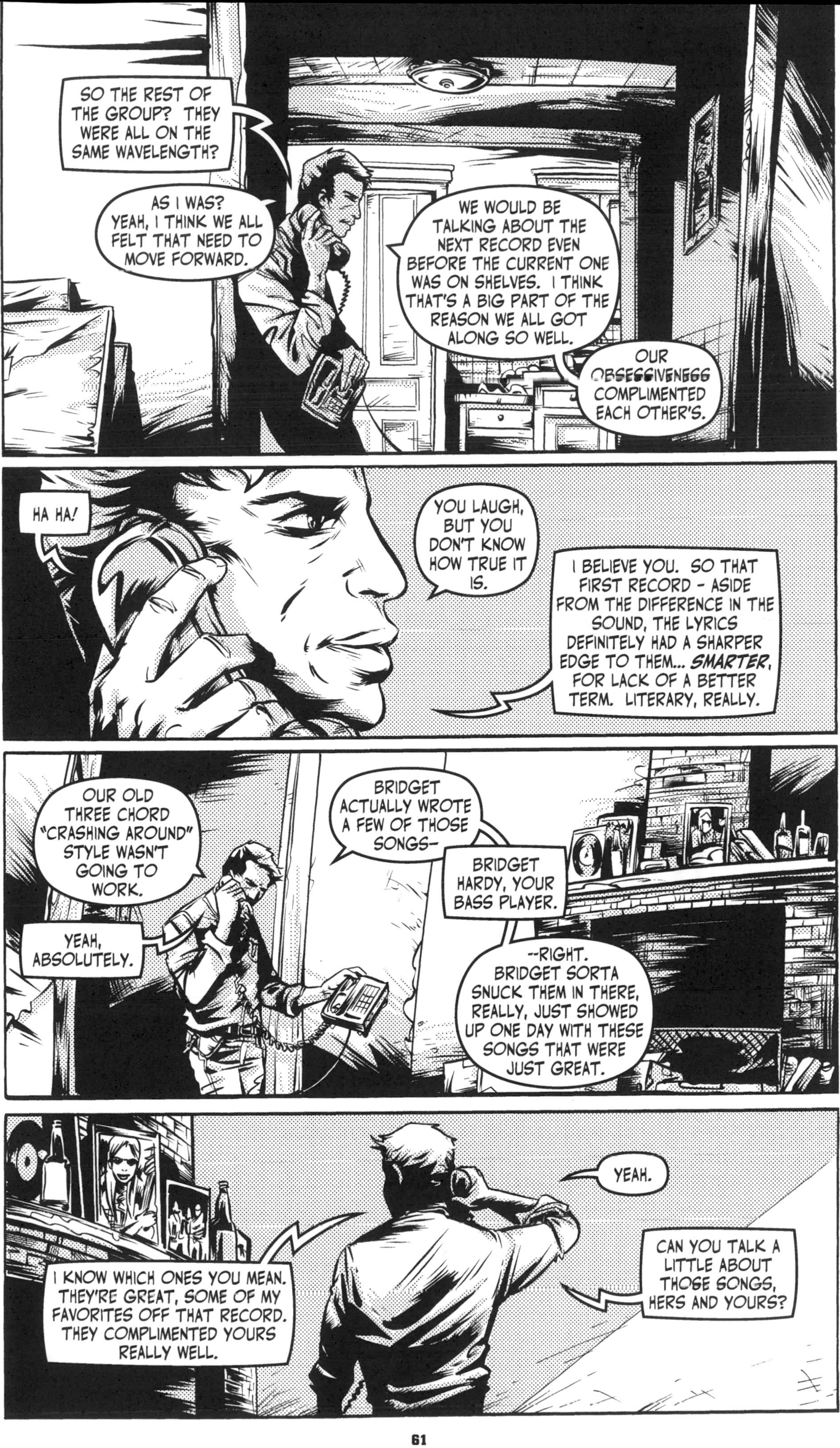
SO THE REST OF THE GROUP? THEY WERE ALL ON THE SAME WAVELENGTH?
AS I WAS? YEAH, I THINK WE ALL FELT THAT NEED TO MOVE FORWARD.
WE WOULD BE TALKING ABOUT THE NEXT RECORD EVEN BEFORE THE CURRENT ONE WAS ON SHELVES. I THINK THAT'S A BIG PART OF THE REASON WE ALL GOT ALONG SO WELL.
OUR OBSESSIVENESS COMPLIMENTED EACH OTHER'S.
HA HA!
YOU LAUGH, BUT YOU DON'T KNOW HOW TRUE IT IS.
I BELIEVE YOU. SO THAT FIRST RECORD - ASIDE FROM THE DIFFERENCE IN THE SOUND, THE LYRICS DEFINITELY HAD A SHARPER EDGE TO THEM... *SMARTER*, FOR LACK OF A BETTER TERM. LITERARY, REALLY.
OUR OLD THREE CHORD "CRASHING AROUND" STYLE WASN'T GOING TO WORK.
YEAH, ABSOLUTELY.
BRIDGET ACTUALLY WROTE A FEW OF THOSE SONGS–
BRIDGET HARDY, YOUR BASS PLAYER.
--RIGHT. BRIDGET SORTA SNUCK THEM IN THERE, REALLY, JUST SHOWED UP ONE DAY WITH THESE SONGS THAT WERE JUST GREAT.
I KNOW WHICH ONES YOU MEAN. THEY'RE GREAT, SOME OF MY FAVORITES OFF THAT RECORD. THEY COMPLIMENTED YOURS REALLY WELL.
YEAH.
CAN YOU TALK A LITTLE ABOUT THOSE SONGS, HERS AND YOURS?

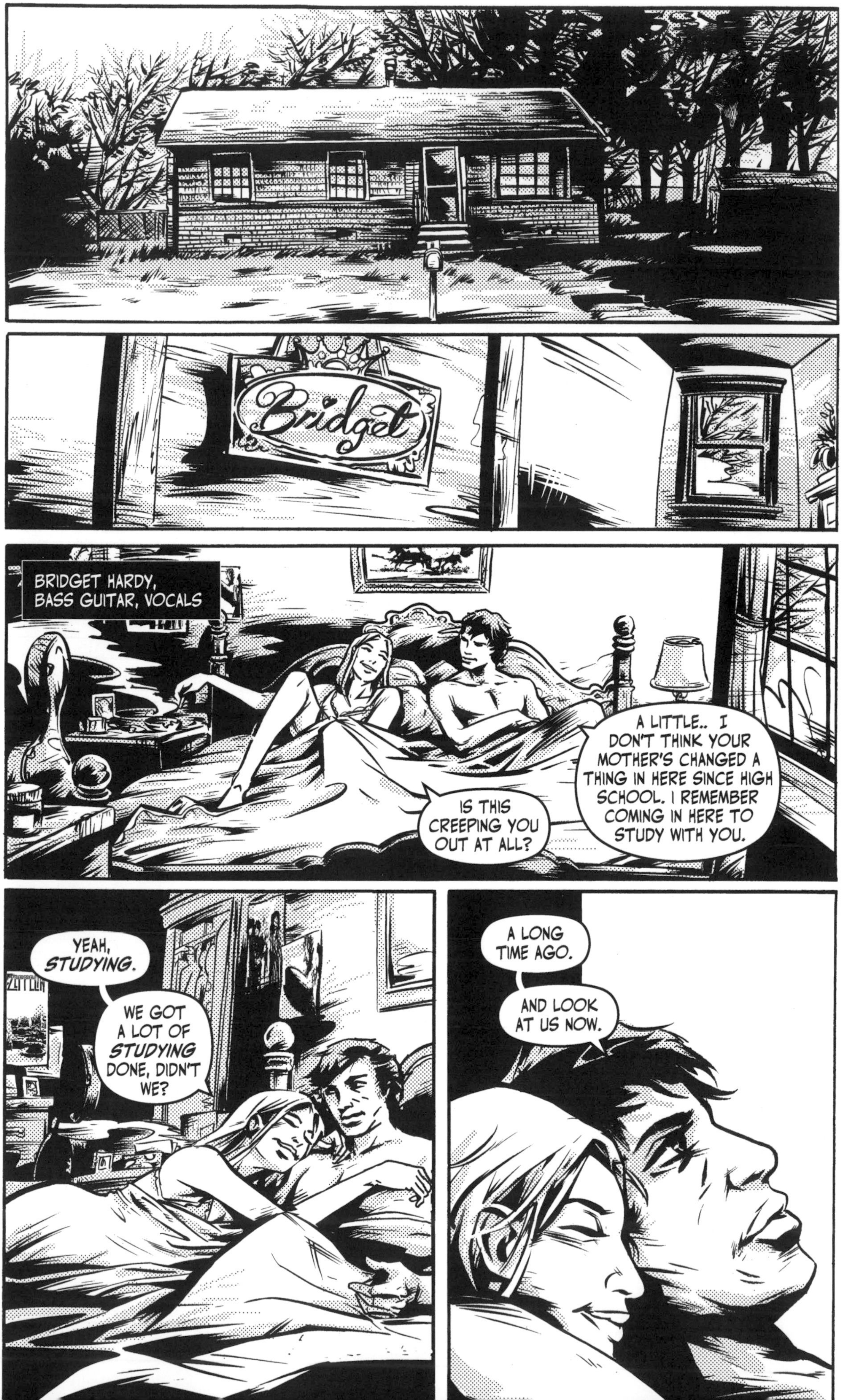
Bridget
BRIDGET HARDY, BASS GUITAR, VOCALS
IS THIS CREEPING YOU OUT AT ALL?
A LITTLE.. I DON'T THINK YOUR MOTHER'S CHANGED A THING IN HERE SINCE HIGH SCHOOL. I REMEMBER COMING IN HERE TO STUDY WITH YOU.
YEAH, *STUDYING*.
WE GOT A LOT OF *STUDYING* DONE, DIDN'T WE?
A LONG TIME AGO.
AND LOOK AT US NOW.

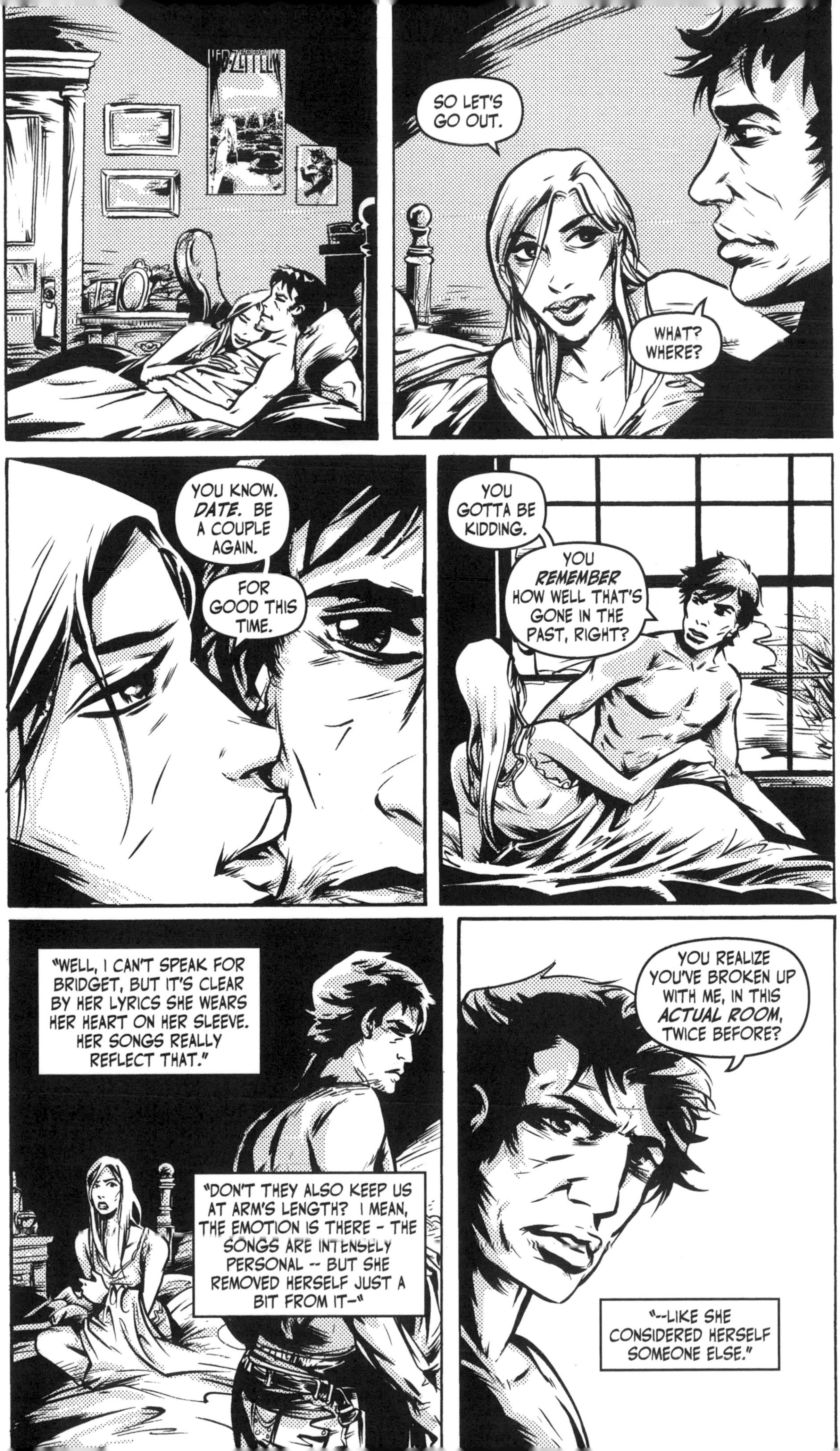

LED ZEPPELIN
SO LET'S GO OUT.
WHAT? WHERE?
YOU KNOW. DATE. BE A COUPLE AGAIN.
FOR GOOD THIS TIME.
YOU GOTTA BE KIDDING.
YOU REMEMBER HOW WELL THAT'S GONE IN THE PAST, RIGHT?
"WELL, I CAN'T SPEAK FOR BRIDGET, BUT IT'S CLEAR BY HER LYRICS SHE WEARS HER HEART ON HER SLEEVE. HER SONGS REALLY REFLECT THAT."
"DON'T THEY ALSO KEEP US AT ARM'S LENGTH? I MEAN, THE EMOTION IS THERE - THE SONGS ARE INTENSELY PERSONAL -- BUT SHE REMOVED HERSELF JUST A BIT FROM IT--"
YOU REALIZE YOU'VE BROKEN UP WITH ME, IN THIS ACTUAL ROOM, TWICE BEFORE?
"--LIKE SHE CONSIDERED HERSELF SOMEONE ELSE."

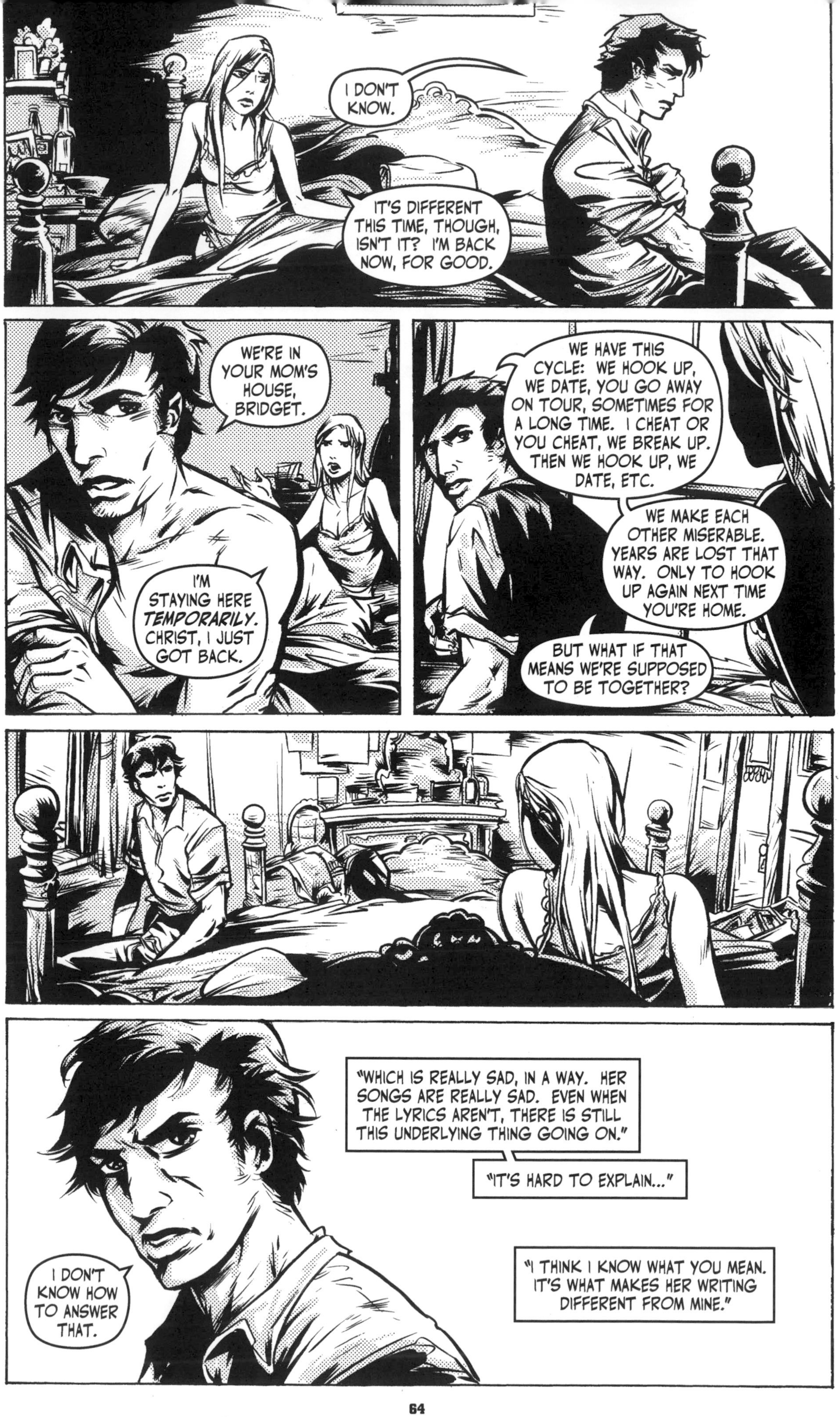
I DON'T KNOW.
IT'S DIFFERENT THIS TIME, THOUGH, ISN'T IT? I'M BACK NOW, FOR GOOD.
WE'RE IN YOUR MOM'S HOUSE, BRIDGET.
I'M STAYING HERE *TEMPORARILY*. CHRIST, I JUST GOT BACK.
WE HAVE THIS CYCLE: WE HOOK UP, WE DATE, YOU GO AWAY ON TOUR, SOMETIMES FOR A LONG TIME. I CHEAT OR YOU CHEAT, WE BREAK UP. THEN WE HOOK UP, WE DATE, ETC.
WE MAKE EACH OTHER MISERABLE. YEARS ARE LOST THAT WAY. ONLY TO HOOK UP AGAIN NEXT TIME YOU'RE HOME.
BUT WHAT IF THAT MEANS WE'RE SUPPOSED TO BE TOGETHER?
"WHICH IS REALLY SAD, IN A WAY. HER SONGS ARE REALLY SAD. EVEN WHEN THE LYRICS AREN'T, THERE IS STILL THIS UNDERLYING THING GOING ON."
"IT'S HARD TO EXPLAIN..."
I DON'T KNOW HOW TO ANSWER THAT.
"I THINK I KNOW WHAT YOU MEAN. IT'S WHAT MAKES HER WRITING DIFFERENT FROM MINE."

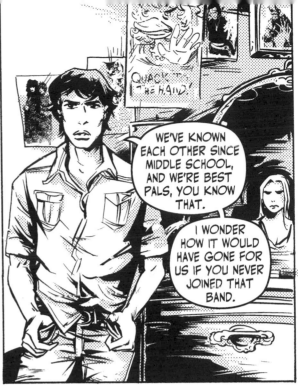

WELL, CAN YOU *TRY* ANYWAY?

WE'VE KNOWN EACH OTHER SINCE MIDDLE SCHOOL, AND WE'RE BEST PALS, YOU KNOW THAT.

I WONDER HOW IT WOULD HAVE GONE FOR US IF YOU NEVER JOINED THAT BAND.

YOU'RE BLAMING MY *MUSIC?*

BRIDGET, I'M BLAMING THE *BAND.*

"DID HER WRITING INFLUENCE YOURS AT ALL? YOU SAID SHE JUST APPEARED AT REHEARSALS ONE DAY WITH THESE SONGS... DID YOUR OWN CHANGE AT ALL AS A RESULT?"

"BRIDGET'S FIRST FEW SONGS HAD A HUGE IMPACT ON THE BAND, FROM THAT POINT ON. I COULD SAY SHE SORT OF DEFINED US AFTER THAT. CLARIFIED OUR DIRECTION."

"BUT WHAT ABOUT *YOU?* HOW DID THEY AFFECT YOU, *PERSONALLY,* AS A SONGWRITER?"

YOU WANT ME TO BE *HONEST,* BRIDGET?

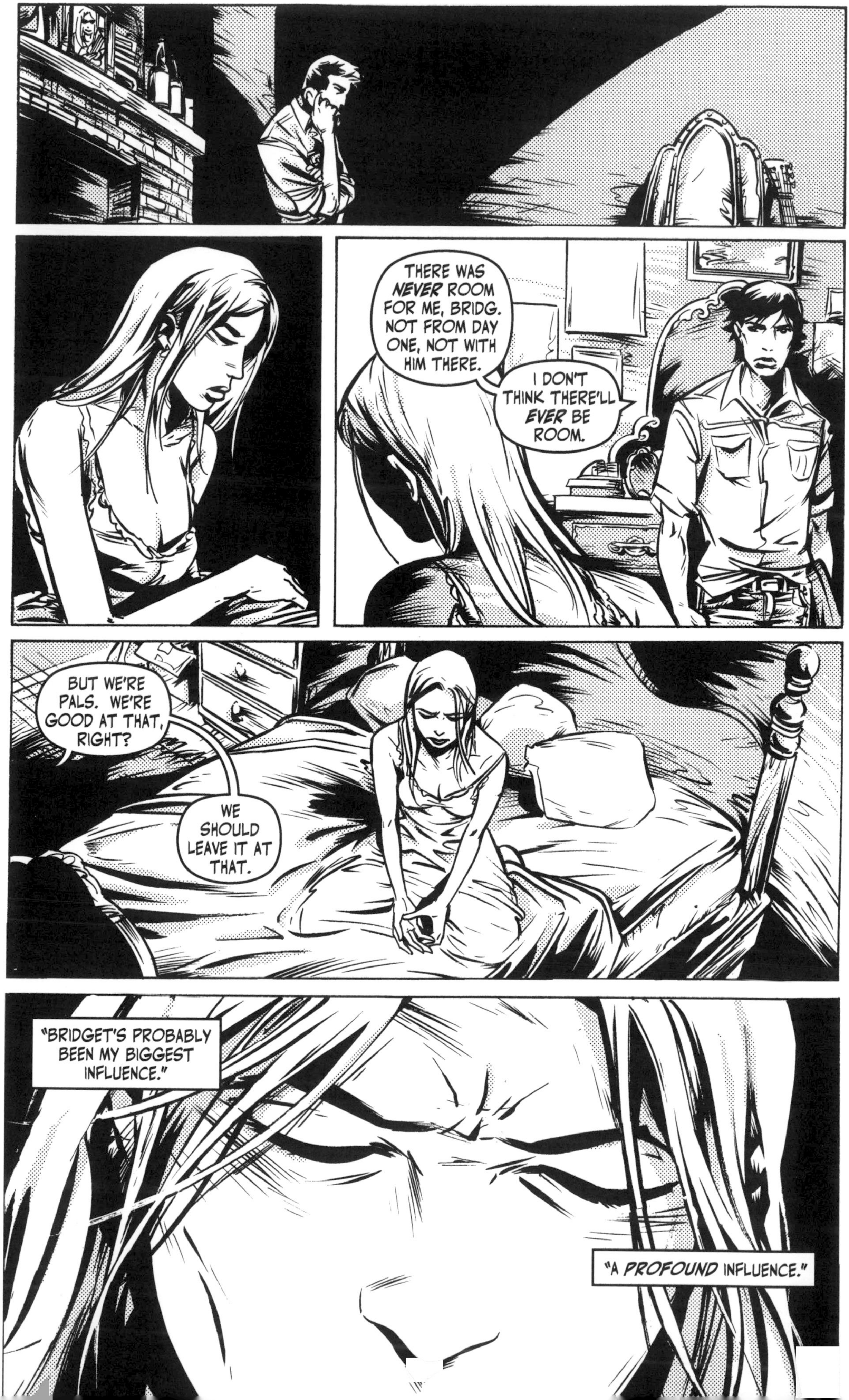
THERE WAS NEVER ROOM FOR ME, BRIDG. NOT FROM DAY ONE, NOT WITH HIM THERE.
I DON'T THINK THERE'LL EVER BE ROOM.
BUT WE'RE PALS. WE'RE GOOD AT THAT, RIGHT?
WE SHOULD LEAVE IT AT THAT.
"BRIDGET'S PROBABLY BEEN MY BIGGEST INFLUENCE."
"A PROFOUND INFLUENCE."

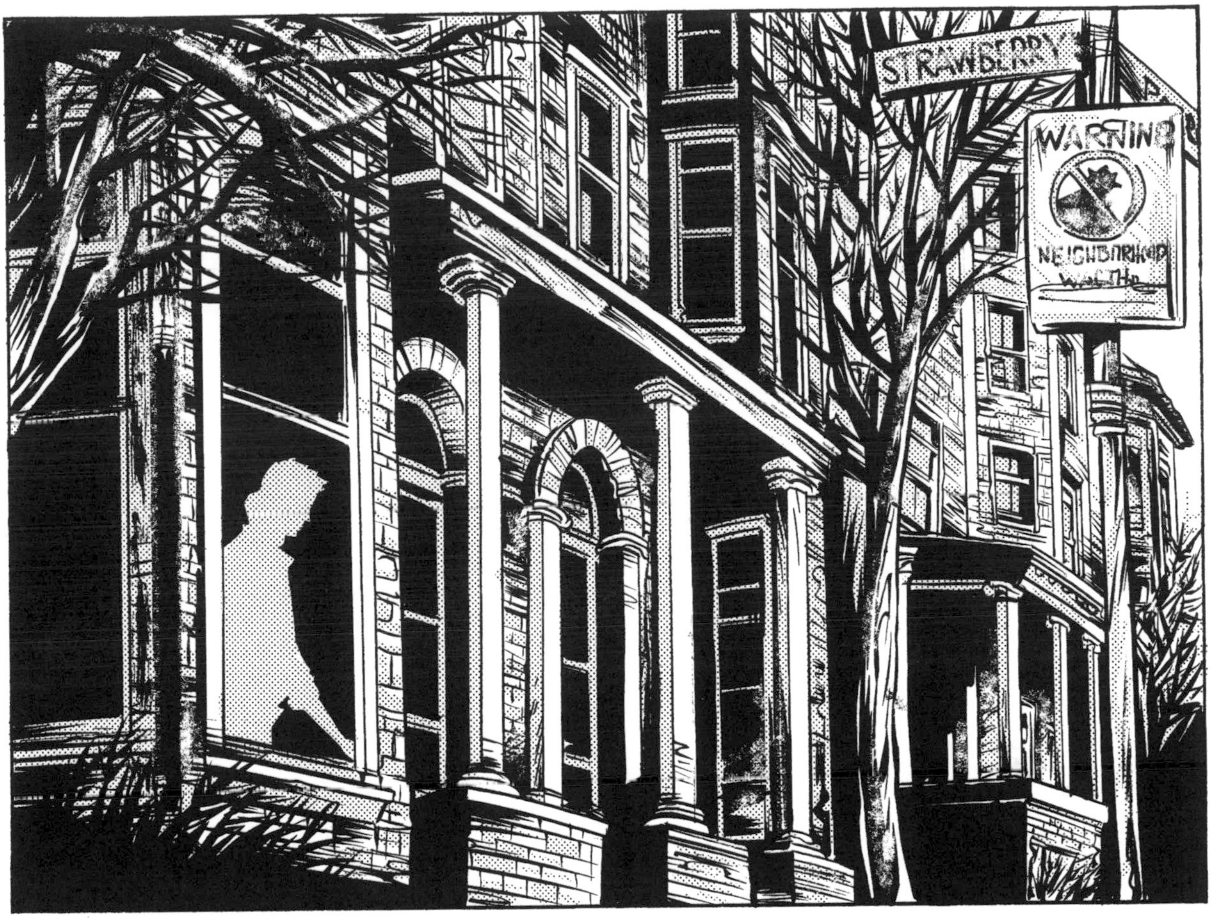
STRAWBERRY
WARNING
NEIGHBORHOOD

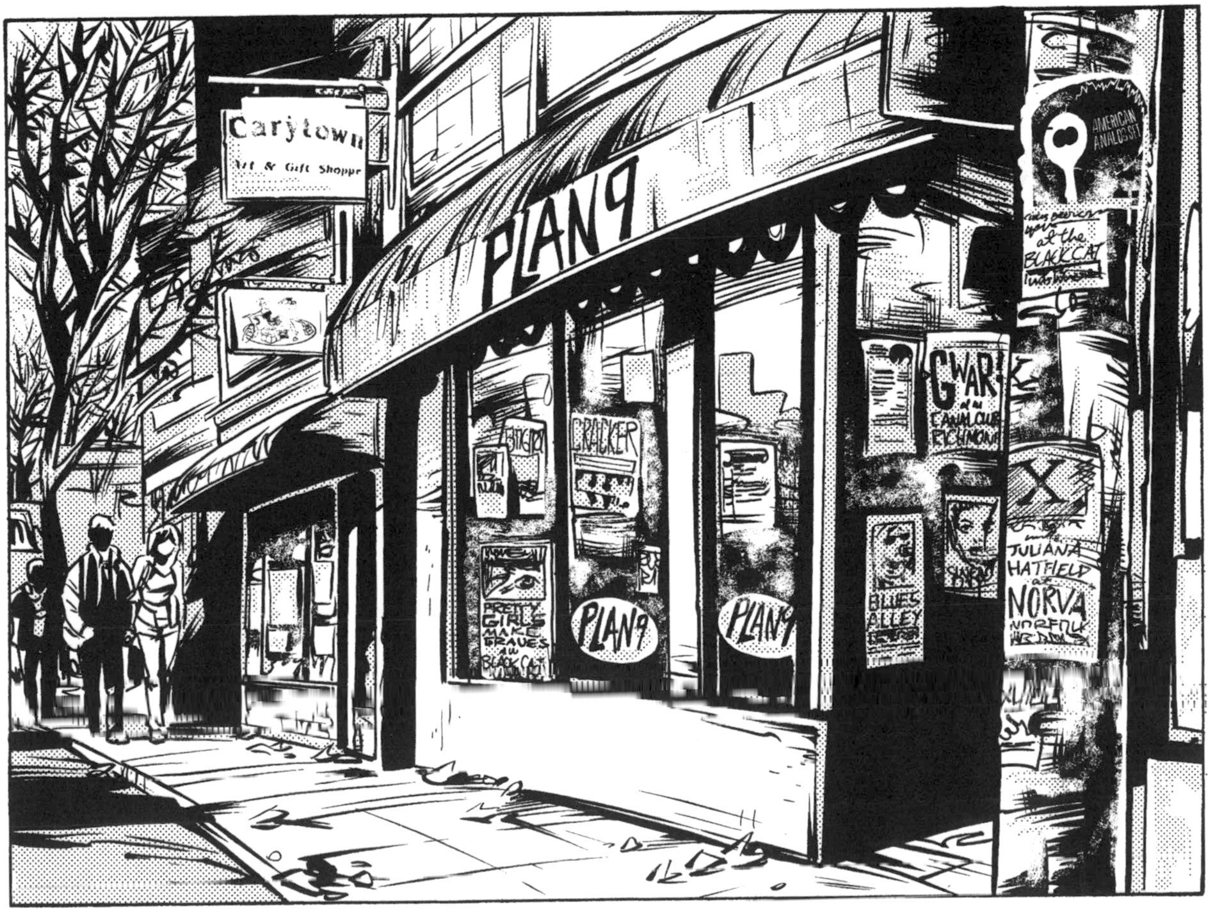
Carytown
Art & Gift Shoppe
PLAN 9
AMERICAN ANALOG SET
at the BLACK CAT
CRACKER
GWAR!
CANAL CLUB RICHMOND
X
JULIANA HATFIELD
at
NORVA
NORFOLK
BLUES ALLEY
PRETTY GIRLS MAKE GRAVES
BLACK CAT
PLAN 9
PLAN 9

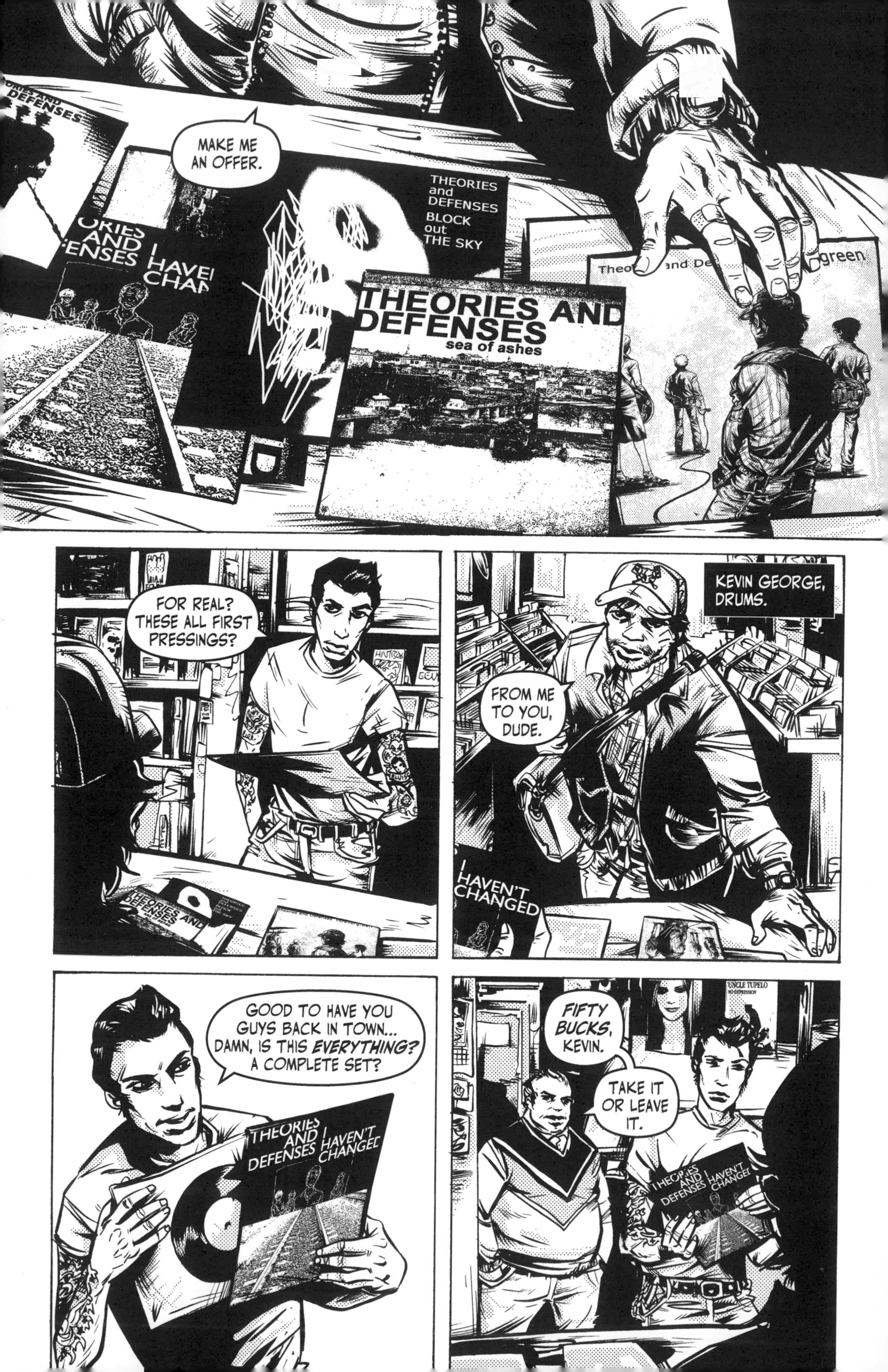
MAKE ME AN OFFER.
THEORIES and DEFENSES BLOCK out THE SKY
THEORIES AND DEFENSES sea of ashes
FOR REAL? THESE ALL FIRST PRESSINGS?
KEVIN GEORGE, DRUMS.
FROM ME TO YOU, DUDE.
I HAVEN'T CHANGED
GOOD TO HAVE YOU GUYS BACK IN TOWN... DAMN, IS THIS *EVERYTHING?* A COMPLETE SET?
THEORIES AND DEFENSES I HAVEN'T CHANGED
UNCLE TUPELO
FIFTY BUCKS, KEVIN.
TAKE IT OR LEAVE IT.

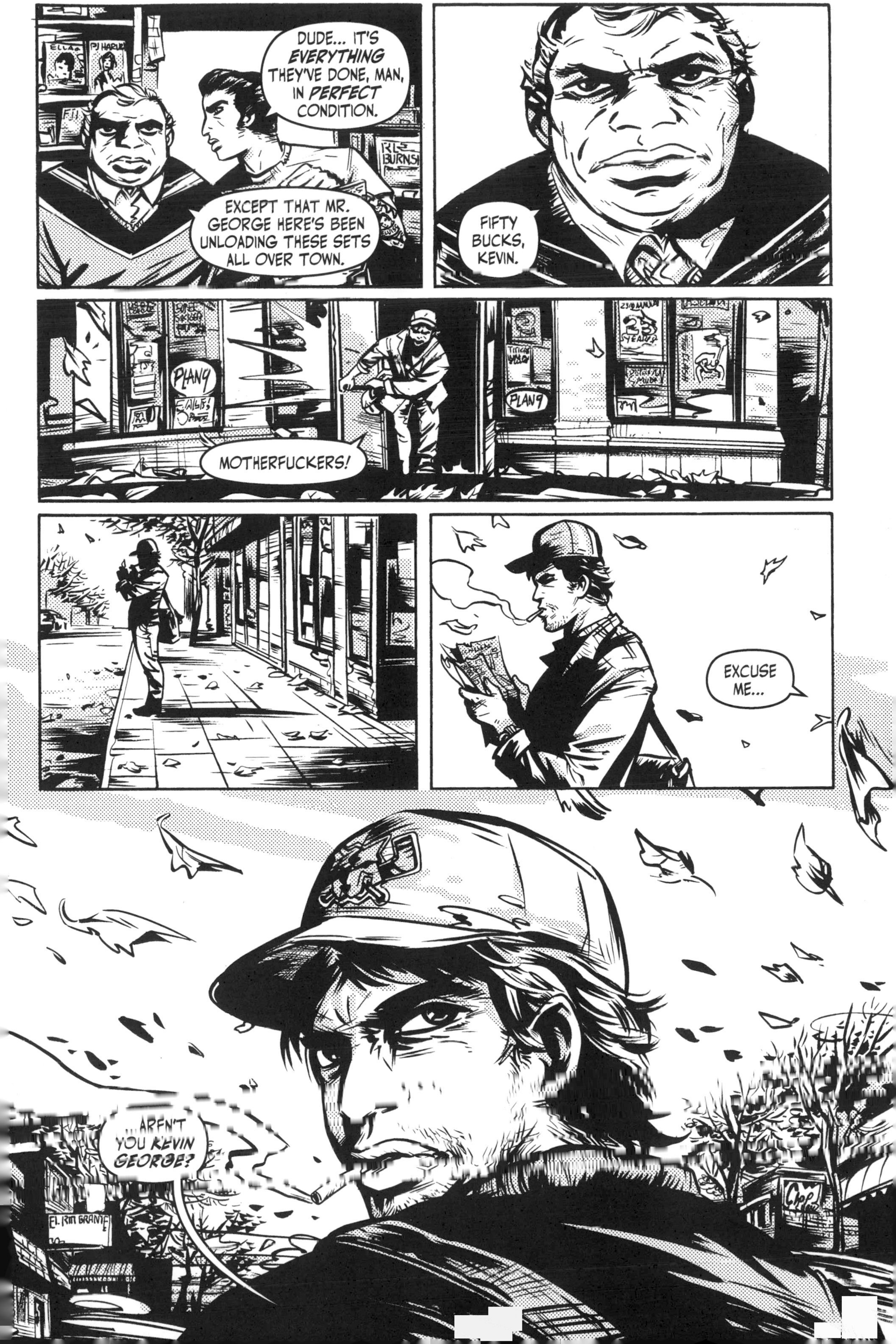
DUDE... IT'S *EVERYTHING* THEY'VE DONE, MAN, IN *PERFECT* CONDITION.
EXCEPT THAT MR. GEORGE HERE'S BEEN UNLOADING THESE SETS ALL OVER TOWN.
FIFTY BUCKS, KEVIN.
MOTHERFUCKERS!
EXCUSE ME...
...AREN'T YOU *KEVIN GEORGE?*

"CAN WE TALK ABOUT FAN REACTION NOW?"

"SURE."

"SPECIFICALLY, THE REACTION TO THE NEW DIRECTION YOU TOOK AROUND THIS TIME, AND ALSO, IF YOU WANT, WHAT WE TOUCHED ON EARLIER--"

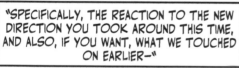

"US ABANDONING RICHMOND."

"--YEAH. IF YOU WANT, IF YOU'RE COMFORTABLE."

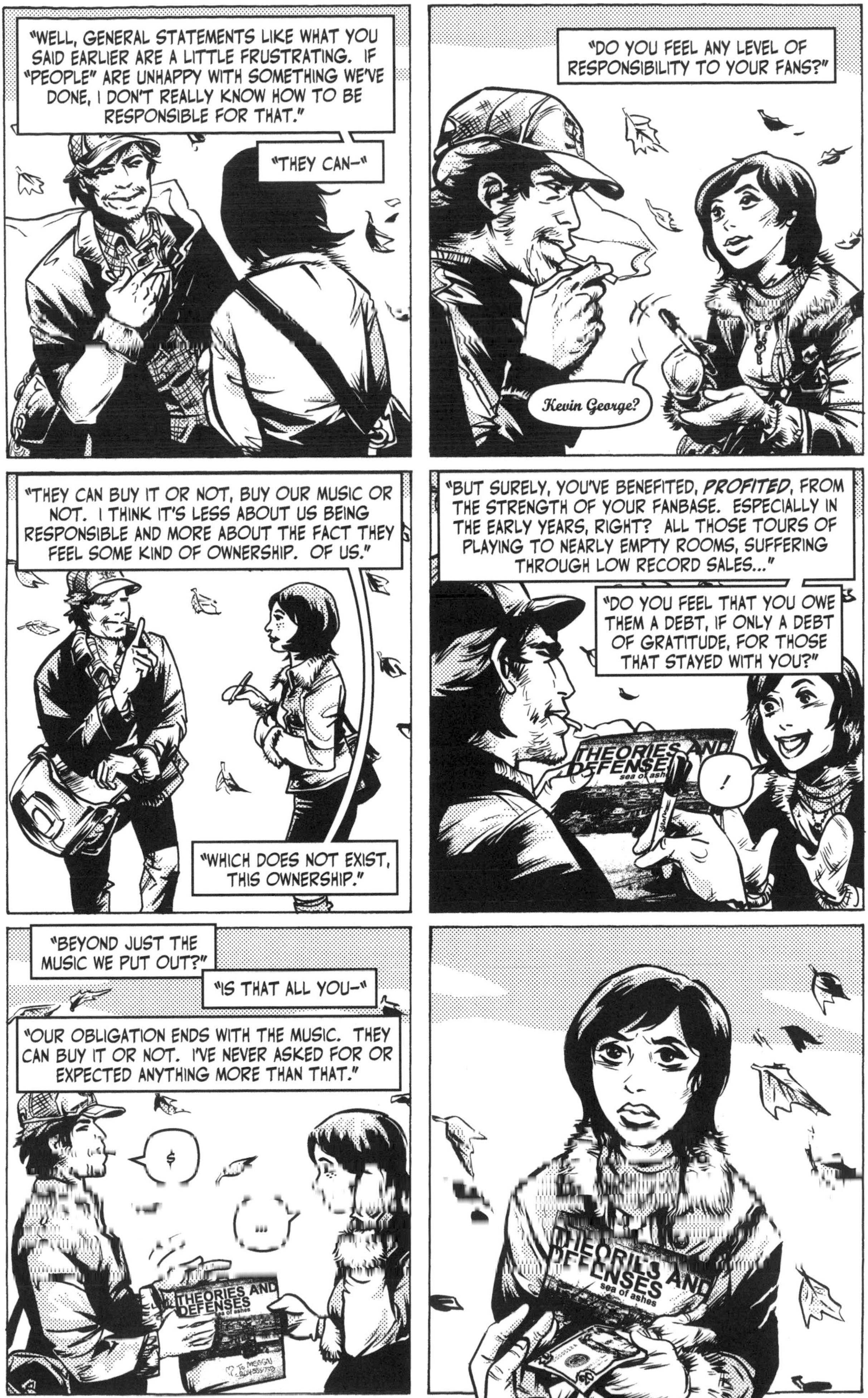
"WELL, GENERAL STATEMENTS LIKE WHAT YOU SAID EARLIER ARE A LITTLE FRUSTRATING. IF "PEOPLE" ARE UNHAPPY WITH SOMETHING WE'VE DONE, I DON'T REALLY KNOW HOW TO BE RESPONSIBLE FOR THAT."
"THEY CAN–"
"DO YOU FEEL ANY LEVEL OF RESPONSIBILITY TO YOUR FANS?"
Kevin George?
"THEY CAN BUY IT OR NOT, BUY OUR MUSIC OR NOT. I THINK IT'S LESS ABOUT US BEING RESPONSIBLE AND MORE ABOUT THE FACT THEY FEEL SOME KIND OF OWNERSHIP. OF US."
"WHICH DOES NOT EXIST, THIS OWNERSHIP."
"BUT SURELY, YOU'VE BENEFITED, *PROFITED*, FROM THE STRENGTH OF YOUR FANBASE. ESPECIALLY IN THE EARLY YEARS, RIGHT? ALL THOSE TOURS OF PLAYING TO NEARLY EMPTY ROOMS, SUFFERING THROUGH LOW RECORD SALES..."
"DO YOU FEEL THAT YOU OWE THEM A DEBT, IF ONLY A DEBT OF GRATITUDE, FOR THOSE THAT STAYED WITH YOU?"
THEORIES AND DEFENSES
sea of ashes
!
"BEYOND JUST THE MUSIC WE PUT OUT?"
"IS THAT ALL YOU–"
"OUR OBLIGATION ENDS WITH THE MUSIC. THEY CAN BUY IT OR NOT. I'VE NEVER ASKED FOR OR EXPECTED ANYTHING MORE THAN THAT."
$
...
THEORIES AND DEFENSES
sea of ashes
THEORIES AND DEFENSES
sea of ashes

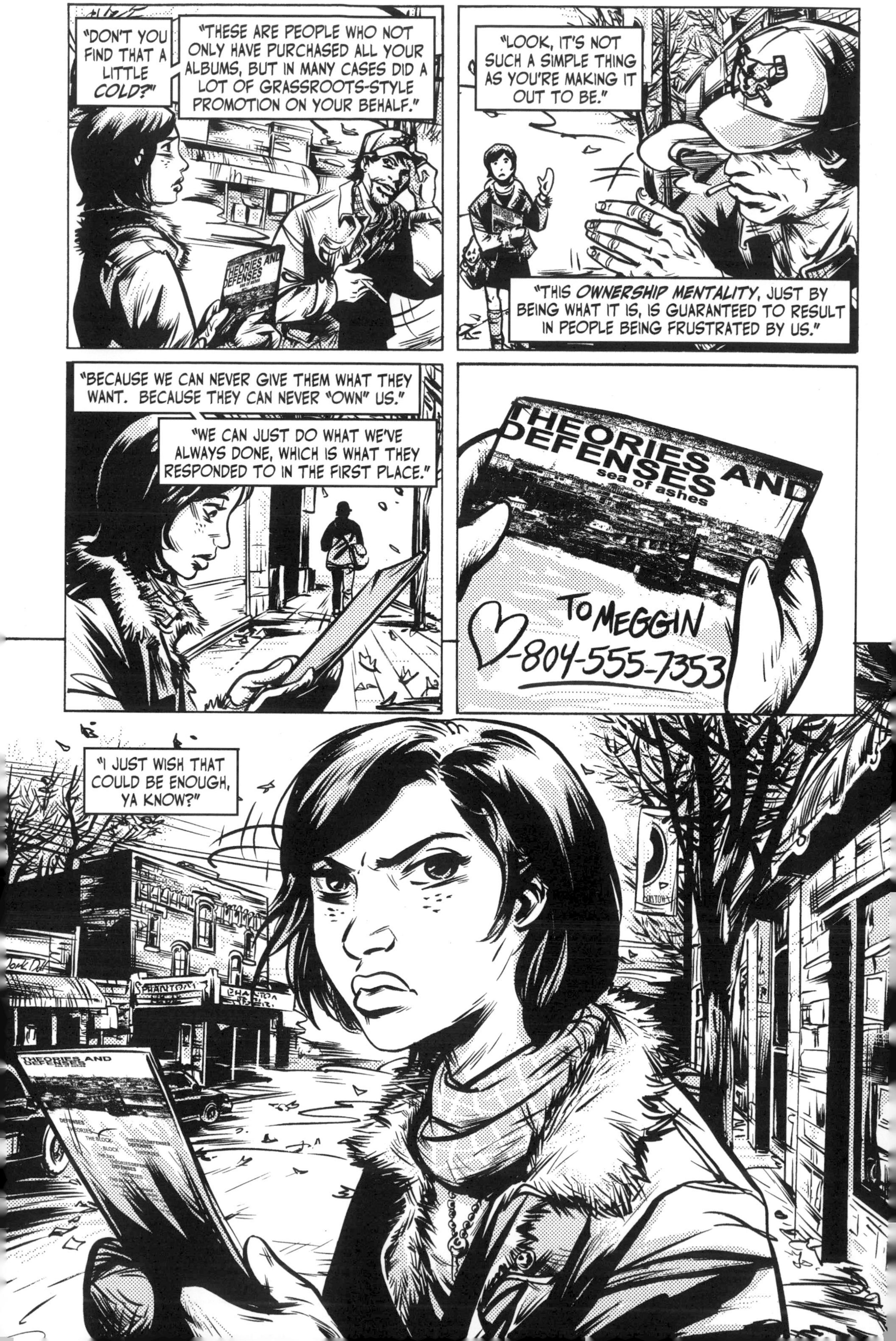
"DON'T YOU FIND THAT A LITTLE *COLD?*"
"THESE ARE PEOPLE WHO NOT ONLY HAVE PURCHASED ALL YOUR ALBUMS, BUT IN MANY CASES DID A LOT OF GRASSROOTS-STYLE PROMOTION ON YOUR BEHALF."
THEORIES AND DEFENSES
"LOOK, IT'S NOT SUCH A SIMPLE THING AS YOU'RE MAKING IT OUT TO BE."
"THIS *OWNERSHIP MENTALITY*, JUST BY BEING WHAT IT IS, IS GUARANTEED TO RESULT IN PEOPLE BEING FRUSTRATED BY US."
"BECAUSE WE CAN NEVER GIVE THEM WHAT THEY WANT. BECAUSE THEY CAN NEVER "OWN" US."
"WE CAN JUST DO WHAT WE'VE ALWAYS DONE, WHICH IS WHAT THEY RESPONDED TO IN THE FIRST PLACE."
THEORIES AND DEFENSES
sea of ashes
TO MEGGIN
804-555-7353
"I JUST WISH THAT COULD BE ENOUGH, YA KNOW?"
PHANTOM
THEORIES AND DEFENSES

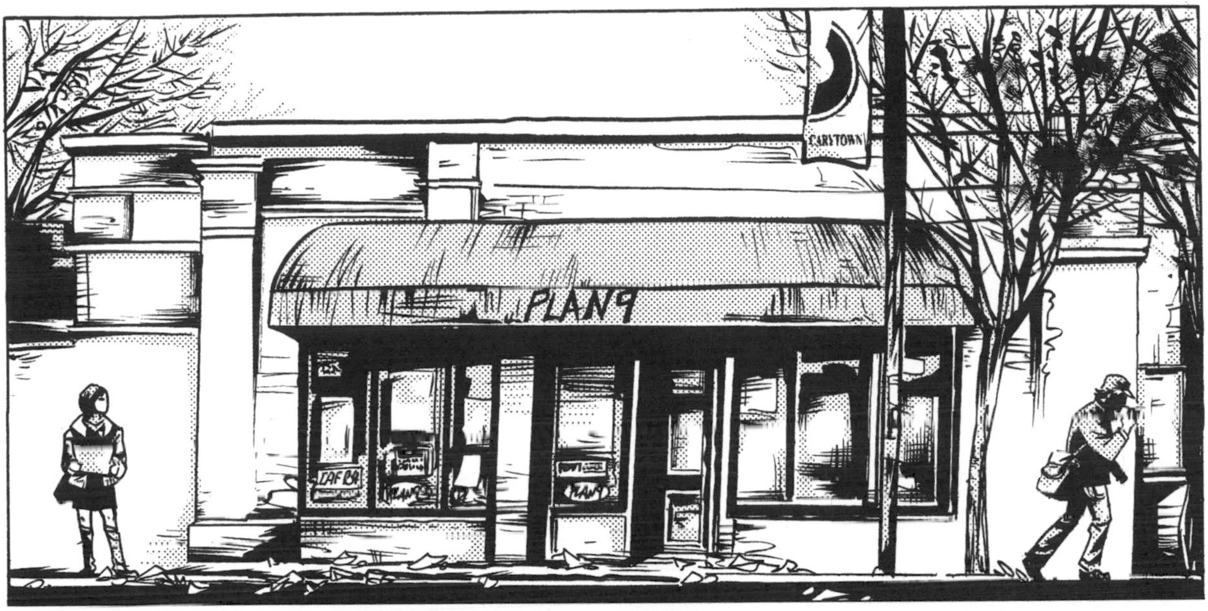
PLAN 9

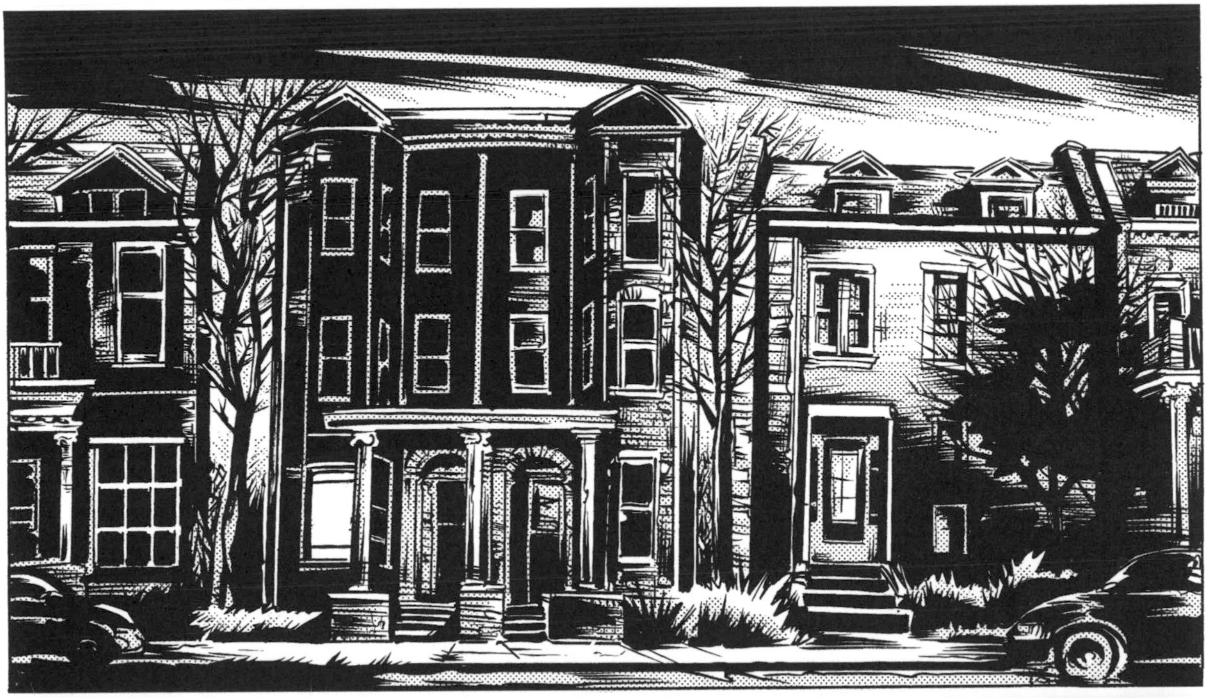

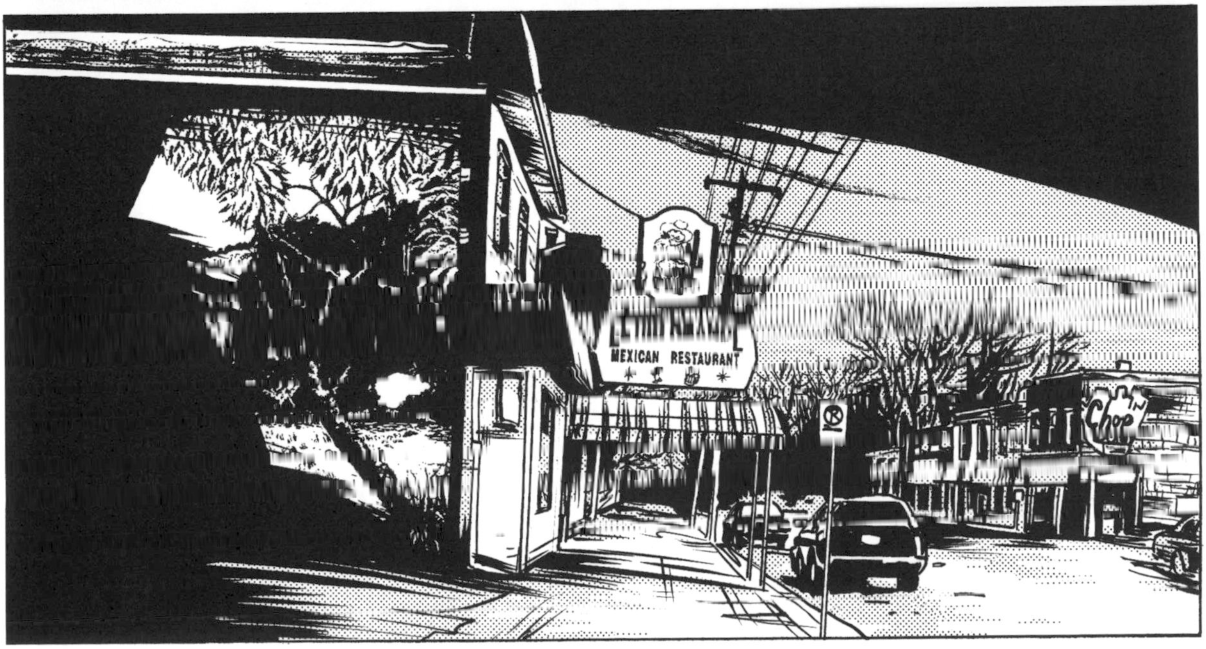
MEXICAN RESTAURANT

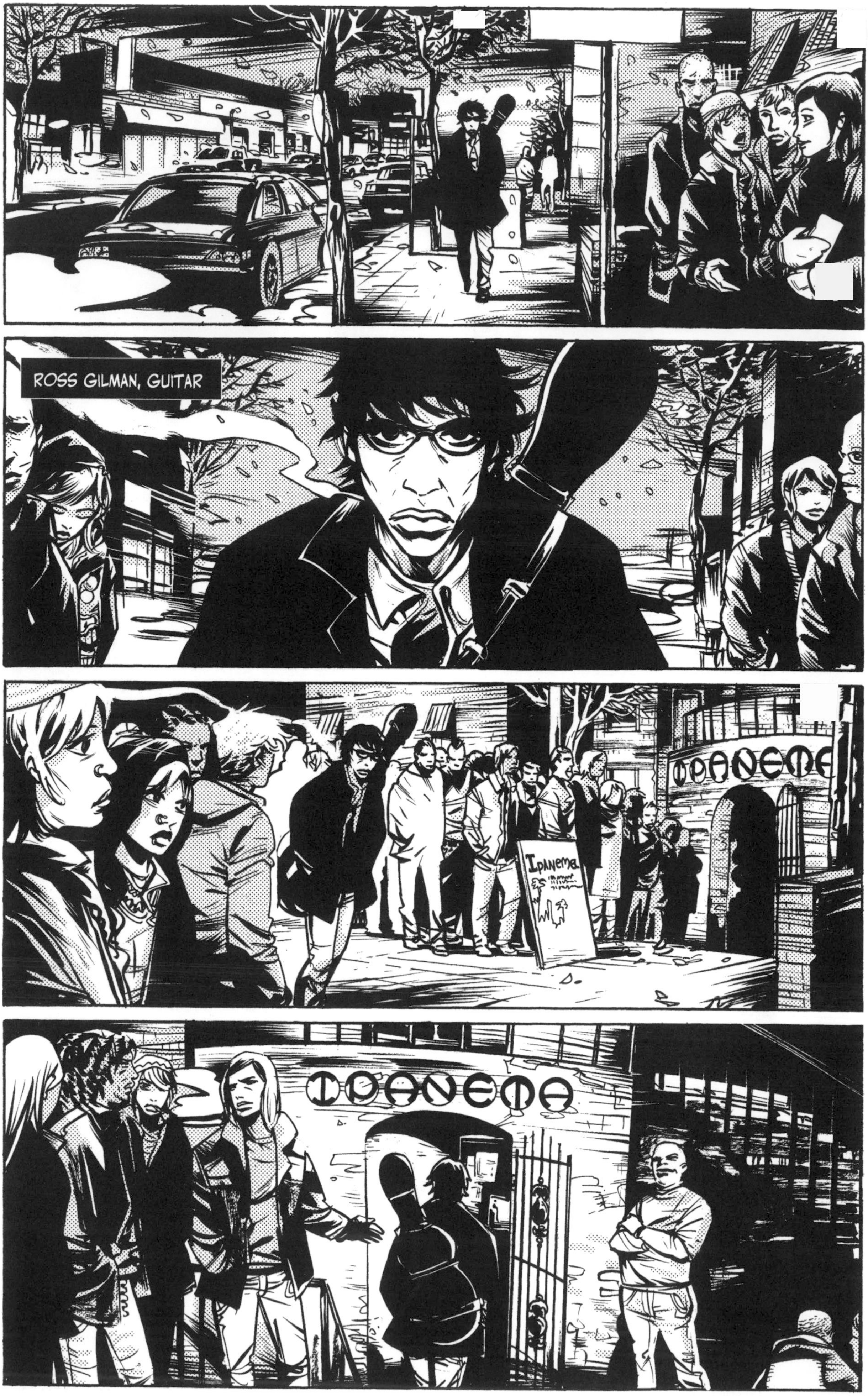
ROSS GILMAN, GUITAR
IPANEMA
Ipanema
IPANEMA

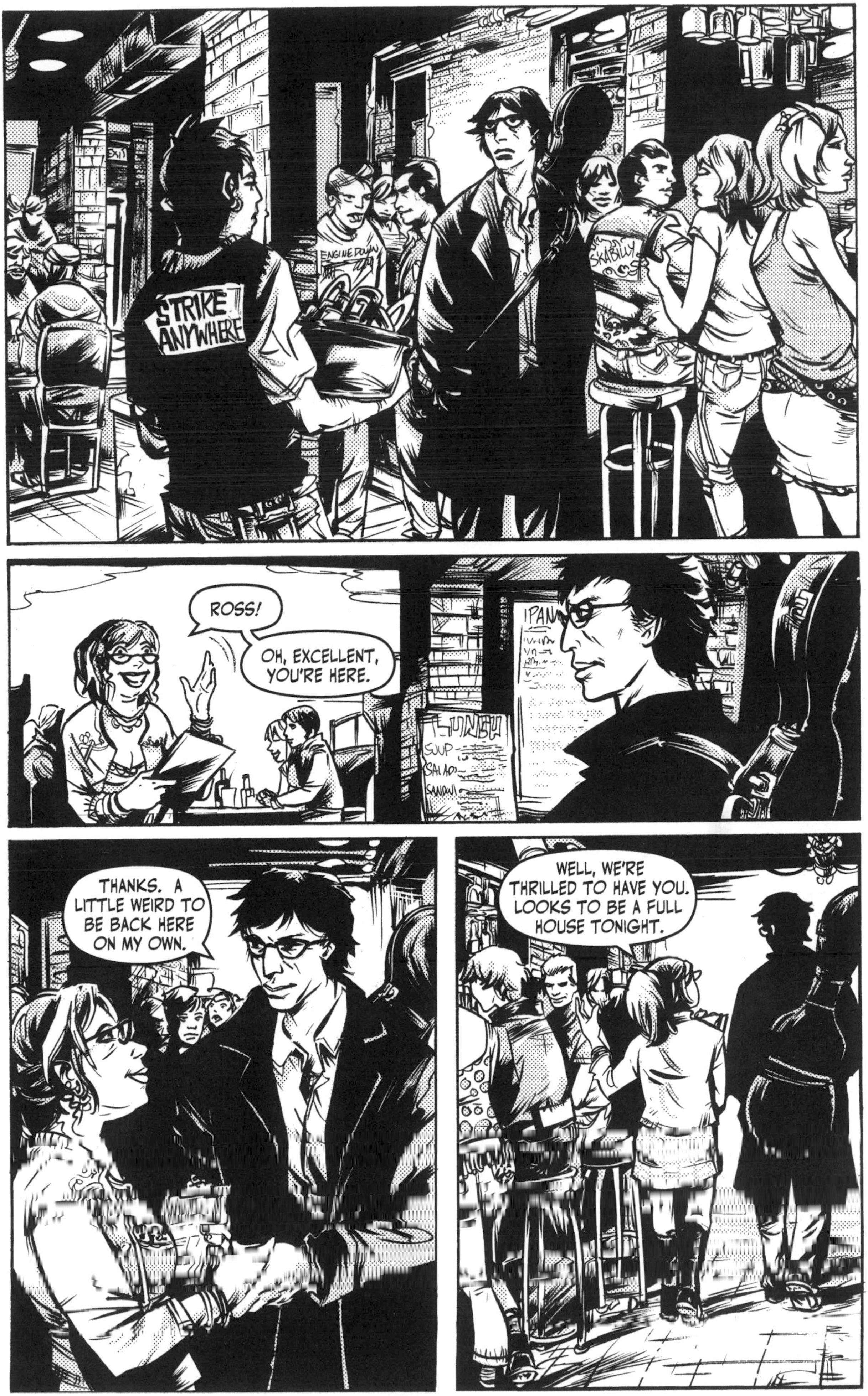
STRIKE ANYWHERE
ENGINE DOWN
SKABILLY
ROSS!
OH, EXCELLENT, YOU'RE HERE.
THANKS. A LITTLE WEIRD TO BE BACK HERE ON MY OWN.
WELL, WE'RE THRILLED TO HAVE YOU. LOOKS TO BE A FULL HOUSE TONIGHT.

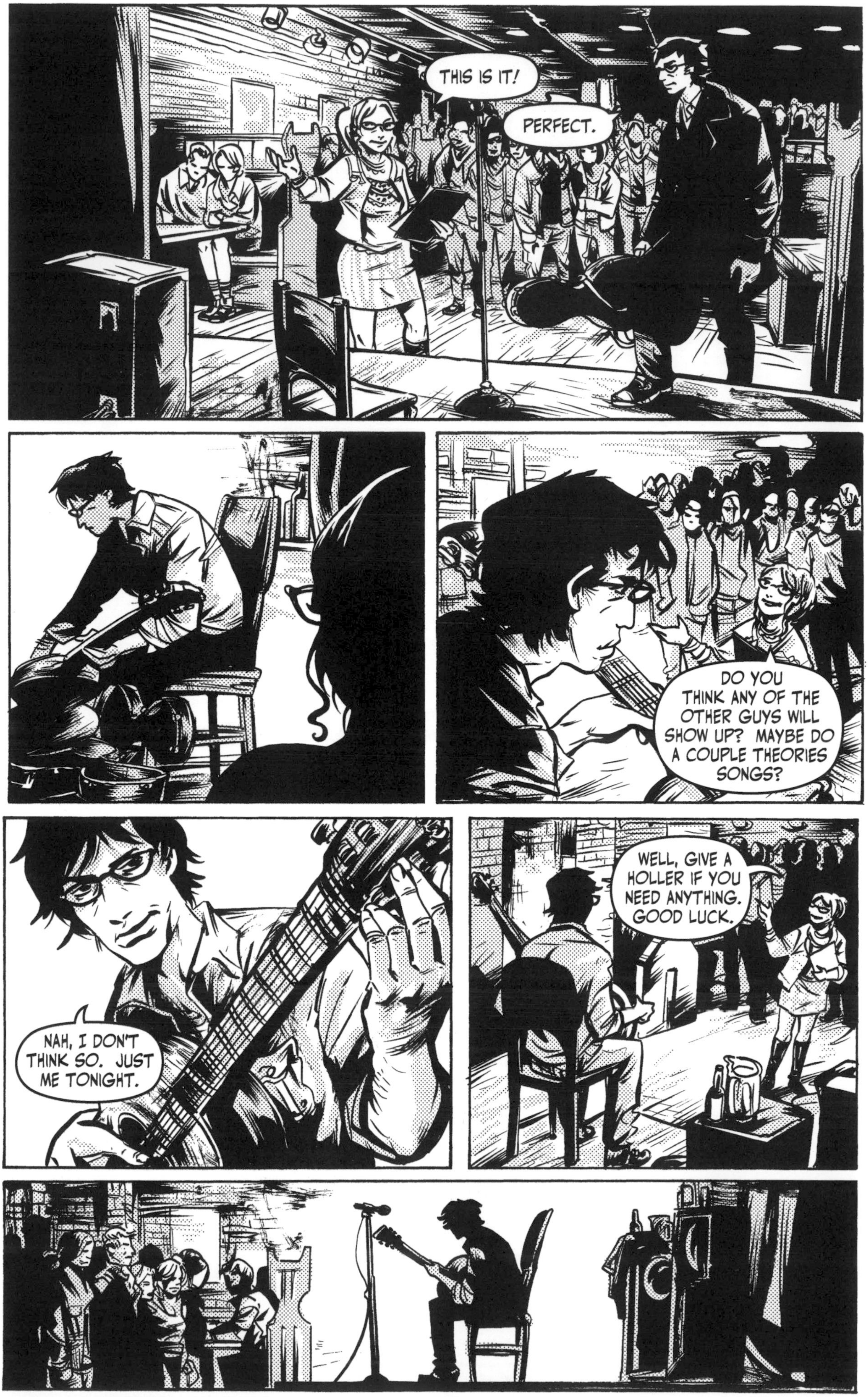
THIS IS IT!
PERFECT.
DO YOU THINK ANY OF THE OTHER GUYS WILL SHOW UP? MAYBE DO A COUPLE THEORIES SONGS?
NAH, I DON'T THINK SO. JUST ME TONIGHT.
WELL, GIVE A HOLLER IF YOU NEED ANYTHING. GOOD LUCK.

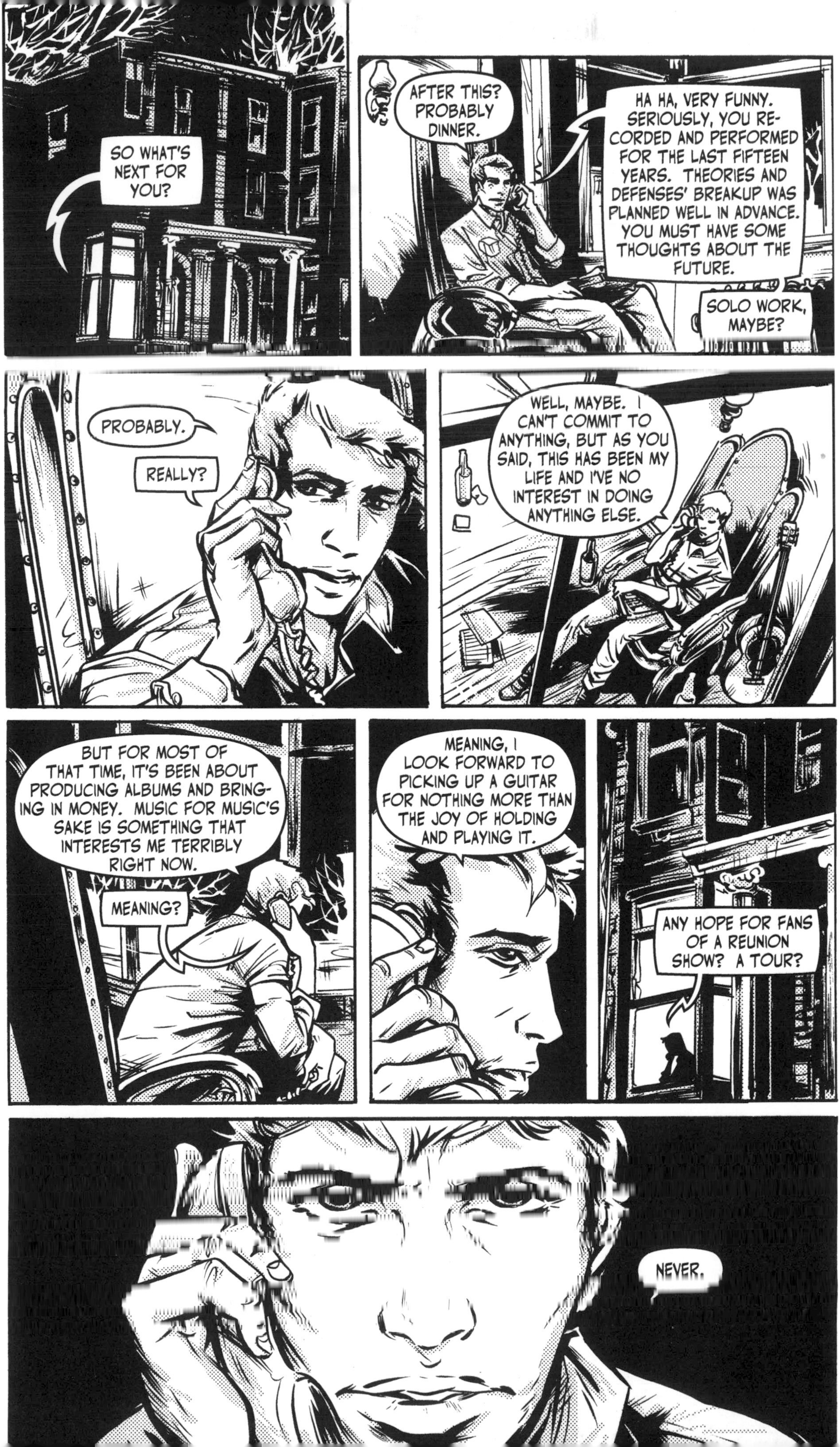
SO WHAT'S NEXT FOR YOU?
AFTER THIS? PROBABLY DINNER.
HA HA, VERY FUNNY. SERIOUSLY, YOU RECORDED AND PERFORMED FOR THE LAST FIFTEEN YEARS. THEORIES AND DEFENSES' BREAKUP WAS PLANNED WELL IN ADVANCE. YOU MUST HAVE SOME THOUGHTS ABOUT THE FUTURE.
SOLO WORK, MAYBE?
PROBABLY.
REALLY?
WELL, MAYBE. I CAN'T COMMIT TO ANYTHING, BUT AS YOU SAID, THIS HAS BEEN MY LIFE AND I'VE NO INTEREST IN DOING ANYTHING ELSE.
BUT FOR MOST OF THAT TIME, IT'S BEEN ABOUT PRODUCING ALBUMS AND BRINGING IN MONEY. MUSIC FOR MUSIC'S SAKE IS SOMETHING THAT INTERESTS ME TERRIBLY RIGHT NOW.
MEANING?
MEANING, I LOOK FORWARD TO PICKING UP A GUITAR FOR NOTHING MORE THAN THE JOY OF HOLDING AND PLAYING IT.
ANY HOPE FOR FANS OF A REUNION SHOW? A TOUR?
NEVER.

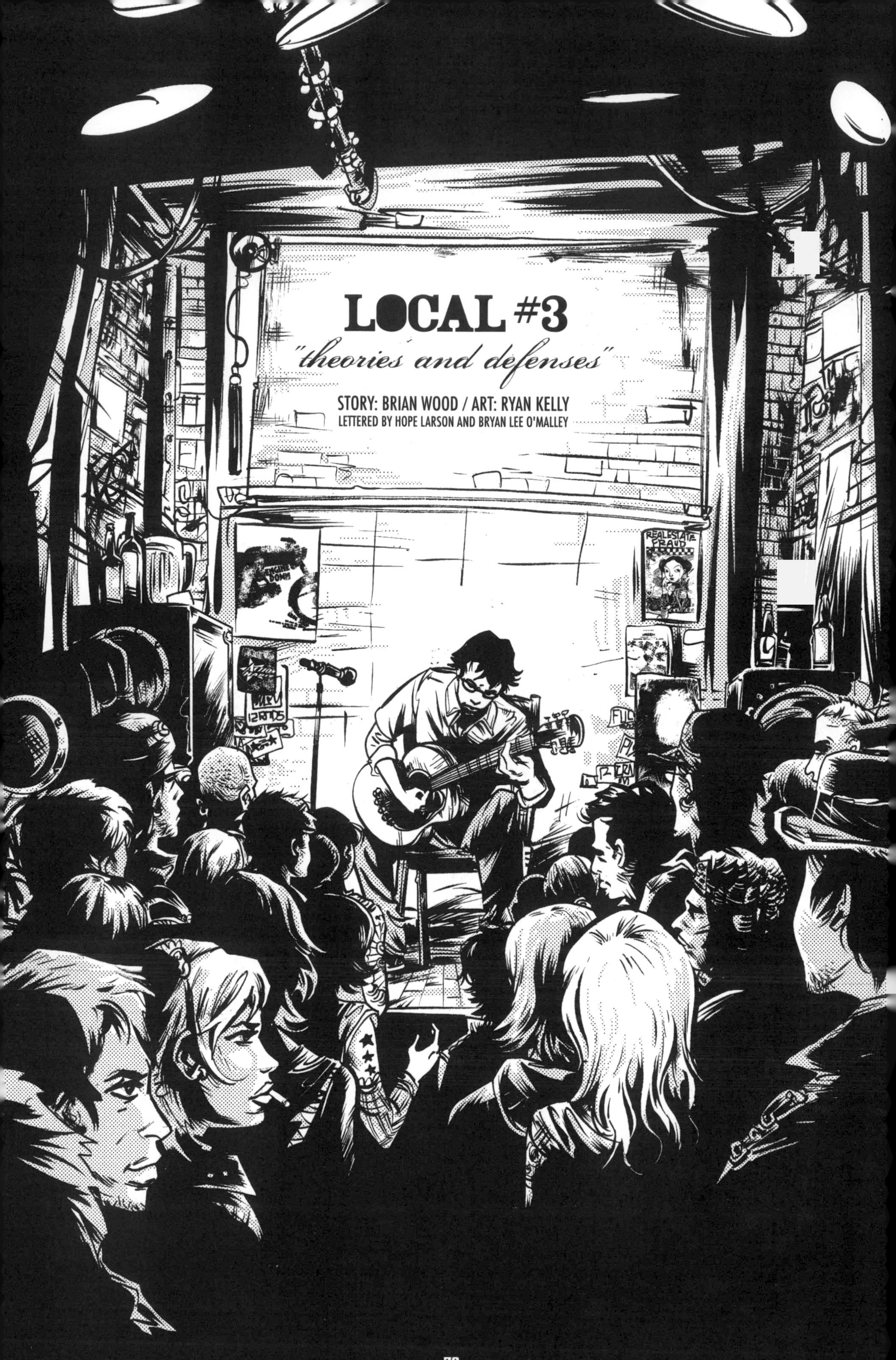
LOCAL #3
"theories and defenses"
STORY: BRIAN WOOD / ART: RYAN KELLY
LETTERED BY HOPE LARSON AND BRYAN LEE O'MALLEY

CHAPTER 4
"TWO BROTHERS"
Missoula, Montana

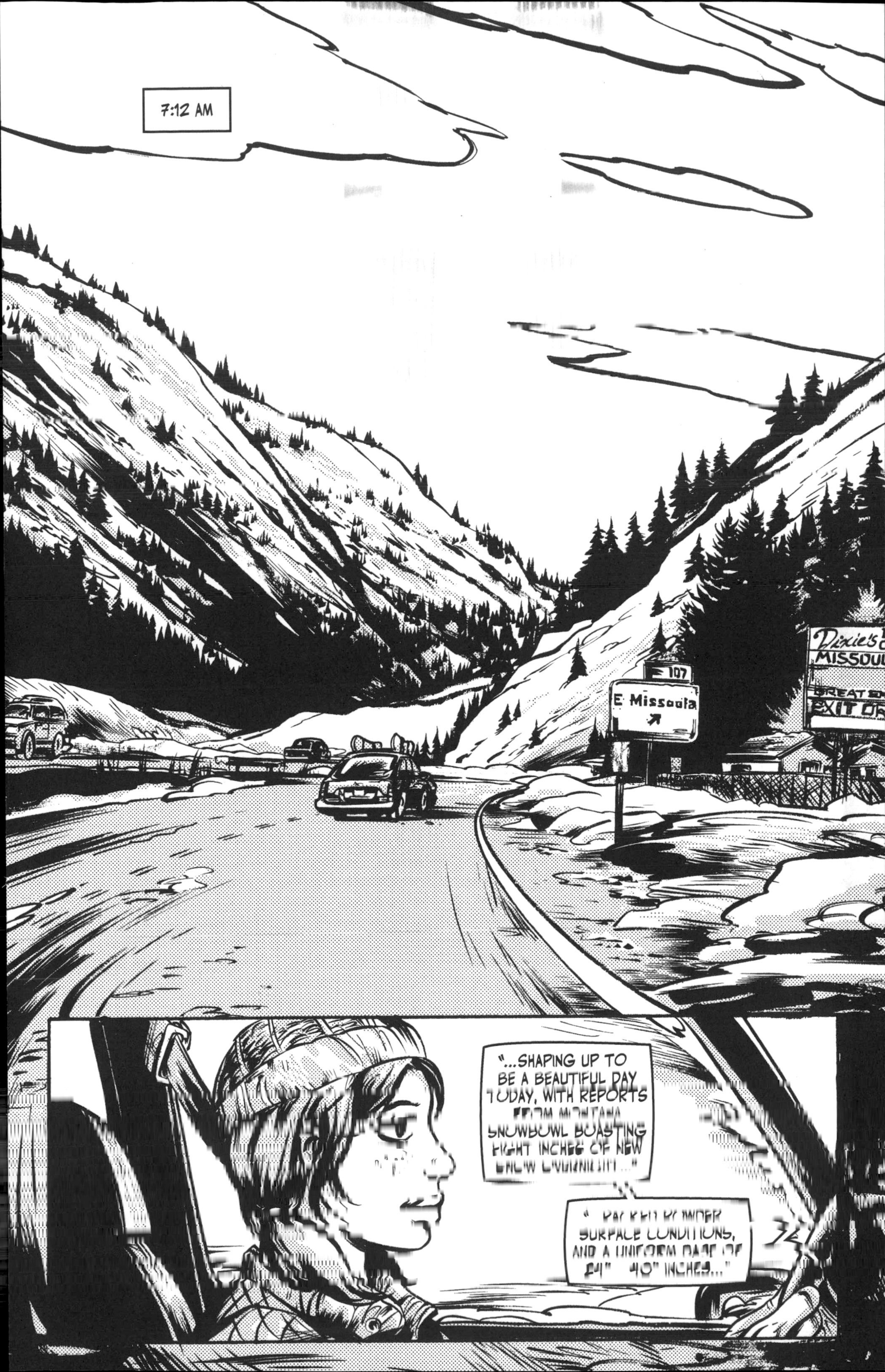
7:12 AM
107
E Missoula
"...SHAPING UP TO BE A BEAUTIFUL DAY TODAY, WITH REPORTS FROM MONTANA SNOWBOWL BOASTING EIGHT INCHES OF NEW SNOW OVERNIGHT..."
"...PACKED POWDER SURFACE CONDITIONS, AND A UNIFORM BASE OF 24"-40" INCHES..."

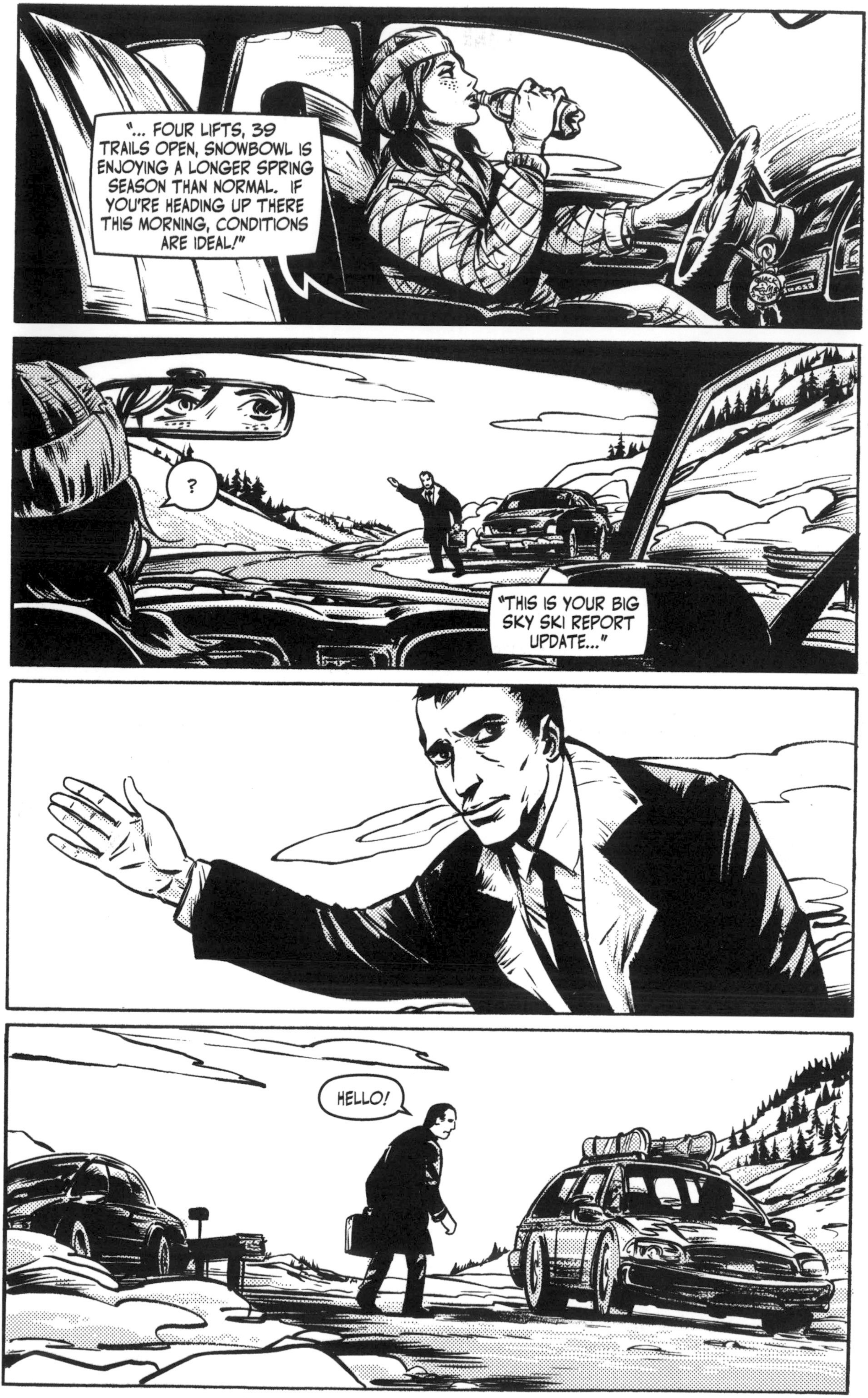
"... FOUR LIFTS, 39 TRAILS OPEN, SNOWBOWL IS ENJOYING A LONGER SPRING SEASON THAN NORMAL. IF YOU'RE HEADING UP THERE THIS MORNING, CONDITIONS ARE IDEAL!"
?
"THIS IS YOUR BIG SKY SKI REPORT UPDATE..."
HELLO!

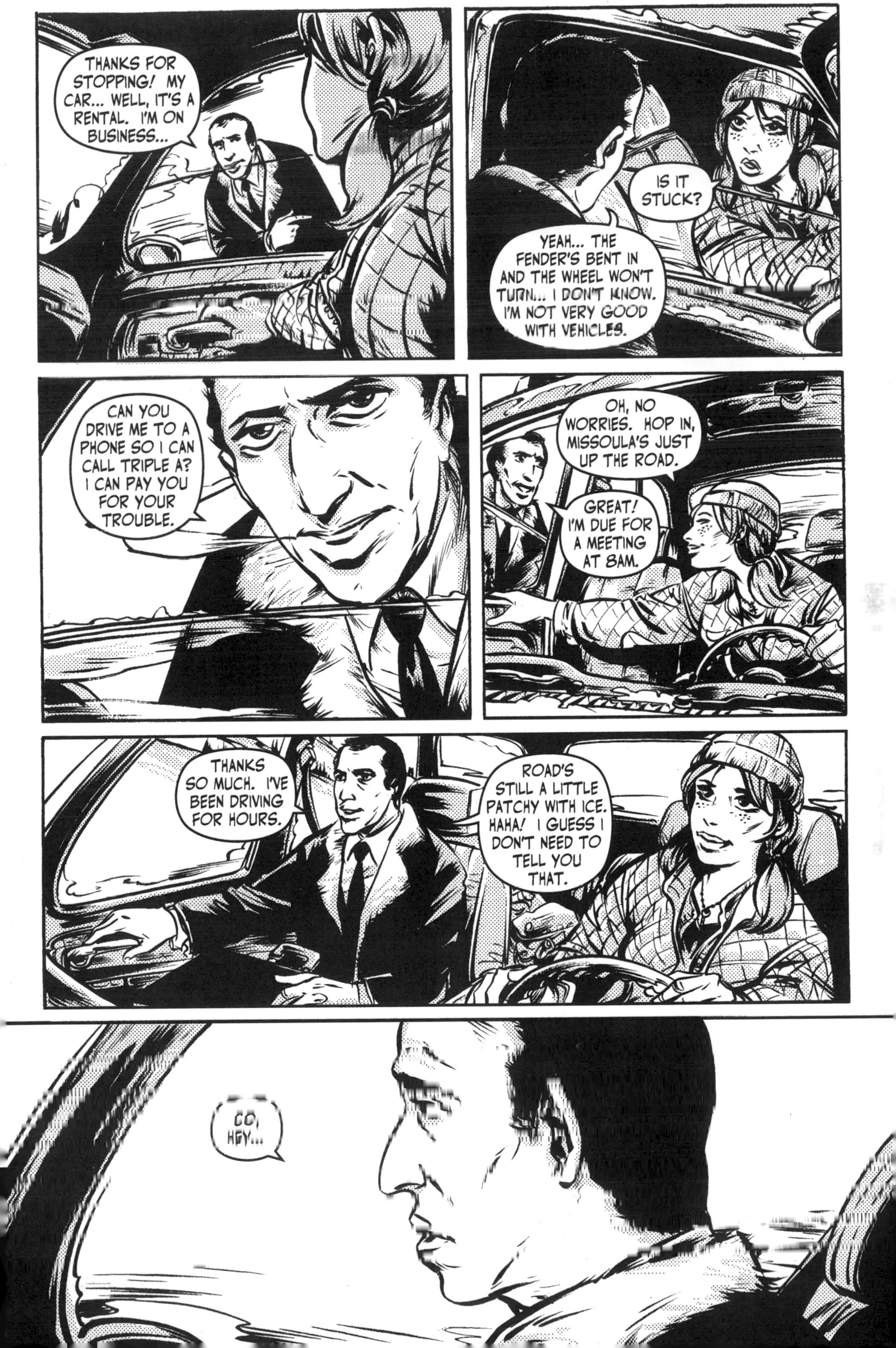
THANKS FOR STOPPING! MY CAR... WELL, IT'S A RENTAL. I'M ON BUSINESS...
IS IT STUCK?
YEAH... THE FENDER'S BENT IN AND THE WHEEL WON'T TURN... I DON'T KNOW. I'M NOT VERY GOOD WITH VEHICLES.
CAN YOU DRIVE ME TO A PHONE SO I CAN CALL TRIPLE A? I CAN PAY YOU FOR YOUR TROUBLE.
OH, NO WORRIES. HOP IN, MISSOULA'S JUST UP THE ROAD.
GREAT! I'M DUE FOR A MEETING AT 8AM.
THANKS SO MUCH. I'VE BEEN DRIVING FOR HOURS.
ROAD'S STILL A LITTLE PATCHY WITH ICE. HAHA! I GUESS I DON'T NEED TO TELL YOU THAT.
SO, HEY...

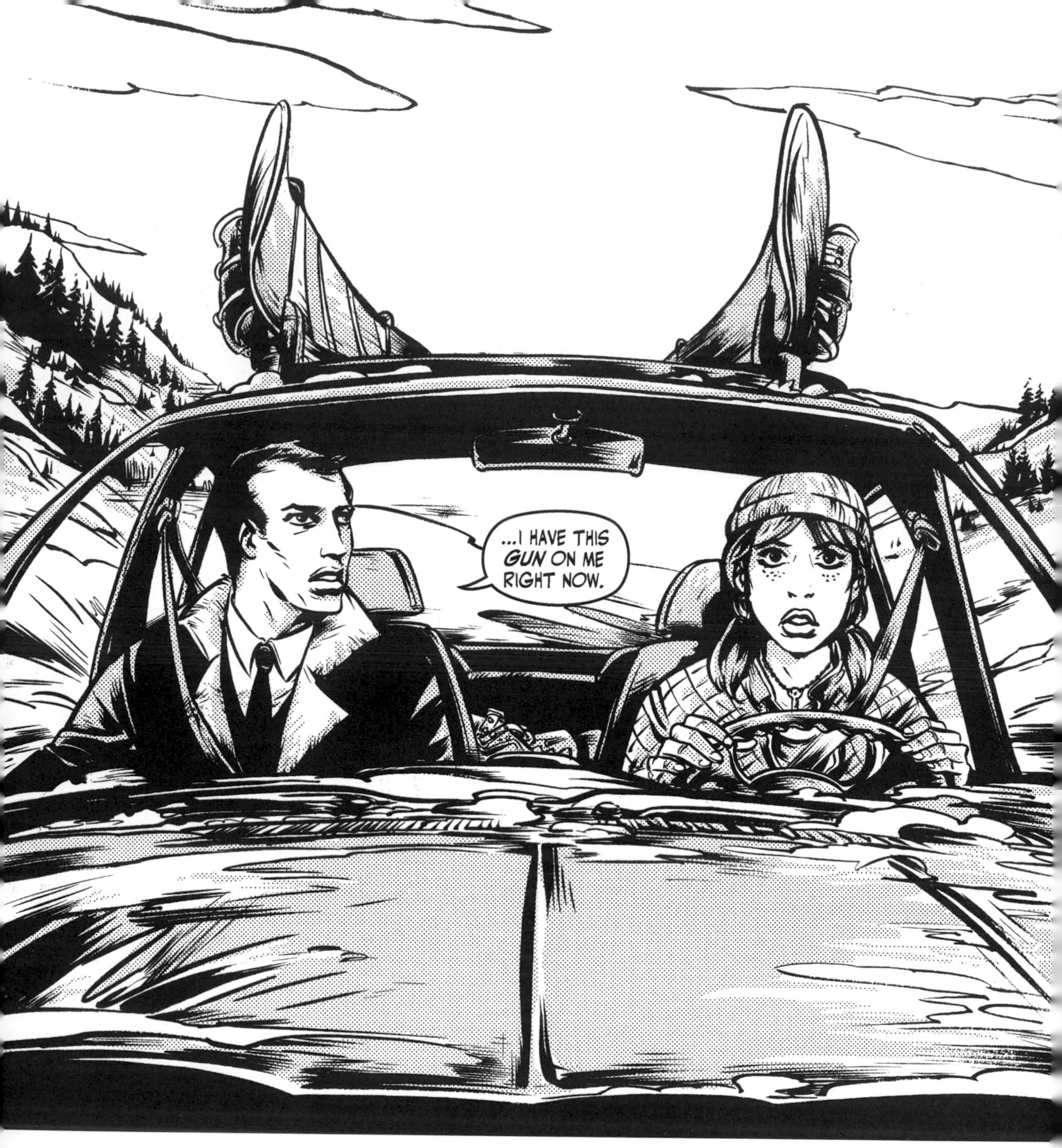
...I HAVE THIS GUN ON ME RIGHT NOW.

LOCAL #4

"two brothers"

STORY: BRIAN WOOD / ART: RYAN KELLY

LETTERED BY HOPE LARSON AND BRYAN LEE O'MALLEY

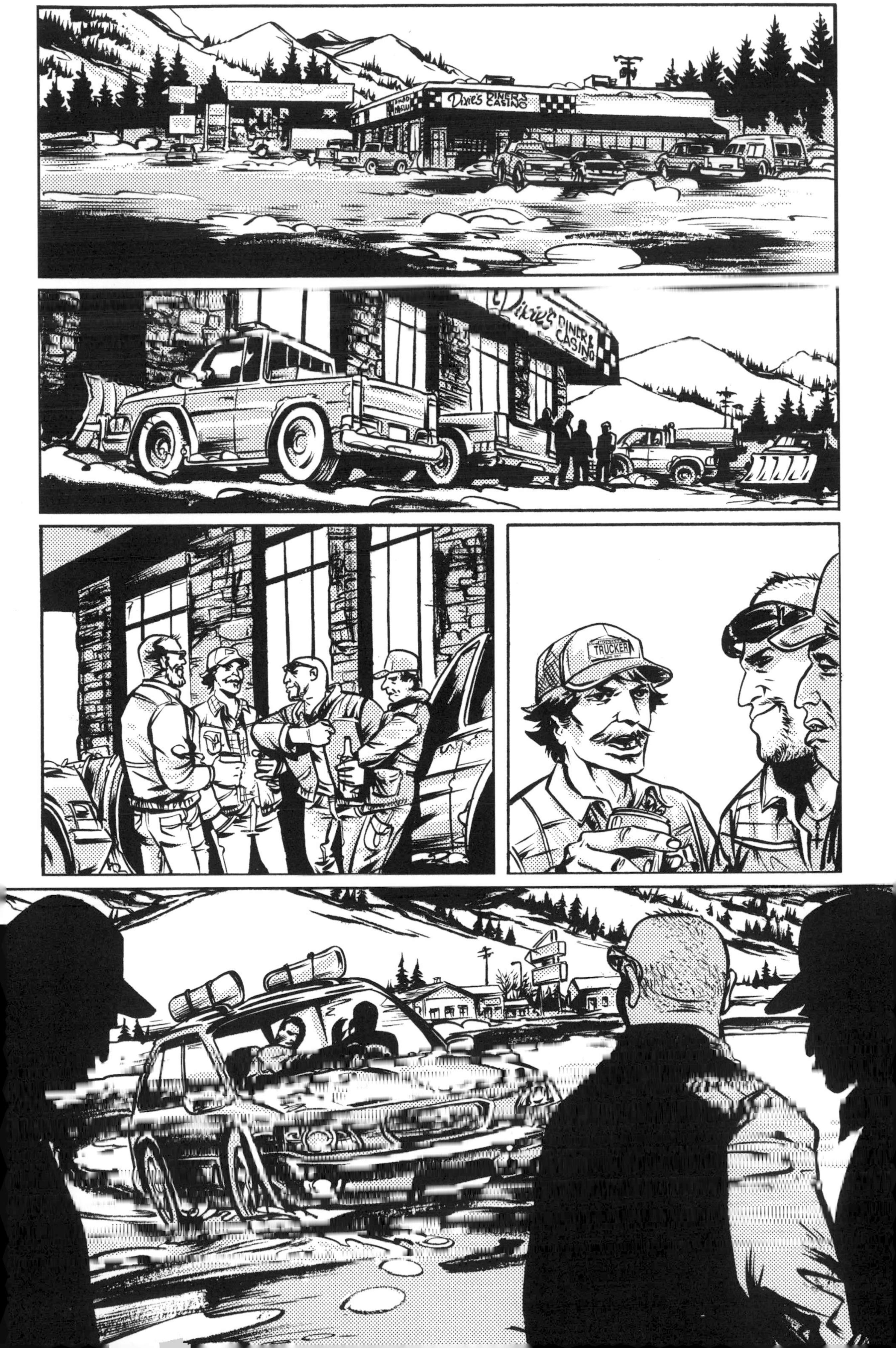
Dixie's DINER & CASINO
Dixie's DINER & CASINO
TRUCKER

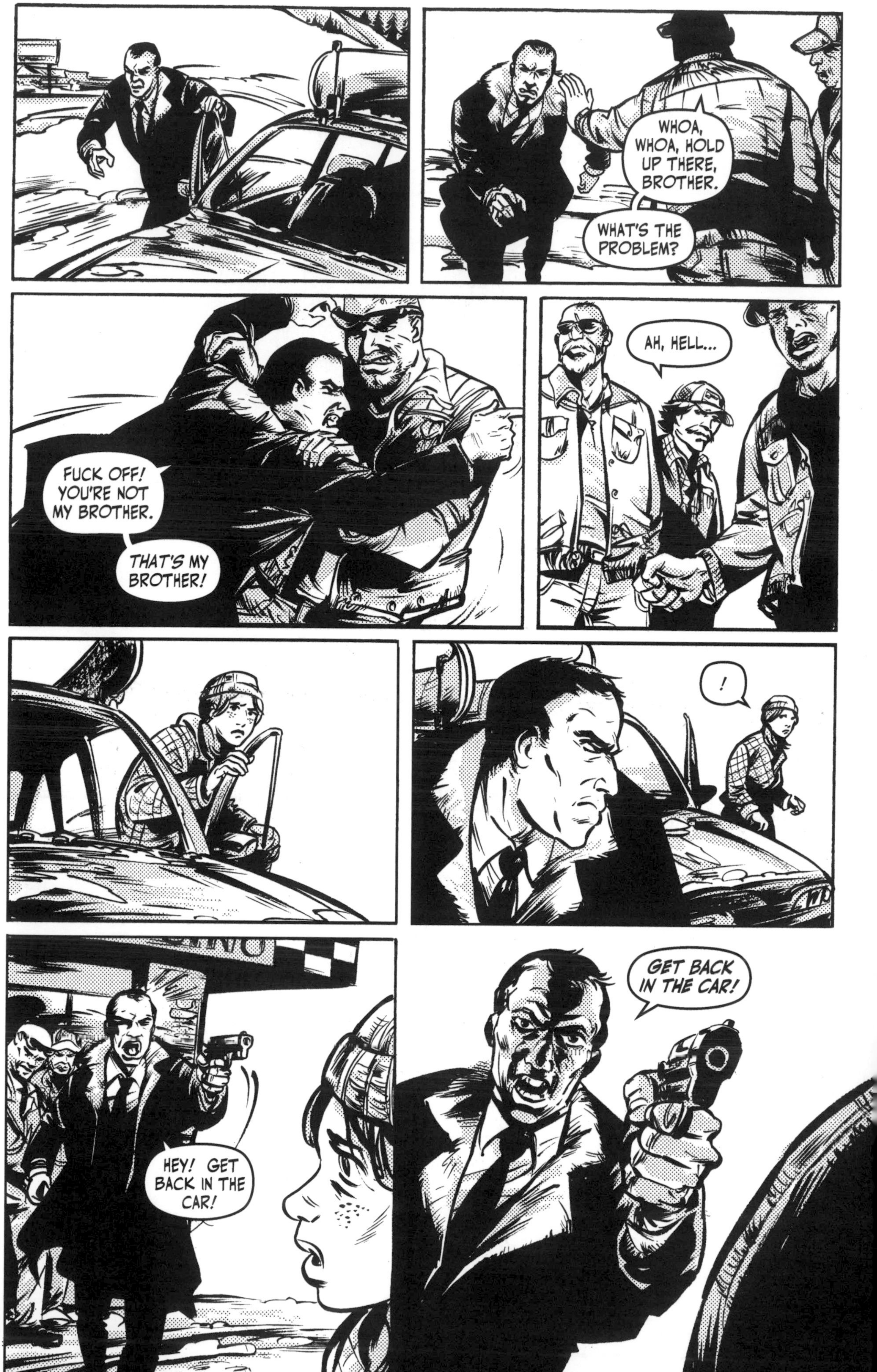
WHOA, WHOA, HOLD UP THERE, BROTHER.
WHAT'S THE PROBLEM?
FUCK OFF! YOU'RE NOT MY BROTHER.
THAT'S MY BROTHER!
AH, HELL...
!
HEY! GET BACK IN THE CAR!
GET BACK IN THE CAR!

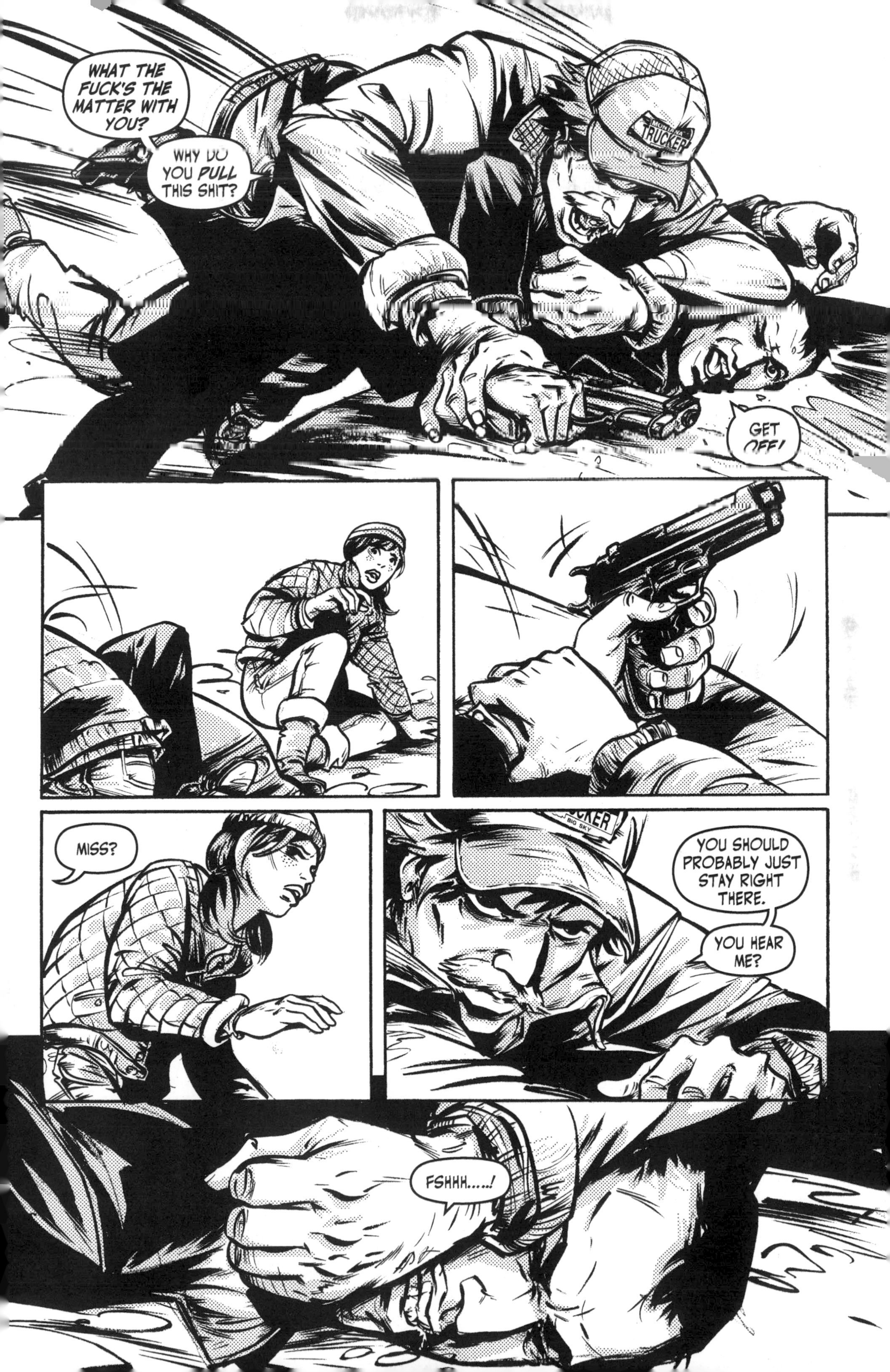
WHAT THE FUCK'S THE MATTER WITH YOU?
WHY DO YOU PULL THIS SHIT?
MONTANA TRUCKER
GET OFF!
MISS?
YOU SHOULD PROBABLY JUST STAY RIGHT THERE.
YOU HEAR ME?
FSHHH.....!

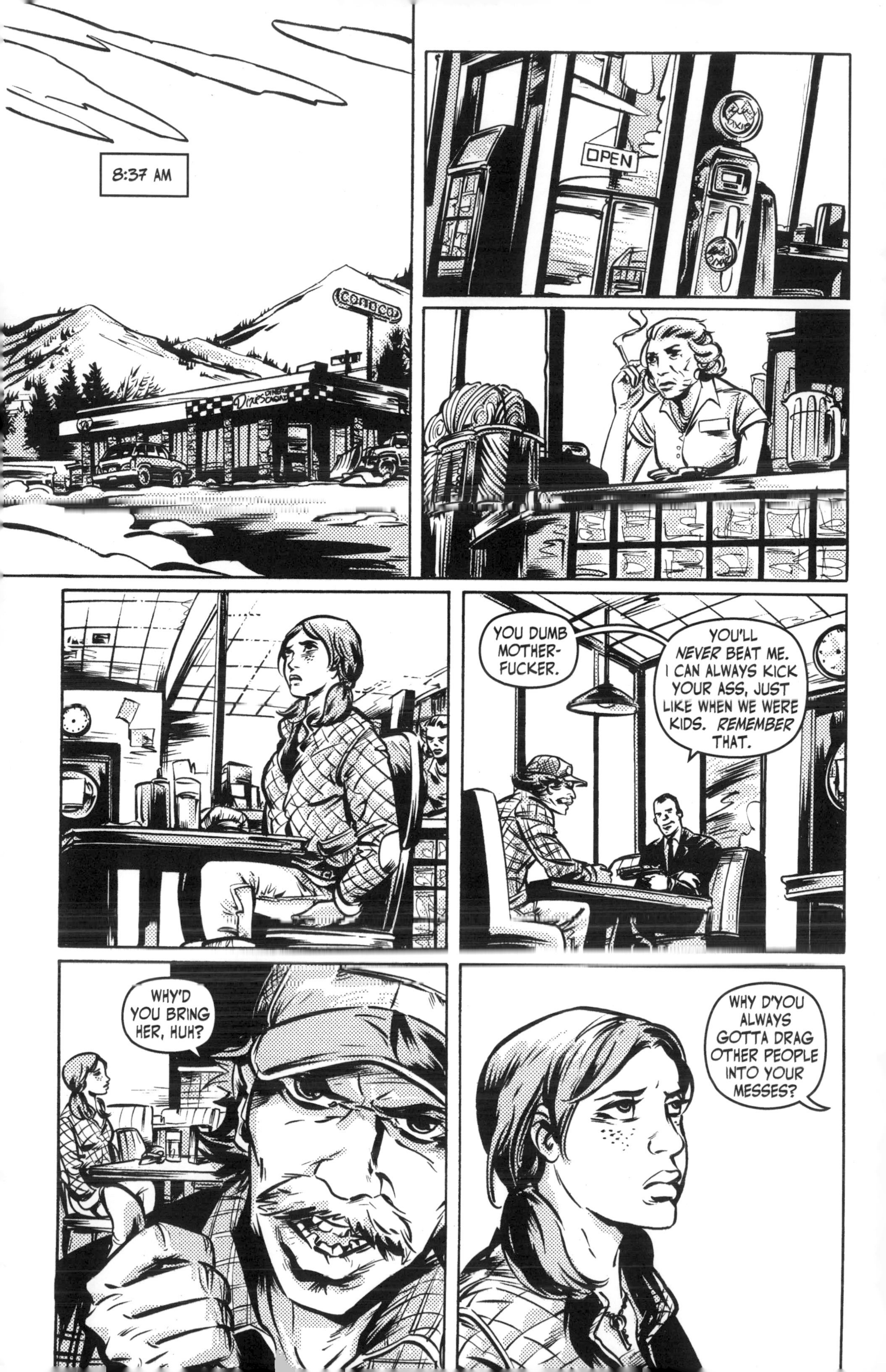

8:37 AM
OPEN
YOU DUMB MOTHER-FUCKER.
YOU'LL *NEVER* BEAT ME. I CAN ALWAYS KICK YOUR ASS, JUST LIKE WHEN WE WERE KIDS. *REMEMBER* THAT.
WHY'D YOU BRING HER, HUH?
WHY D'YOU ALWAYS GOTTA DRAG OTHER PEOPLE INTO YOUR MESSES?

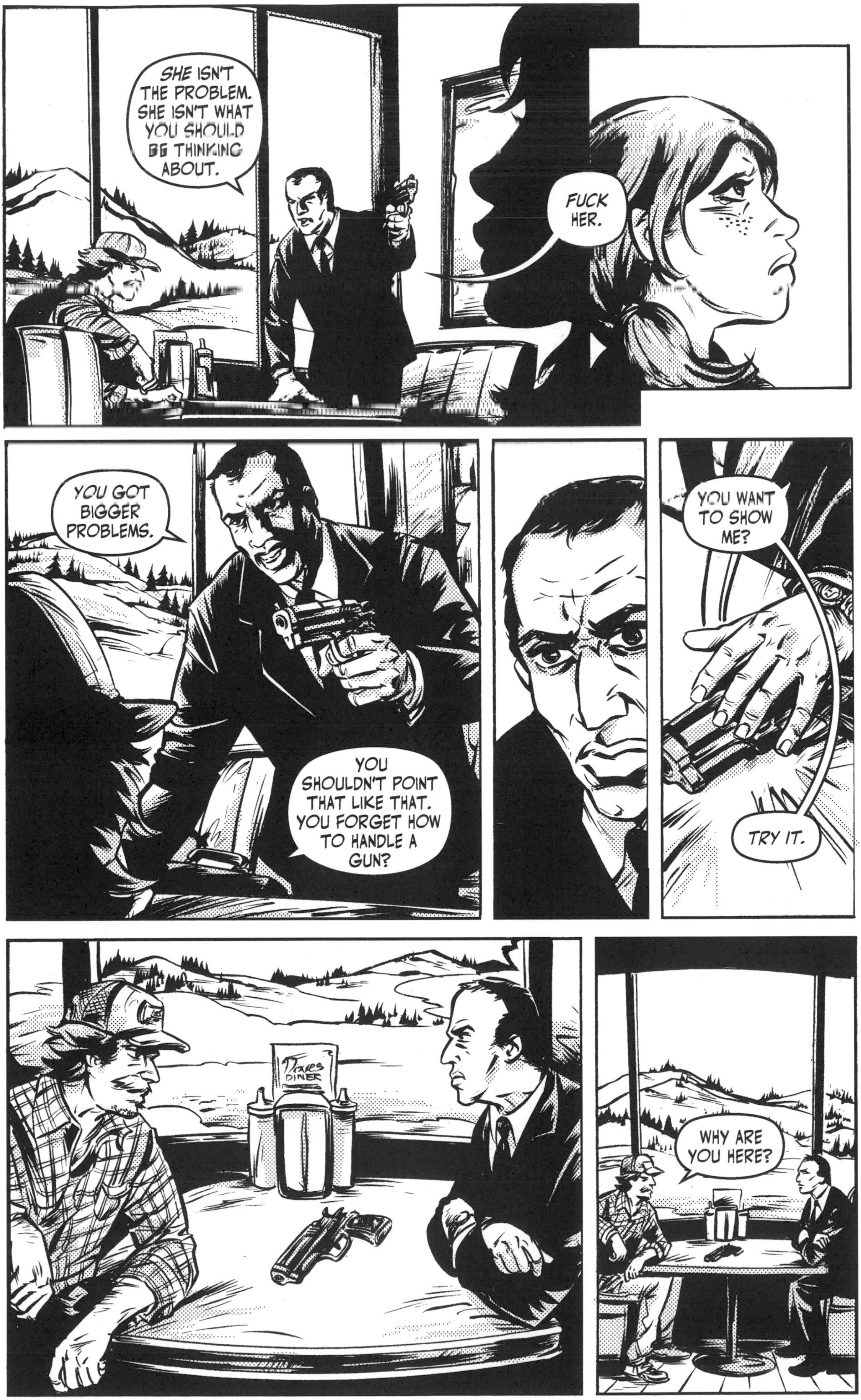
SHE ISN'T THE PROBLEM. SHE ISN'T WHAT YOU SHOULD BE THINKING ABOUT.
FUCK HER.
YOU GOT BIGGER PROBLEMS.
YOU SHOULDN'T POINT THAT LIKE THAT. YOU FORGET HOW TO HANDLE A GUN?
YOU WANT TO SHOW ME?
TRY IT.
DINER
WHY ARE YOU HERE?

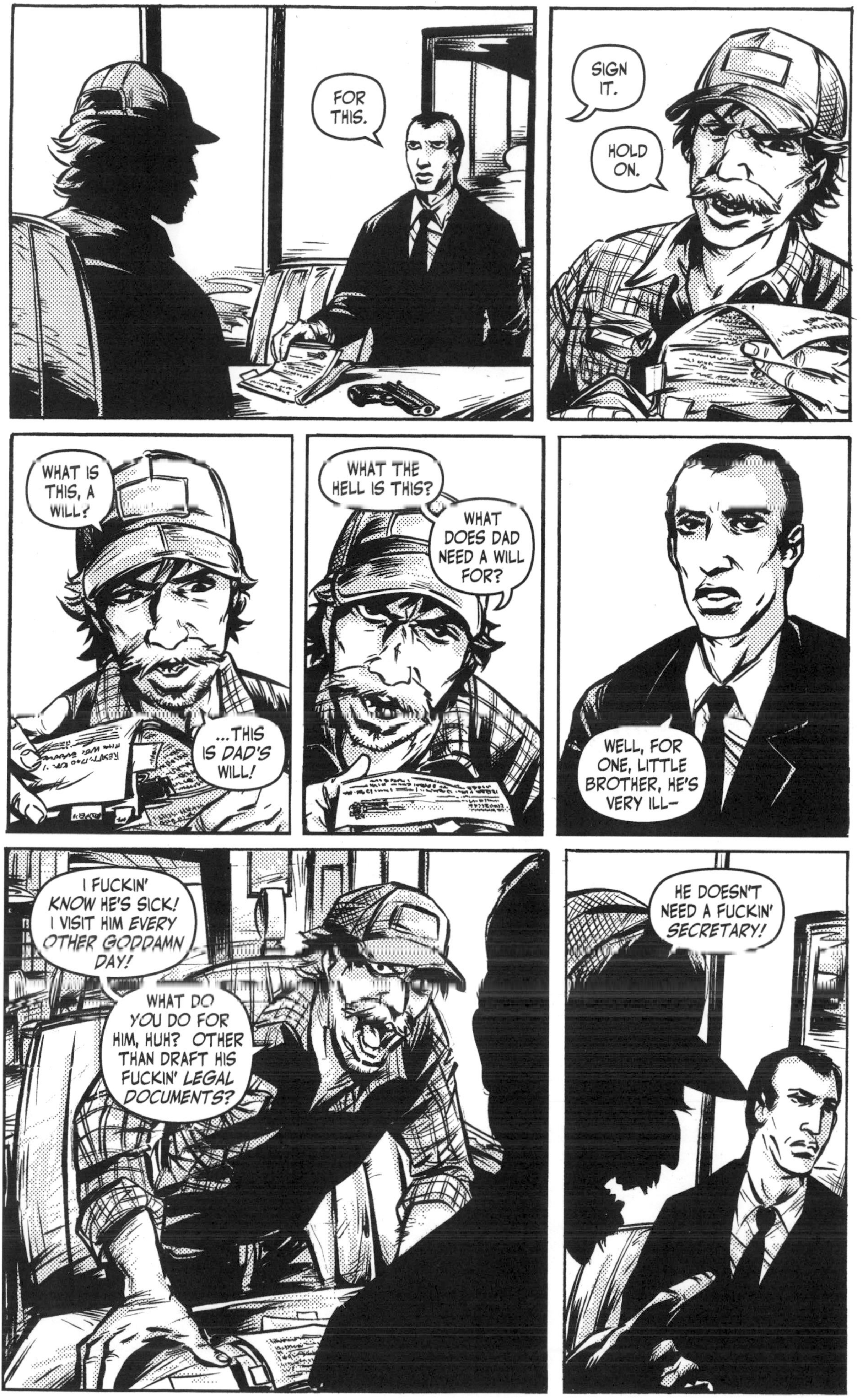

FOR THIS.
SIGN IT.
HOLD ON.
WHAT IS THIS, A WILL?
...THIS IS DAD'S WILL!
WHAT THE HELL IS THIS?
WHAT DOES DAD NEED A WILL FOR?
WELL, FOR ONE, LITTLE BROTHER, HE'S VERY ILL–
I FUCKIN' KNOW HE'S SICK! I VISIT HIM EVERY OTHER GODDAMN DAY!
WHAT DO YOU DO FOR HIM, HUH? OTHER THAN DRAFT HIS FUCKIN' LEGAL DOCUMENTS?
HE DOESN'T NEED A FUCKIN' SECRETARY!

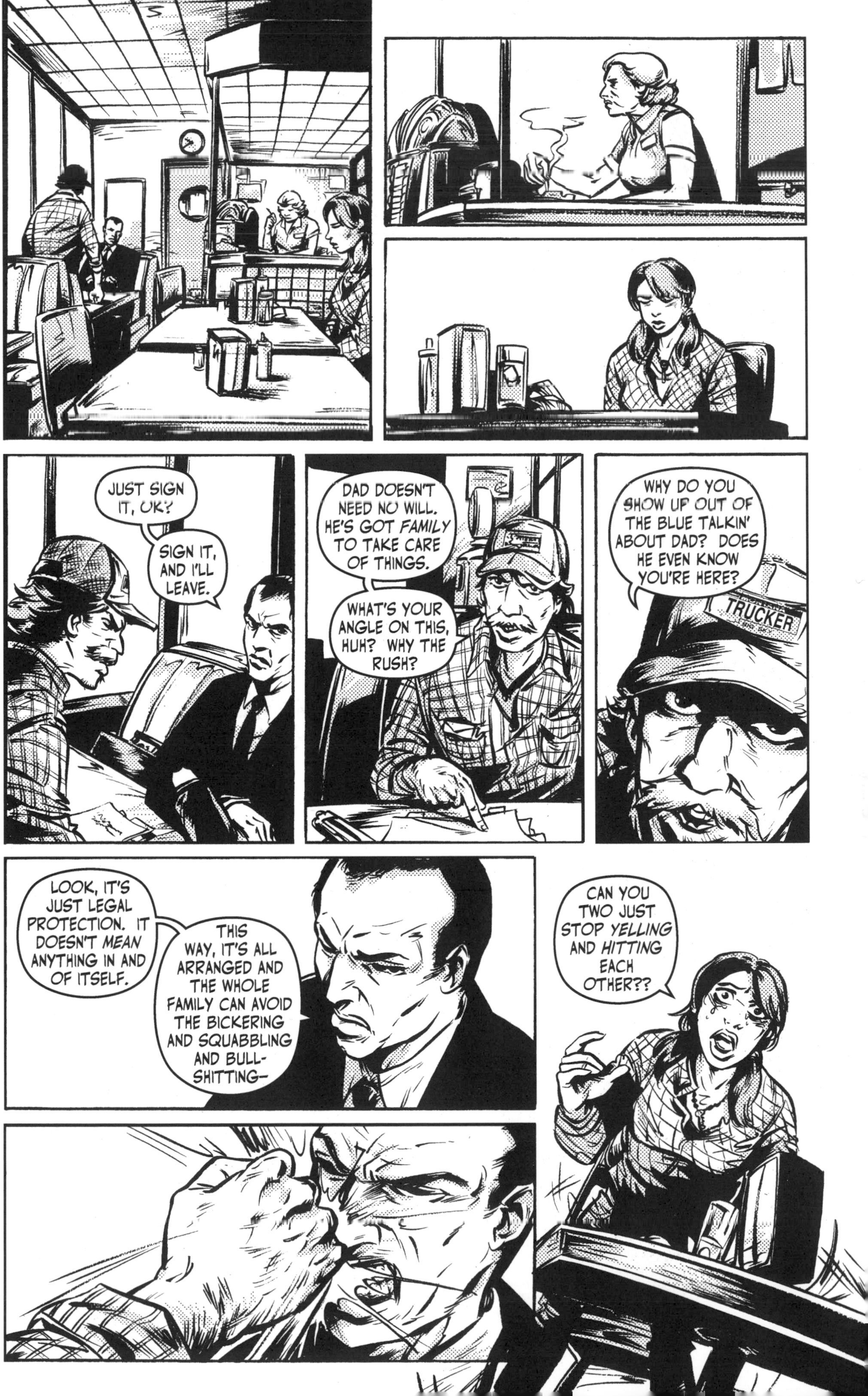
JUST SIGN IT, OK?
SIGN IT, AND I'LL LEAVE.
DAD DOESN'T NEED NO WILL. HE'S GOT *FAMILY* TO TAKE CARE OF THINGS.
WHAT'S YOUR ANGLE ON THIS, HUH? WHY THE RUSH?
WHY DO YOU SHOW UP OUT OF THE BLUE TALKIN' ABOUT DAD? DOES HE EVEN KNOW YOU'RE HERE?
TRUCKER
LOOK, IT'S JUST LEGAL PROTECTION. IT DOESN'T *MEAN* ANYTHING IN AND OF ITSELF.
THIS WAY, IT'S ALL ARRANGED AND THE WHOLE FAMILY CAN AVOID THE BICKERING AND SQUABBLING AND BULL-SHITTING–
CAN YOU TWO JUST STOP *YELLING* AND *HITTING* EACH OTHER??

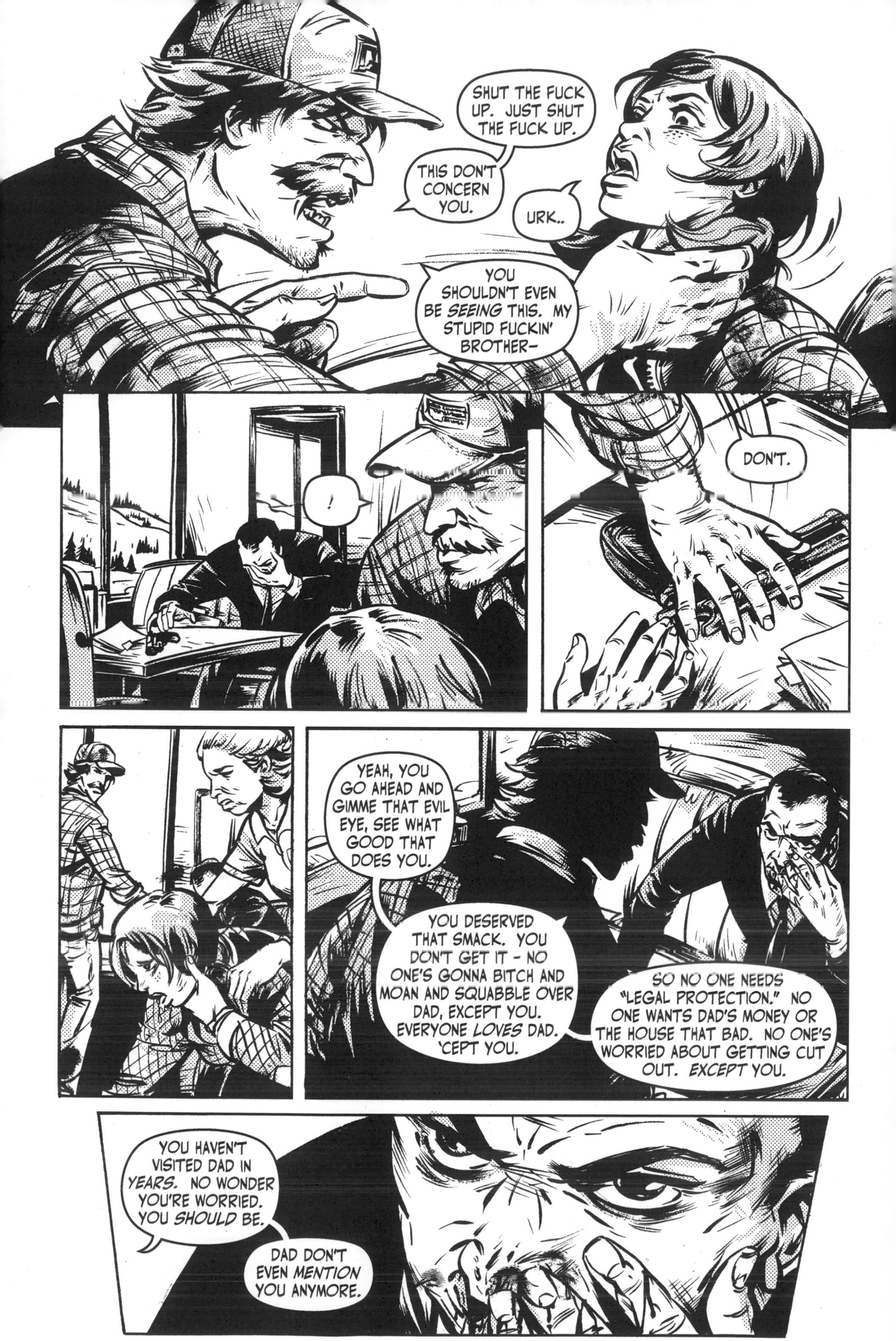
SHUT THE FUCK UP. JUST SHUT THE FUCK UP.
THIS DON'T CONCERN YOU.
URK..
YOU SHOULDN'T EVEN BE *SEEING* THIS. MY STUPID FUCKIN' BROTHER–
!
DON'T.
YEAH, YOU GO AHEAD AND GIMME THAT EVIL EYE, SEE WHAT GOOD THAT DOES YOU.
YOU DESERVED THAT SMACK. YOU DON'T GET IT - NO ONE'S GONNA BITCH AND MOAN AND SQUABBLE OVER DAD, EXCEPT YOU. EVERYONE *LOVES* DAD. 'CEPT YOU.
SO NO ONE NEEDS "LEGAL PROTECTION." NO ONE WANTS DAD'S MONEY OR THE HOUSE THAT BAD. NO ONE'S WORRIED ABOUT GETTING CUT OUT. *EXCEPT* YOU.
YOU HAVEN'T VISITED DAD IN *YEARS*. NO WONDER YOU'RE WORRIED. YOU *SHOULD* BE.
DAD DON'T EVEN *MENTION* YOU ANYMORE.

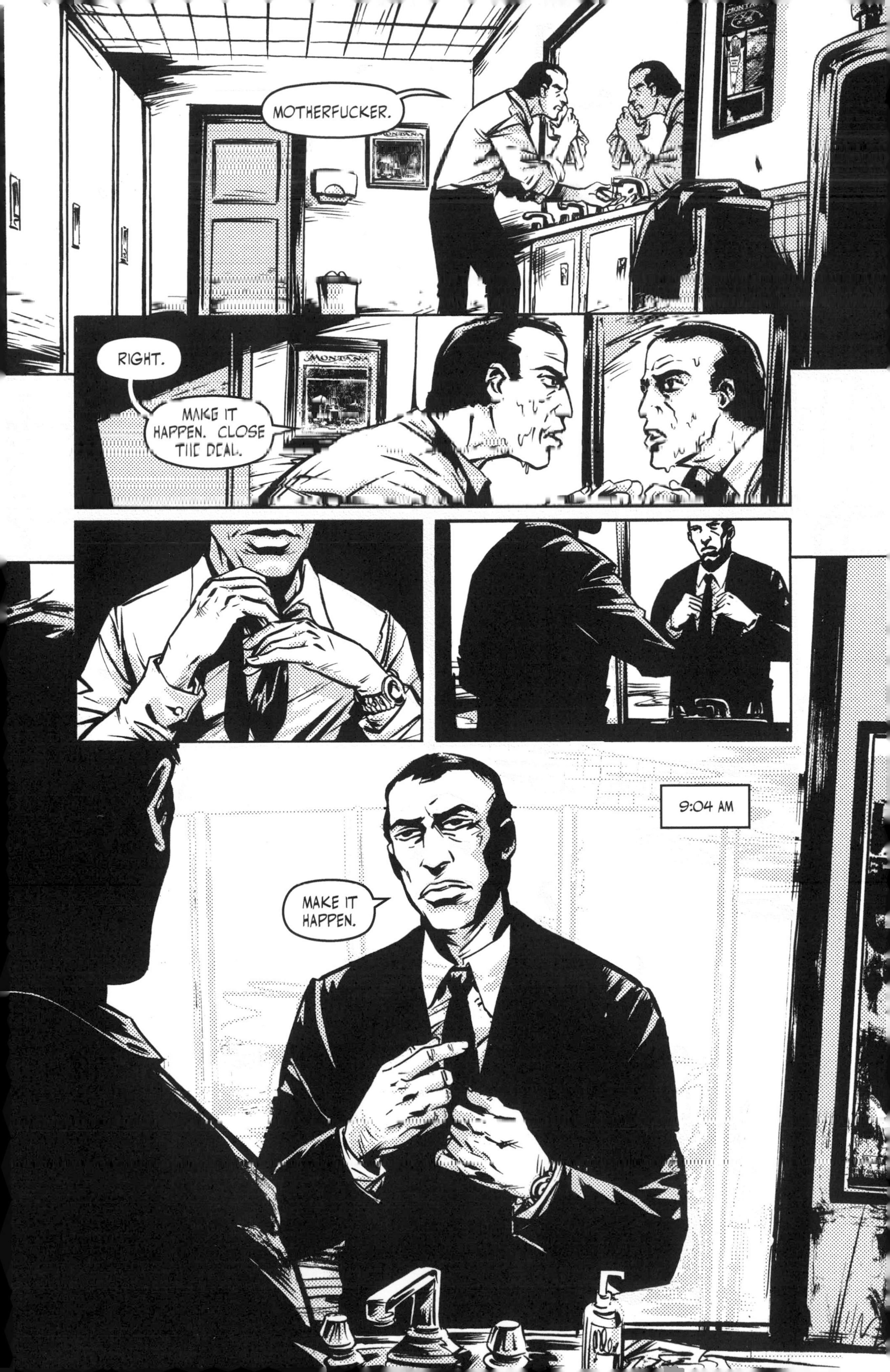
MOTHERFUCKER.
RIGHT.
MAKE IT HAPPEN. CLOSE THE DEAL.
9:04 AM
MAKE IT HAPPEN.

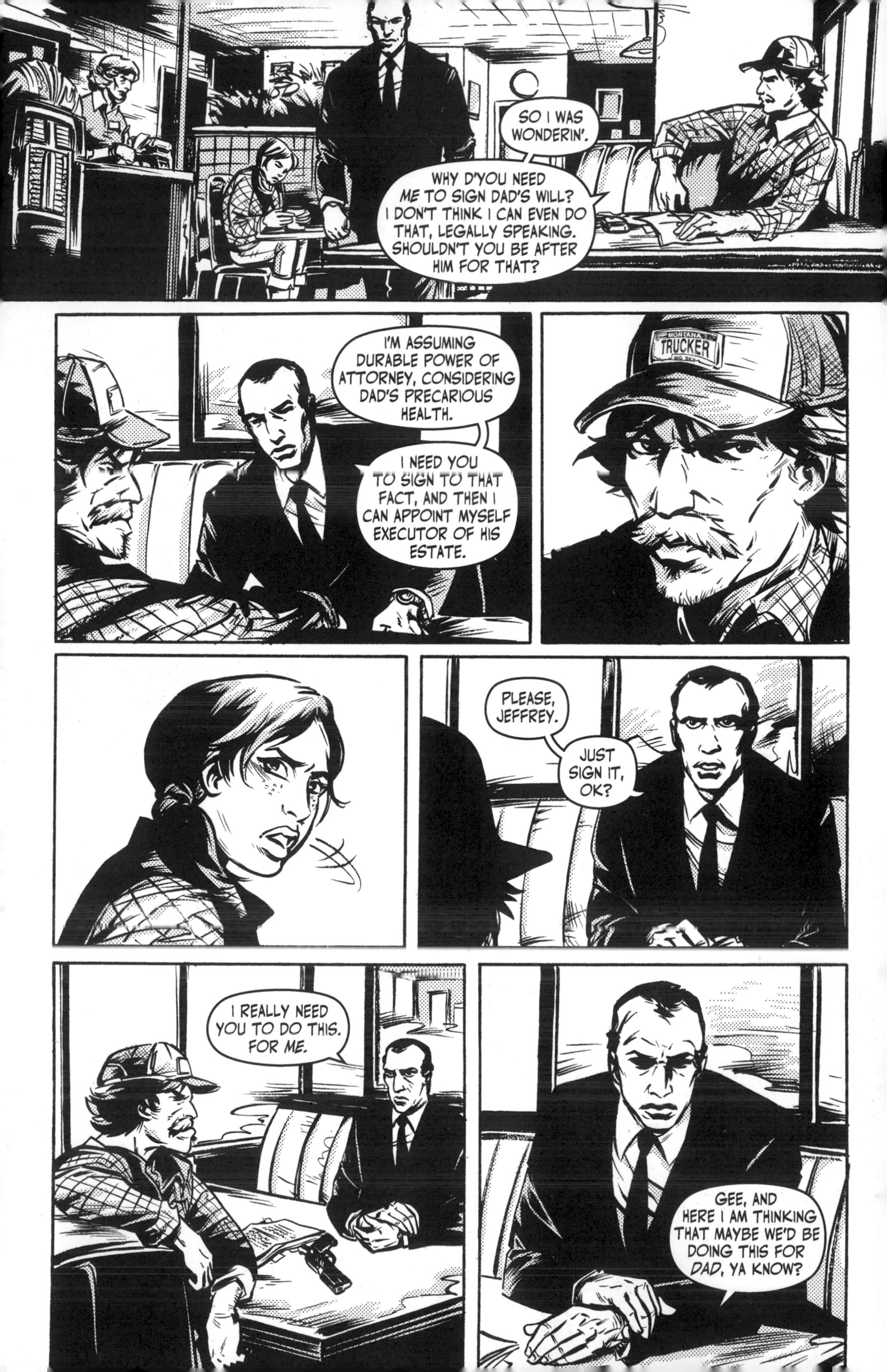
SO I WAS WONDERIN'.
WHY D'YOU NEED ME TO SIGN DAD'S WILL? I DON'T THINK I CAN EVEN DO THAT, LEGALLY SPEAKING. SHOULDN'T YOU BE AFTER HIM FOR THAT?
I'M ASSUMING DURABLE POWER OF ATTORNEY, CONSIDERING DAD'S PRECARIOUS HEALTH.
I NEED YOU TO SIGN TO THAT FACT, AND THEN I CAN APPOINT MYSELF EXECUTOR OF HIS ESTATE.
MONTANA TRUCKER BIG SKY
PLEASE, JEFFREY.
JUST SIGN IT, OK?
I REALLY NEED YOU TO DO THIS. FOR ME.
GEE, AND HERE I AM THINKING THAT MAYBE WE'D BE DOING THIS FOR DAD, YA KNOW?

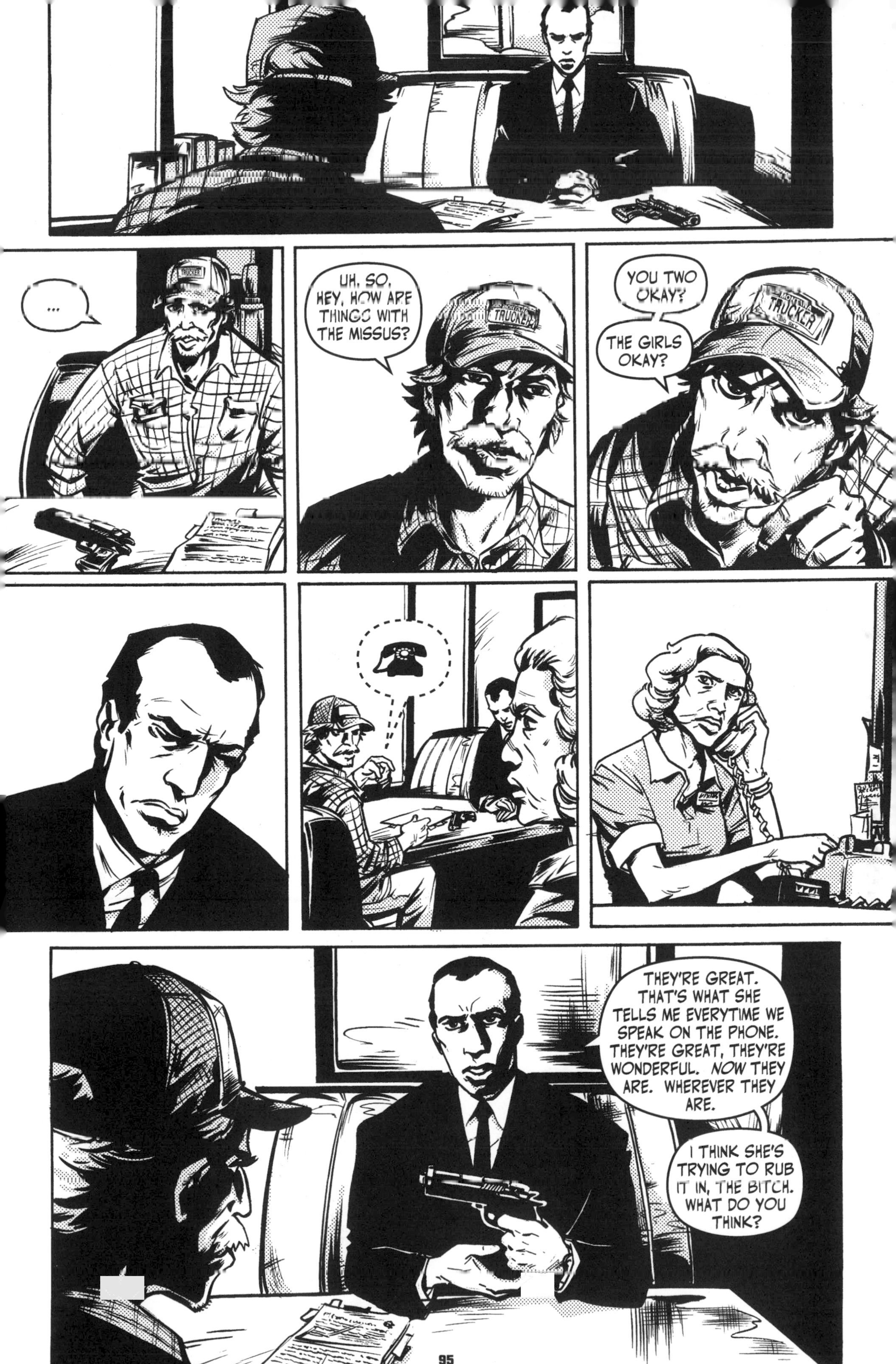
...
UH, SO, HEY, HOW ARE THINGS WITH THE MISSUS?
YOU TWO OKAY?
THE GIRLS OKAY?
THEY'RE GREAT. THAT'S WHAT SHE TELLS ME EVERYTIME WE SPEAK ON THE PHONE. THEY'RE GREAT, THEY'RE WONDERFUL. *NOW* THEY ARE. WHEREVER THEY ARE.
I THINK SHE'S TRYING TO RUB IT IN, THE BITCH. WHAT DO YOU THINK?

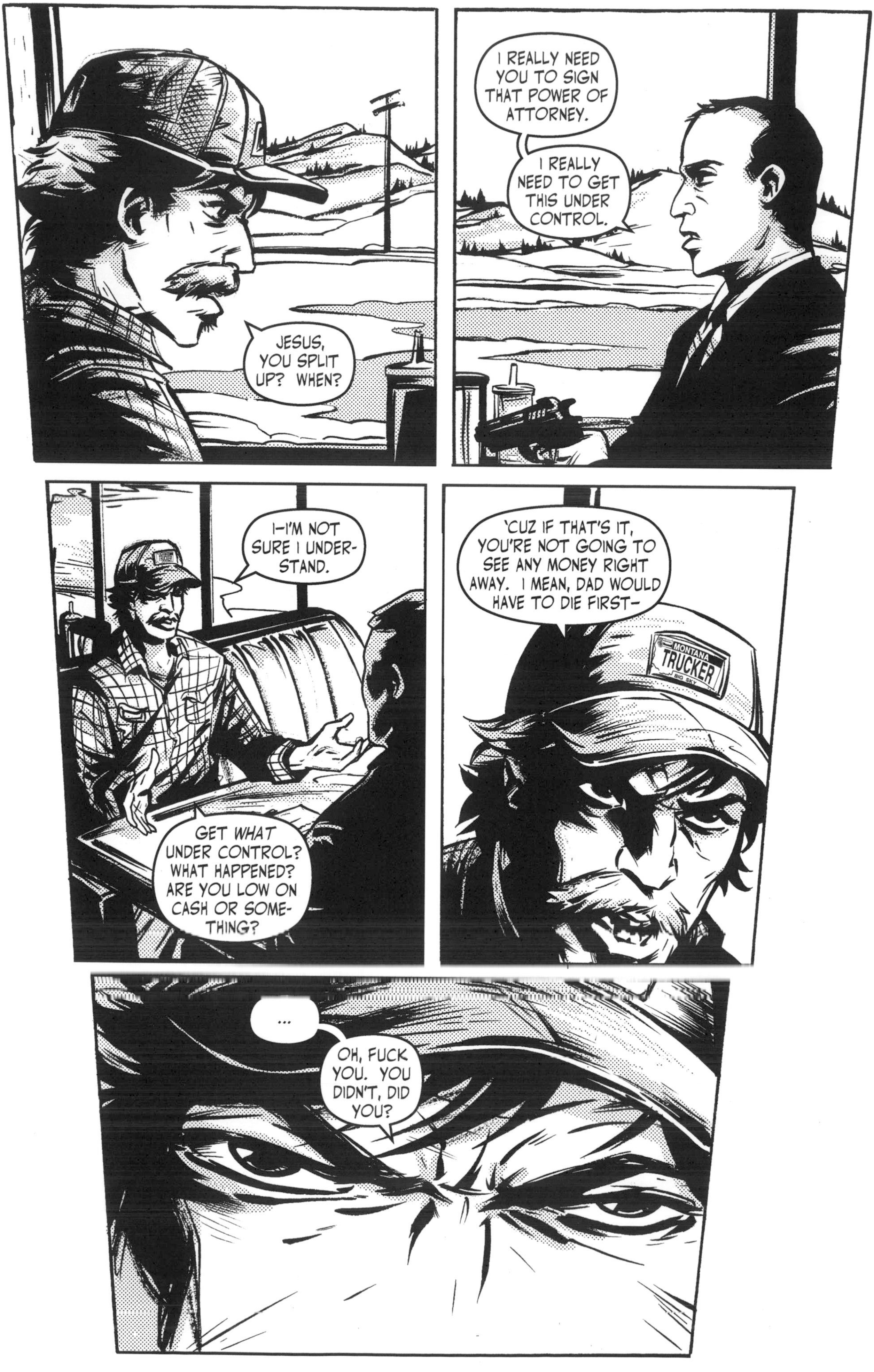
JESUS, YOU SPLIT UP? WHEN?
I REALLY NEED YOU TO SIGN THAT POWER OF ATTORNEY.
I REALLY NEED TO GET THIS UNDER CONTROL.
I-I'M NOT SURE I UNDER-STAND.
GET WHAT UNDER CONTROL? WHAT HAPPENED? ARE YOU LOW ON CASH OR SOME-THING?
'CUZ IF THAT'S IT, YOU'RE NOT GOING TO SEE ANY MONEY RIGHT AWAY. I MEAN, DAD WOULD HAVE TO DIE FIRST—
MONTANA
TRUCKER
BIG SKY
...
OH, FUCK YOU. YOU DIDN'T, DID YOU?

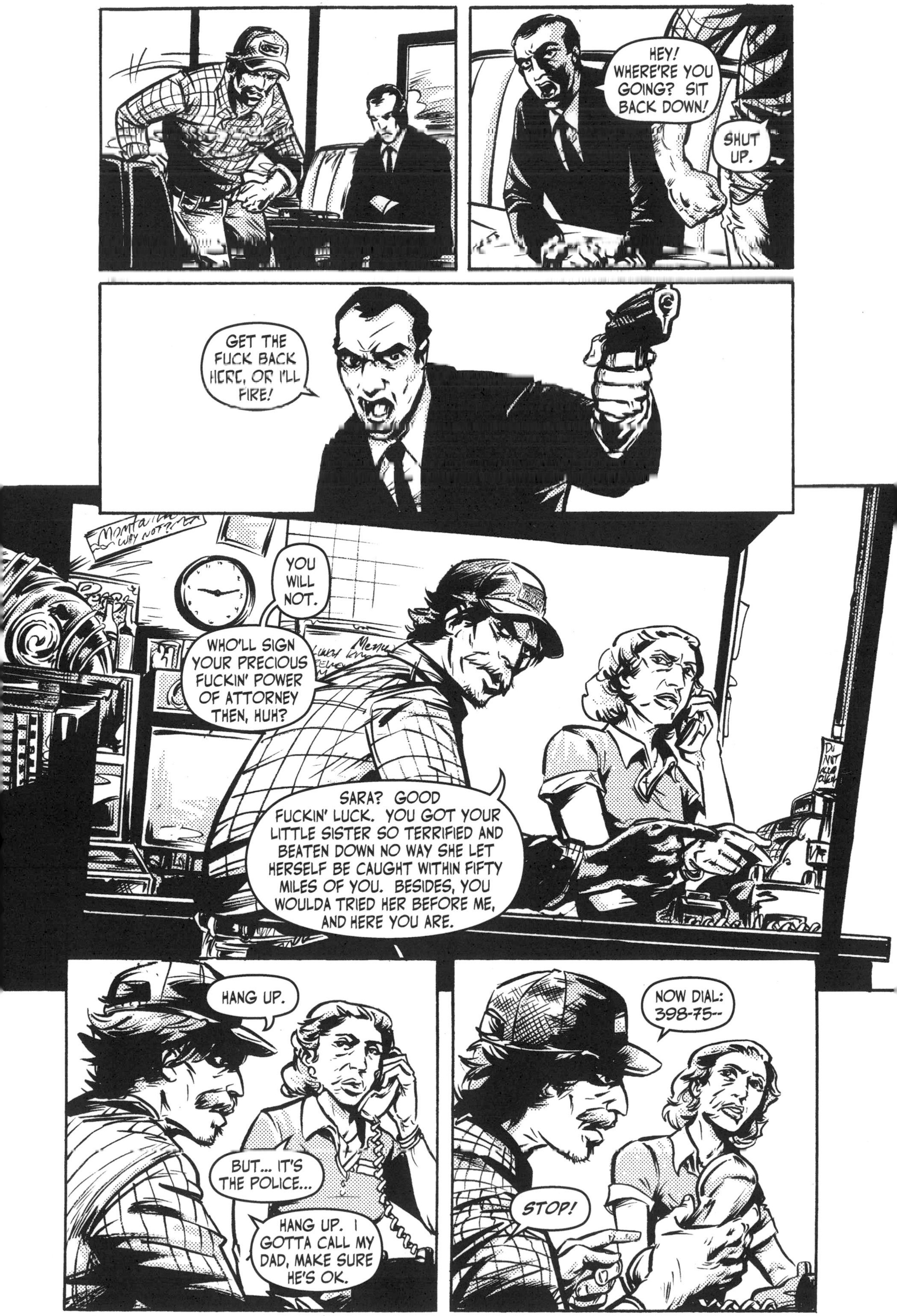
HEY! WHERE'RE YOU GOING? SIT BACK DOWN!
SHUT UP.
GET THE FUCK BACK HERE, OR I'LL FIRE!
YOU WILL NOT.
WHO'LL SIGN YOUR PRECIOUS FUCKIN' POWER OF ATTORNEY THEN, HUH?
SARA? GOOD FUCKIN' LUCK. YOU GOT YOUR LITTLE SISTER SO TERRIFIED AND BEATEN DOWN NO WAY SHE LET HERSELF BE CAUGHT WITHIN FIFTY MILES OF YOU. BESIDES, YOU WOULDA TRIED HER BEFORE ME, AND HERE YOU ARE.
HANG UP.
BUT... IT'S THE POLICE...
HANG UP. I GOTTA CALL MY DAD, MAKE SURE HE'S OK.
NOW DIAL: 398-75--
STOP!

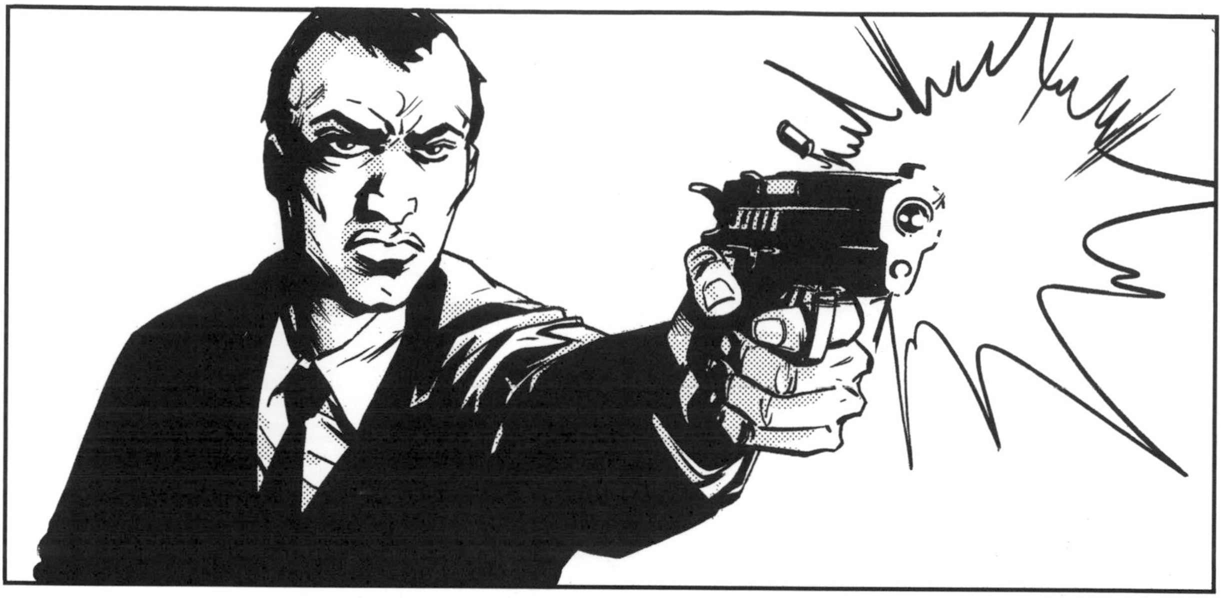

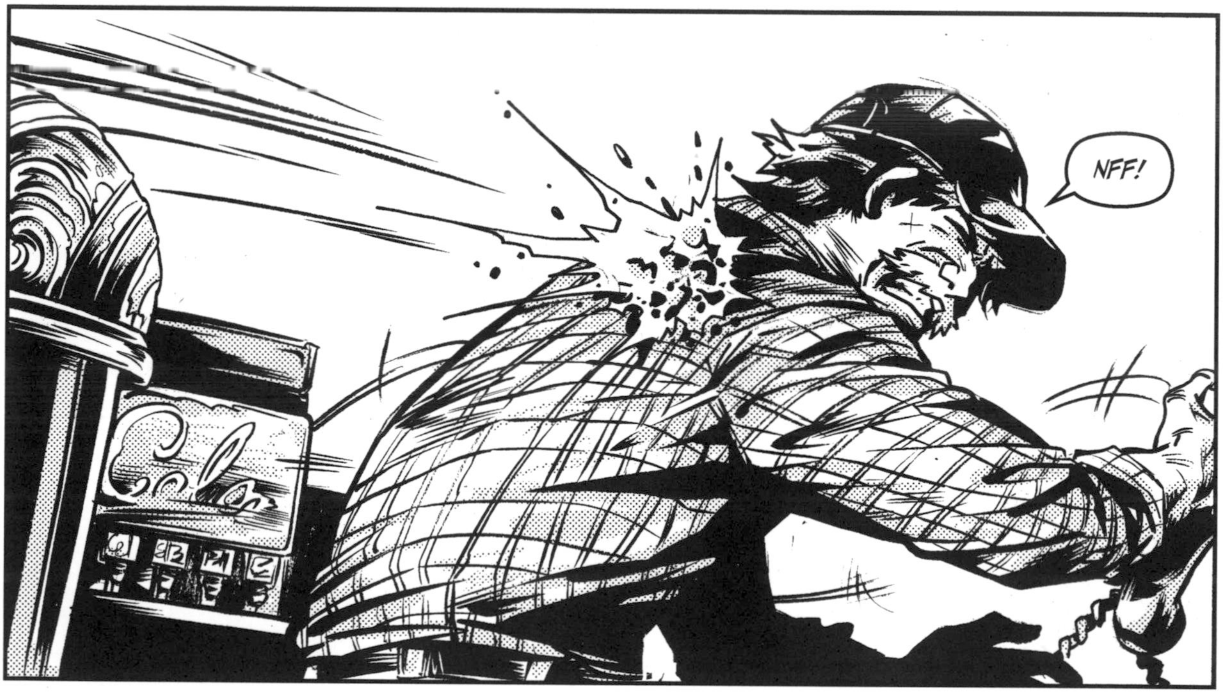
NFF!

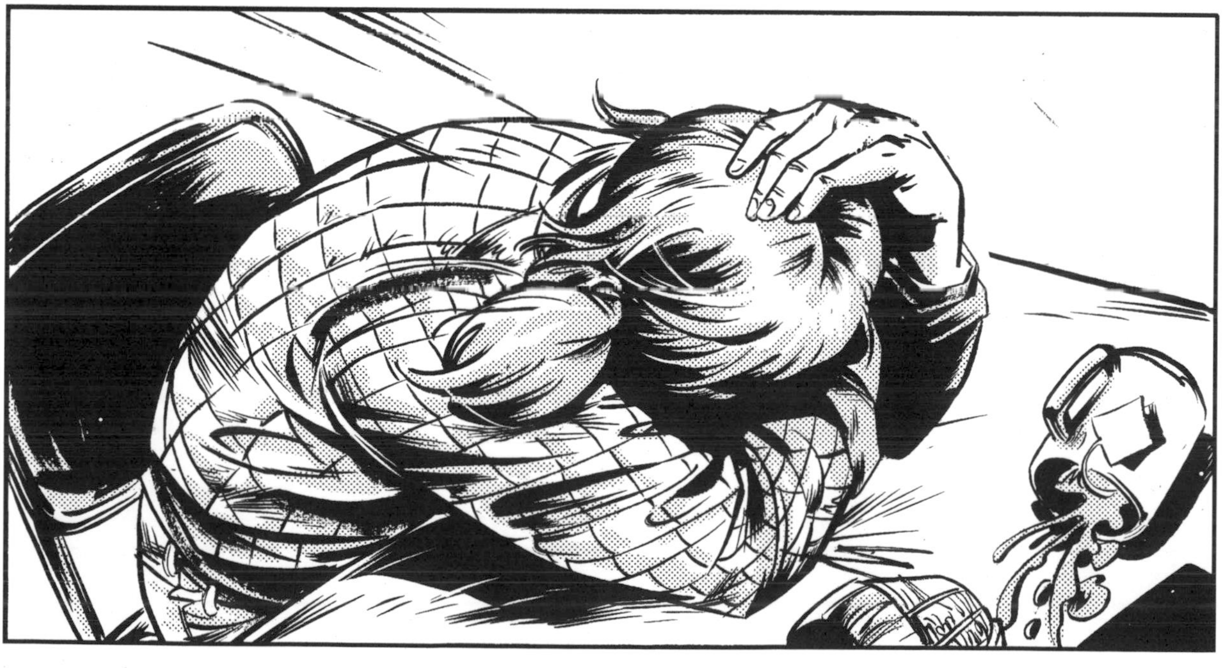

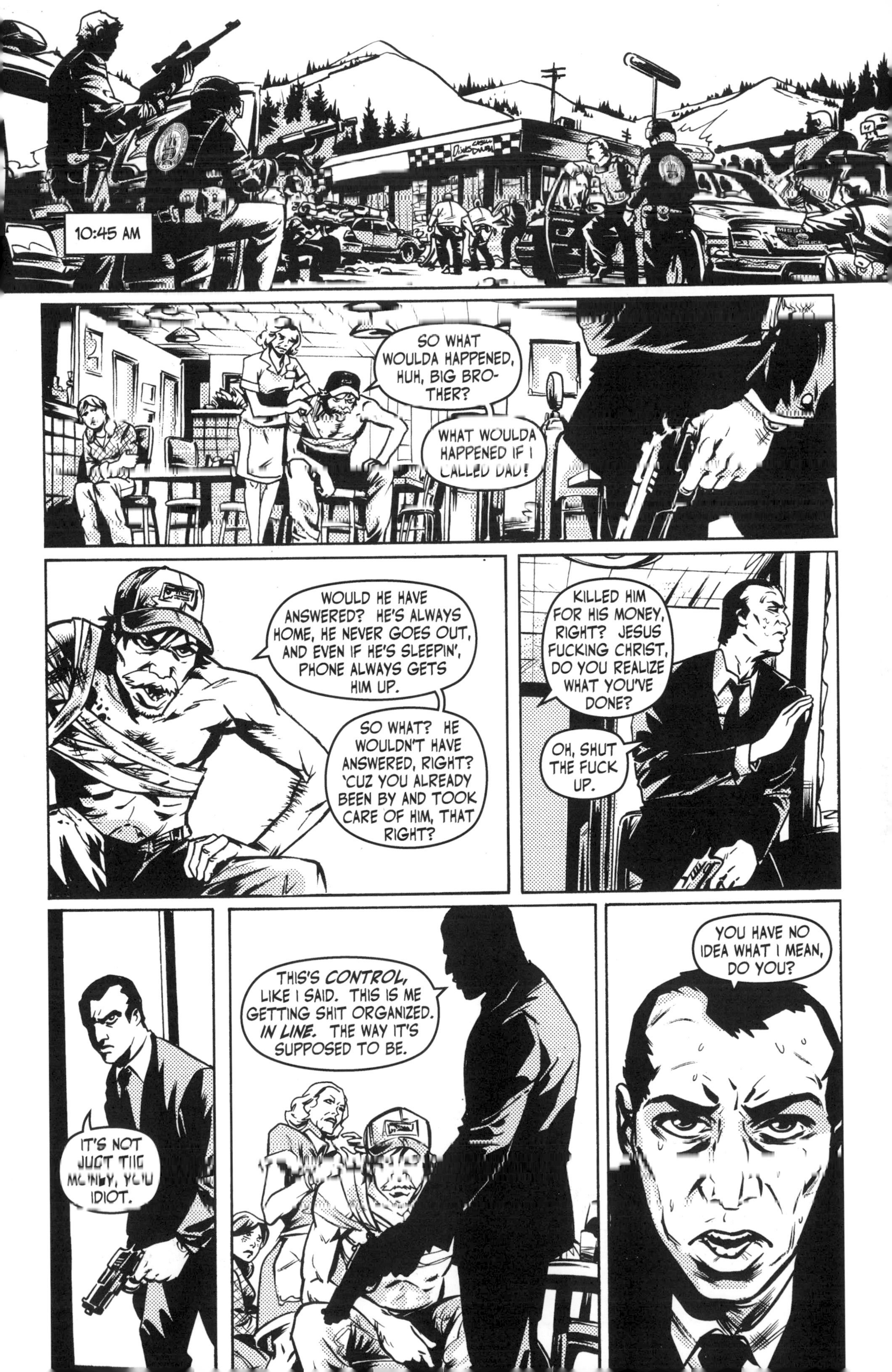
10:45 AM
SO WHAT WOULDA HAPPENED, HUH, BIG BROTHER?
WHAT WOULDA HAPPENED IF I CALLED DAD!
WOULD HE HAVE ANSWERED? HE'S ALWAYS HOME, HE NEVER GOES OUT, AND EVEN IF HE'S SLEEPIN', PHONE ALWAYS GETS HIM UP.
SO WHAT? HE WOULDN'T HAVE ANSWERED, RIGHT? 'CUZ YOU ALREADY BEEN BY AND TOOK CARE OF HIM, THAT RIGHT?
KILLED HIM FOR HIS MONEY, RIGHT? JESUS FUCKING CHRIST, DO YOU REALIZE WHAT YOU'VE DONE?
OH, SHUT THE FUCK UP.
IT'S NOT JUST THE MONEY, YOU IDIOT.
THIS'S *CONTROL*, LIKE I SAID. THIS IS ME GETTING SHIT ORGANIZED. *IN LINE.* THE WAY IT'S SUPPOSED TO BE.
YOU HAVE NO IDEA WHAT I MEAN, DO YOU?

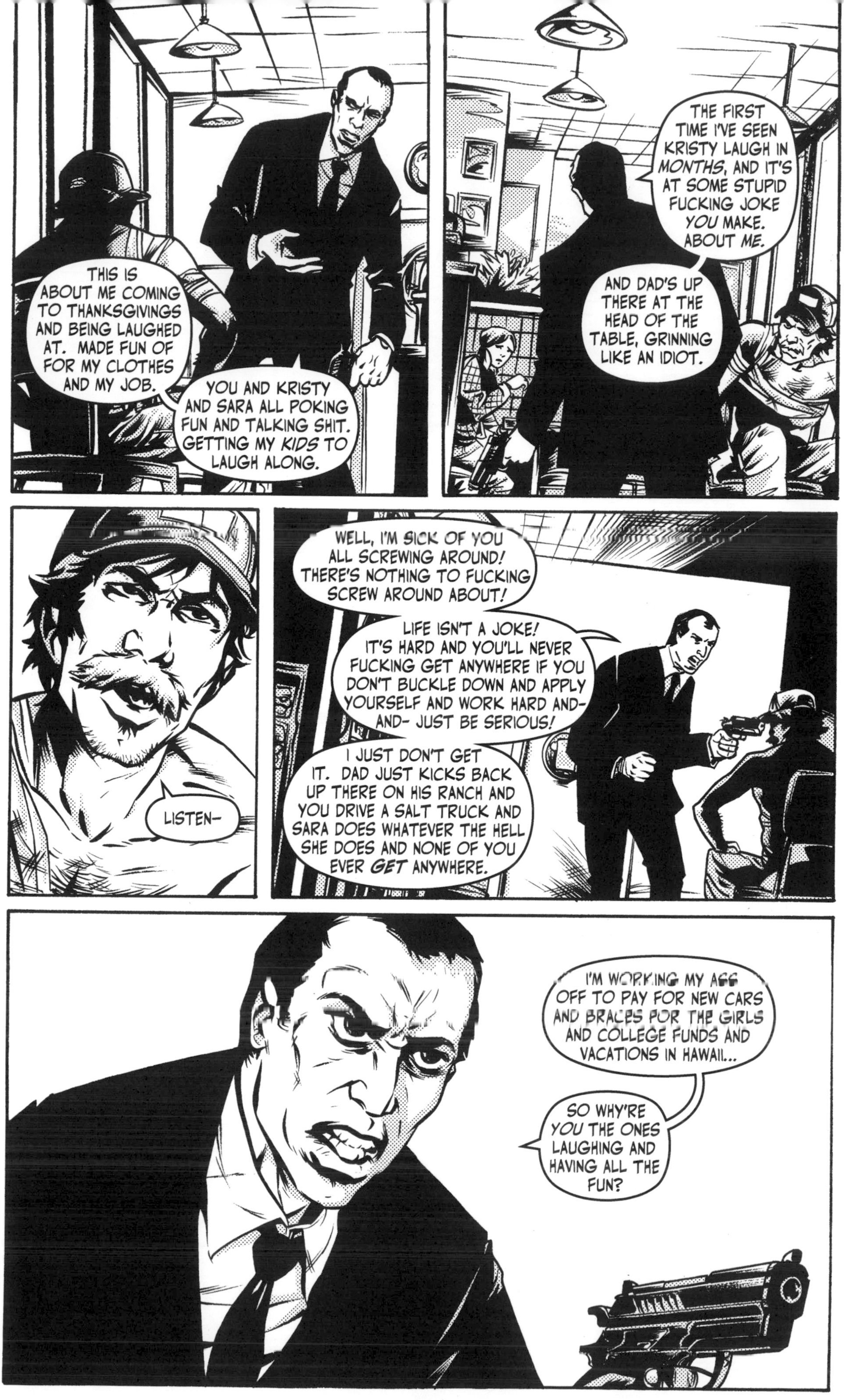
THIS IS ABOUT ME COMING TO THANKSGIVINGS AND BEING LAUGHED AT. MADE FUN OF FOR MY CLOTHES AND MY JOB.
YOU AND KRISTY AND SARA ALL POKING FUN AND TALKING SHIT. GETTING MY *KIDS* TO LAUGH ALONG.
THE FIRST TIME I'VE SEEN KRISTY LAUGH IN *MONTHS*, AND IT'S AT SOME STUPID FUCKING JOKE *YOU* MAKE. ABOUT *ME*.
AND DAD'S UP THERE AT THE HEAD OF THE TABLE, GRINNING LIKE AN IDIOT.
LISTEN-
WELL, I'M SICK OF YOU ALL SCREWING AROUND! THERE'S NOTHING TO FUCKING SCREW AROUND ABOUT!
LIFE ISN'T A JOKE! IT'S HARD AND YOU'LL NEVER FUCKING GET ANYWHERE IF YOU DON'T BUCKLE DOWN AND APPLY YOURSELF AND WORK HARD AND- AND- JUST BE SERIOUS!
I JUST DON'T GET IT. DAD JUST KICKS BACK UP THERE ON HIS RANCH AND YOU DRIVE A SALT TRUCK AND SARA DOES WHATEVER THE HELL SHE DOES AND NONE OF YOU EVER *GET* ANYWHERE.
I'M WORKING MY ASS OFF TO PAY FOR NEW CARS AND BRACES FOR THE GIRLS AND COLLEGE FUNDS AND VACATIONS IN HAWAII...
SO WHY'RE *YOU* THE ONES LAUGHING AND HAVING ALL THE FUN?

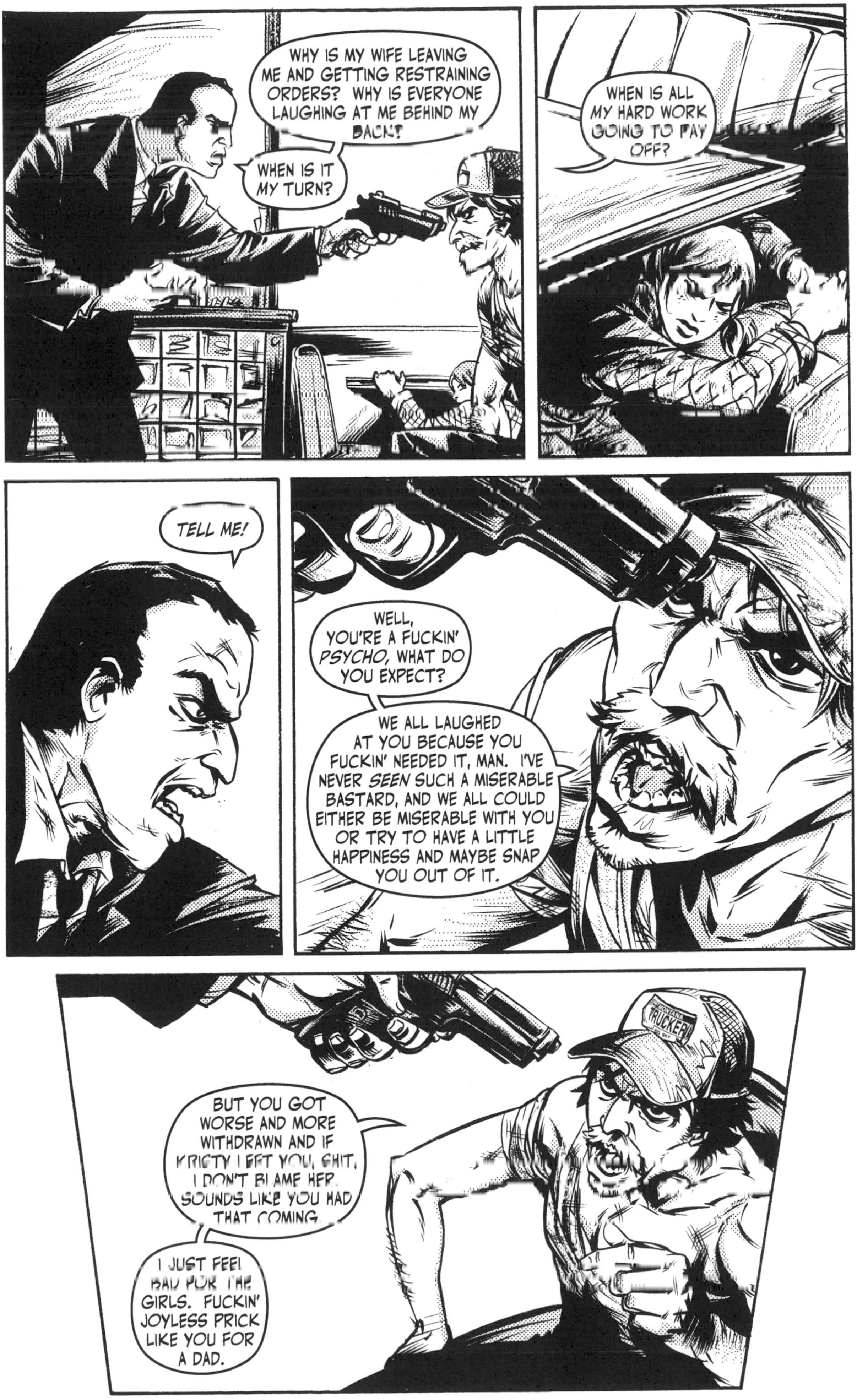
WHY IS MY WIFE LEAVING ME AND GETTING RESTRAINING ORDERS? WHY IS EVERYONE LAUGHING AT ME BEHIND MY BACK?
WHEN IS IT MY TURN?
WHEN IS ALL MY HARD WORK GOING TO PAY OFF?
TELL ME!
WELL, YOU'RE A FUCKIN' *PSYCHO*, WHAT DO YOU EXPECT?
WE ALL LAUGHED AT YOU BECAUSE YOU FUCKIN' NEEDED IT, MAN. I'VE NEVER *SEEN* SUCH A MISERABLE BASTARD, AND WE ALL COULD EITHER BE MISERABLE WITH YOU OR TRY TO HAVE A LITTLE HAPPINESS AND MAYBE SNAP YOU OUT OF IT.
BUT YOU GOT WORSE AND MORE WITHDRAWN AND IF KRISTY LEFT YOU, SHIT, I DON'T BLAME HER. SOUNDS LIKE YOU HAD THAT COMING.
I JUST FEEL BAD FOR THE GIRLS. FUCKIN' JOYLESS PRICK LIKE YOU FOR A DAD.

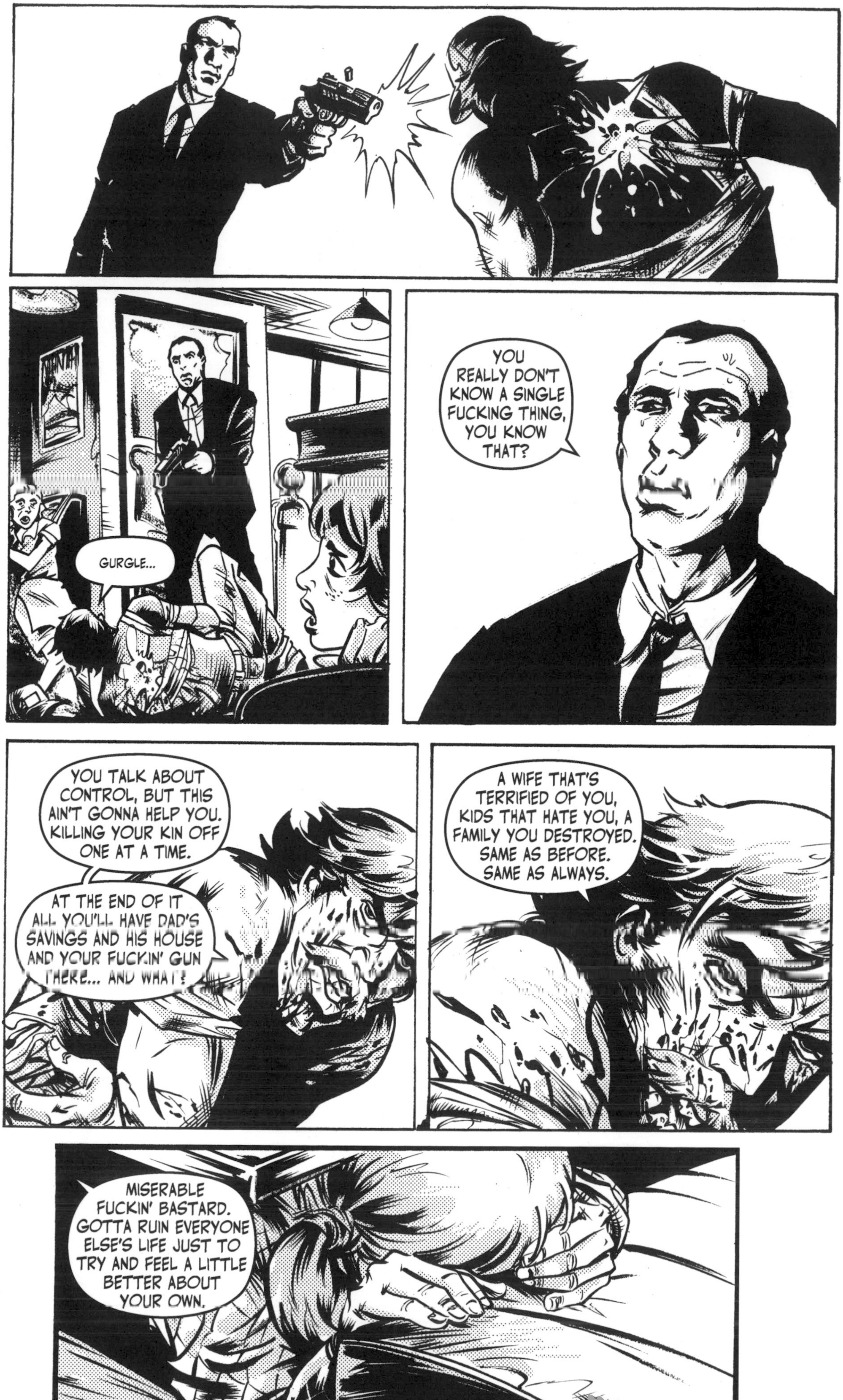
GURGLE...
YOU REALLY DON'T KNOW A SINGLE FUCKING THING, YOU KNOW THAT?
YOU TALK ABOUT CONTROL, BUT THIS AIN'T GONNA HELP YOU. KILLING YOUR KIN OFF ONE AT A TIME.
AT THE END OF IT ALL YOU'LL HAVE DAD'S SAVINGS AND HIS HOUSE AND YOUR FUCKIN' GUN THERE... AND WHAT?
A WIFE THAT'S TERRIFIED OF YOU, KIDS THAT HATE YOU, A FAMILY YOU DESTROYED. SAME AS BEFORE. SAME AS ALWAYS.
MISERABLE FUCKIN' BASTARD. GOTTA RUIN EVERYONE ELSE'S LIFE JUST TO TRY AND FEEL A LITTLE BETTER ABOUT YOUR OWN.

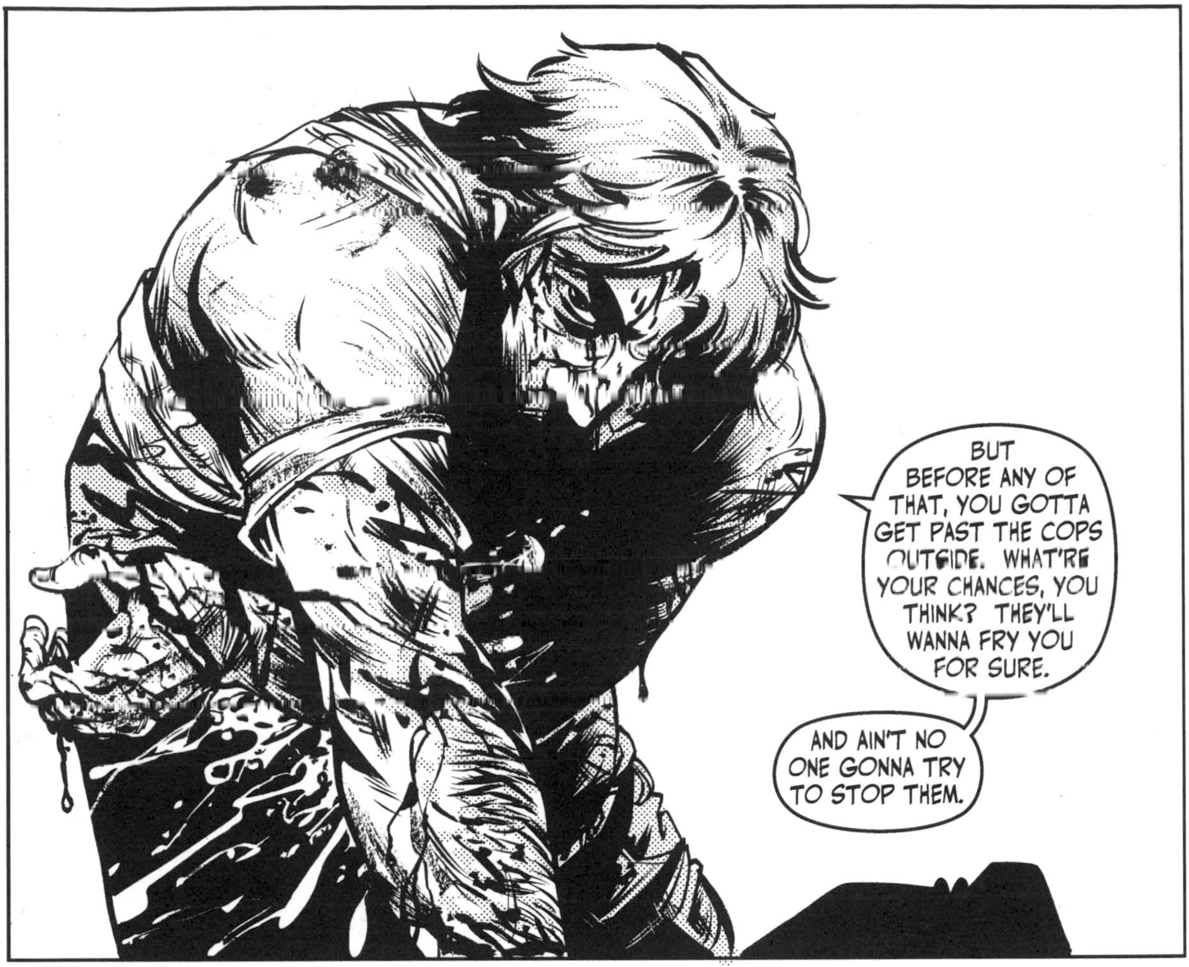
BUT BEFORE ANY OF THAT, YOU GOTTA GET PAST THE COPS OUTSIDE. WHAT'RE YOUR CHANCES, YOU THINK? THEY'LL WANNA FRY YOU FOR SURE.
AND AIN'T NO ONE GONNA TRY TO STOP THEM.

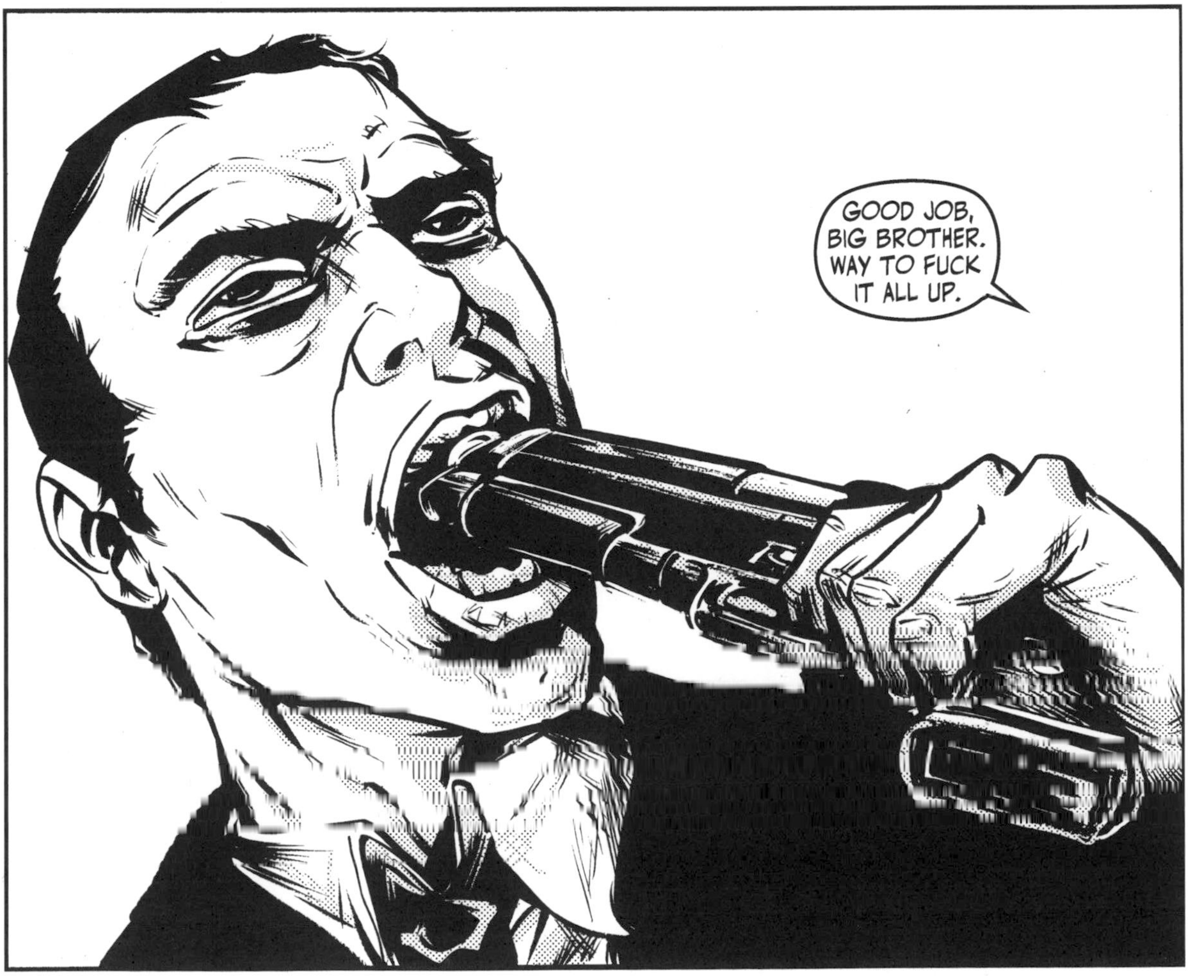
GOOD JOB, BIG BROTHER. WAY TO FUCK IT ALL UP.

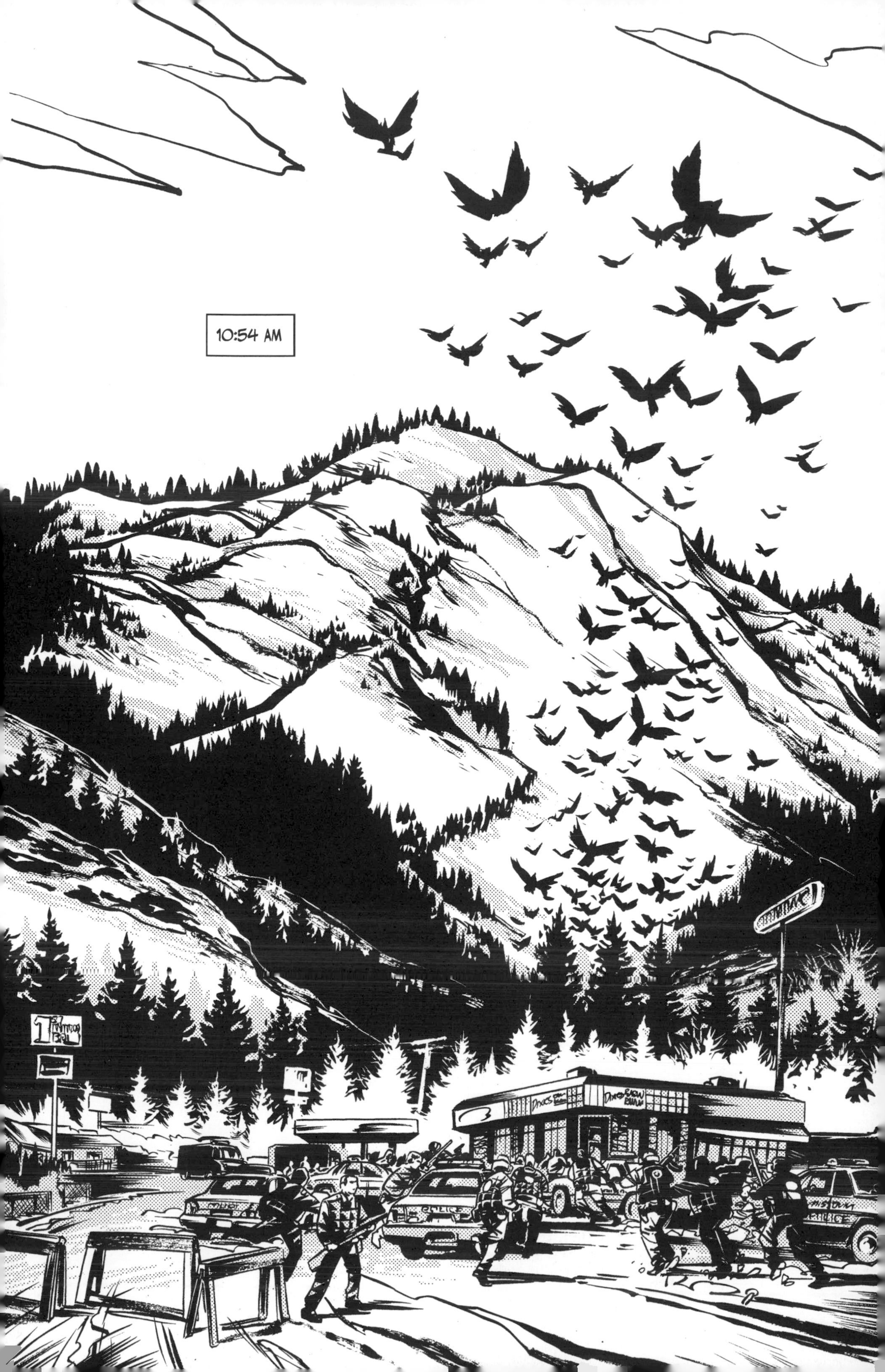
10:54 AM

CHAPTER 5
"THE LAST LONELY DAYS AT THE OXFORD THEATRE"
Halifax, Nova Scotia

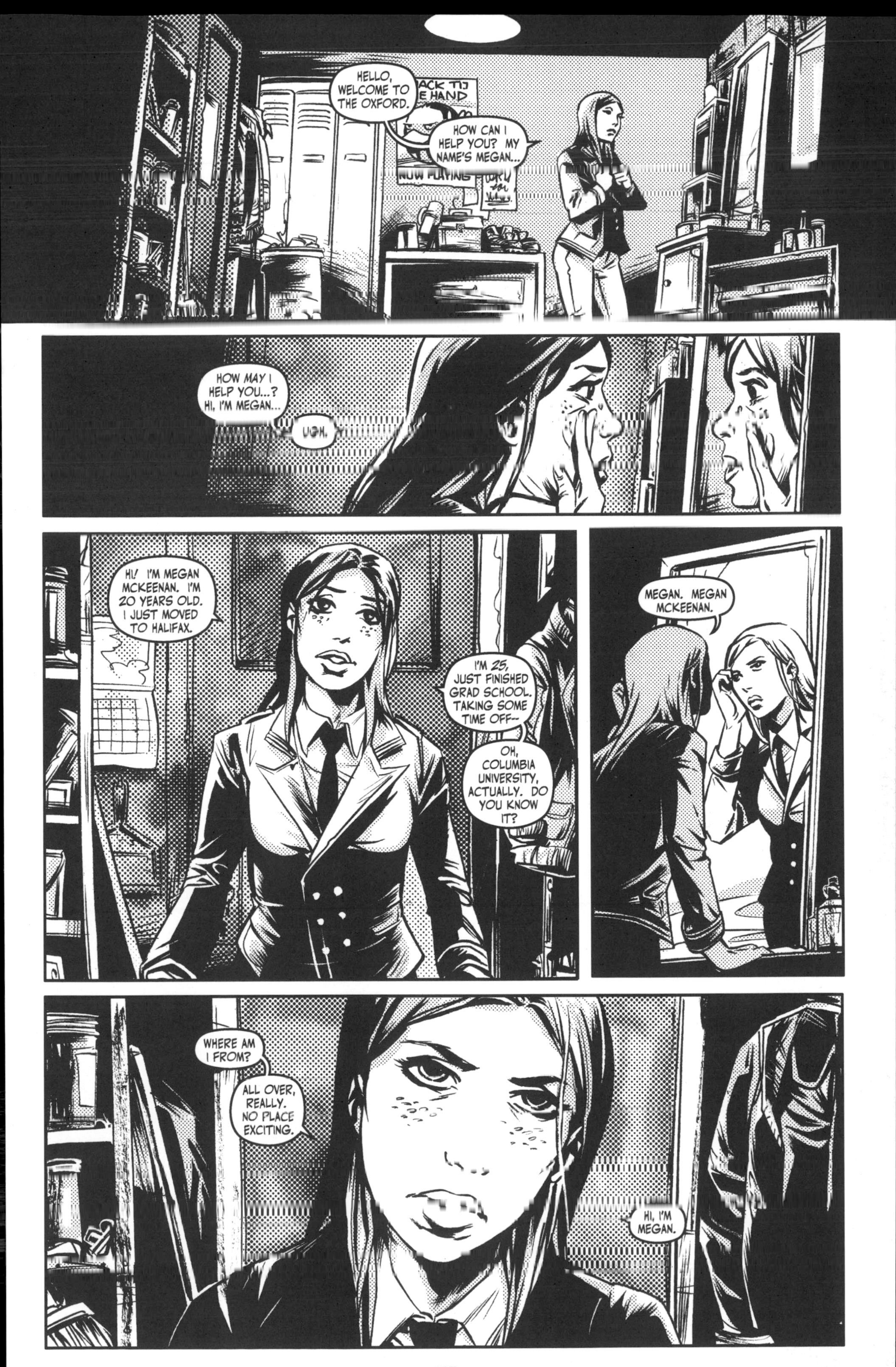
HELLO, WELCOME TO THE OXFORD.
HOW CAN I HELP YOU? MY NAME'S MEGAN...
NOW PLAYING
HOW MAY I HELP YOU...? HI, I'M MEGAN...
UGH.
HI! I'M MEGAN MCKEENAN. I'M 20 YEARS OLD. I JUST MOVED TO HALIFAX.
I'M 25, JUST FINISHED GRAD SCHOOL. TAKING SOME TIME OFF--
OH, COLUMBIA UNIVERSITY, ACTUALLY. DO YOU KNOW IT?
MEGAN. MEGAN MCKEENAN.
WHERE AM I FROM?
ALL OVER, REALLY. NO PLACE EXCITING.
HI, I'M MEGAN.

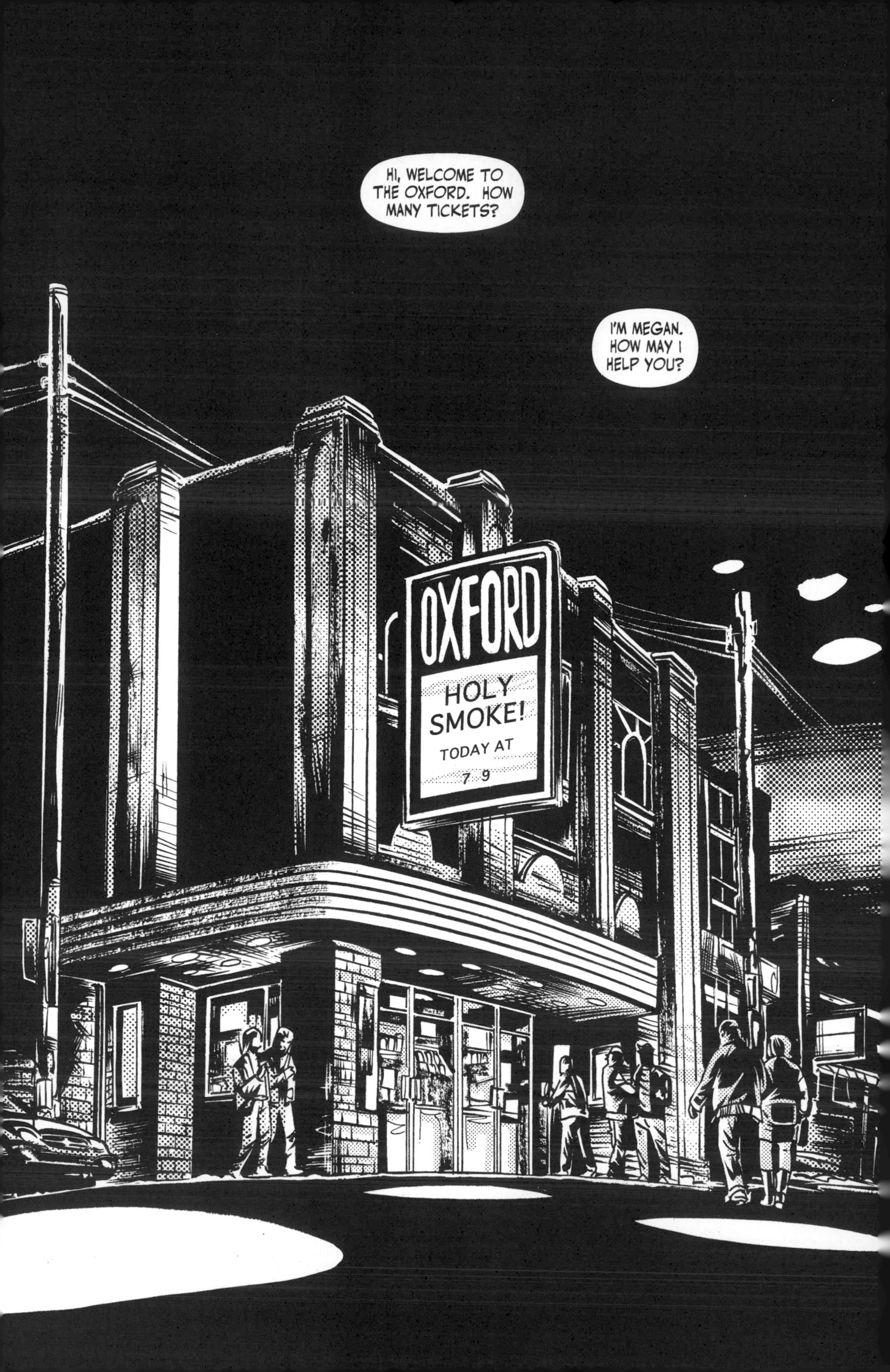
HI, WELCOME TO THE OXFORD. HOW MANY TICKETS?
I'M MEGAN. HOW MAY I HELP YOU?
OXFORD
HOLY SMOKE!
TODAY AT
7 9

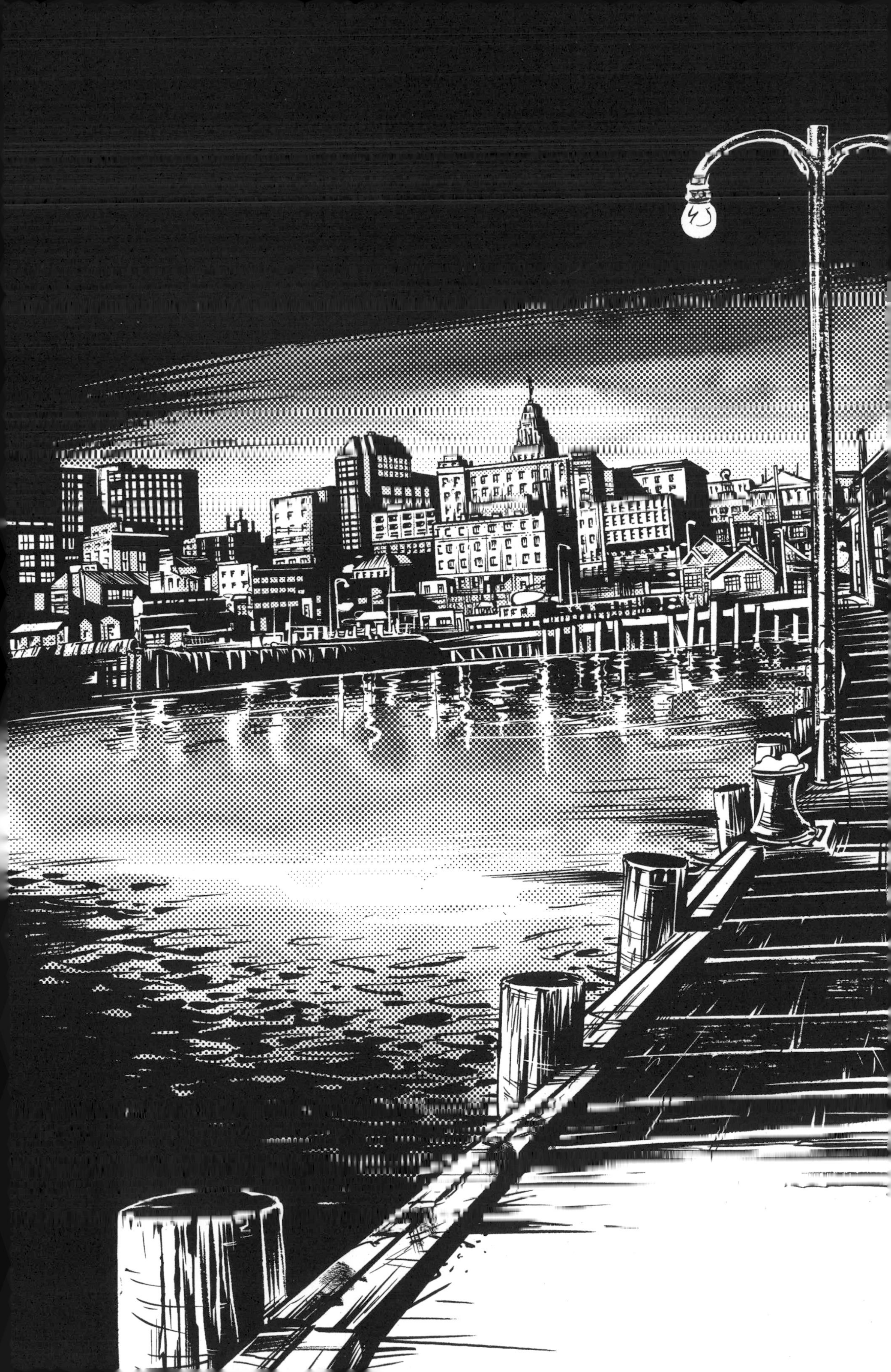

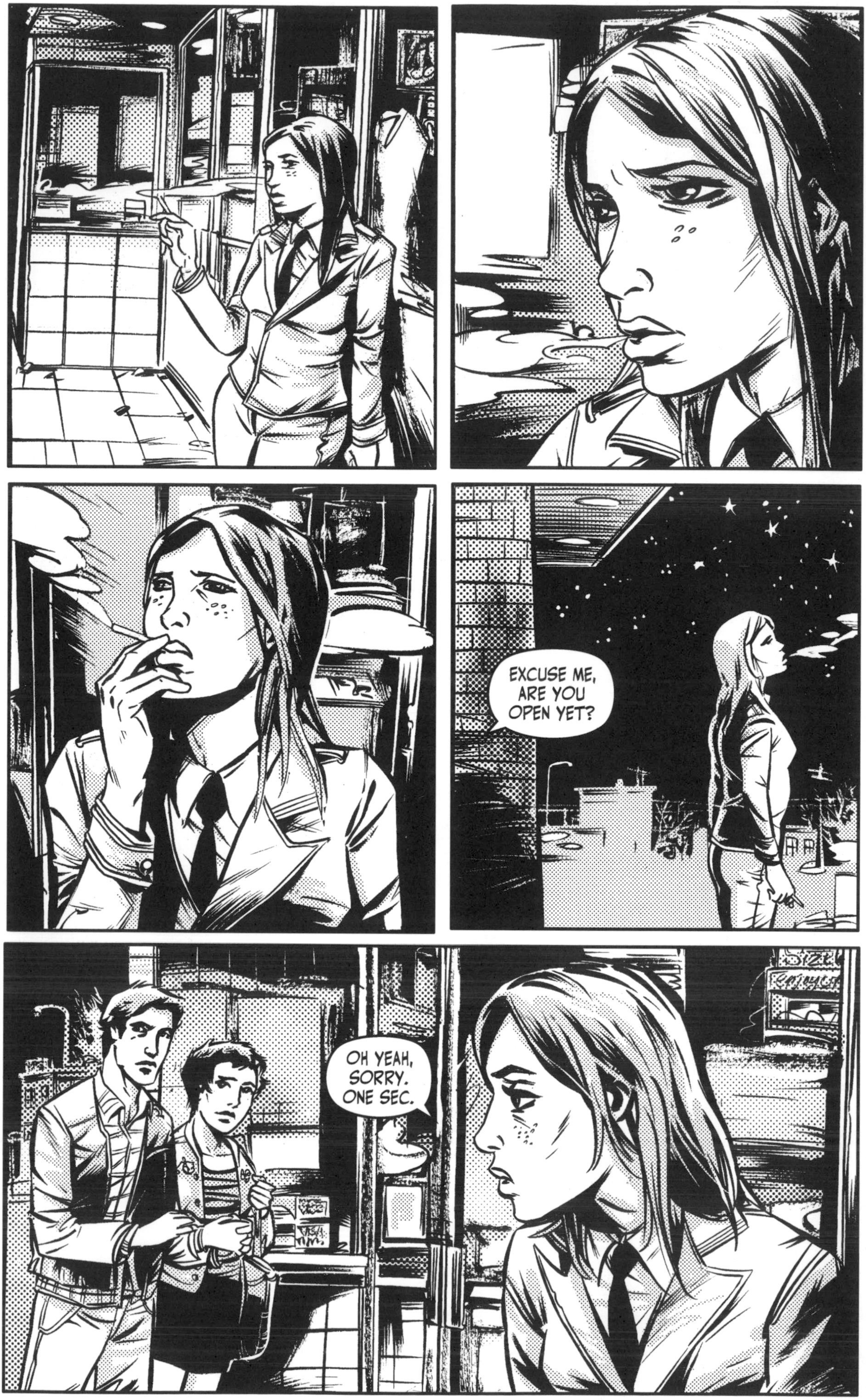
EXCUSE ME, ARE YOU OPEN YET?
OH YEAH, SORRY. ONE SEC.

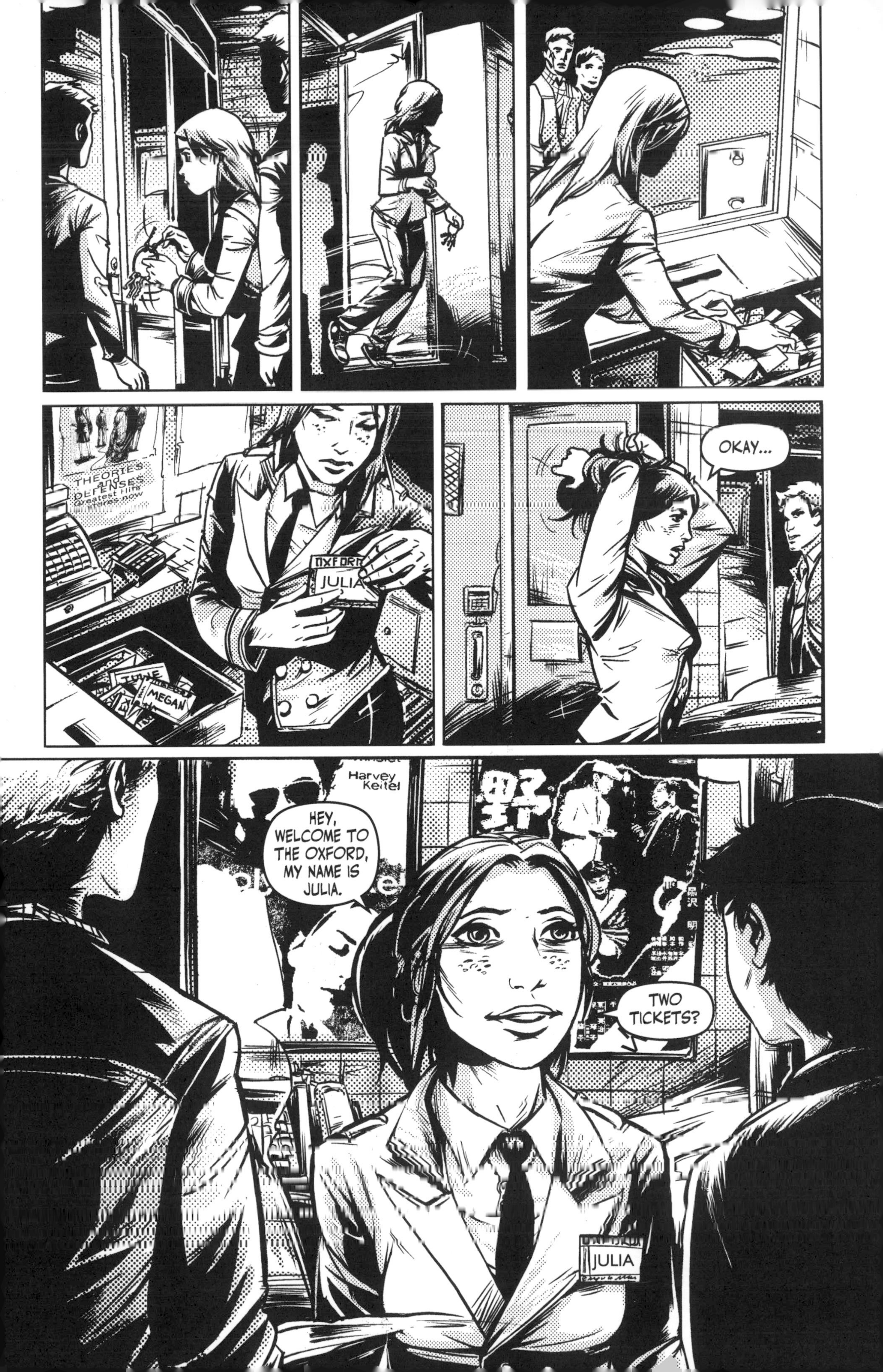

THEORIES and DEFENSES
Greatest Hits
OXFORD
JULIA
MEGAN
OKAY...
Harvey Keitel
HEY, WELCOME TO THE OXFORD, MY NAME IS JULIA.
TWO TICKETS?
JULIA

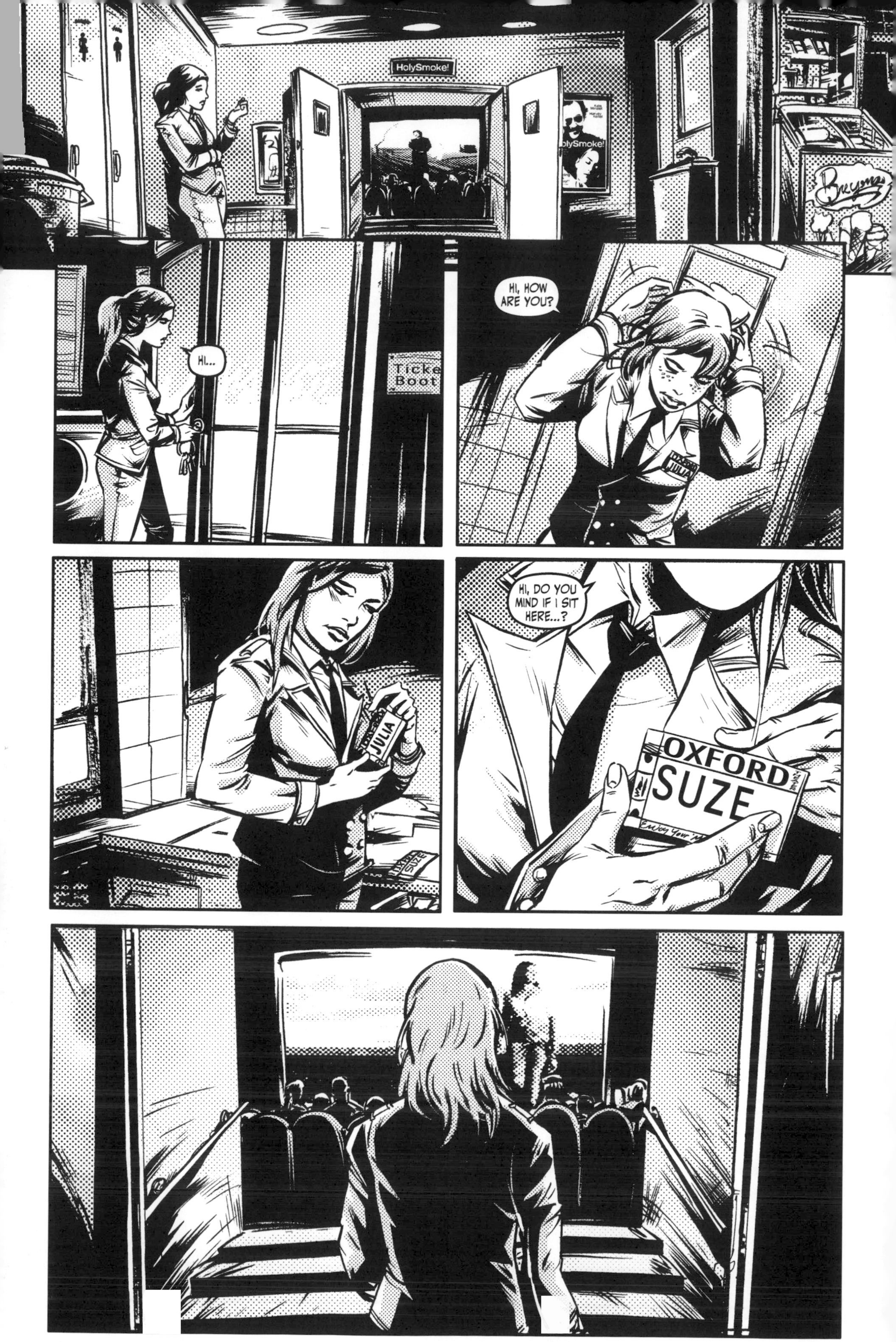
HolySmoke!
HolySmoke!
HI...
Ticke
Boot
HI, HOW ARE YOU?
JULIA
JULIA
HI, DO YOU MIND IF I SIT HERE...?
OXFORD
SUZE

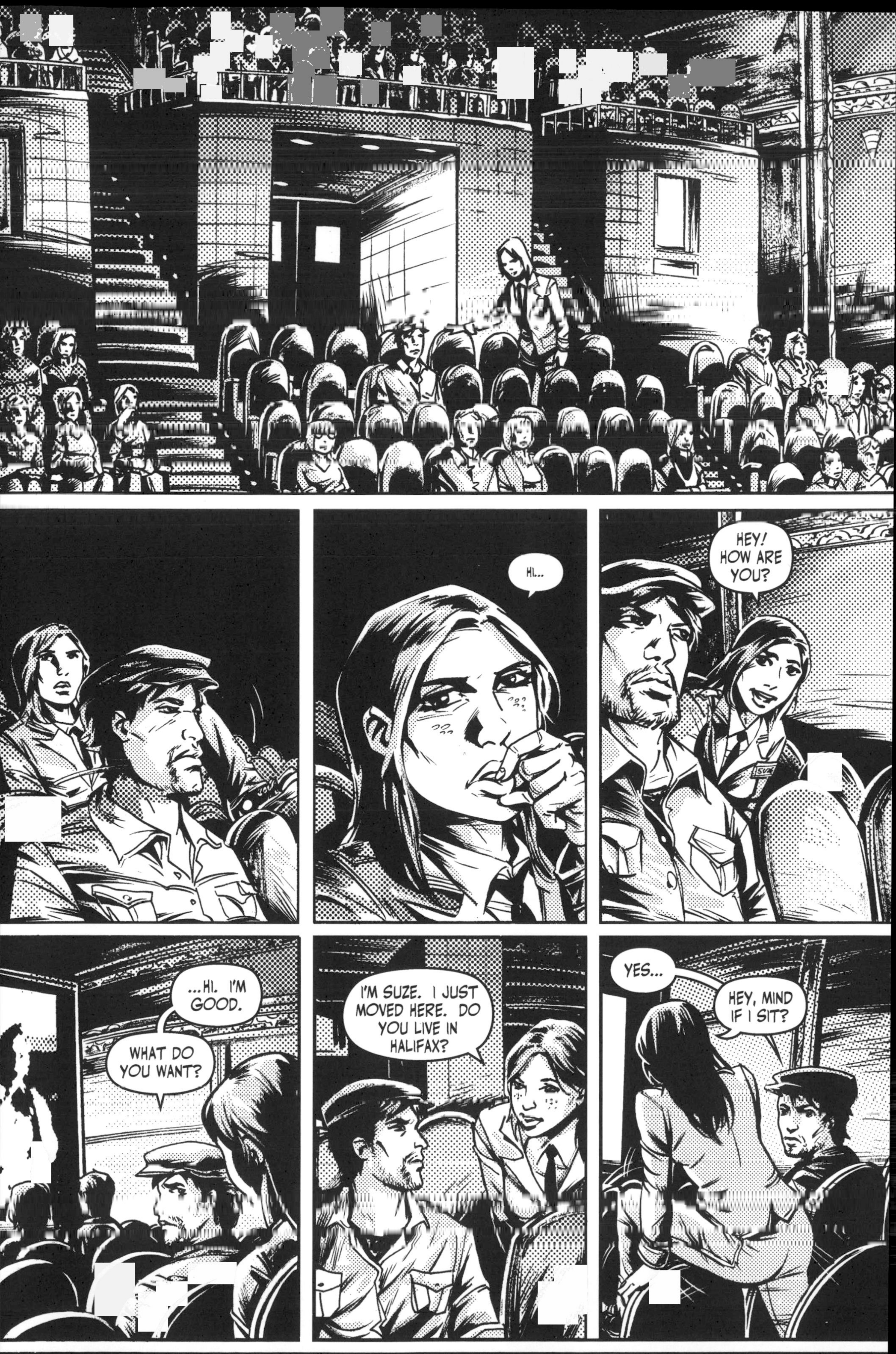
HI...
HEY! HOW ARE YOU?
...HI. I'M GOOD.
WHAT DO YOU WANT?
I'M SUZE. I JUST MOVED HERE. DO YOU LIVE IN HALIFAX?
YES...
HEY, MIND IF I SIT?

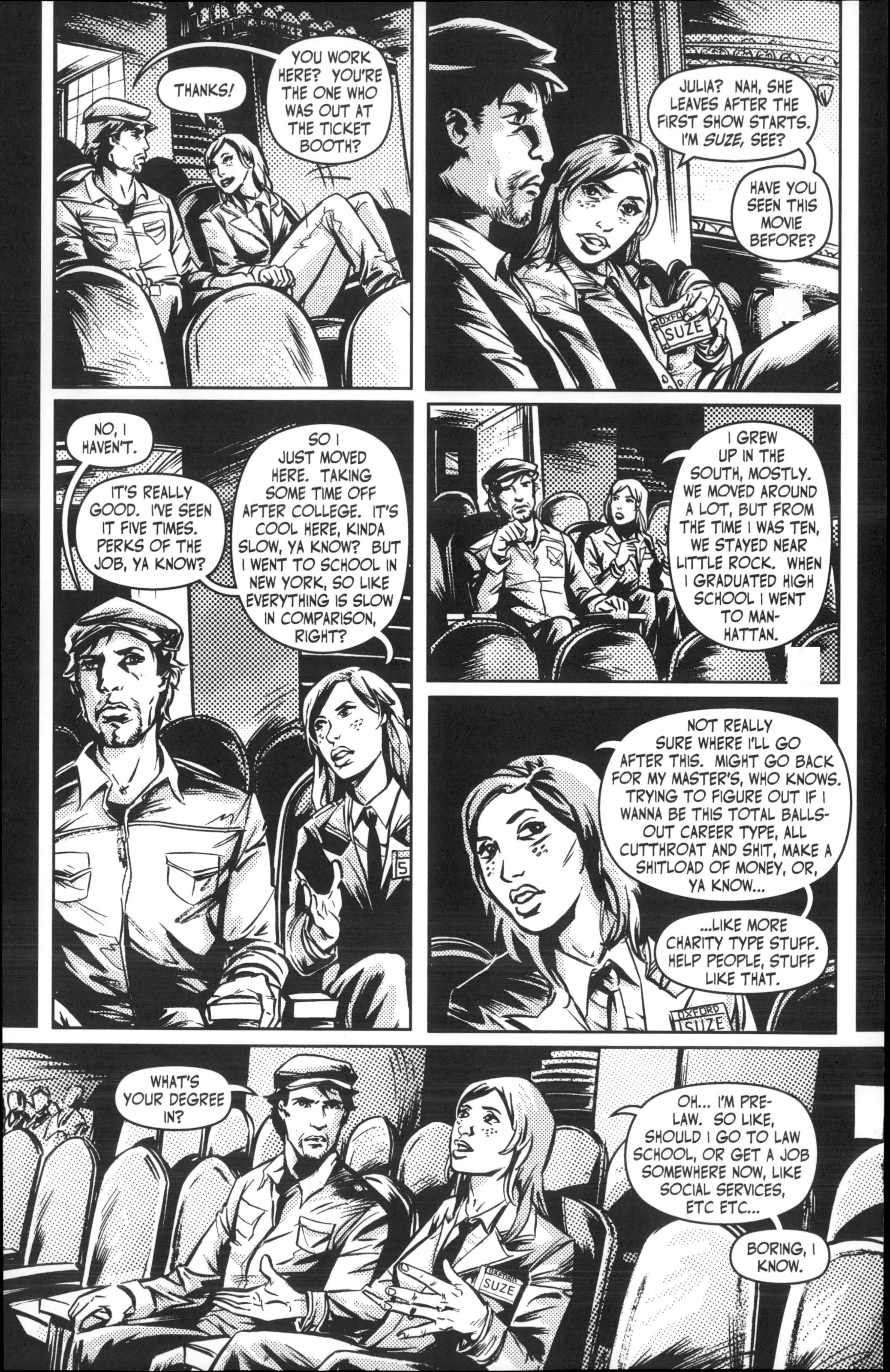
THANKS!
YOU WORK HERE? YOU'RE THE ONE WHO WAS OUT AT THE TICKET BOOTH?
JULIA? NAH, SHE LEAVES AFTER THE FIRST SHOW STARTS. I'M SUZE, SEE?
HAVE YOU SEEN THIS MOVIE BEFORE?
OXFORD
SUZE
NO, I HAVEN'T.
IT'S REALLY GOOD. I'VE SEEN IT FIVE TIMES. PERKS OF THE JOB, YA KNOW?
SO I JUST MOVED HERE. TAKING SOME TIME OFF AFTER COLLEGE. IT'S COOL HERE, KINDA SLOW, YA KNOW? BUT I WENT TO SCHOOL IN NEW YORK, SO LIKE EVERYTHING IS SLOW IN COMPARISON, RIGHT?
I GREW UP IN THE SOUTH, MOSTLY. WE MOVED AROUND A LOT, BUT FROM THE TIME I WAS TEN, WE STAYED NEAR LITTLE ROCK. WHEN I GRADUATED HIGH SCHOOL I WENT TO MAN-HATTAN.
NOT REALLY SURE WHERE I'LL GO AFTER THIS. MIGHT GO BACK FOR MY MASTER'S, WHO KNOWS. TRYING TO FIGURE OUT IF I WANNA BE THIS TOTAL BALLS-OUT CAREER TYPE, ALL CUTTHROAT AND SHIT, MAKE A SHITLOAD OF MONEY, OR, YA KNOW...
...LIKE MORE CHARITY TYPE STUFF. HELP PEOPLE, STUFF LIKE THAT.
OXFORD
SUZE
WHAT'S YOUR DEGREE IN?
OH... I'M PRE-LAW. SO LIKE, SHOULD I GO TO LAW SCHOOL, OR GET A JOB SOMEWHERE NOW, LIKE SOCIAL SERVICES, ETC ETC...
BORING, I KNOW.
OXFORD
SUZE

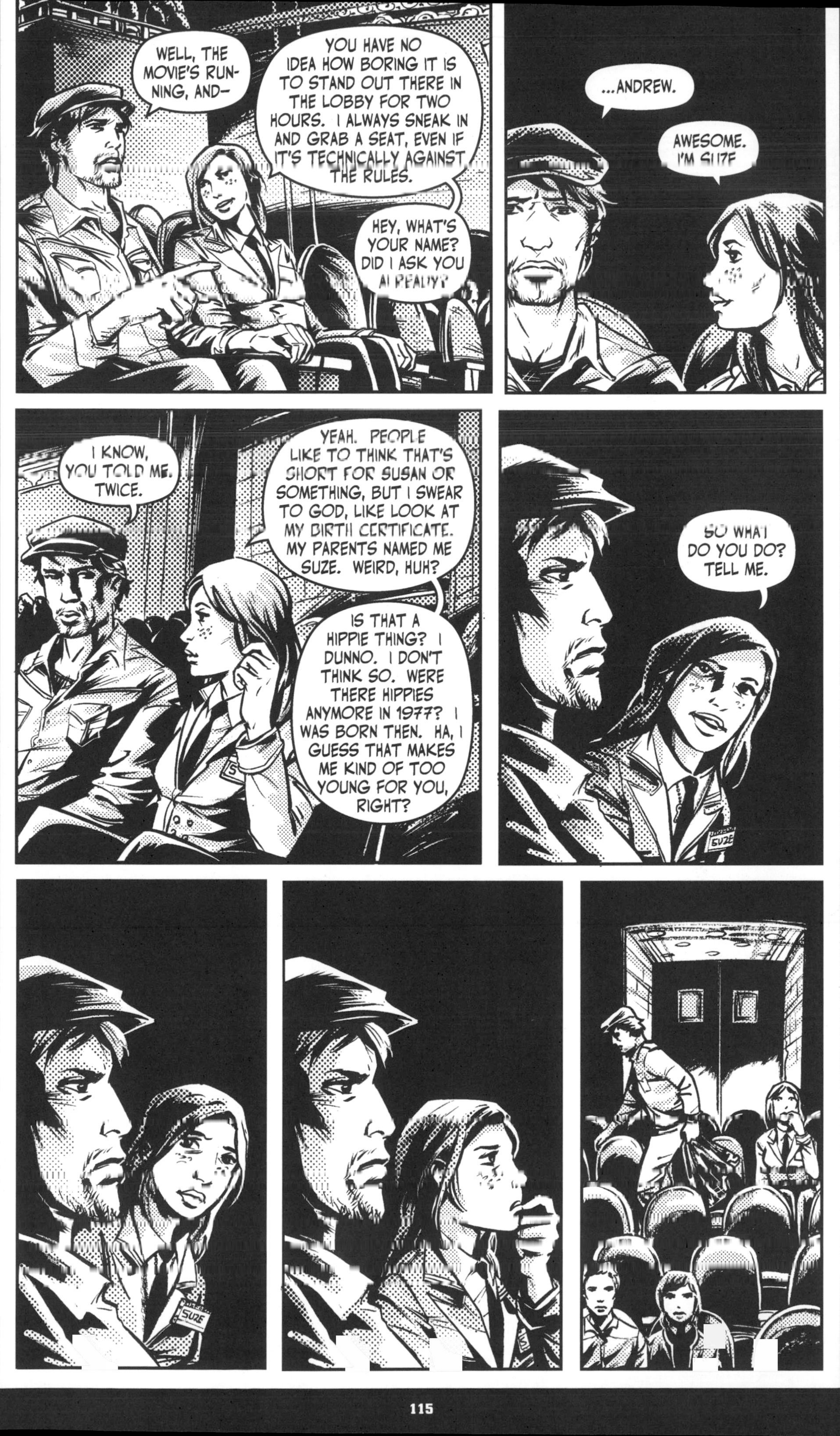
WELL, THE MOVIE'S RUN- NING, AND–
YOU HAVE NO IDEA HOW BORING IT IS TO STAND OUT THERE IN THE LOBBY FOR TWO HOURS. I ALWAYS SNEAK IN AND GRAB A SEAT, EVEN IF IT'S TECHNICALLY AGAINST THE RULES.
HEY, WHAT'S YOUR NAME? DID I ASK YOU ALREADY?
...ANDREW.
AWESOME. I'M SUZE.
I KNOW, YOU TOLD ME. TWICE.
YEAH. PEOPLE LIKE TO THINK THAT'S SHORT FOR SUSAN OR SOMETHING, BUT I SWEAR TO GOD, LIKE LOOK AT MY BIRTH CERTIFICATE. MY PARENTS NAMED ME SUZE. WEIRD, HUH?
IS THAT A HIPPIE THING? I DUNNO. I DON'T THINK SO. WERE THERE HIPPIES ANYMORE IN 1977? I WAS BORN THEN. HA, I GUESS THAT MAKES ME KIND OF TOO YOUNG FOR YOU, RIGHT?
SO WHAT DO YOU DO? TELL ME.
SUZE

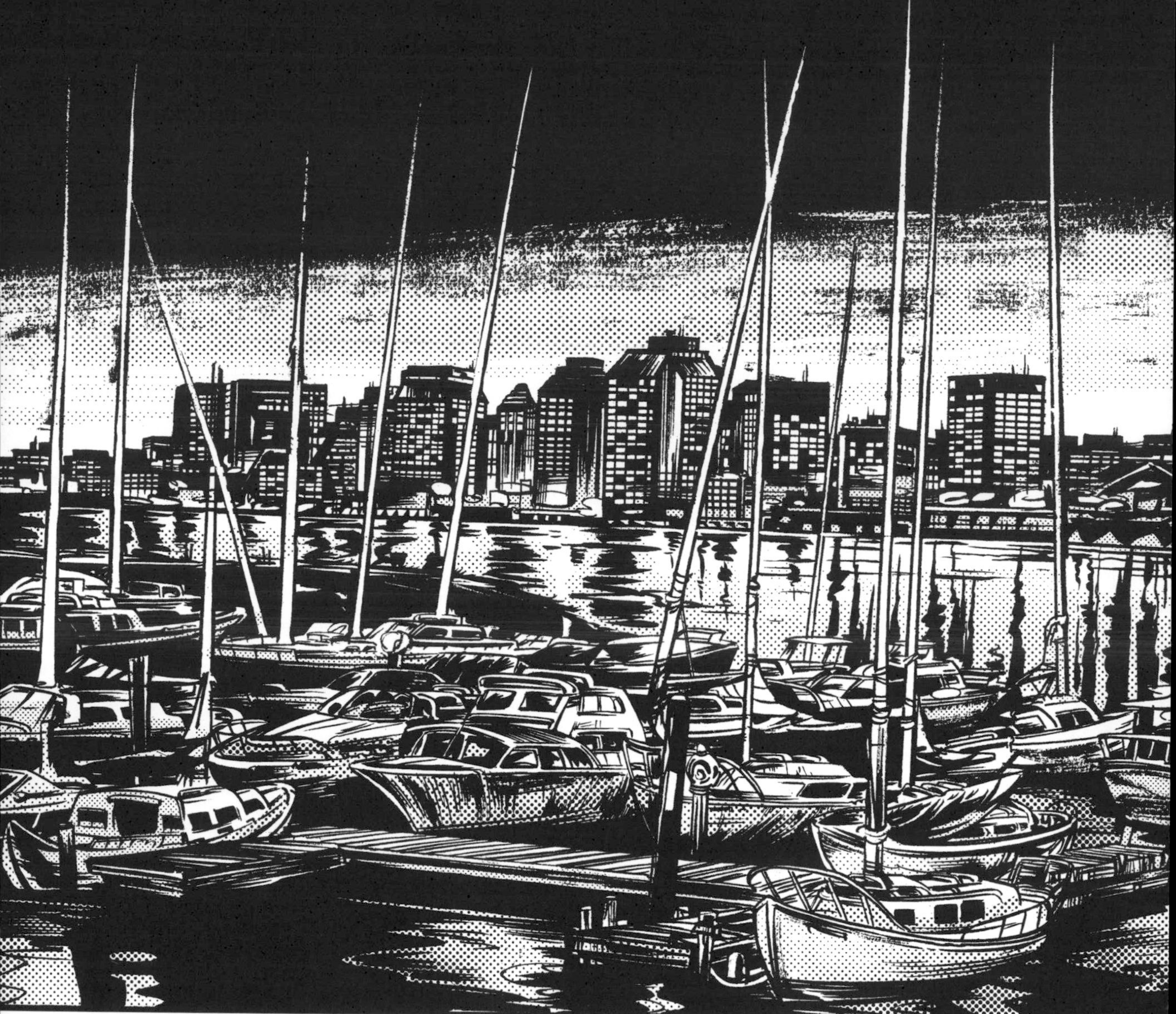

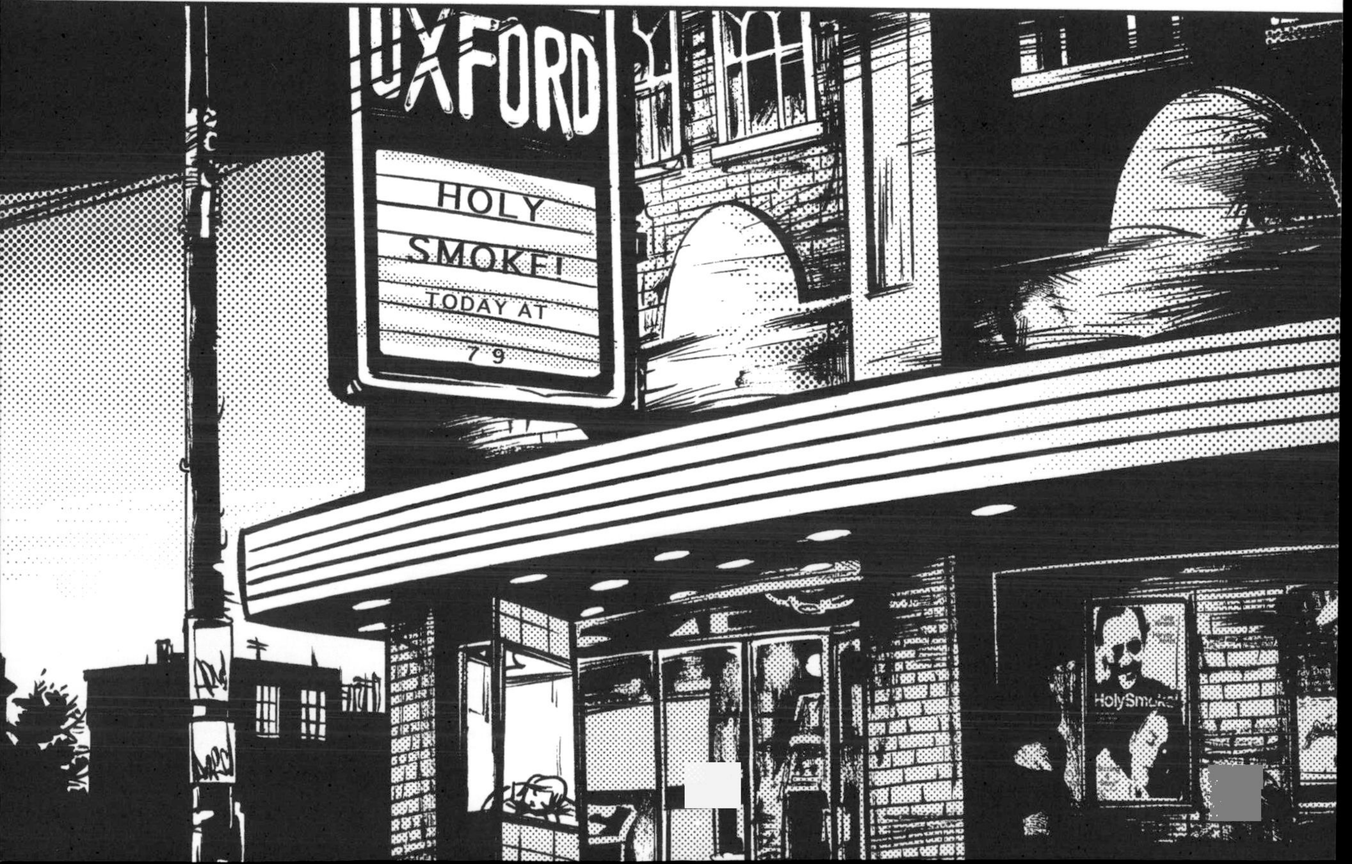
HOLY
SMOKE!
TODAY AT
7 9

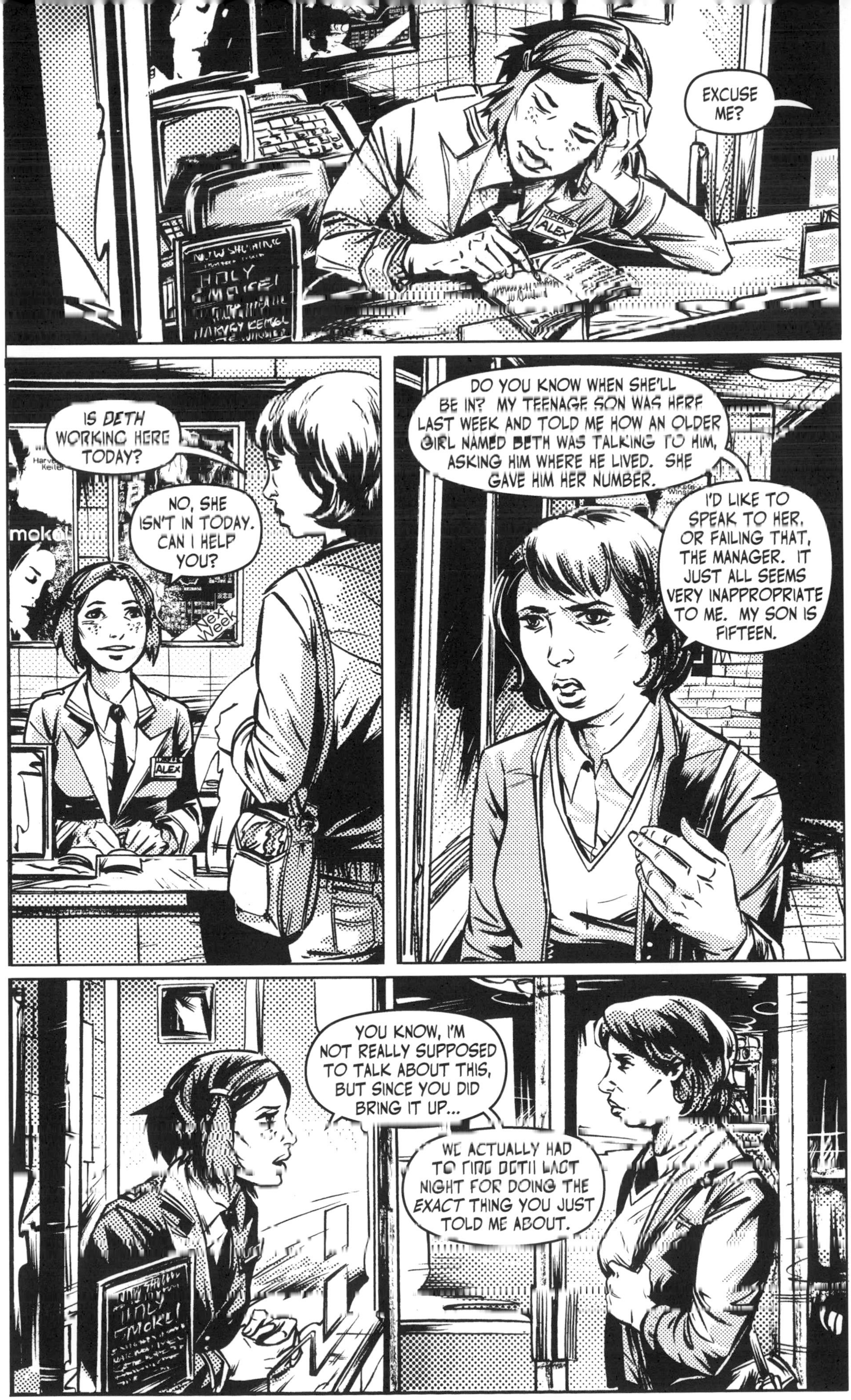
EXCUSE ME?
NOW SHOWING
HOLY SMOKE!
HARVEY KEITEL
IS BETH WORKING HERE TODAY?
NO, SHE ISN'T IN TODAY. CAN I HELP YOU?
DO YOU KNOW WHEN SHE'LL BE IN? MY TEENAGE SON WAS HERE LAST WEEK AND TOLD ME HOW AN OLDER GIRL NAMED BETH WAS TALKING TO HIM, ASKING HIM WHERE HE LIVED. SHE GAVE HIM HER NUMBER.
I'D LIKE TO SPEAK TO HER, OR FAILING THAT, THE MANAGER. IT JUST ALL SEEMS VERY INAPPROPRIATE TO ME. MY SON IS FIFTEEN.
YOU KNOW, I'M NOT REALLY SUPPOSED TO TALK ABOUT THIS, BUT SINCE YOU DID BRING IT UP...
WE ACTUALLY HAD TO FIRE BETH LAST NIGHT FOR DOING THE *EXACT* THING YOU JUST TOLD ME ABOUT.

REALLY? YOU DID?

I DON'T WISH ANYONE TO LOSE THEIR JOB; I MAINLY JUST HAD A COUPLE OF QUESTIONS I WANTED TO ASK HER...

OH NO, YOU HAVE NO IDEA. SHE WAS *TOTALLY* OUT OF CONTROL.

WE HAD A LOT OF COMPLAINTS, PLUS SHE WOULD DO THINGS LIKE LOCK THE FRONT DOOR WHEN THE MOVIE WAS ON, AND THAT'S TOTALLY A FIRE HAZARD.

REALLY?

WELL, I SUPPOSE IT'S JUST AS WELL, THEN.

I'M REALLY SORRY SHE BOTHERED YOUR SON. DID HE TELL HER WHERE YOU LIVE?

NO, THANK GOD.

MY SON WAS MORE ANNOYED THAN ANYTHING ELSE, BUT HE DID TELL ME ABOUT IT, SO I SUSPECT SHE DID MAKE HIM PRETTY NERVOUS.

HE REALLY MADE HER SOUND LIKE SHE WAS CRAZY. IS SHE, DO YOU KNOW? MAYBE A LITTLE OFF?

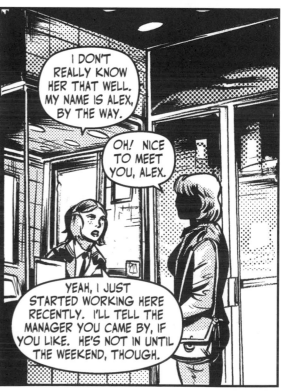

I DON'T REALLY KNOW HER THAT WELL. MY NAME IS ALEX, BY THE WAY.

OH! NICE TO MEET YOU, ALEX.

YEAH, I JUST STARTED WORKING HERE RECENTLY. I'LL TELL THE MANAGER YOU CAME BY, IF YOU LIKE. HE'S NOT IN UNTIL THE WEEKEND, THOUGH.

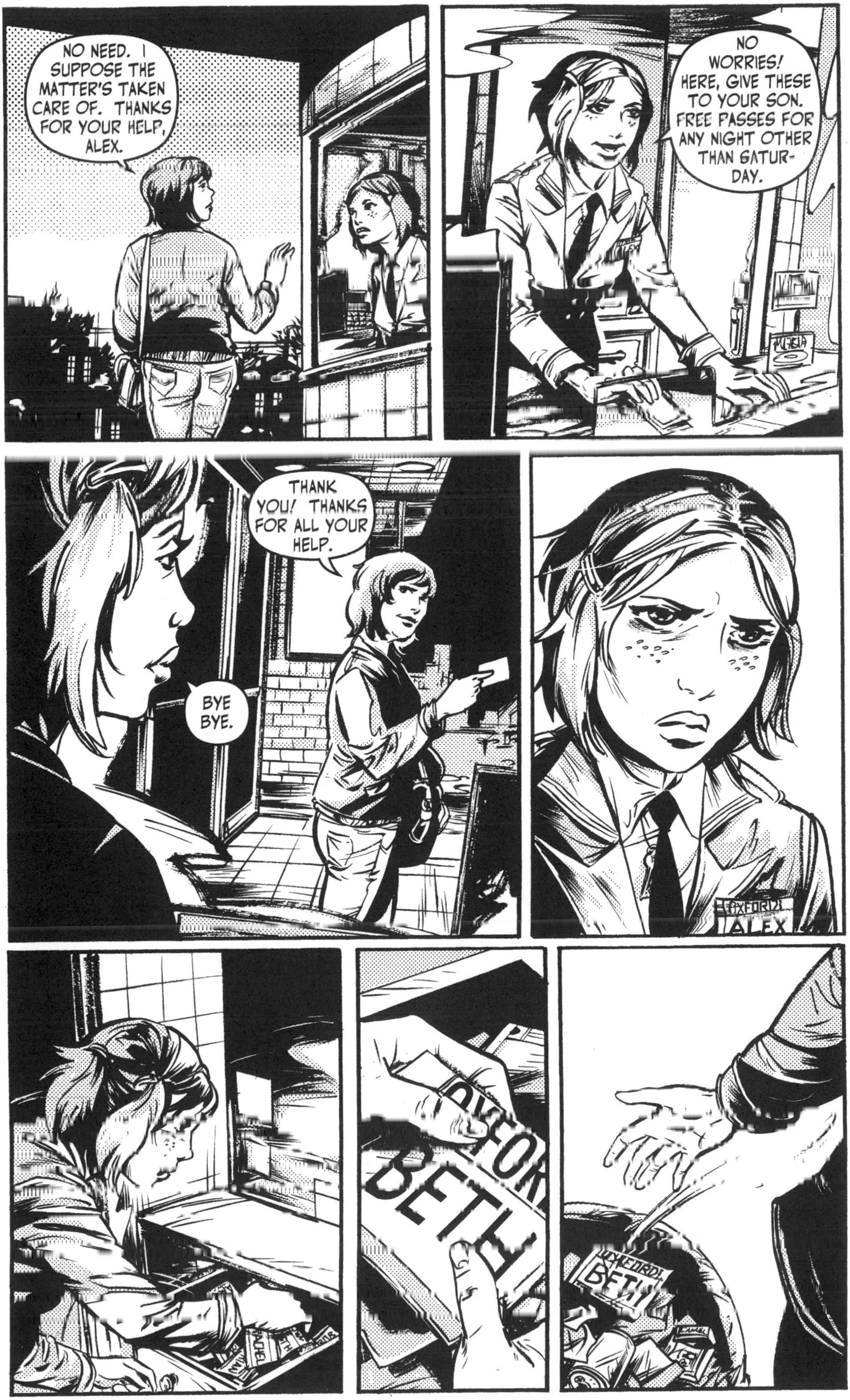
NO NEED. I SUPPOSE THE MATTER'S TAKEN CARE OF. THANKS FOR YOUR HELP, ALEX.
NO WORRIES! HERE, GIVE THESE TO YOUR SON. FREE PASSES FOR ANY NIGHT OTHER THAN SATUR-DAY.
THANK YOU! THANKS FOR ALL YOUR HELP.
BYE BYE.
OXFORD
ALEX
BETH

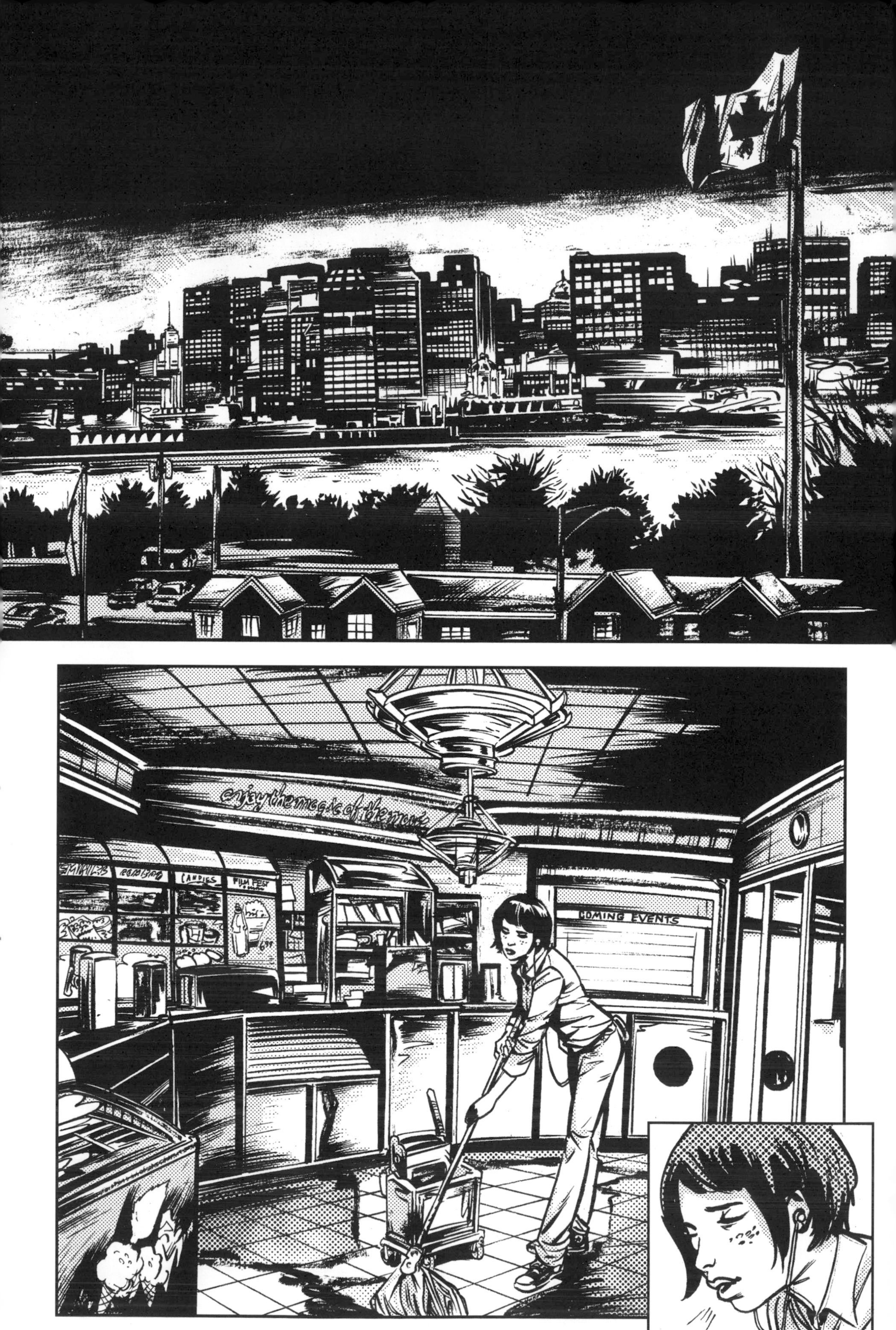
CANDIES
FILM FEST
COMING EVENTS

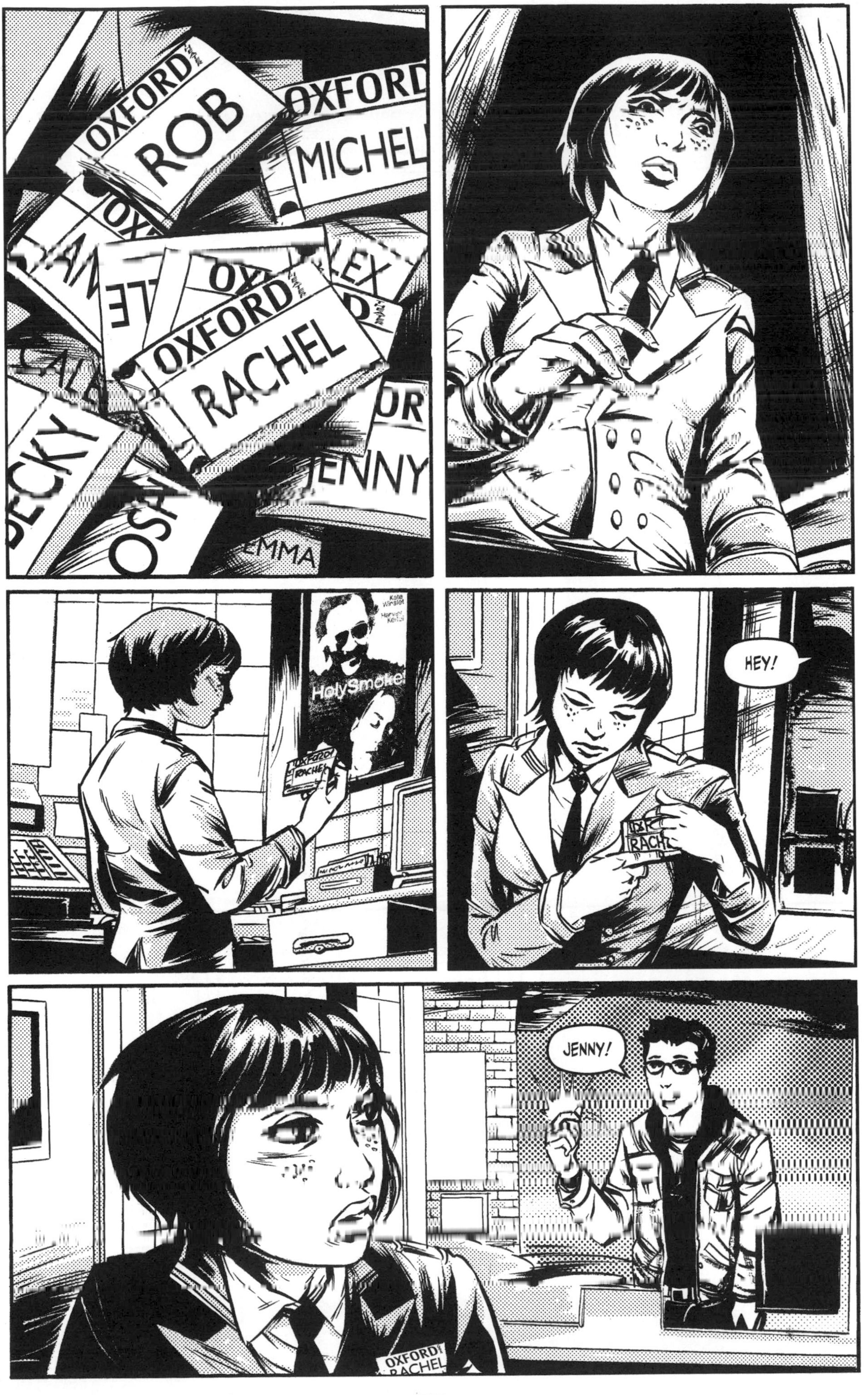
OXFORD
ROB
OXFORD
MICHEL
OXFORD
RACHEL
BECKY
JENNY
EMMA
Kate Winslet
Harvey Keitel
HolySmoke!
HEY!
JENNY!
OXFORD
RACHEL

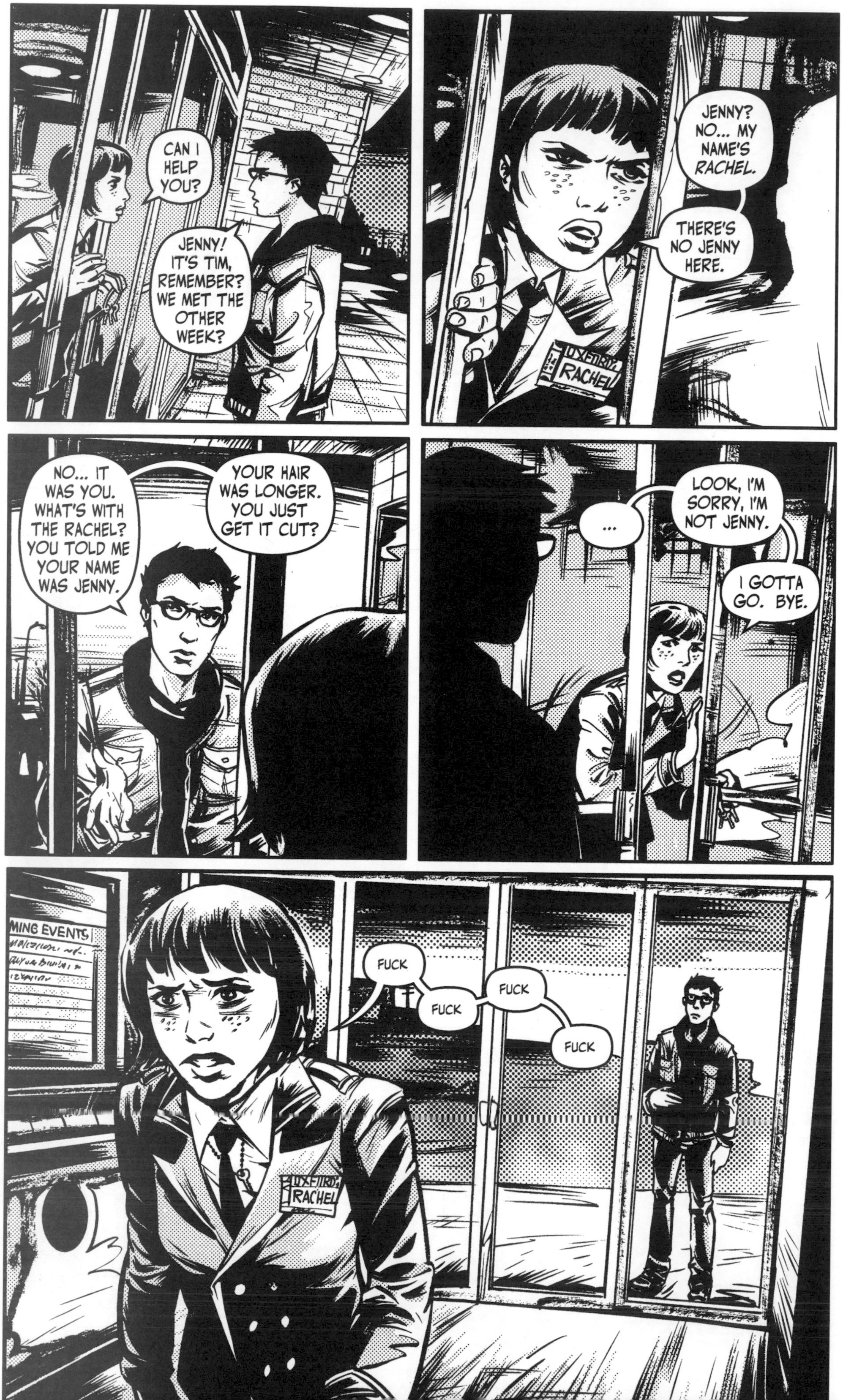
CAN I HELP YOU?
JENNY! IT'S TIM, REMEMBER? WE MET THE OTHER WEEK?
JENNY? NO... MY NAME'S RACHEL.
THERE'S NO JENNY HERE.
NO... IT WAS YOU. WHAT'S WITH THE RACHEL? YOU TOLD ME YOUR NAME WAS JENNY.
YOUR HAIR WAS LONGER. YOU JUST GET IT CUT?
...
LOOK, I'M SORRY, I'M NOT JENNY.
I GOTTA GO. BYE.
MING EVENTS
FUCK
FUCK
FUCK
FUCK

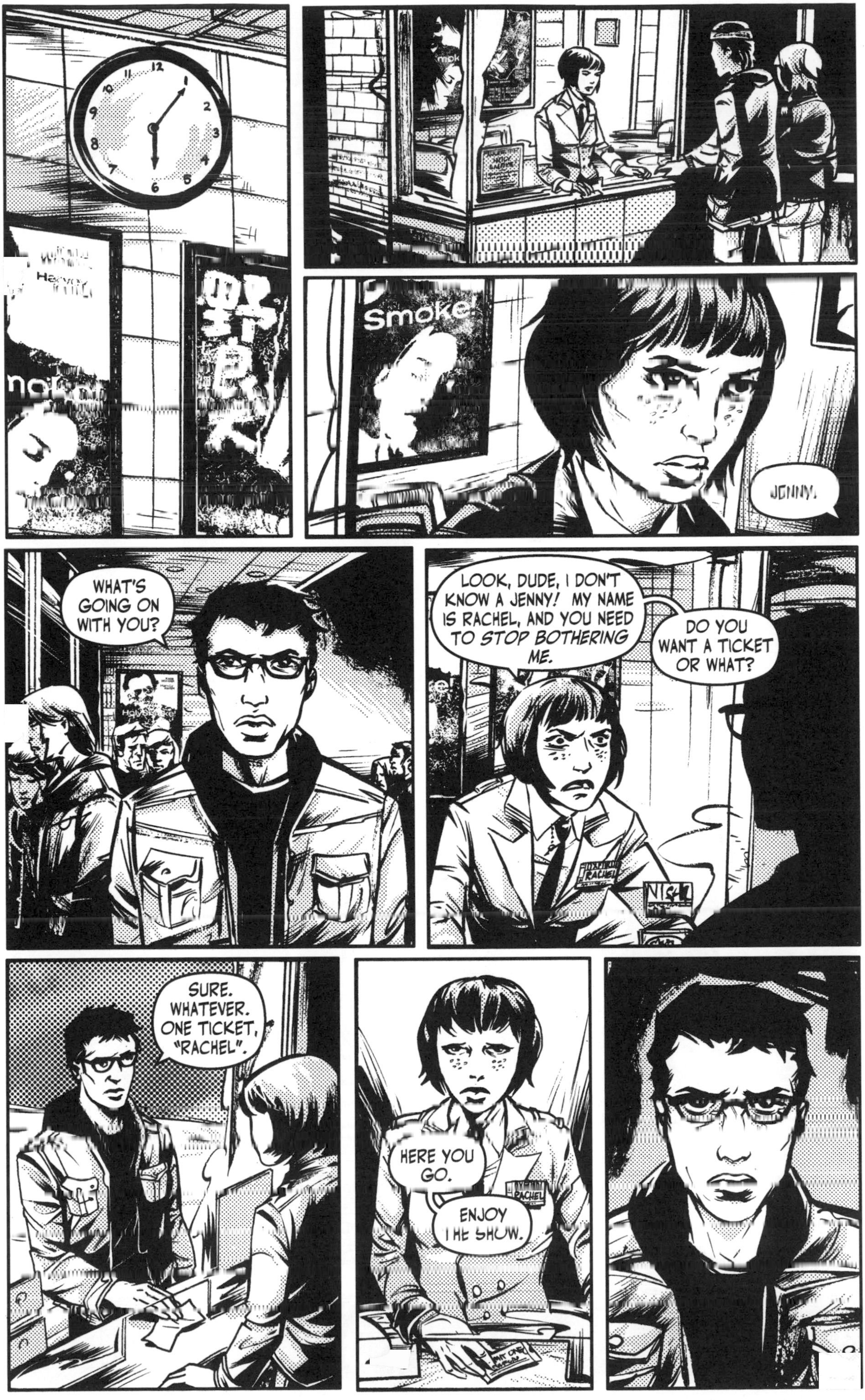
Smoke!
JENNY!
WHAT'S GOING ON WITH YOU?
LOOK, DUDE, I DON'T KNOW A JENNY! MY NAME IS RACHEL, AND YOU NEED TO STOP BOTHERING ME.
DO YOU WANT A TICKET OR WHAT?
RACHEL
SURE. WHATEVER. ONE TICKET, "RACHEL".
HERE YOU GO.
RACHEL
ENJOY THE SHOW.

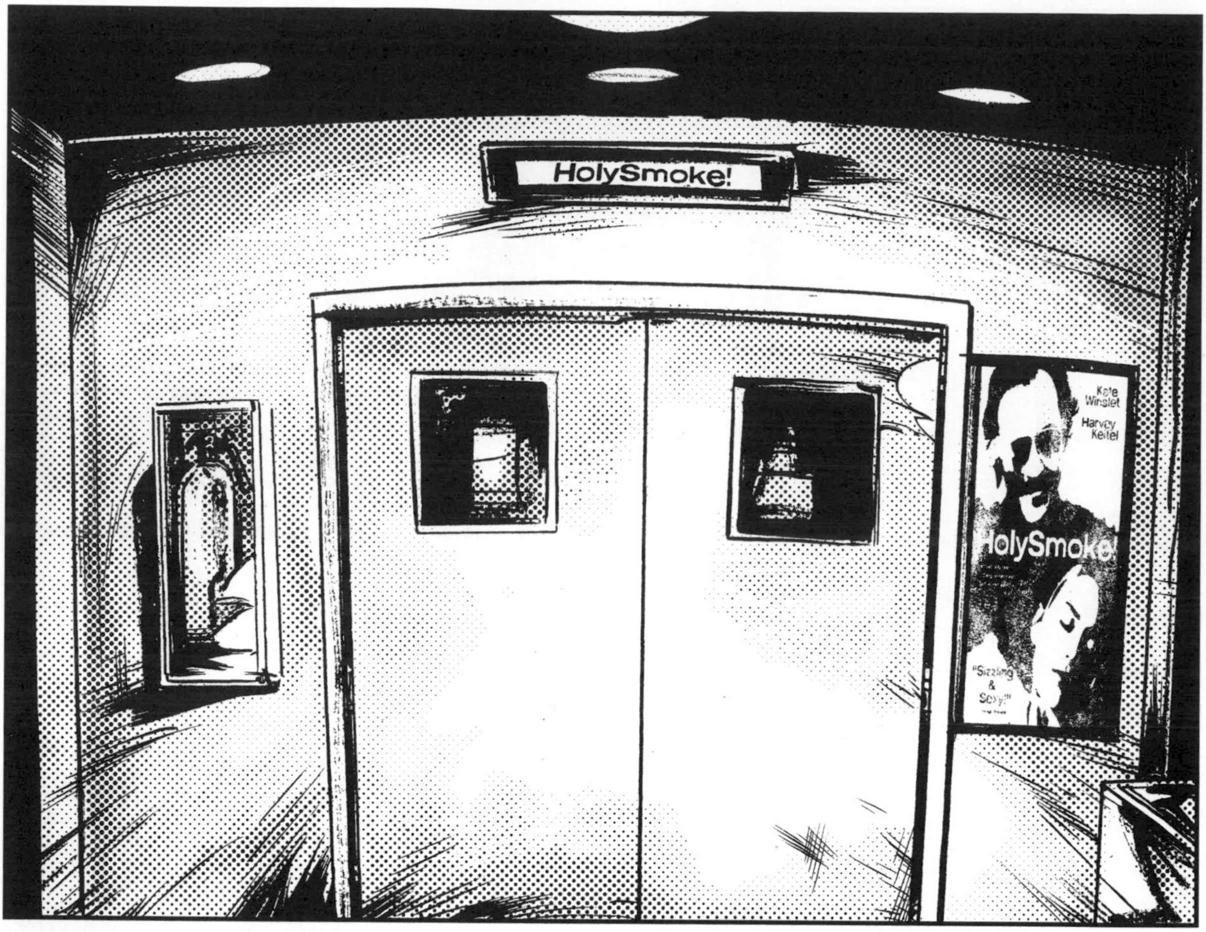
HolySmoke!
Kate Winslet
Harvey Keitel
HolySmoke!
"Sizzling & Sexy!"

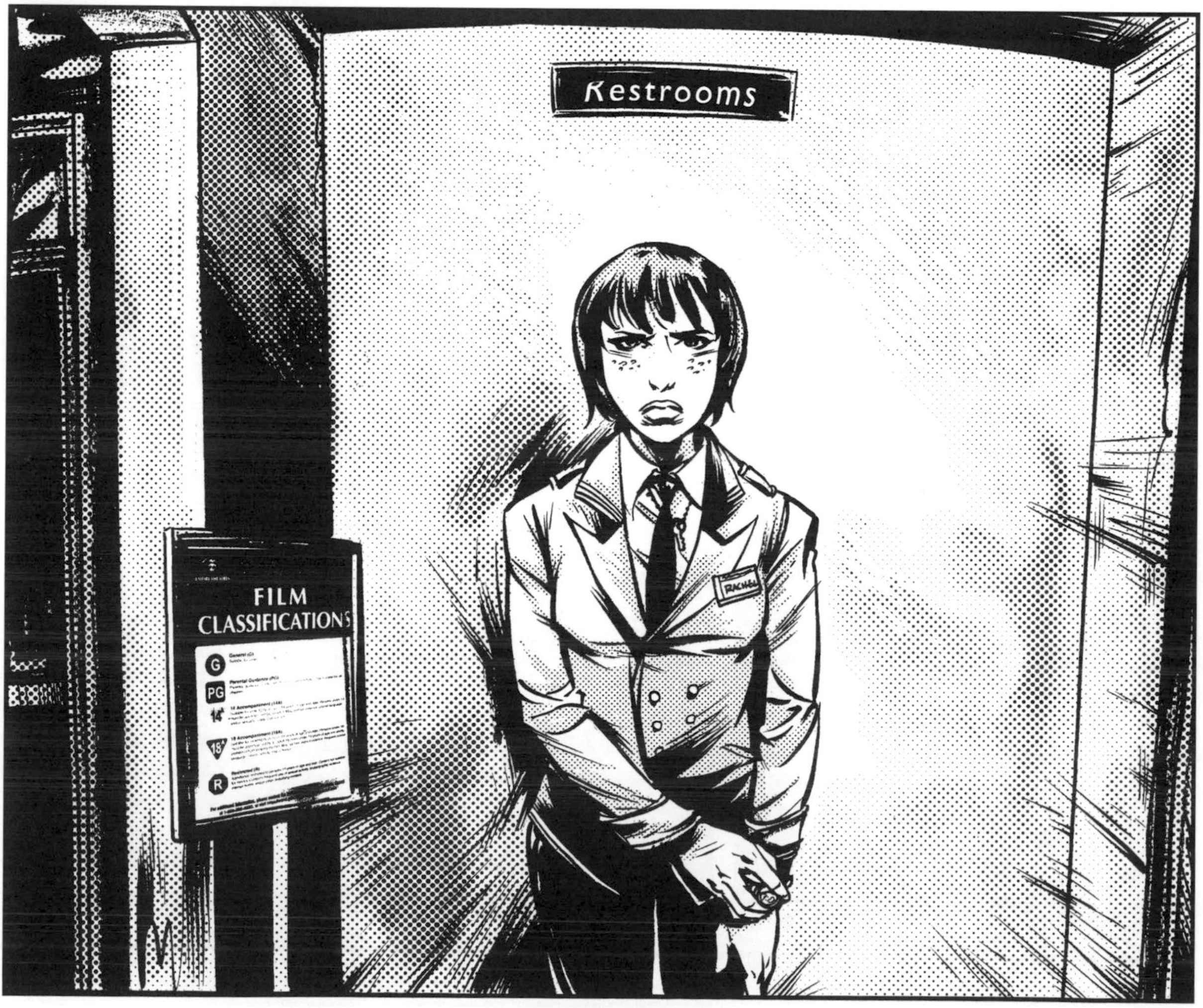
Restrooms
FILM CLASSIFICATIONS

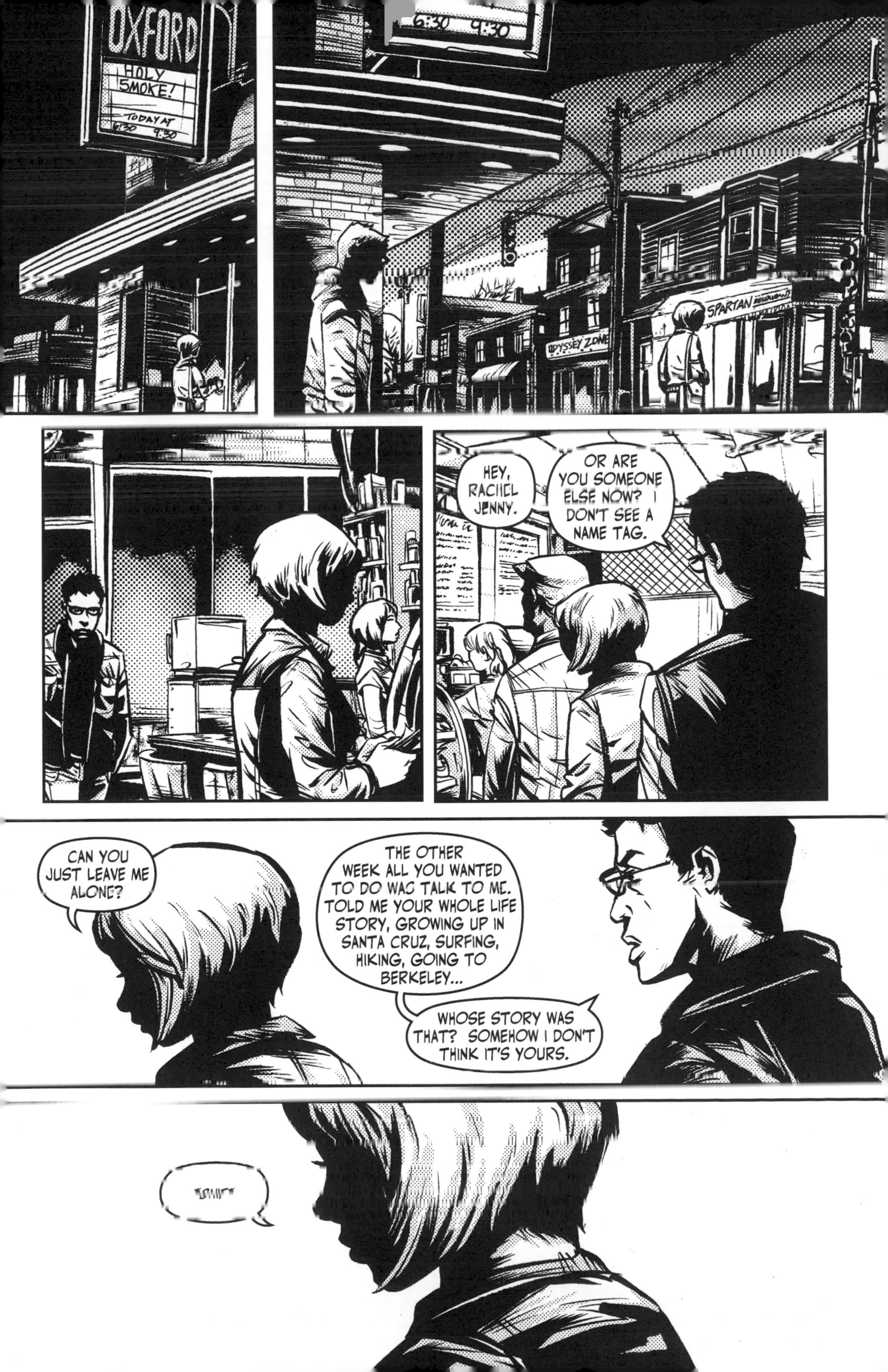
OXFORD
HOLY SMOKE!
TODAY AT 6:30 9:30
6:30 9:30
ODYSSEY ZONE
SPARTAN
HEY, RACHEL JENNY.
OR ARE YOU SOMEONE ELSE NOW? I DON'T SEE A NAME TAG.
CAN YOU JUST LEAVE ME ALONE?
THE OTHER WEEK ALL YOU WANTED TO DO WAS TALK TO ME. TOLD ME YOUR WHOLE LIFE STORY, GROWING UP IN SANTA CRUZ, SURFING, HIKING, GOING TO BERKELEY...
WHOSE STORY WAS THAT? SOMEHOW I DON'T THINK IT'S YOURS.

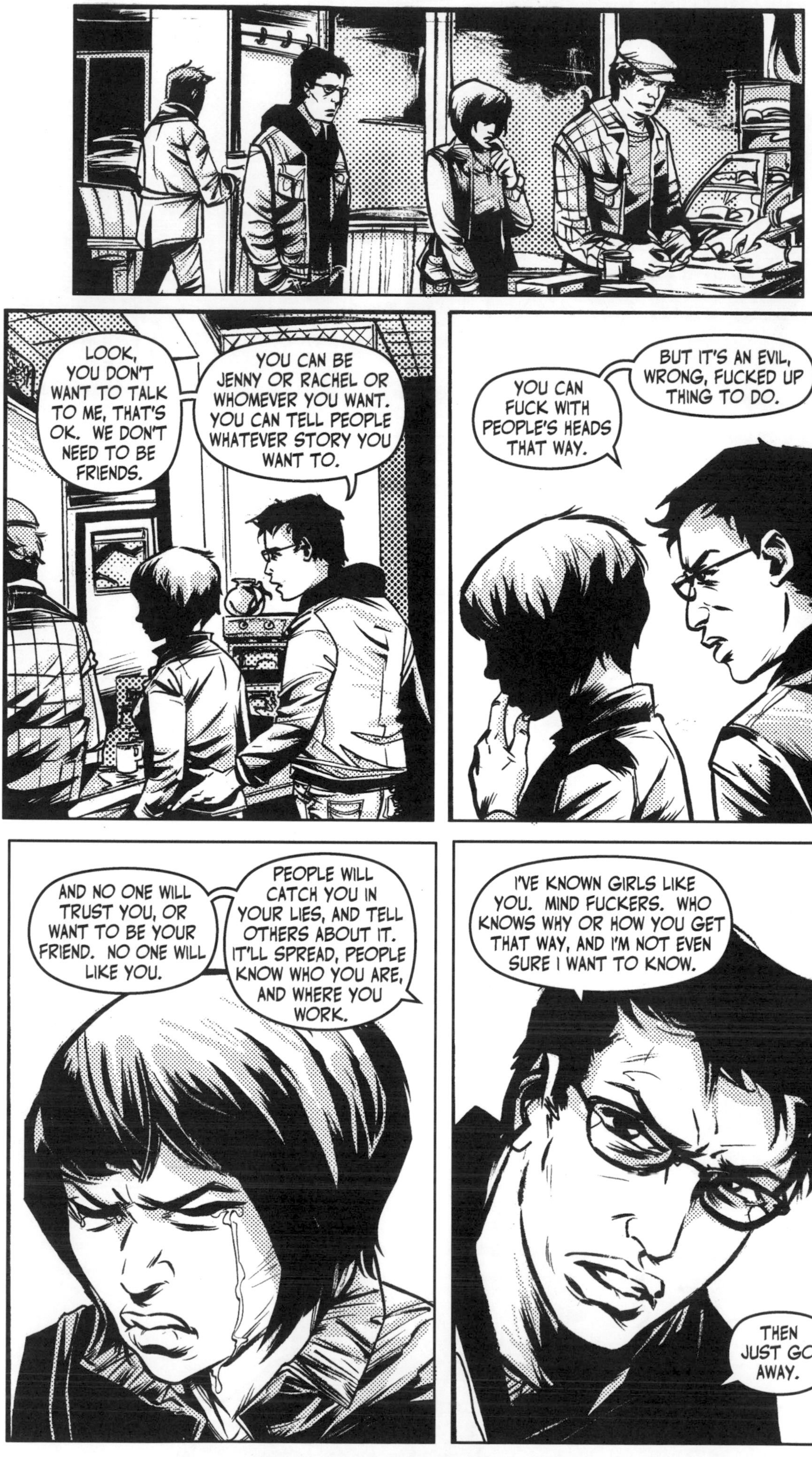
LOOK, YOU DON'T WANT TO TALK TO ME, THAT'S OK. WE DON'T NEED TO BE FRIENDS.
YOU CAN BE JENNY OR RACHEL OR WHOMEVER YOU WANT. YOU CAN TELL PEOPLE WHATEVER STORY YOU WANT TO.
YOU CAN FUCK WITH PEOPLE'S HEADS THAT WAY.
BUT IT'S AN EVIL, WRONG, FUCKED UP THING TO DO.
AND NO ONE WILL TRUST YOU, OR WANT TO BE YOUR FRIEND. NO ONE WILL LIKE YOU.
PEOPLE WILL CATCH YOU IN YOUR LIES, AND TELL OTHERS ABOUT IT. IT'LL SPREAD, PEOPLE KNOW WHO YOU ARE, AND WHERE YOU WORK.
I'VE KNOWN GIRLS LIKE YOU. MIND FUCKERS. WHO KNOWS WHY OR HOW YOU GET THAT WAY, AND I'M NOT EVEN SURE I WANT TO KNOW.
THEN JUST GO AWAY.

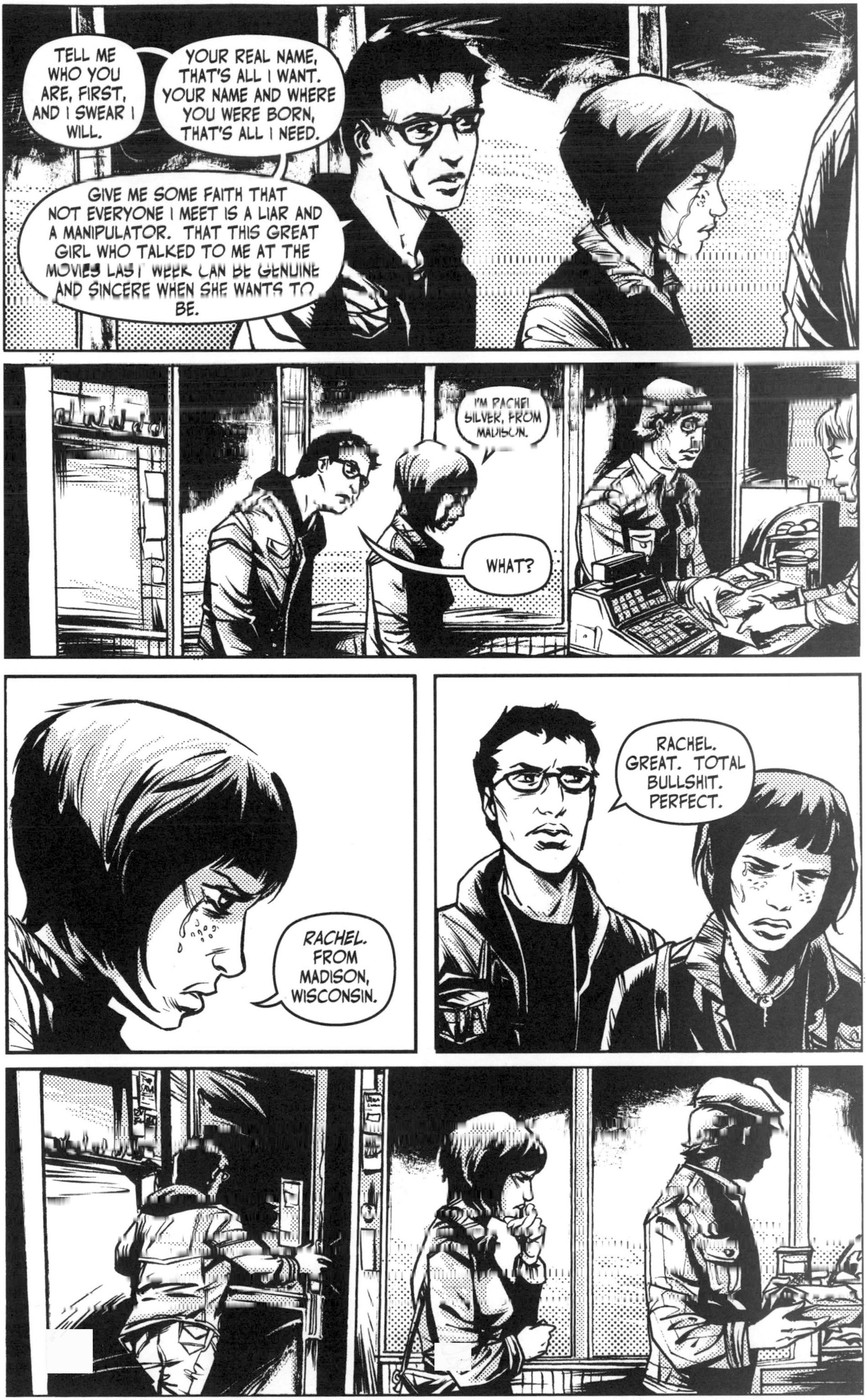
TELL ME WHO YOU ARE, FIRST, AND I SWEAR I WILL.
YOUR REAL NAME, THAT'S ALL I WANT. YOUR NAME AND WHERE YOU WERE BORN, THAT'S ALL I NEED.
GIVE ME SOME FAITH THAT NOT EVERYONE I MEET IS A LIAR AND A MANIPULATOR. THAT THIS GREAT GIRL WHO TALKED TO ME AT THE MOVIES LAST WEEK CAN BE GENUINE AND SINCERE WHEN SHE WANTS TO BE.
I'M RACHEL SILVER, FROM MADISON.
WHAT?
RACHEL. FROM MADISON, WISCONSIN.
RACHEL. GREAT. TOTAL BULLSHIT. PERFECT.

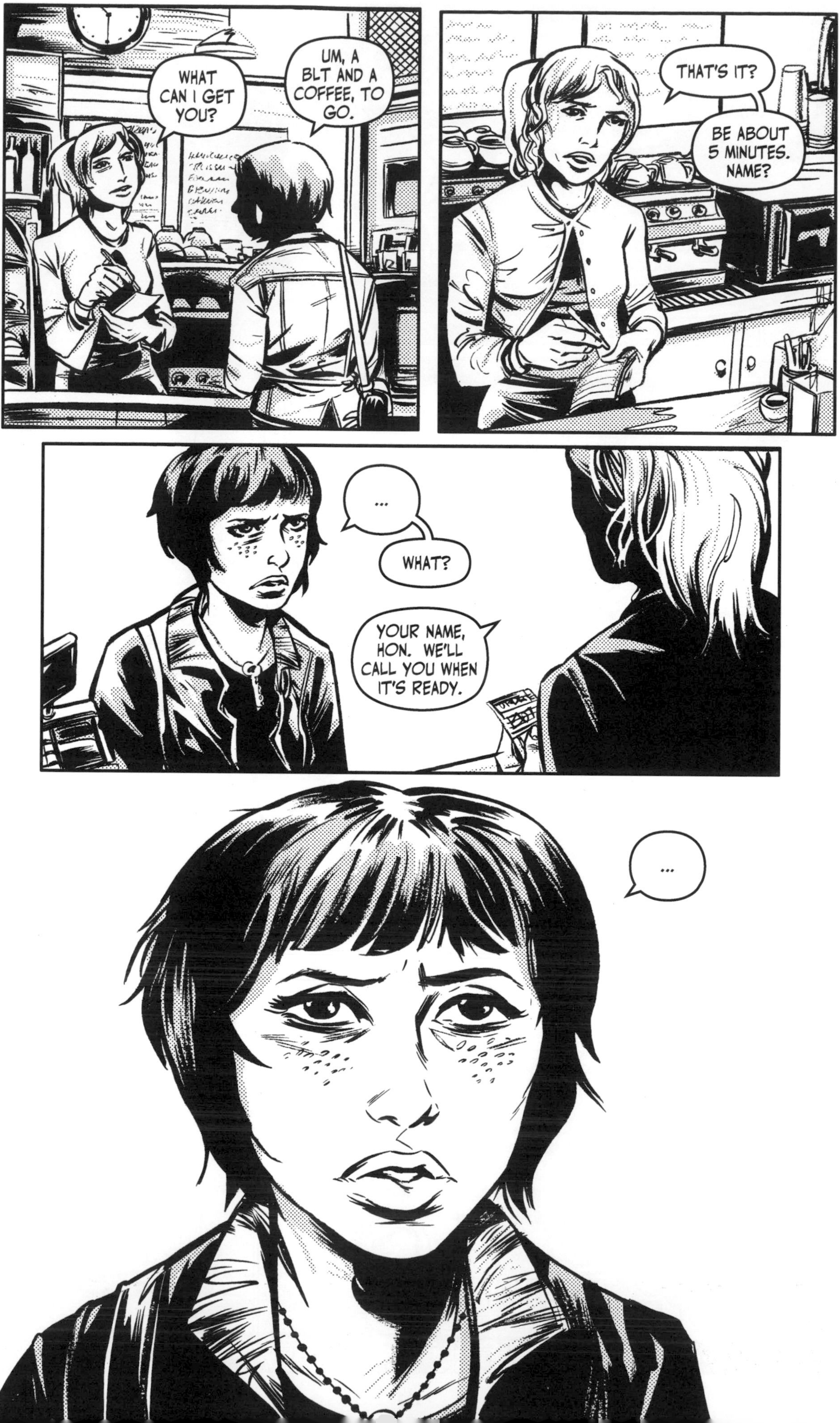
WHAT CAN I GET YOU?
UM, A BLT AND A COFFEE, TO GO.
THAT'S IT?
BE ABOUT 5 MINUTES. NAME?
...
WHAT?
YOUR NAME, HON. WE'LL CALL YOU WHEN IT'S READY.
...

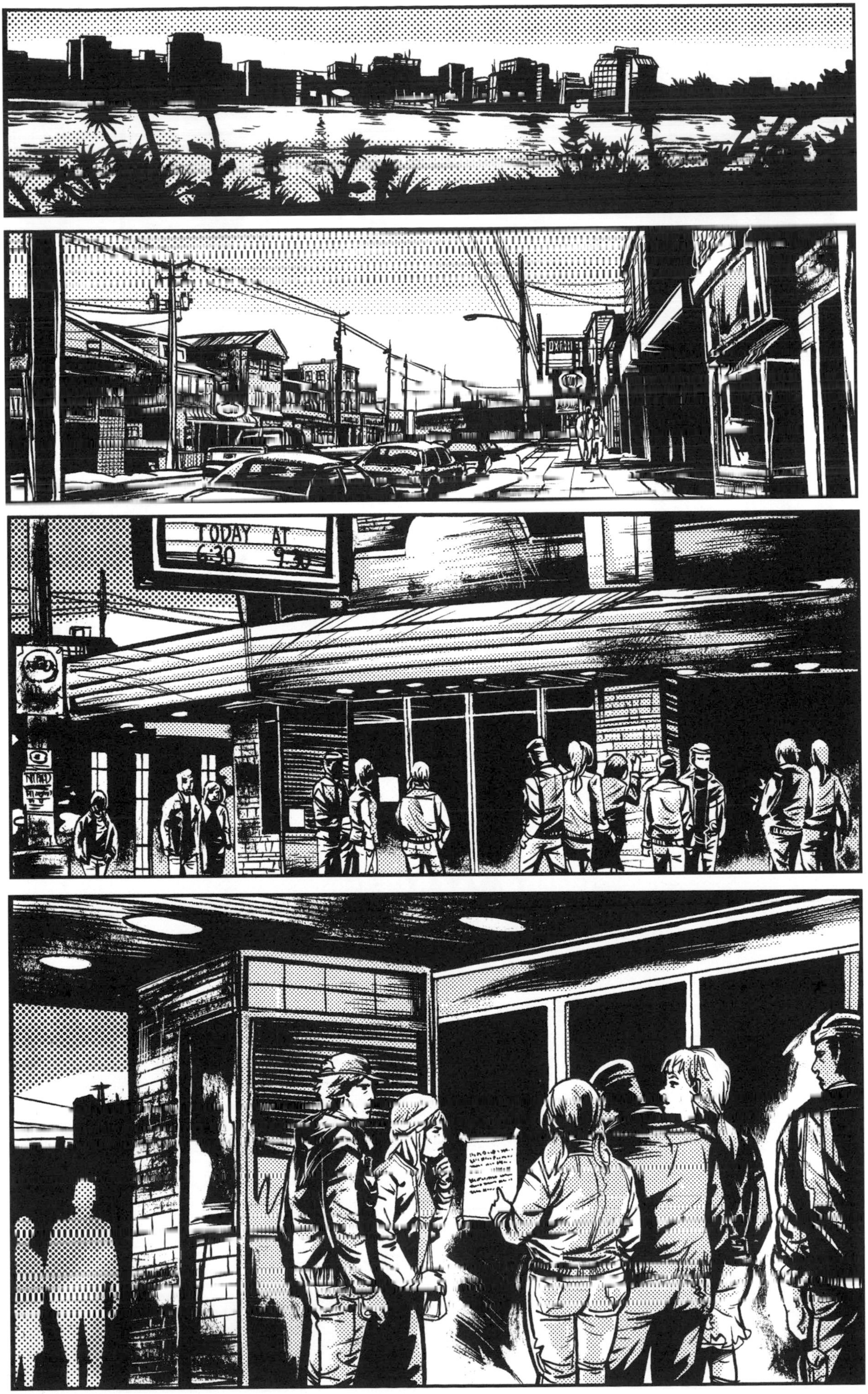
TODAY AT
6:30 9:30

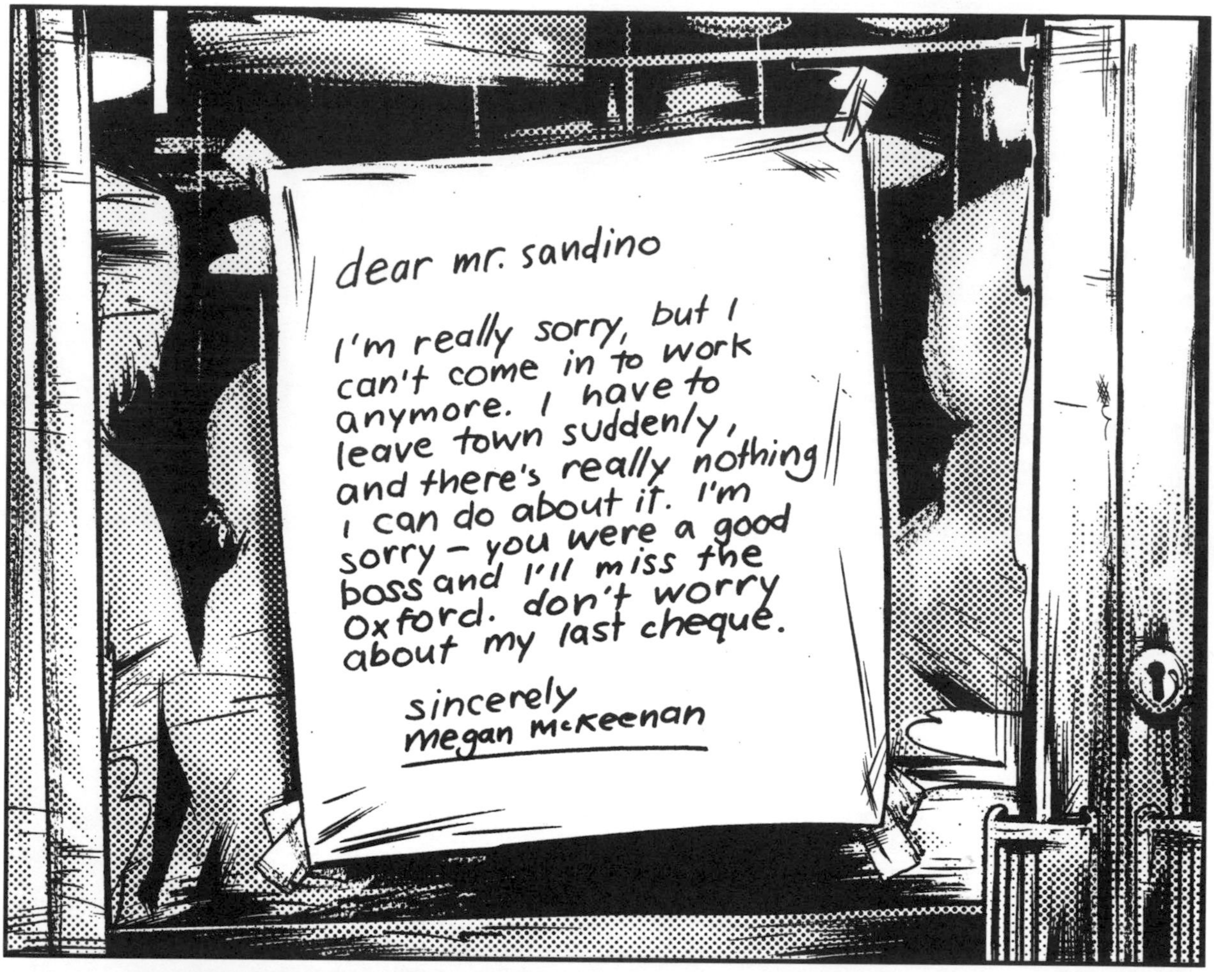
dear mr. sandino
I'm really sorry, but I can't come in to work anymore. I have to leave town suddenly, and there's really nothing I can do about it. I'm sorry - you were a good boss and I'll miss the Oxford. don't worry about my last cheque.
sincerely
megan McKeenan

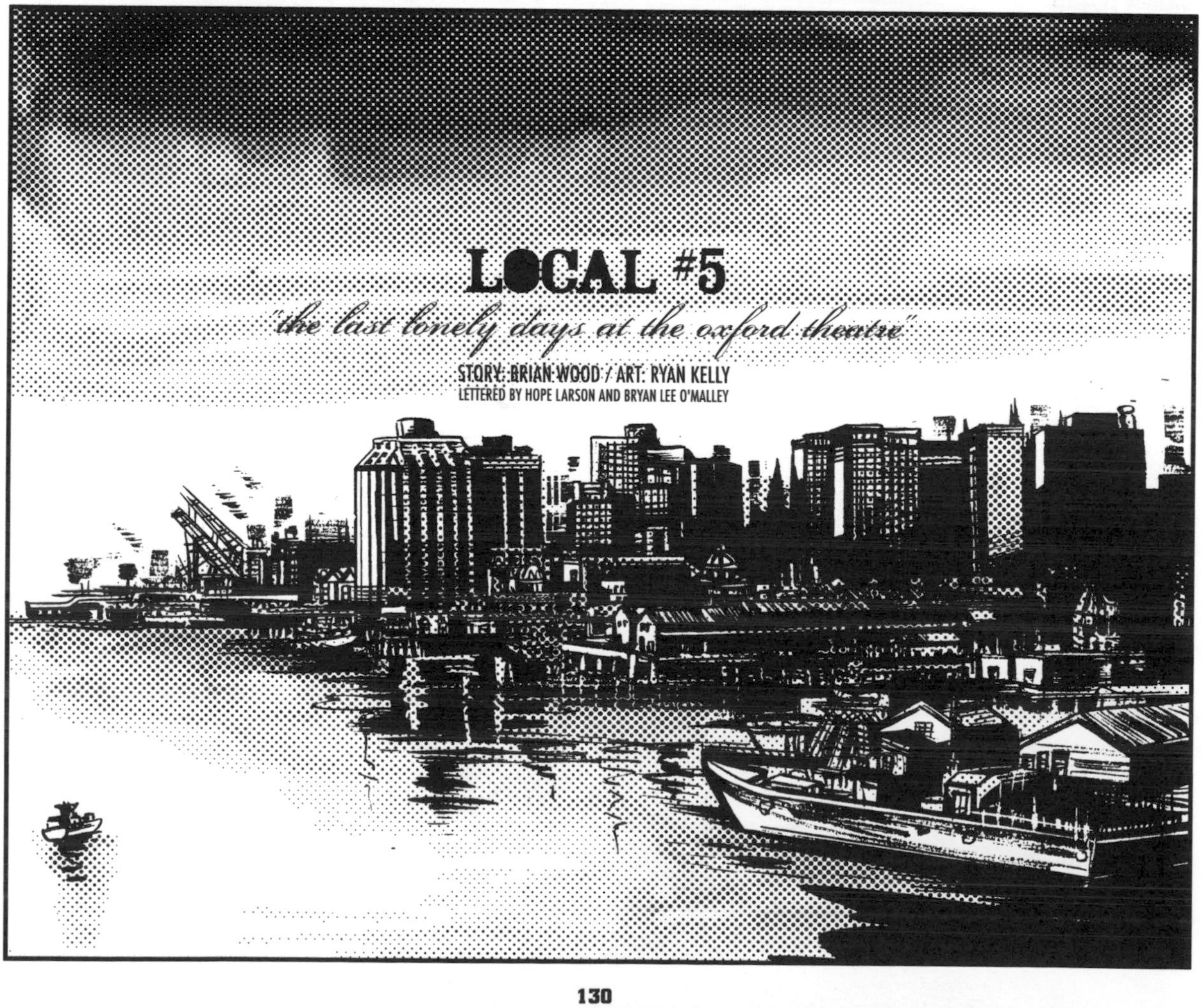
LOCAL #5
"the last lonely days at the oxford theatre"
STORY: BRIAN WOOD / ART: RYAN KELLY
LETTERED BY HOPE LARSON AND BRYAN LEE O'MALLEY

CHAPTER 6
"MEGAN AND GLORIA, APARTMENT 5A"
Park Slope, Brooklyn, New York

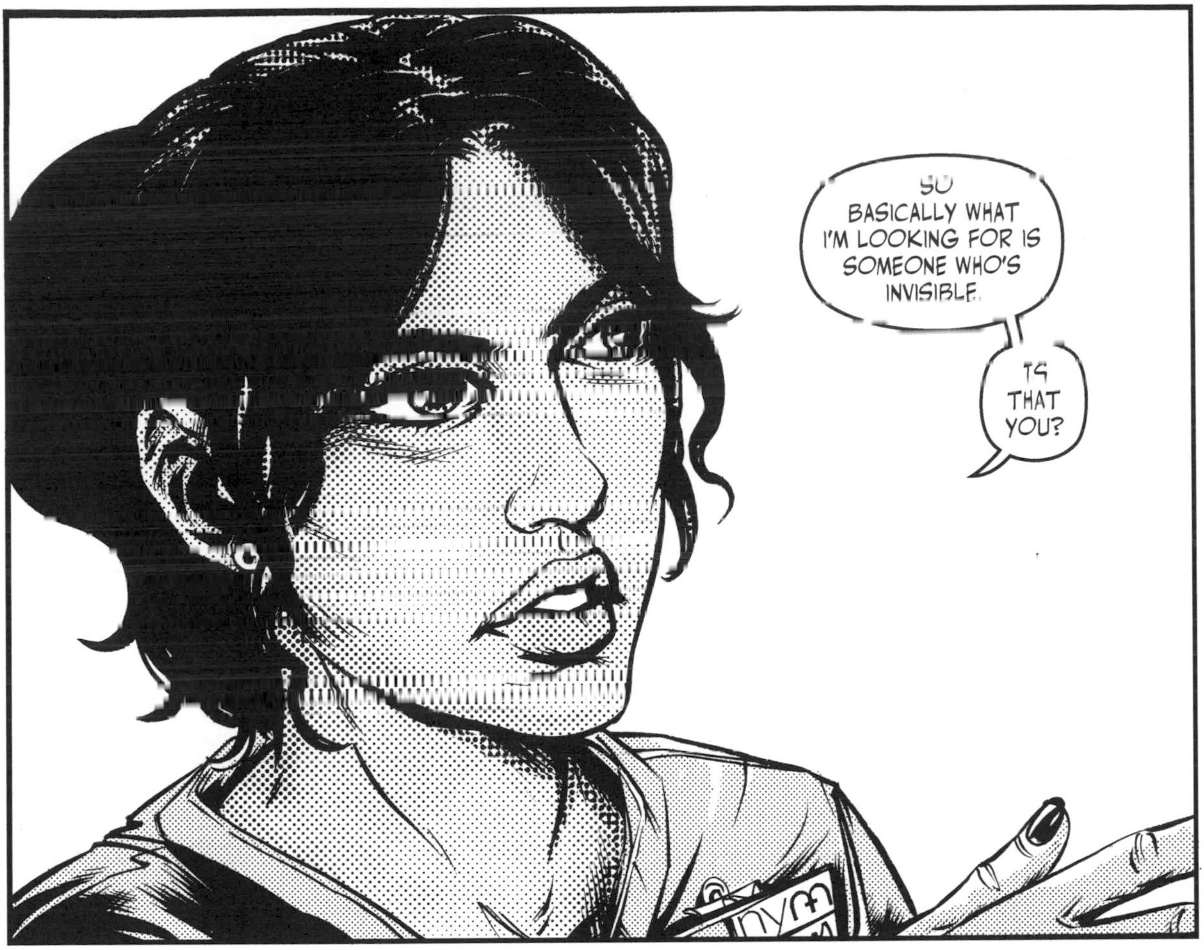
SO BASICALLY WHAT I'M LOOKING FOR IS SOMEONE WHO'S INVISIBLE.
IS THAT YOU?

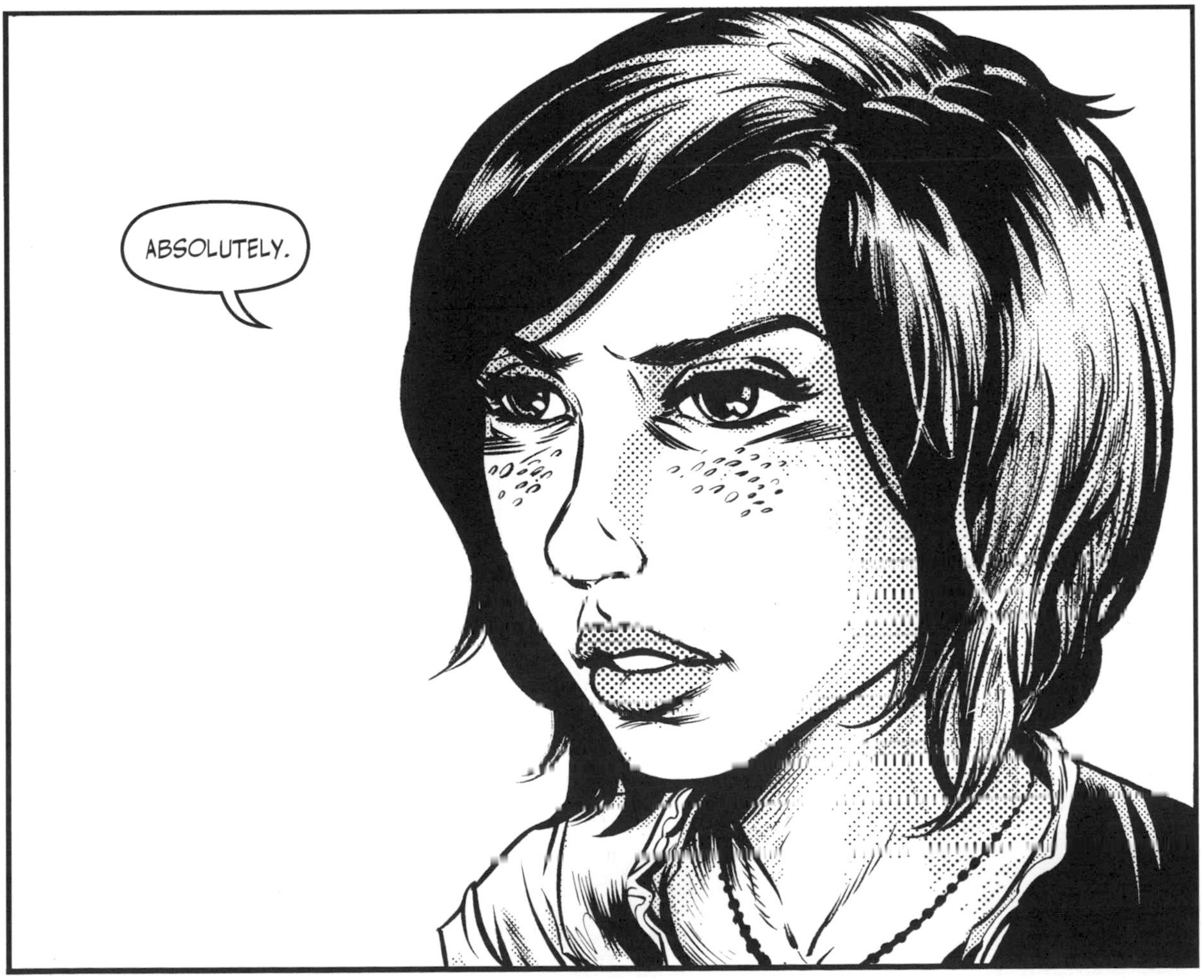
ABSOLUTELY.

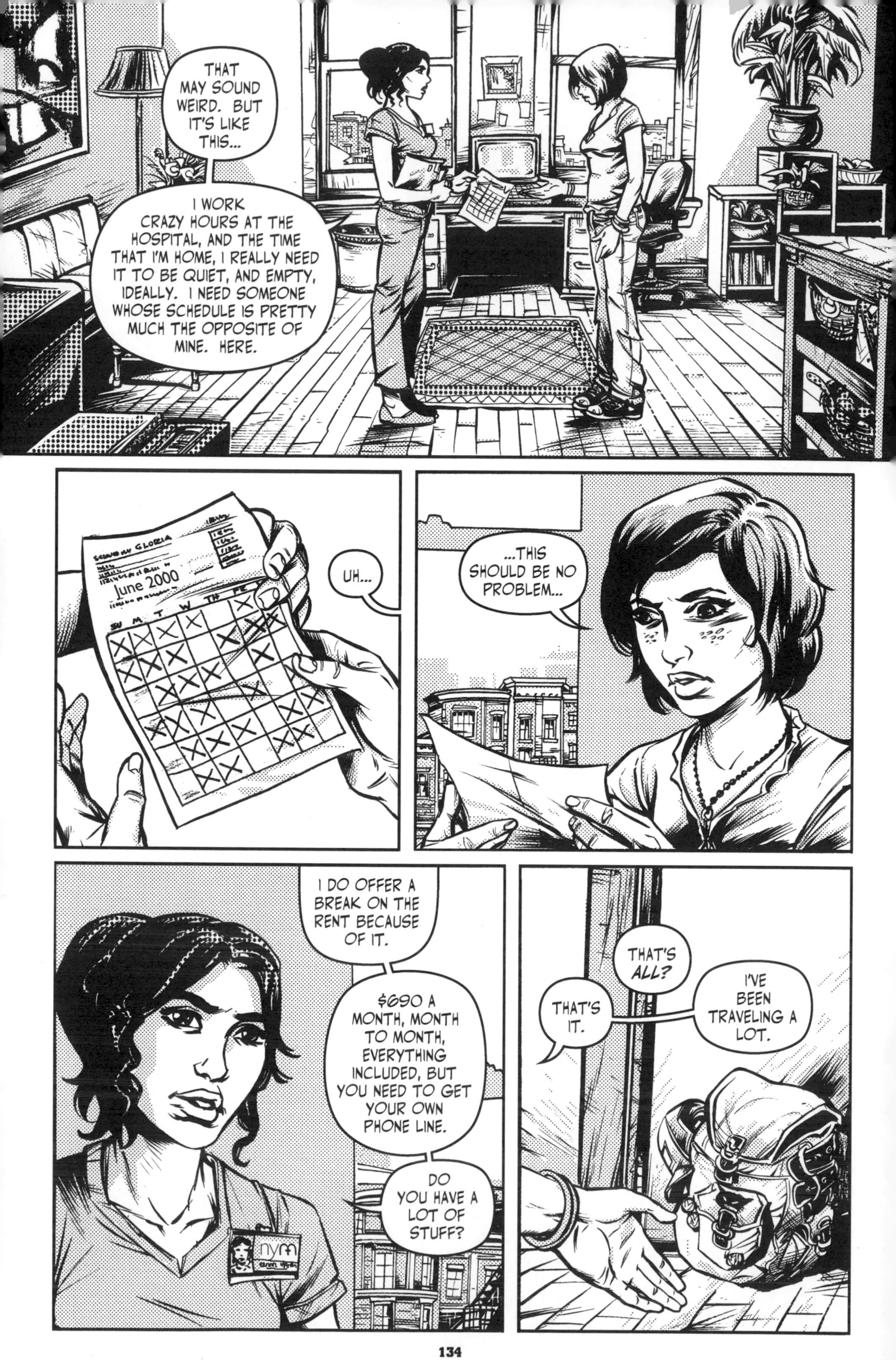
THAT MAY SOUND WEIRD. BUT IT'S LIKE THIS...
I WORK CRAZY HOURS AT THE HOSPITAL, AND THE TIME THAT I'M HOME, I REALLY NEED IT TO BE QUIET, AND EMPTY, IDEALLY. I NEED SOMEONE WHOSE SCHEDULE IS PRETTY MUCH THE OPPOSITE OF MINE. HERE.
June 2000
UH...
...THIS SHOULD BE NO PROBLEM...
I DO OFFER A BREAK ON THE RENT BECAUSE OF IT.
$690 A MONTH, MONTH TO MONTH, EVERYTHING INCLUDED, BUT YOU NEED TO GET YOUR OWN PHONE LINE.
DO YOU HAVE A LOT OF STUFF?
THAT'S IT.
THAT'S *ALL?*
I'VE BEEN TRAVELING A LOT.

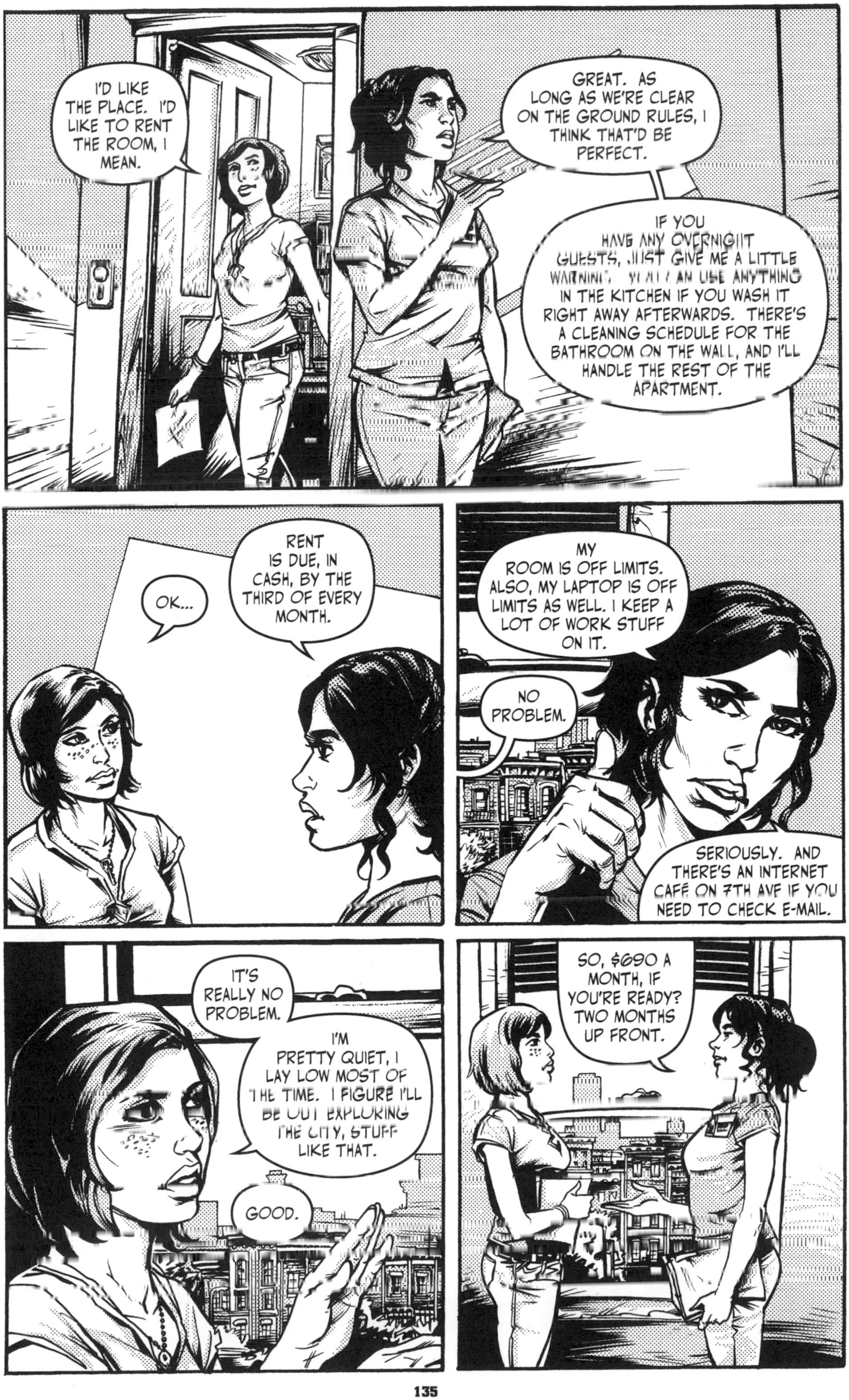
I'D LIKE THE PLACE. I'D LIKE TO RENT THE ROOM, I MEAN.
GREAT. AS LONG AS WE'RE CLEAR ON THE GROUND RULES, I THINK THAT'D BE PERFECT.
IF YOU HAVE ANY OVERNIGHT GUESTS, JUST GIVE ME A LITTLE WARNING. YOU CAN USE ANYTHING IN THE KITCHEN IF YOU WASH IT RIGHT AWAY AFTERWARDS. THERE'S A CLEANING SCHEDULE FOR THE BATHROOM ON THE WALL, AND I'LL HANDLE THE REST OF THE APARTMENT.
RENT IS DUE, IN CASH, BY THE THIRD OF EVERY MONTH.
OK...
MY ROOM IS OFF LIMITS. ALSO, MY LAPTOP IS OFF LIMITS AS WELL. I KEEP A LOT OF WORK STUFF ON IT.
NO PROBLEM.
SERIOUSLY. AND THERE'S AN INTERNET CAFE ON 7TH AVE IF YOU NEED TO CHECK E-MAIL.
IT'S REALLY NO PROBLEM.
I'M PRETTY QUIET, I LAY LOW MOST OF THE TIME. I FIGURE I'LL BE OUT EXPLORING THE CITY, STUFF LIKE THAT.
GOOD.
SO, $690 A MONTH, IF YOU'RE READY? TWO MONTHS UP FRONT.

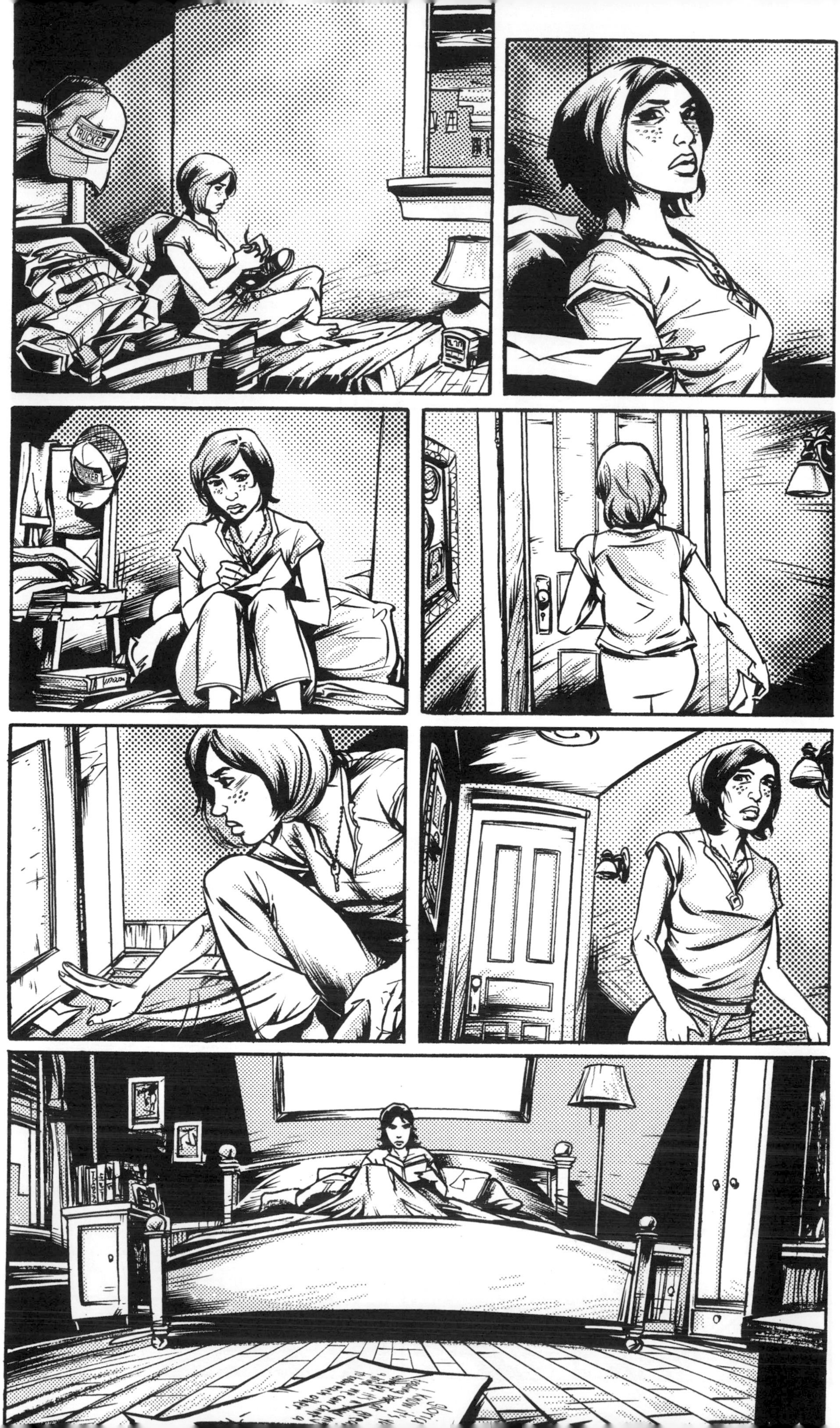
TRUCKER

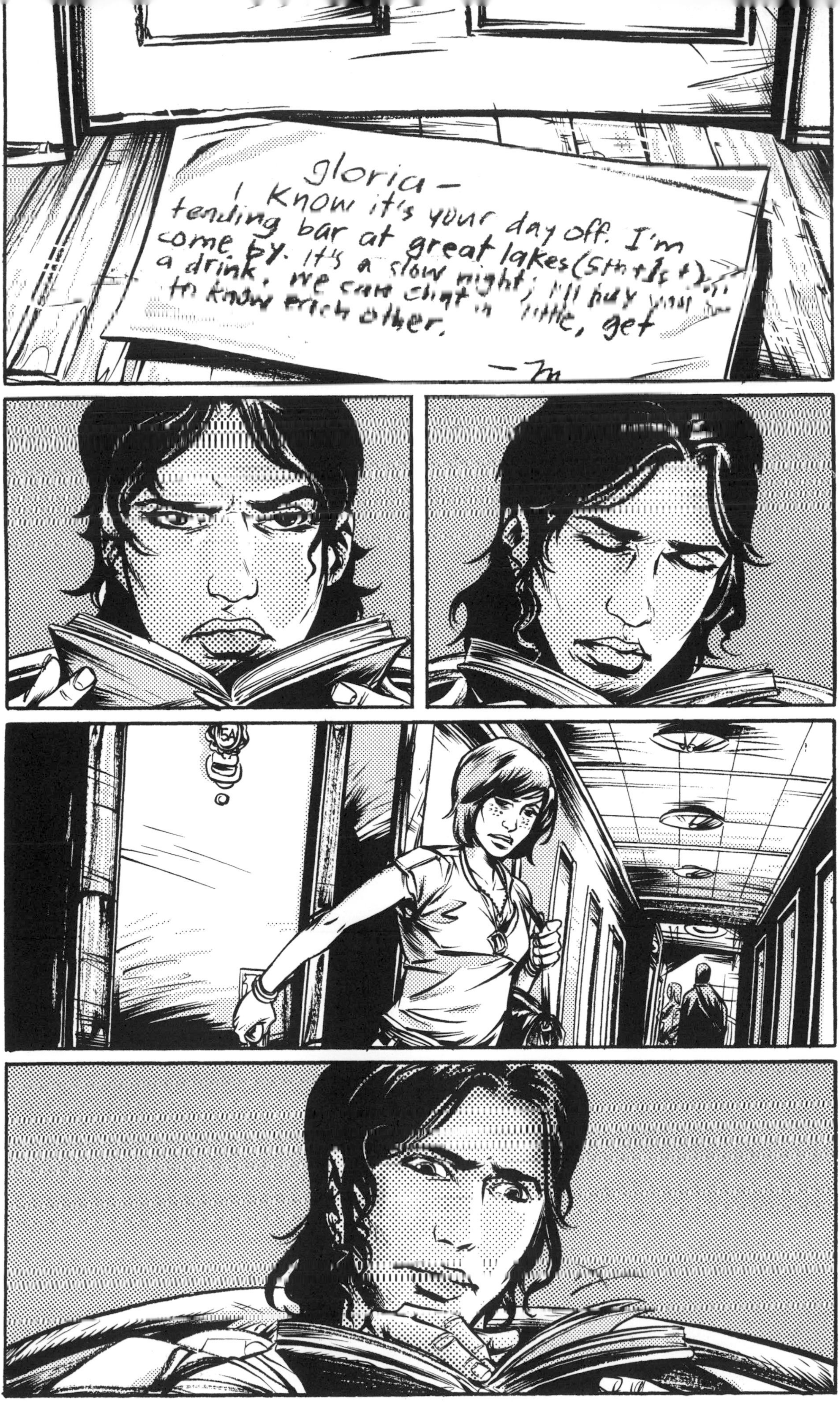
gloria—
I know it's your day off. I'm
tending bar at great lakes
come by. It's a slow night; I'll buy you
a drink.
other.
—M

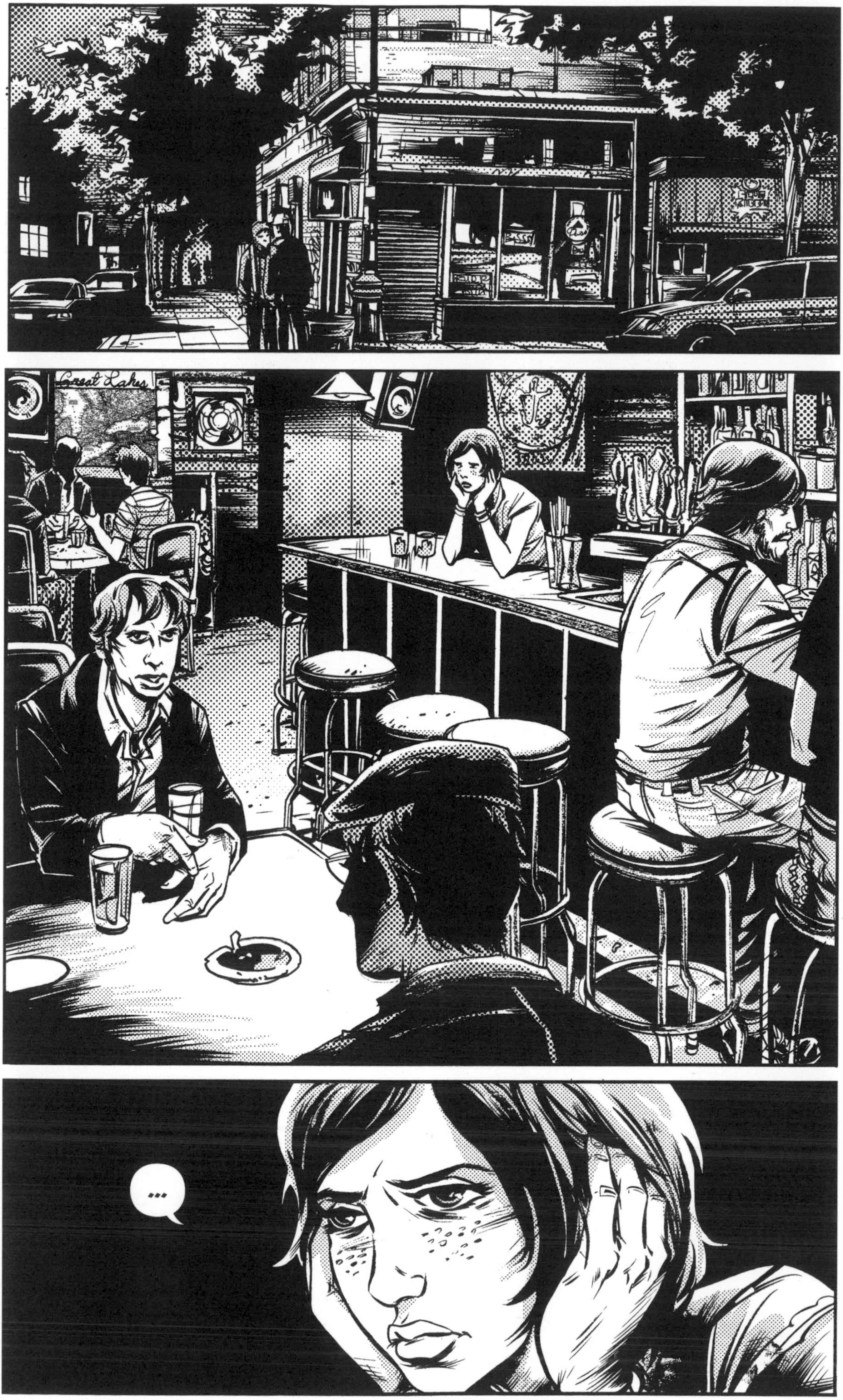

Great Lakes
...

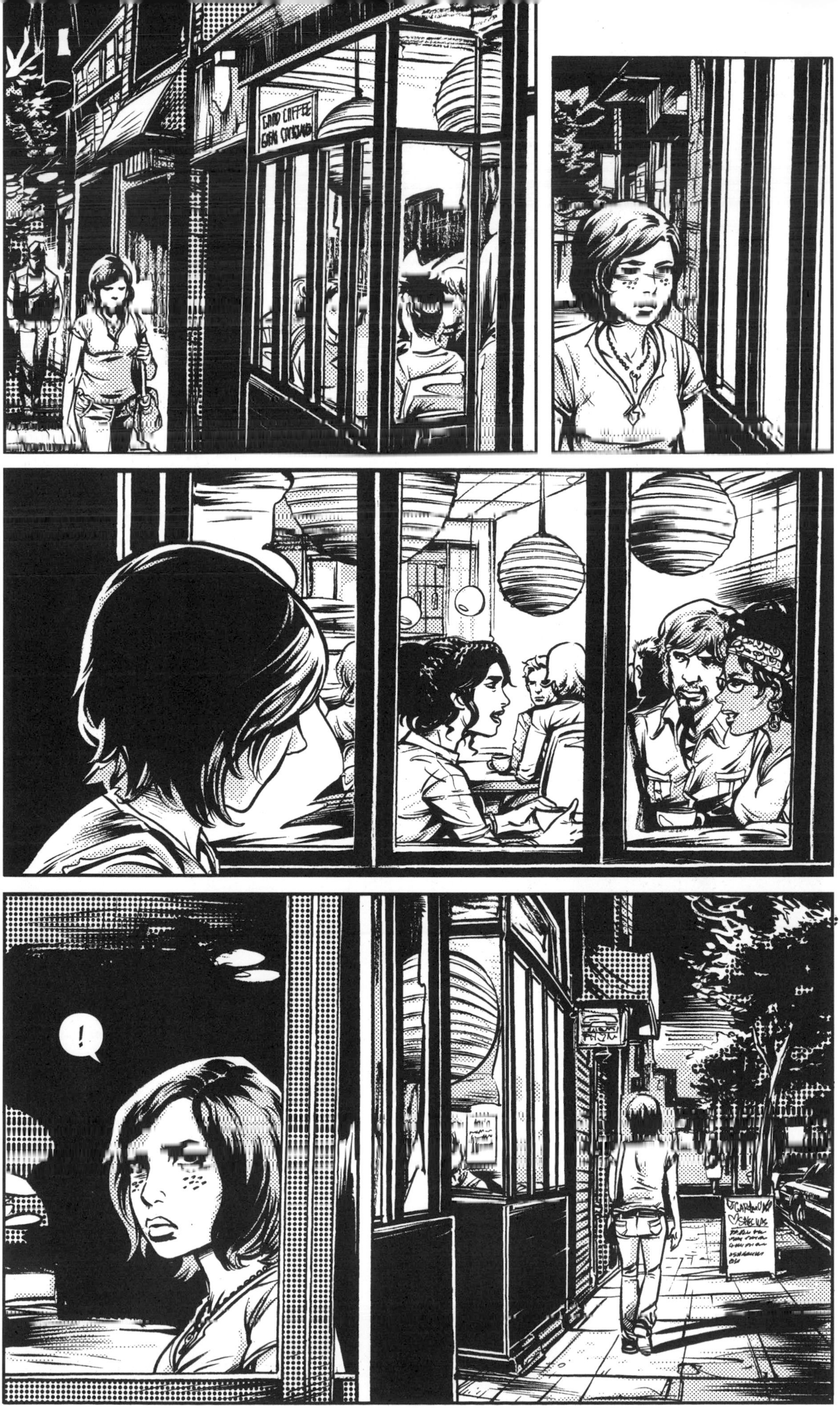
!

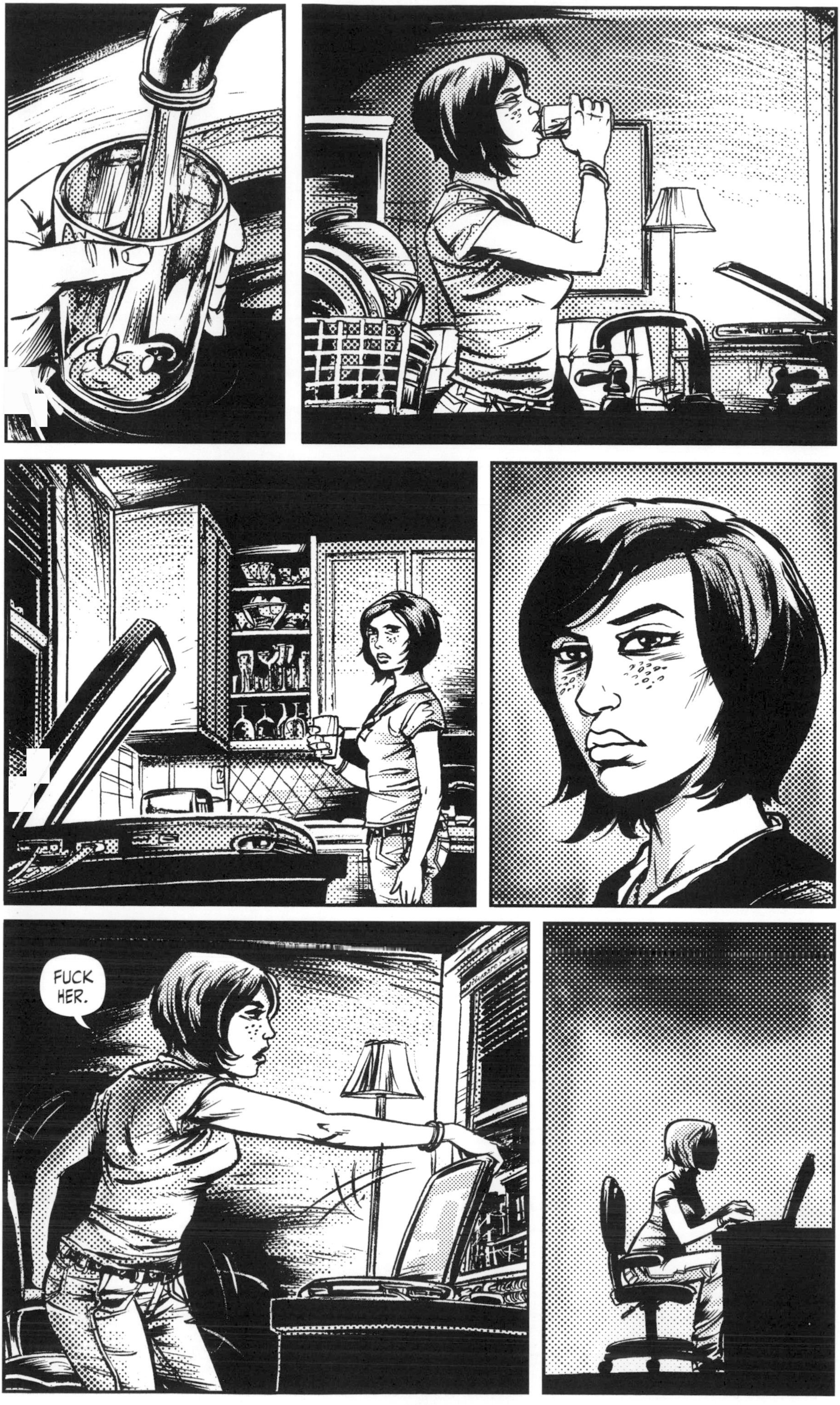
FUCK HER.

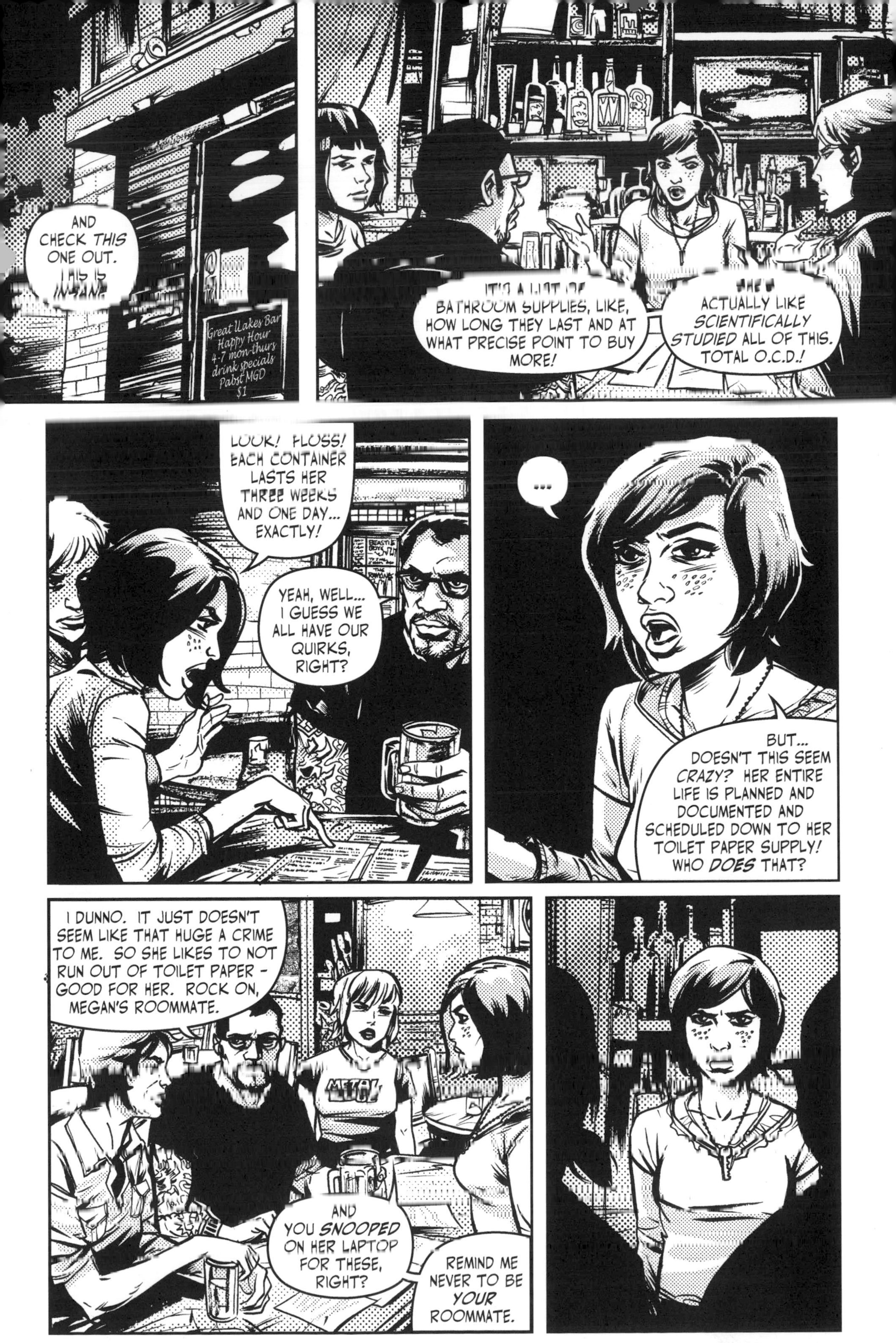
AND CHECK THIS ONE OUT. THIS IS
Great Lakes Bar Happy Hour 4-7 mon-thurs drink specials Pabst MGD $1
BATHROOM SUPPLIES, LIKE, HOW LONG THEY LAST AND AT WHAT PRECISE POINT TO BUY MORE!
ACTUALLY LIKE SCIENTIFICALLY STUDIED ALL OF THIS. TOTAL O.C.D.!
LOOK! FLOSS! EACH CONTAINER LASTS HER THREE WEEKS AND ONE DAY... EXACTLY!
YEAH, WELL... I GUESS WE ALL HAVE OUR QUIRKS, RIGHT?
...
BUT... DOESN'T THIS SEEM CRAZY? HER ENTIRE LIFE IS PLANNED AND DOCUMENTED AND SCHEDULED DOWN TO HER TOILET PAPER SUPPLY! WHO DOES THAT?
I DUNNO. IT JUST DOESN'T SEEM LIKE THAT HUGE A CRIME TO ME. SO SHE LIKES TO NOT RUN OUT OF TOILET PAPER - GOOD FOR HER. ROCK ON, MEGAN'S ROOMMATE.
AND YOU SNOOPED ON HER LAPTOP FOR THESE, RIGHT?
REMIND ME NEVER TO BE YOUR ROOMMATE.

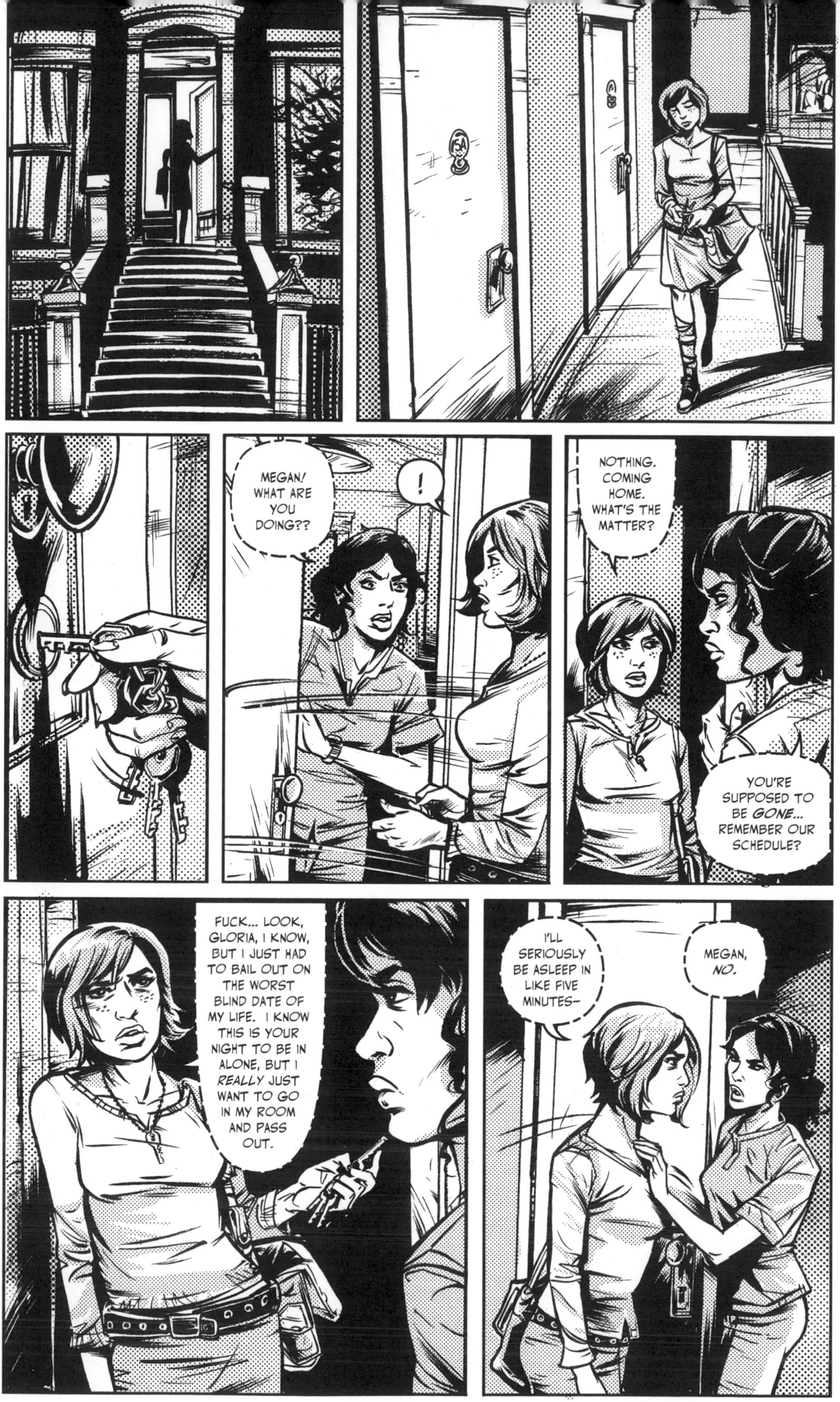

MEGAN! WHAT ARE YOU DOING??
!
NOTHING. COMING HOME. WHAT'S THE MATTER?
YOU'RE SUPPOSED TO BE *GONE*... REMEMBER OUR SCHEDULE?
FUCK... LOOK, GLORIA, I KNOW, BUT I JUST HAD TO BAIL OUT ON THE WORST BLIND DATE OF MY LIFE. I KNOW THIS IS YOUR NIGHT TO BE IN ALONE, BUT I *REALLY* JUST WANT TO GO IN MY ROOM AND PASS OUT.
I'LL SERIOUSLY BE ASLEEP IN LIKE FIVE MINUTES–
MEGAN, *NO*.

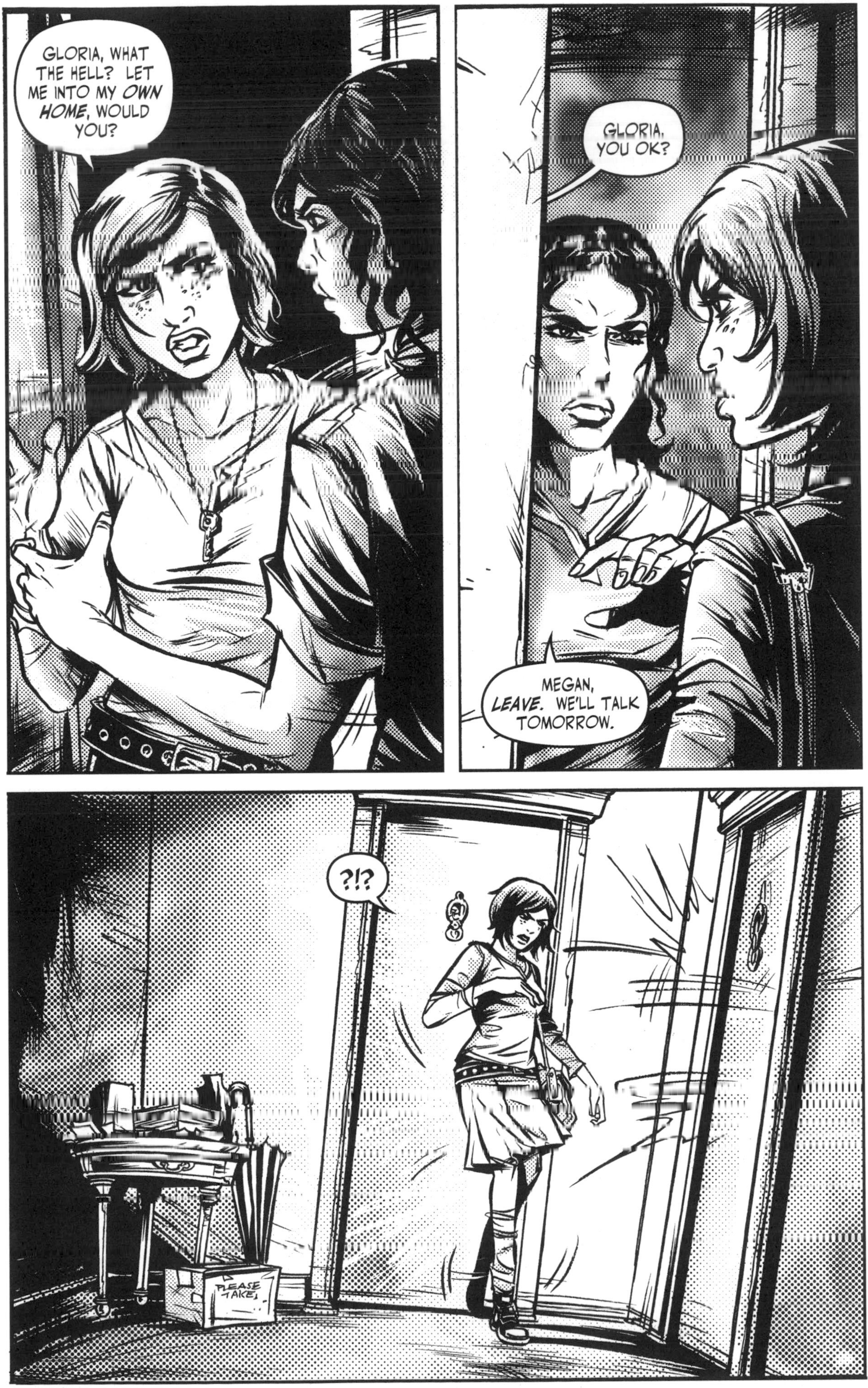
GLORIA, WHAT THE HELL? LET ME INTO MY *OWN HOME*, WOULD YOU?
GLORIA, YOU OK?
MEGAN, *LEAVE*. WE'LL TALK TOMORROW.
?!?
PLEASE TAKE!

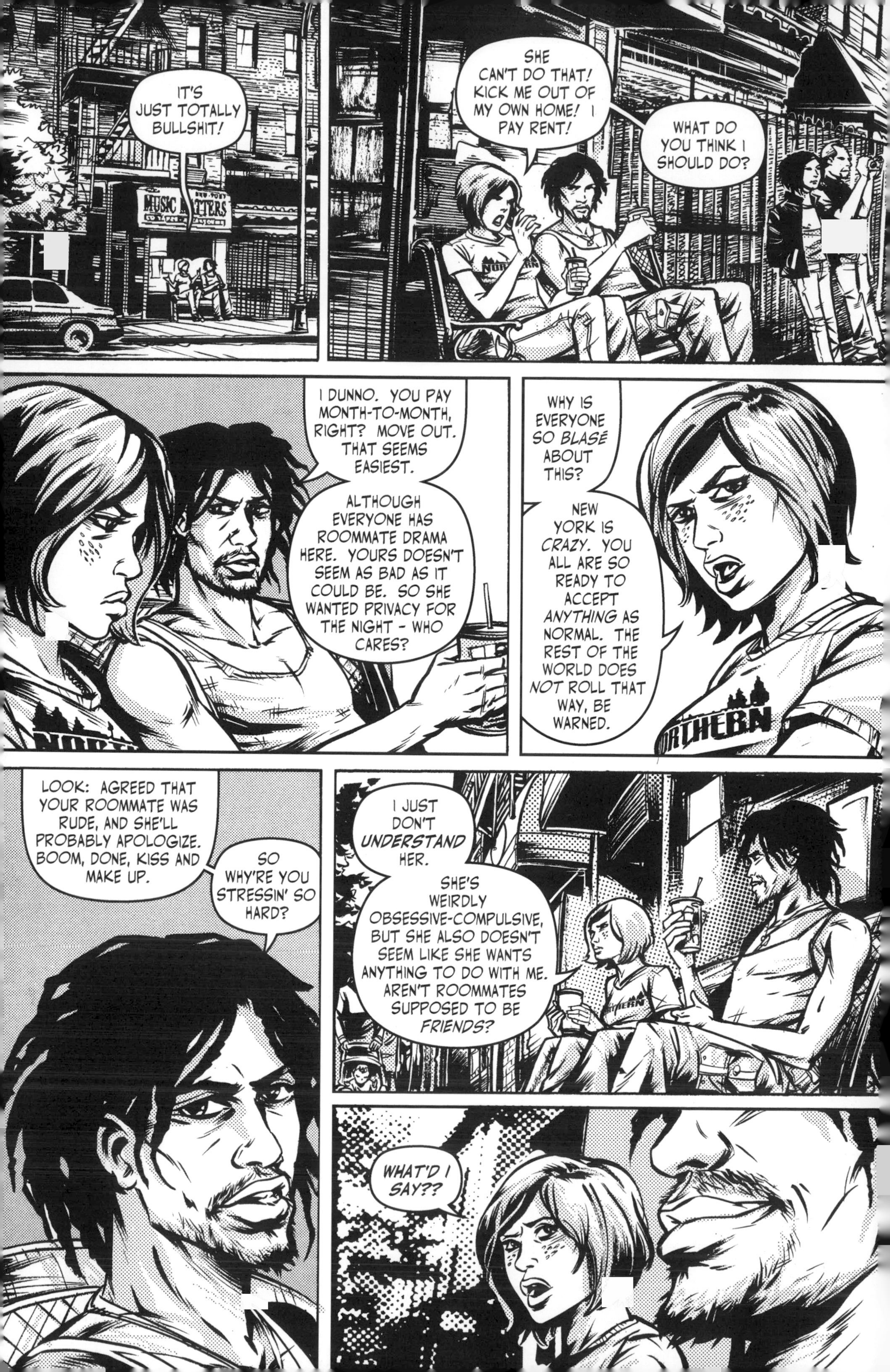
IT'S JUST TOTALLY BULLSHIT!
MUSIC MATTERS
SHE CAN'T DO THAT! KICK ME OUT OF MY OWN HOME! I PAY RENT!
WHAT DO YOU THINK I SHOULD DO?
I DUNNO. YOU PAY MONTH-TO-MONTH, RIGHT? MOVE OUT. THAT SEEMS EASIEST.
ALTHOUGH EVERYONE HAS ROOMMATE DRAMA HERE. YOURS DOESN'T SEEM AS BAD AS IT COULD BE. SO SHE WANTED PRIVACY FOR THE NIGHT – WHO CARES?
WHY IS EVERYONE SO *BLASÉ* ABOUT THIS?
NEW YORK IS *CRAZY*. YOU ALL ARE SO READY TO ACCEPT *ANYTHING* AS NORMAL. THE REST OF THE WORLD DOES *NOT* ROLL THAT WAY, BE WARNED.
NORTHERN
LOOK: AGREED THAT YOUR ROOMMATE WAS RUDE, AND SHE'LL PROBABLY APOLOGIZE. BOOM, DONE, KISS AND MAKE UP.
SO WHY'RE YOU STRESSIN' SO HARD?
I JUST DON'T *UNDERSTAND* HER.
SHE'S WEIRDLY OBSESSIVE-COMPULSIVE, BUT SHE ALSO DOESN'T SEEM LIKE SHE WANTS ANYTHING TO DO WITH ME. AREN'T ROOMMATES SUPPOSED TO BE *FRIENDS*?
WHAT'D I SAY??

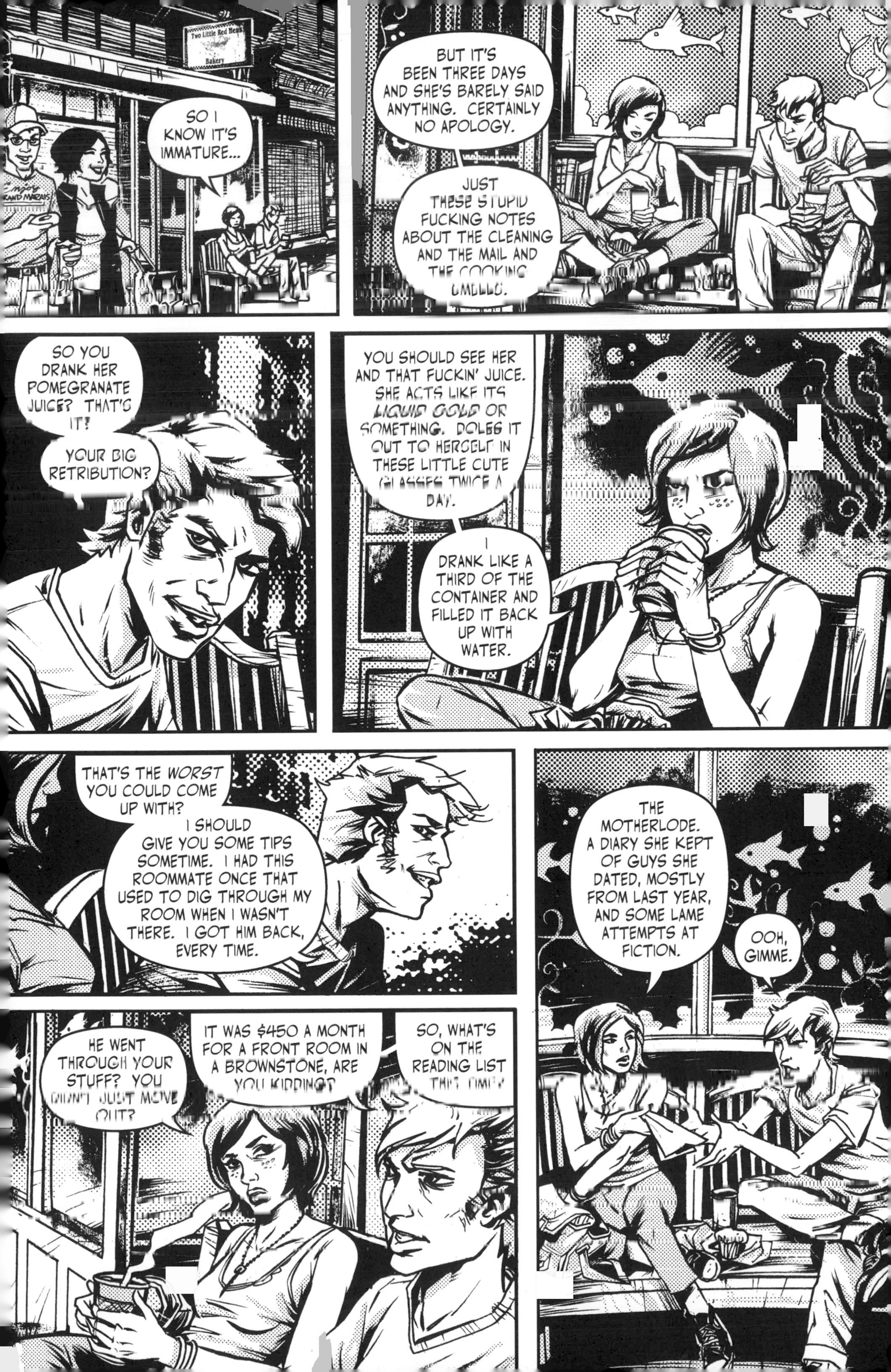

Two Little Red Hens Bakery
SO I KNOW IT'S IMMATURE...
BUT IT'S BEEN THREE DAYS AND SHE'S BARELY SAID ANYTHING. CERTAINLY NO APOLOGY.
JUST THESE STUPID FUCKING NOTES ABOUT THE CLEANING AND THE MAIL AND THE COOKING SMELLS.
SO YOU DRANK HER POMEGRANATE JUICE? THAT'S IT?
YOUR BIG RETRIBUTION?
YOU SHOULD SEE HER AND THAT FUCKIN' JUICE. SHE ACTS LIKE ITS *LIQUID GOLD* OR SOMETHING. DOLES IT OUT TO HERSELF IN THESE LITTLE CUTE GLASSES TWICE A DAY.
I DRANK LIKE A THIRD OF THE CONTAINER AND FILLED IT BACK UP WITH WATER.
THAT'S THE *WORST* YOU COULD COME UP WITH?
I SHOULD GIVE YOU SOME TIPS SOMETIME. I HAD THIS ROOMMATE ONCE THAT USED TO DIG THROUGH MY ROOM WHEN I WASN'T THERE. I GOT HIM BACK, EVERY TIME.
HE WENT THROUGH YOUR STUFF? YOU DIDN'T JUST MOVE OUT?
IT WAS $450 A MONTH FOR A FRONT ROOM IN A BROWNSTONE, ARE YOU KIDDING?
SO, WHAT'S ON THE READING LIST THIS TIME?
THE MOTHERLODE. A DIARY SHE KEPT OF GUYS SHE DATED, MOSTLY FROM LAST YEAR, AND SOME LAME ATTEMPTS AT FICTION.
OOH, GIMME.

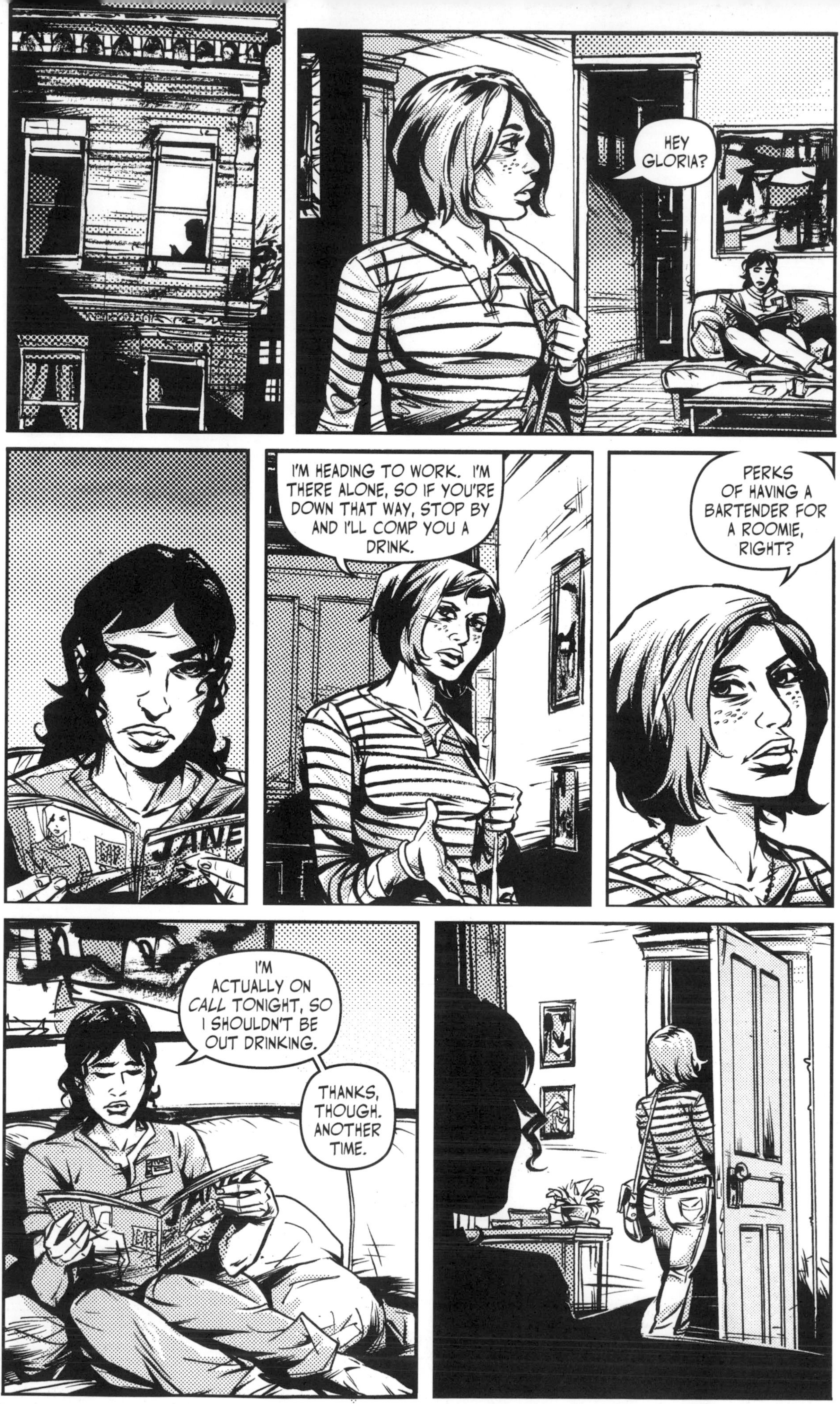
HEY GLORIA?
I'M HEADING TO WORK. I'M THERE ALONE, SO IF YOU'RE DOWN THAT WAY, STOP BY AND I'LL COMP YOU A DRINK.
PERKS OF HAVING A BARTENDER FOR A ROOMIE, RIGHT?
I'M ACTUALLY ON CALL TONIGHT, SO I SHOULDN'T BE OUT DRINKING.
THANKS, THOUGH. ANOTHER TIME.

STOP THE WAR NOW
Gloria Liriano
Shopping List
for the week of July 5-12, 2000
Scheduled shopping date:
Wednesday, July 7, 5:45 pm
LIQUID MEASURE
DRY MEASURE
WEIGHT
KITCHEN MEASUREMENTS
1.LEMONS, midsize, 4, darker yellow than last time
2.KALE, bundle, organic(?), no brown on edges, 1 pound
3.PEANUT BUTTER, natural, no salt
4.BABY CARROTS, pre-packaged, in water if possible, check ingredients first
5.APPLES, organic, bag of 6, packaged upstate.
6.ORANGE JUICE, no pulp. Not Florida's Select-awful taste.
7.AVOCADO, organic, Non-ripe, 2-3 days ripe time on these.
8.BANANAS, organic, from Ecuador if possible
8.CORNMEAL, COURSE ,100% ground, 1 lb bag.
9. Olive Oil, EXTRA virgin, get from Cossettas or any Italian grocer.
10 CHEESE, cheddar, extra sharp, aged 6 months atleast.
11.CANNED WHOLE TOMATOES, peeled, 3, 14oz cans.
14. TELLICHERRY PEPPERCORNS, whole, 4oz size.
15. WHITE PASTRY FLOUR, unbleached, not all-purpose.
16. PASTA, fusilli, whole wheat.
17.ALASKAN SALMON STEAK, 2 pounds.
Living Room
Bathroom
Kitchen
TASKS
Cleaning
Gloria Liriano
Clothing Organization
Pro and Con
Organize by Color
Organize by Style
PRO
CON
OH.
HEY GABE.
MEN
HEY, CAN I CRASH ON YOUR COUCH TONIGHT?

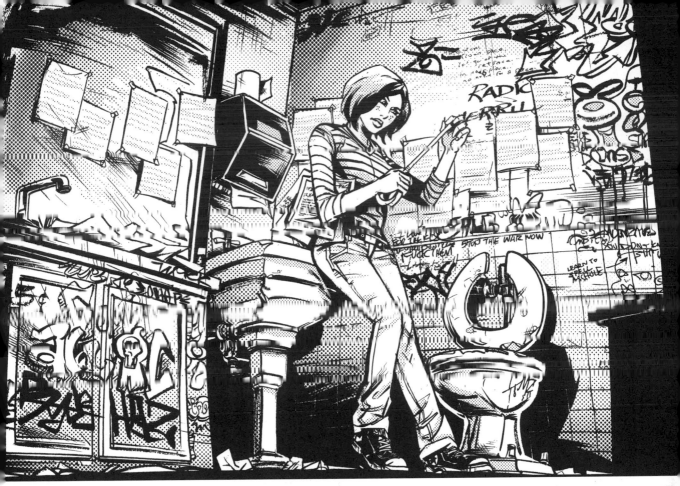

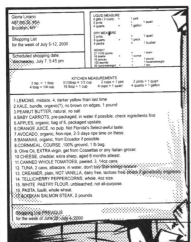

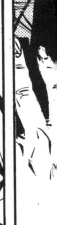

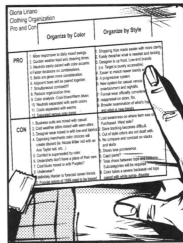

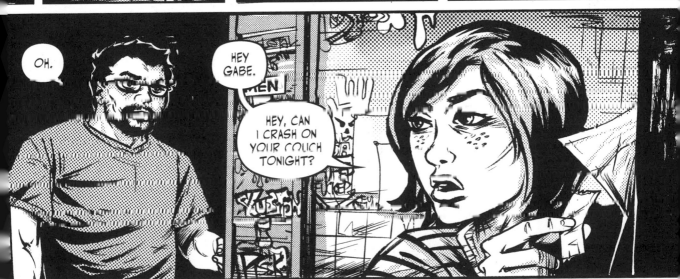

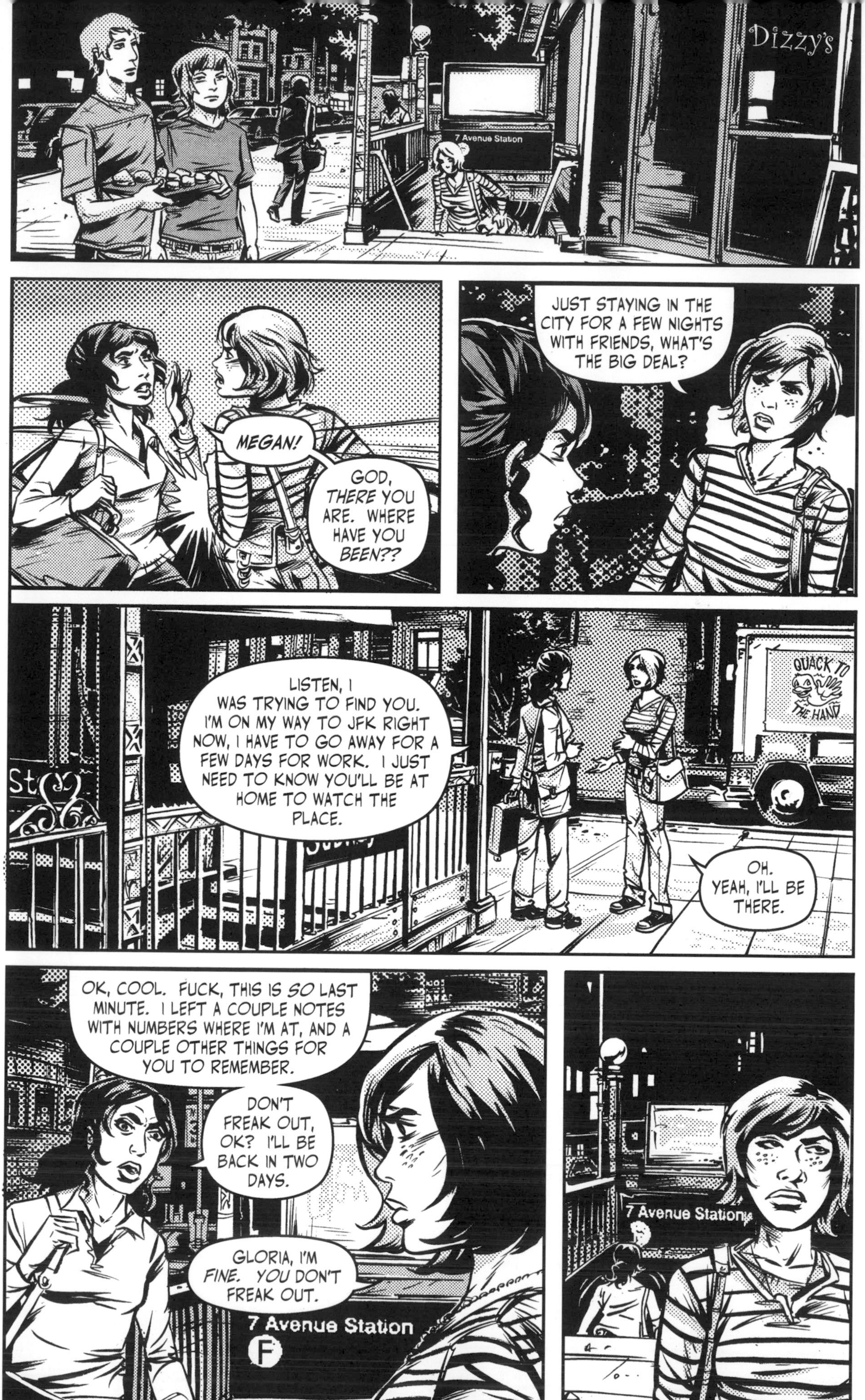
Dizzy's
7 Avenue Station
MEGAN!
GOD, THERE YOU ARE. WHERE HAVE YOU BEEN??
JUST STAYING IN THE CITY FOR A FEW NIGHTS WITH FRIENDS, WHAT'S THE BIG DEAL?
LISTEN, I WAS TRYING TO FIND YOU. I'M ON MY WAY TO JFK RIGHT NOW, I HAVE TO GO AWAY FOR A FEW DAYS FOR WORK. I JUST NEED TO KNOW YOU'LL BE AT HOME TO WATCH THE PLACE.
QUACK TO THE HAND
OH. YEAH, I'LL BE THERE.
OK, COOL. FUCK, THIS IS SO LAST MINUTE. I LEFT A COUPLE NOTES WITH NUMBERS WHERE I'M AT, AND A COUPLE OTHER THINGS FOR YOU TO REMEMBER.
DON'T FREAK OUT, OK? I'LL BE BACK IN TWO DAYS.
GLORIA, I'M FINE. YOU DON'T FREAK OUT.
7 Avenue Station
F
7 Avenue Station

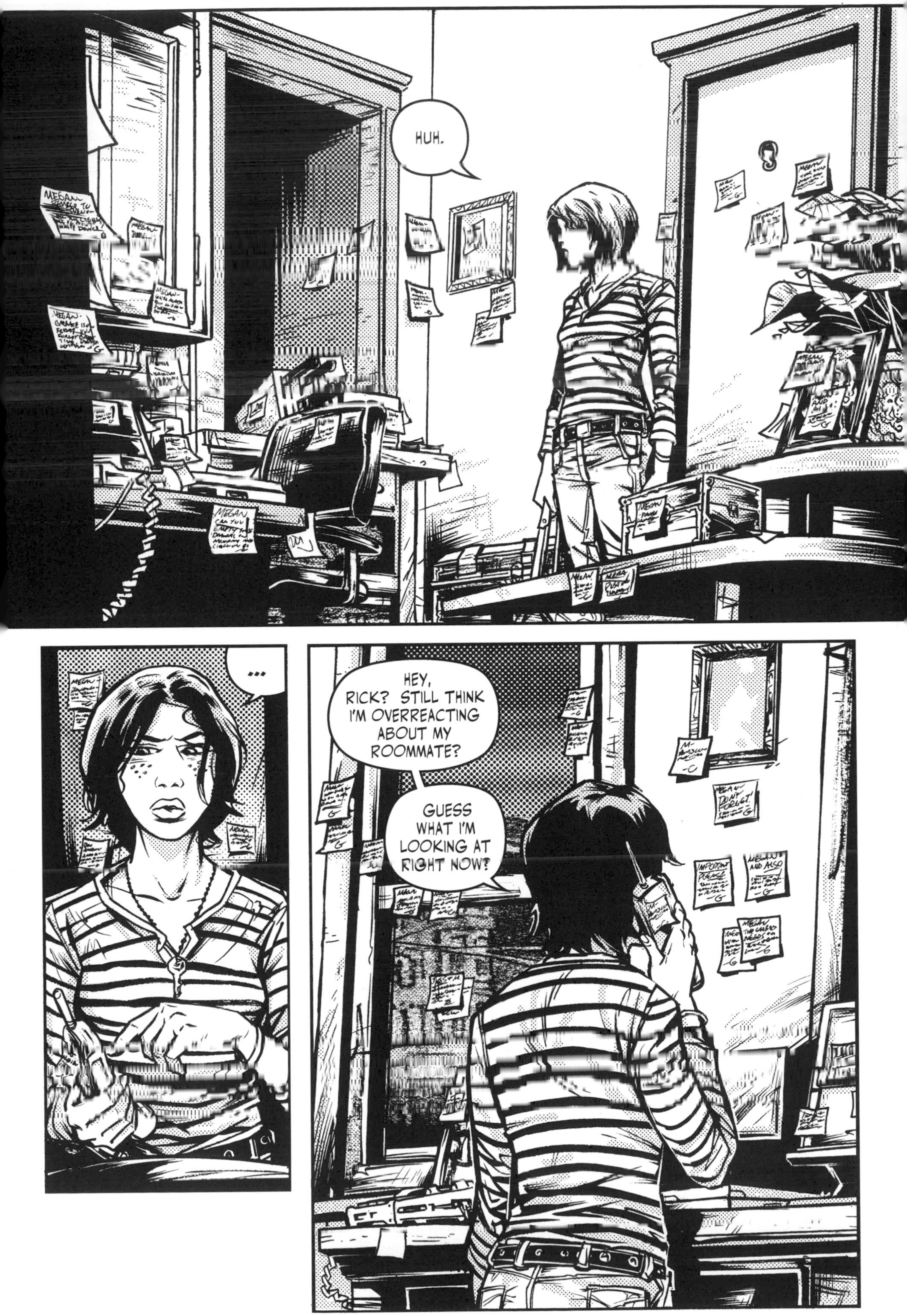
HUH.
...
HEY, RICK? STILL THINK I'M OVERREACTING ABOUT MY ROOMMATE?
GUESS WHAT I'M LOOKING AT RIGHT NOW?

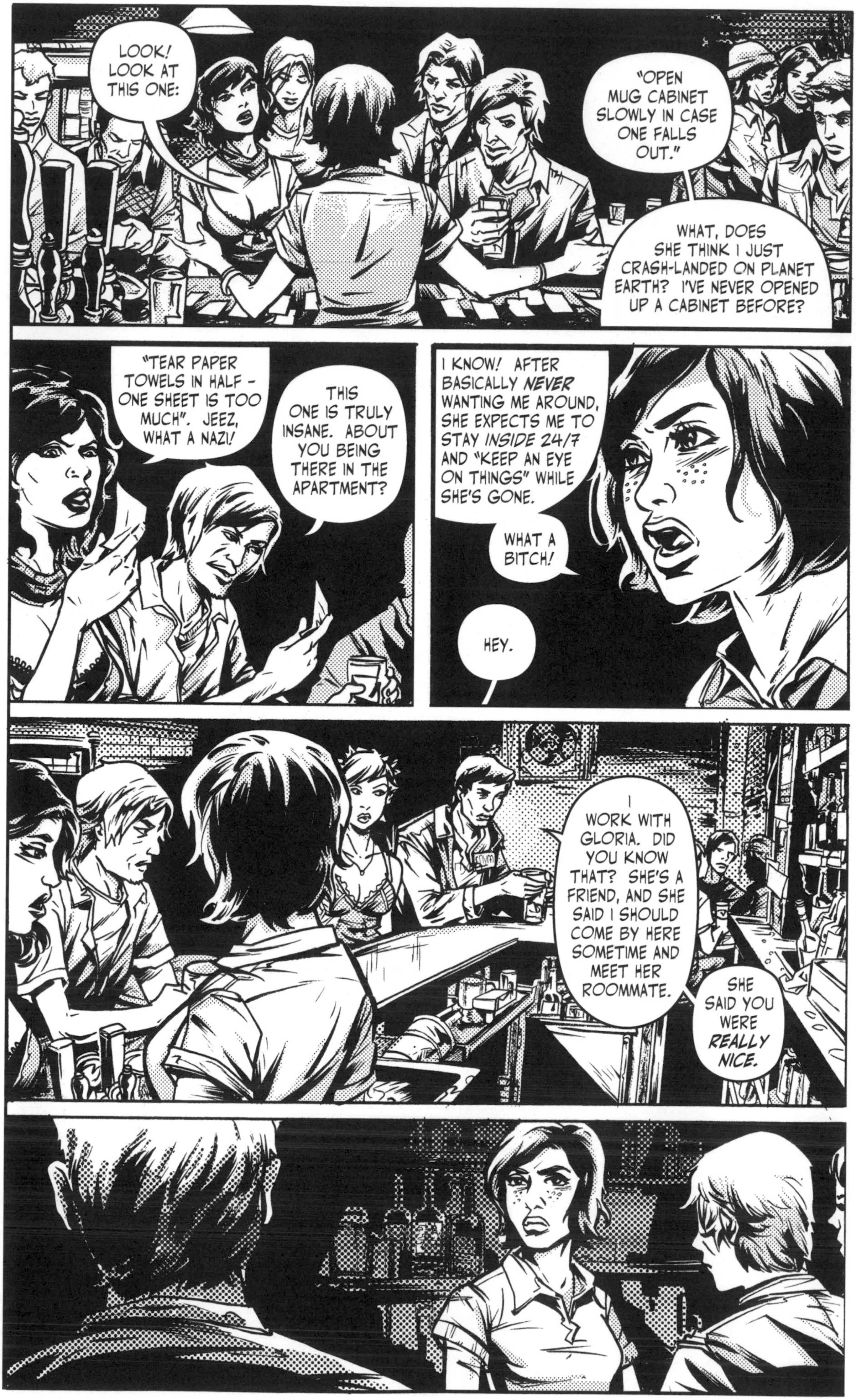
LOOK! LOOK AT THIS ONE:
"OPEN MUG CABINET SLOWLY IN CASE ONE FALLS OUT."
WHAT, DOES SHE THINK I JUST CRASH-LANDED ON PLANET EARTH? I'VE NEVER OPENED UP A CABINET BEFORE?
"TEAR PAPER TOWELS IN HALF - ONE SHEET IS TOO MUCH". JEEZ, WHAT A NAZI!
THIS ONE IS TRULY INSANE. ABOUT YOU BEING THERE IN THE APARTMENT?
I KNOW! AFTER BASICALLY *NEVER* WANTING ME AROUND, SHE EXPECTS ME TO STAY *INSIDE* 24/7 AND "KEEP AN EYE ON THINGS" WHILE SHE'S GONE.
WHAT A BITCH!
HEY.
I WORK WITH GLORIA. DID YOU KNOW THAT? SHE'S A FRIEND, AND SHE SAID I SHOULD COME BY HERE SOMETIME AND MEET HER ROOMMATE.
SHE SAID YOU WERE *REALLY NICE.*

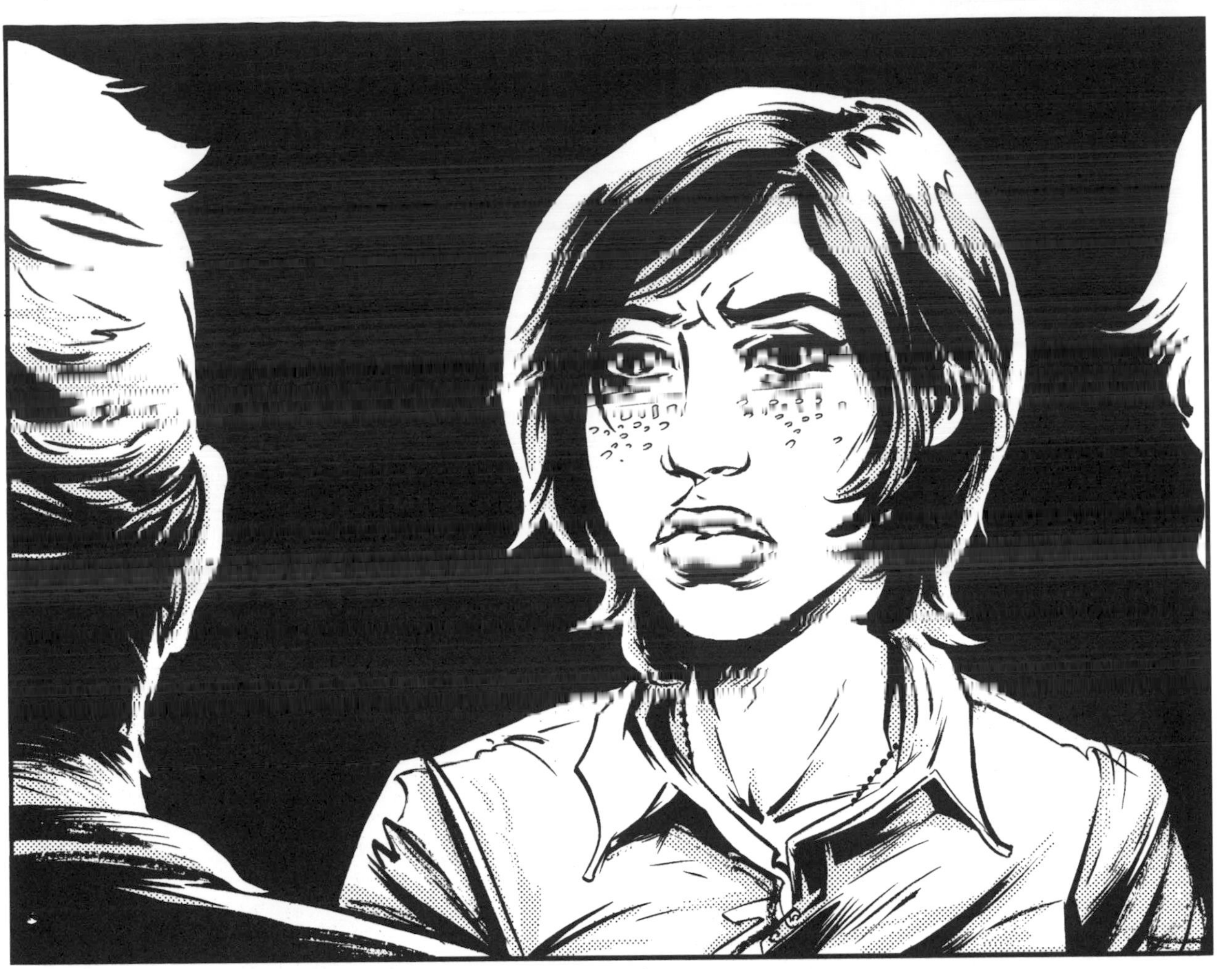

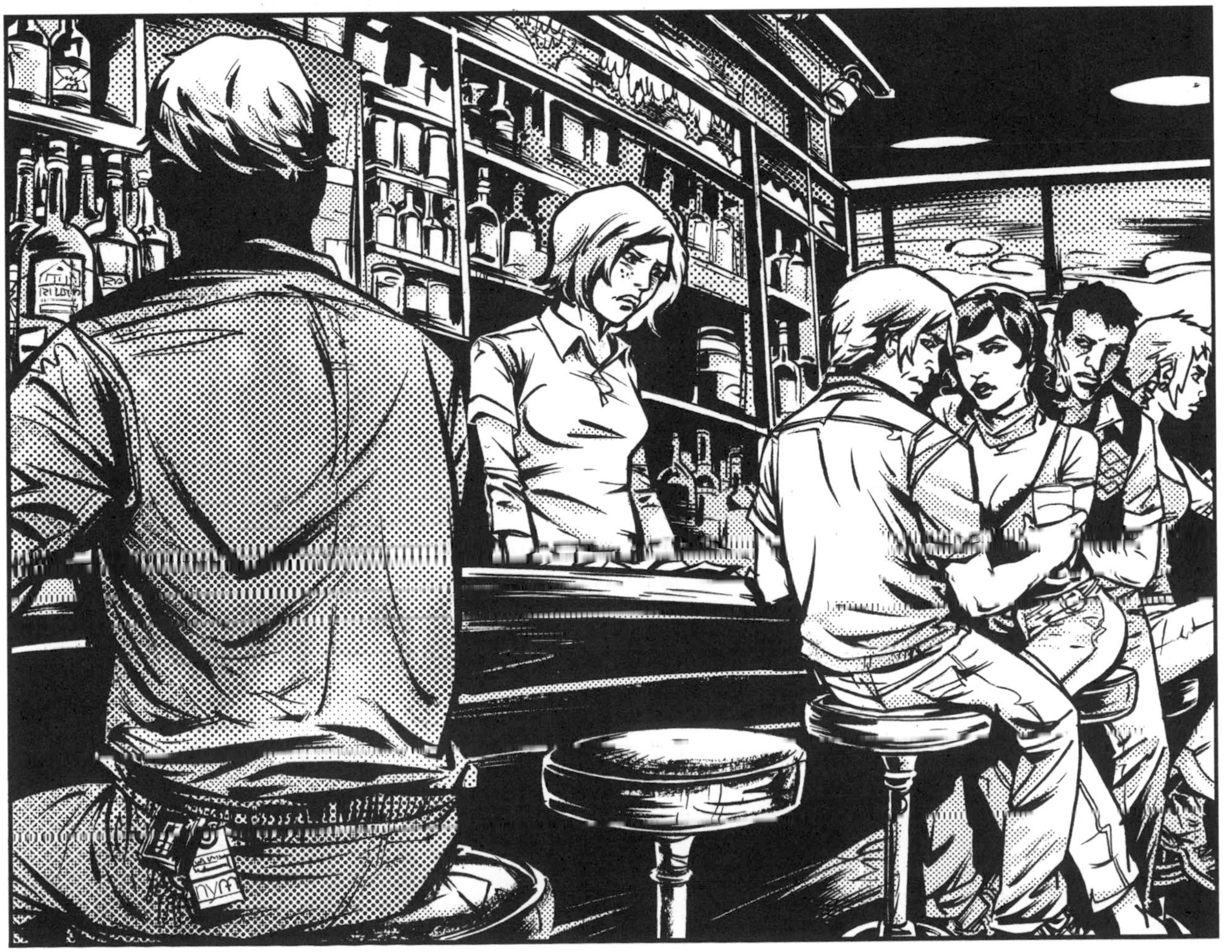

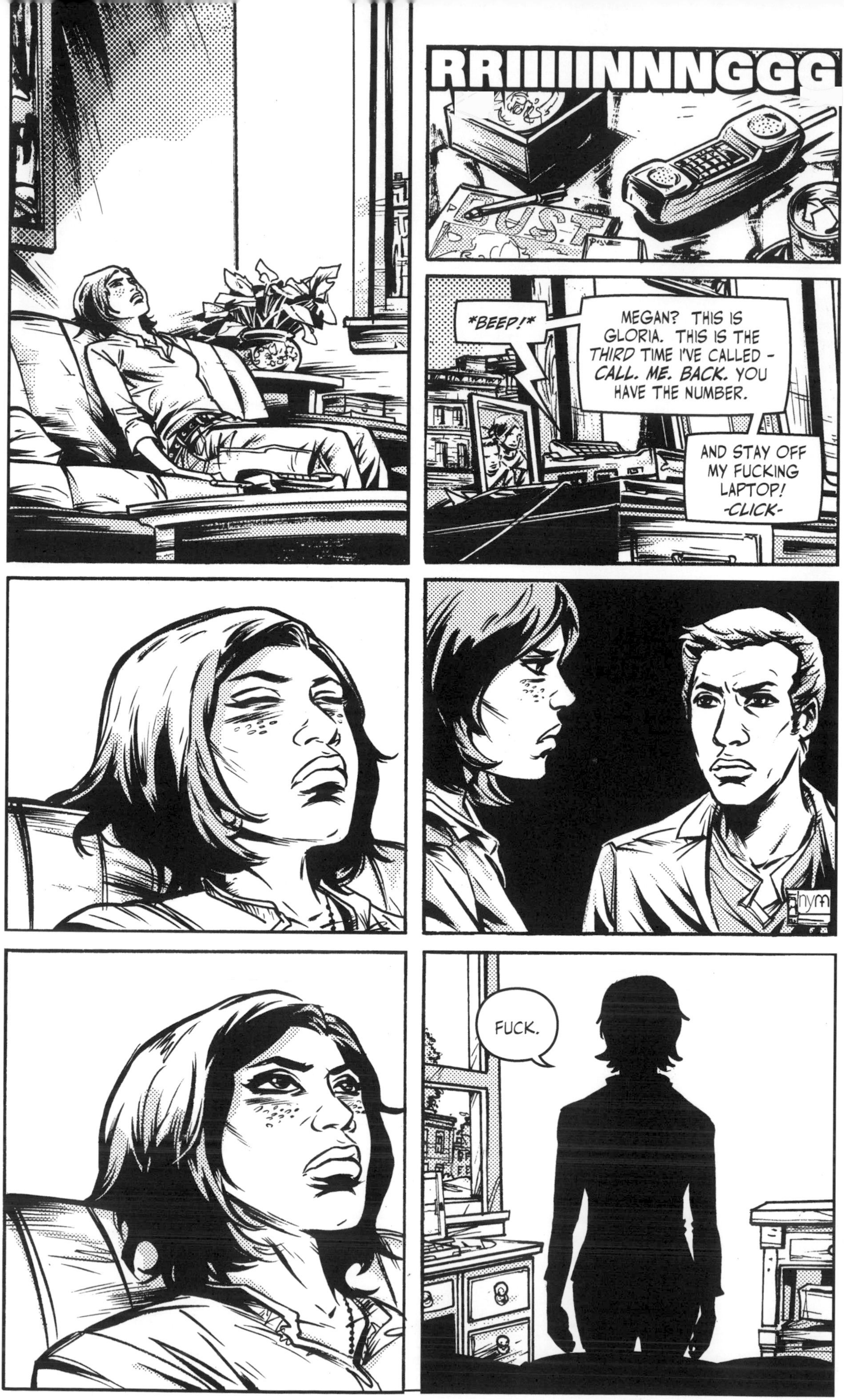
RRIIIIINNNNGGG
BEEP!
MEGAN? THIS IS GLORIA. THIS IS THE THIRD TIME I'VE CALLED - CALL. ME. BACK. YOU HAVE THE NUMBER.
AND STAY OFF MY FUCKING LAPTOP! -CLICK-
FUCK.

WHY DO YOU DO THIS?

WHY DO YOU PICK THESE SITUATIONS WHERE YOU KNOW YOU'LL SCREW YOURSELF OVER?

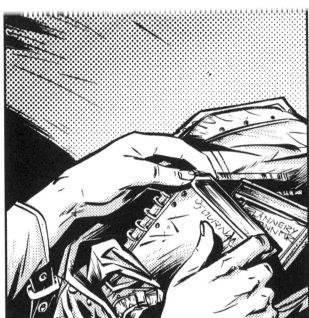

ARE YOU THAT DESPERATE?

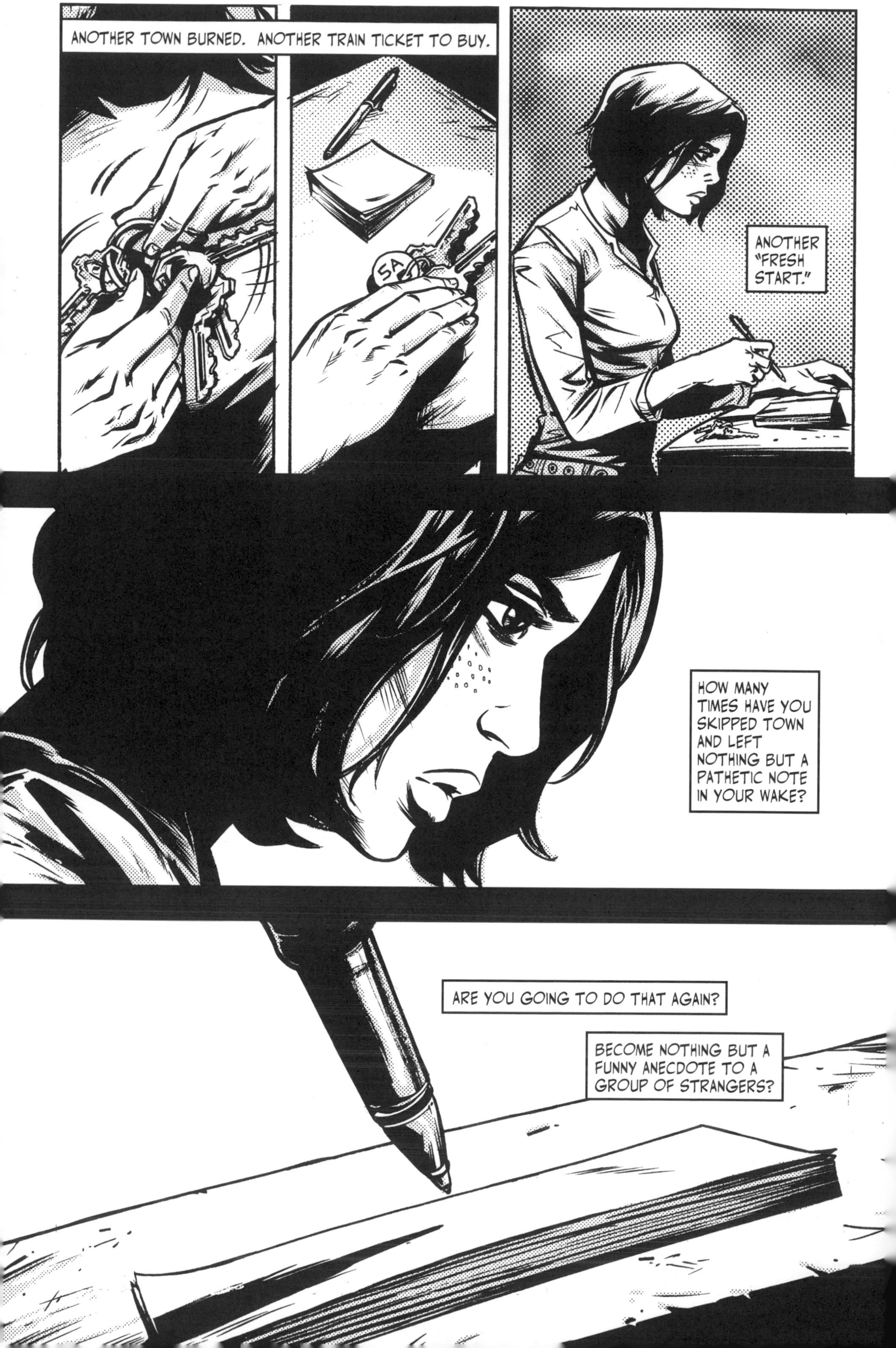
ANOTHER TOWN BURNED. ANOTHER TRAIN TICKET TO BUY.
5A
ANOTHER "FRESH START."
HOW MANY TIMES HAVE YOU SKIPPED TOWN AND LEFT NOTHING BUT A PATHETIC NOTE IN YOUR WAKE?
ARE YOU GOING TO DO THAT AGAIN?
BECOME NOTHING BUT A FUNNY ANECDOTE TO A GROUP OF STRANGERS?

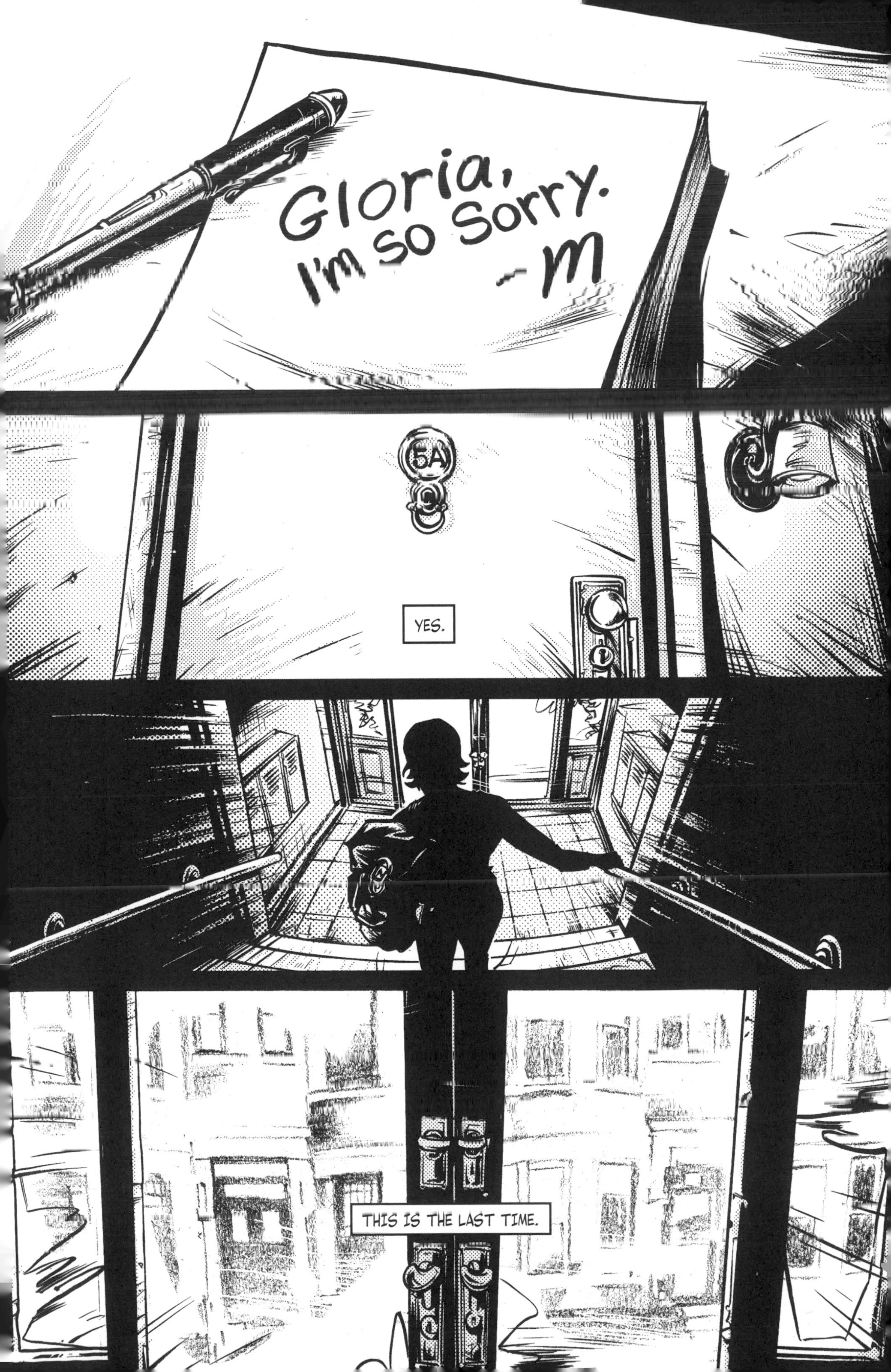
Gloria, I'm so Sorry. -M
5A
YES.
THIS IS THE LAST TIME.

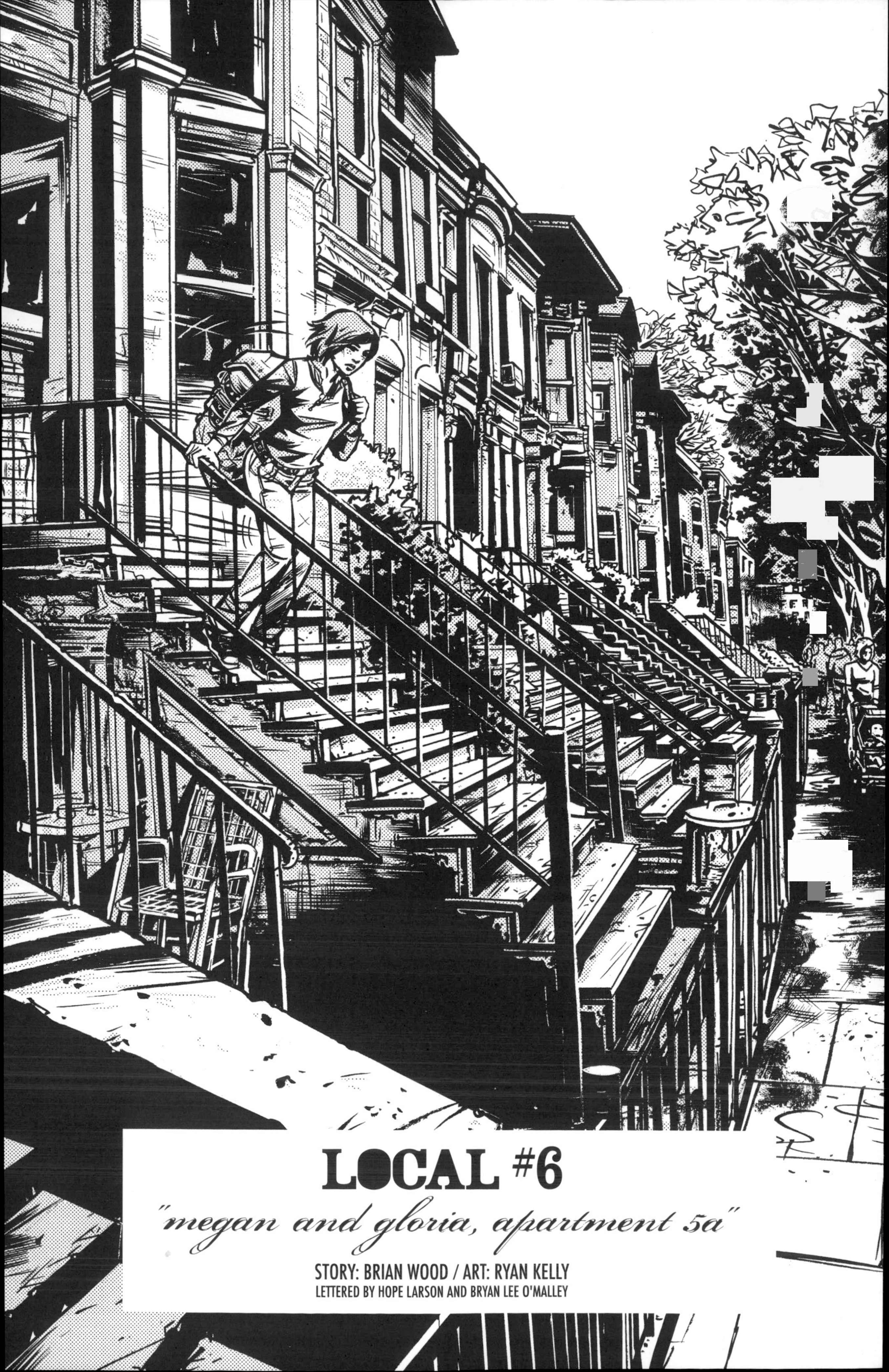
LOCAL #6
"megan and gloria, apartment 5a"
STORY: BRIAN WOOD / ART: RYAN KELLY
LETTERED BY HOPE LARSON AND BRYAN LEE O'MALLEY

CHAPTER 7
"HAZARDOUS YOUTH"
Tempe, Arizona

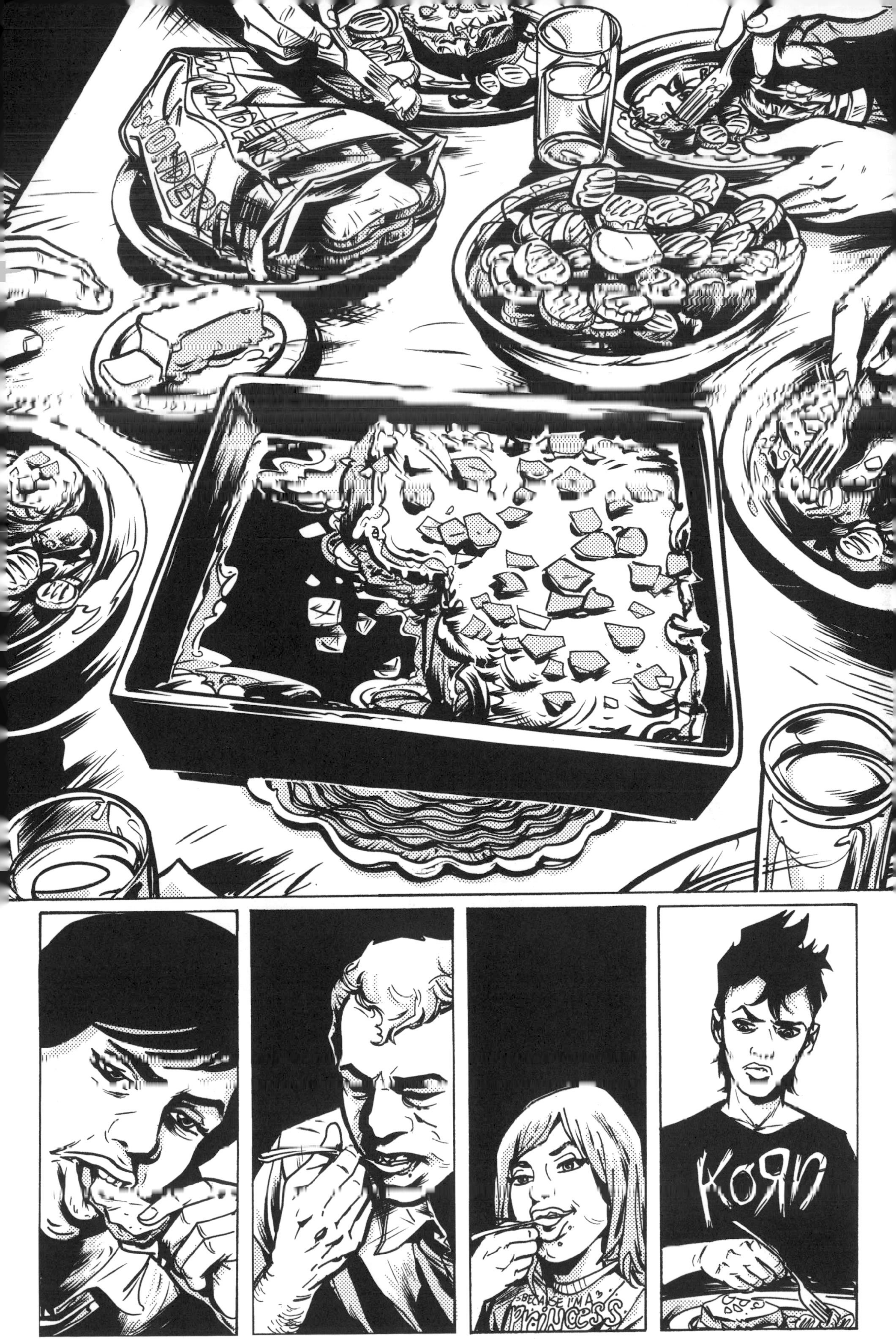
WONDER
BECAUSE I'M A PRINCESS
KORN

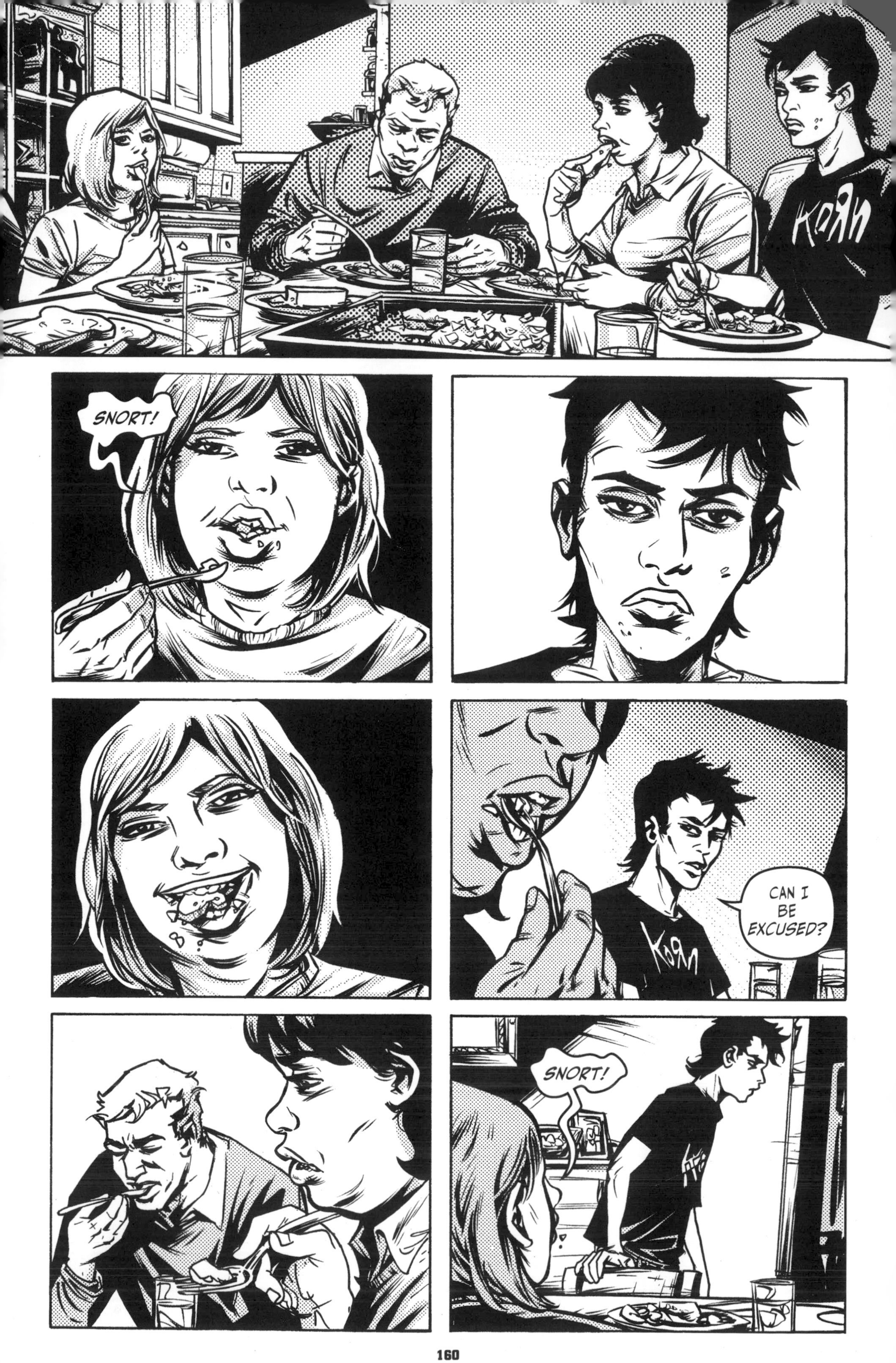
KoЯn
SNORT!
CAN I BE EXCUSED?
SNORT!

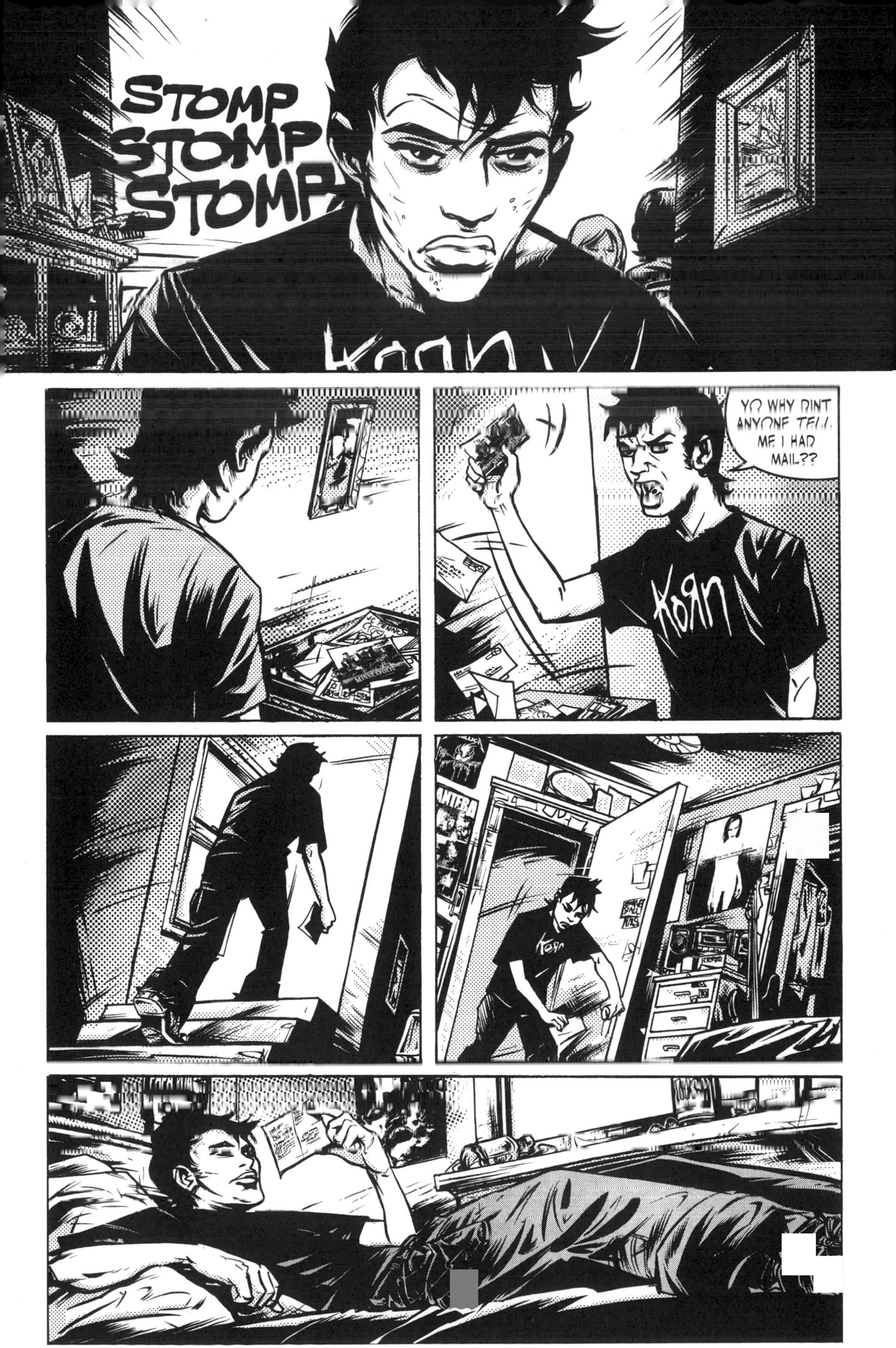
STOMP STOMP STOMP
YO WHY DINT ANYONE TELL ME I HAD MAIL??

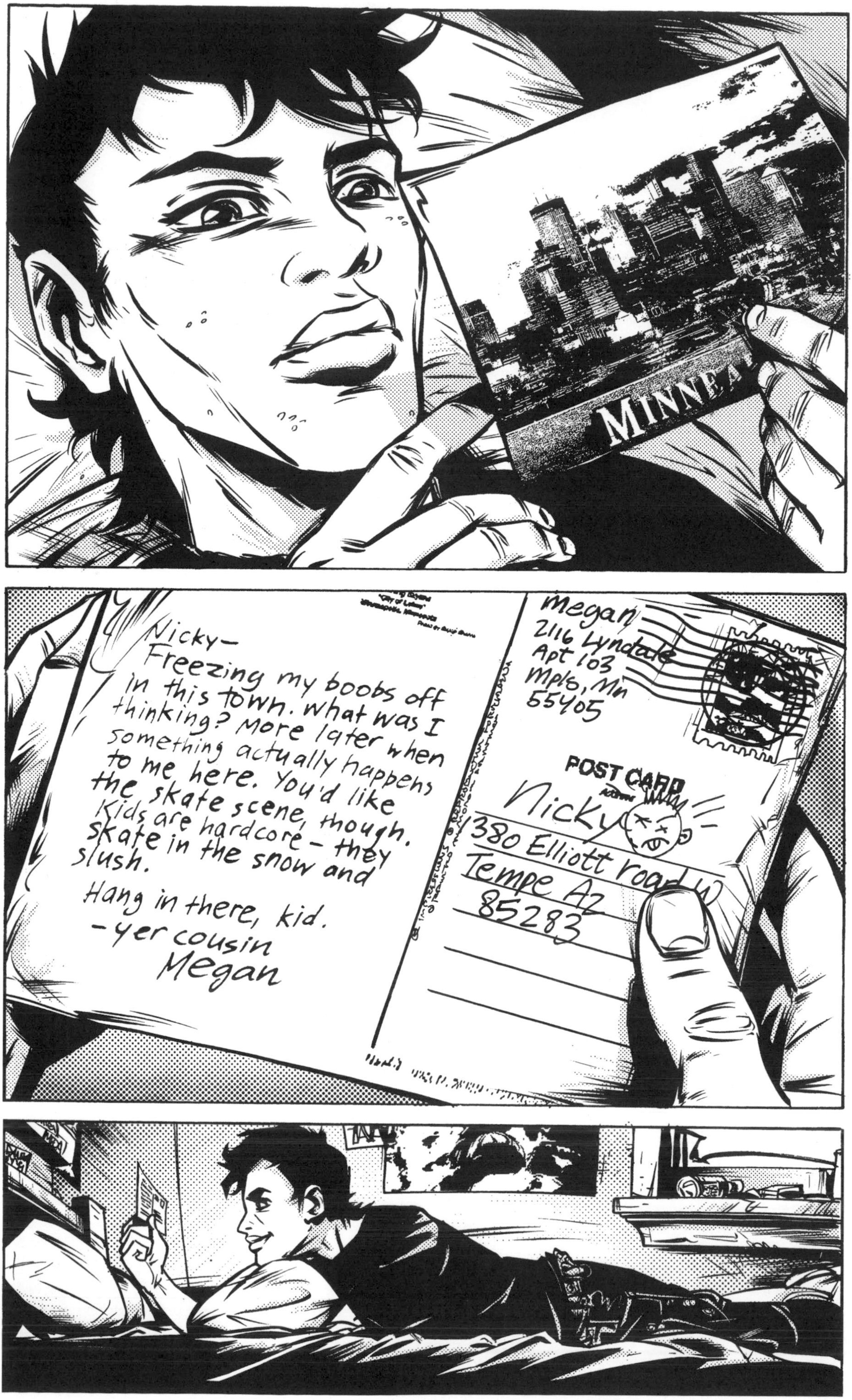
MINNEA
Nicky—
Freezing my boobs off in this town. what was I thinking? More later when something actually happens to me here. You'd like the skate scene, though. Kids are hardcore— they skate in the snow and slush.
Hang in there, kid.
-yer cousin
Megan
Megan
2116 Lyndale
Apt 103
Mpls, Mn
55405
POST CARD
Nicky
1380 Elliott road W
Tempe Az
85283

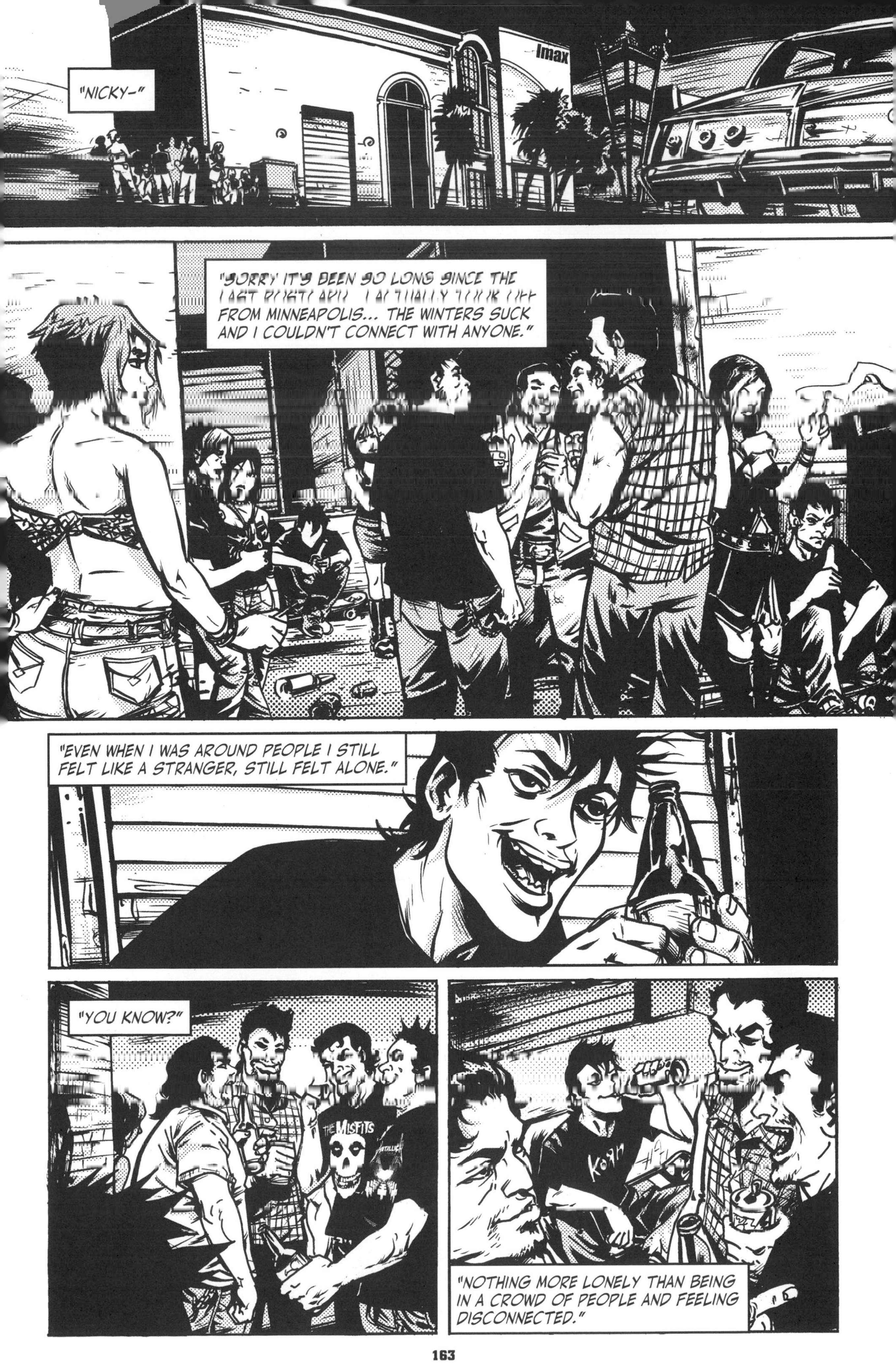
"NICKY-"
"SORRY IT'S BEEN SO LONG SINCE THE LAST POSTCARD. I ACTUALLY TOOK OFF FROM MINNEAPOLIS... THE WINTERS SUCK AND I COULDN'T CONNECT WITH ANYONE."
"EVEN WHEN I WAS AROUND PEOPLE I STILL FELT LIKE A STRANGER, STILL FELT ALONE."
"YOU KNOW?"
"NOTHING MORE LONELY THAN BEING IN A CROWD OF PEOPLE AND FEELING DISCONNECTED."

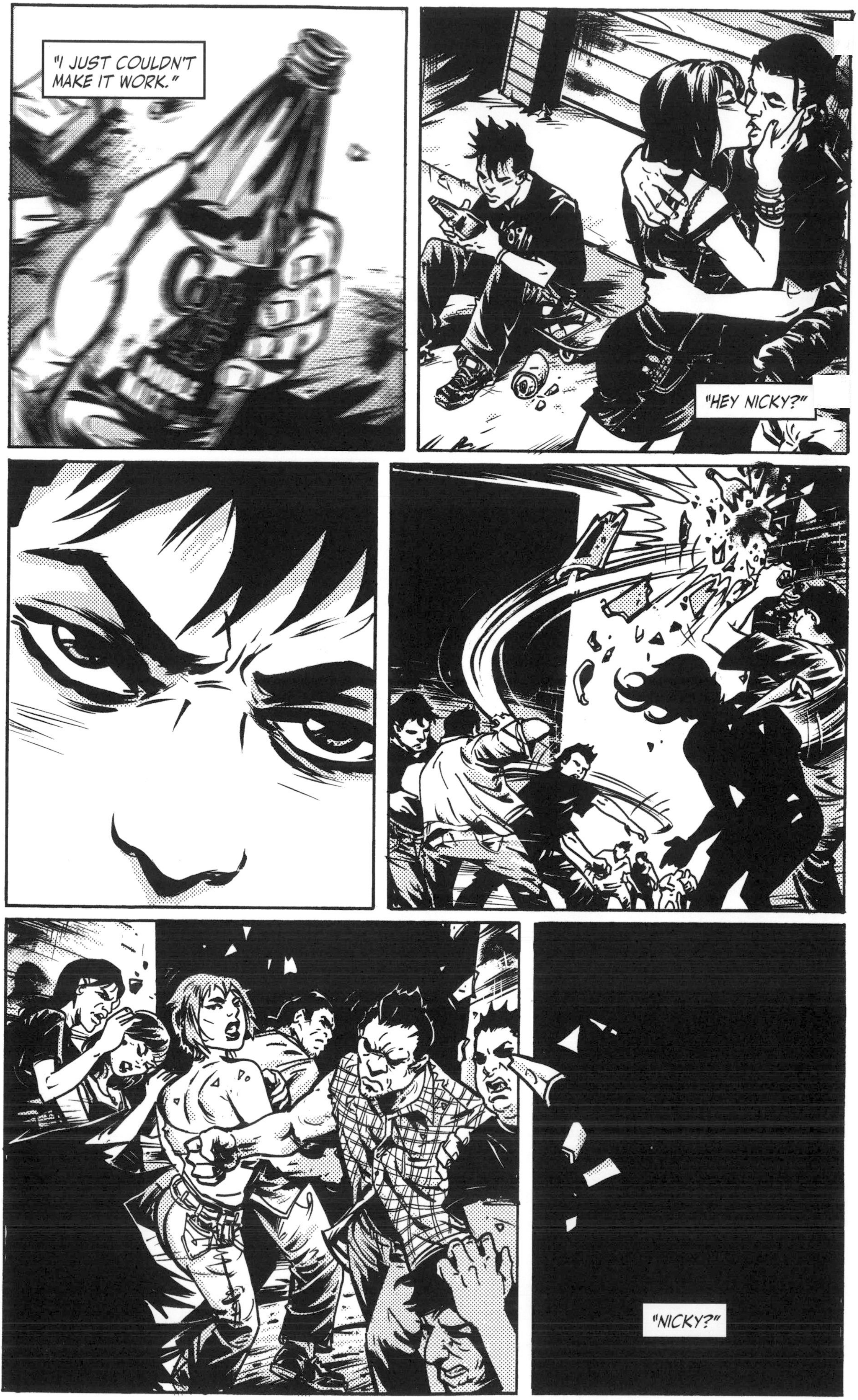
"I JUST COULDN'T MAKE IT WORK."
"HEY NICKY?"
"NICKY?"

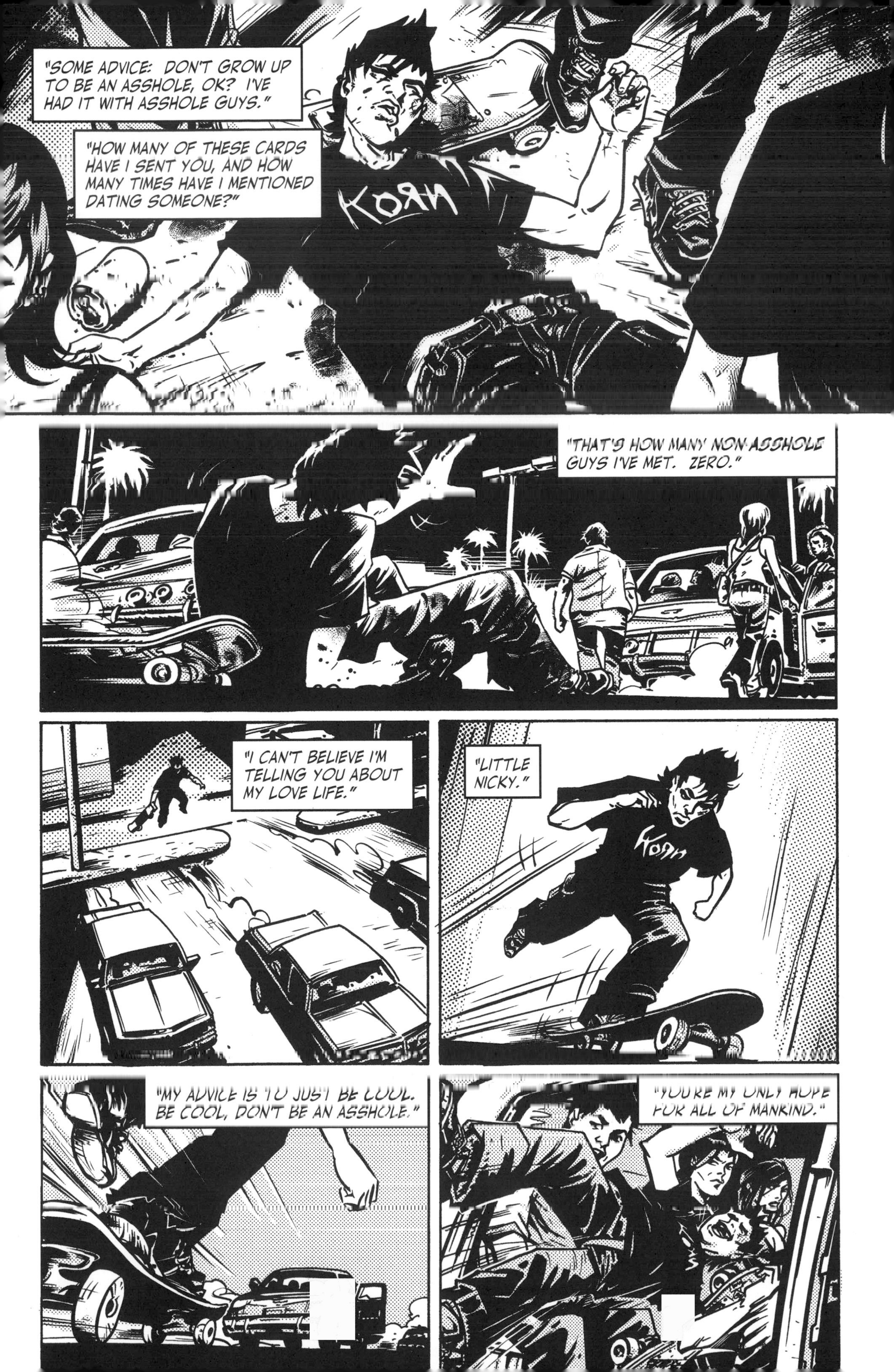
"SOME ADVICE: DON'T GROW UP TO BE AN ASSHOLE, OK? I'VE HAD IT WITH ASSHOLE GUYS."
"HOW MANY OF THESE CARDS HAVE I SENT YOU, AND HOW MANY TIMES HAVE I MENTIONED DATING SOMEONE?"
"THAT'S HOW MANY NON-ASSHOLE GUYS I'VE MET. ZERO."
"I CAN'T BELIEVE I'M TELLING YOU ABOUT MY LOVE LIFE."
"LITTLE NICKY."
"MY ADVICE IS TO JUST BE COOL. BE COOL, DON'T BE AN ASSHOLE."
"YOU'RE MY ONLY HOPE FOR ALL OF MANKIND."

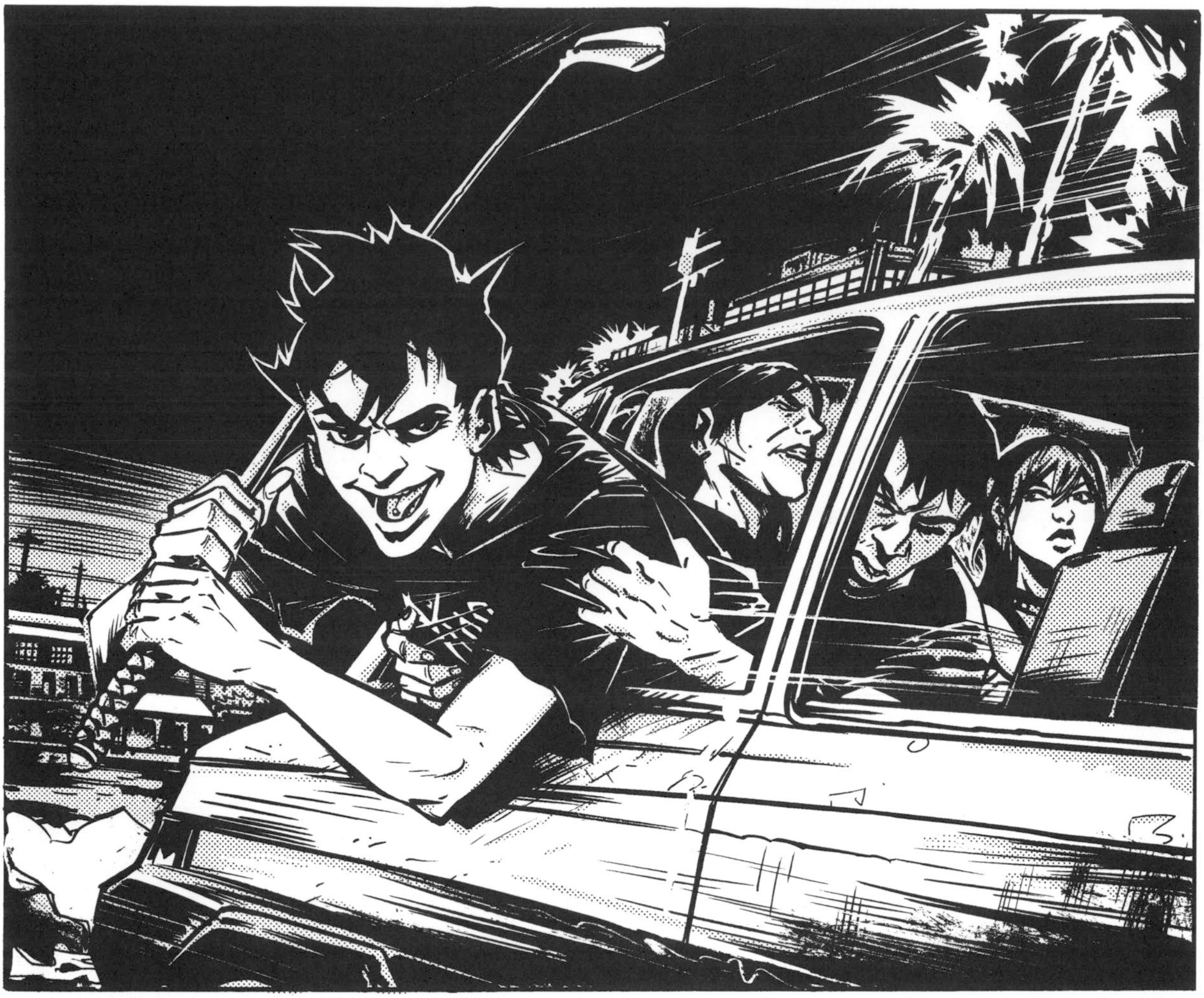

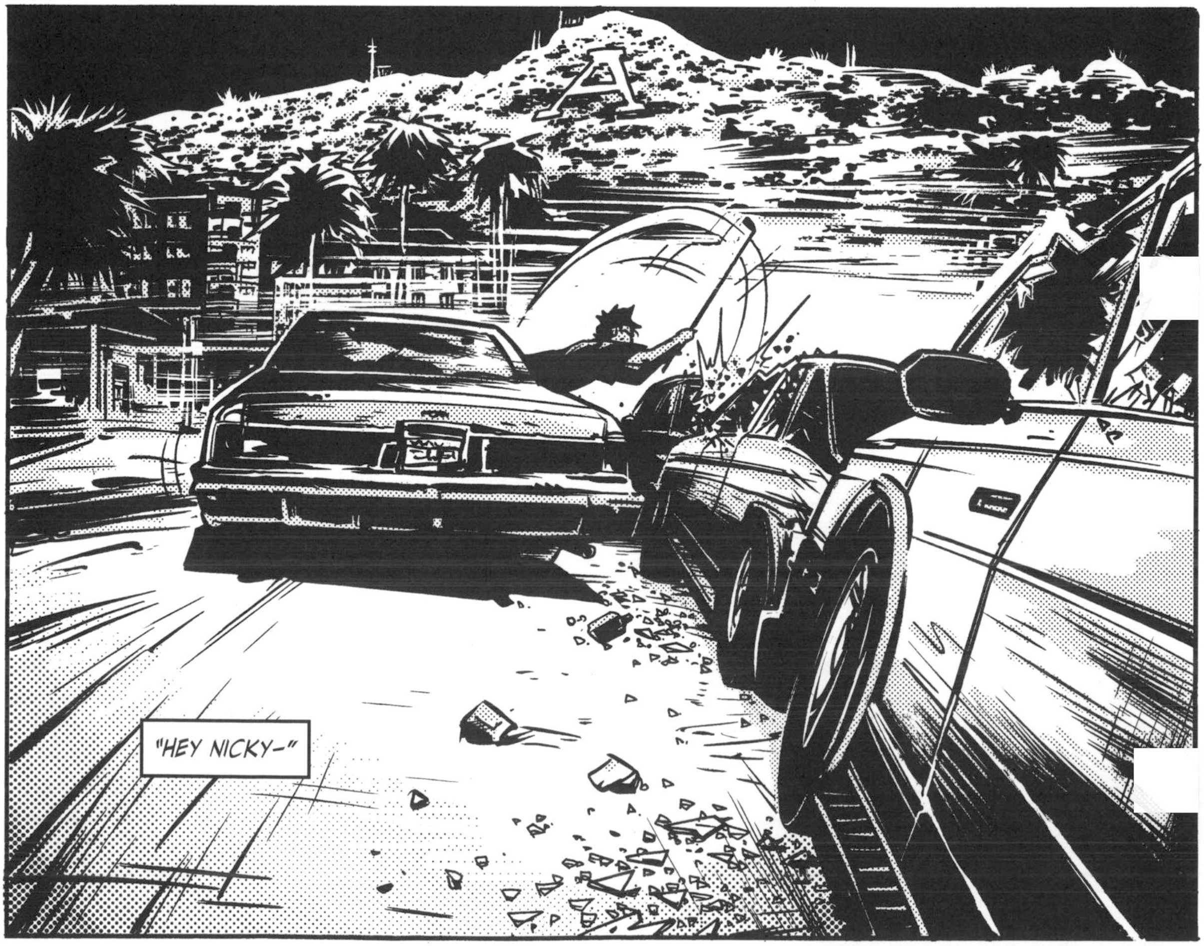
"HEY NICKY-"

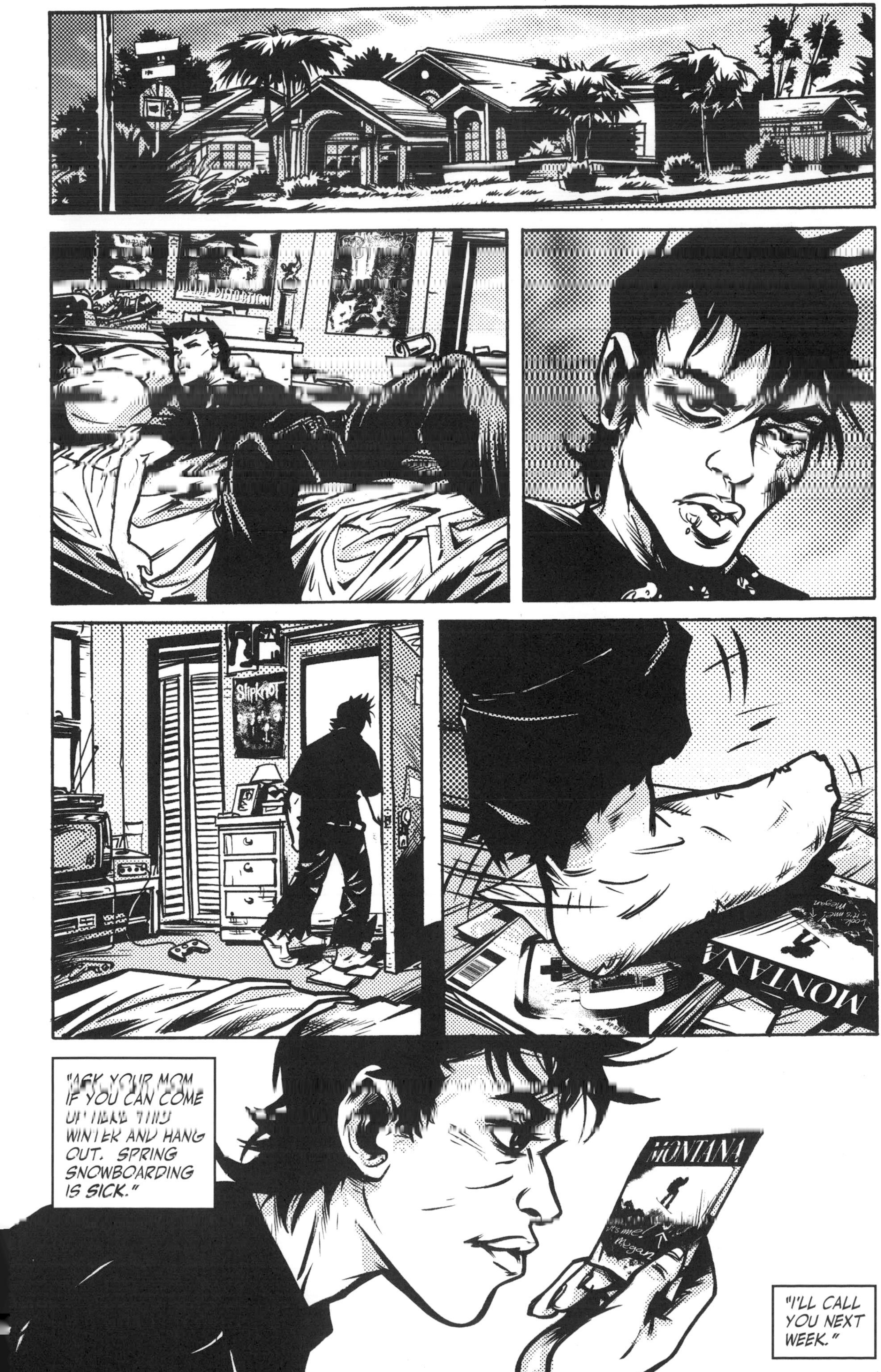
Slipknot
Look, it's me! Megan
MONTANA
"ASK YOUR MOM IF YOU CAN COME UP HERE THIS WINTER AND HANG OUT. SPRING SNOWBOARDING IS SICK."
MONTANA
It's me! Megan
"I'LL CALL YOU NEXT WEEK."

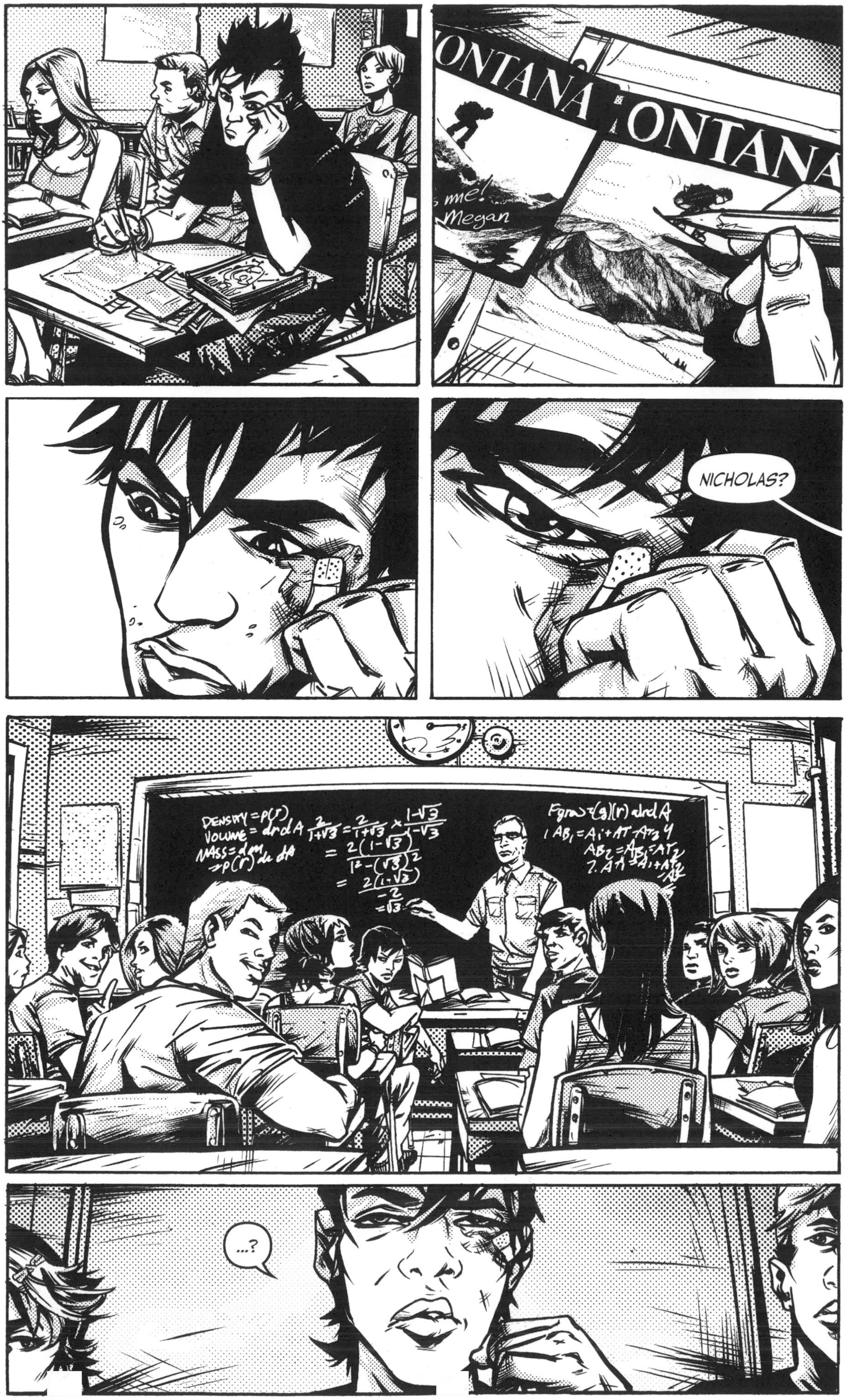
ONTANA
s me!
Megan
ONTANA
NICHOLAS?
...?

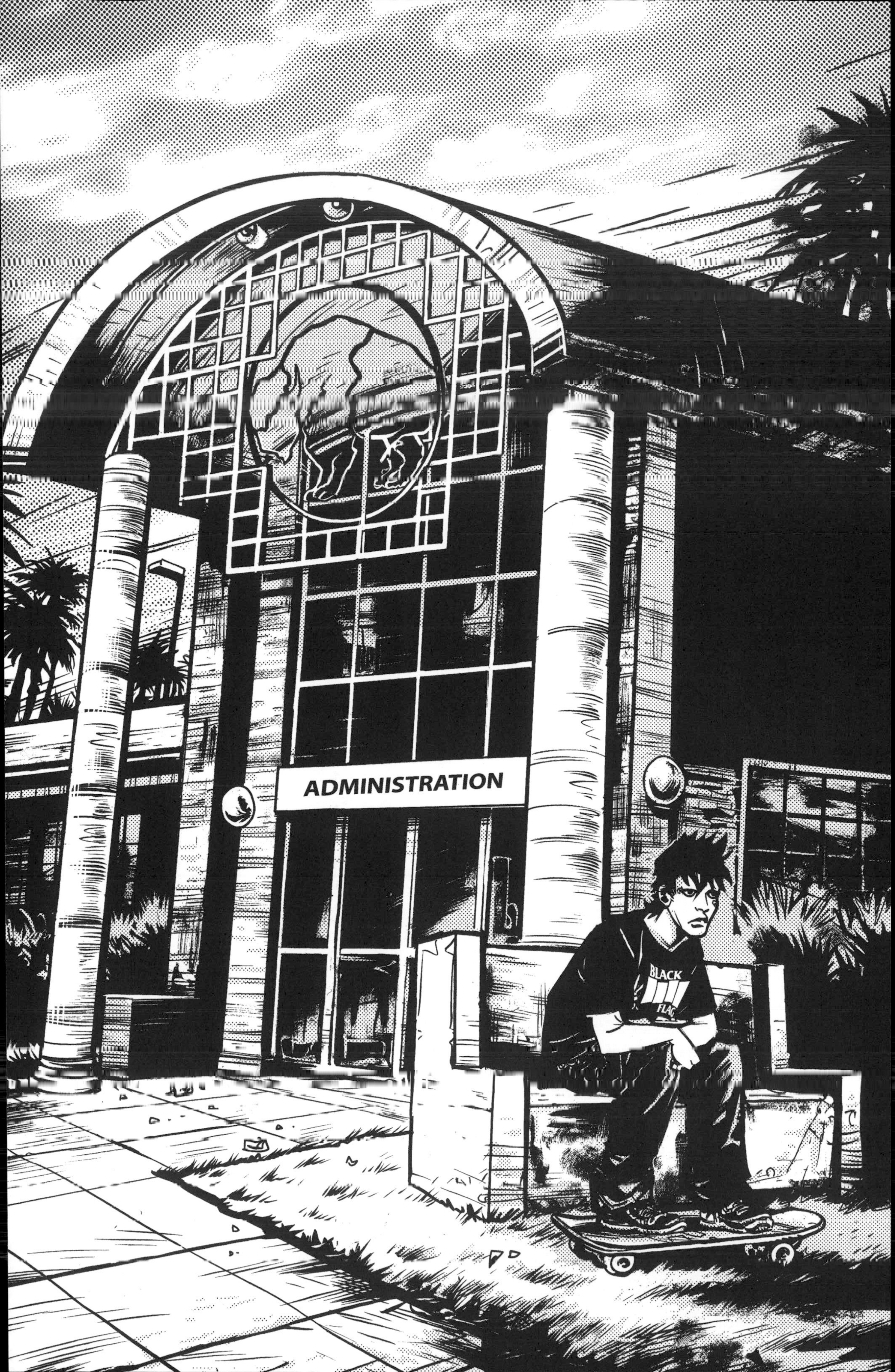
ADMINISTRATION
BLACK
FLAG

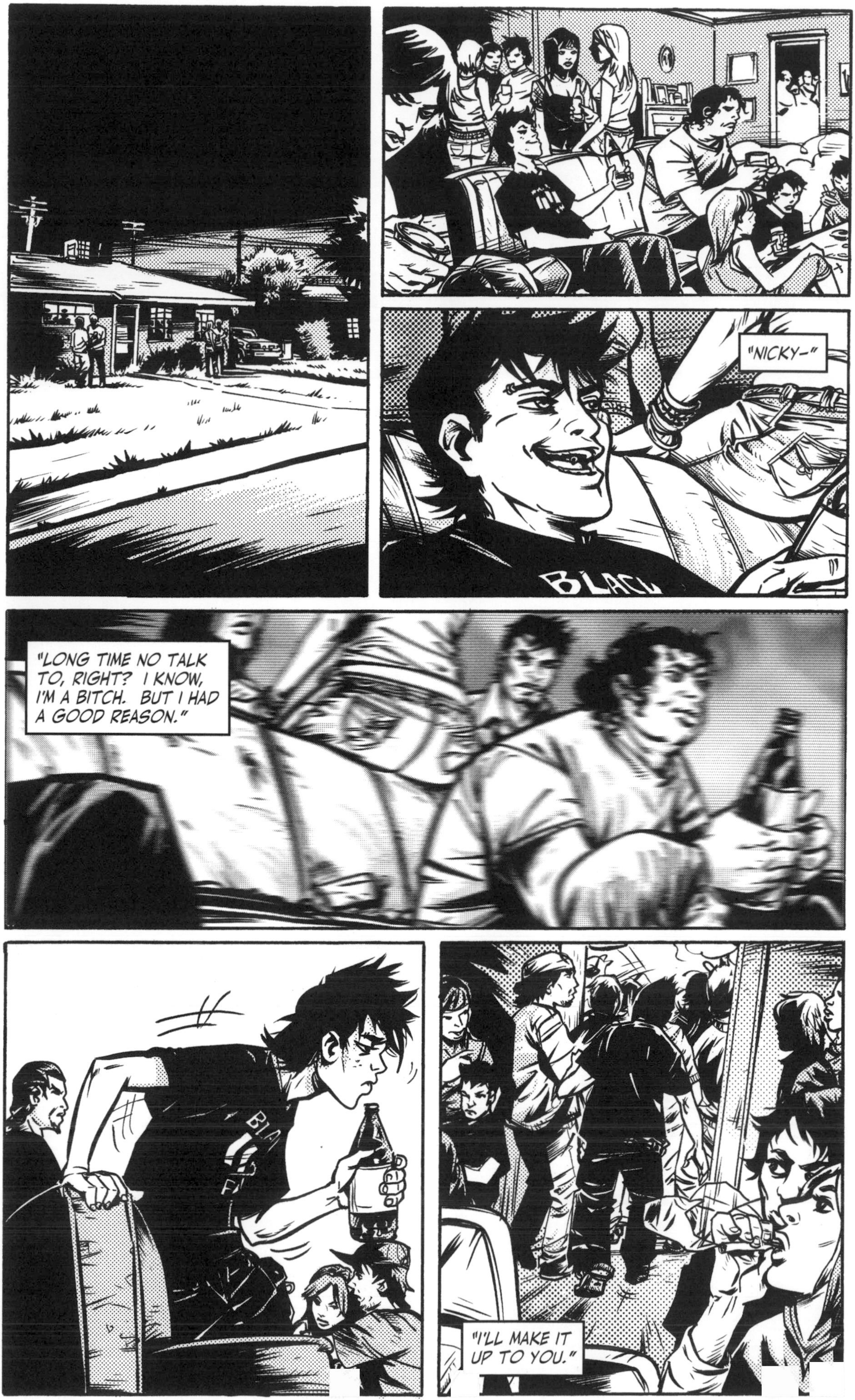
"NICKY-"
"LONG TIME NO TALK TO, RIGHT? I KNOW, I'M A BITCH. BUT I HAD A GOOD REASON."
"I'LL MAKE IT UP TO YOU."

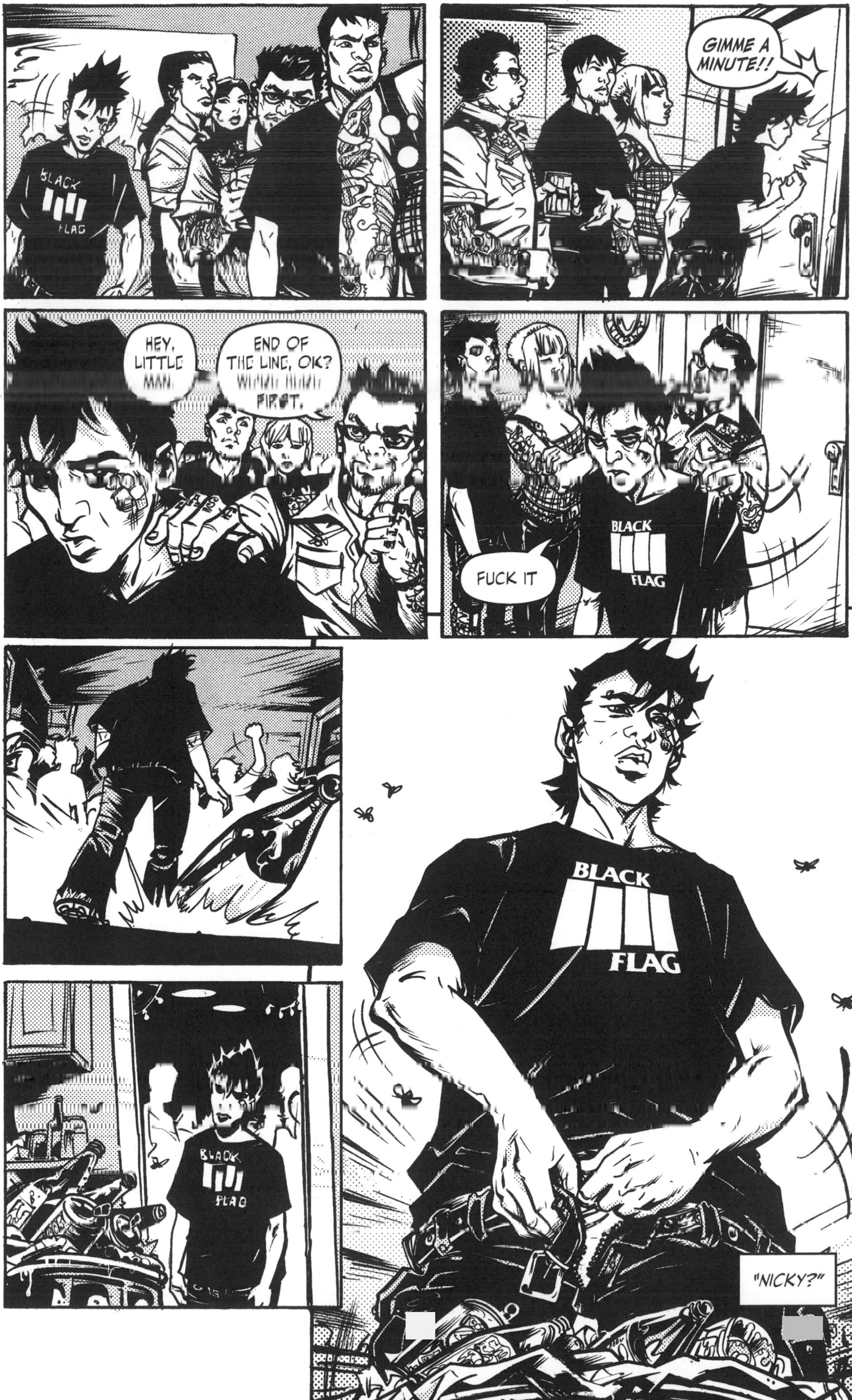
BLACK FLAG
GIMME A MINUTE!!
HEY, LITTLE MAN
END OF THE LINE, OK?
FUCK IT
"NICKY?"

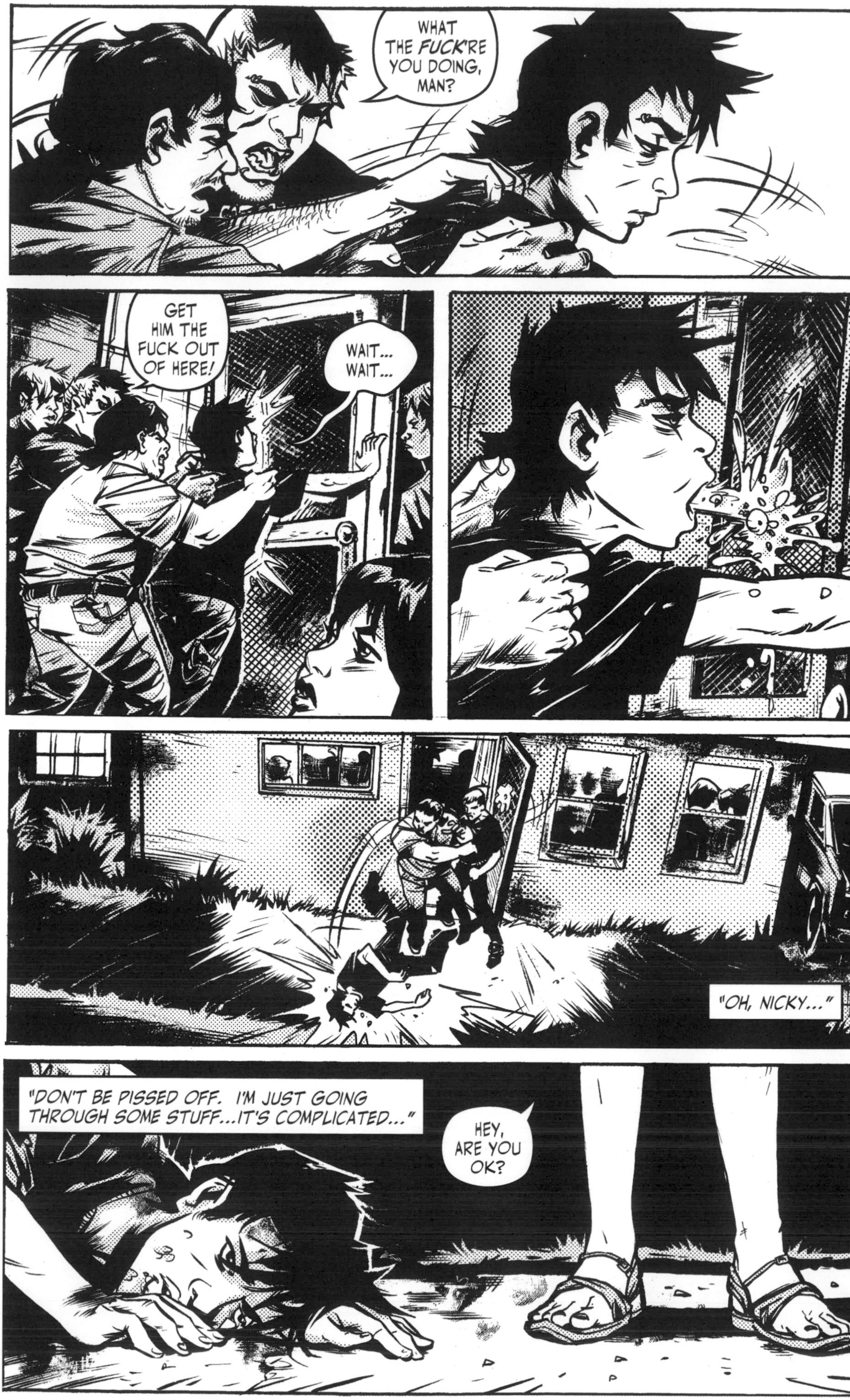
WHAT THE FUCK'RE YOU DOING, MAN?
GET HIM THE FUCK OUT OF HERE!
WAIT... WAIT...
"OH, NICKY..."
"DON'T BE PISSED OFF. I'M JUST GOING THROUGH SOME STUFF...IT'S COMPLICATED..."
HEY, ARE YOU OK?

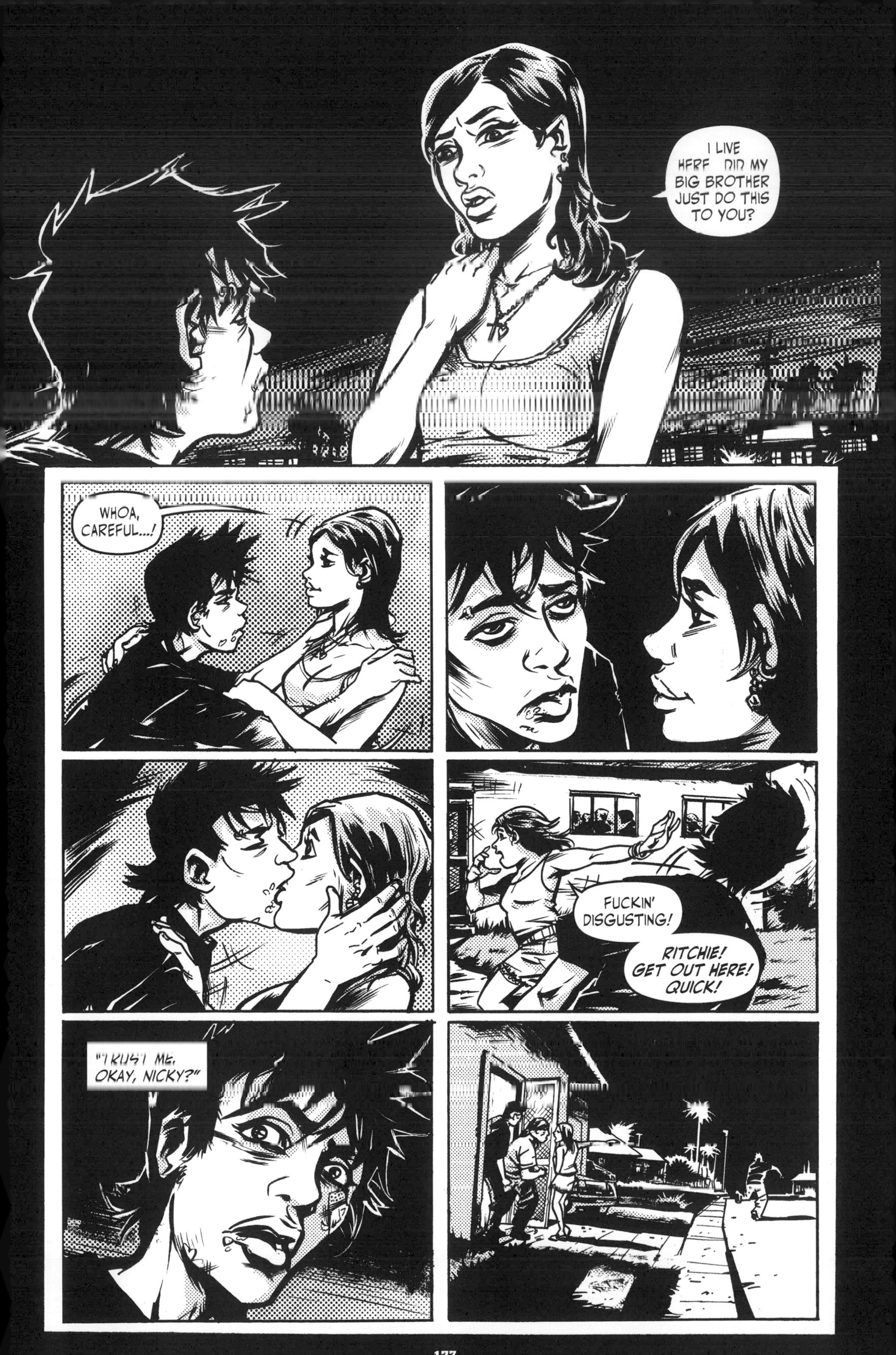
I LIVE HERE. DID MY BIG BROTHER JUST DO THIS TO YOU?
WHOA, CAREFUL...!
FUCKIN' DISGUSTING!
RITCHIE! GET OUT HERE! QUICK!
"TRUST ME, OKAY, NICKY?"

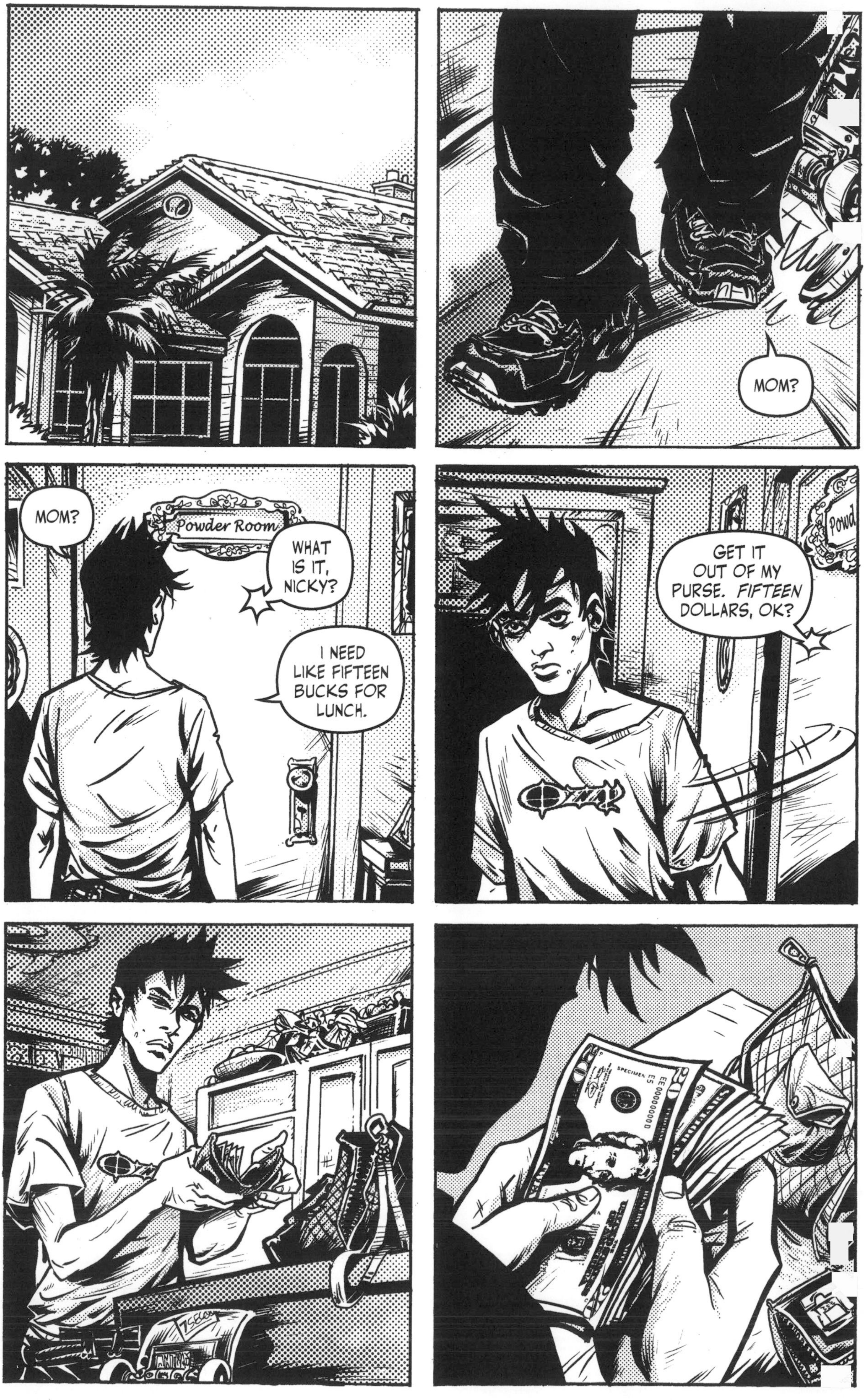
MOM?
MOM?
WHAT IS IT, NICKY?
I NEED LIKE FIFTEEN BUCKS FOR LUNCH.
GET IT OUT OF MY PURSE. *FIFTEEN* DOLLARS, OK?
Powder Room

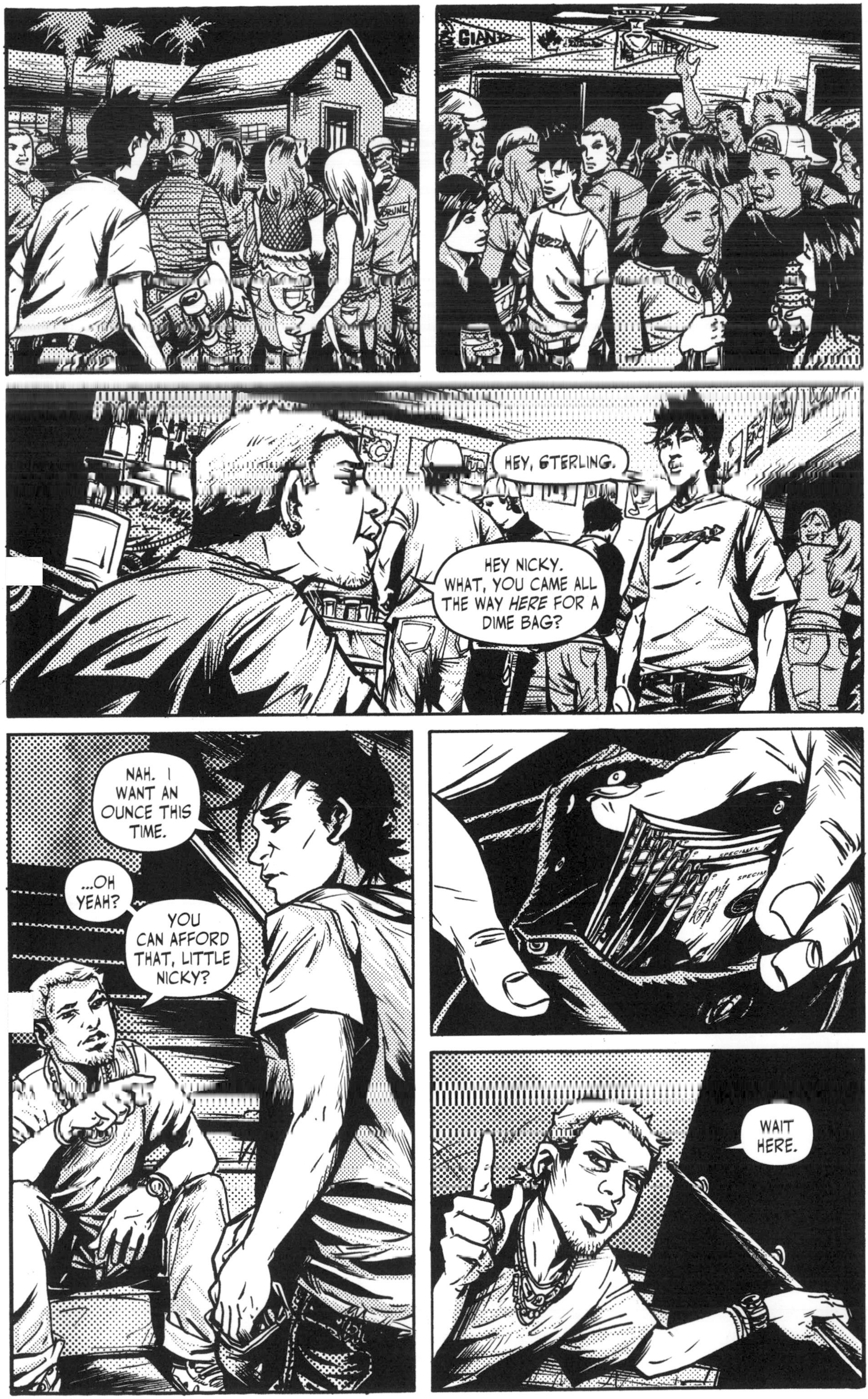
HEY, STERLING.
HEY NICKY. WHAT, YOU CAME ALL THE WAY *HERE* FOR A DIME BAG?
NAH. I WANT AN OUNCE THIS TIME.
...OH YEAH?
YOU CAN AFFORD THAT, LITTLE NICKY?
WAIT HERE.

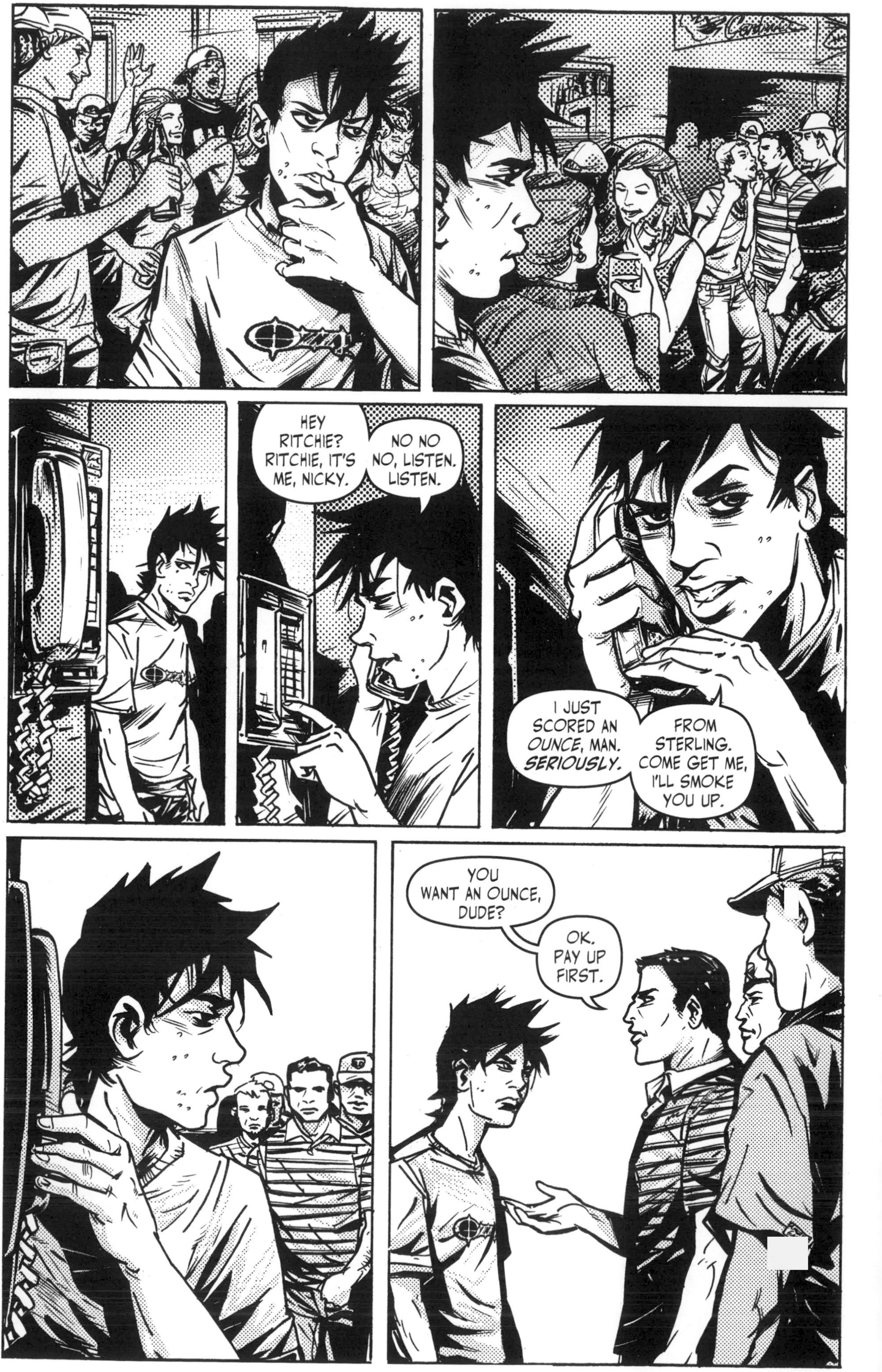

HEY RITCHIE? RITCHIE, IT'S ME, NICKY.
NO NO NO, LISTEN. LISTEN.
I JUST SCORED AN OUNCE, MAN. SERIOUSLY.
FROM STERLING. COME GET ME, I'LL SMOKE YOU UP.
YOU WANT AN OUNCE, DUDE?
OK. PAY UP FIRST.

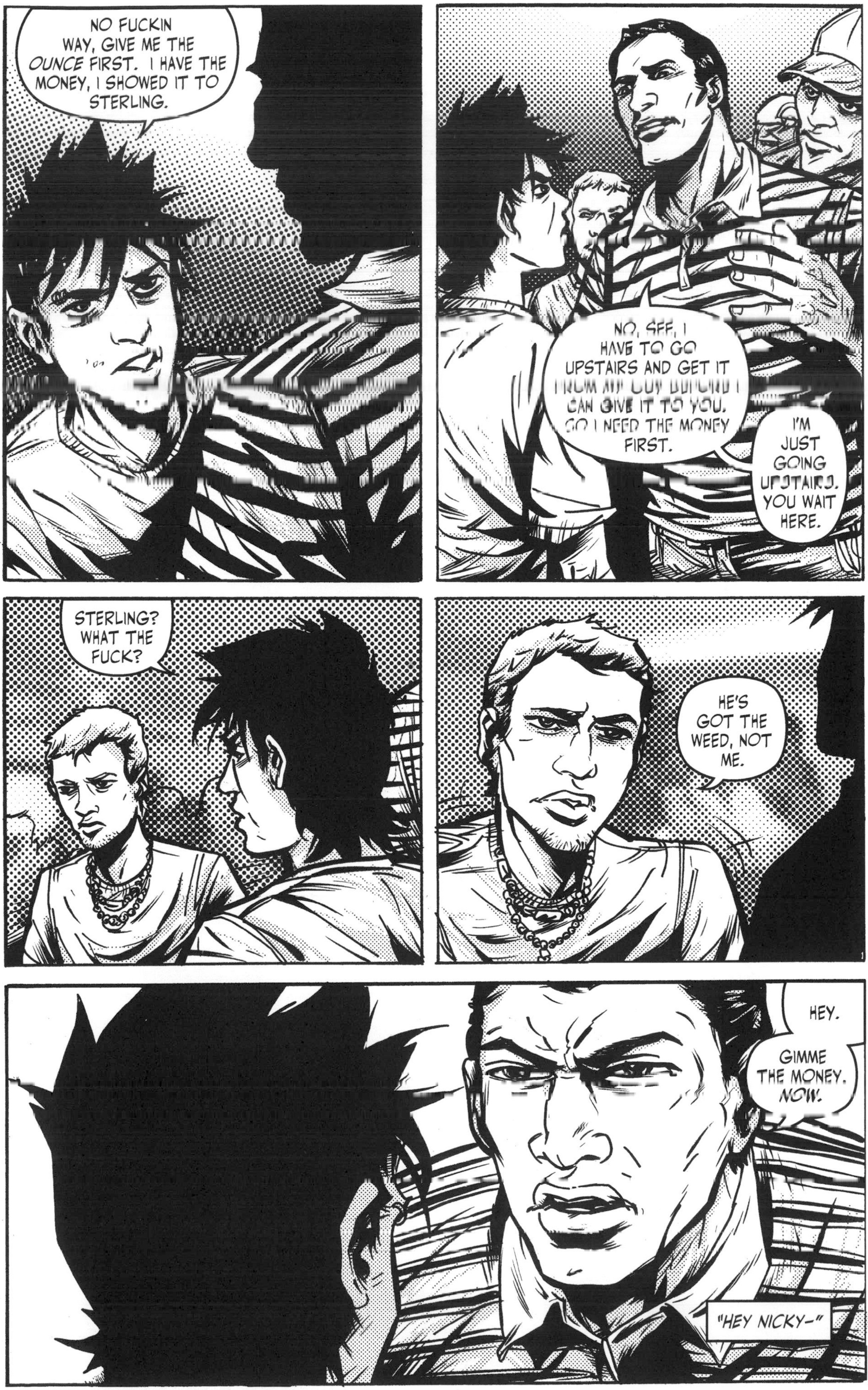
NO FUCKIN WAY, GIVE ME THE *OUNCE* FIRST. I HAVE THE MONEY, I SHOWED IT TO STERLING.
NO, SEE, I HAVE TO GO UPSTAIRS AND GET IT FROM MY GUY BEFORE I CAN GIVE IT TO YOU. SO I NEED THE MONEY FIRST.
I'M JUST GOING UPSTAIRS. YOU WAIT HERE.
STERLING? WHAT THE FUCK?
HE'S GOT THE WEED, NOT ME.
HEY.
GIMME THE MONEY. *NOW.*
"HEY NICKY-"

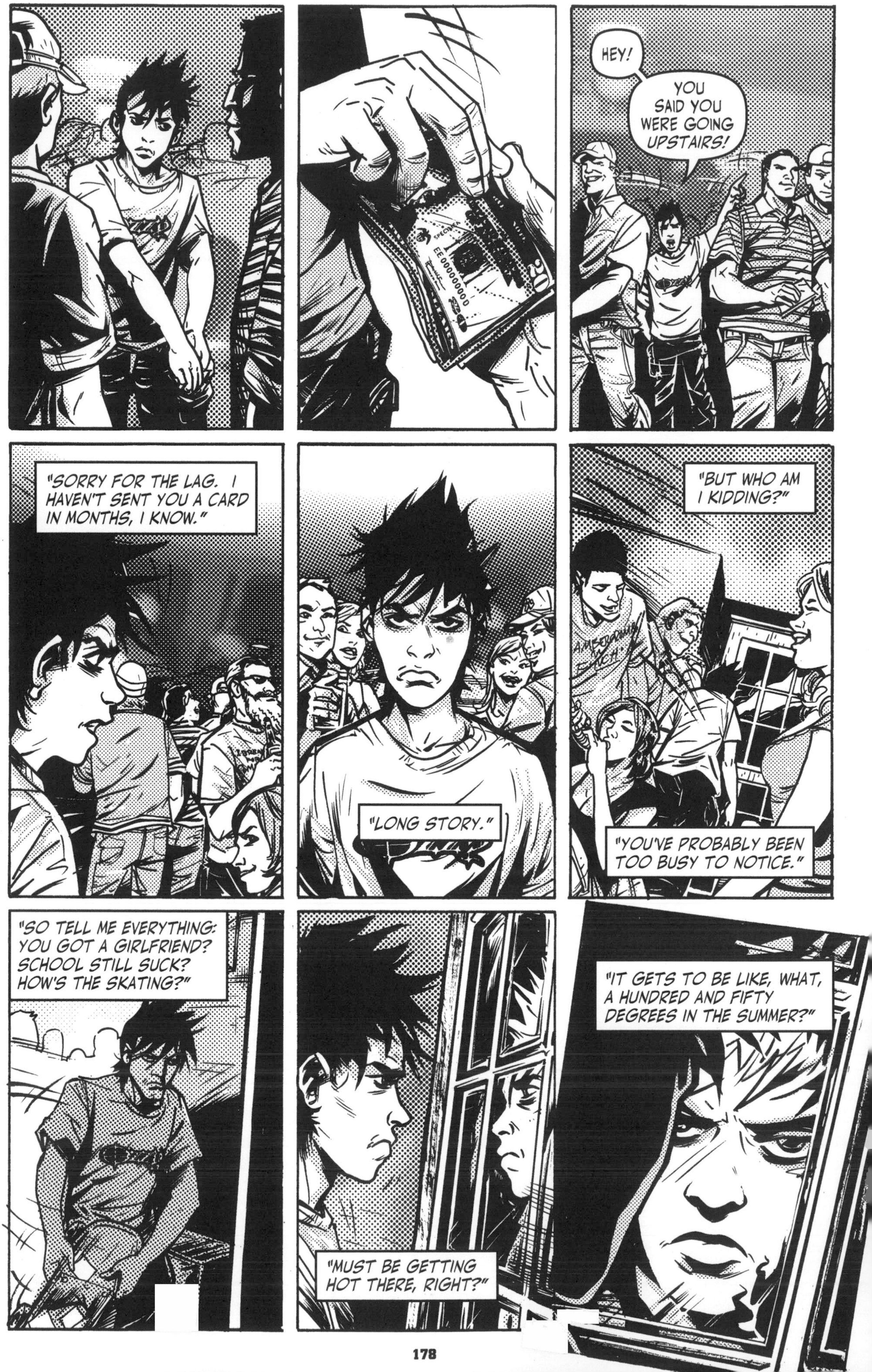
HEY!
YOU SAID YOU WERE GOING UPSTAIRS!
"SORRY FOR THE LAG. I HAVEN'T SENT YOU A CARD IN MONTHS, I KNOW."
"LONG STORY."
"BUT WHO AM I KIDDING?"
"YOU'VE PROBABLY BEEN TOO BUSY TO NOTICE."
"SO TELL ME EVERYTHING: YOU GOT A GIRLFRIEND? SCHOOL STILL SUCK? HOW'S THE SKATING?"
"MUST BE GETTING HOT THERE, RIGHT?"
"IT GETS TO BE LIKE, WHAT, A HUNDRED AND FIFTY DEGREES IN THE SUMMER?"

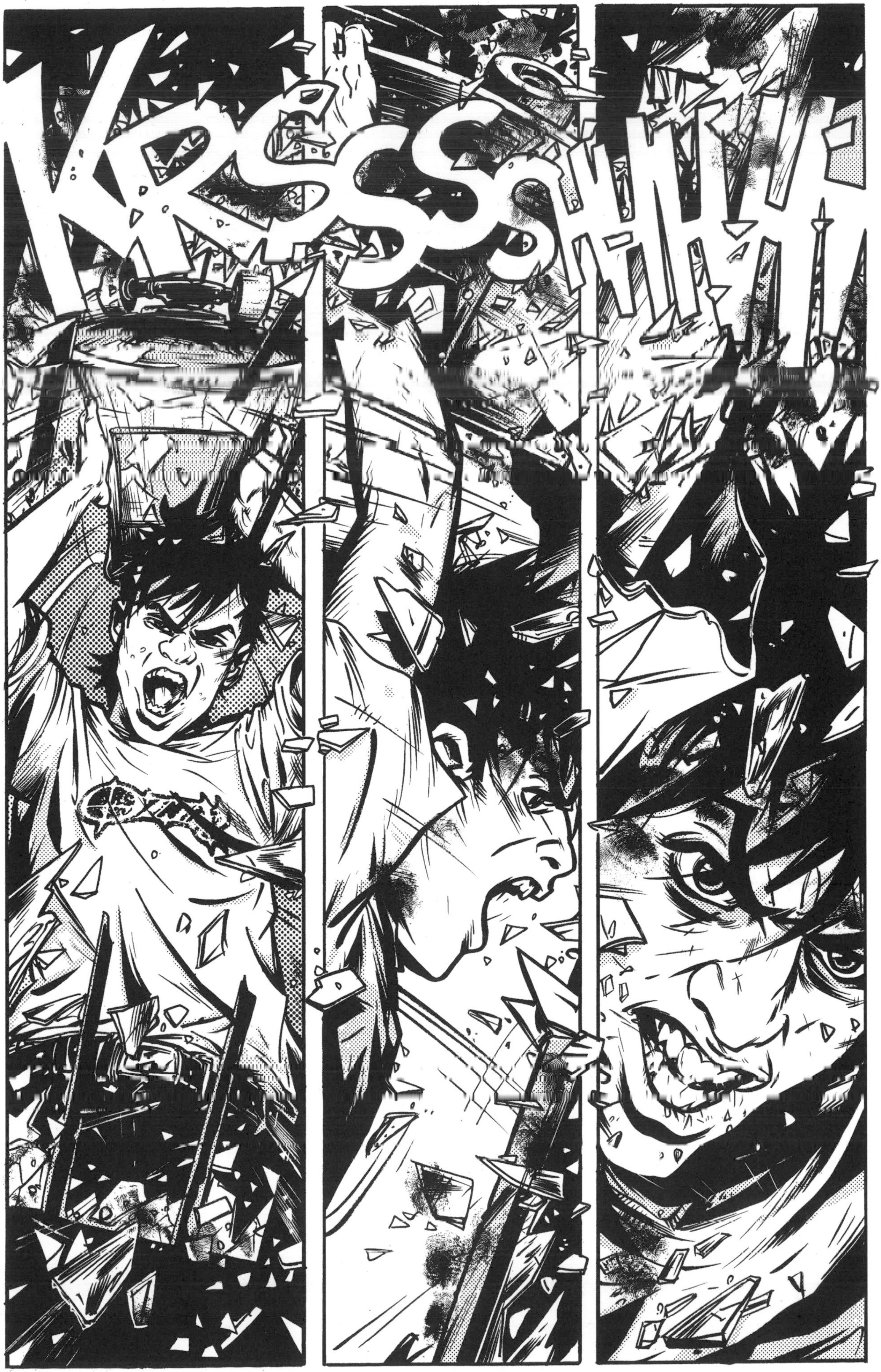
KRSSSHHH

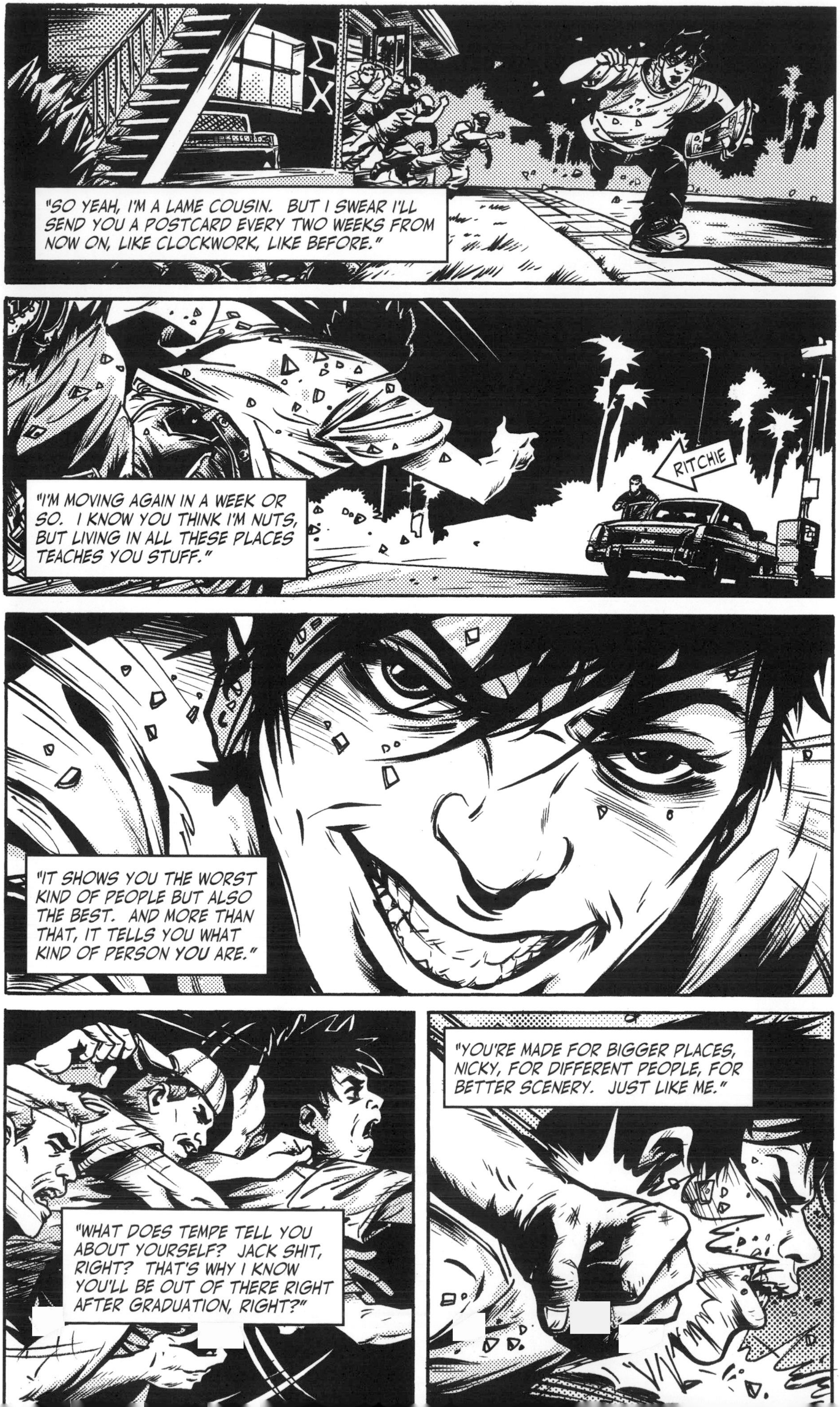
"SO YEAH, I'M A LAME COUSIN. BUT I SWEAR I'LL SEND YOU A POSTCARD EVERY TWO WEEKS FROM NOW ON, LIKE CLOCKWORK, LIKE BEFORE."
"I'M MOVING AGAIN IN A WEEK OR SO. I KNOW YOU THINK I'M NUTS, BUT LIVING IN ALL THESE PLACES TEACHES YOU STUFF."
RITCHIE
"IT SHOWS YOU THE WORST KIND OF PEOPLE BUT ALSO THE BEST. AND MORE THAN THAT, IT TELLS YOU WHAT KIND OF PERSON YOU ARE."
"WHAT DOES TEMPE TELL YOU ABOUT YOURSELF? JACK SHIT, RIGHT? THAT'S WHY I KNOW YOU'LL BE OUT OF THERE RIGHT AFTER GRADUATION, RIGHT?"
"YOU'RE MADE FOR BIGGER PLACES, NICKY, FOR DIFFERENT PEOPLE, FOR BETTER SCENERY. JUST LIKE ME."

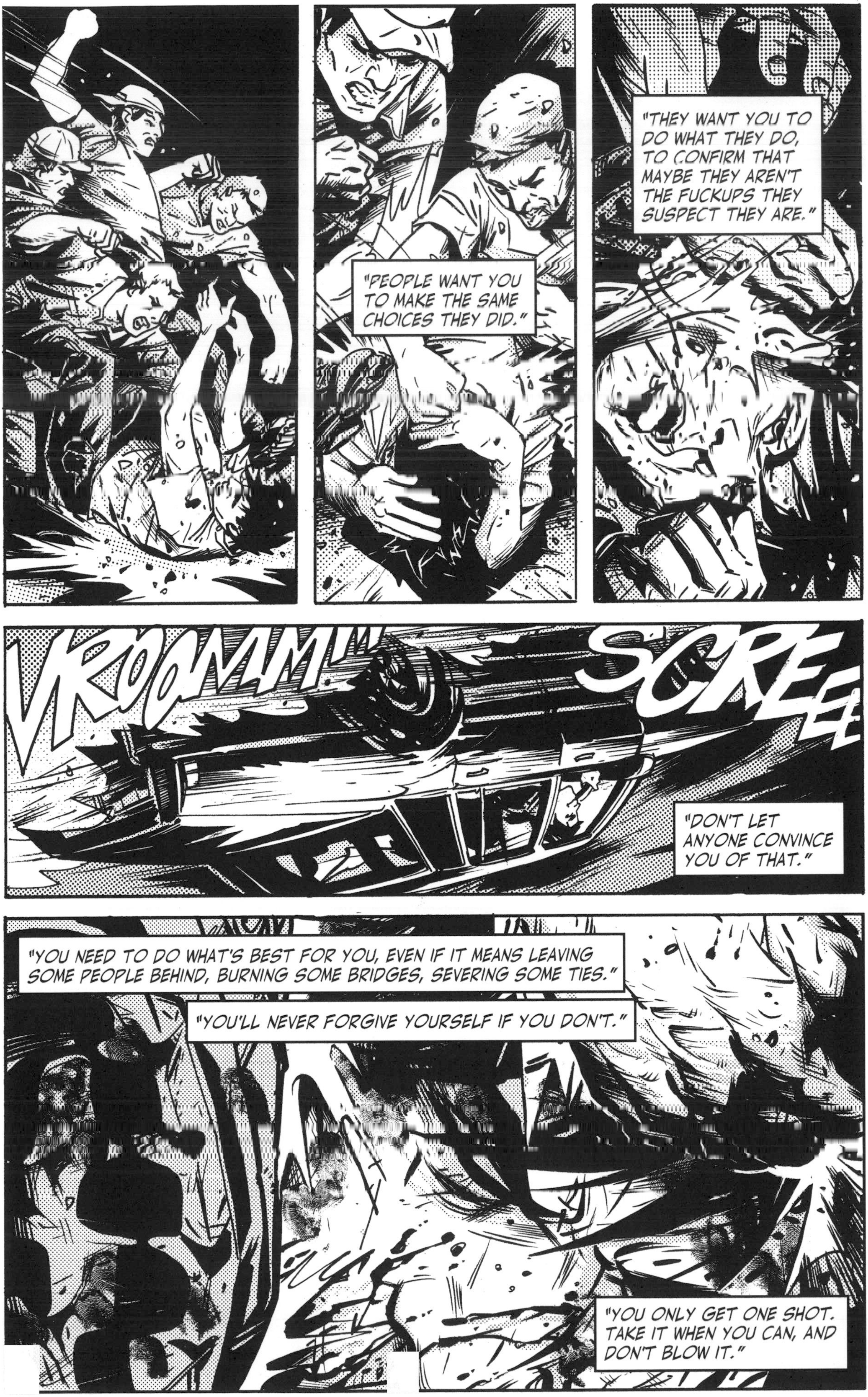
"PEOPLE WANT YOU TO MAKE THE SAME CHOICES THEY DID."
"THEY WANT YOU TO DO WHAT THEY DO, TO CONFIRM THAT MAYBE THEY AREN'T THE FUCKUPS THEY SUSPECT THEY ARE."
VROOMMM
SCREEE
"DON'T LET ANYONE CONVINCE YOU OF THAT."
"YOU NEED TO DO WHAT'S BEST FOR YOU, EVEN IF IT MEANS LEAVING SOME PEOPLE BEHIND, BURNING SOME BRIDGES, SEVERING SOME TIES."
"YOU'LL NEVER FORGIVE YOURSELF IF YOU DON'T."
"YOU ONLY GET ONE SHOT. TAKE IT WHEN YOU CAN, AND DON'T BLOW IT."

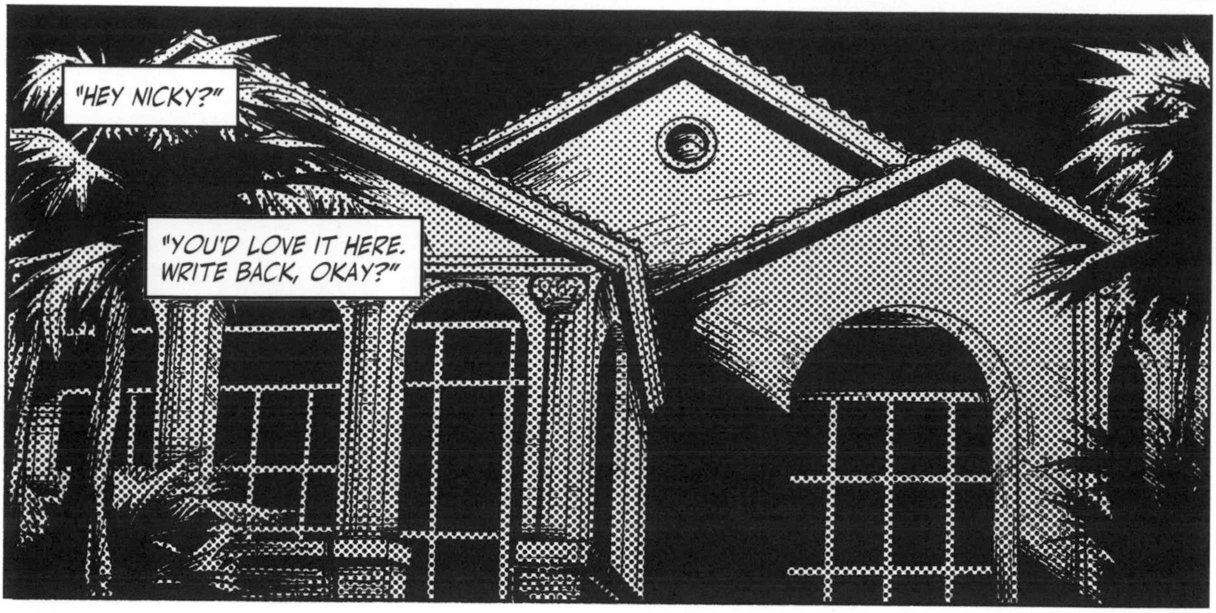
"HEY NICKY?"
"YOU'D LOVE IT HERE. WRITE BACK, OKAY?"

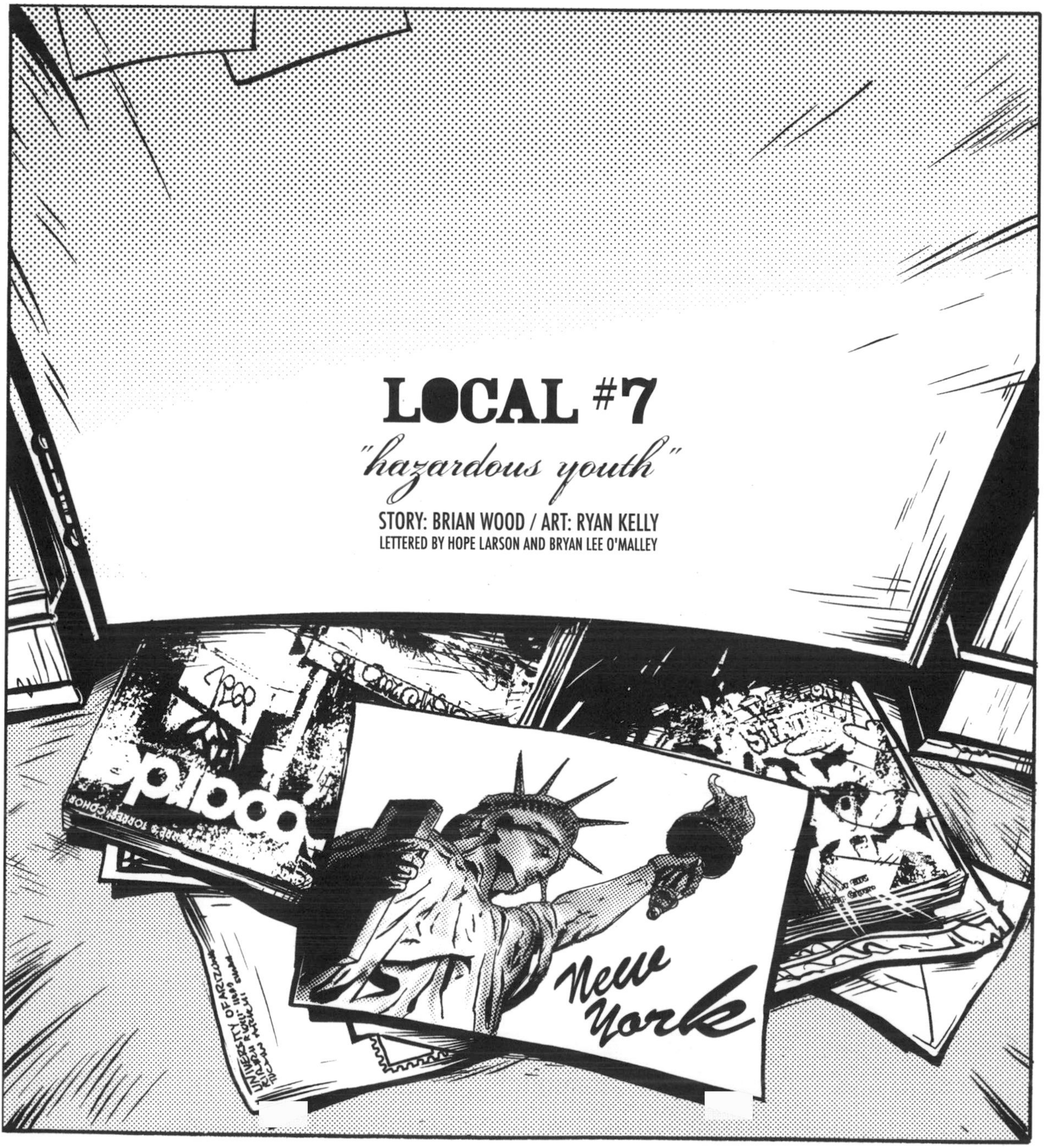
LOCAL #7
"hazardous youth"
STORY: BRIAN WOOD / ART: RYAN KELLY
LETTERED BY HOPE LARSON AND BRYAN LEE O'MALLEY
New York

CHAPTER 8
"FOOD AS SUBSTITUTE"
Wicker Park, Chicago, Illinois

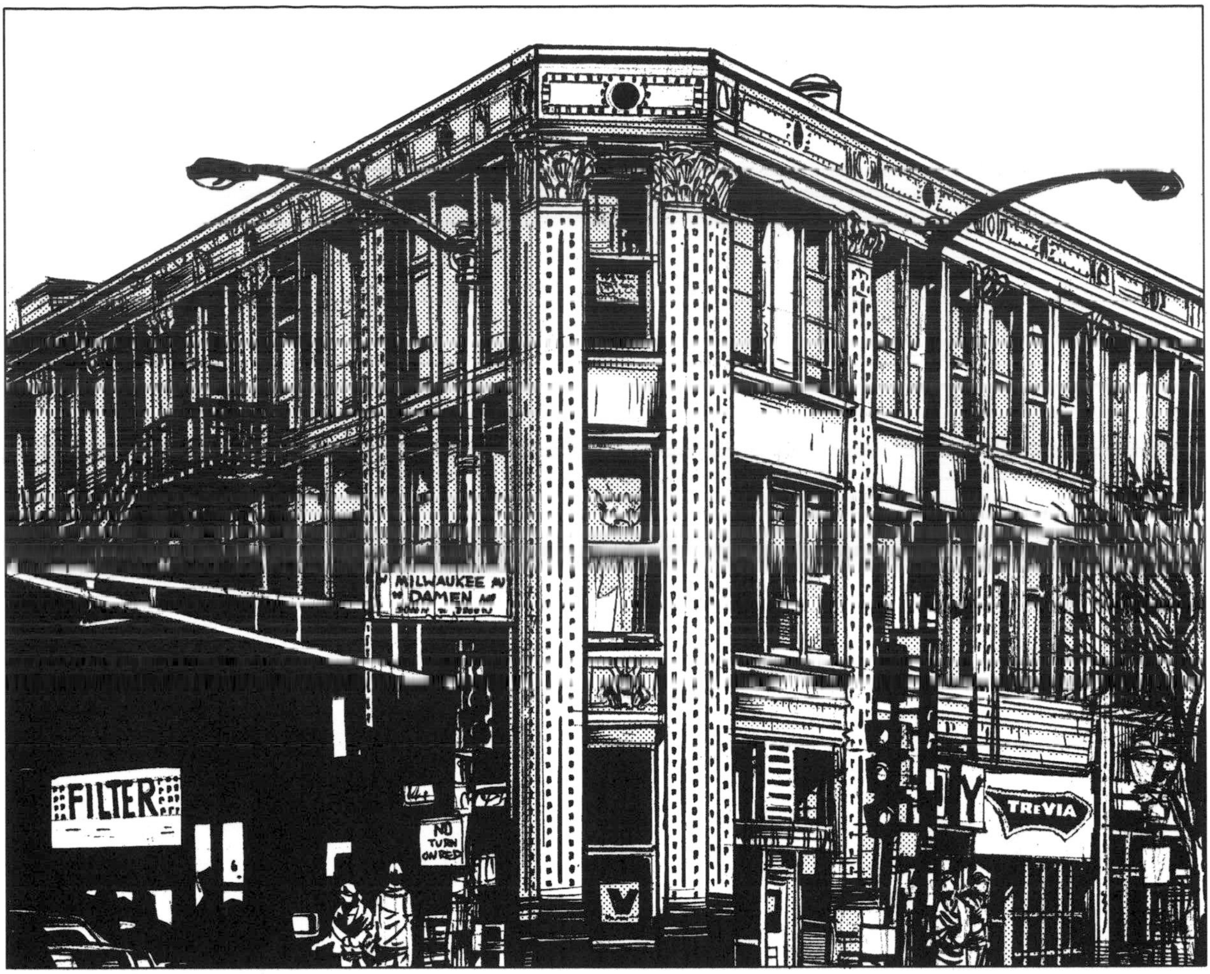
MILWAUKEE AV
DAMEN AV
FILTER
NO TURN ON RED
TREVIA

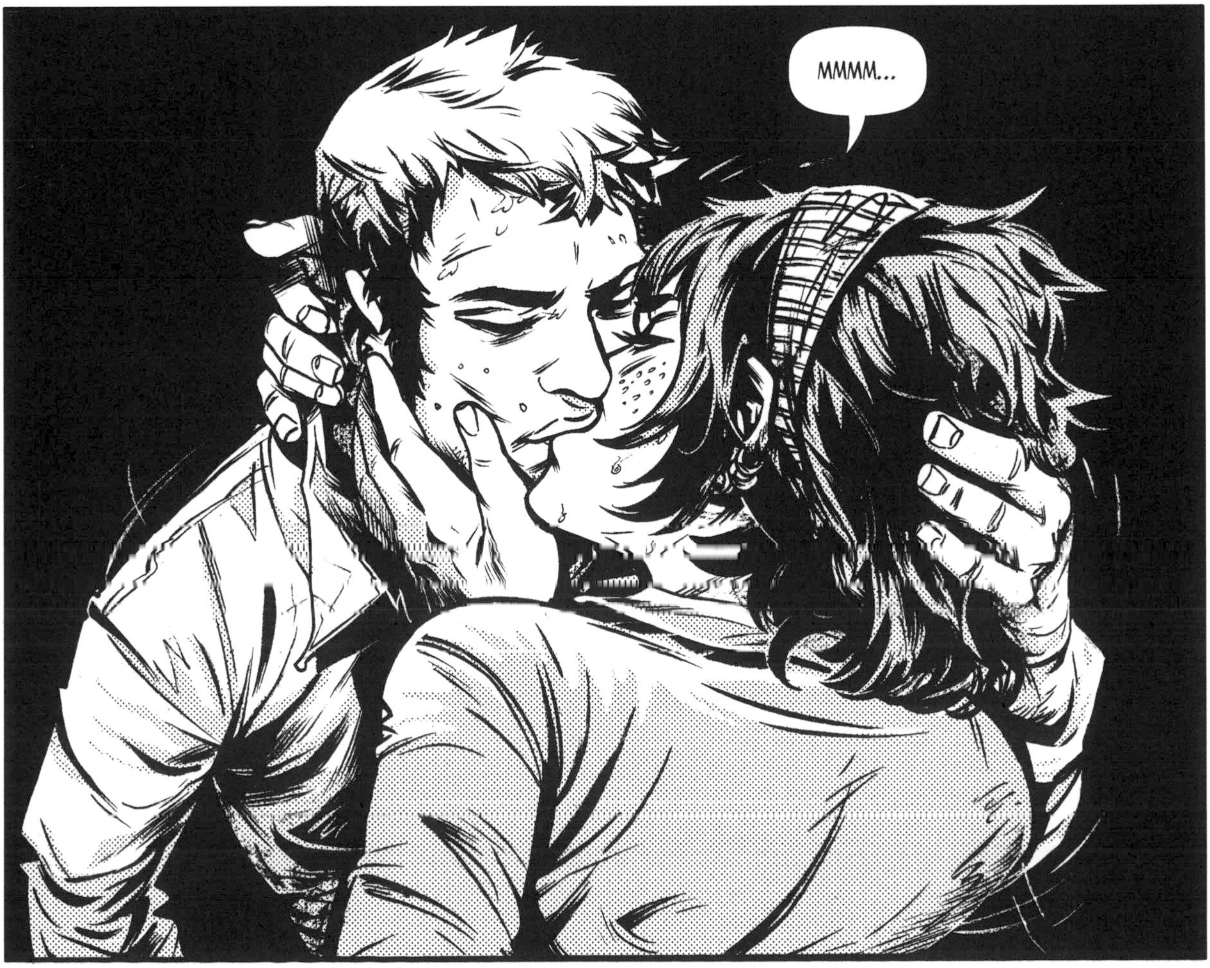
MMMM...

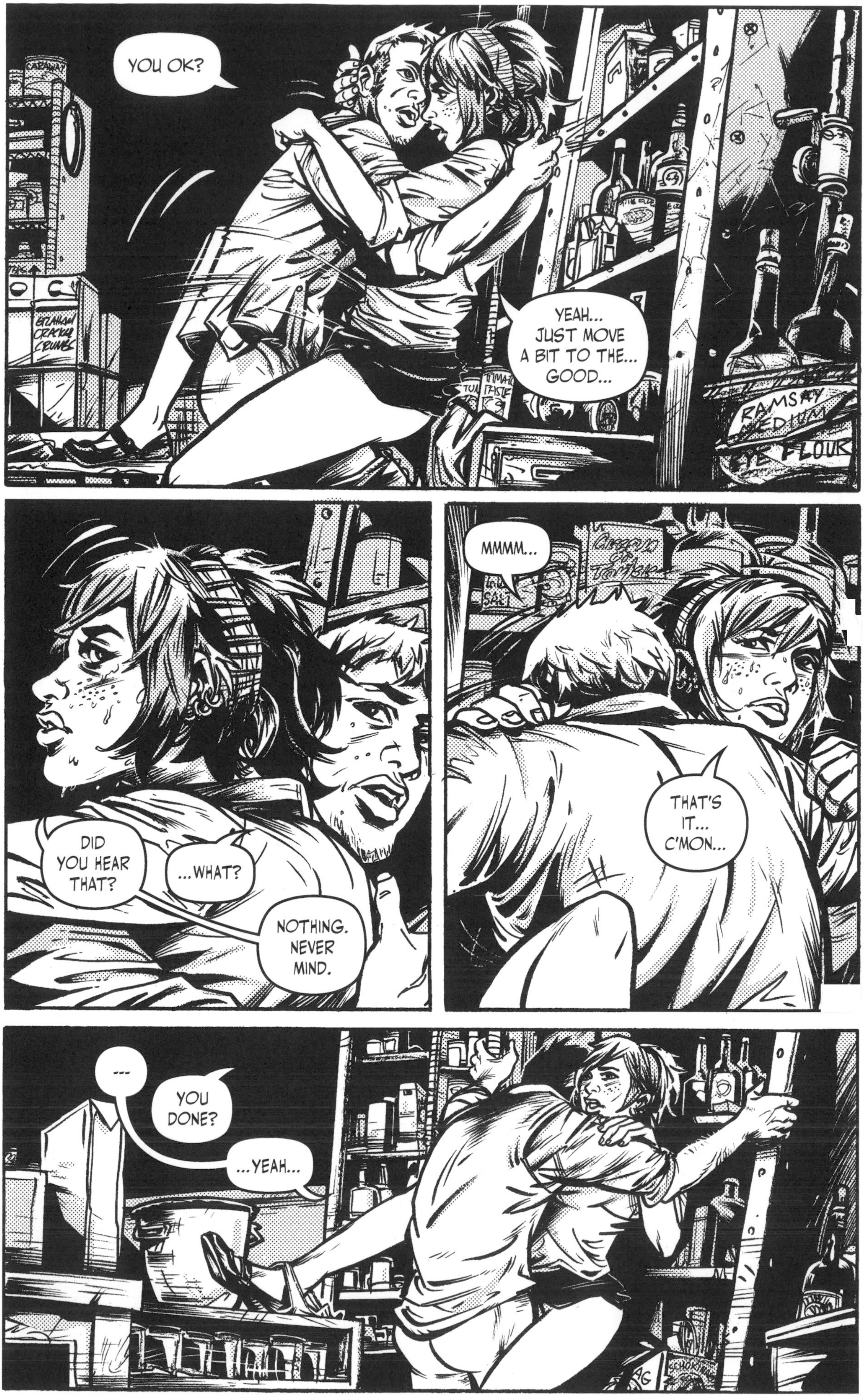
YOU OK?
YEAH... JUST MOVE A BIT TO THE... GOOD...
RAMSAY MEDIUM RYE FLOUR
DID YOU HEAR THAT?
...WHAT?
NOTHING. NEVER MIND.
MMMM...
THAT'S IT... C'MON...
...
YOU DONE?
...YEAH...

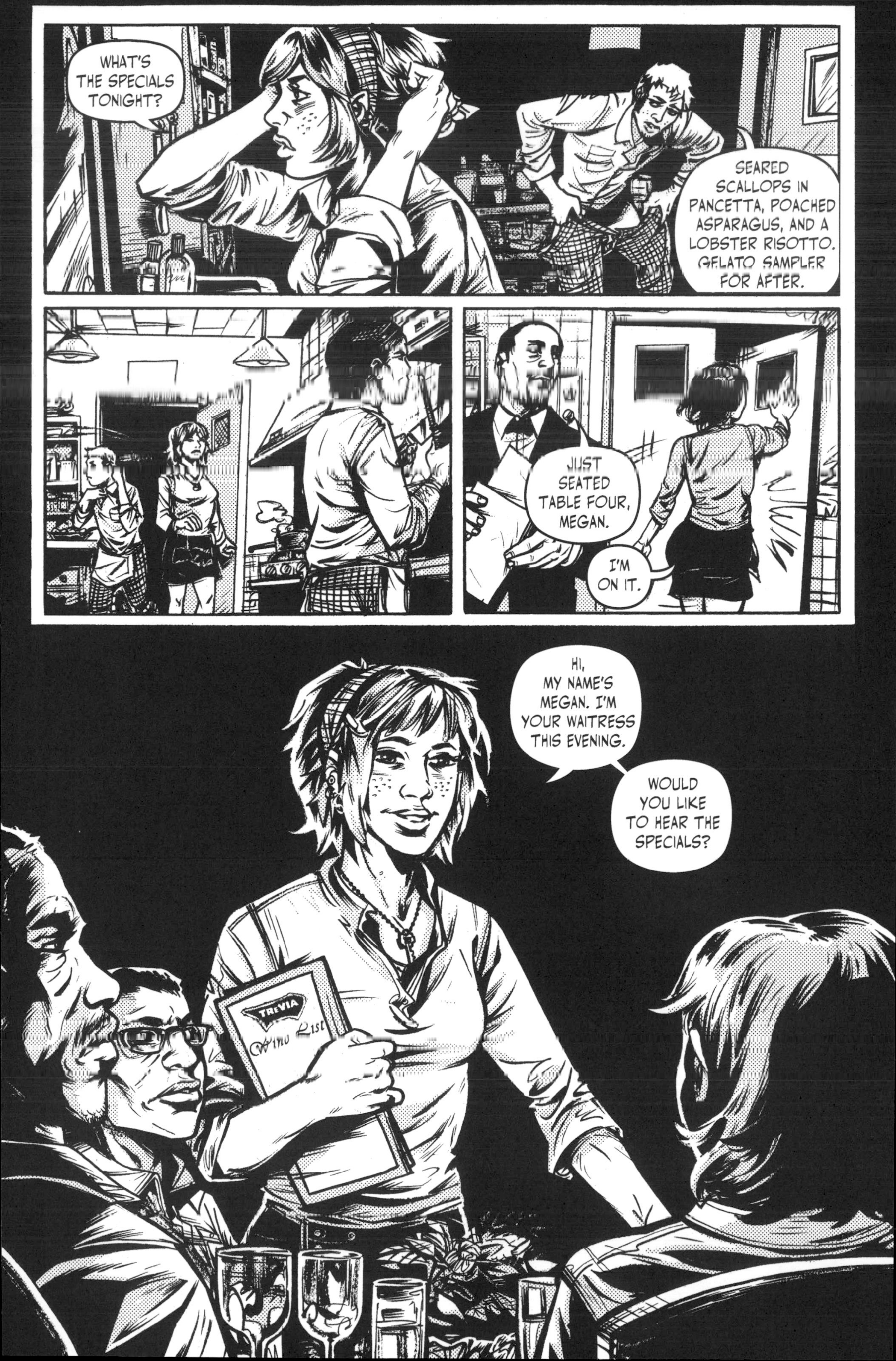
WHAT'S THE SPECIALS TONIGHT?
SEARED SCALLOPS IN PANCETTA, POACHED ASPARAGUS, AND A LOBSTER RISOTTO. GELATO SAMPLER FOR AFTER.
JUST SEATED TABLE FOUR, MEGAN.
I'M ON IT.
HI, MY NAME'S MEGAN. I'M YOUR WAITRESS THIS EVENING.
WOULD YOU LIKE TO HEAR THE SPECIALS?
TREVIA
Wine List

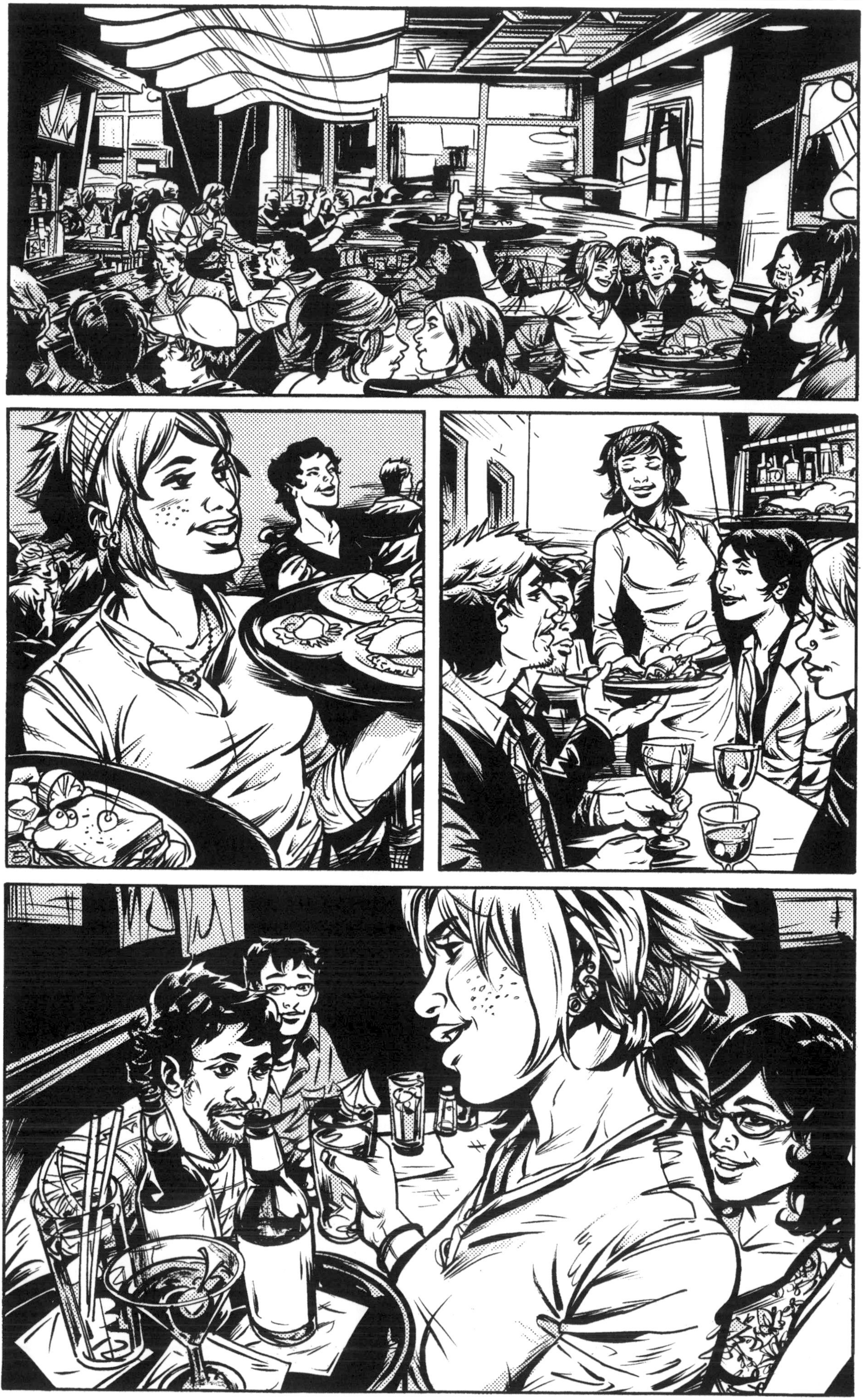

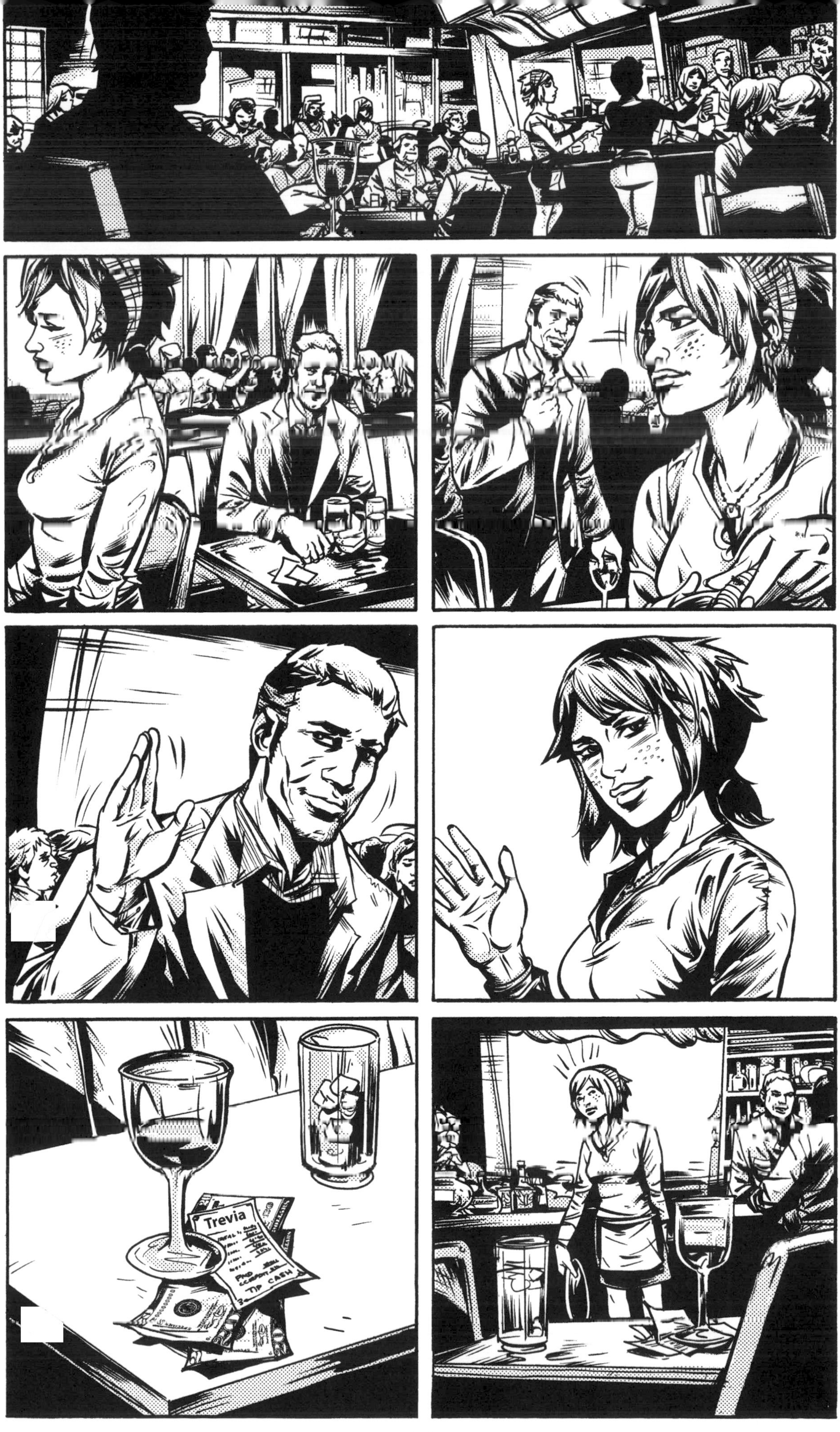
Trevia
TIP CASH

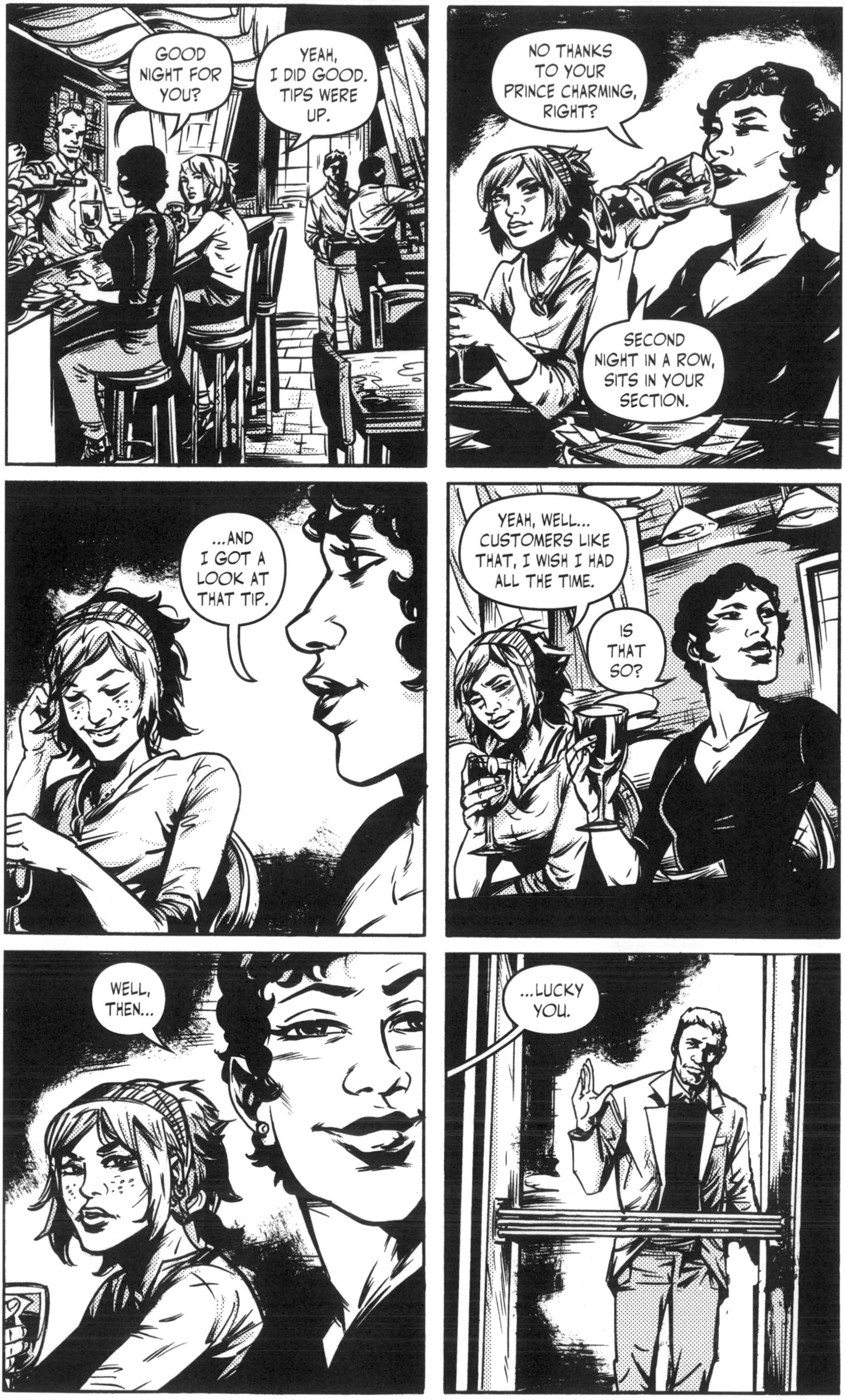
GOOD NIGHT FOR YOU?
YEAH, I DID GOOD. TIPS WERE UP.
NO THANKS TO YOUR PRINCE CHARMING, RIGHT?
SECOND NIGHT IN A ROW, SITS IN YOUR SECTION.
...AND I GOT A LOOK AT THAT TIP.
YEAH, WELL... CUSTOMERS LIKE THAT, I WISH I HAD ALL THE TIME.
IS THAT SO?
WELL, THEN...
...LUCKY YOU.

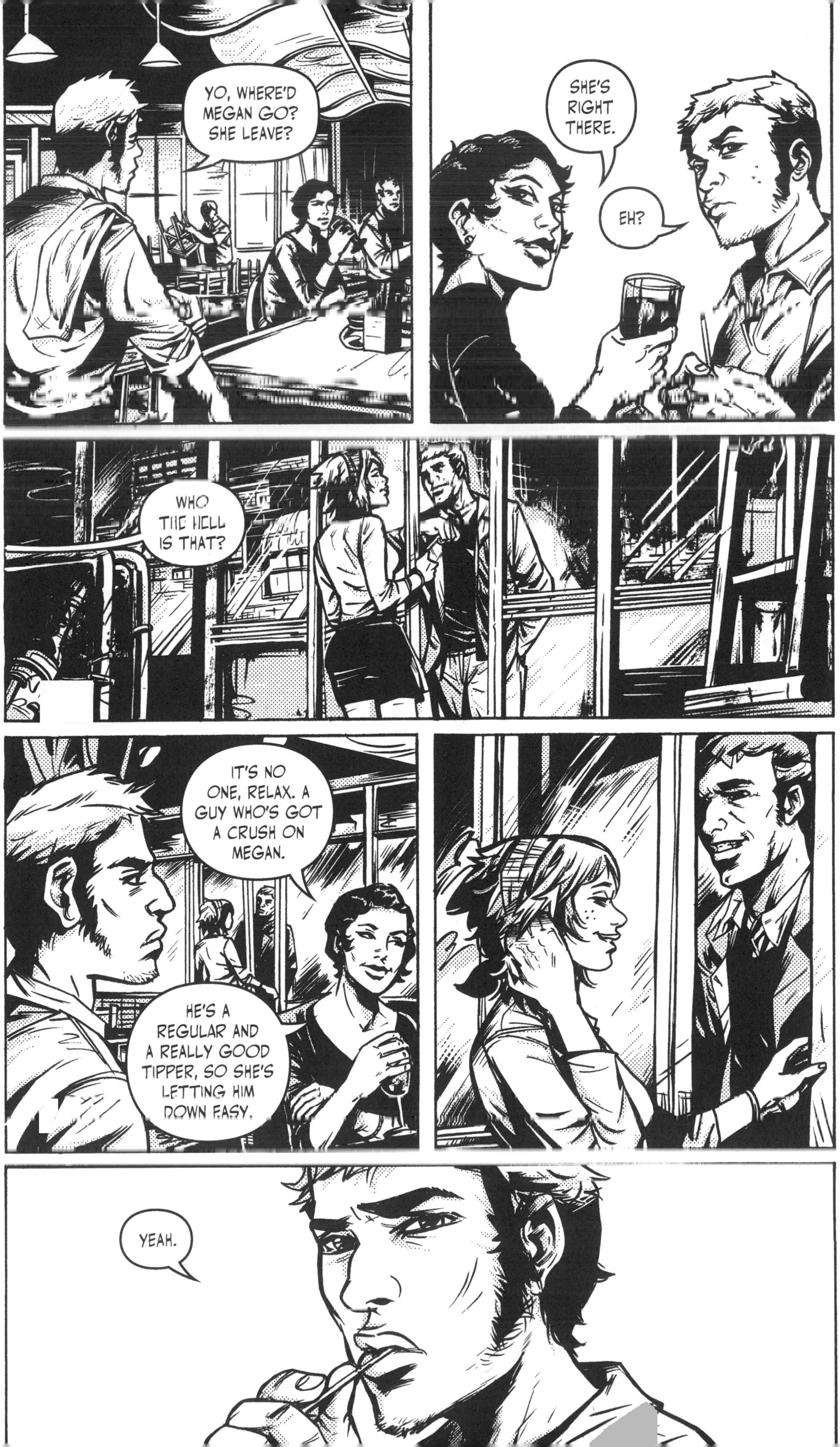
YO, WHERE'D MEGAN GO? SHE LEAVE?
SHE'S RIGHT THERE.
EH?
WHO THE HELL IS THAT?
IT'S NO ONE, RELAX. A GUY WHO'S GOT A CRUSH ON MEGAN.
HE'S A REGULAR AND A REALLY GOOD TIPPER, SO SHE'S LETTING HIM DOWN EASY.
YEAH.

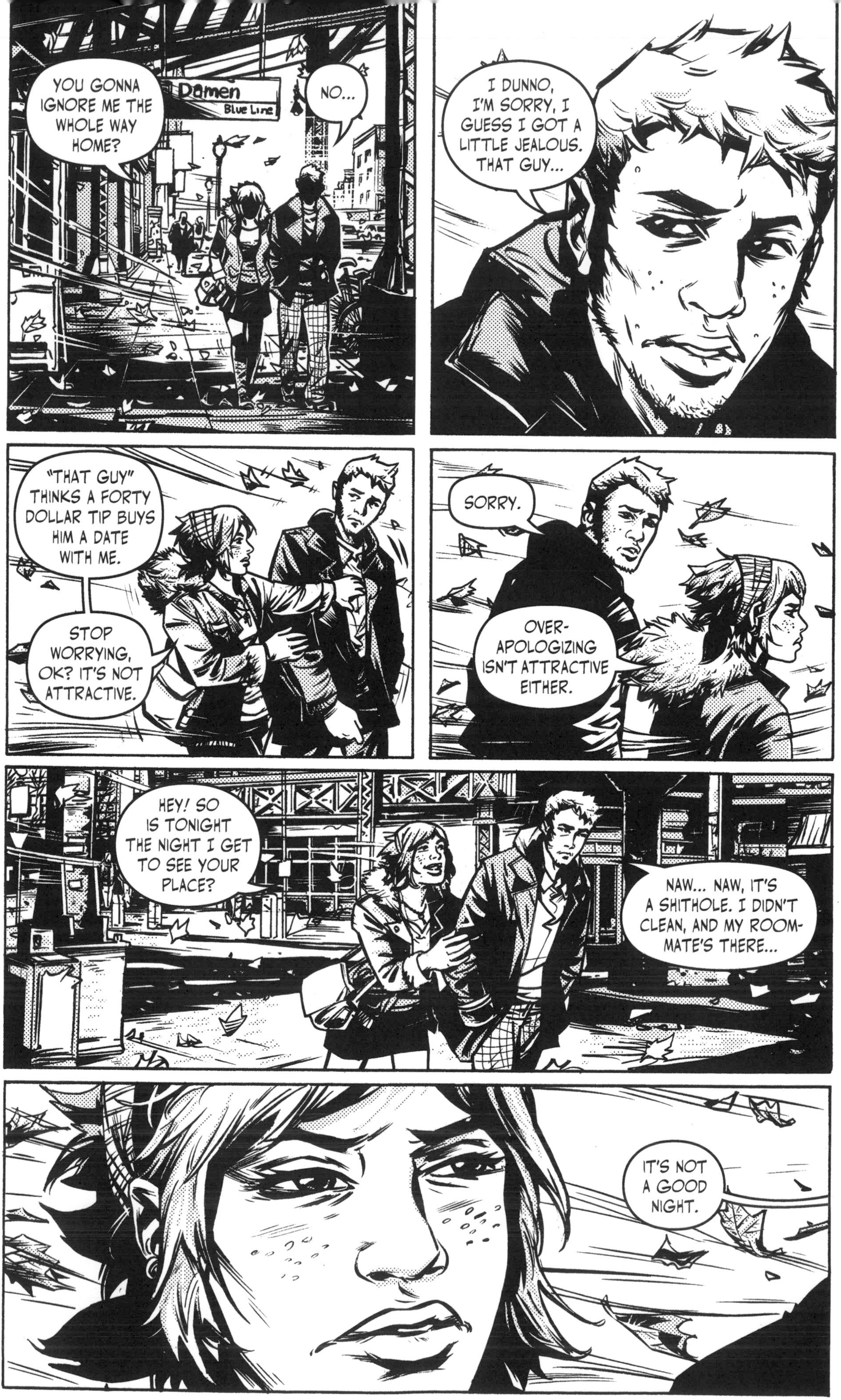
Damen
Blue Line
YOU GONNA IGNORE ME THE WHOLE WAY HOME?
NO...
I DUNNO, I'M SORRY, I GUESS I GOT A LITTLE JEALOUS. THAT GUY...
"THAT GUY" THINKS A FORTY DOLLAR TIP BUYS HIM A DATE WITH ME.
STOP WORRYING, OK? IT'S NOT ATTRACTIVE.
SORRY.
OVER-APOLOGIZING ISN'T ATTRACTIVE EITHER.
HEY! SO IS TONIGHT THE NIGHT I GET TO SEE YOUR PLACE?
NAW... NAW, IT'S A SHITHOLE. I DIDN'T CLEAN, AND MY ROOM-MATE'S THERE...
IT'S NOT A GOOD NIGHT.

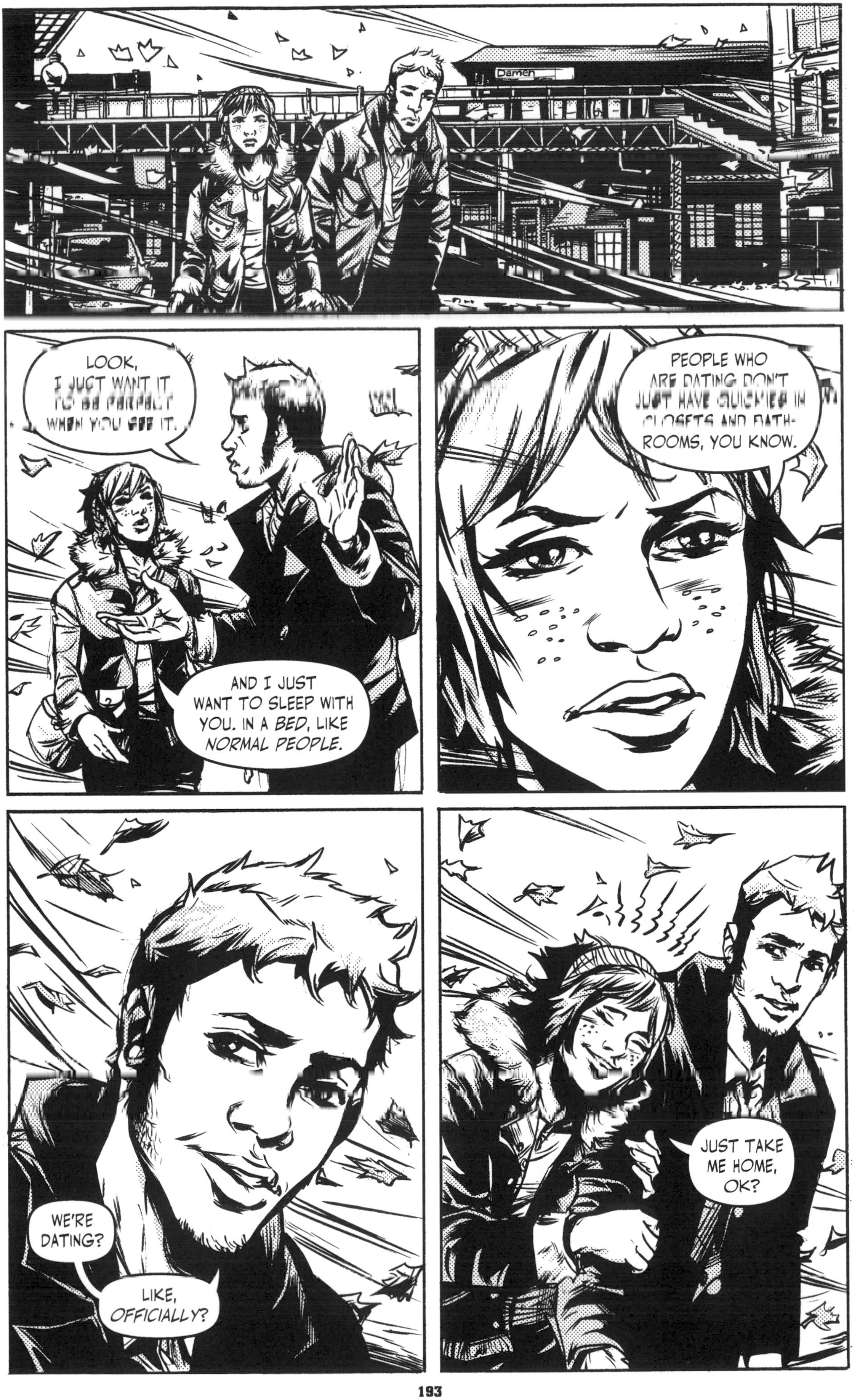
Damen
LOOK, I JUST WANT IT TO BE PERFECT WHEN YOU SEE IT.
AND I JUST WANT TO SLEEP WITH YOU. IN A *BED*, LIKE *NORMAL PEOPLE*.
PEOPLE WHO ARE DATING DON'T JUST HAVE QUICKIES IN CLOSETS AND BATH-ROOMS, YOU KNOW.
WE'RE DATING?
LIKE, *OFFICIALLY*?
JUST TAKE ME HOME, OK?

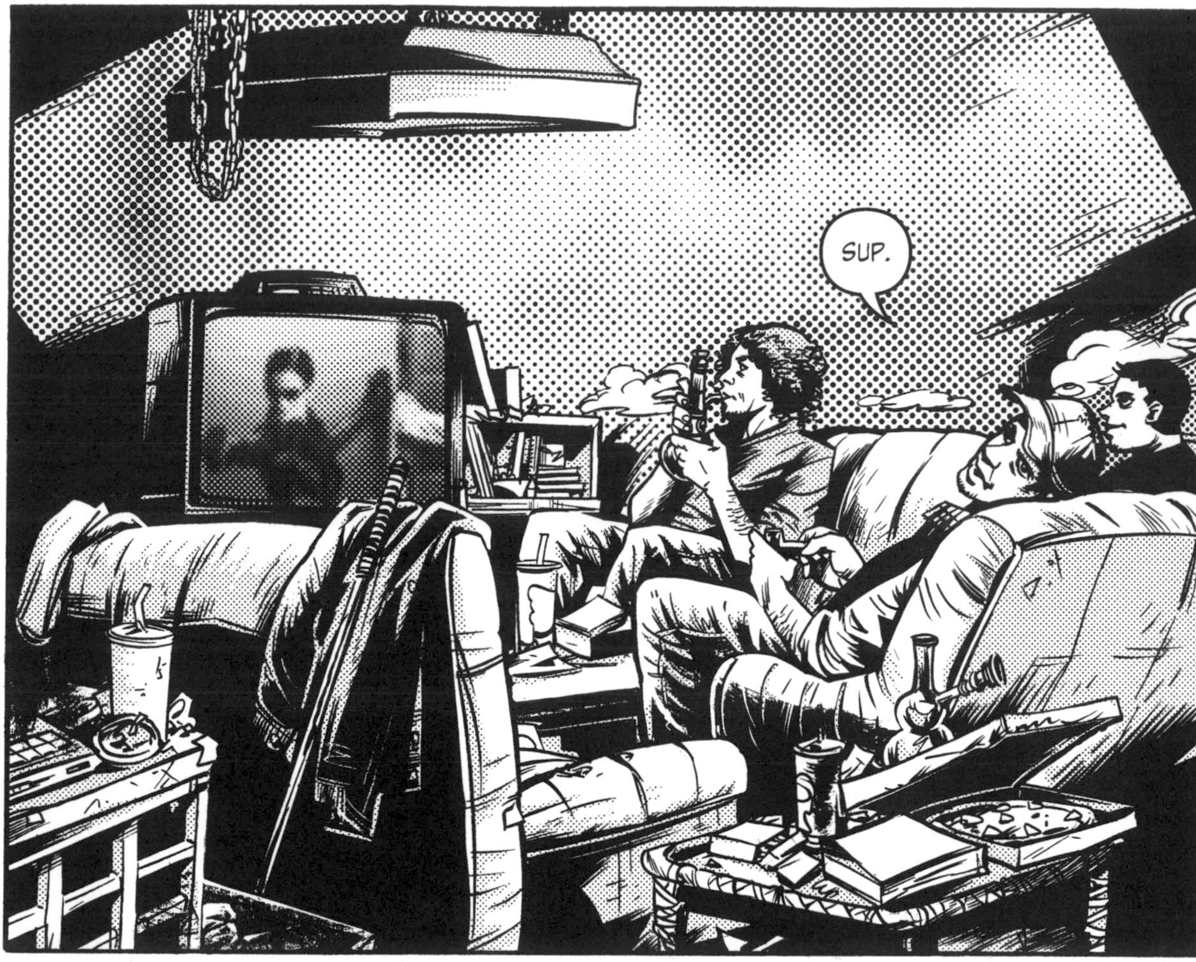
SUP.

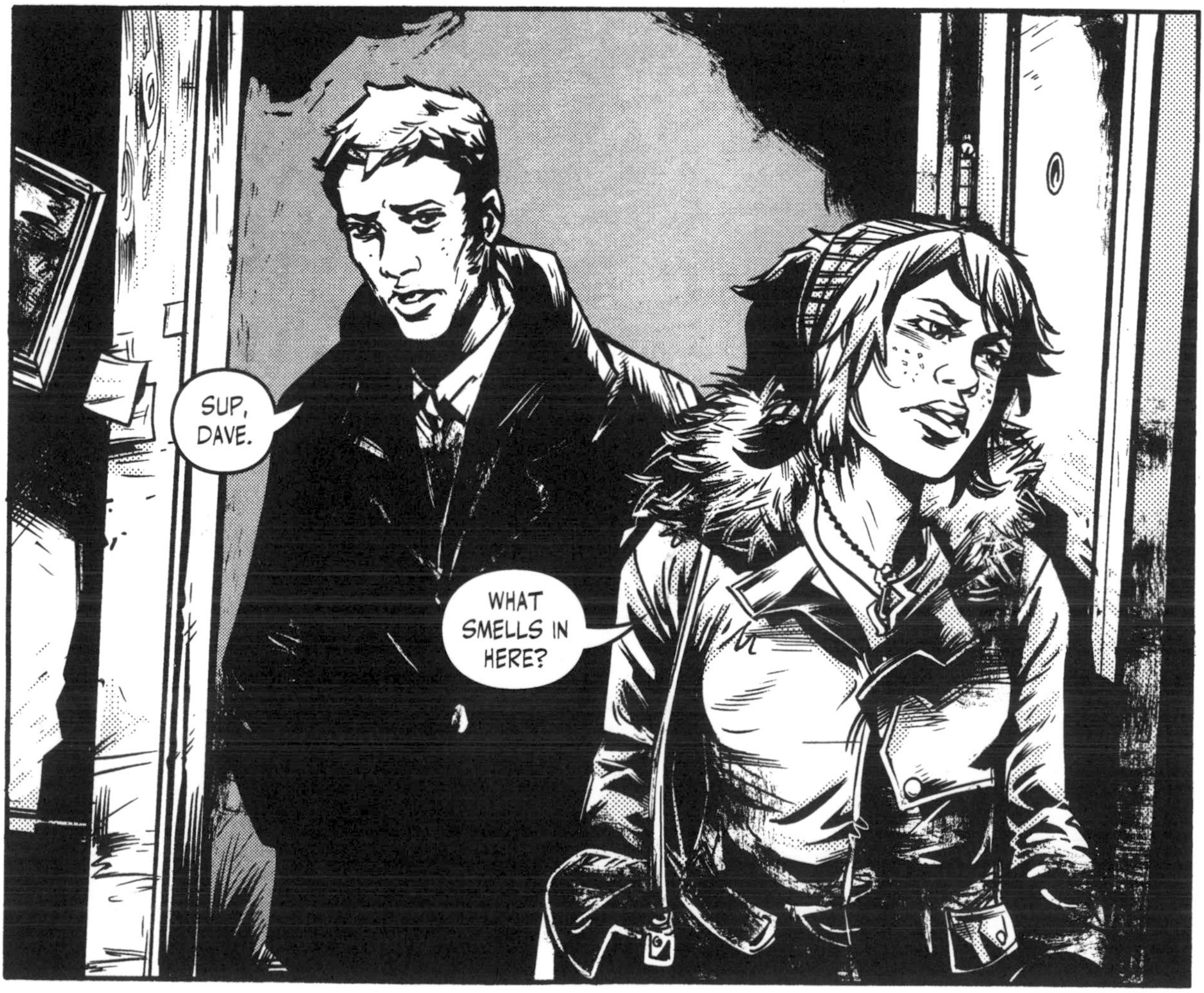
SUP, DAVE.
WHAT SMELLS IN HERE?

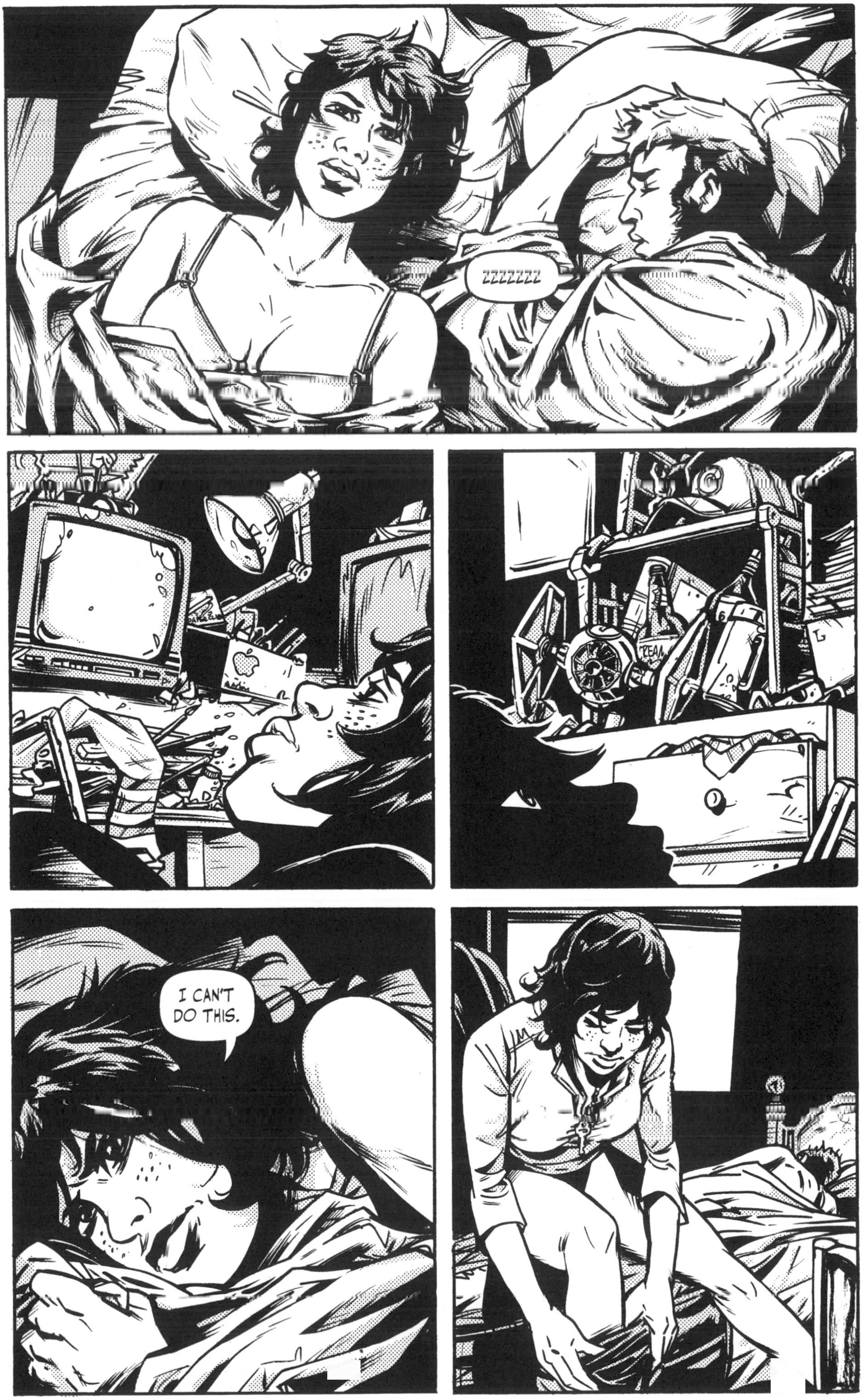
ZZZZZZZ
I CAN'T DO THIS.

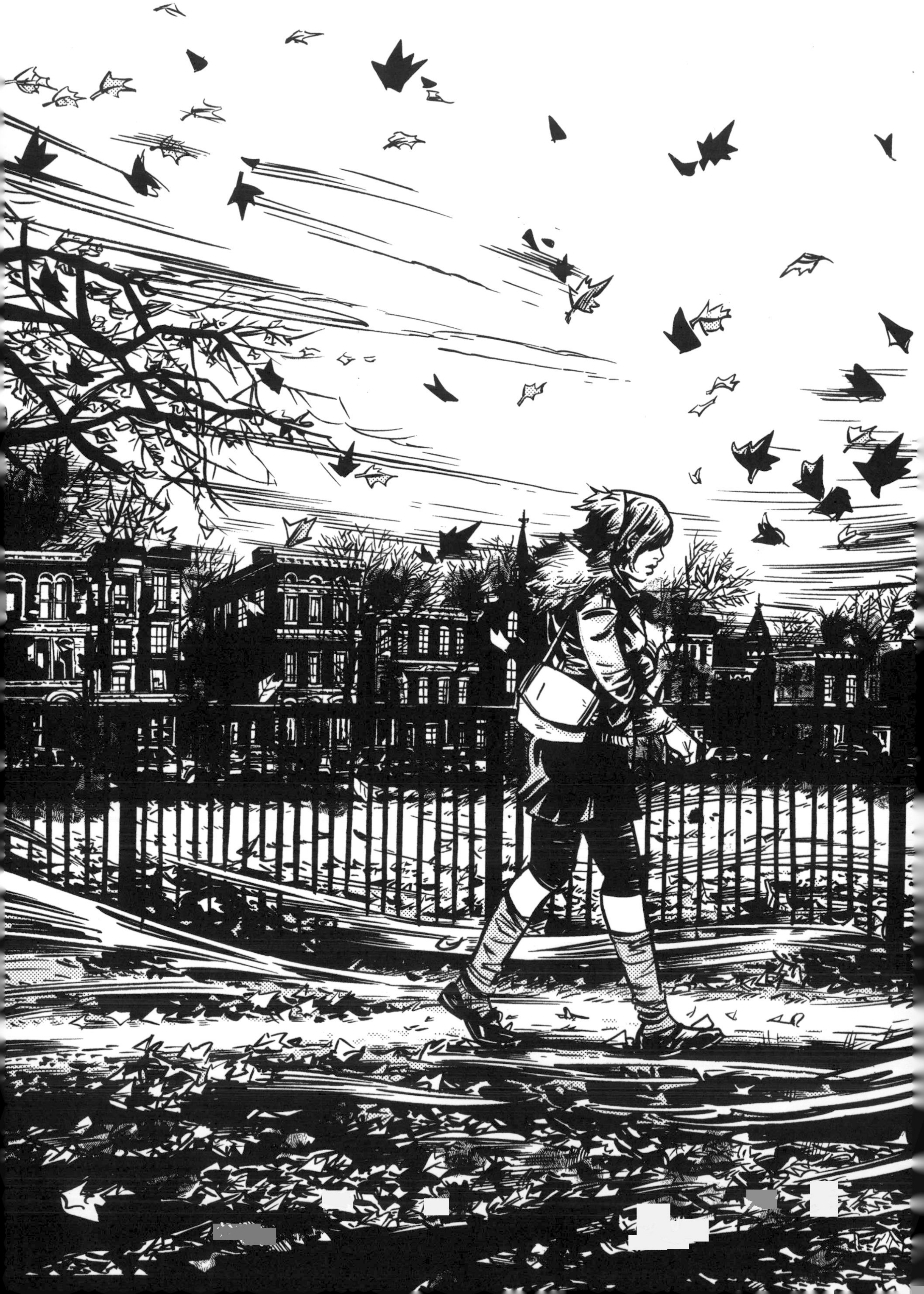

755 1999 VELLETRI RISERVA Lazio 35
750 2001 FAUNUS PRIMITIVO Puglia 26
780 2004 ANTINORI SANTA CRISTINA Tuscany 32
710 1998 FATTORIA DI BIBBIANI PULIGNANO Tuscany 71
790 2002 AVIGNONESI ROSSO Tuscany 32
720 2003 CA... Tuscany 19
745 ... SANGIOVESE/CABERNE...
...P... CHIANTI Tuscany 30
...AZIAN... Tuscany 34
...O Tuscany 41
...CLASSICO Tuscany 60

WHAT DO YOU SUGGEST?

OH...I DON'T KNOW MUCH ABOUT THE WINE, TO BE HONEST.

THE PRIMITIVO, THEN.

BUT I'M RELYING ON YOU FOR THE ENTRÉE. I DON'T EVEN WANT TO HEAR THE SPECIALS... JUST BRING ME WHAT YOU'D LIKE.

R-REALLY? HOW DO YOU KNOW YOU'LL LIKE WHAT I LIKE?

I DON'T. I DON'T KNOW ANYTHING ABOUT YOU, ACTUALLY.

BUT THIS SEEMS LIKE AS GOOD A PLACE TO START AS ANY.

DON'T YOU AGREE?

197

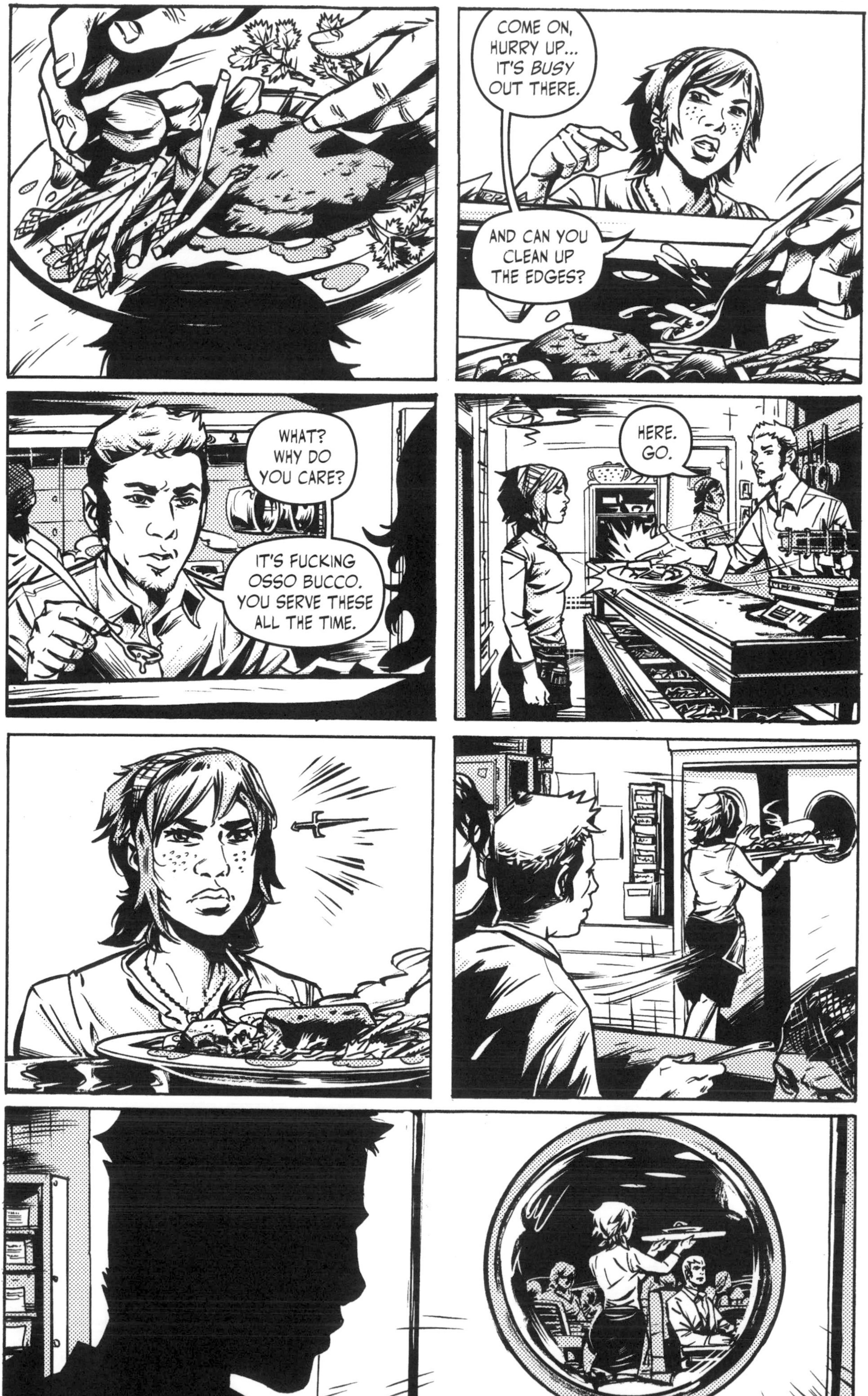
COME ON, HURRY UP... IT'S BUSY OUT THERE.
AND CAN YOU CLEAN UP THE EDGES?
WHAT? WHY DO YOU CARE?
IT'S FUCKING OSSO BUCCO. YOU SERVE THESE ALL THE TIME.
HERE. GO.

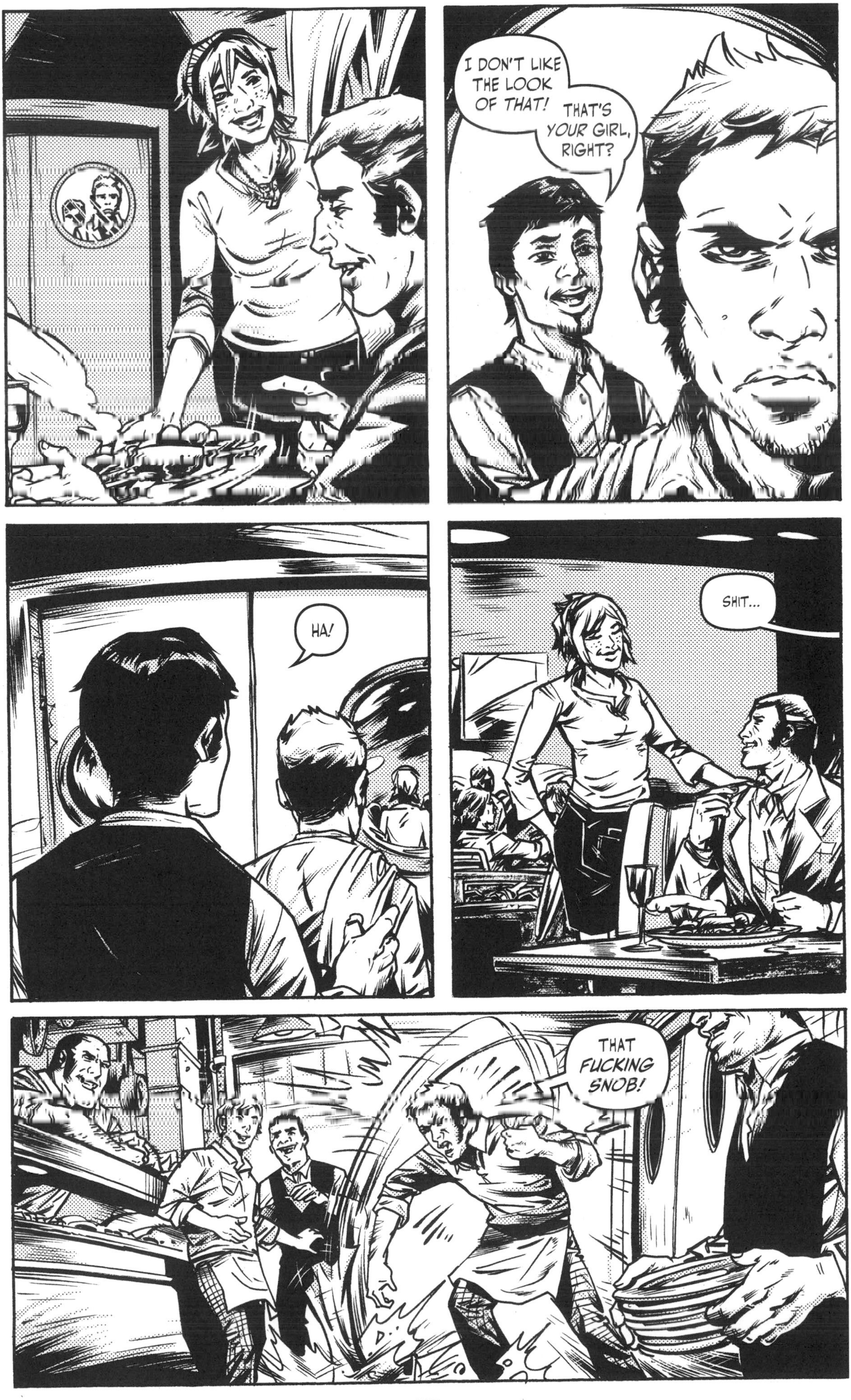
I DON'T LIKE THE LOOK OF THAT!
THAT'S YOUR GIRL, RIGHT?
HA!
SHIT...
THAT FUCKING SNOB!

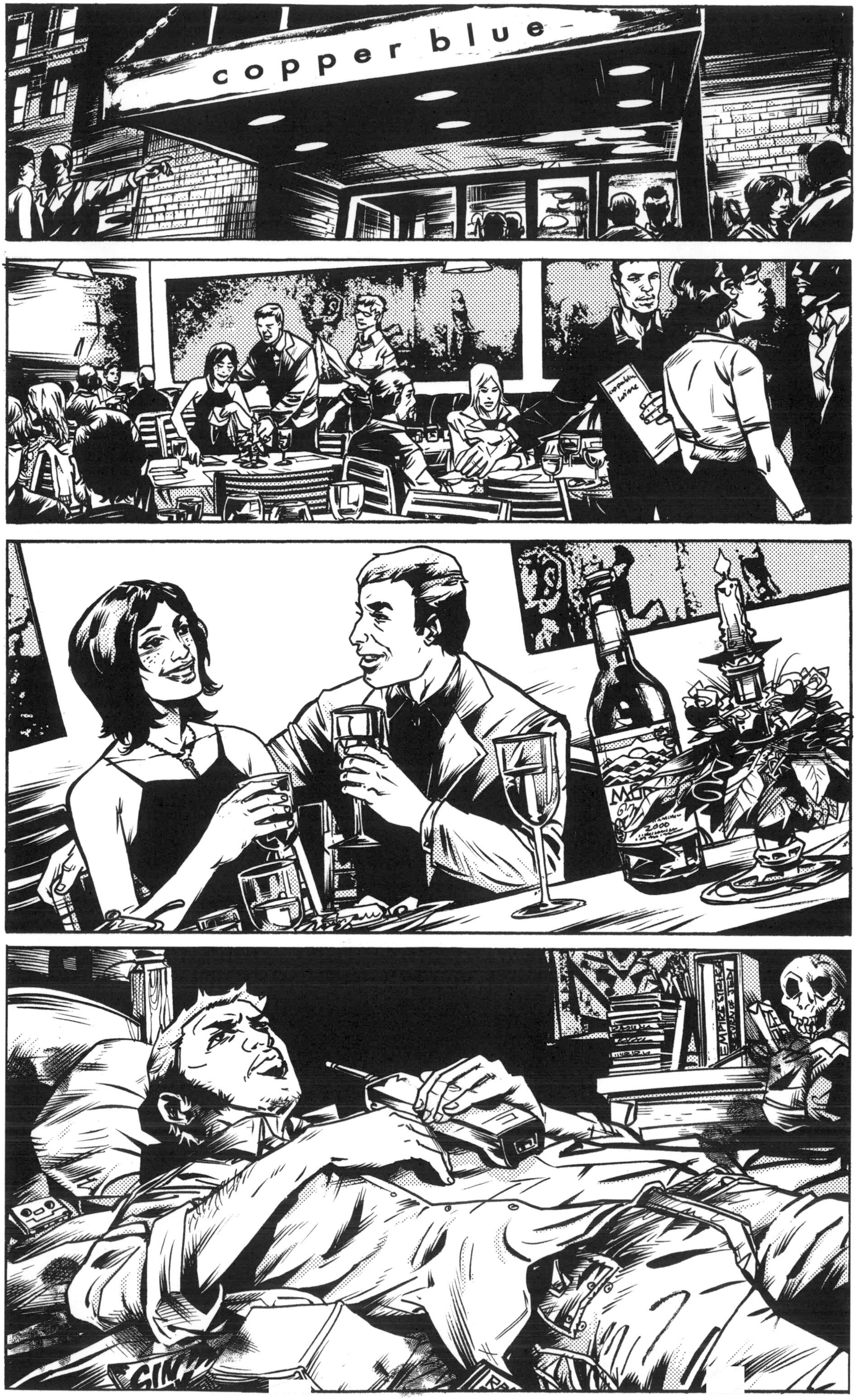
copper blue

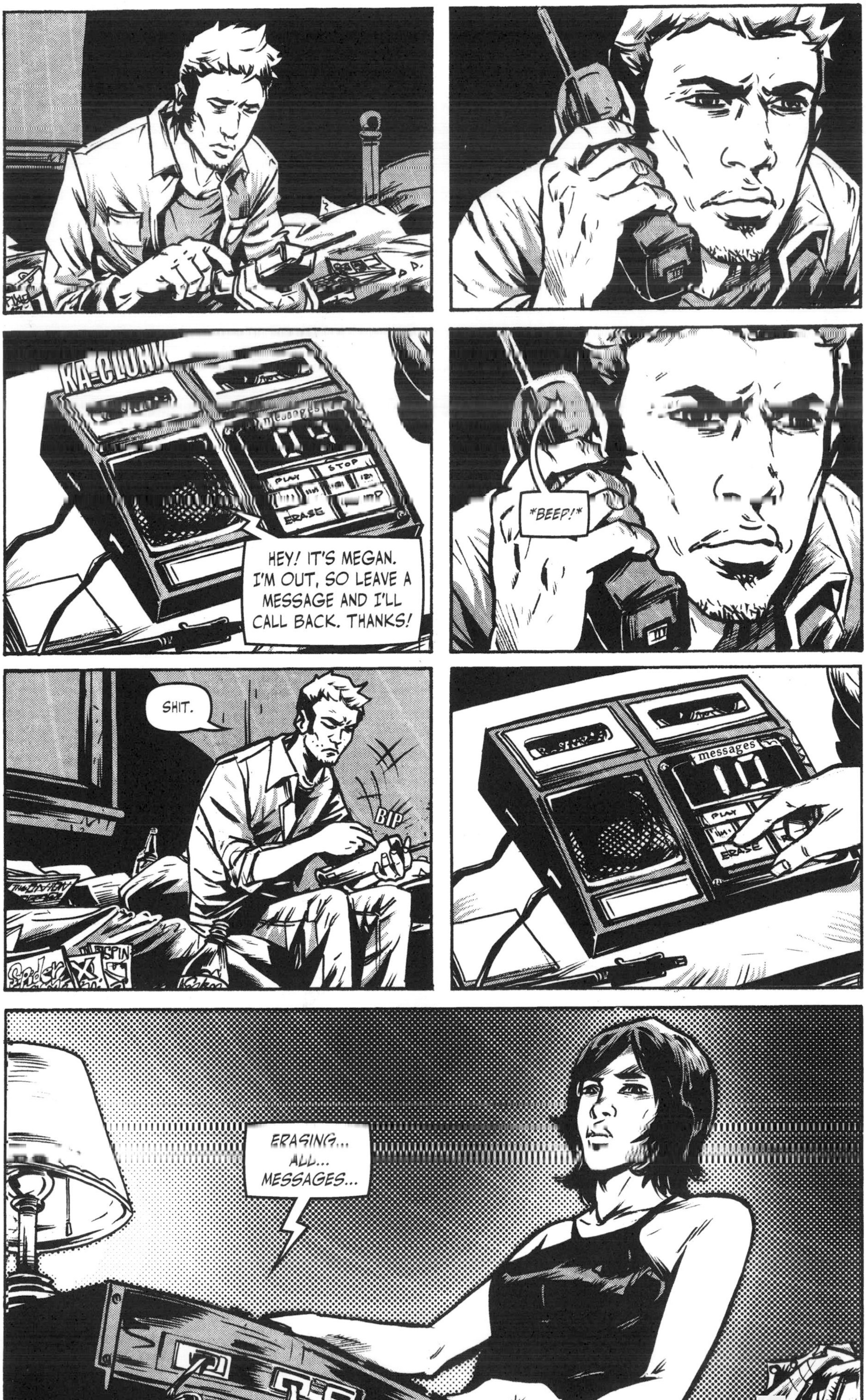
RA-CLUNK
HEY! IT'S MEGAN. I'M OUT, SO LEAVE A MESSAGE AND I'LL CALL BACK. THANKS!
BEEP!
SHIT.
BIP
messages
ERASING... ALL... MESSAGES...

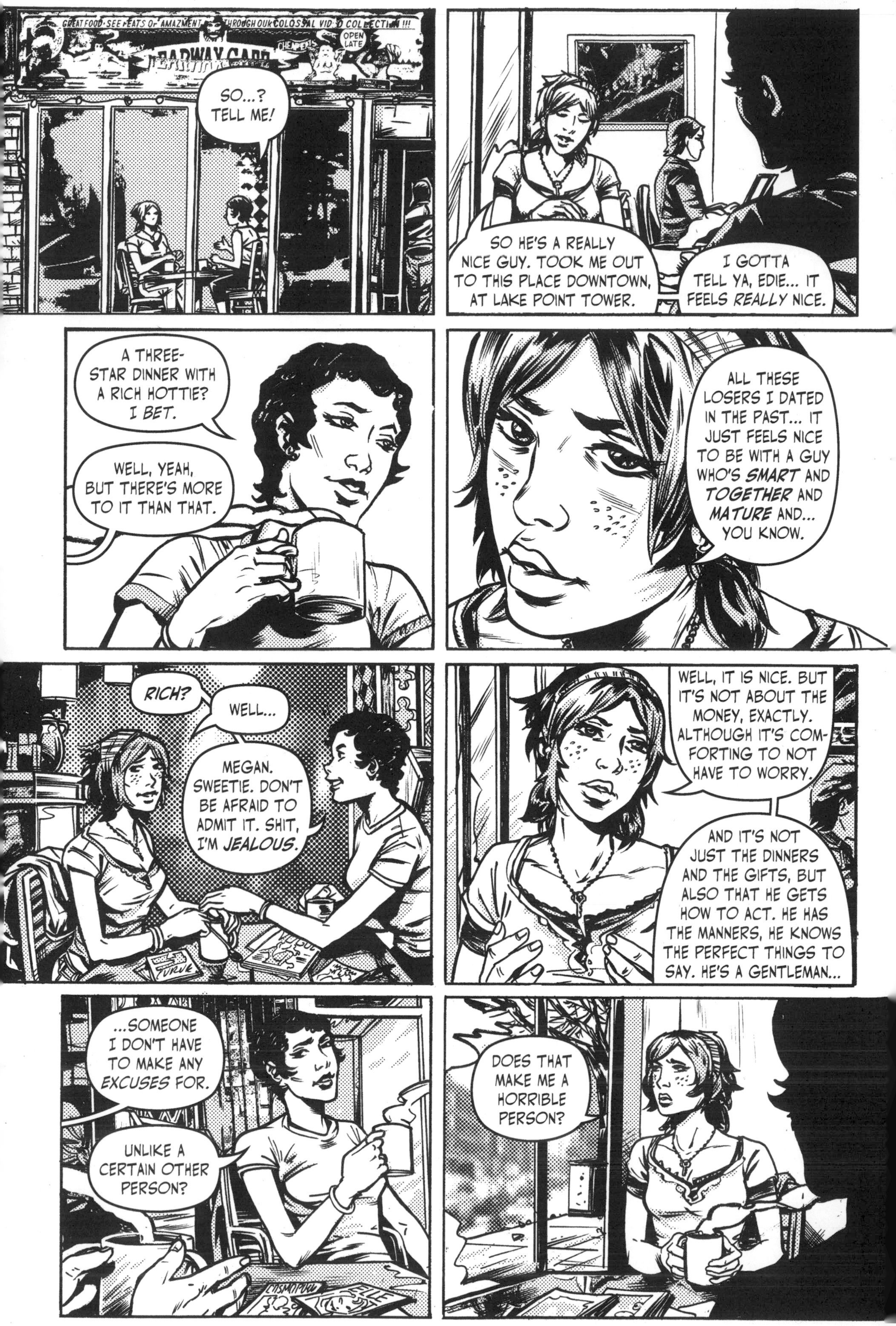
GREAT FOOD · SEE FEATS OF AMAZMENT THROUGH OUR COLOSSAL VIDEO COLLECTION !!!
OPEN LATE
SO...? TELL ME!
SO HE'S A REALLY NICE GUY. TOOK ME OUT TO THIS PLACE DOWNTOWN, AT LAKE POINT TOWER.
I GOTTA TELL YA, EDIE... IT FEELS *REALLY* NICE.
A THREE-STAR DINNER WITH A RICH HOTTIE? I *BET*.
WELL, YEAH, BUT THERE'S MORE TO IT THAN THAT.
ALL THESE LOSERS I DATED IN THE PAST... IT JUST FEELS NICE TO BE WITH A GUY WHO'S ***SMART*** AND ***TOGETHER*** AND ***MATURE*** AND... YOU KNOW.
RICH?
WELL...
MEGAN. SWEETIE. DON'T BE AFRAID TO ADMIT IT. SHIT, I'M ***JEALOUS***.
WELL, IT IS NICE. BUT IT'S NOT ABOUT THE MONEY, EXACTLY. ALTHOUGH IT'S COMFORTING TO NOT HAVE TO WORRY.
AND IT'S NOT JUST THE DINNERS AND THE GIFTS, BUT ALSO THAT HE GETS HOW TO ACT. HE HAS THE MANNERS, HE KNOWS THE PERFECT THINGS TO SAY. HE'S A GENTLEMAN...
...SOMEONE I DON'T HAVE TO MAKE ANY *EXCUSES* FOR.
UNLIKE A CERTAIN OTHER PERSON?
DOES THAT MAKE ME A HORRIBLE PERSON?

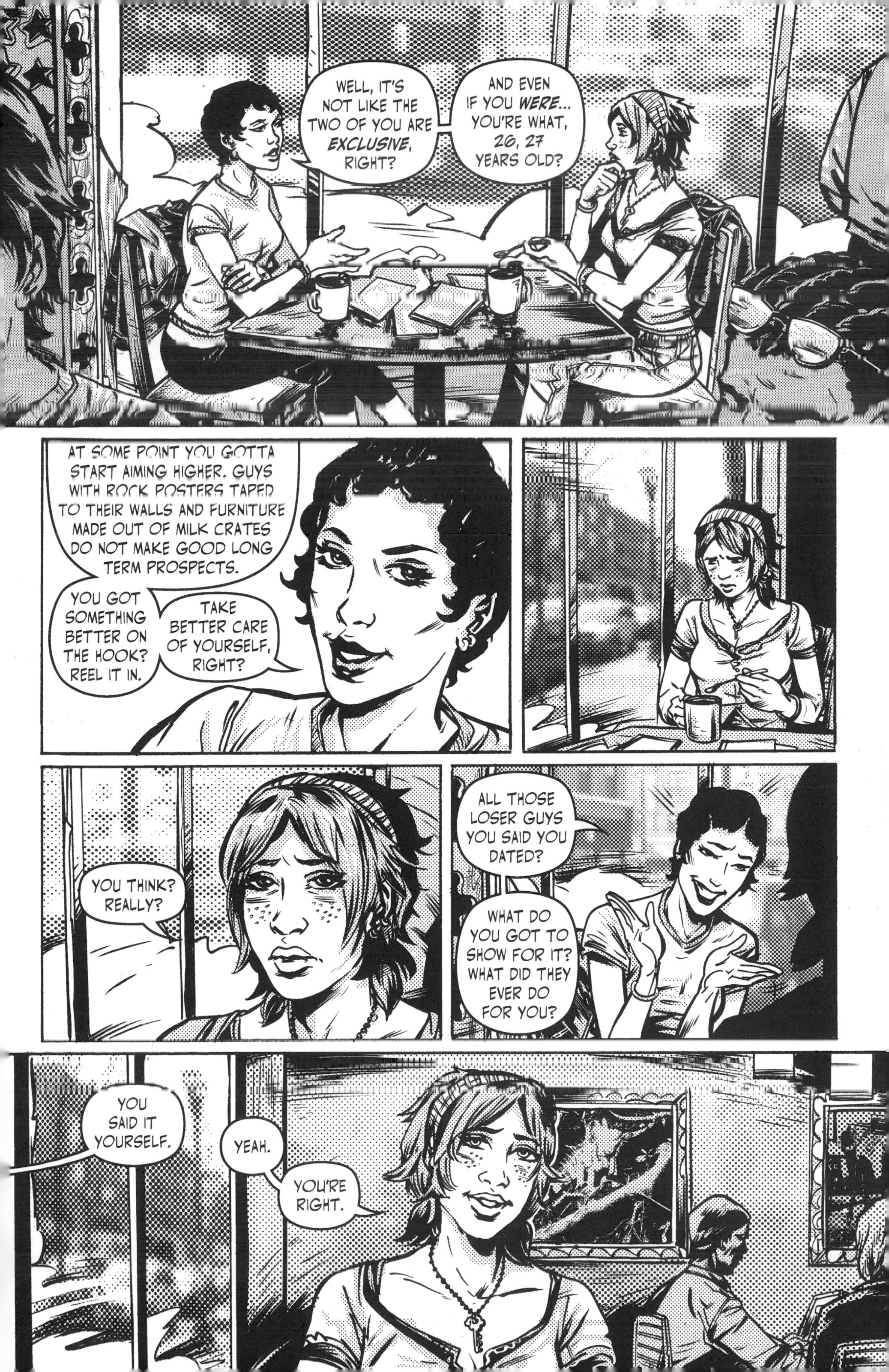
WELL, IT'S NOT LIKE THE TWO OF YOU ARE *EXCLUSIVE*, RIGHT?
AND EVEN IF YOU *WERE*... YOU'RE WHAT, 26, 27 YEARS OLD?
AT SOME POINT YOU GOTTA START AIMING HIGHER. GUYS WITH ROCK POSTERS TAPED TO THEIR WALLS AND FURNITURE MADE OUT OF MILK CRATES DO NOT MAKE GOOD LONG TERM PROSPECTS.
YOU GOT SOMETHING BETTER ON THE HOOK? REEL IT IN.
TAKE BETTER CARE OF YOURSELF, RIGHT?
YOU THINK? REALLY?
ALL THOSE LOSER GUYS YOU SAID YOU DATED?
WHAT DO YOU GOT TO SHOW FOR IT? WHAT DID THEY EVER DO FOR YOU?
YOU SAID IT YOURSELF.
YEAH.
YOU'RE RIGHT.

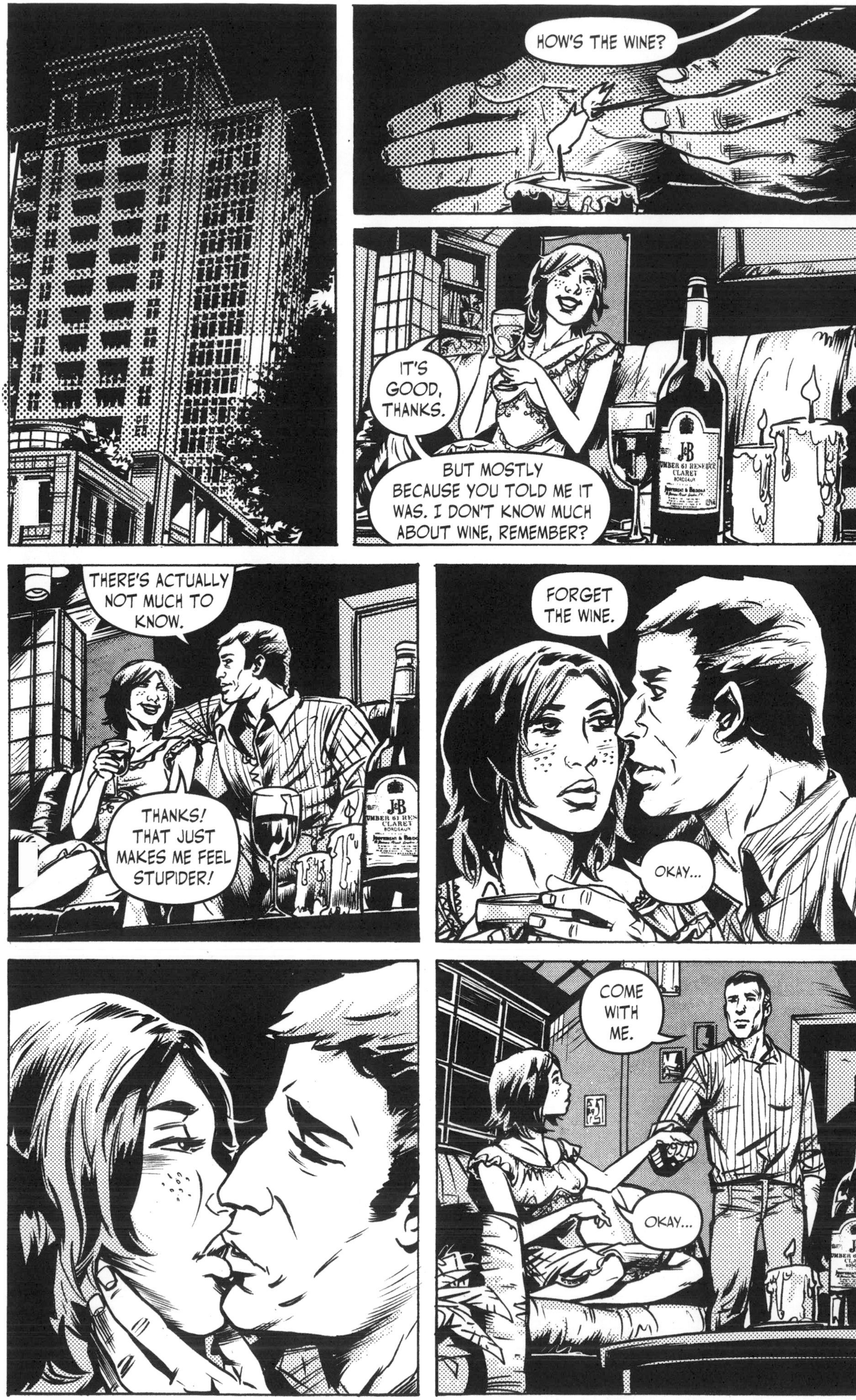

HOW'S THE WINE?
IT'S GOOD, THANKS.
BUT MOSTLY BECAUSE YOU TOLD ME IT WAS. I DON'T KNOW MUCH ABOUT WINE, REMEMBER?
THERE'S ACTUALLY NOT MUCH TO KNOW.
THANKS! THAT JUST MAKES ME FEEL STUPIDER!
FORGET THE WINE.
OKAY...
COME WITH ME.
OKAY...

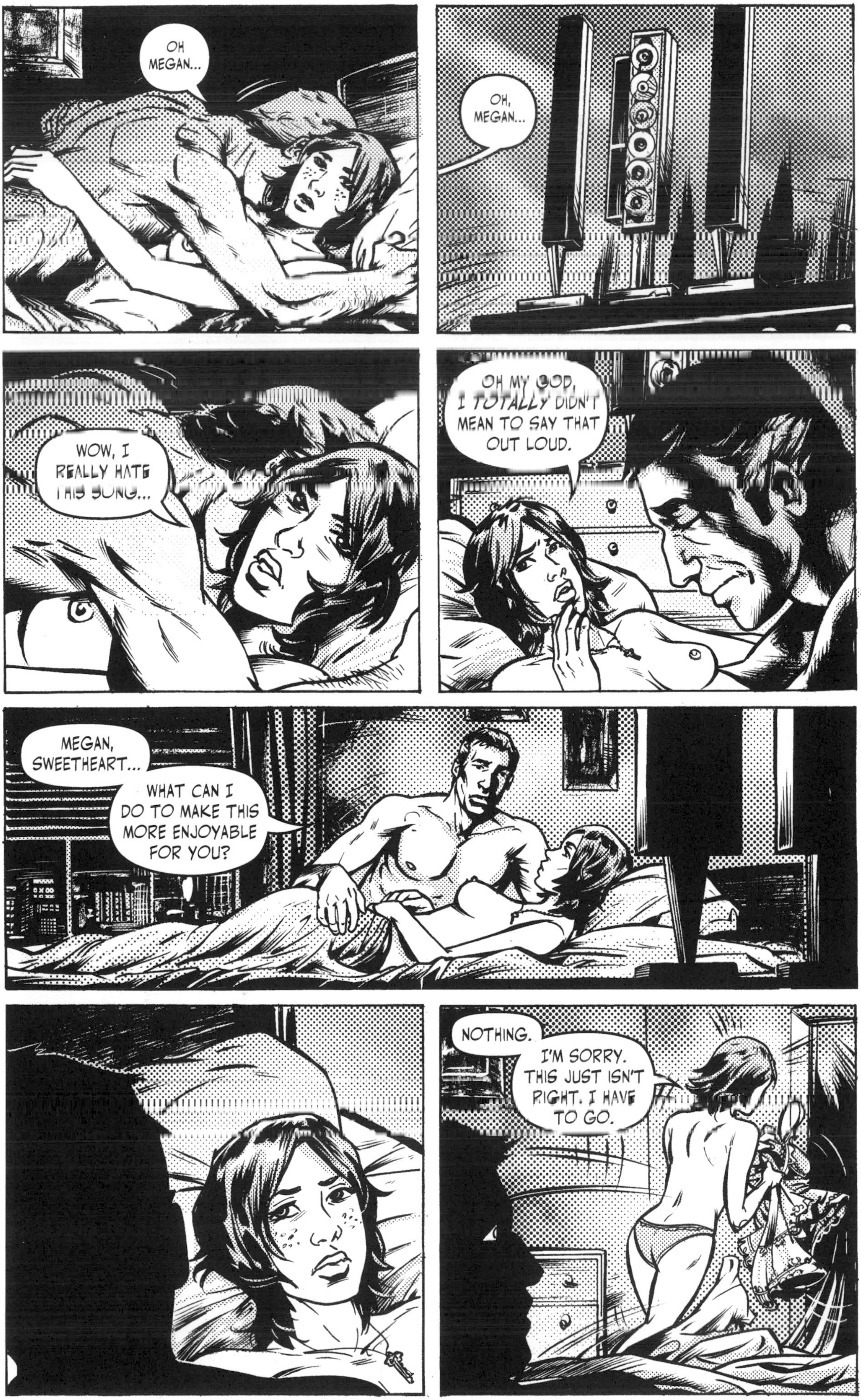
OH MEGAN...
OH, MEGAN...
WOW, I REALLY HATE THIS SONG...
OH MY GOD, I TOTALLY DIDN'T MEAN TO SAY THAT OUT LOUD.
MEGAN, SWEETHEART...
WHAT CAN I DO TO MAKE THIS MORE ENJOYABLE FOR YOU?
NOTHING.
I'M SORRY. THIS JUST ISN'T RIGHT. I HAVE TO GO.

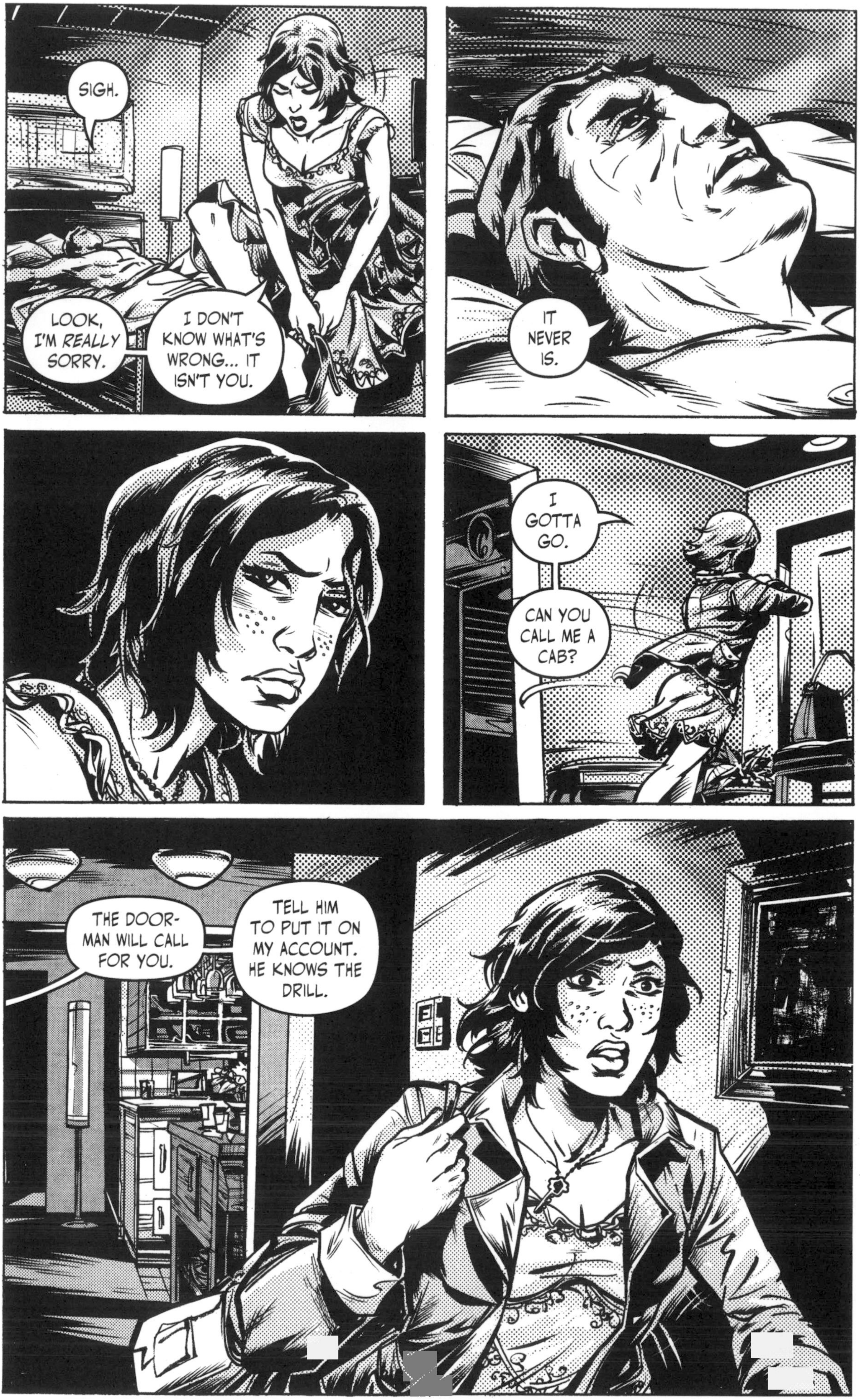
SIGH.
LOOK, I'M *REALLY* SORRY.
I DON'T KNOW WHAT'S WRONG... IT ISN'T YOU.
IT NEVER IS.
I GOTTA GO.
CAN YOU CALL ME A CAB?
THE DOOR-MAN WILL CALL FOR YOU.
TELL HIM TO PUT IT ON MY ACCOUNT. HE KNOWS THE DRILL.

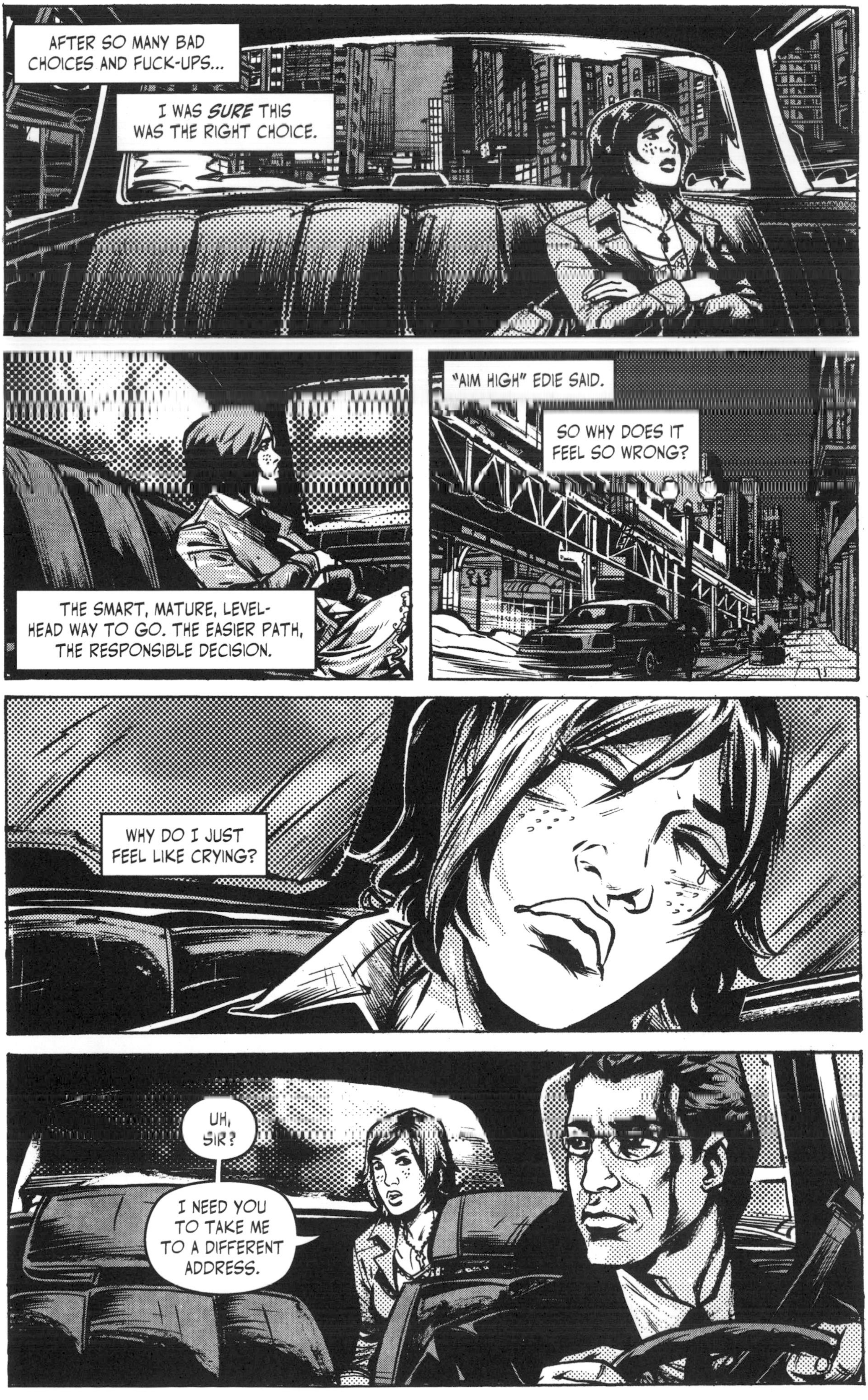
AFTER SO MANY BAD CHOICES AND FUCK-UPS...
I WAS *SURE* THIS WAS THE RIGHT CHOICE.
THE SMART, MATURE, LEVEL-HEAD WAY TO GO. THE EASIER PATH, THE RESPONSIBLE DECISION.
"AIM HIGH" EDIE SAID.
SO WHY DOES IT FEEL SO WRONG?
WHY DO I JUST FEEL LIKE CRYING?
UH, SIR?
I NEED YOU TO TAKE ME TO A DIFFERENT ADDRESS.

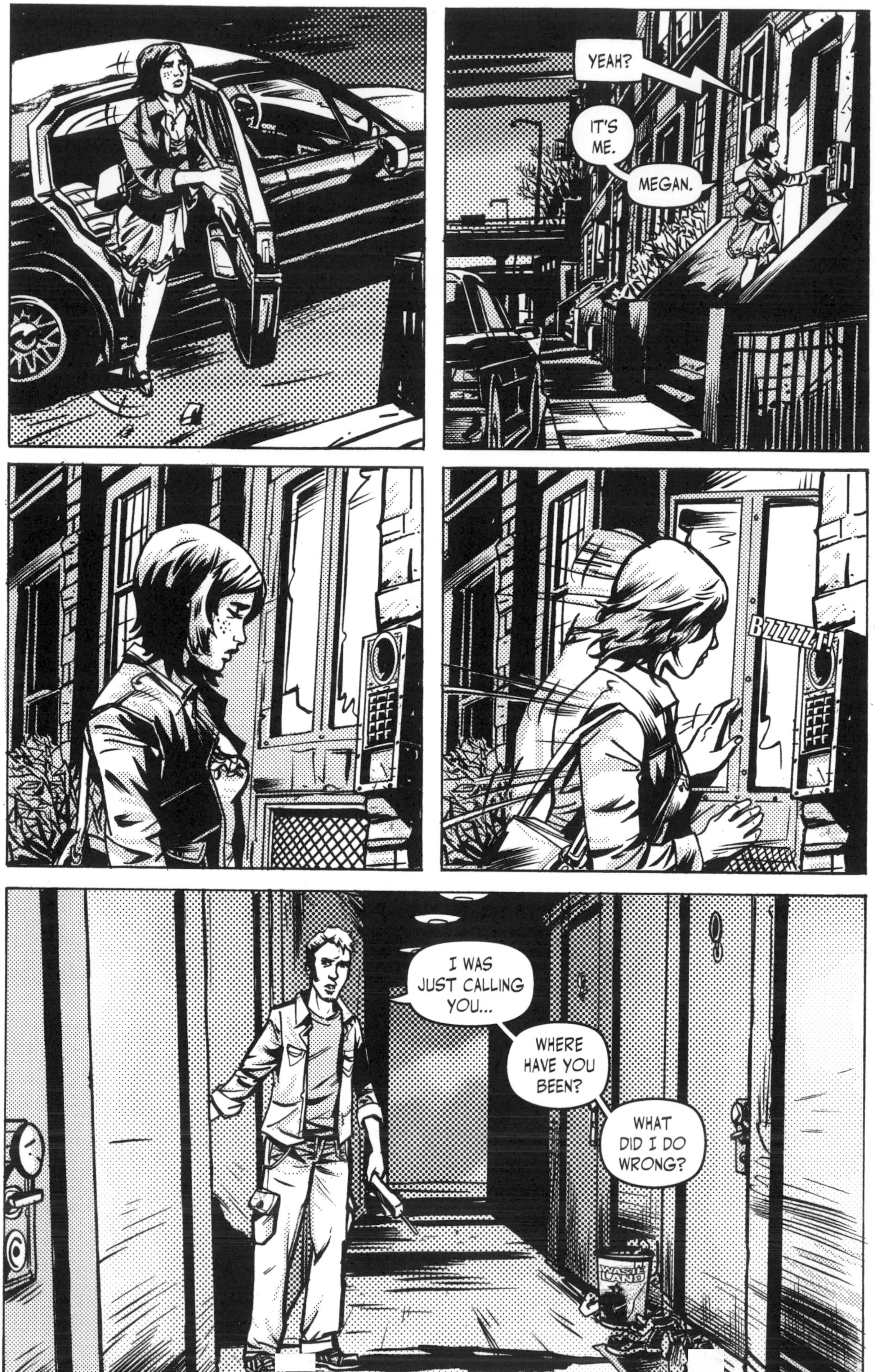
YEAH?
IT'S ME.
MEGAN.
BZZZZZT!
I WAS JUST CALLING YOU...
WHERE HAVE YOU BEEN?
WHAT DID I DO WRONG?

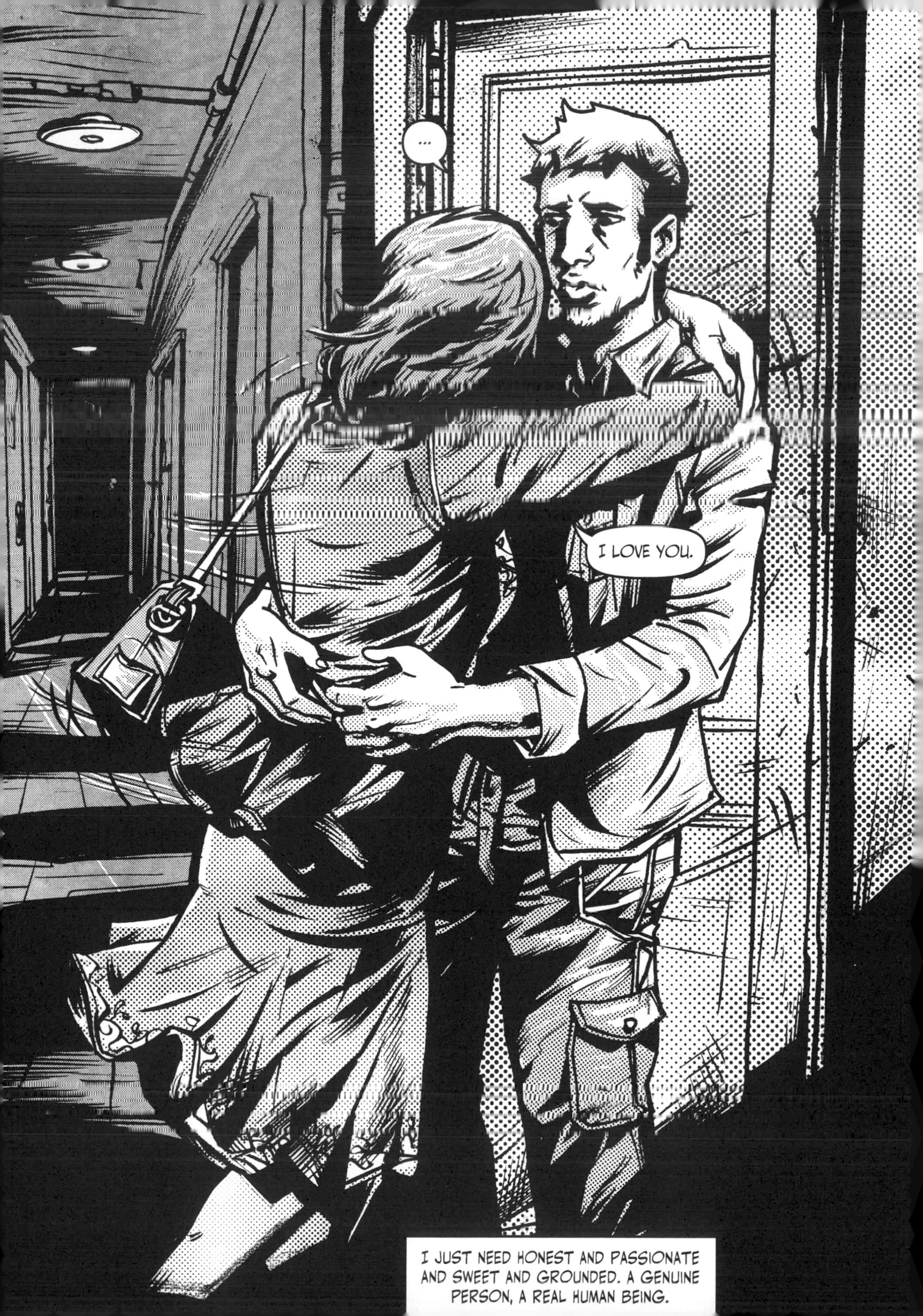
...
I LOVE YOU.
I JUST NEED HONEST AND PASSIONATE AND SWEET AND GROUNDED. A GENUINE PERSON, A REAL HUMAN BEING.

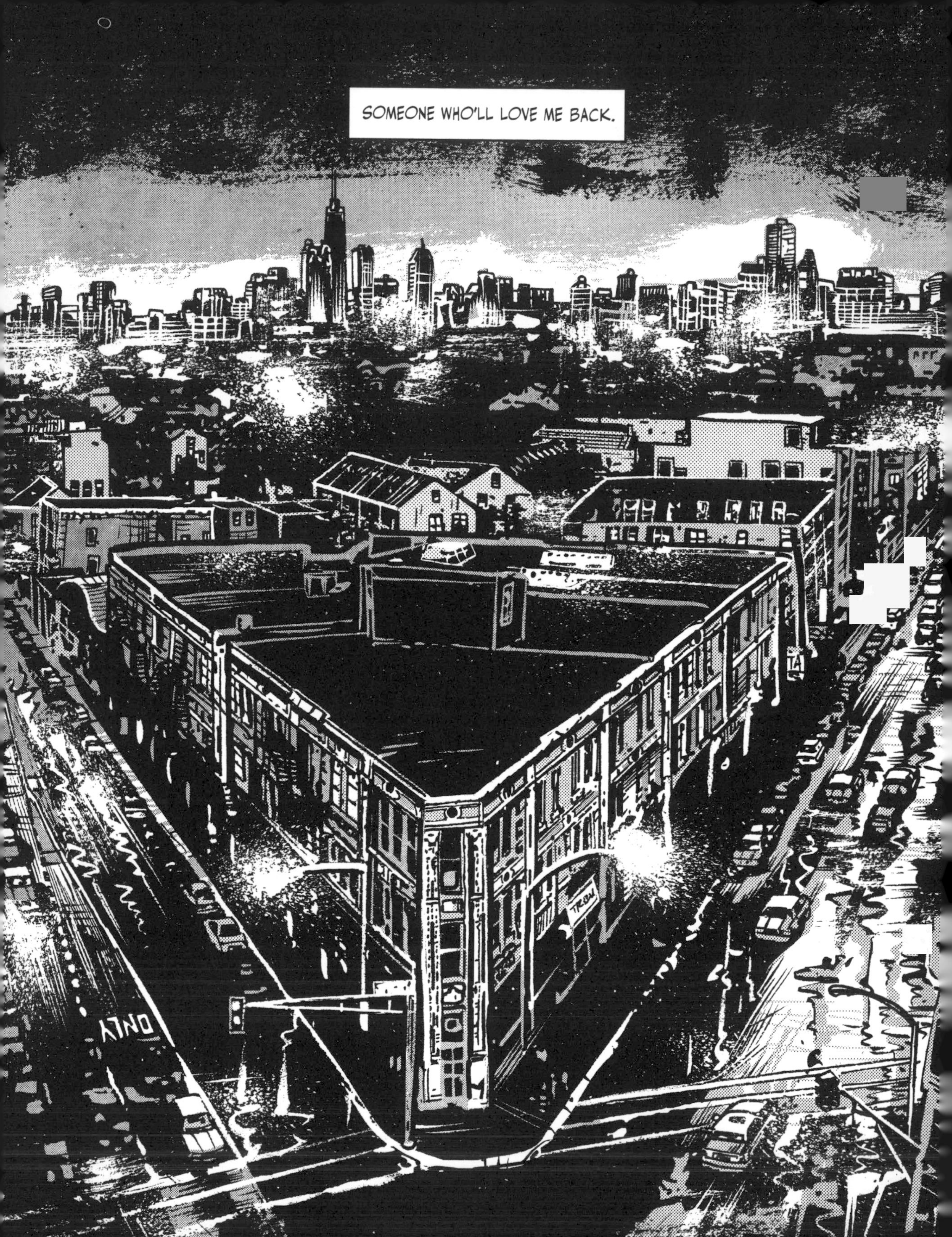
SOMEONE WHO'LL LOVE ME BACK.

LOCAL #8

"food as substitute"

STORY: BRIAN WOOD / ART: RYAN KELLY

LETTERED BY DOUGLAS E. SHERWOOD

CHAPTER 9
"WISH YOU WERE HERE"
Norman, Oklahoma

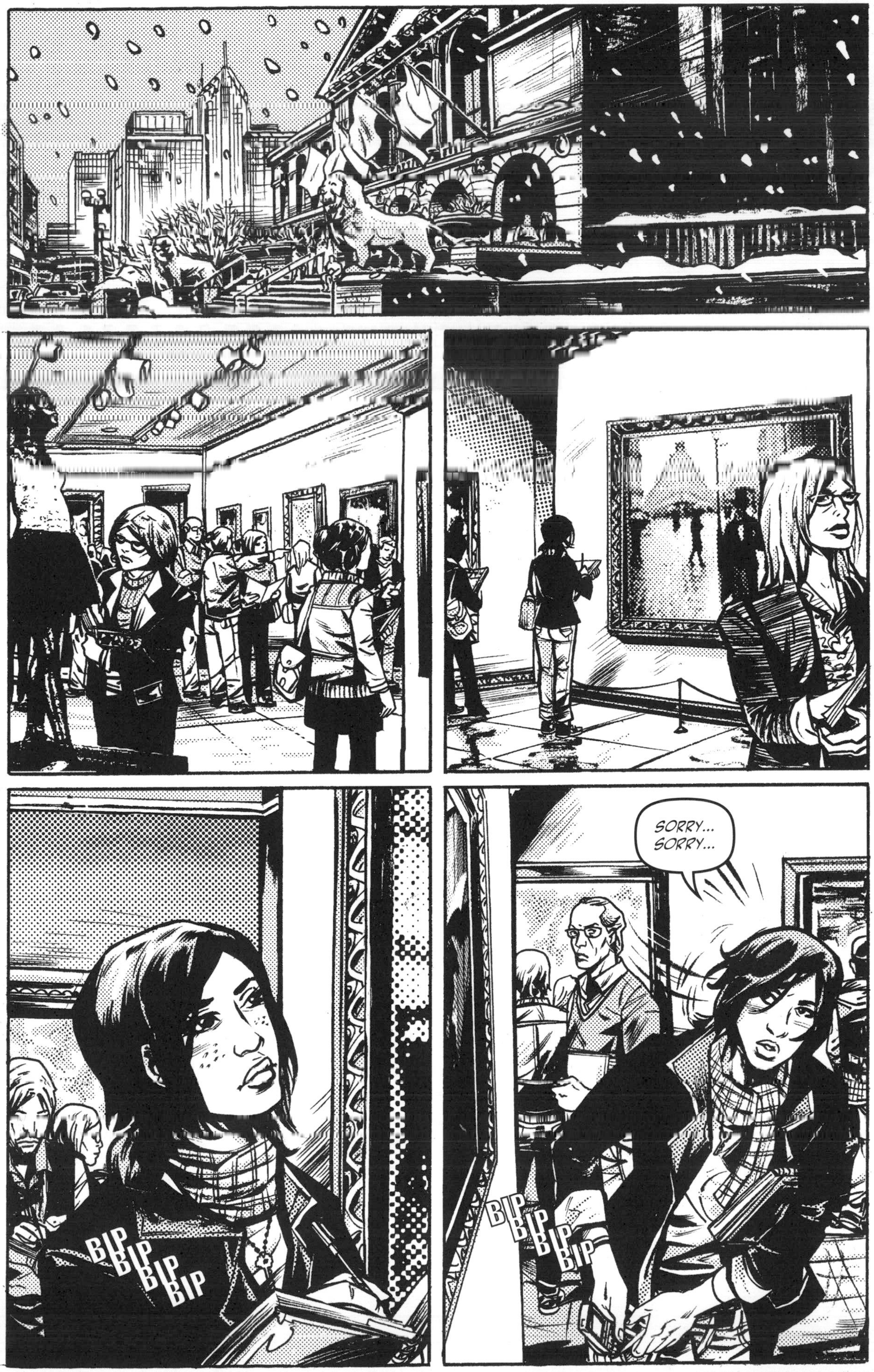
BIP BIP BIP BIP
SORRY... SORRY...
BIP BIP BIP BIP

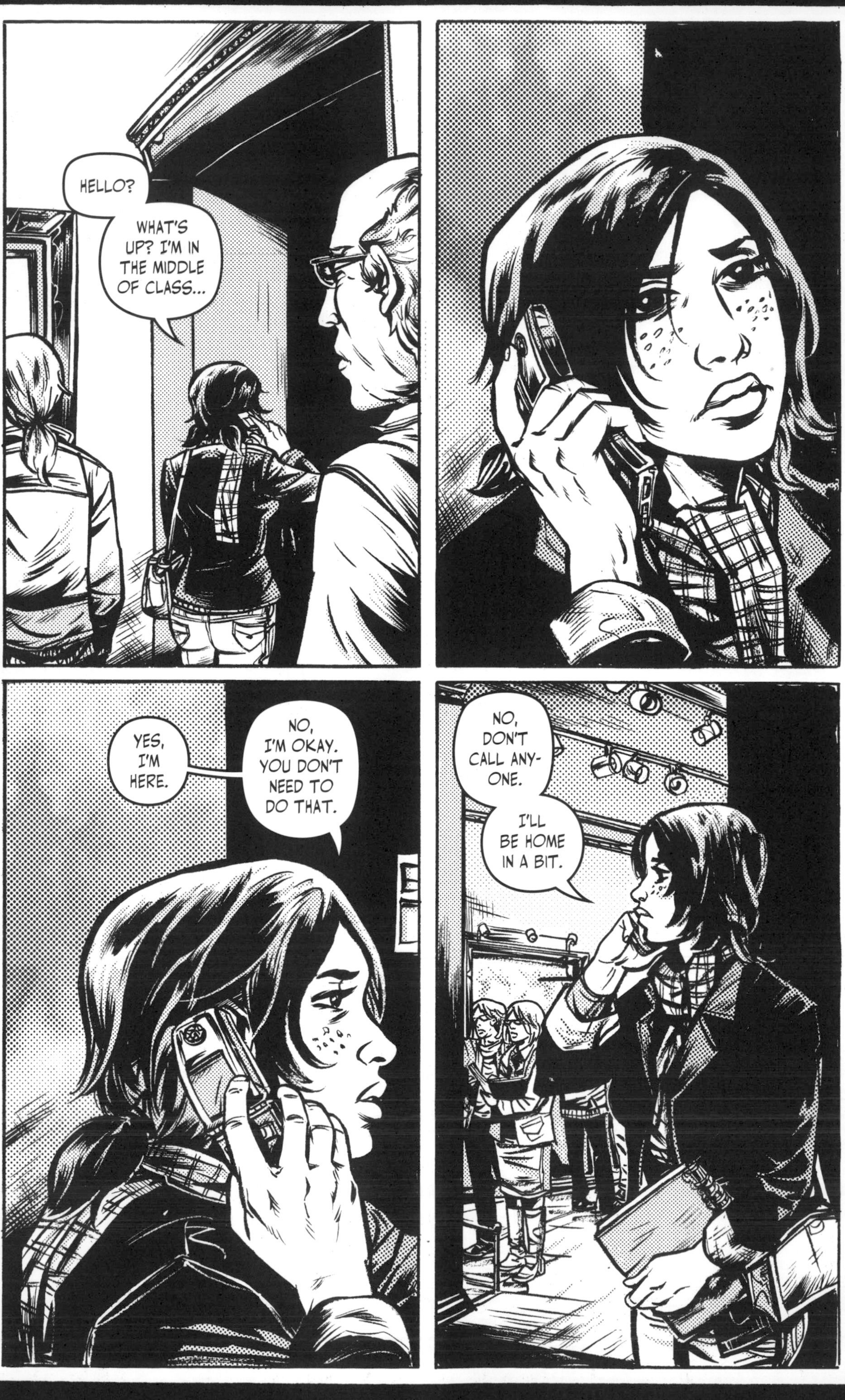
HELLO?
WHAT'S UP? I'M IN THE MIDDLE OF CLASS...
YES, I'M HERE.
NO, I'M OKAY. YOU DON'T NEED TO DO THAT.
NO, DON'T CALL ANY-ONE.
I'LL BE HOME IN A BIT.

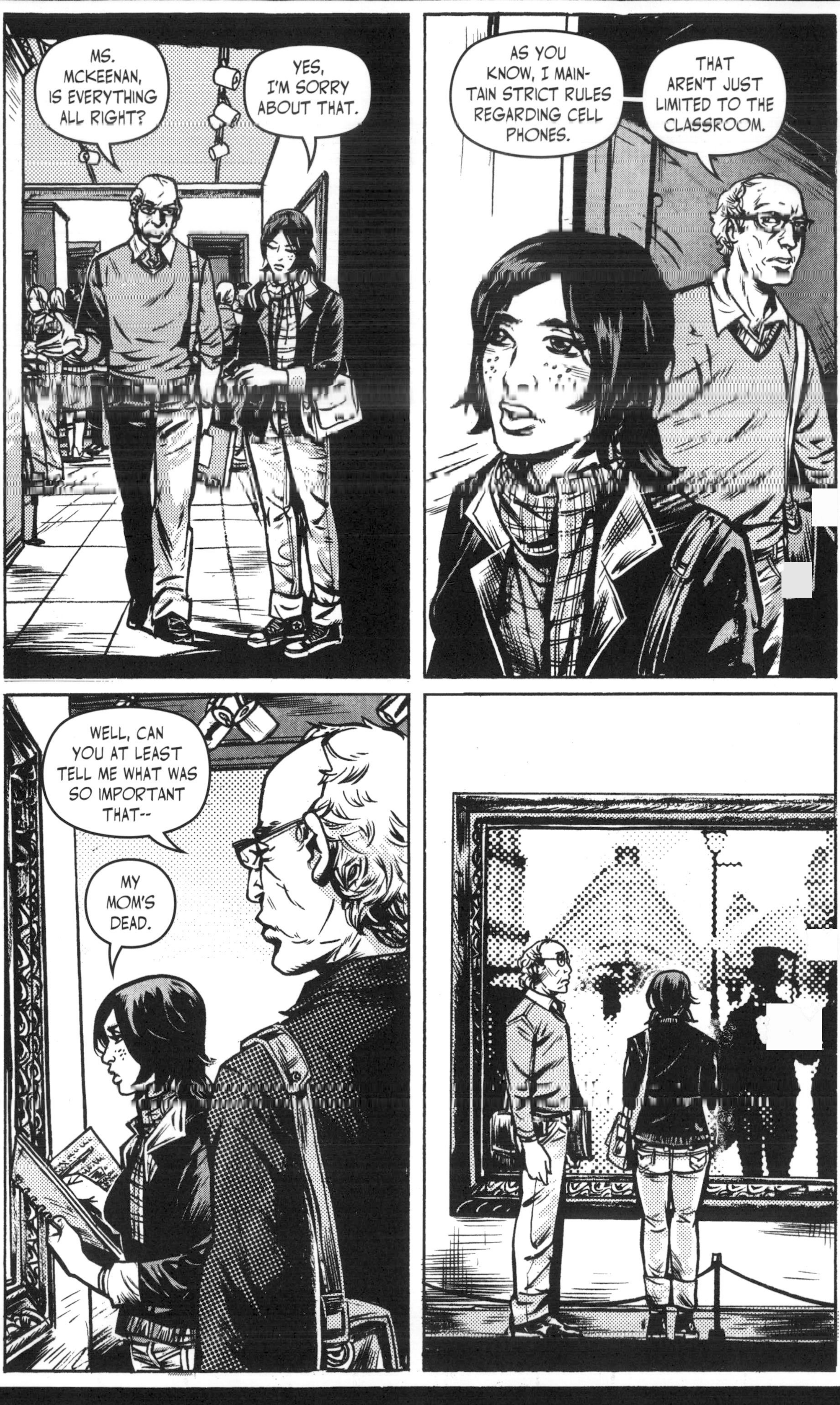
MS. MCKEENAN, IS EVERYTHING ALL RIGHT?
YES, I'M SORRY ABOUT THAT.
AS YOU KNOW, I MAIN-TAIN STRICT RULES REGARDING CELL PHONES.
THAT AREN'T JUST LIMITED TO THE CLASSROOM.
WELL, CAN YOU AT LEAST TELL ME WHAT WAS SO IMPORTANT THAT--
MY MOM'S DEAD.

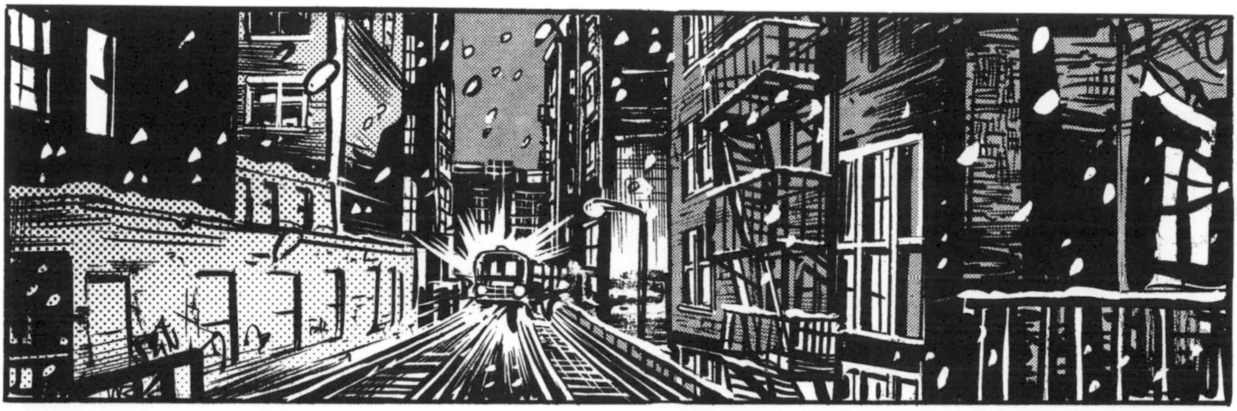

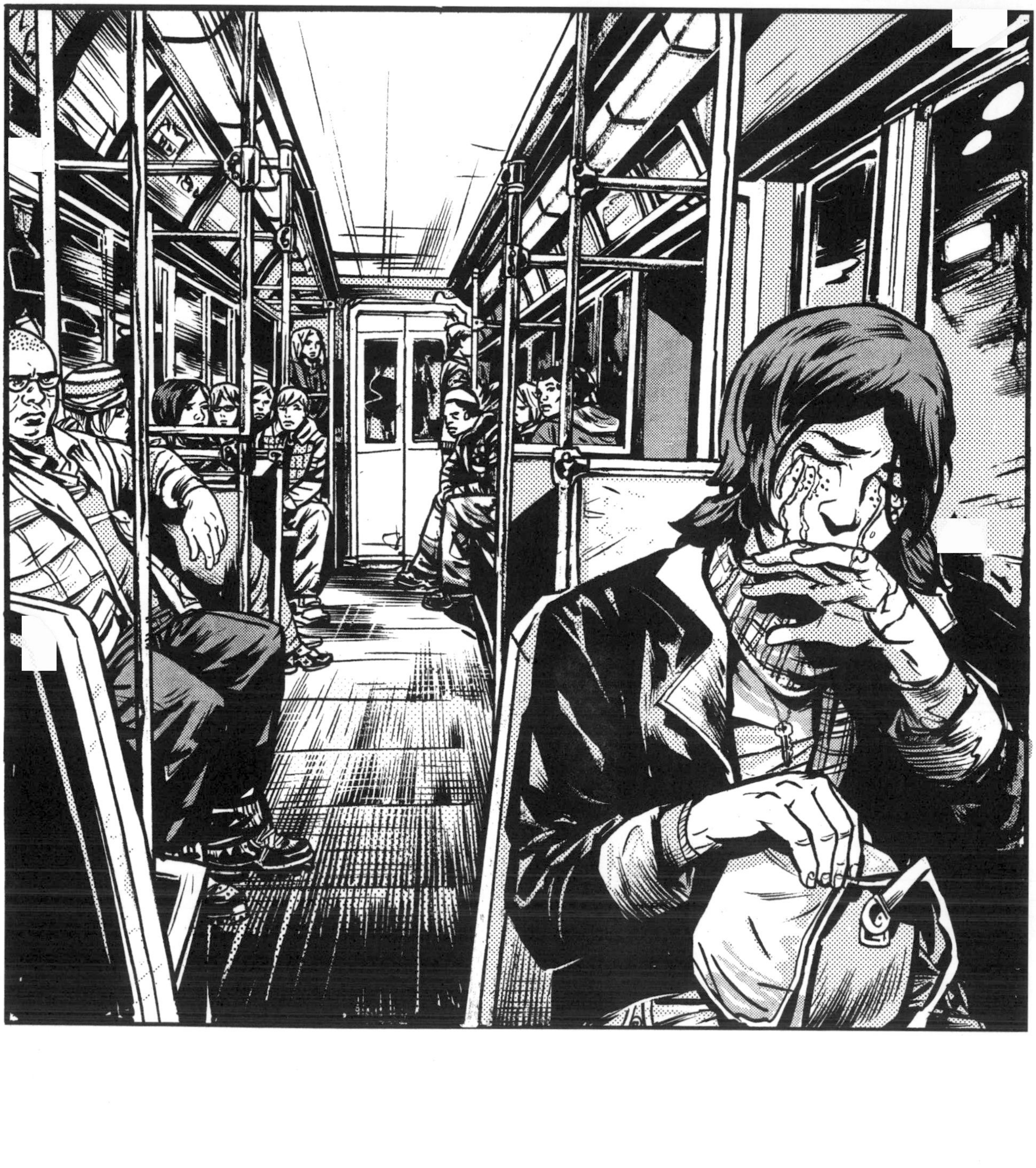

LOCAL #9

"wish you were here"

STORY: BRIAN WOOD / ART: RYAN KELLY
LETTERED BY DOUGLAS E. SHERWOOD

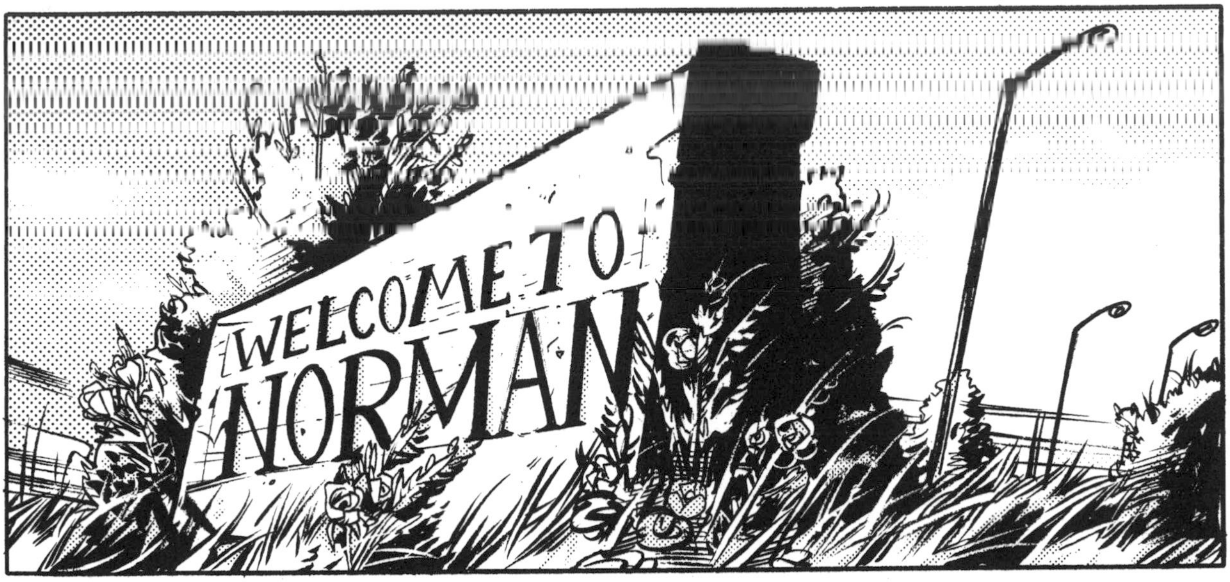
WELCOME TO NORMAN

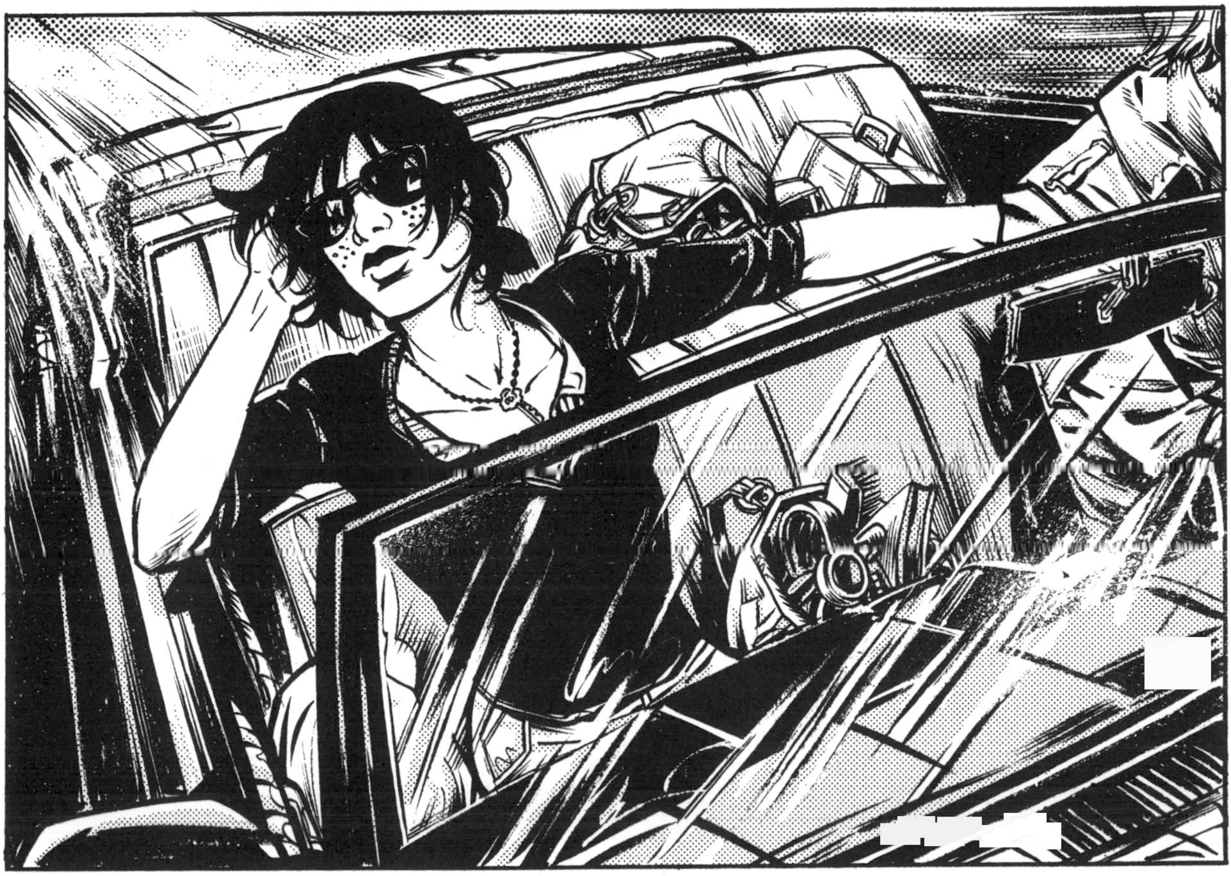

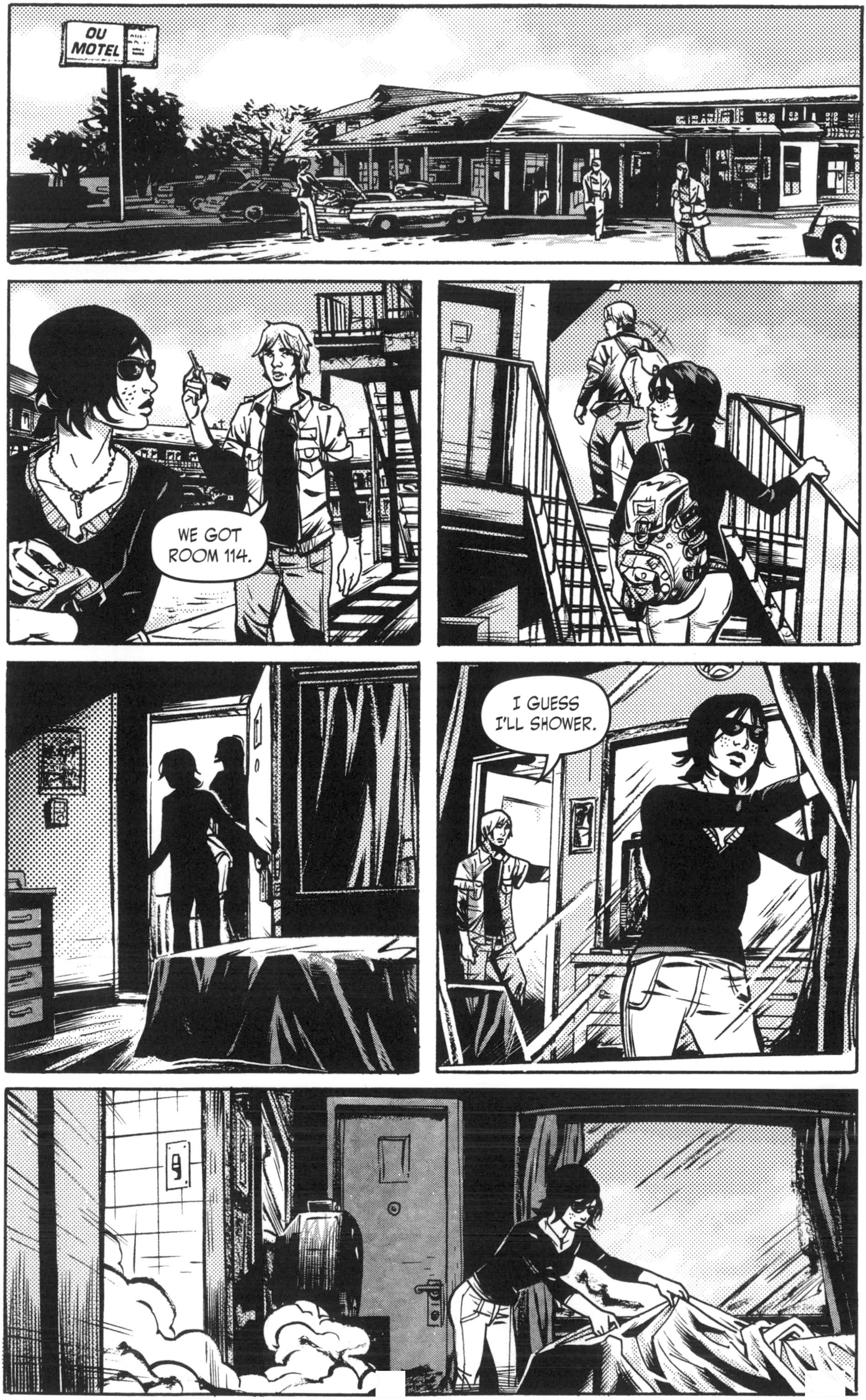

OU MOTEL
WE GOT ROOM 114.
I GUESS I'LL SHOWER.

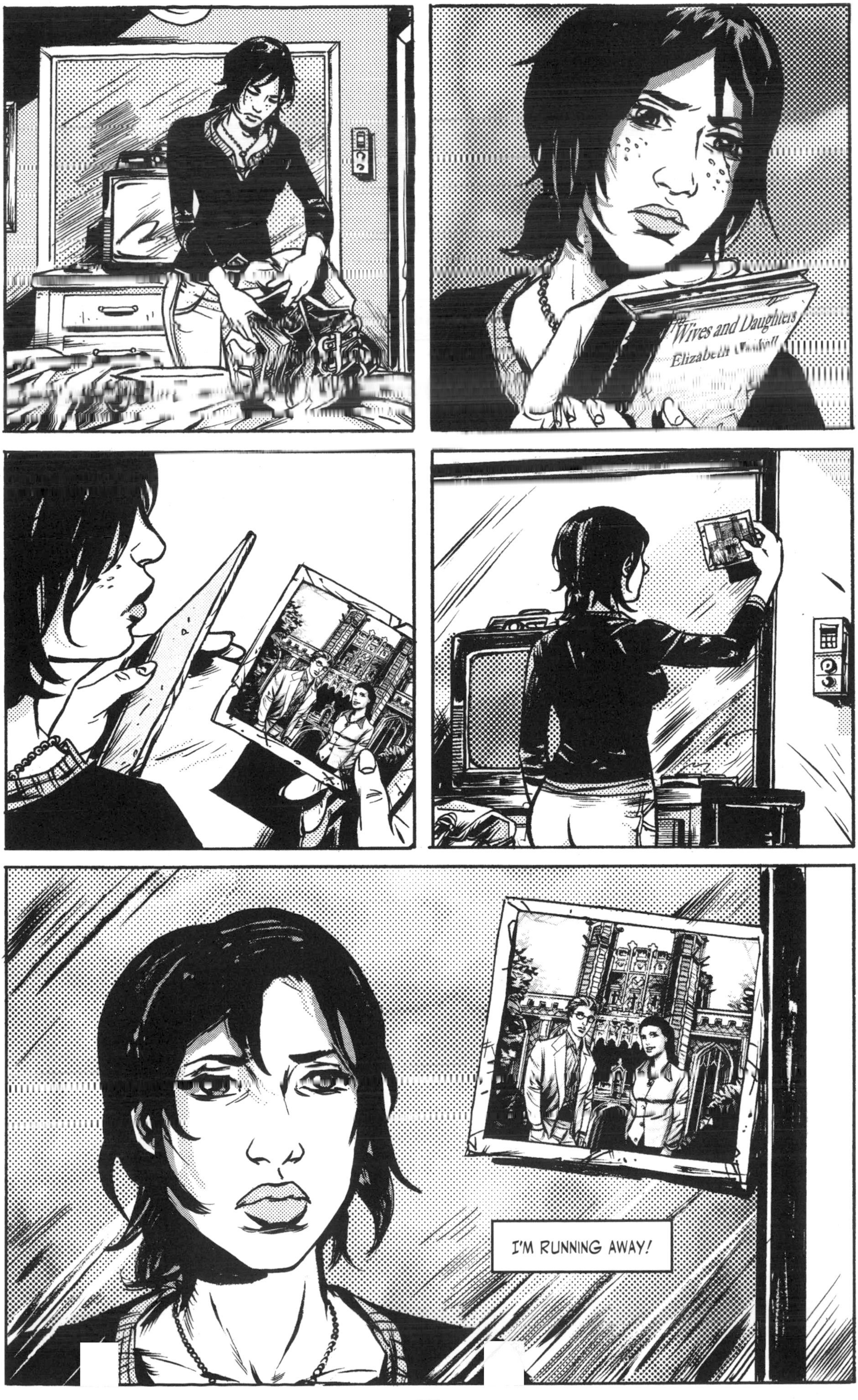
Wives and Daughters
Elizabeth
I'M RUNNING AWAY!

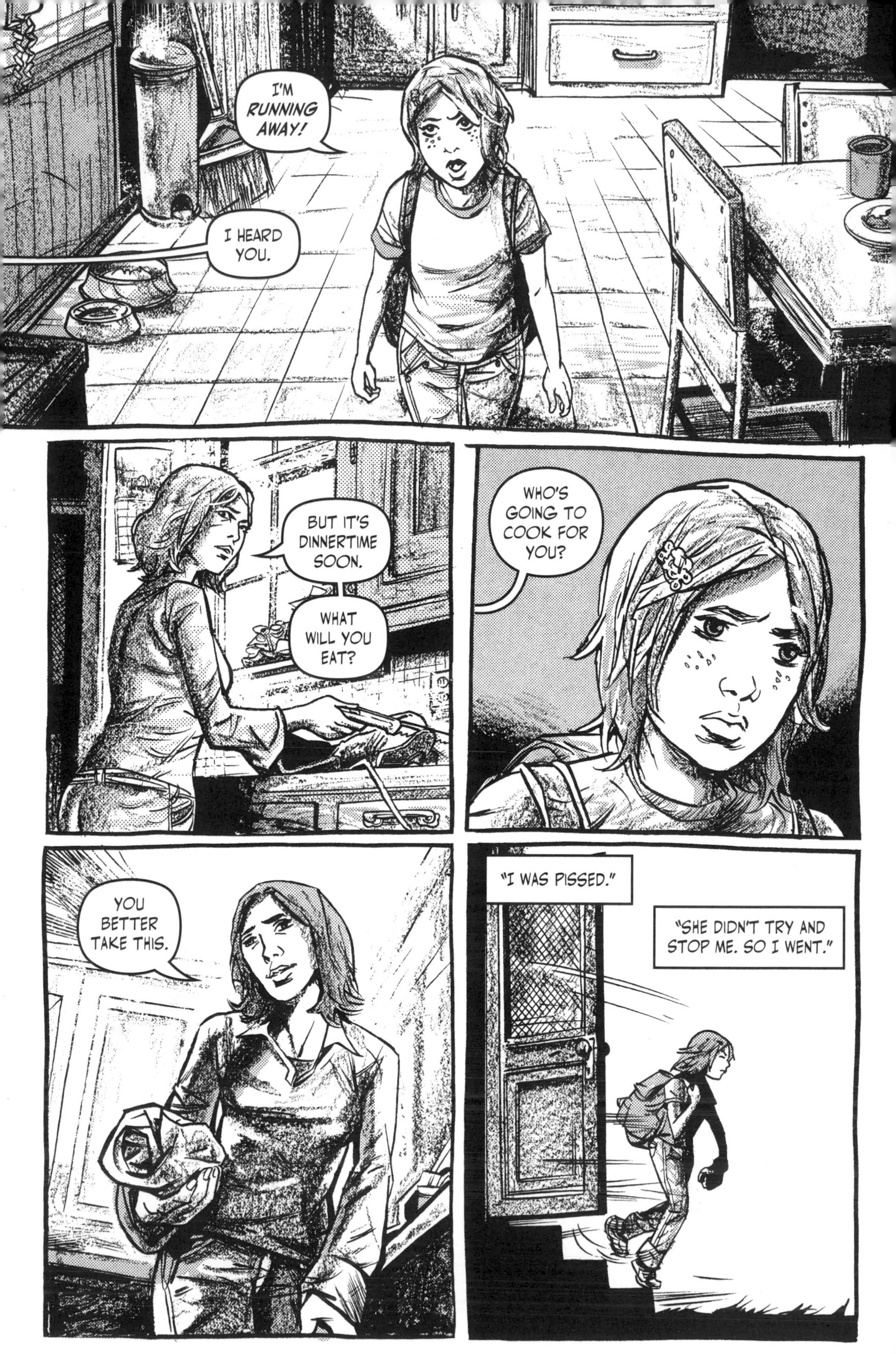
I'M RUNNING AWAY!
I HEARD YOU.
BUT IT'S DINNERTIME SOON.
WHAT WILL YOU EAT?
WHO'S GOING TO COOK FOR YOU?
YOU BETTER TAKE THIS.
"I WAS PISSED."
"SHE DIDN'T TRY AND STOP ME. SO I WENT."

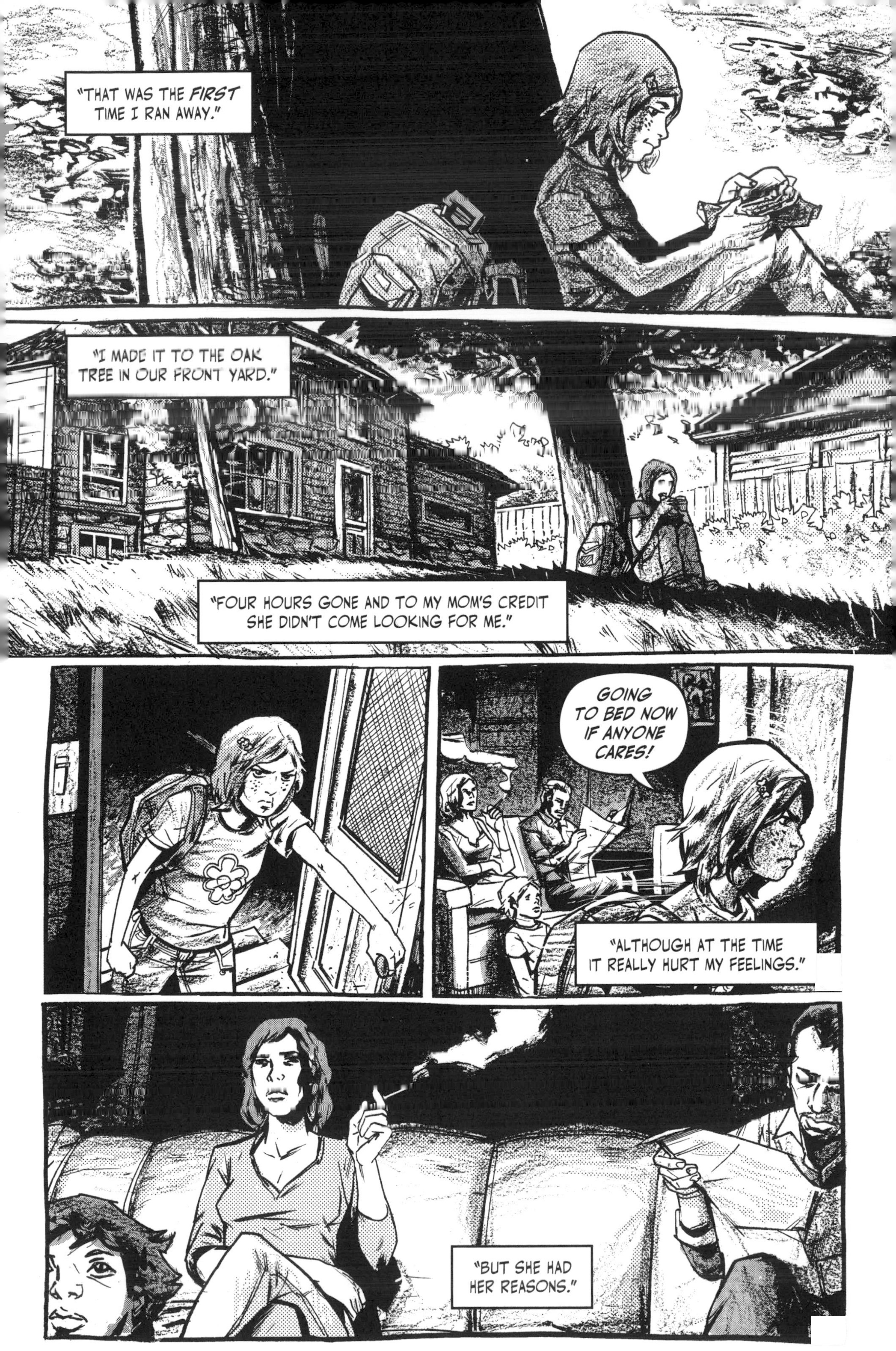
"THAT WAS THE FIRST TIME I RAN AWAY."
"I MADE IT TO THE OAK TREE IN OUR FRONT YARD."
"FOUR HOURS GONE AND TO MY MOM'S CREDIT SHE DIDN'T COME LOOKING FOR ME."
GOING TO BED NOW IF ANYONE CARES!
"ALTHOUGH AT THE TIME IT REALLY HURT MY FEELINGS."
"BUT SHE HAD HER REASONS."

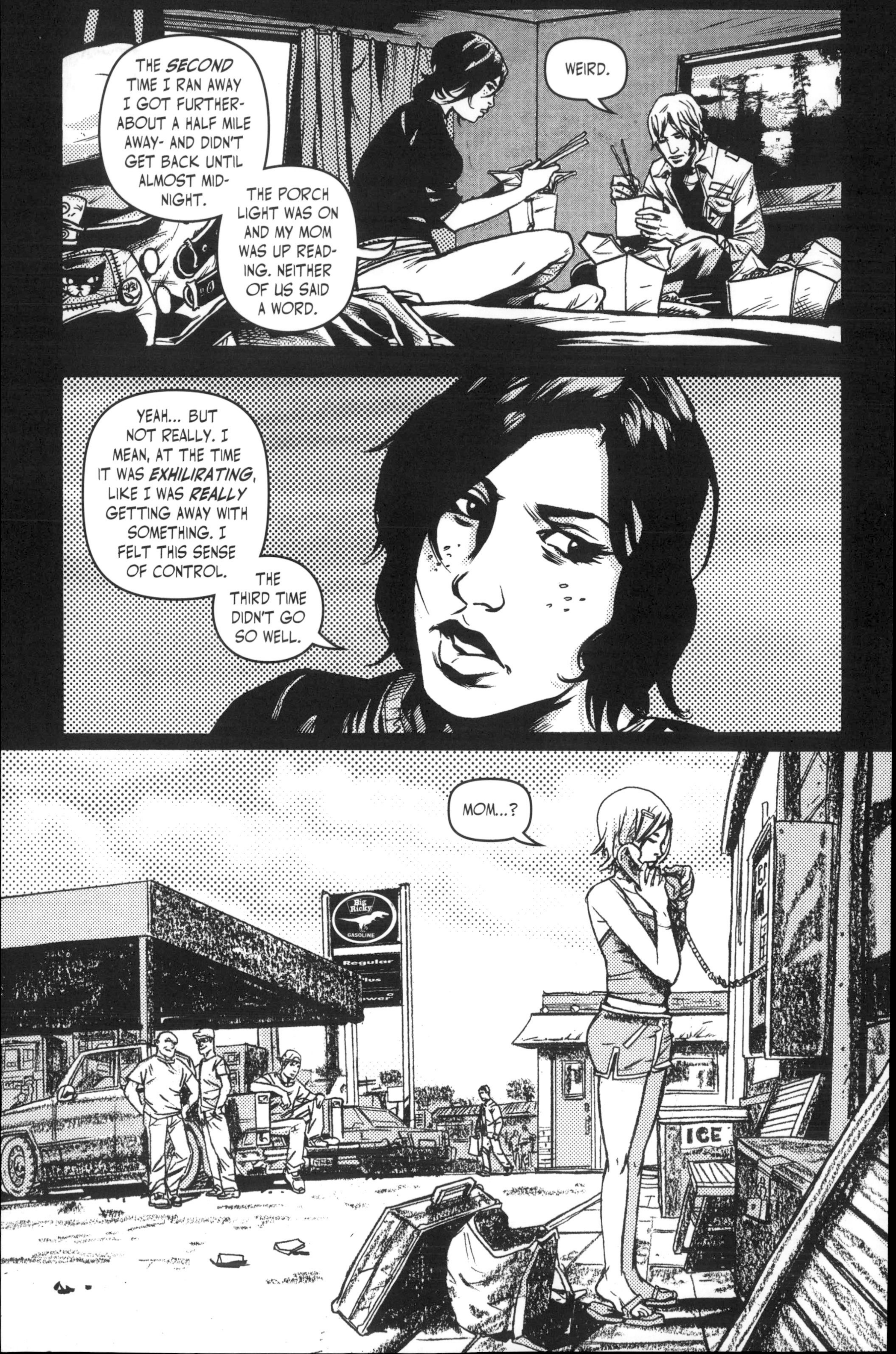
THE *SECOND* TIME I RAN AWAY I GOT FURTHER- ABOUT A HALF MILE AWAY- AND DIDN'T GET BACK UNTIL ALMOST MID-NIGHT.
THE PORCH LIGHT WAS ON AND MY MOM WAS UP READ-ING. NEITHER OF US SAID A WORD.
WEIRD.
YEAH... BUT NOT REALLY. I MEAN, AT THE TIME IT WAS *EXHILIRATING*, LIKE I WAS *REALLY* GETTING AWAY WITH SOMETHING. I FELT THIS SENSE OF CONTROL.
THE THIRD TIME DIDN'T GO SO WELL.
MOM...?
Big Ricky
GASOLINE
Regular
ICE

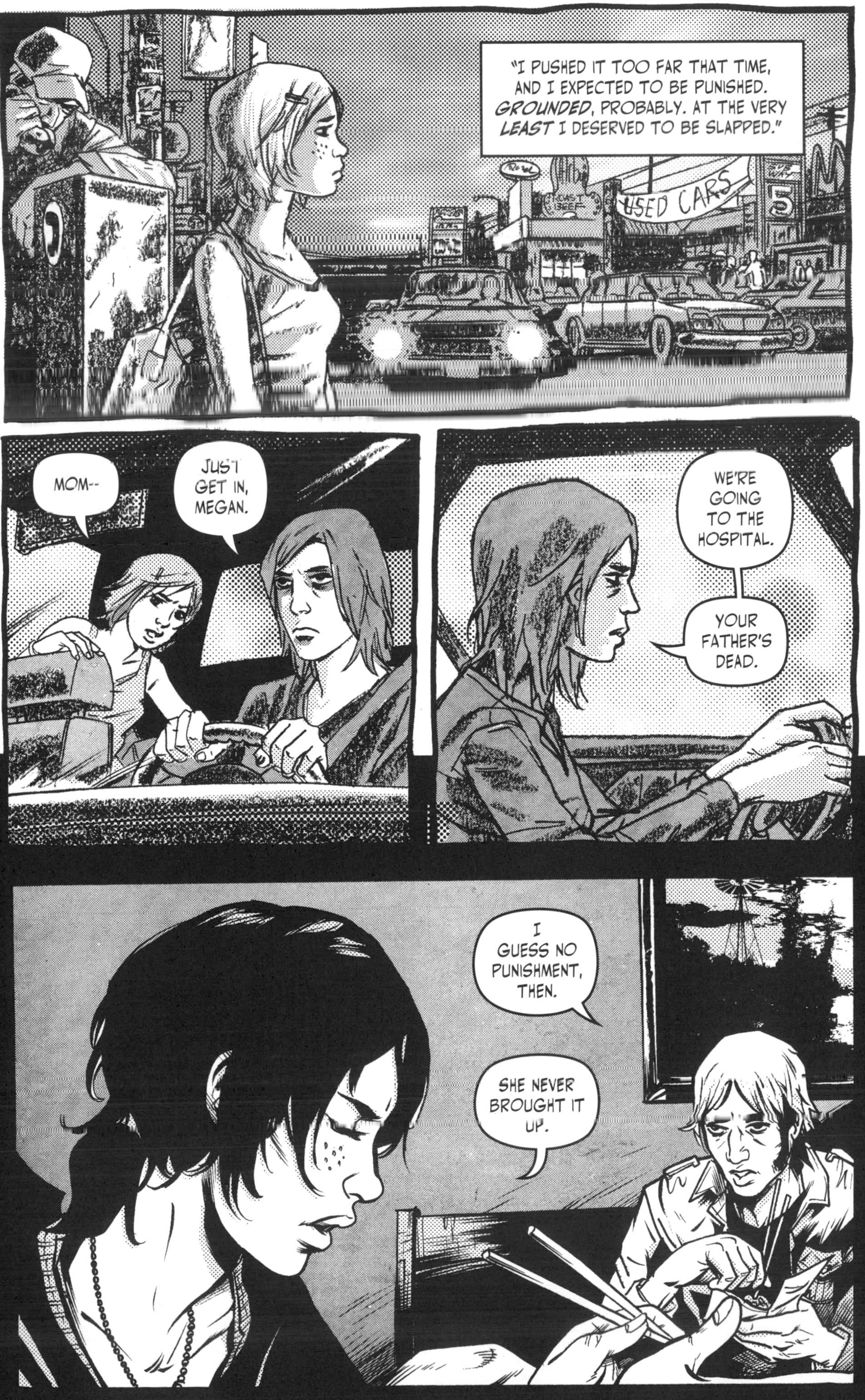
"I PUSHED IT TOO FAR THAT TIME, AND I EXPECTED TO BE PUNISHED. GROUNDED, PROBABLY. AT THE VERY LEAST I DESERVED TO BE SLAPPED."
USED CARS
MOM--
JUST GET IN, MEGAN.
WE'RE GOING TO THE HOSPITAL.
YOUR FATHER'S DEAD.
I GUESS NO PUNISHMENT, THEN.
SHE NEVER BROUGHT IT UP.

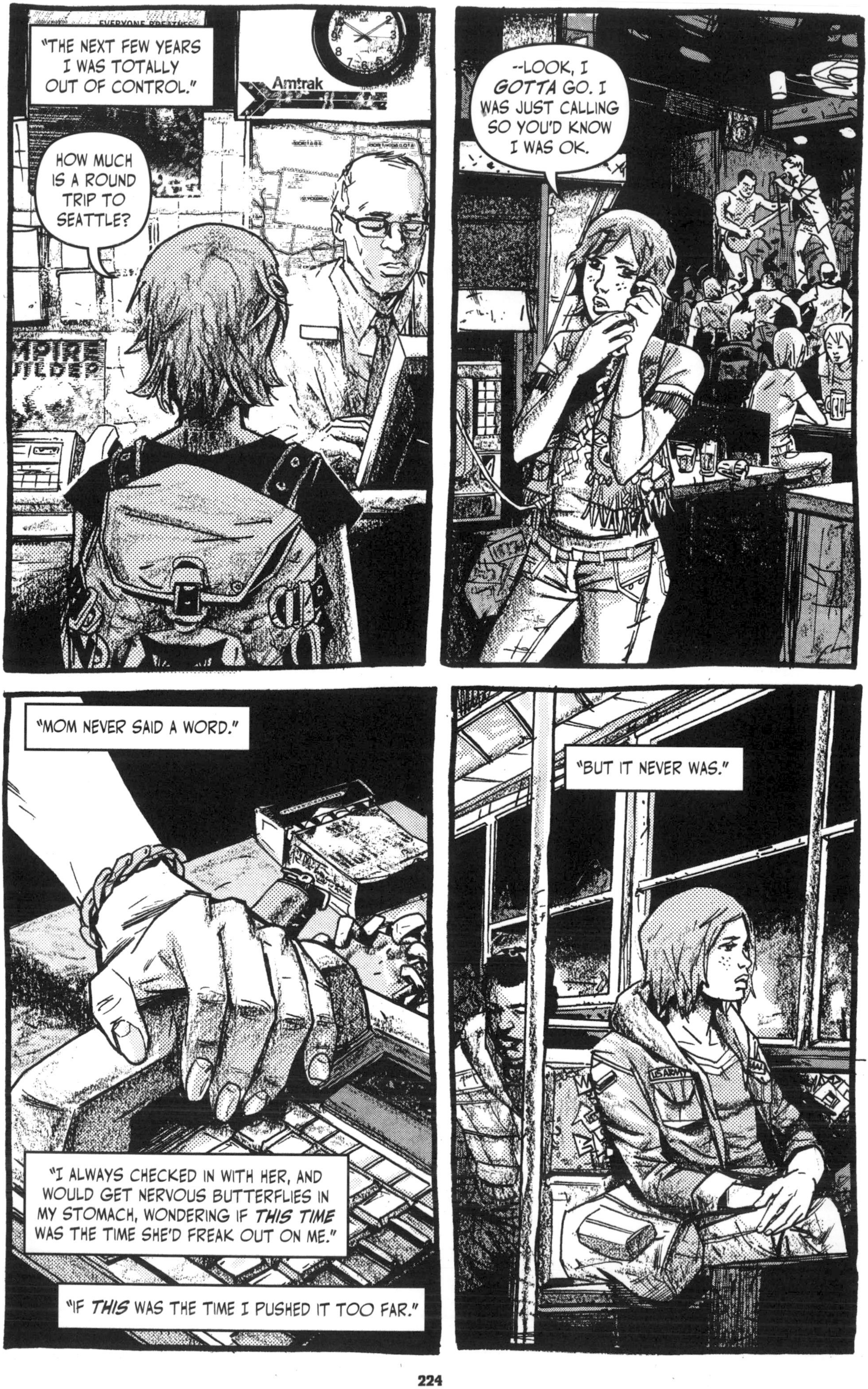
EVERYONE BREATHES
"THE NEXT FEW YEARS I WAS TOTALLY OUT OF CONTROL."
Amtrak
HOW MUCH IS A ROUND TRIP TO SEATTLE?
EMPIRE BUILDER
--LOOK, I *GOTTA* GO. I WAS JUST CALLING SO YOU'D KNOW I WAS OK.
"MOM NEVER SAID A WORD."
"I ALWAYS CHECKED IN WITH HER, AND WOULD GET NERVOUS BUTTERFLIES IN MY STOMACH, WONDERING IF *THIS TIME* WAS THE TIME SHE'D FREAK OUT ON ME."
"IF *THIS* WAS THE TIME I PUSHED IT TOO FAR."
"BUT IT NEVER WAS."
US ARMY

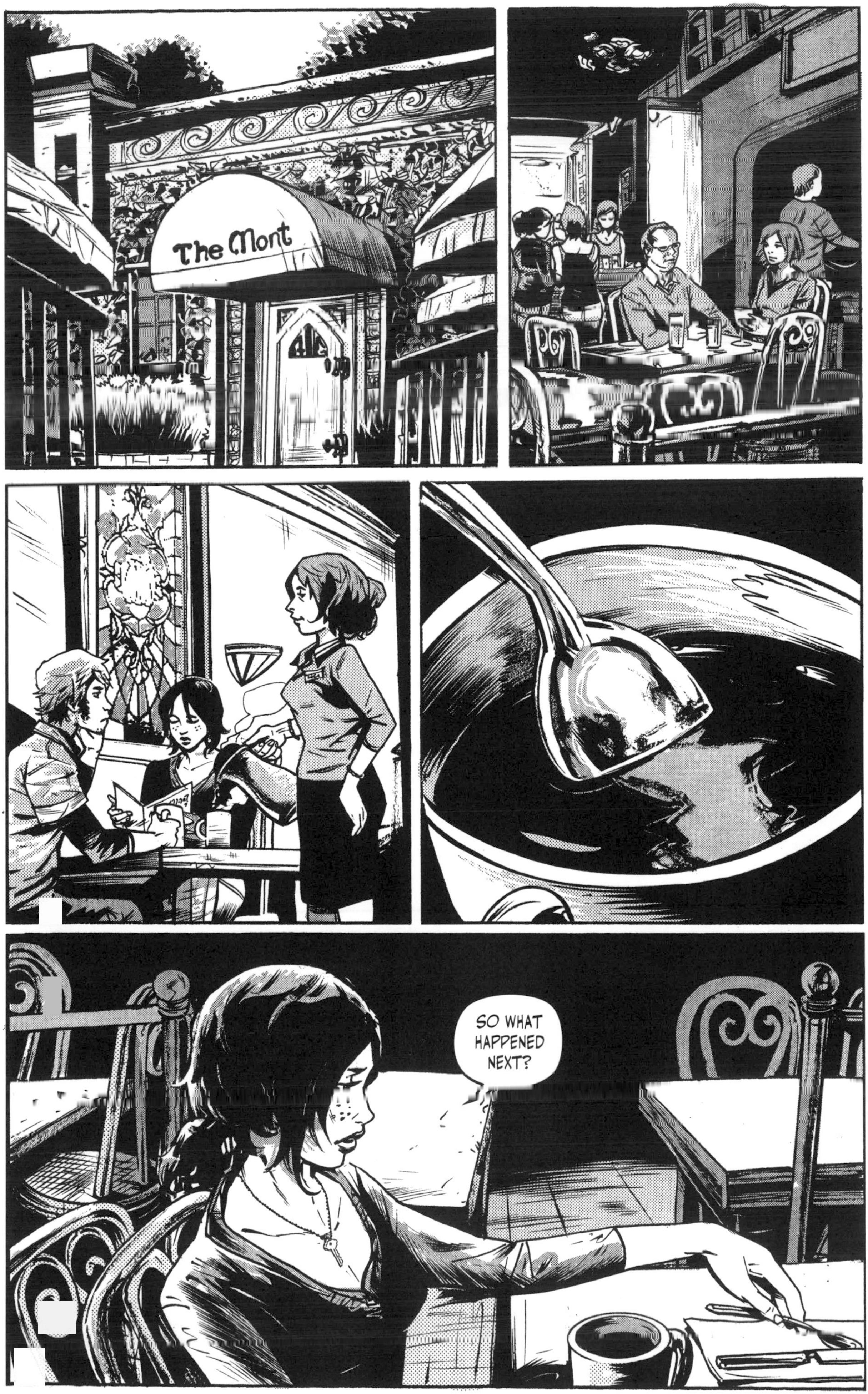
The Mont
SO WHAT HAPPENED NEXT?

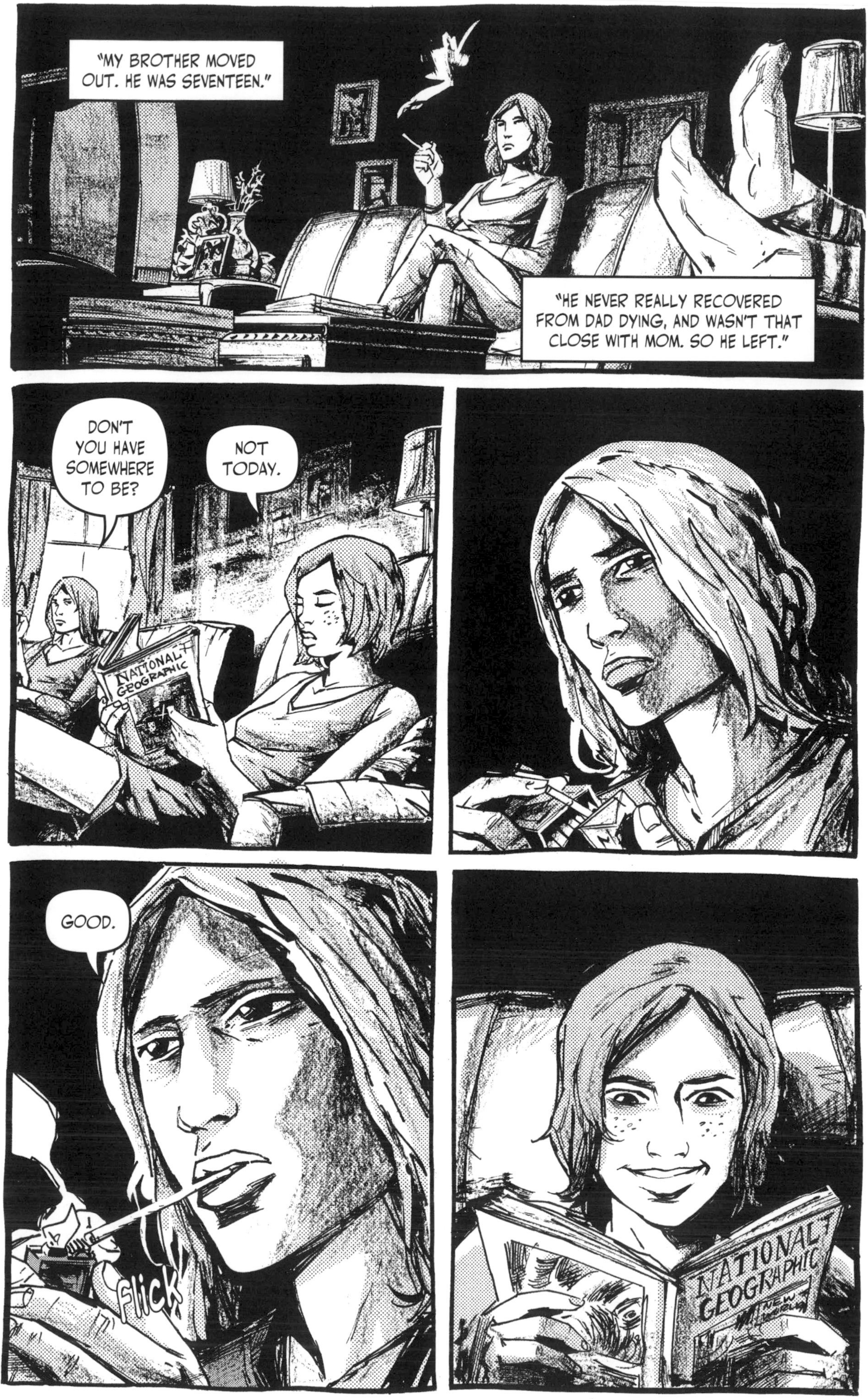
"MY BROTHER MOVED OUT. HE WAS SEVENTEEN."
"HE NEVER REALLY RECOVERED FROM DAD DYING, AND WASN'T THAT CLOSE WITH MOM. SO HE LEFT."
DON'T YOU HAVE SOMEWHERE TO BE?
NOT TODAY.
NATIONAL GEOGRAPHIC
GOOD.
flick
NATIONAL GEOGRAPHIC

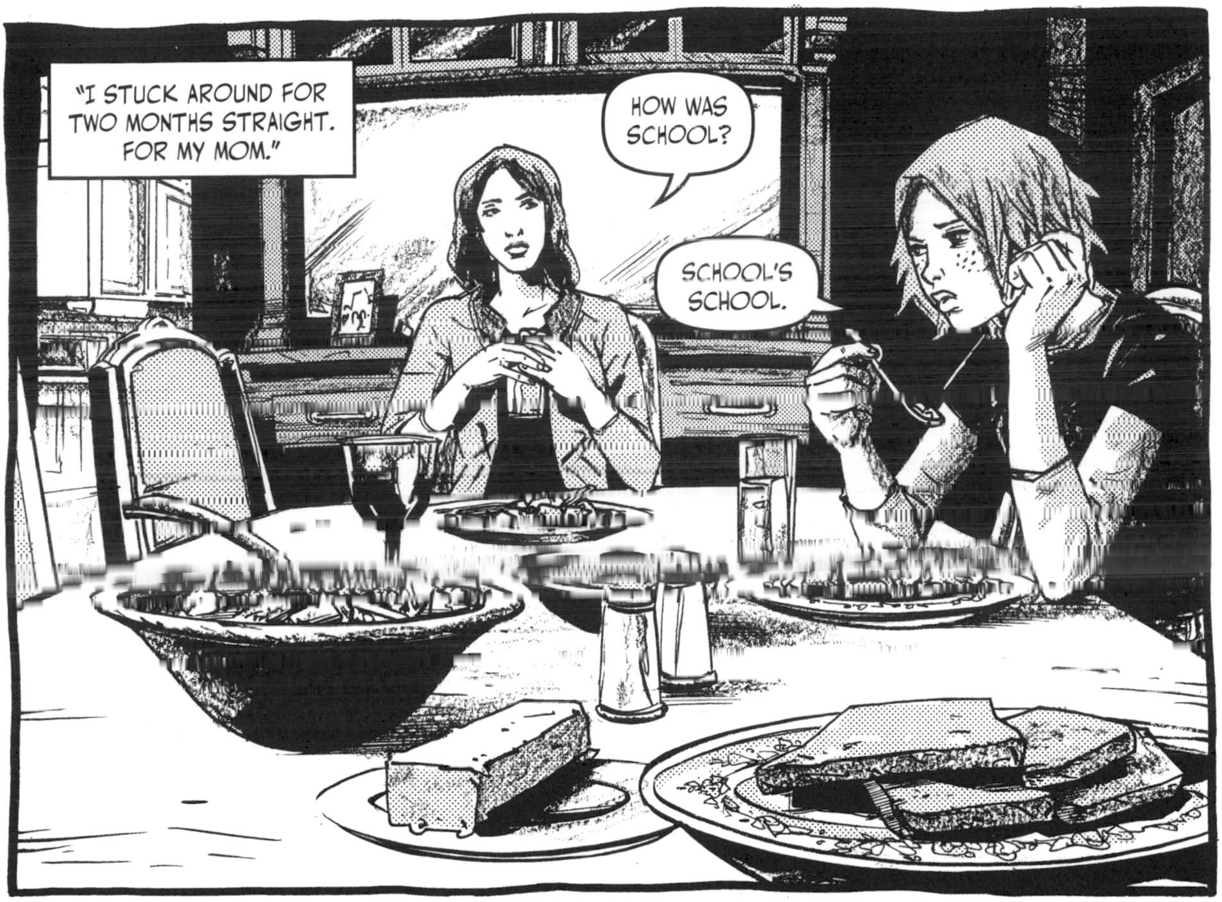
"I STUCK AROUND FOR TWO MONTHS STRAIGHT. FOR MY MOM."
HOW WAS SCHOOL?
SCHOOL'S SCHOOL.

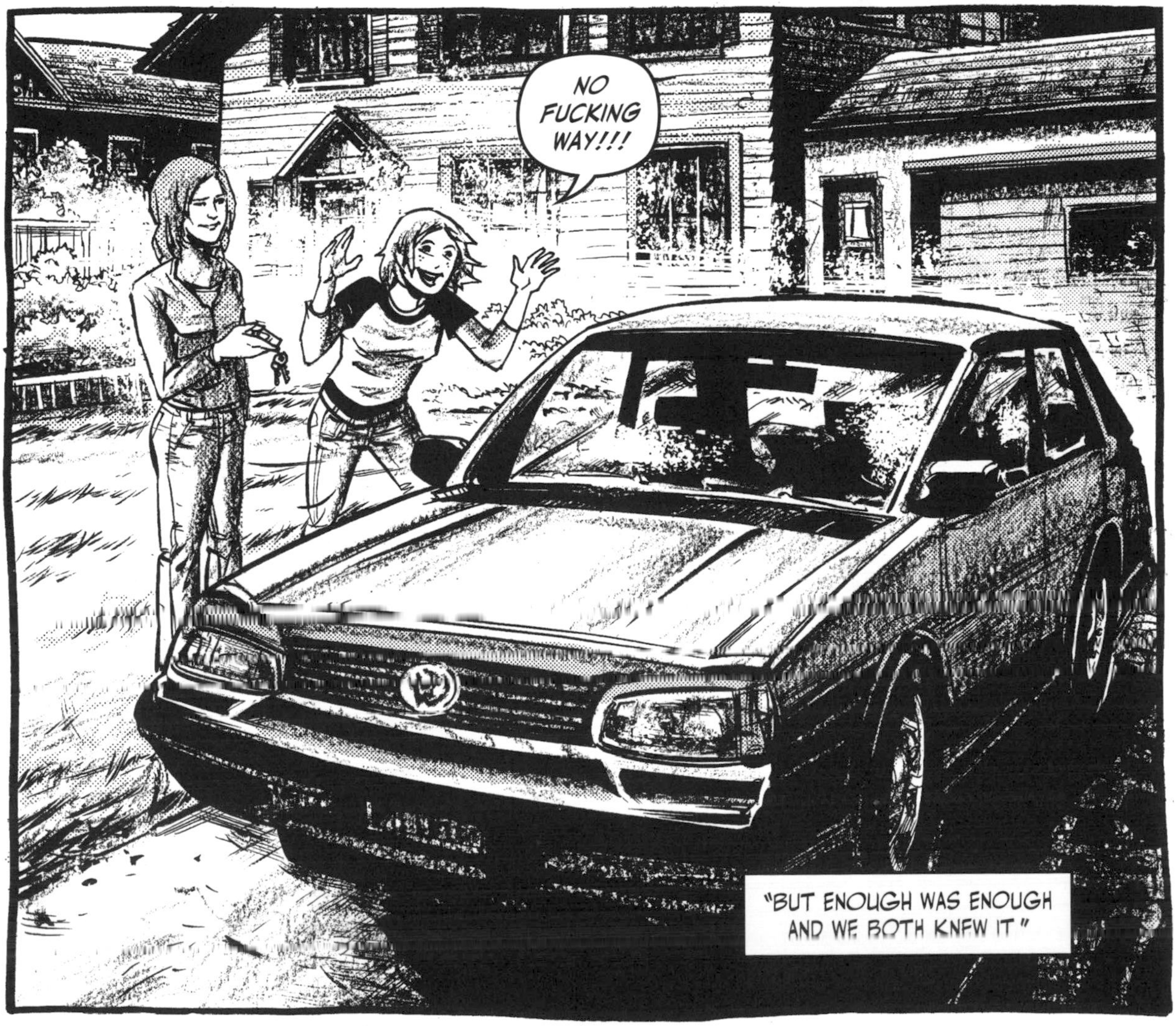
NO FUCKING WAY!!!
"BUT ENOUGH WAS ENOUGH AND WE BOTH KNEW IT"

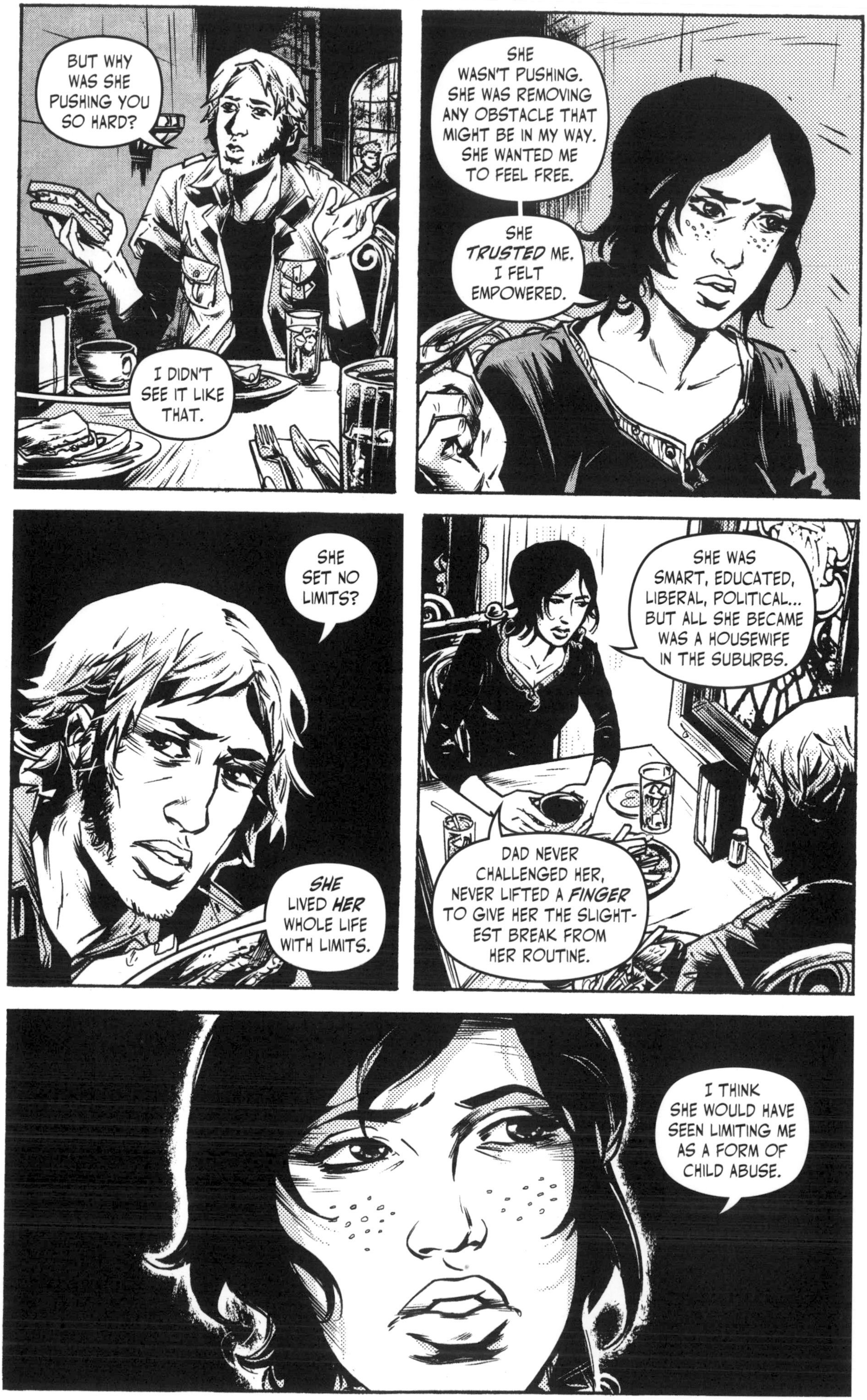
BUT WHY WAS SHE PUSHING YOU SO HARD?
I DIDN'T SEE IT LIKE THAT.
SHE WASN'T PUSHING. SHE WAS REMOVING ANY OBSTACLE THAT MIGHT BE IN MY WAY. SHE WANTED ME TO FEEL FREE.
SHE TRUSTED ME. I FELT EMPOWERED.
SHE SET NO LIMITS?
SHE LIVED HER WHOLE LIFE WITH LIMITS.
SHE WAS SMART, EDUCATED, LIBERAL, POLITICAL... BUT ALL SHE BECAME WAS A HOUSEWIFE IN THE SUBURBS.
DAD NEVER CHALLENGED HER, NEVER LIFTED A FINGER TO GIVE HER THE SLIGHT-EST BREAK FROM HER ROUTINE.
I THINK SHE WOULD HAVE SEEN LIMITING ME AS A FORM OF CHILD ABUSE.

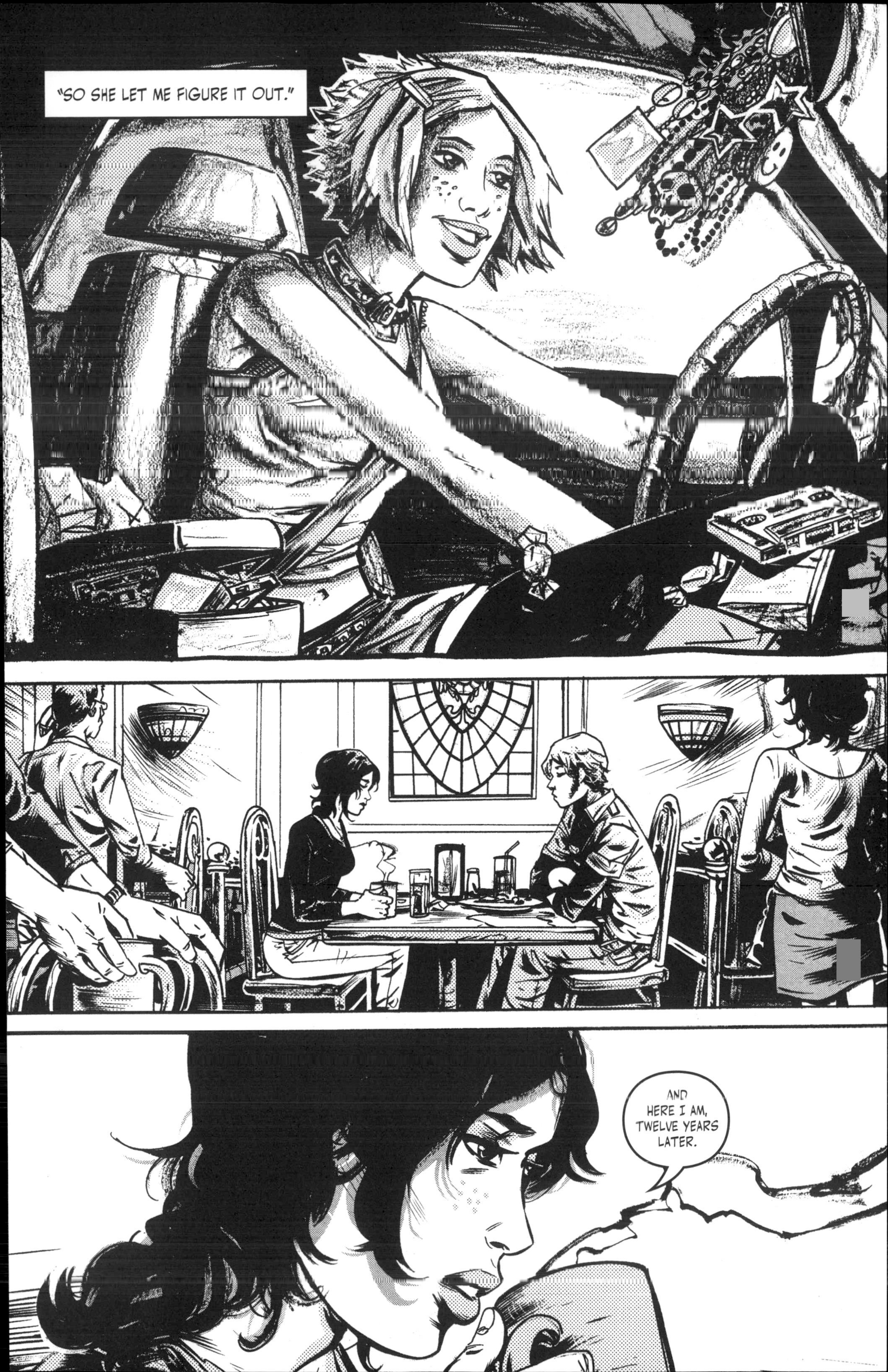
"SO SHE LET ME FIGURE IT OUT."
AND HERE I AM, TWELVE YEARS LATER.

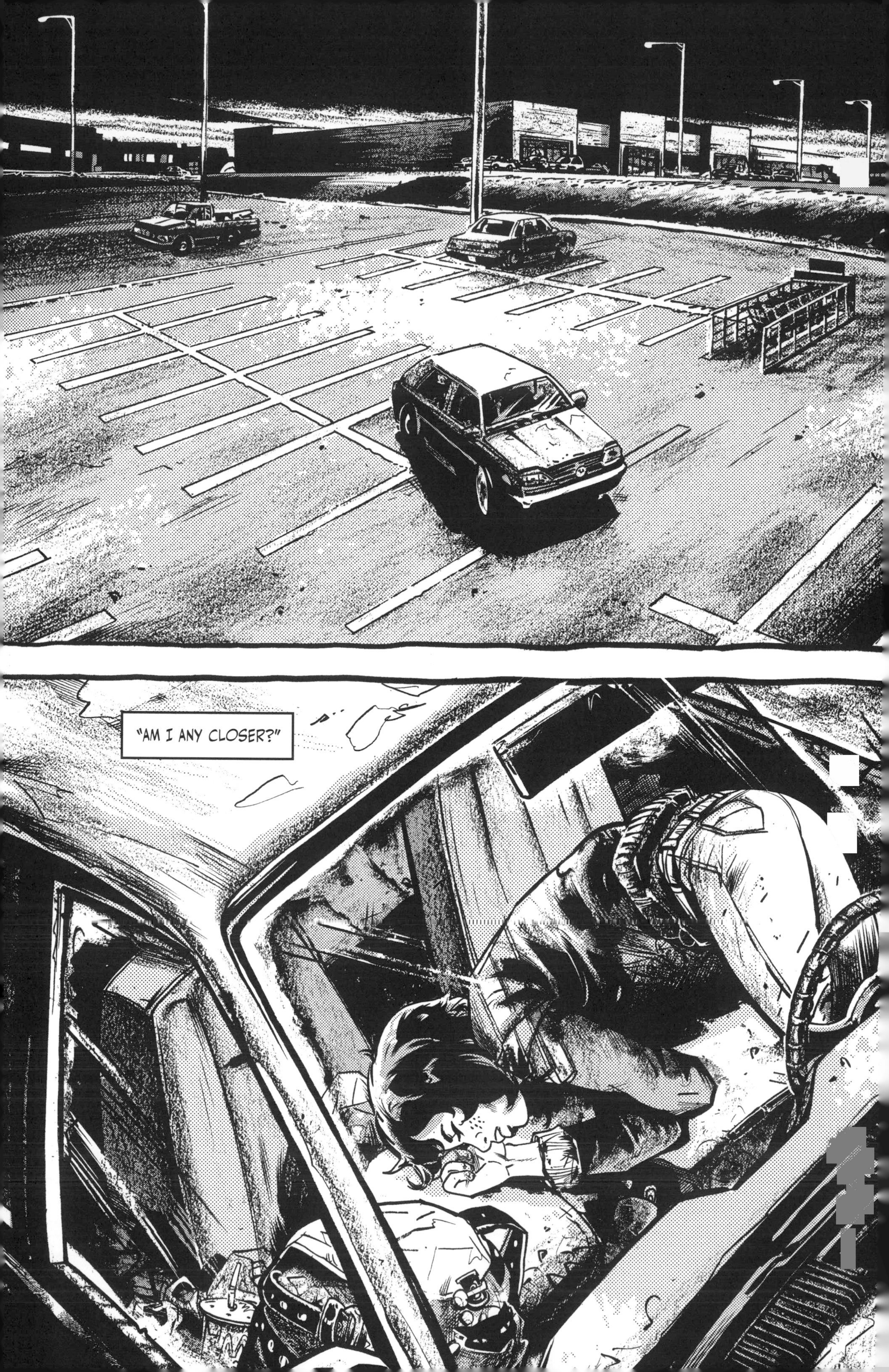
"AM I ANY CLOSER?"

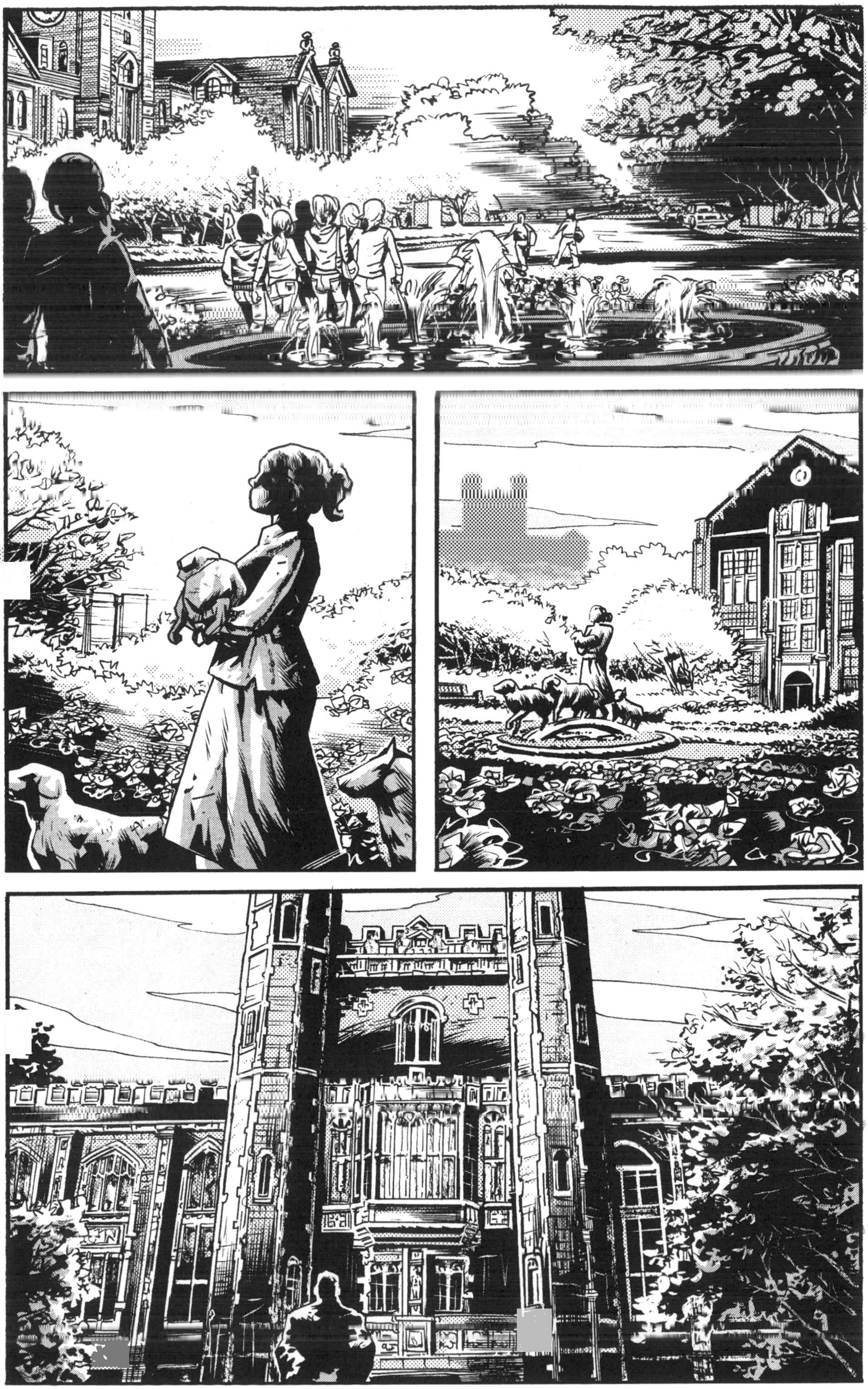

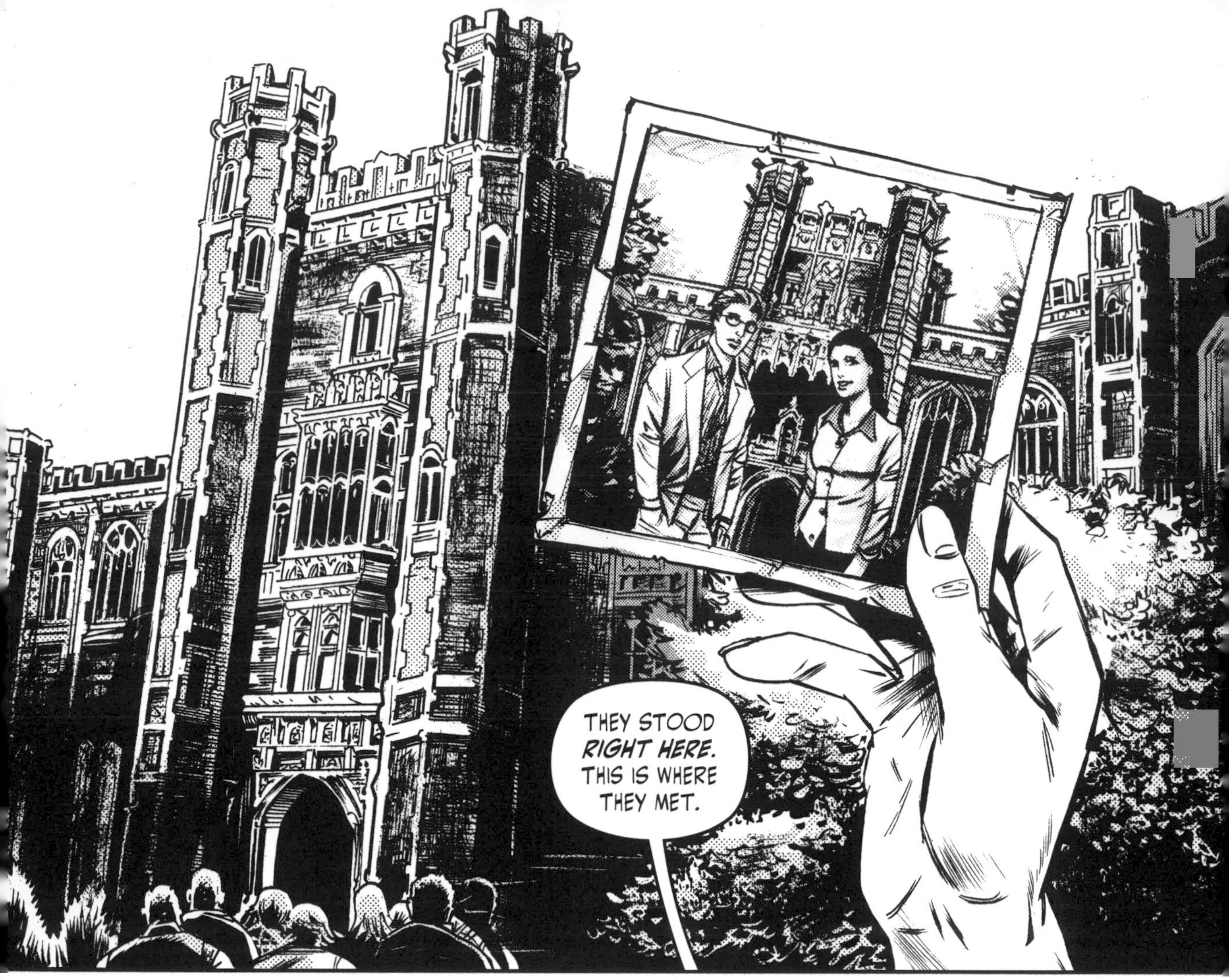
THEY STOOD *RIGHT HERE*. THIS IS WHERE THEY MET.

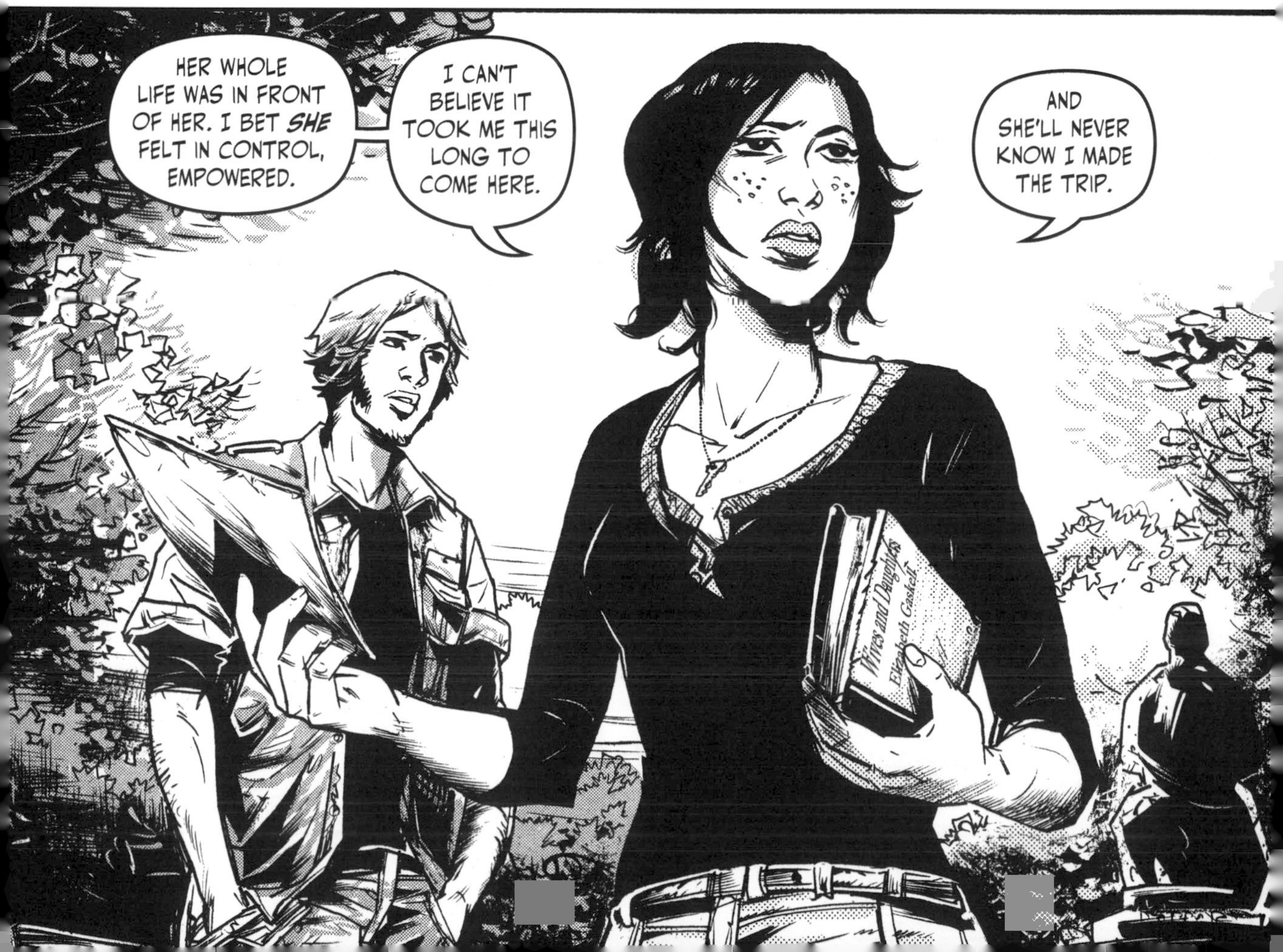
HER WHOLE LIFE WAS IN FRONT OF HER. I BET *SHE* FELT IN CONTROL, EMPOWERED.
I CAN'T BELIEVE IT TOOK ME THIS LONG TO COME HERE.
AND SHE'LL NEVER KNOW I MADE THE TRIP.
Wives and Daughters
Elizabeth Gaskell

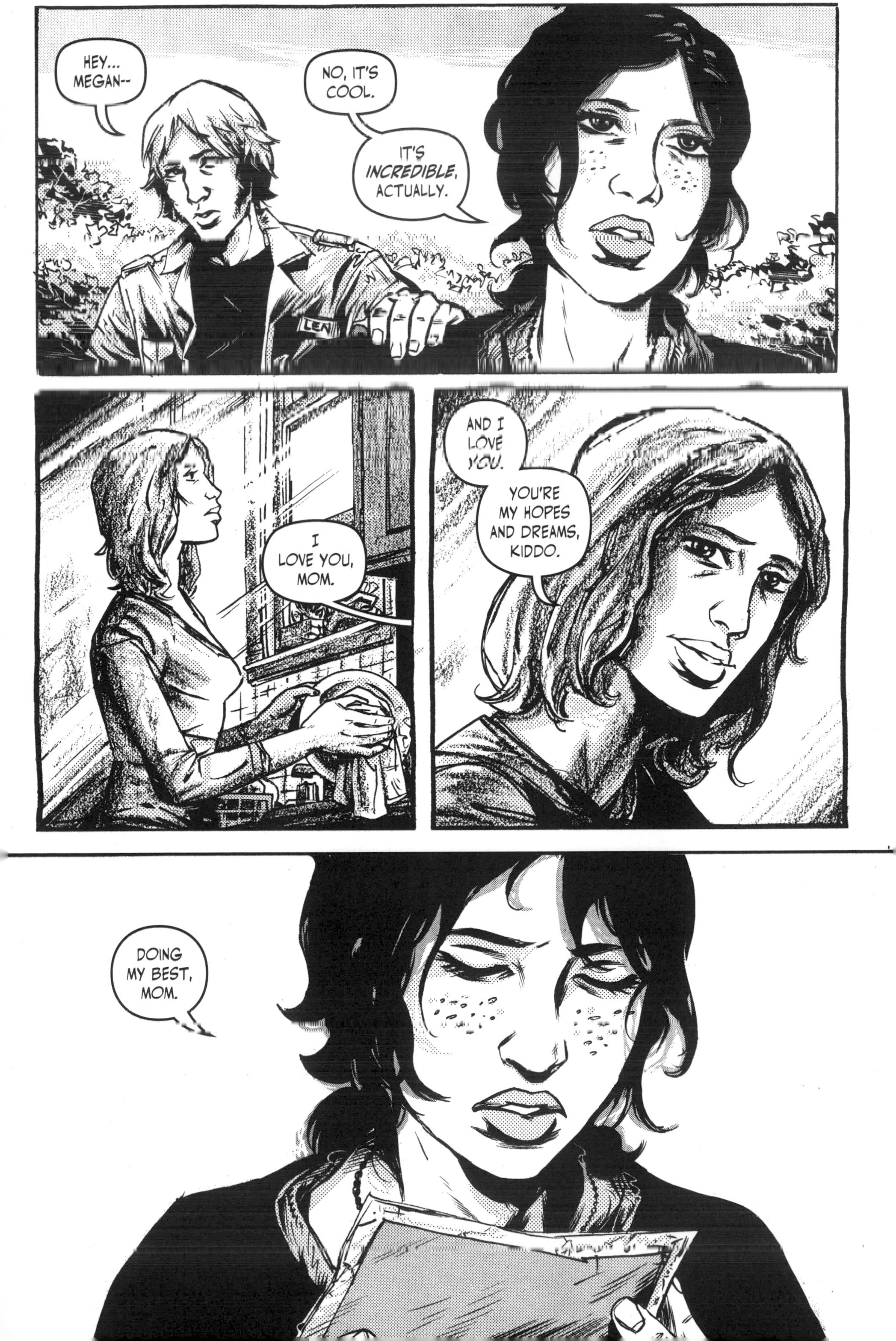
HEY... MEGAN--
NO, IT'S COOL.
IT'S *INCREDIBLE*, ACTUALLY.
LEN
I LOVE YOU, MOM.
AND I LOVE *YOU*.
YOU'RE MY HOPES AND DREAMS, KIDDO.
DOING MY BEST, MOM.

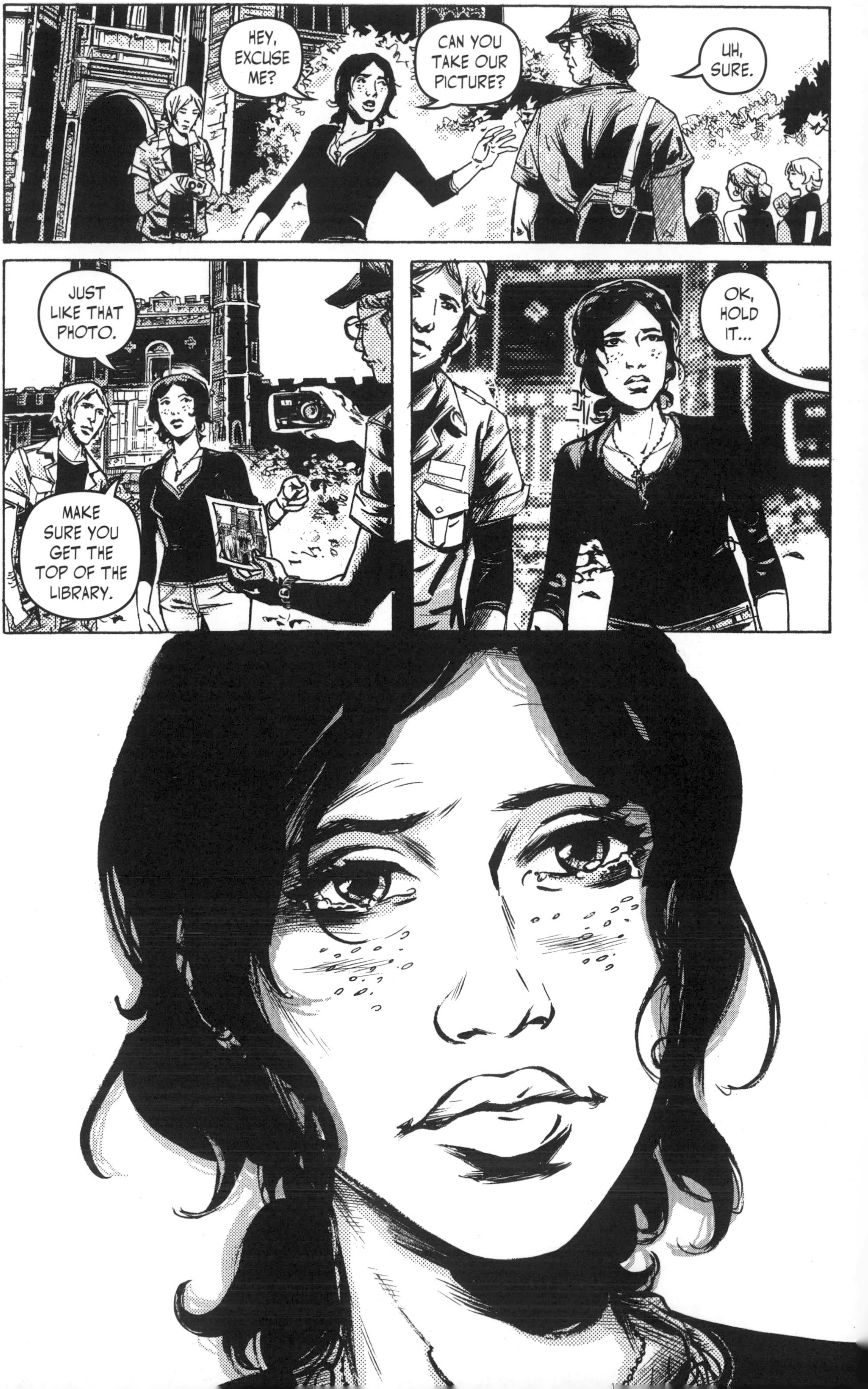
HEY, EXCUSE ME?
CAN YOU TAKE OUR PICTURE?
UH, SURE.
JUST LIKE THAT PHOTO.
MAKE SURE YOU GET THE TOP OF THE LIBRARY.
OK, HOLD IT...

CHAPTER 10
"BAR CRAWL"
Austin, Texas

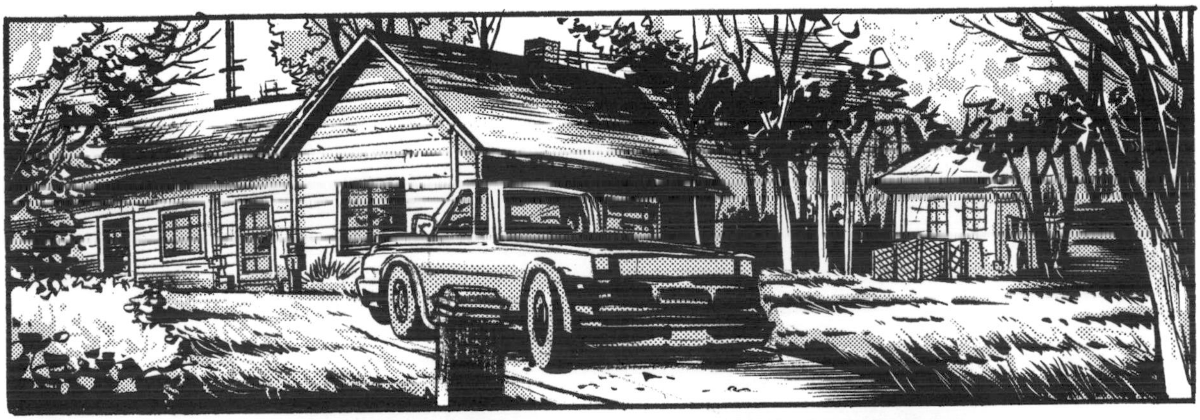

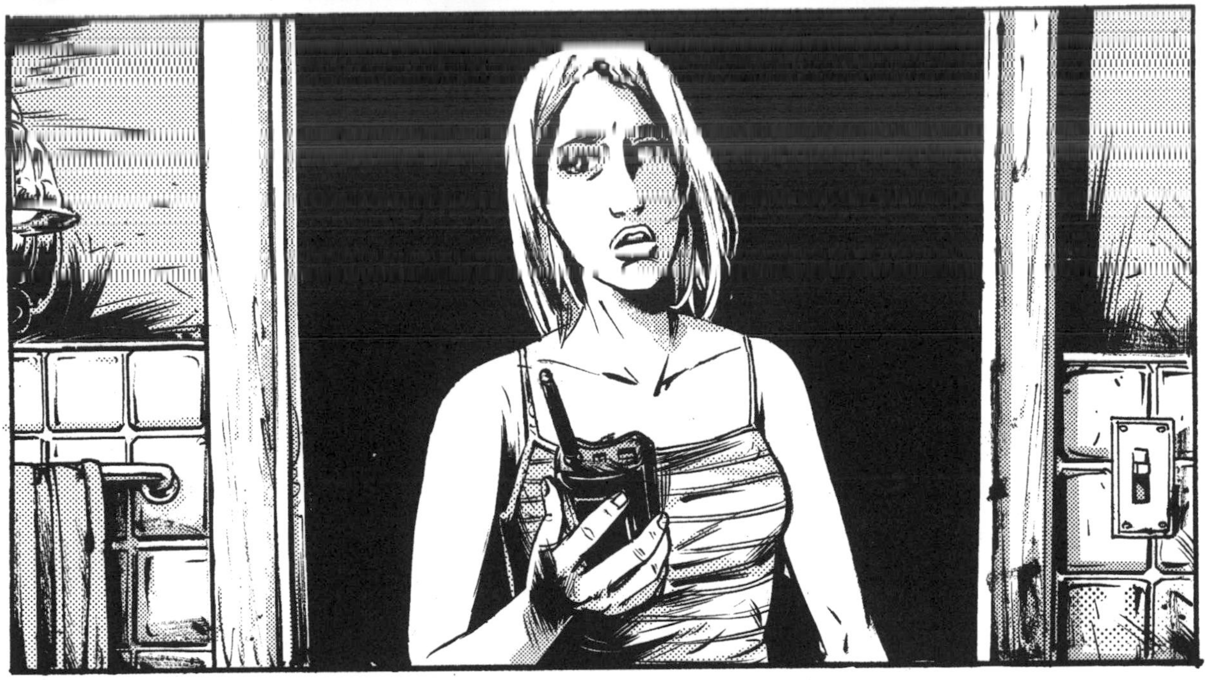

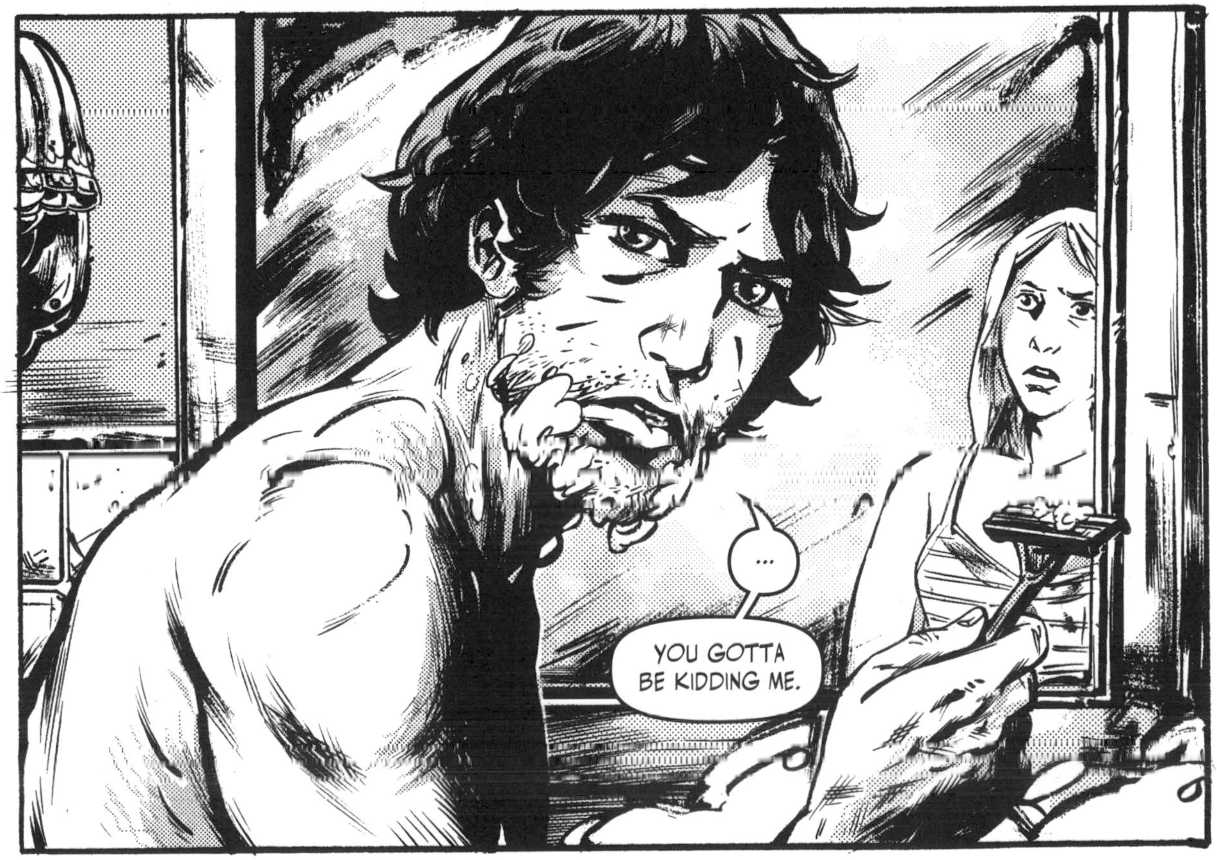
...
YOU GOTTA BE KIDDING ME.

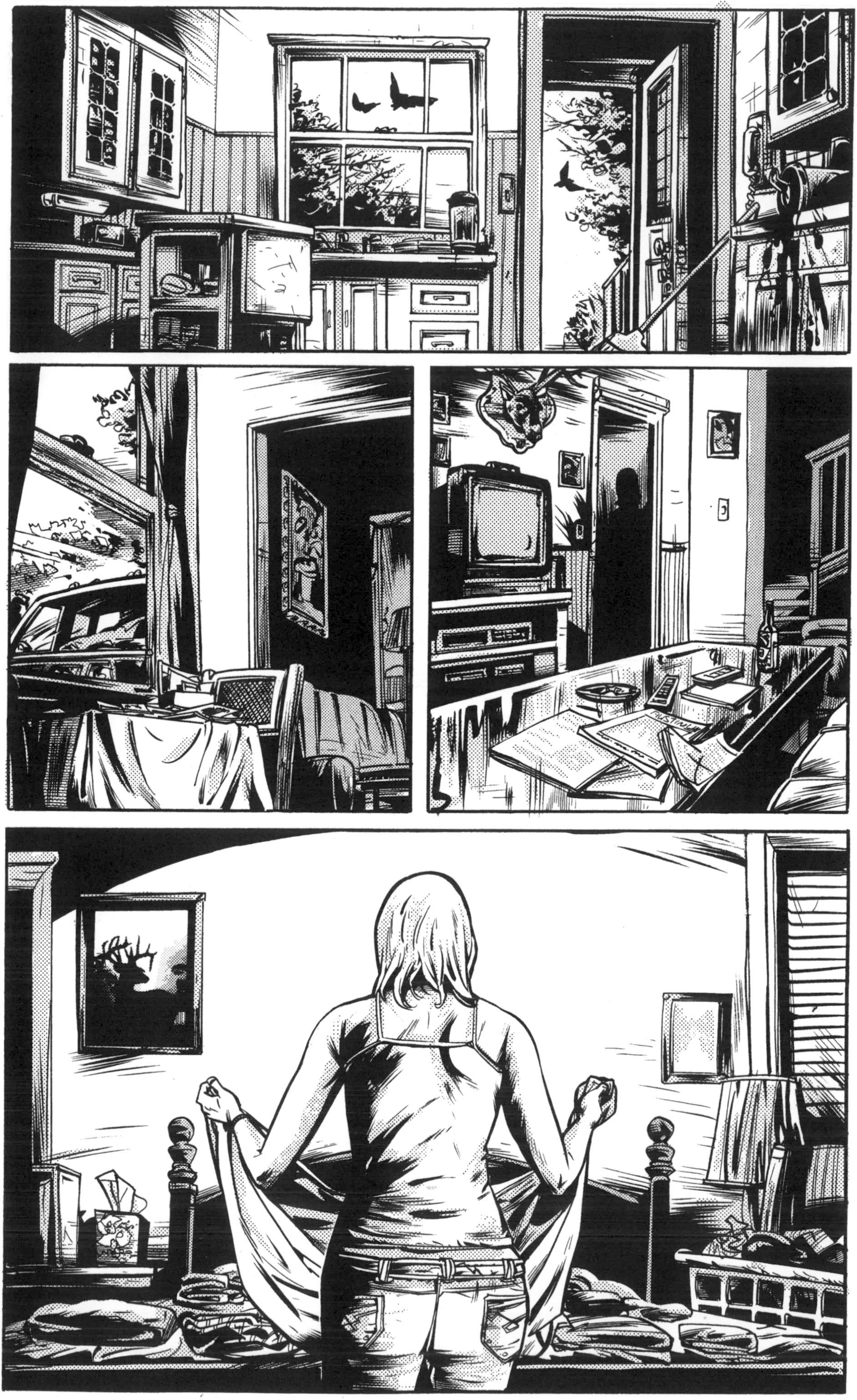

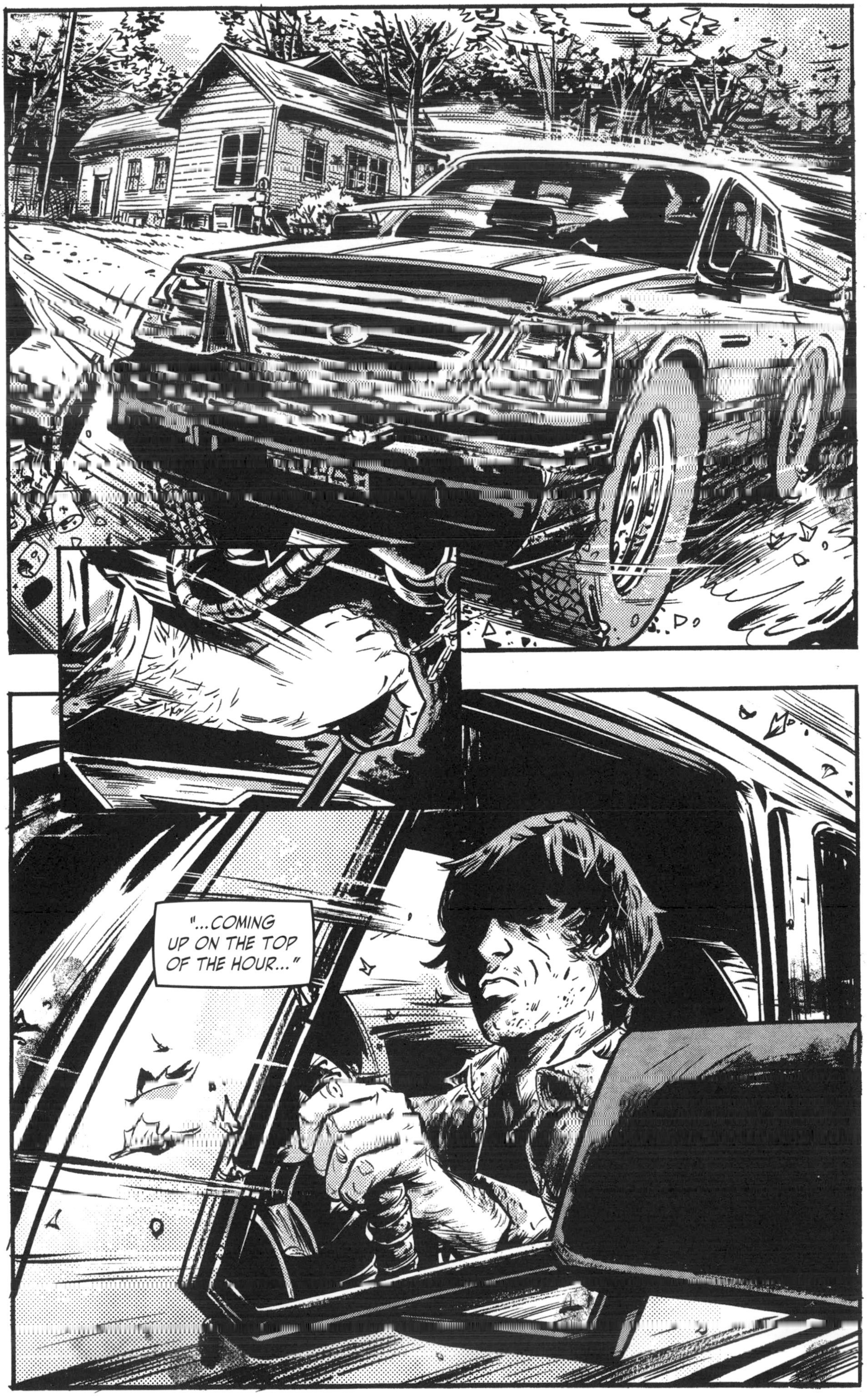
"...COMING UP ON THE TOP OF THE HOUR..."

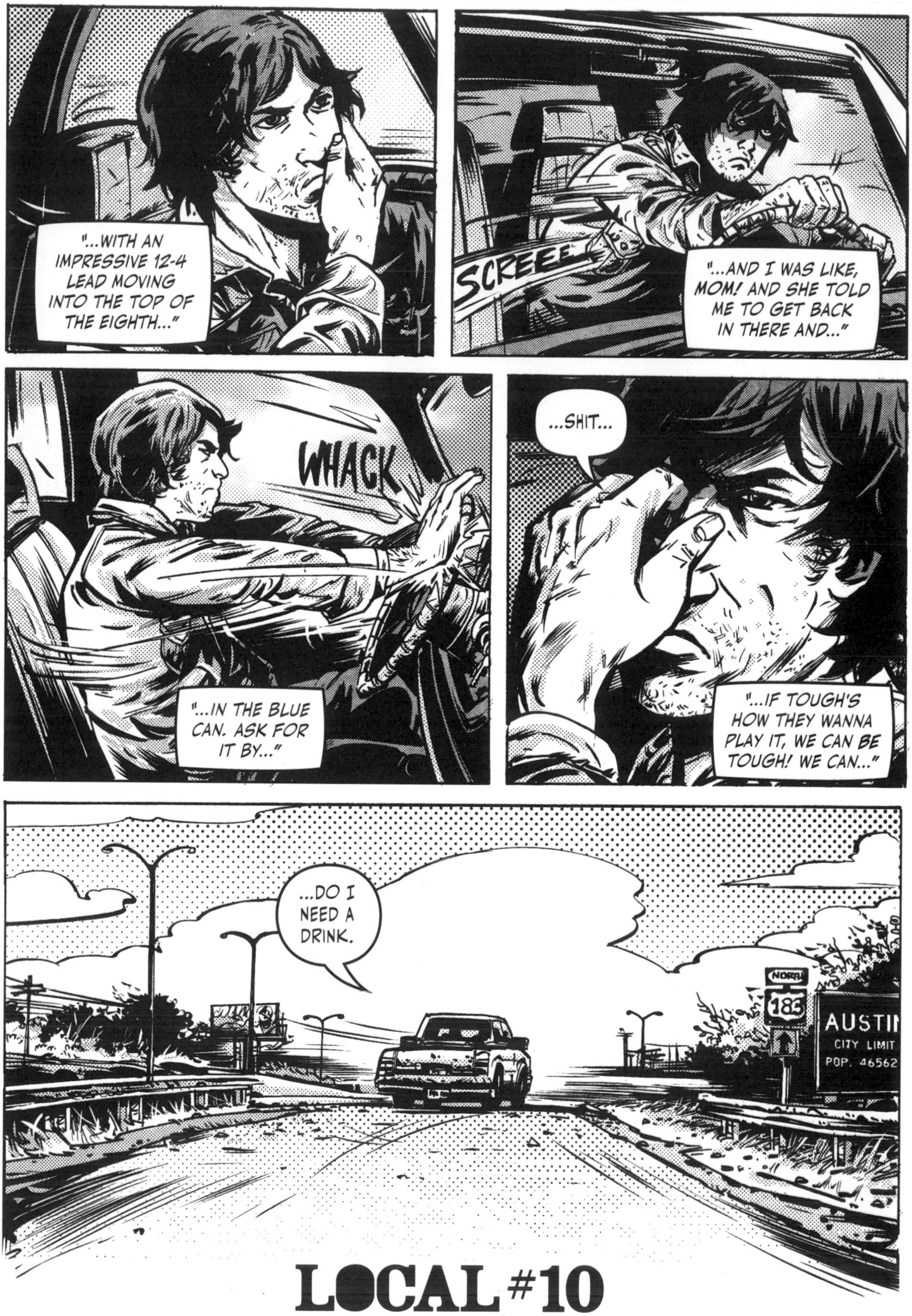
"...WITH AN IMPRESSIVE 12-4 LEAD MOVING INTO THE TOP OF THE EIGHTH..."
SCREEE
"...AND I WAS LIKE, MOM! AND SHE TOLD ME TO GET BACK IN THERE AND..."
WHACK
"...IN THE BLUE CAN. ASK FOR IT BY..."
...SHIT...
"...IF TOUGH'S HOW THEY WANNA PLAY IT, WE CAN BE TOUGH! WE CAN..."
...DO I NEED A DRINK.
183
AUSTIN
CITY LIMIT
POP. 46562

LOCAL #10

"bar crawl"

STORY: BRIAN WOOD / ART: RYAN KELLY
LETTERED BY DOUGLAS E. SHERWOOD

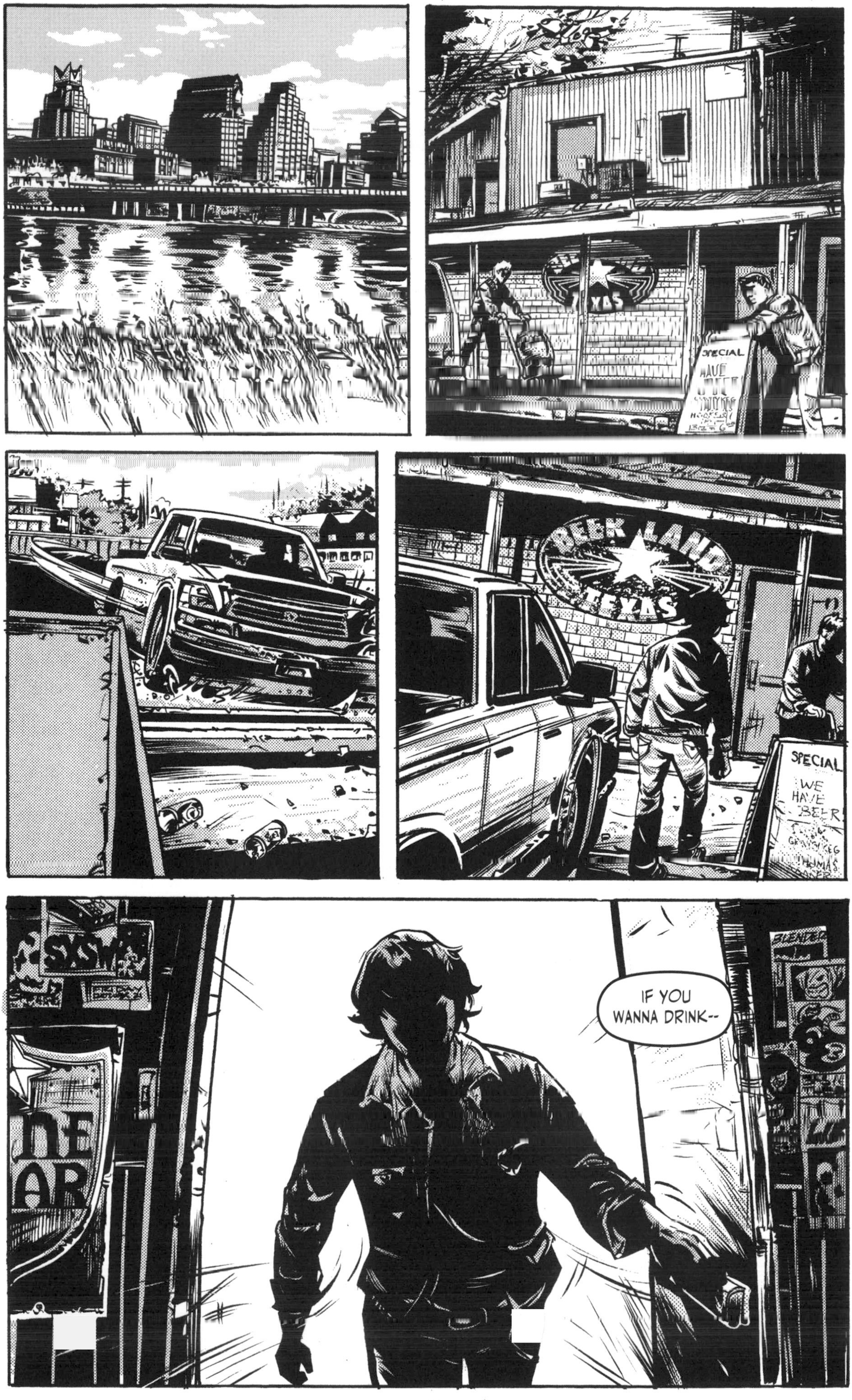
SPECIAL
BEER LAND
TEXAS
SPECIAL
WE HAVE BEER
SXSW
IF YOU WANNA DRINK--

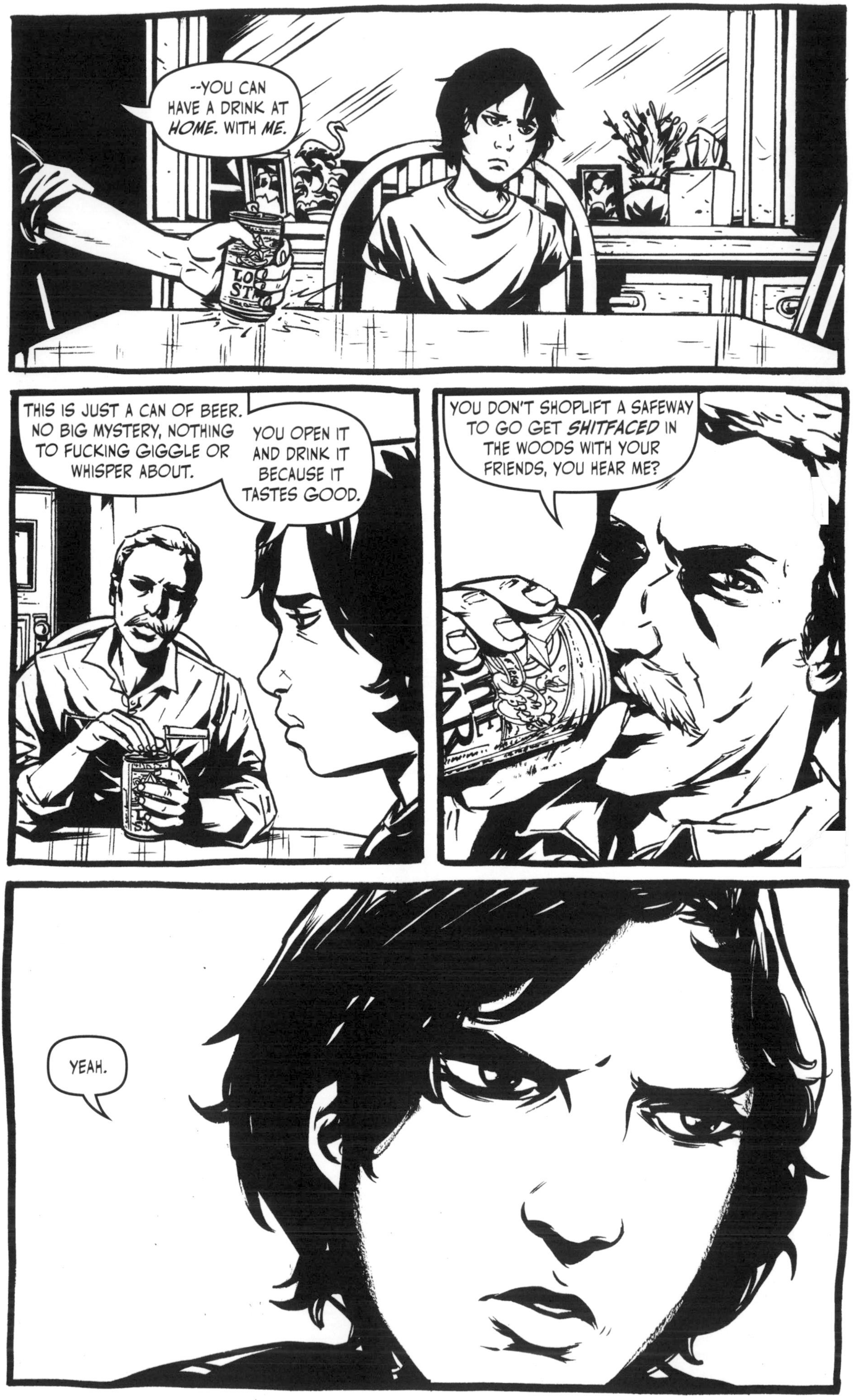
--YOU CAN HAVE A DRINK AT *HOME*. WITH *ME*.
THIS IS JUST A CAN OF BEER. NO BIG MYSTERY, NOTHING TO FUCKING GIGGLE OR WHISPER ABOUT.
YOU OPEN IT AND DRINK IT BECAUSE IT TASTES GOOD.
YOU DON'T SHOPLIFT A SAFEWAY TO GO GET *SHITFACED* IN THE WOODS WITH YOUR FRIENDS, YOU HEAR ME?
YEAH.

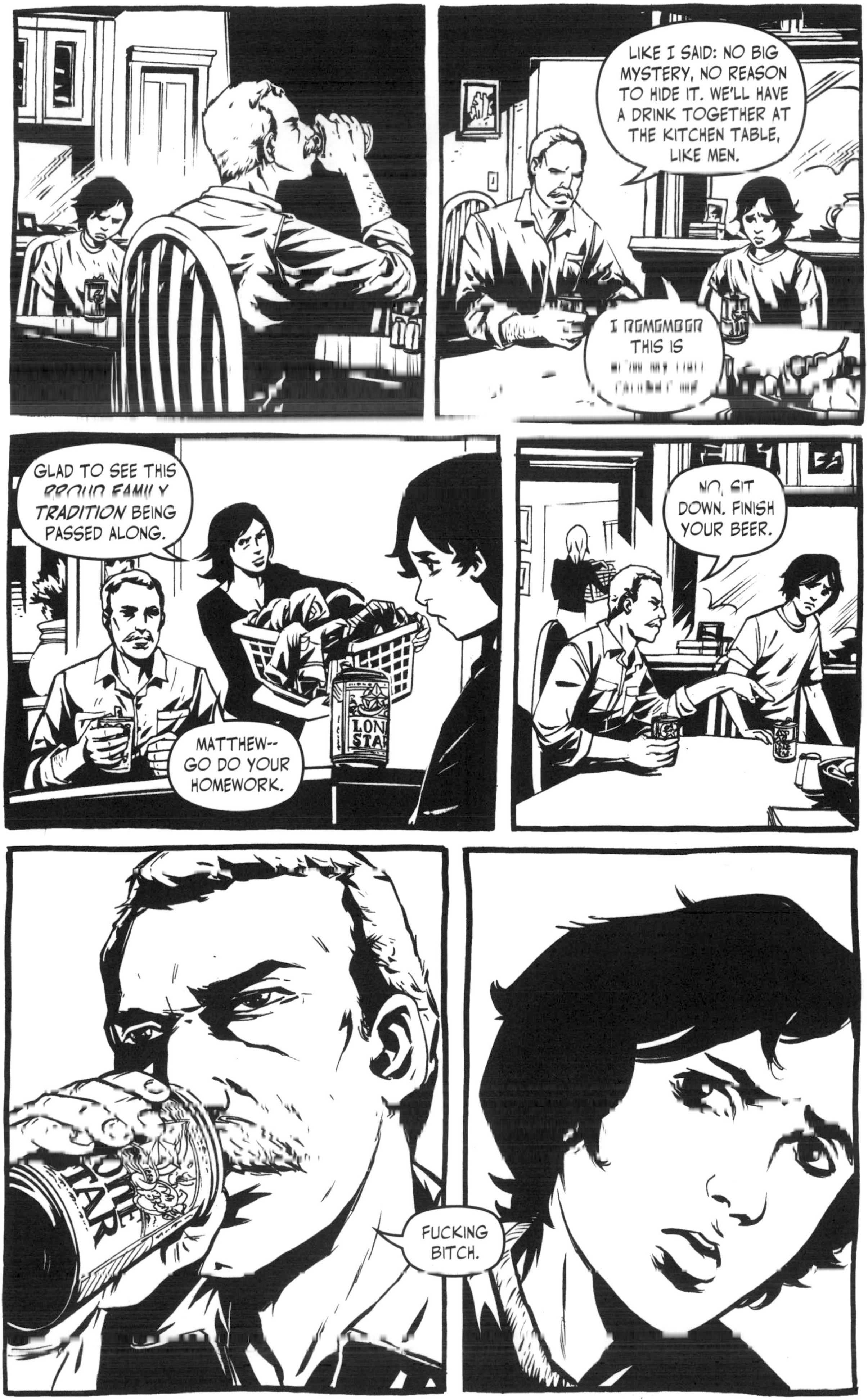
LIKE I SAID: NO BIG MYSTERY, NO REASON TO HIDE IT. WE'LL HAVE A DRINK TOGETHER AT THE KITCHEN TABLE, LIKE MEN.
I REMEMBER THIS IS
GLAD TO SEE THIS PROUD FAMILY TRADITION BEING PASSED ALONG.
MATTHEW-- GO DO YOUR HOMEWORK.
NO, SIT DOWN. FINISH YOUR BEER.
FUCKING BITCH.

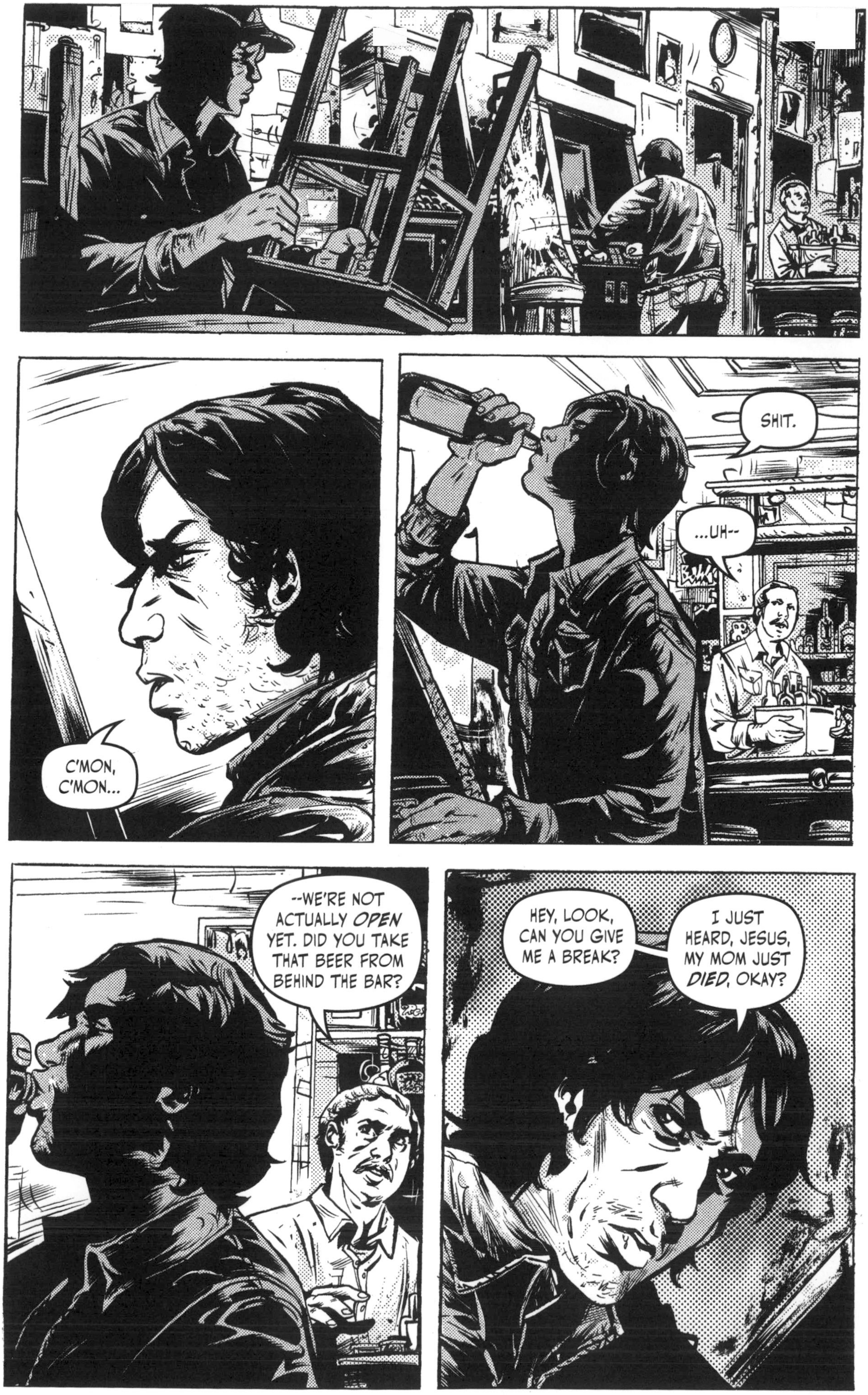

C'MON,
C'MON...
SHIT.
...UH--
--WE'RE NOT ACTUALLY *OPEN* YET. DID YOU TAKE THAT BEER FROM BEHIND THE BAR?
HEY, LOOK, CAN YOU GIVE ME A BREAK?
I JUST HEARD, JESUS, MY MOM JUST *DIED*, OKAY?

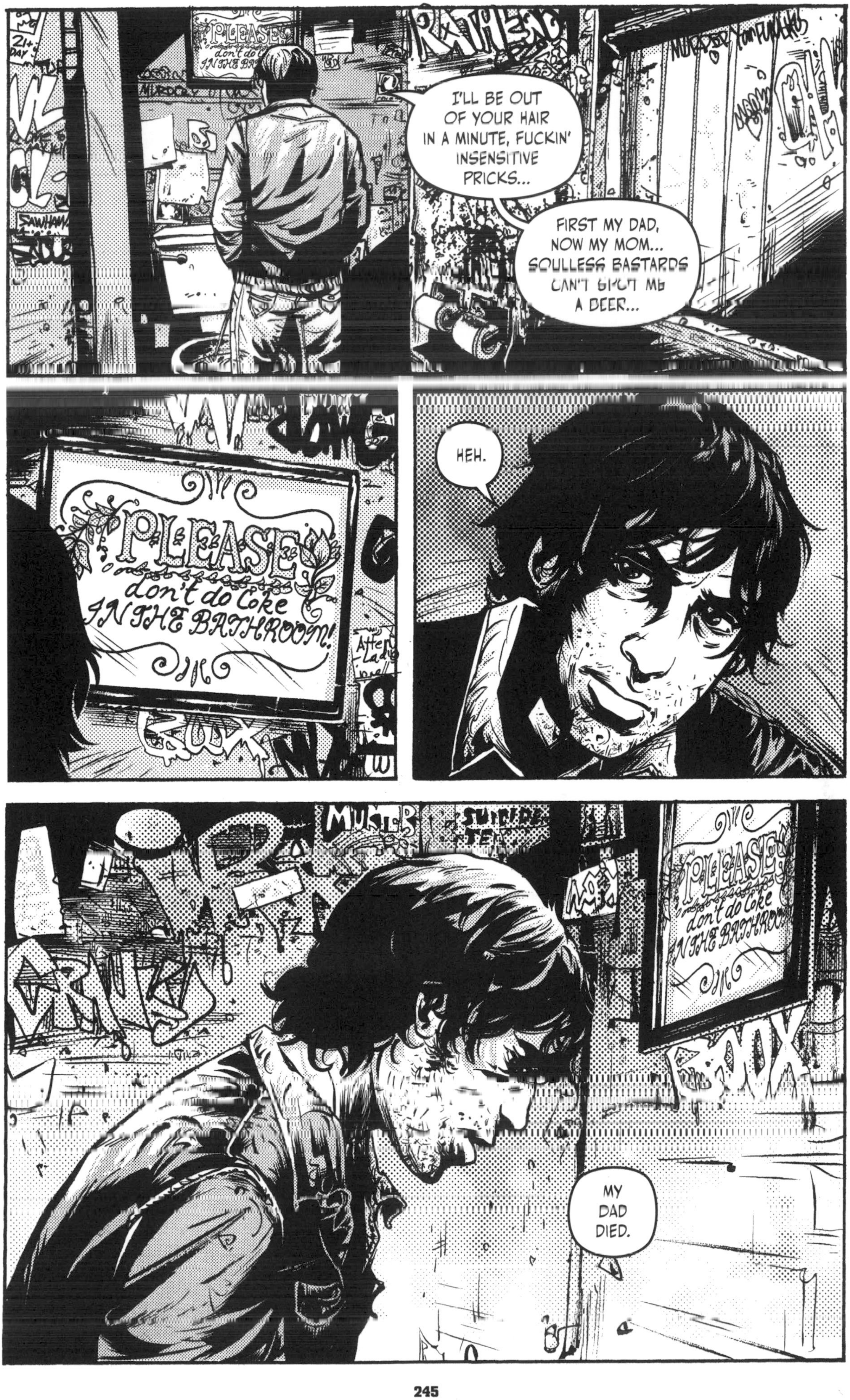
I'LL BE OUT OF YOUR HAIR IN A MINUTE, FUCKIN' INSENSITIVE PRICKS...
FIRST MY DAD, NOW MY MOM... SOULLESS BASTARDS CAN'T SPOT ME A BEER...
PLEASE don't do Coke IN THE BATHROOM!
HEH.
MY DAD DIED.

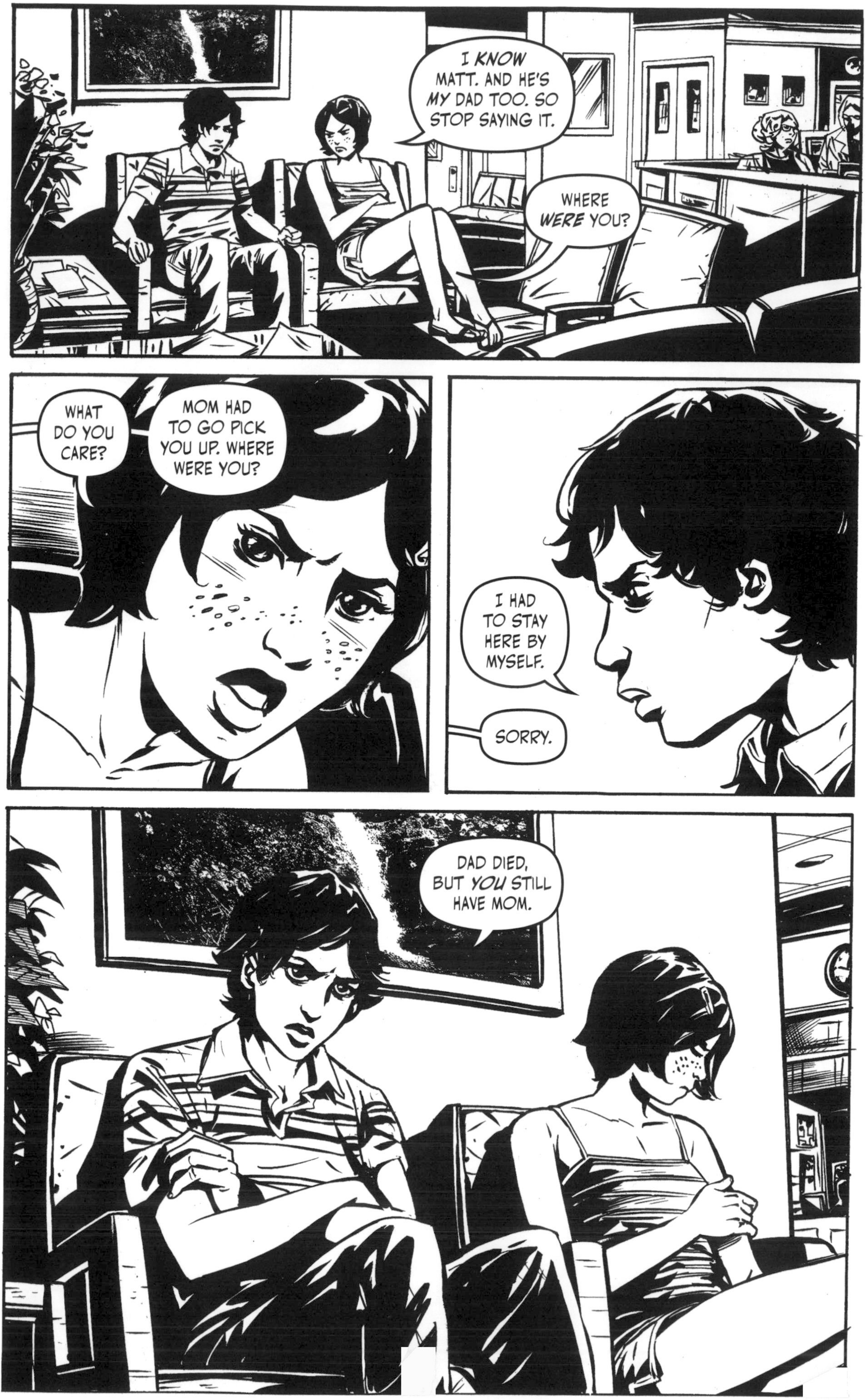
I KNOW MATT. AND HE'S MY DAD TOO. SO STOP SAYING IT.
WHERE WERE YOU?
WHAT DO YOU CARE?
MOM HAD TO GO PICK YOU UP. WHERE WERE YOU?
I HAD TO STAY HERE BY MYSELF.
SORRY.
DAD DIED, BUT YOU STILL HAVE MOM.

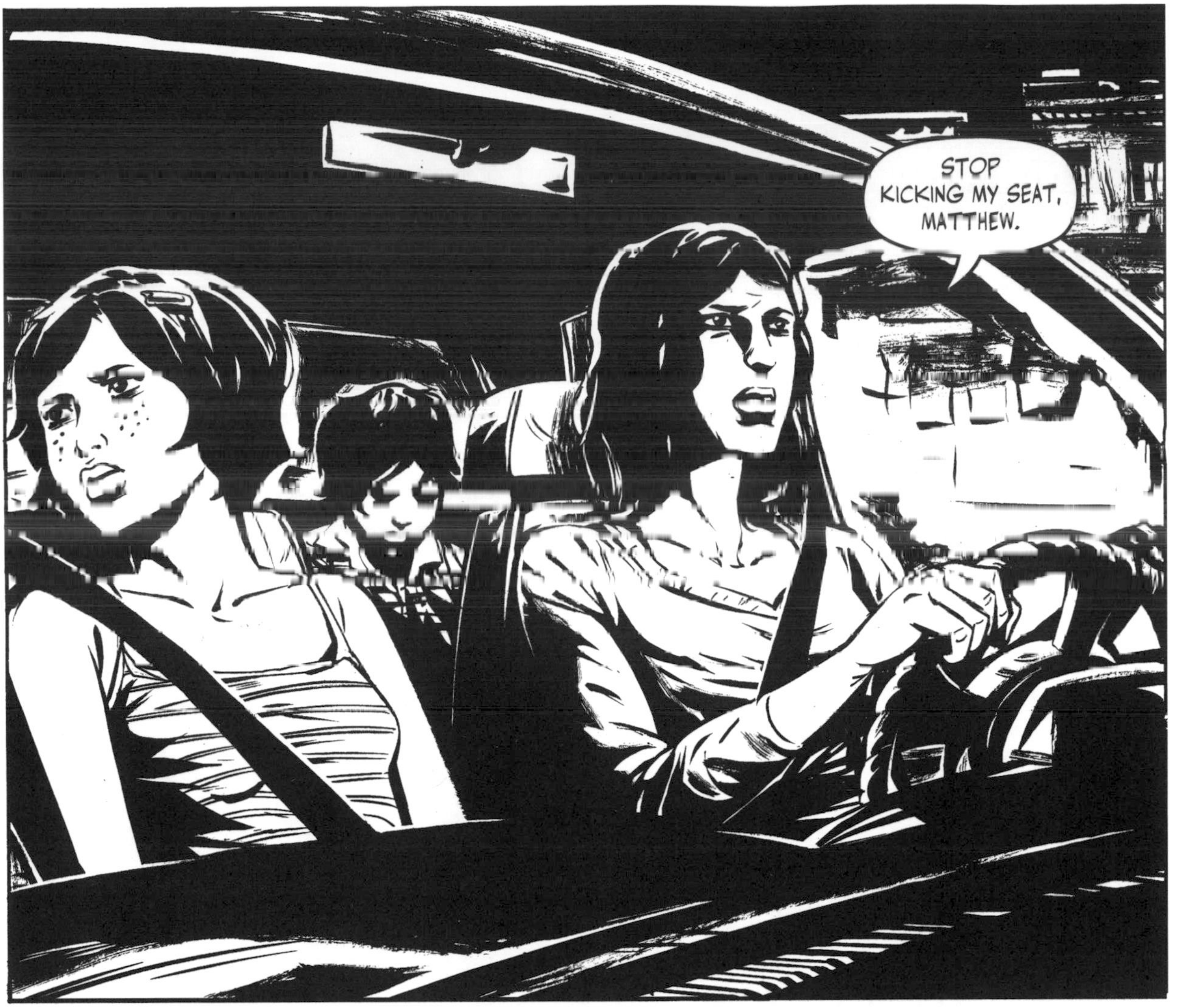
STOP KICKING MY SEAT, MATTHEW.

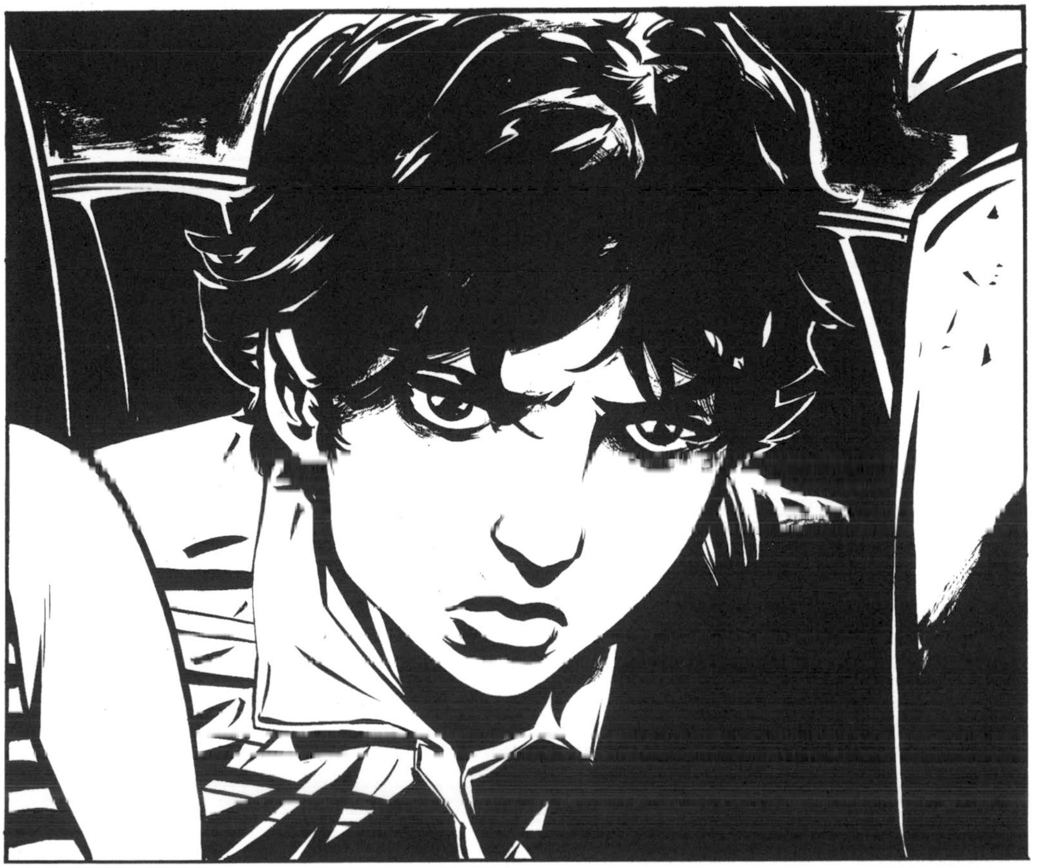

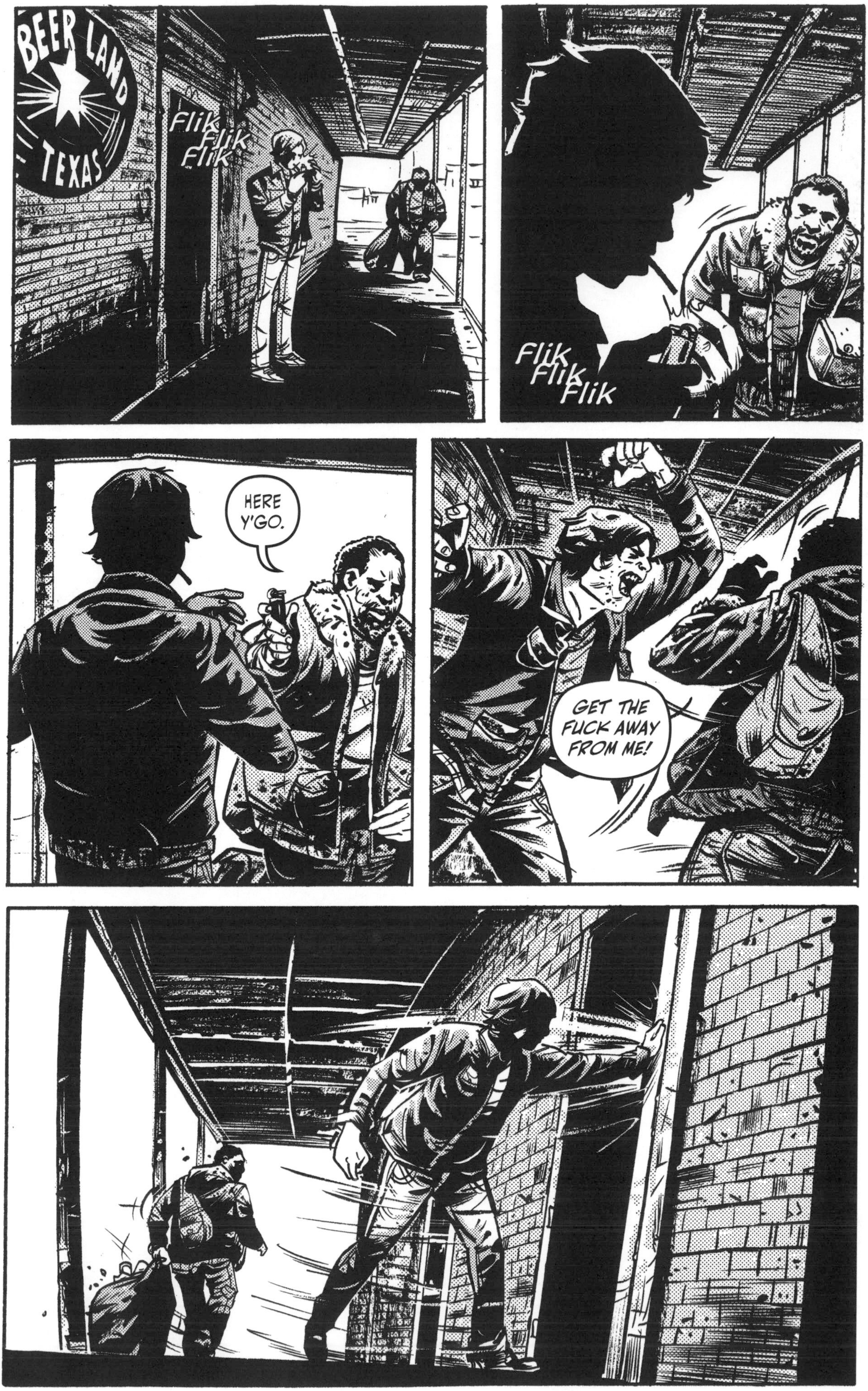
BEER LAND TEXAS
Flik Flik Flik
Flik Flik Flik
HERE Y'GO.
GET THE FUCK AWAY FROM ME!

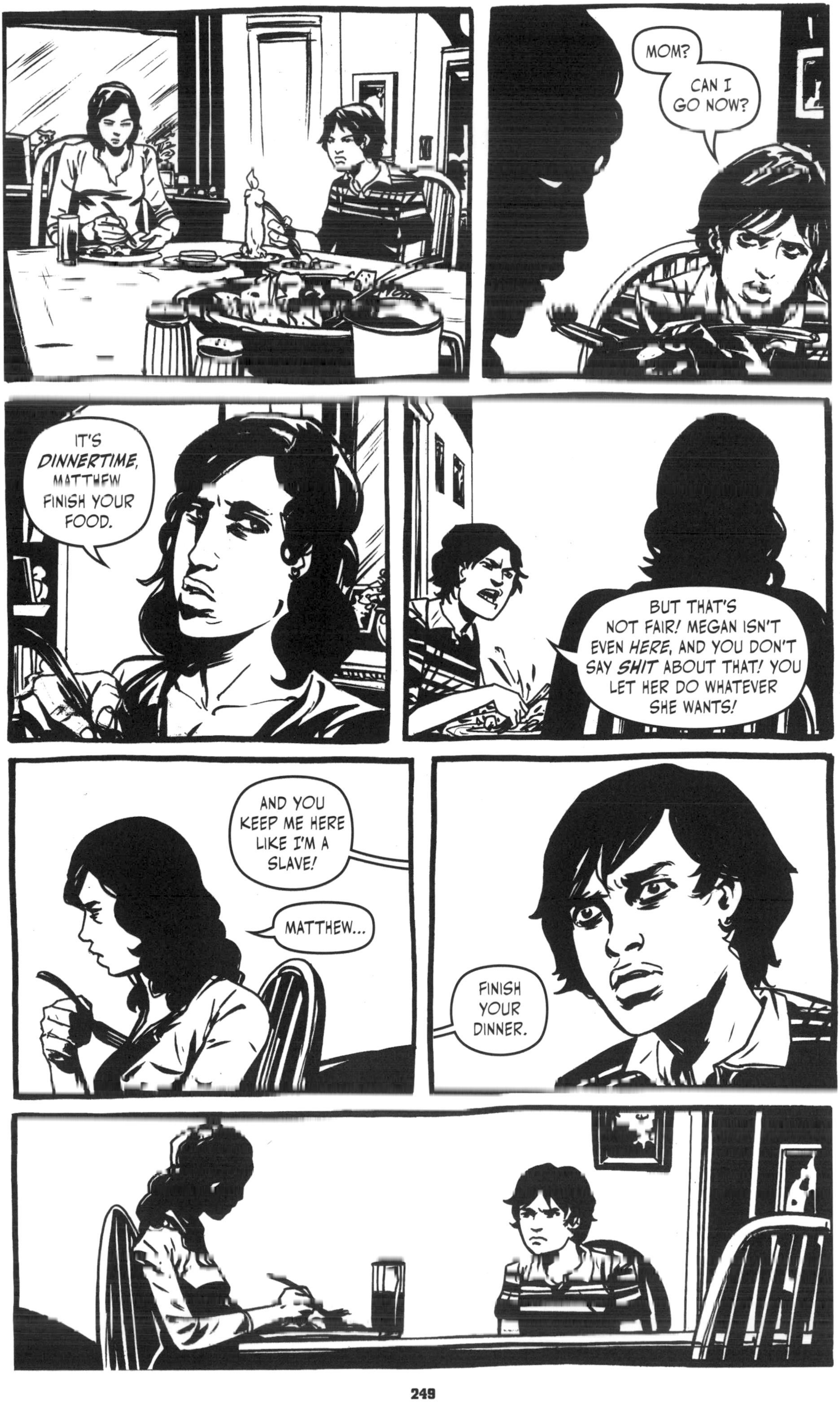
MOM?
CAN I GO NOW?
IT'S DINNERTIME, MATTHEW FINISH YOUR FOOD.
BUT THAT'S NOT FAIR! MEGAN ISN'T EVEN HERE, AND YOU DON'T SAY SHIT ABOUT THAT! YOU LET HER DO WHATEVER SHE WANTS!
AND YOU KEEP ME HERE LIKE I'M A SLAVE!
MATTHEW...
FINISH YOUR DINNER.

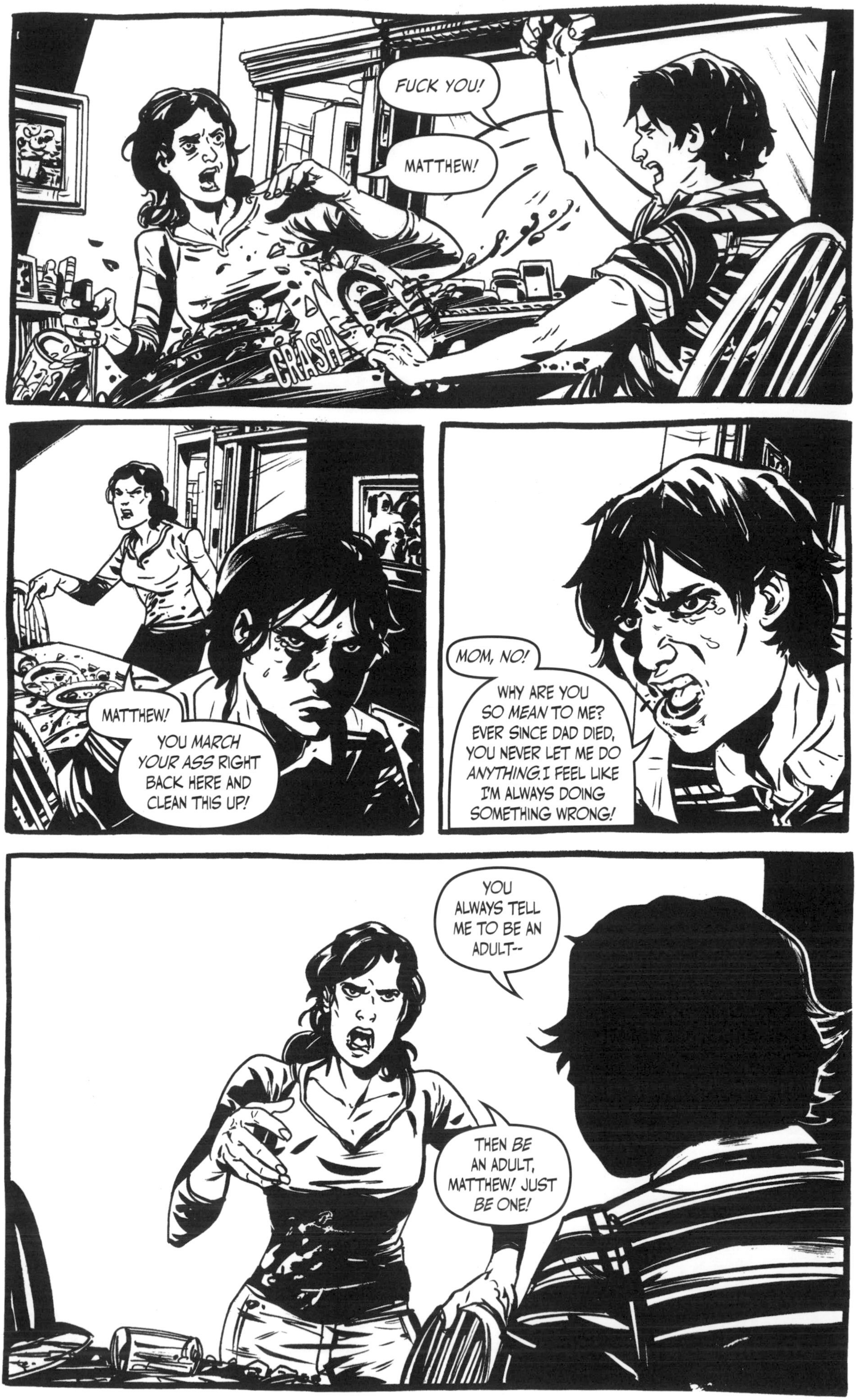
FUCK YOU!
MATTHEW!
CRASH
MATTHEW!
YOU MARCH YOUR ASS RIGHT BACK HERE AND CLEAN THIS UP!
MOM, NO!
WHY ARE YOU SO MEAN TO ME? EVER SINCE DAD DIED, YOU NEVER LET ME DO ANYTHING. I FEEL LIKE I'M ALWAYS DOING SOMETHING WRONG!
YOU ALWAYS TELL ME TO BE AN ADULT--
THEN BE AN ADULT, MATTHEW! JUST BE ONE!

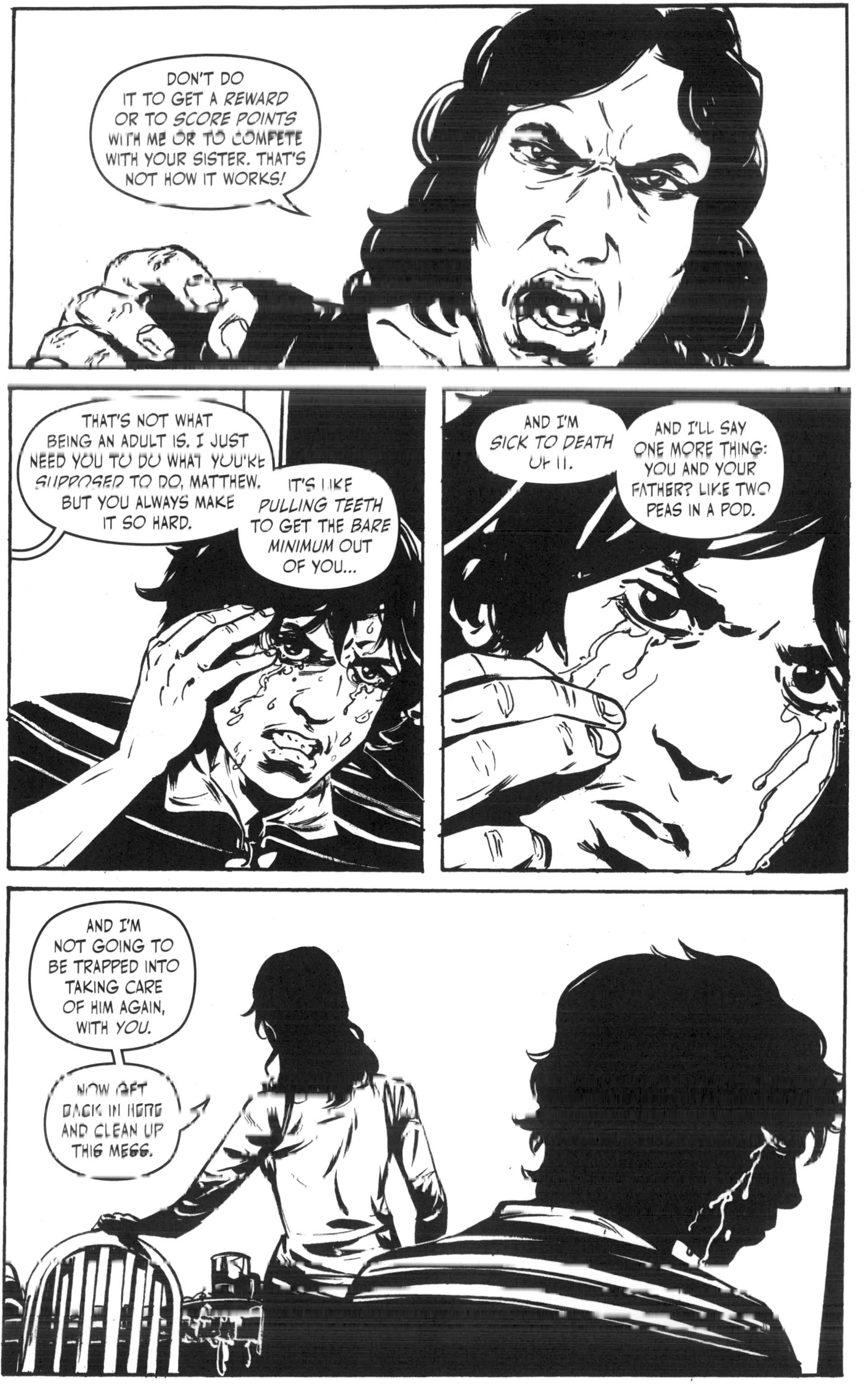
DON'T DO IT TO GET A REWARD OR TO SCORE POINTS WITH ME OR TO COMPETE WITH YOUR SISTER. THAT'S NOT HOW IT WORKS!
THAT'S NOT WHAT BEING AN ADULT IS. I JUST NEED YOU TO DO WHAT YOU'RE SUPPOSED TO DO, MATTHEW. BUT YOU ALWAYS MAKE IT SO HARD.
IT'S LIKE PULLING TEETH TO GET THE BARE MINIMUM OUT OF YOU...
AND I'M SICK TO DEATH OF IT.
AND I'LL SAY ONE MORE THING: YOU AND YOUR FATHER? LIKE TWO PEAS IN A POD.
AND I'M NOT GOING TO BE TRAPPED INTO TAKING CARE OF HIM AGAIN, WITH YOU.
NOW GET BACK IN HERE AND CLEAN UP THIS MESS.

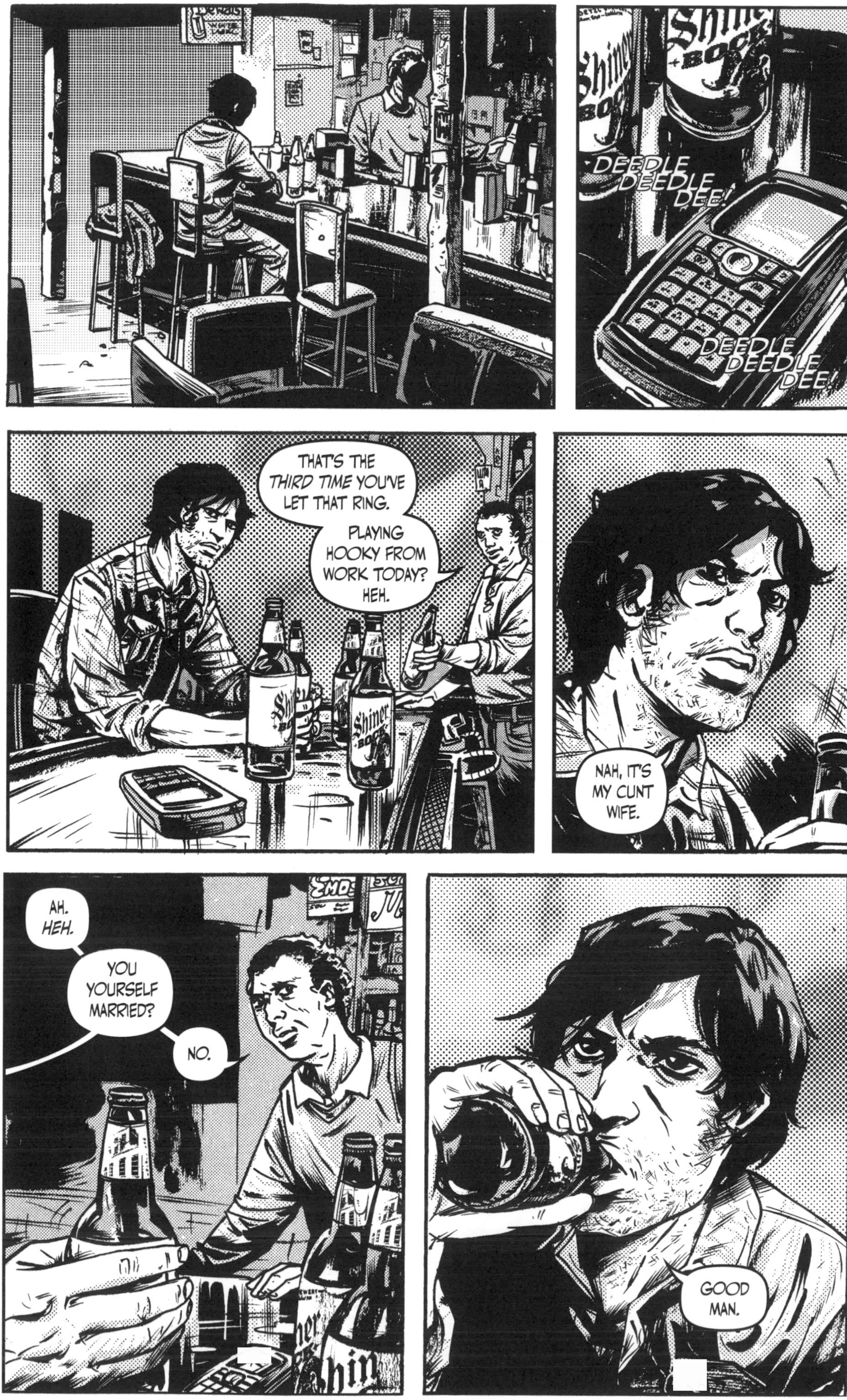
DEEDLE DEEDLE DEE!
DEEDLE DEEDLE DEE!
THAT'S THE *THIRD TIME* YOU'VE LET THAT RING.
PLAYING HOOKY FROM WORK TODAY? HEH.
NAH, IT'S MY CUNT WIFE.
AH. HEH.
YOU YOURSELF MARRIED?
NO.
GOOD MAN.

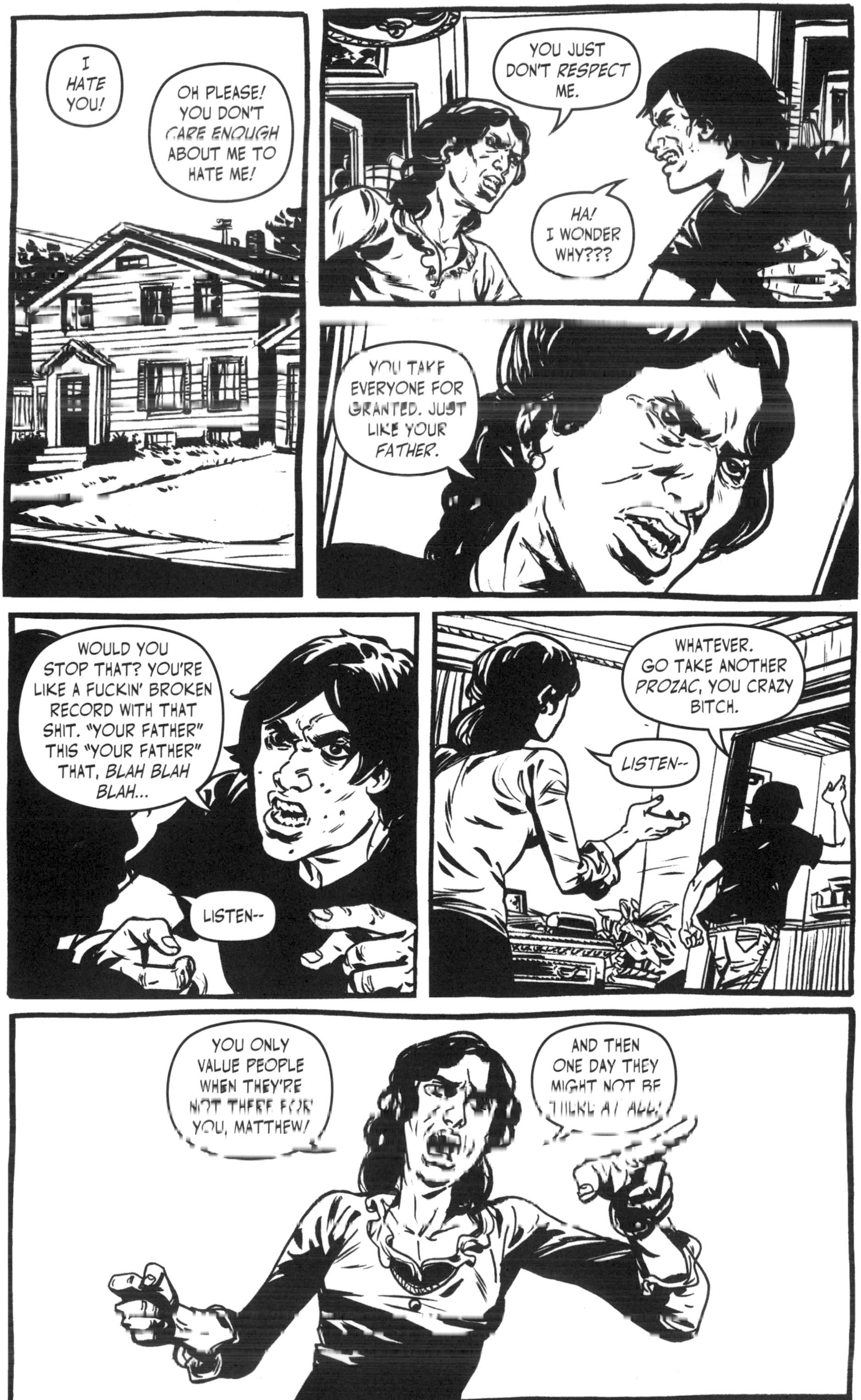
I HATE YOU!
OH PLEASE! YOU DON'T CARE ENOUGH ABOUT ME TO HATE ME!
YOU JUST DON'T RESPECT ME.
HA! I WONDER WHY???
YOU TAKE EVERYONE FOR GRANTED. JUST LIKE YOUR FATHER.
WOULD YOU STOP THAT? YOU'RE LIKE A FUCKIN' BROKEN RECORD WITH THAT SHIT. "YOUR FATHER" THIS "YOUR FATHER" THAT, BLAH BLAH BLAH...
LISTEN--
WHATEVER. GO TAKE ANOTHER PROZAC, YOU CRAZY BITCH.
LISTEN--
YOU ONLY VALUE PEOPLE WHEN THEY'RE NOT THERE FOR YOU, MATTHEW!
AND THEN ONE DAY THEY MIGHT NOT BE THERE AT ALL!

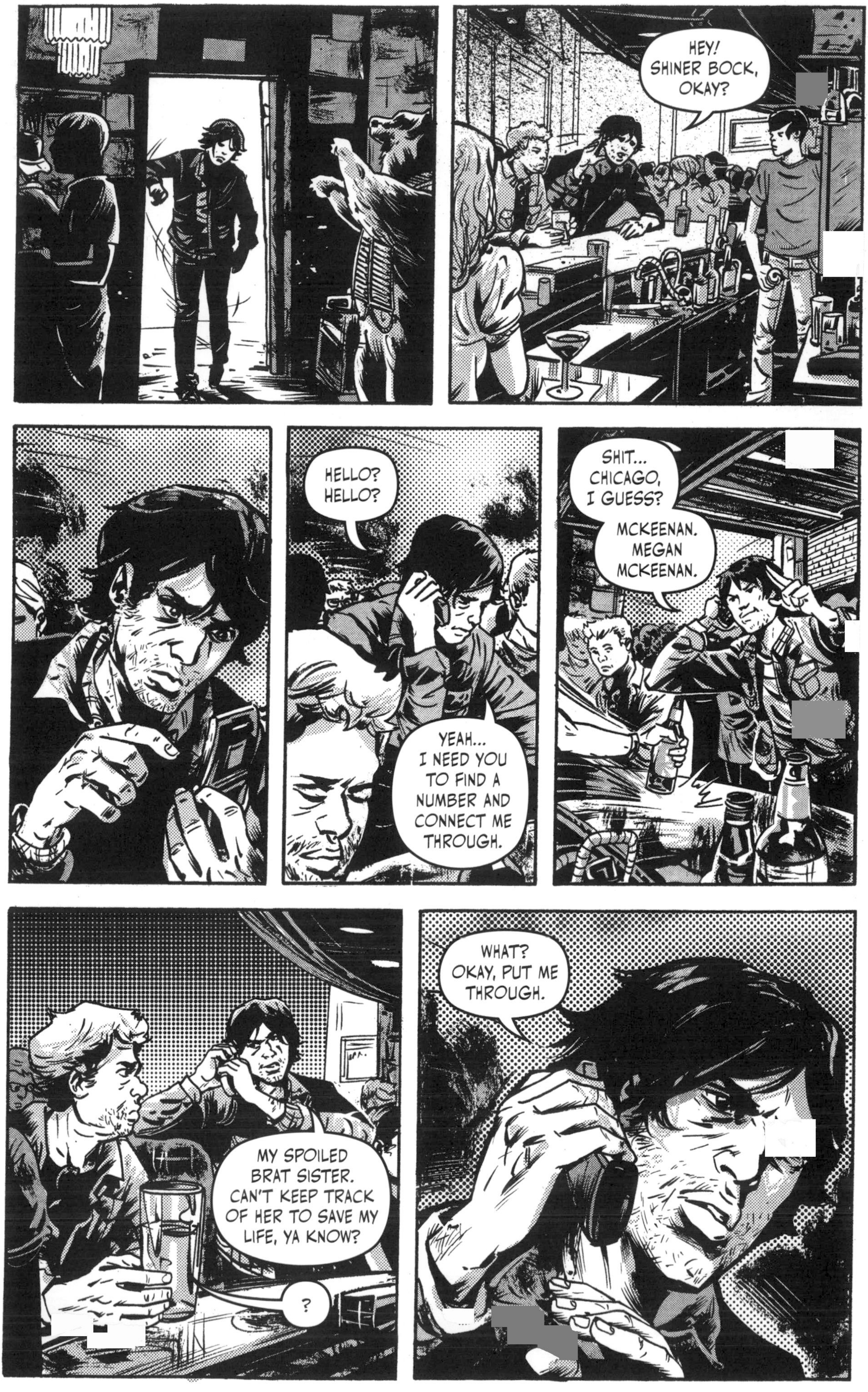
HEY! SHINER BOCK, OKAY?
HELLO? HELLO?
YEAH... I NEED YOU TO FIND A NUMBER AND CONNECT ME THROUGH.
SHIT... CHICAGO, I GUESS?
MCKEENAN. MEGAN MCKEENAN.
MY SPOILED BRAT SISTER. CAN'T KEEP TRACK OF HER TO SAVE MY LIFE, YA KNOW?
?
WHAT? OKAY, PUT ME THROUGH.

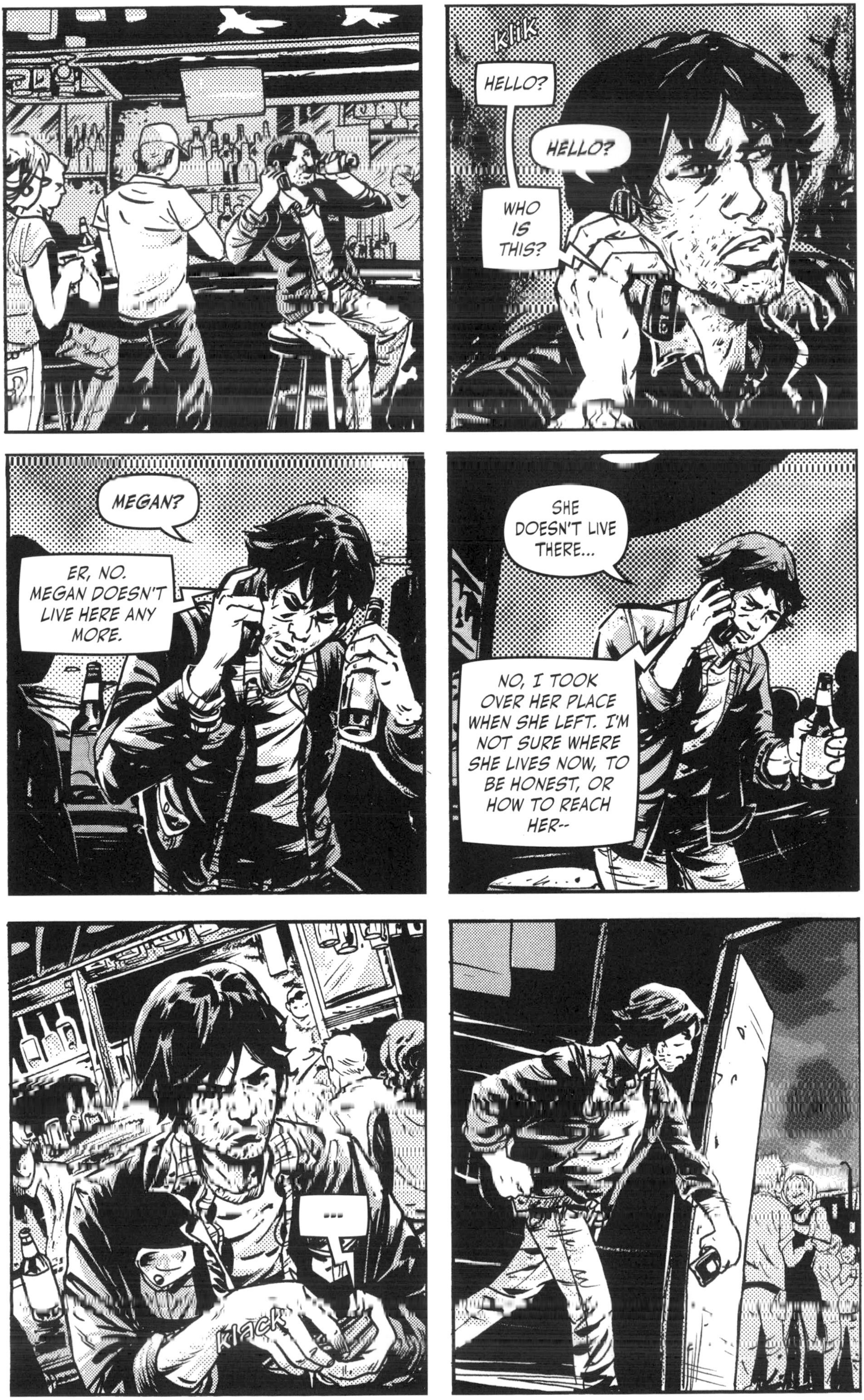
Klik
HELLO?
HELLO?
WHO IS THIS?
MEGAN?
ER, NO. MEGAN DOESN'T LIVE HERE ANY MORE.
SHE DOESN'T LIVE THERE...
NO, I TOOK OVER HER PLACE WHEN SHE LEFT. I'M NOT SURE WHERE SHE LIVES NOW, TO BE HONEST, OR HOW TO REACH HER--
...
klack

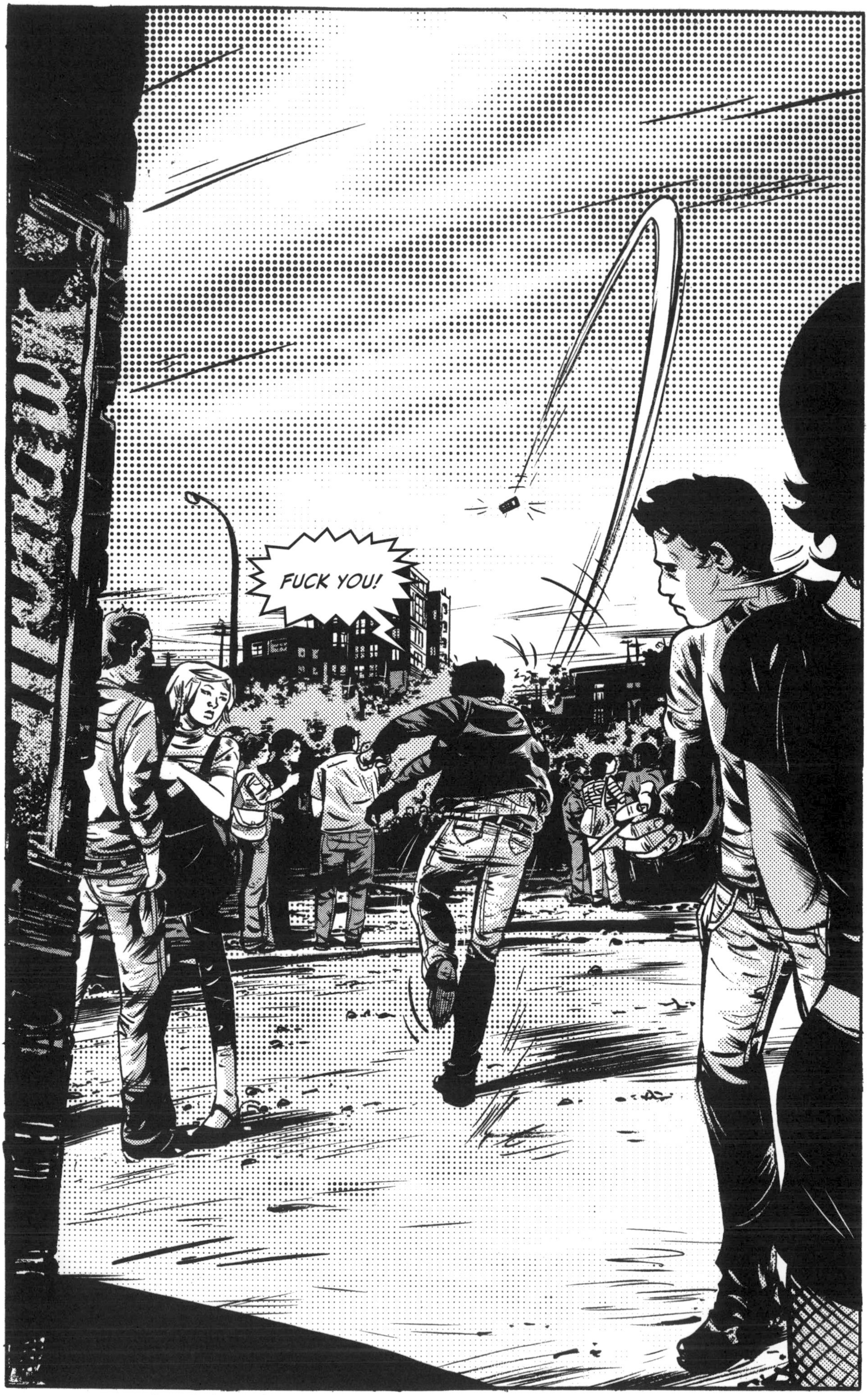
FUCK YOU!

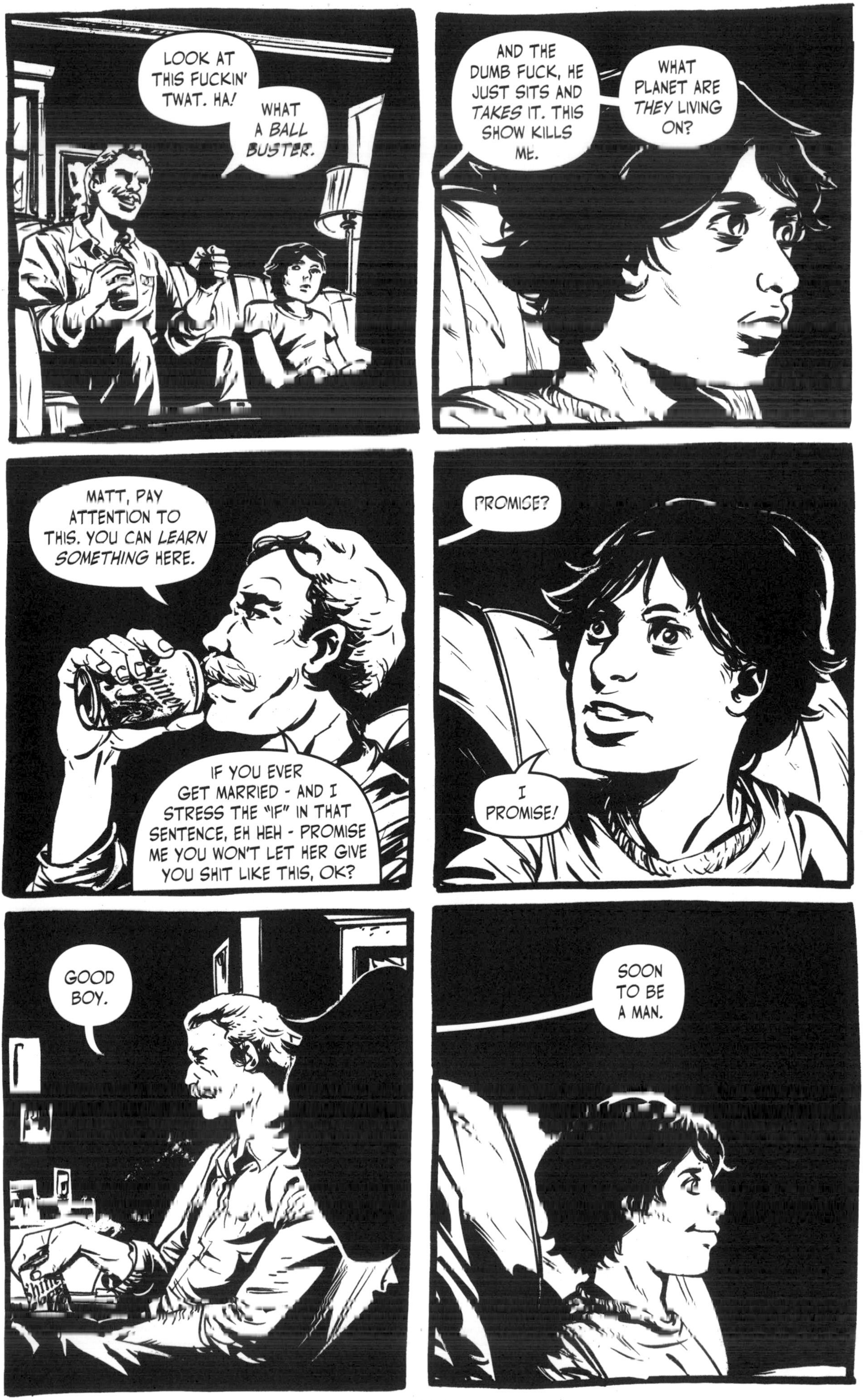
LOOK AT THIS FUCKIN' TWAT. HA!
WHAT A BALL BUSTER.
AND THE DUMB FUCK, HE JUST SITS AND TAKES IT. THIS SHOW KILLS ME.
WHAT PLANET ARE THEY LIVING ON?
MATT, PAY ATTENTION TO THIS. YOU CAN LEARN SOMETHING HERE.
IF YOU EVER GET MARRIED - AND I STRESS THE "IF" IN THAT SENTENCE, EH HEH - PROMISE ME YOU WON'T LET HER GIVE YOU SHIT LIKE THIS, OK?
PROMISE?
I PROMISE!
GOOD BOY.
SOON TO BE A MAN.

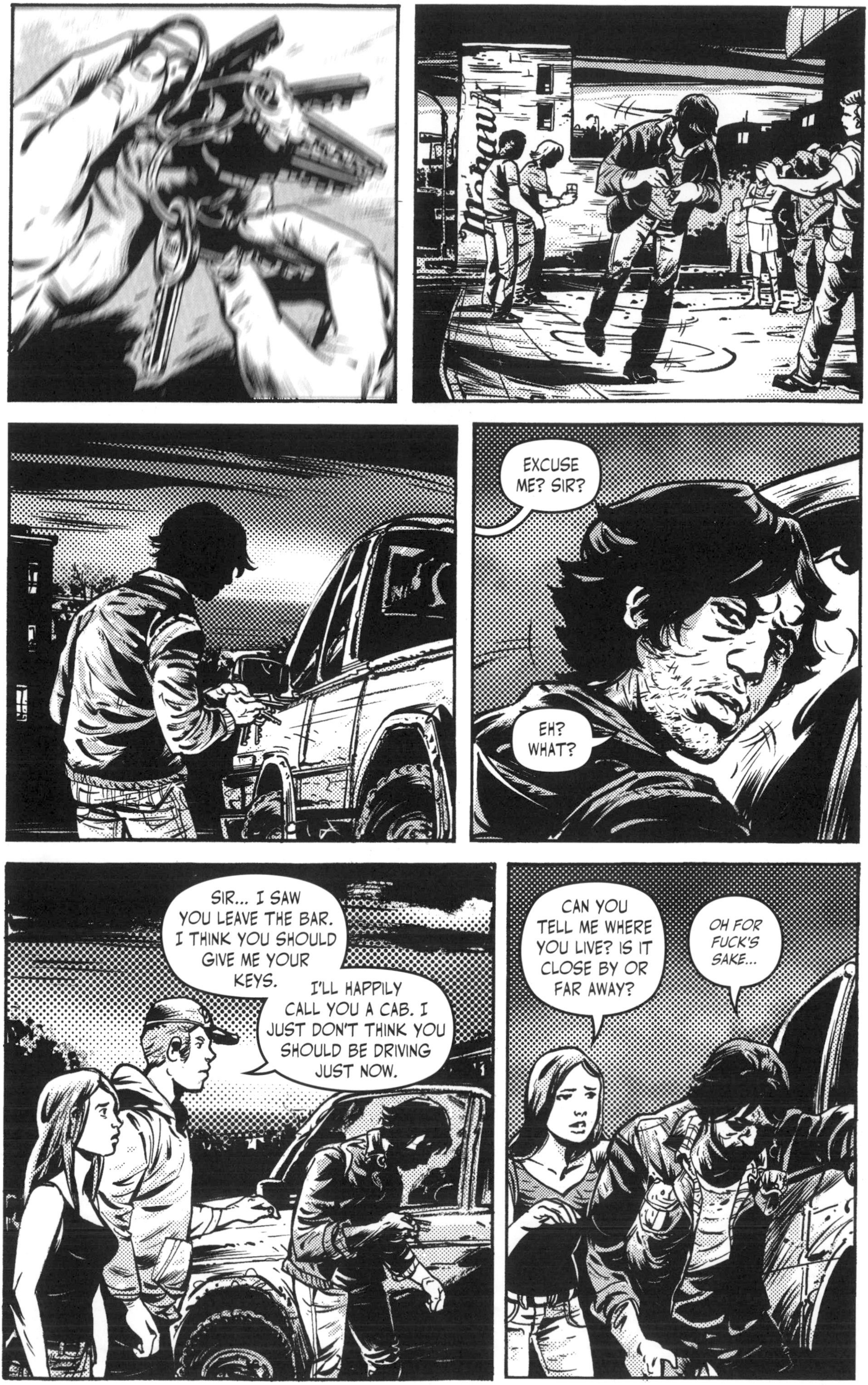

EXCUSE ME? SIR?
EH? WHAT?
SIR... I SAW YOU LEAVE THE BAR. I THINK YOU SHOULD GIVE ME YOUR KEYS.
I'LL HAPPILY CALL YOU A CAB. I JUST DON'T THINK YOU SHOULD BE DRIVING JUST NOW.
CAN YOU TELL ME WHERE YOU LIVE? IS IT CLOSE BY OR FAR AWAY?
OH FOR FUCK'S SAKE...

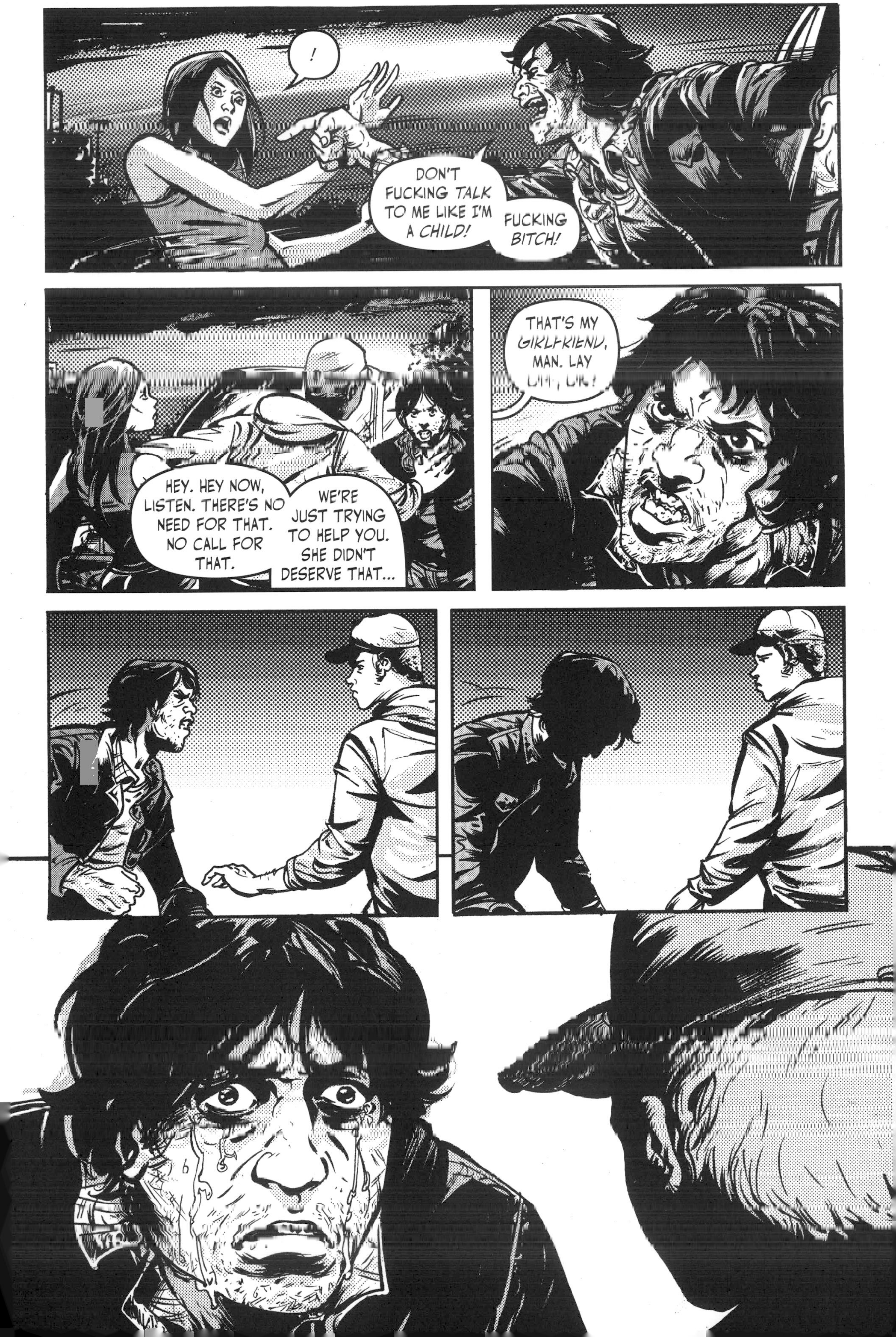
!
DON'T FUCKING TALK TO ME LIKE I'M A CHILD!
FUCKING BITCH!
HEY. HEY NOW, LISTEN. THERE'S NO NEED FOR THAT. NO CALL FOR THAT.
WE'RE JUST TRYING TO HELP YOU. SHE DIDN'T DESERVE THAT...
THAT'S MY GIRLFRIEND, MAN. LAY

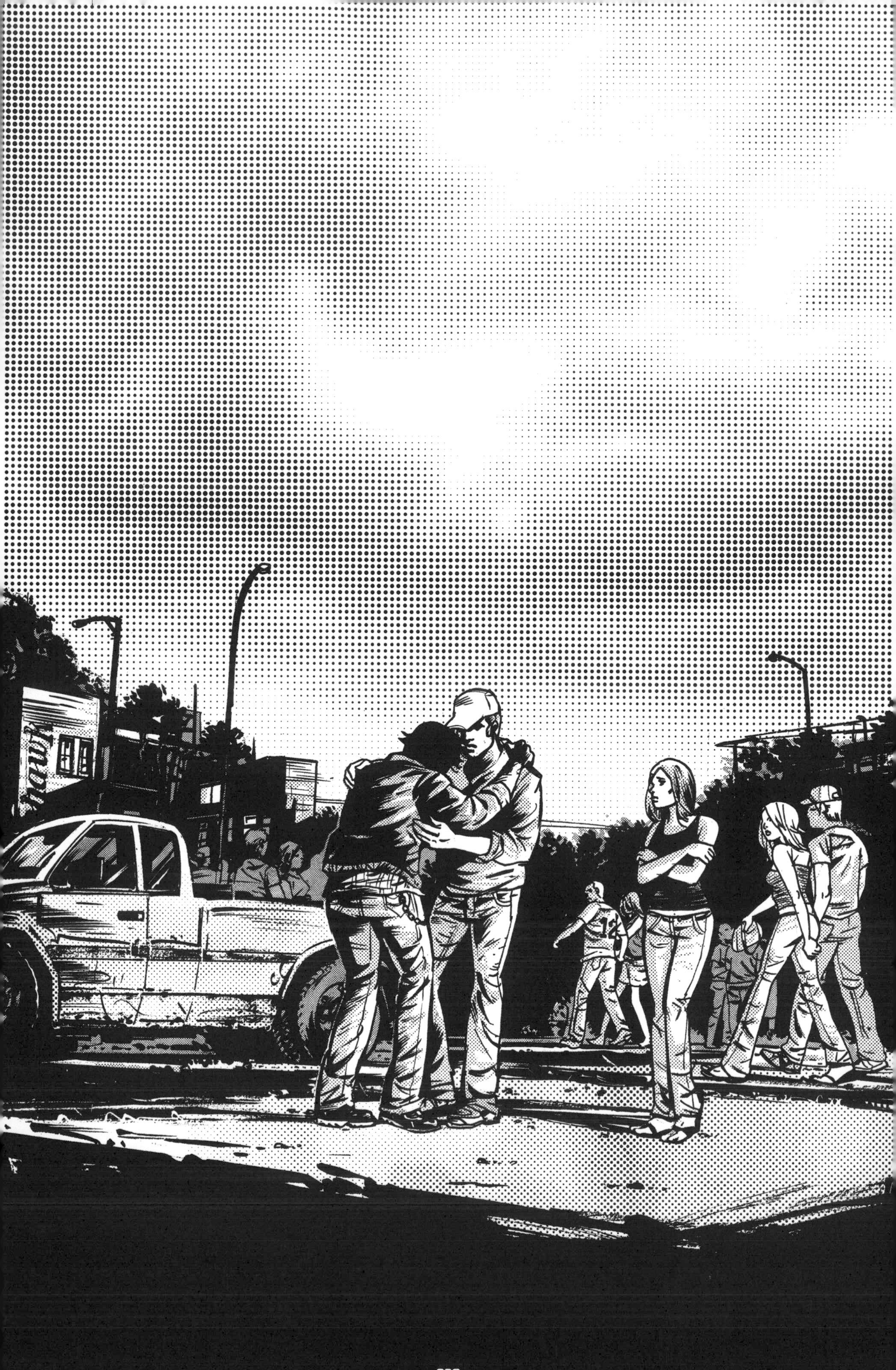

CHAPTER 11
"THE YOUNGER GENERATION"
Toronto, Ontario

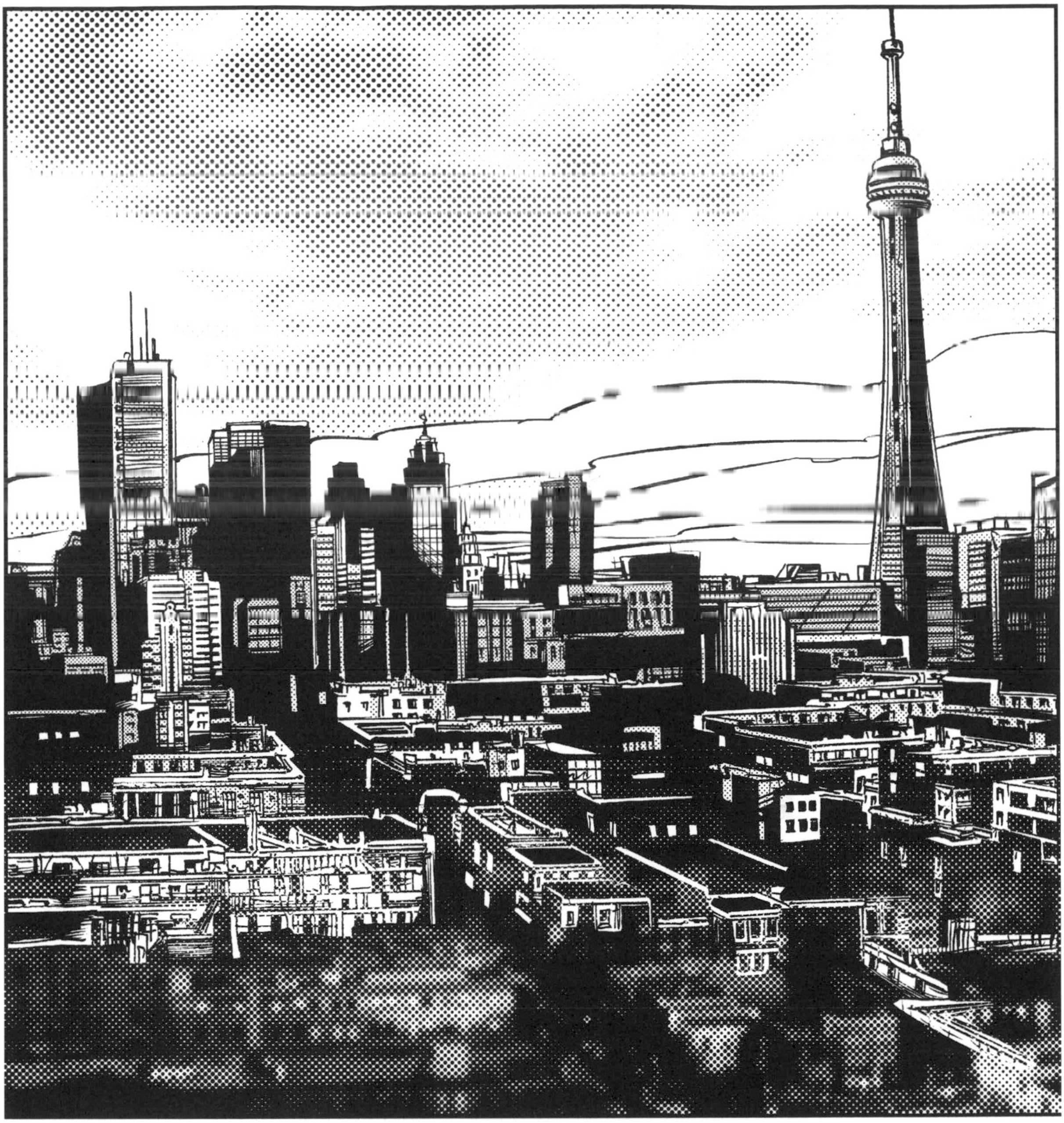

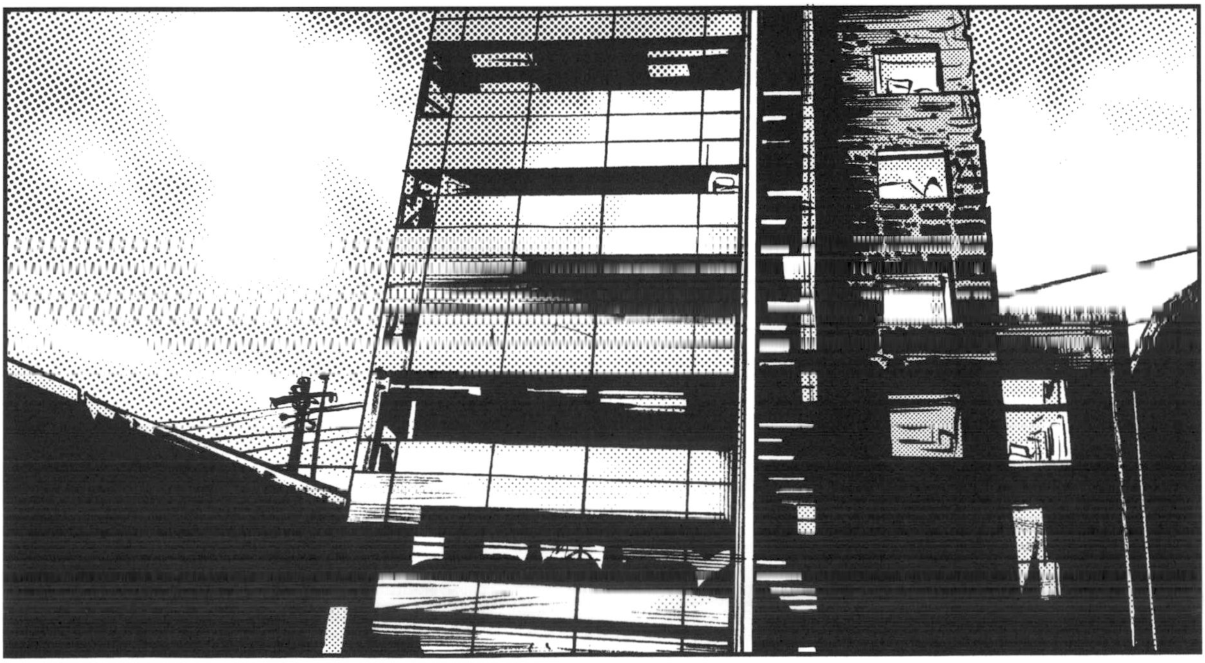

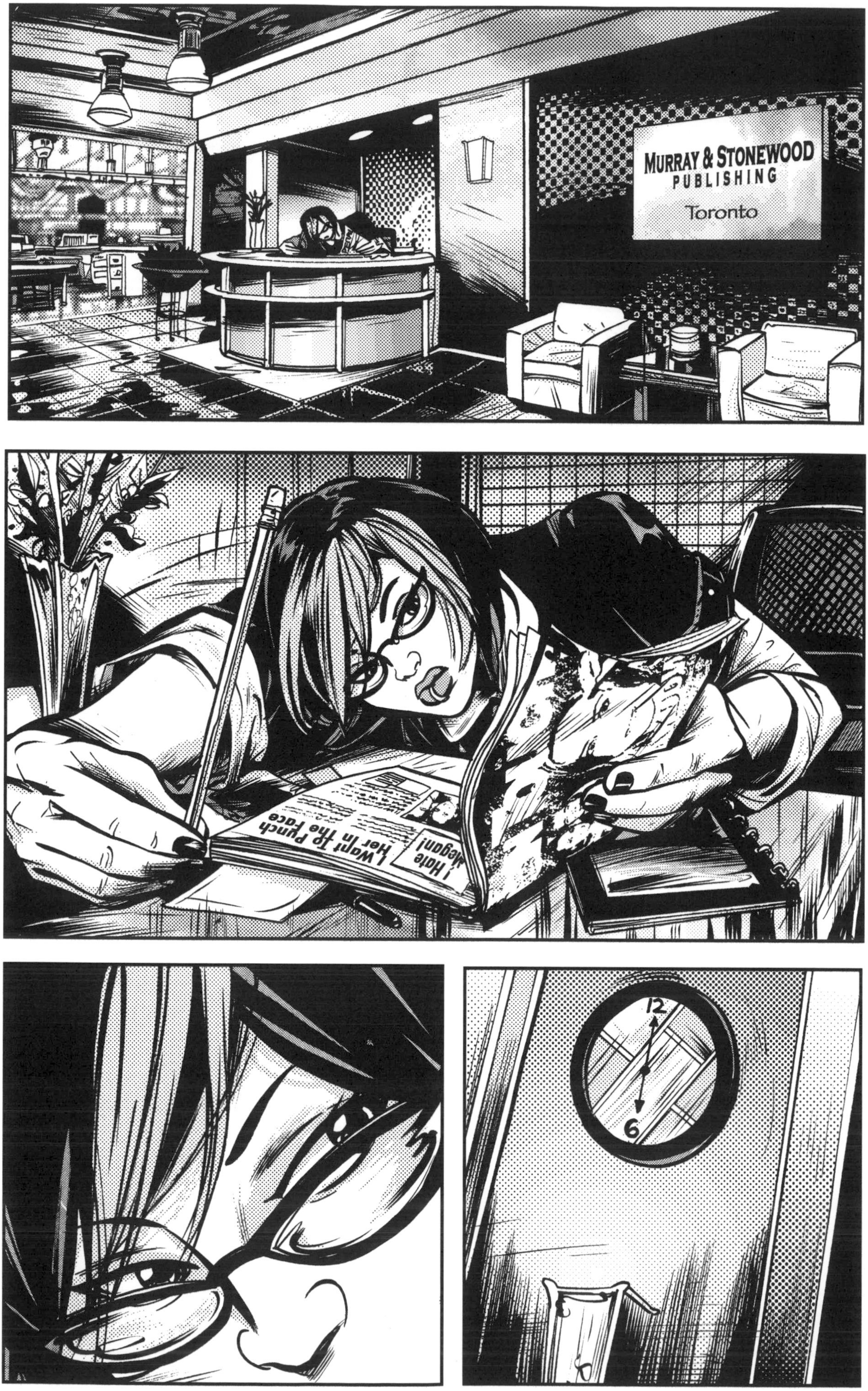
MURRAY & STONEWOOD
PUBLISHING
Toronto
I Hate Megan!
I Want To Punch Her In The Face

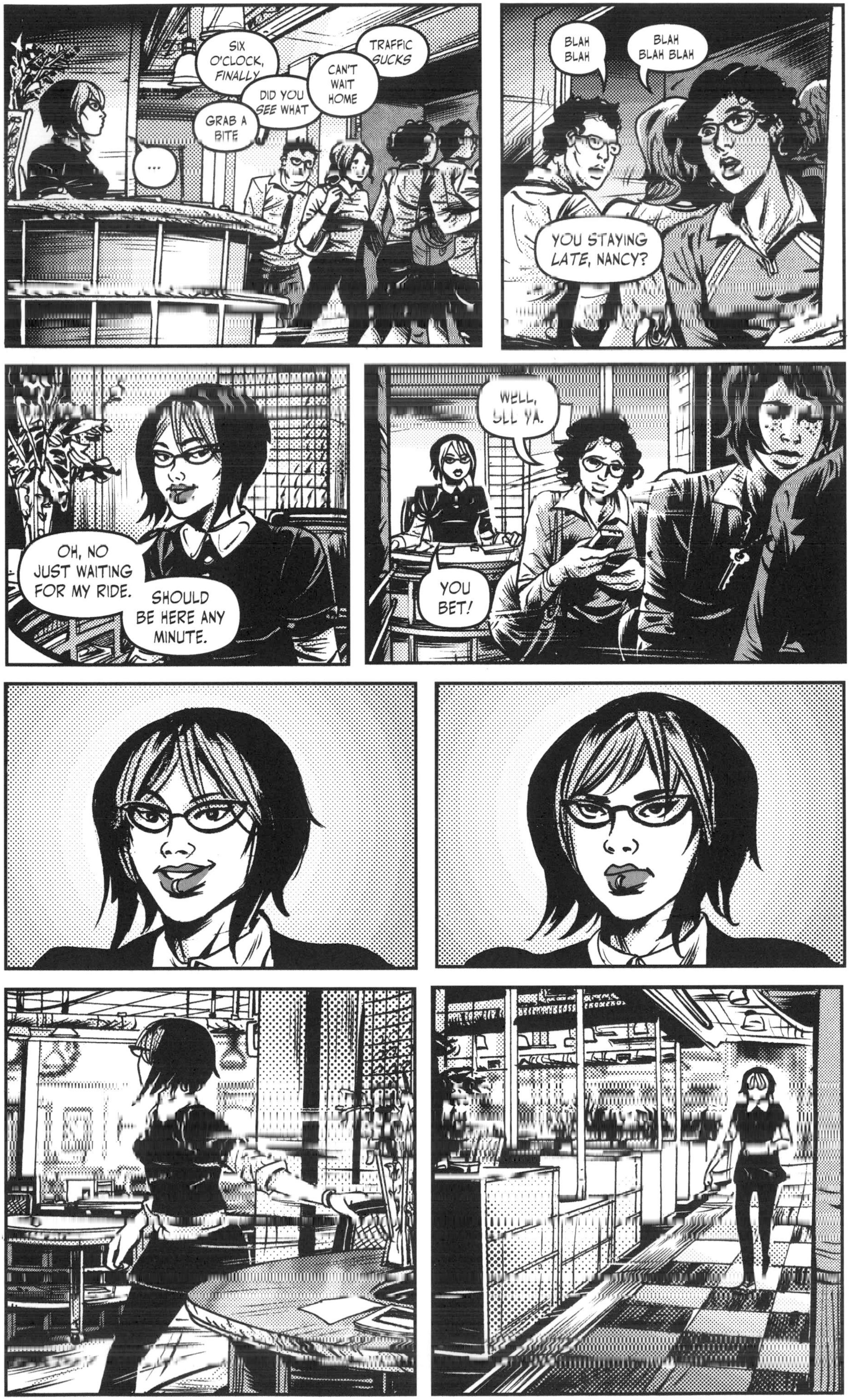
SIX O'CLOCK, FINALLY
TRAFFIC SUCKS
CAN'T WAIT HOME
DID YOU SEE WHAT
GRAB A BITE
...
BLAH BLAH
BLAH BLAH BLAH
YOU STAYING LATE, NANCY?
OH, NO JUST WAITING FOR MY RIDE.
SHOULD BE HERE ANY MINUTE.
WELL, SEE YA.
YOU BET!

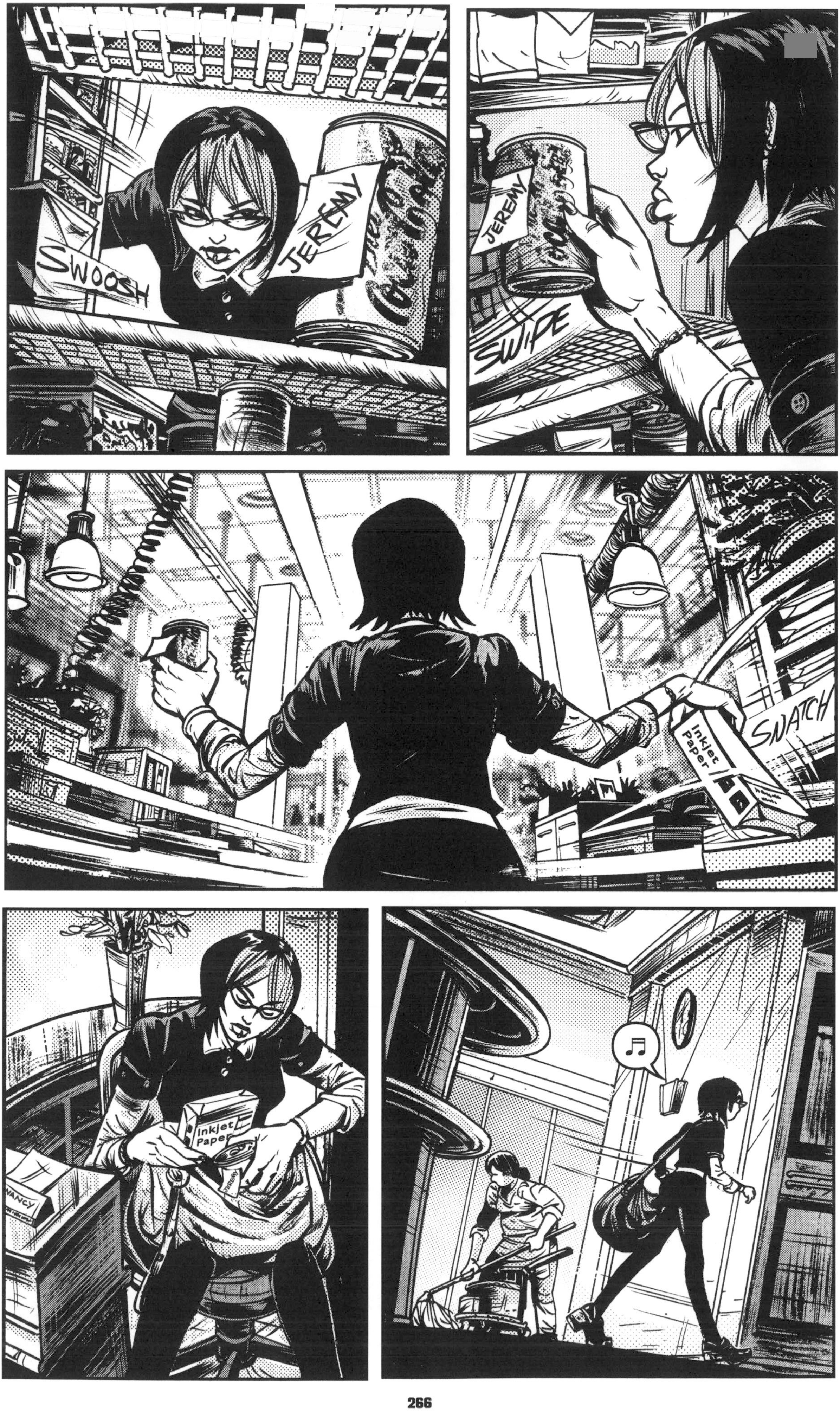
SWOOSH
JEREMY
JEREMY
SWIPE
SNATCH
Inkjet Paper
Inkjet Paper
NANCY
JEREMY
♫

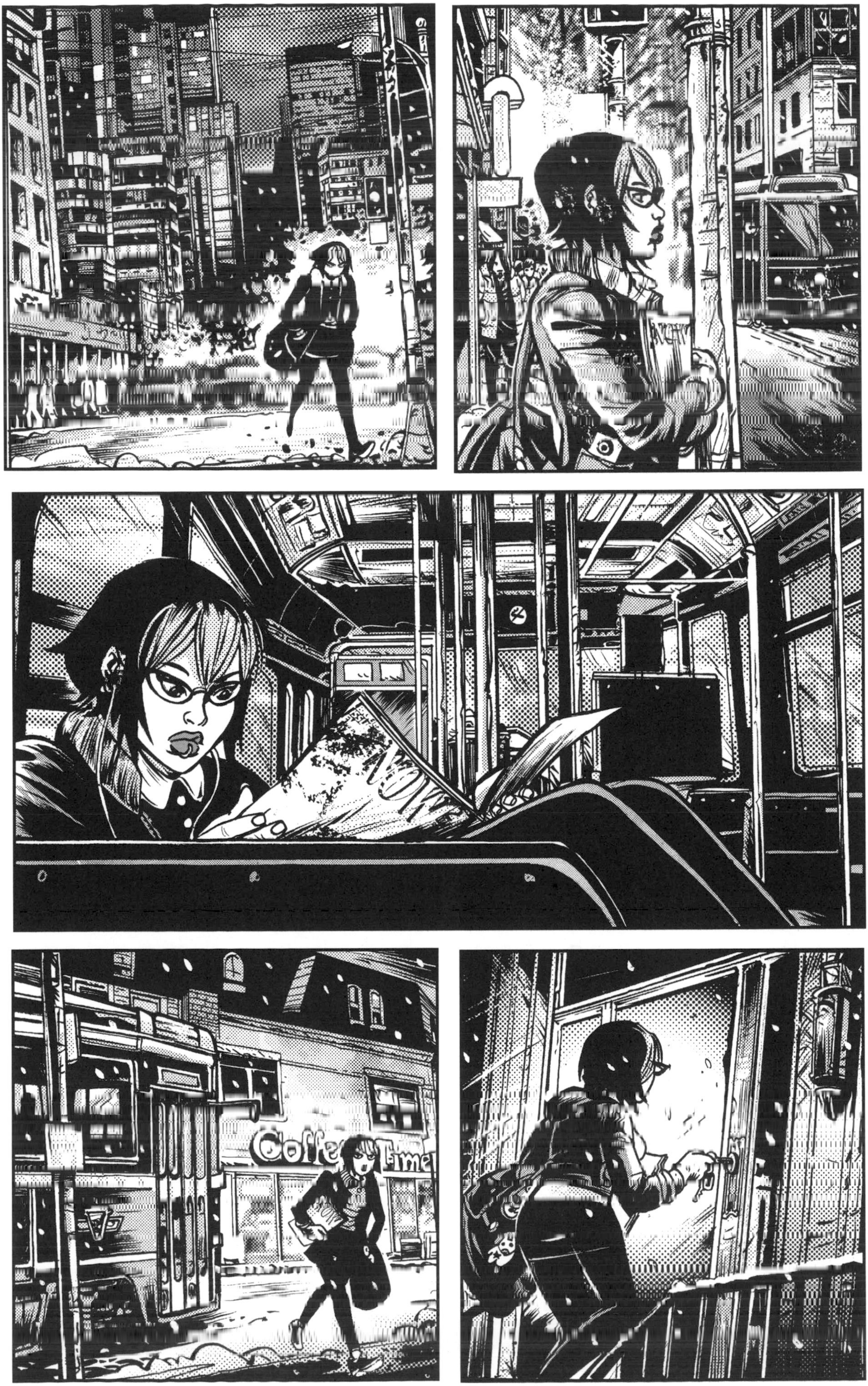

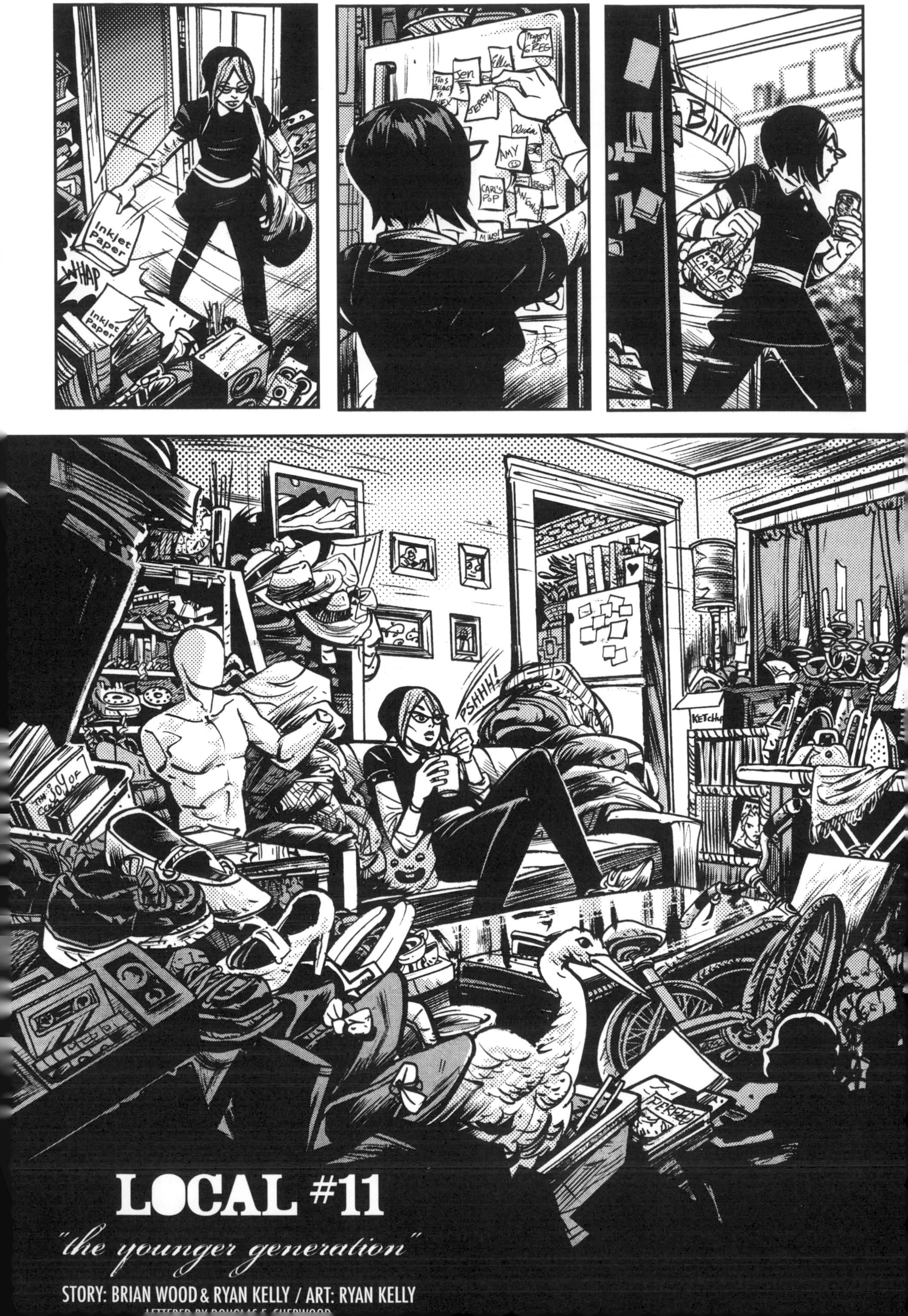
Inkjet Paper
WHAP
Inkjet Paper
PROPERTY OF GREG
Ellen
Jen
THIS BELONGS TO ALEX
JEREMY
Olivia
AMY
CARL'S POP
ANTONIO
Robert
MINE!
BAM!
PSHHH!
LOCAL #11
"the younger generation"
STORY: BRIAN WOOD & RYAN KELLY / ART: RYAN KELLY

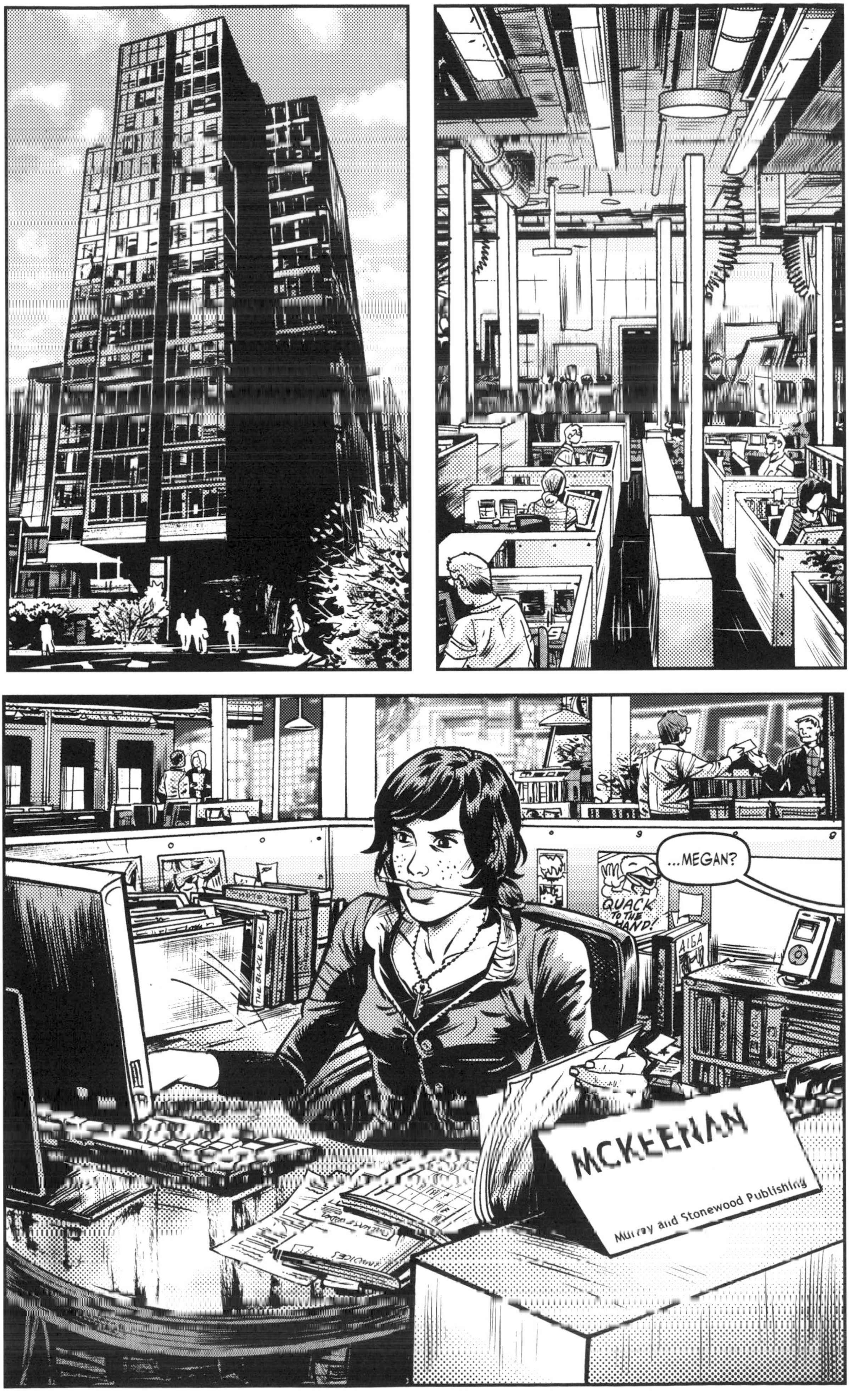
...MEGAN?
QUACK TO THE HAND!
AIGA
MCKEENAN
Murray and Stonewood Publishing
INVOICES

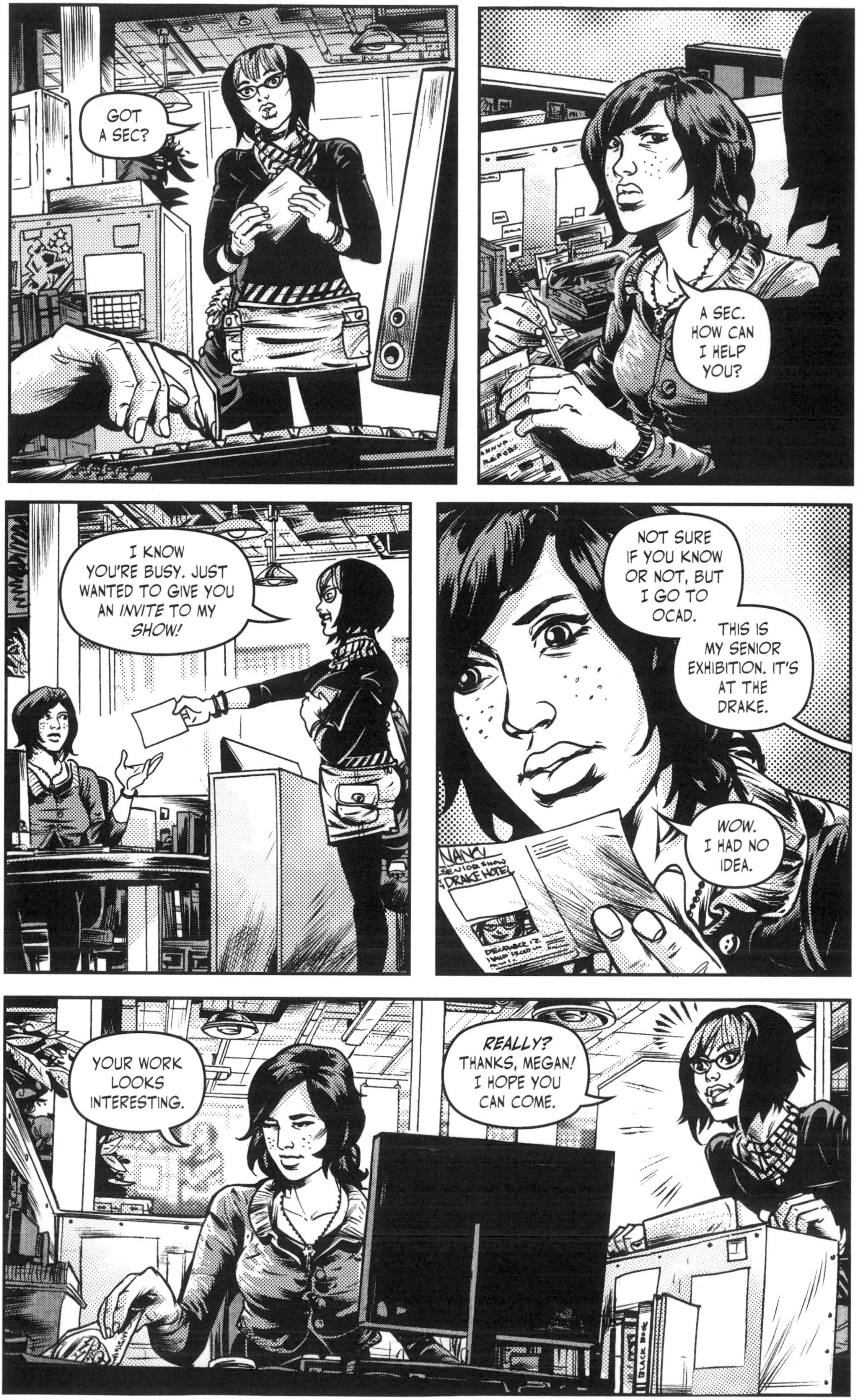
GOT A SEC?
A SEC. HOW CAN I HELP YOU?
I KNOW YOU'RE BUSY. JUST WANTED TO GIVE YOU AN *INVITE* TO MY *SHOW!*
NOT SURE IF YOU KNOW OR NOT, BUT I GO TO OCAD.
THIS IS MY SENIOR EXHIBITION. IT'S AT THE DRAKE.
NANCY SENIOR SHOW DRAKE HOTEL
WOW. I HAD NO IDEA.
YOUR WORK LOOKS INTERESTING.
REALLY? THANKS, MEGAN! I HOPE YOU CAN COME.

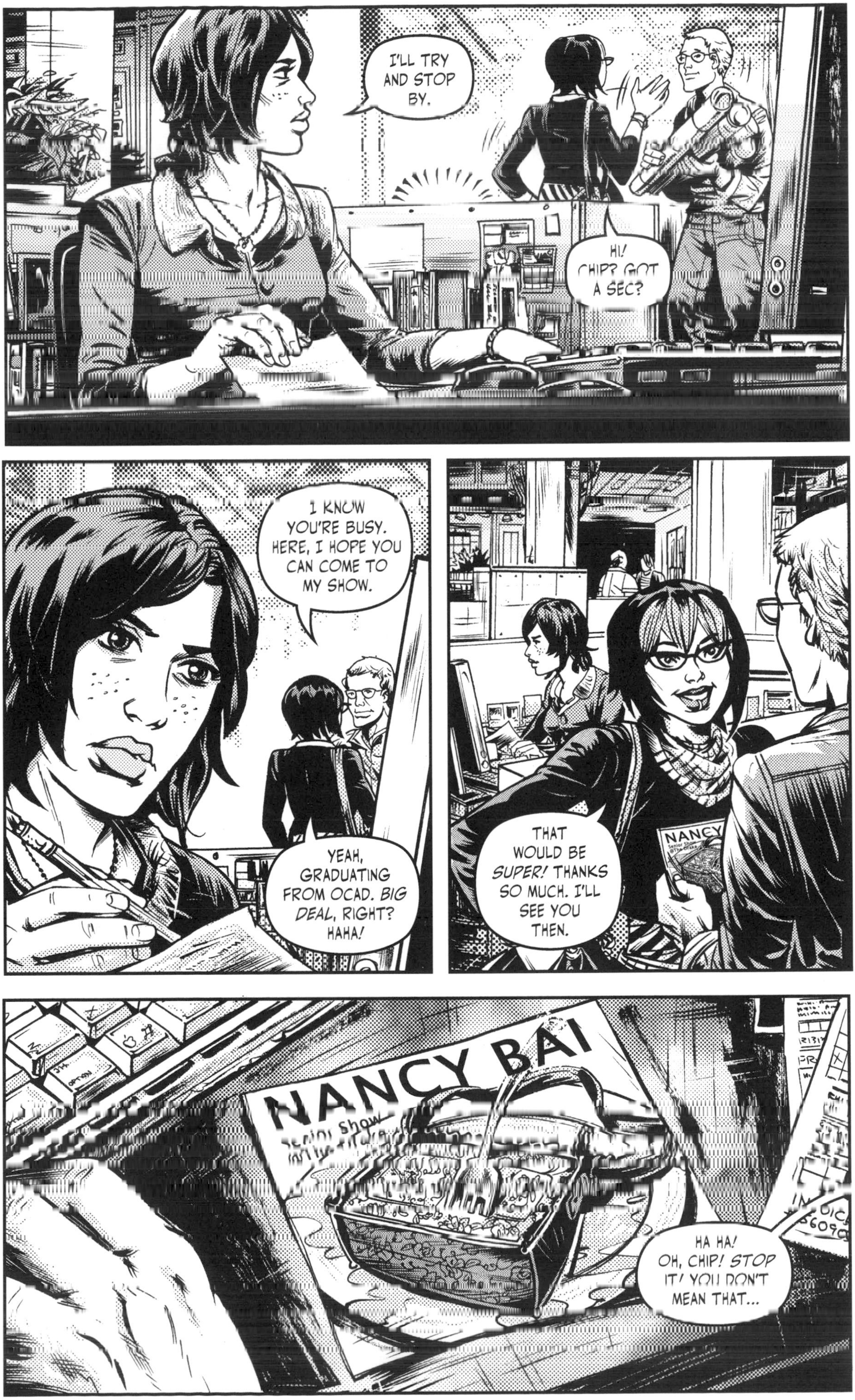
I'LL TRY AND STOP BY.
HI! CHIP? GOT A SEC?
I KNOW YOU'RE BUSY. HERE, I HOPE YOU CAN COME TO MY SHOW.
YEAH, GRADUATING FROM OCAD. *BIG DEAL*, RIGHT? HAHA!
NANCY
THAT WOULD BE *SUPER!* THANKS SO MUCH. I'LL SEE YOU THEN.
NANCY BAI
Senior Show
HA HA! OH, CHIP! *STOP IT!* YOU DON'T MEAN THAT...

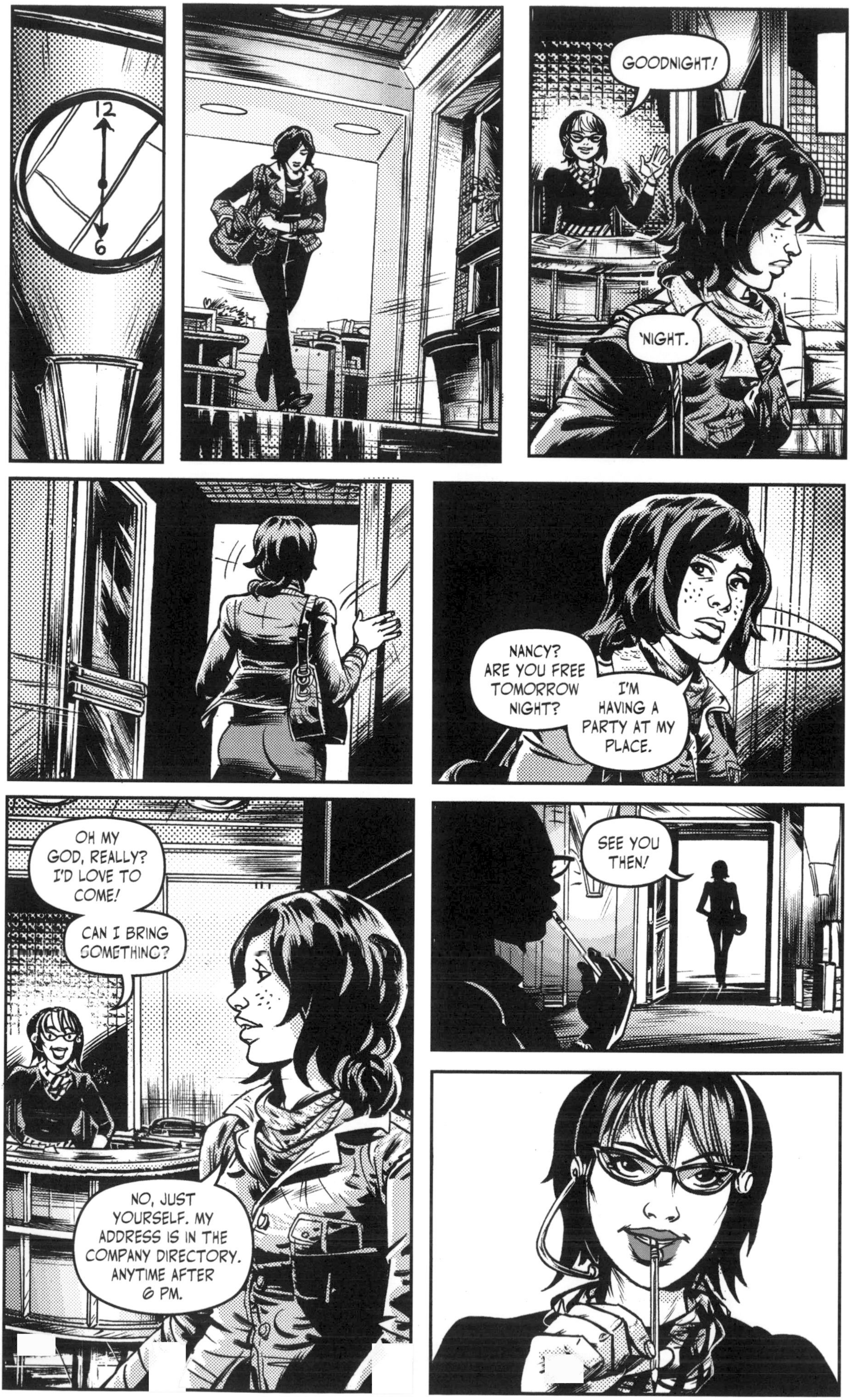

GOODNIGHT!
'NIGHT.
NANCY? ARE YOU FREE TOMORROW NIGHT?
I'M HAVING A PARTY AT MY PLACE.
OH MY GOD, REALLY? I'D LOVE TO COME!
CAN I BRING SOMETHING?
NO, JUST YOURSELF. MY ADDRESS IS IN THE COMPANY DIRECTORY. ANYTIME AFTER 6 PM.
SEE YOU THEN!

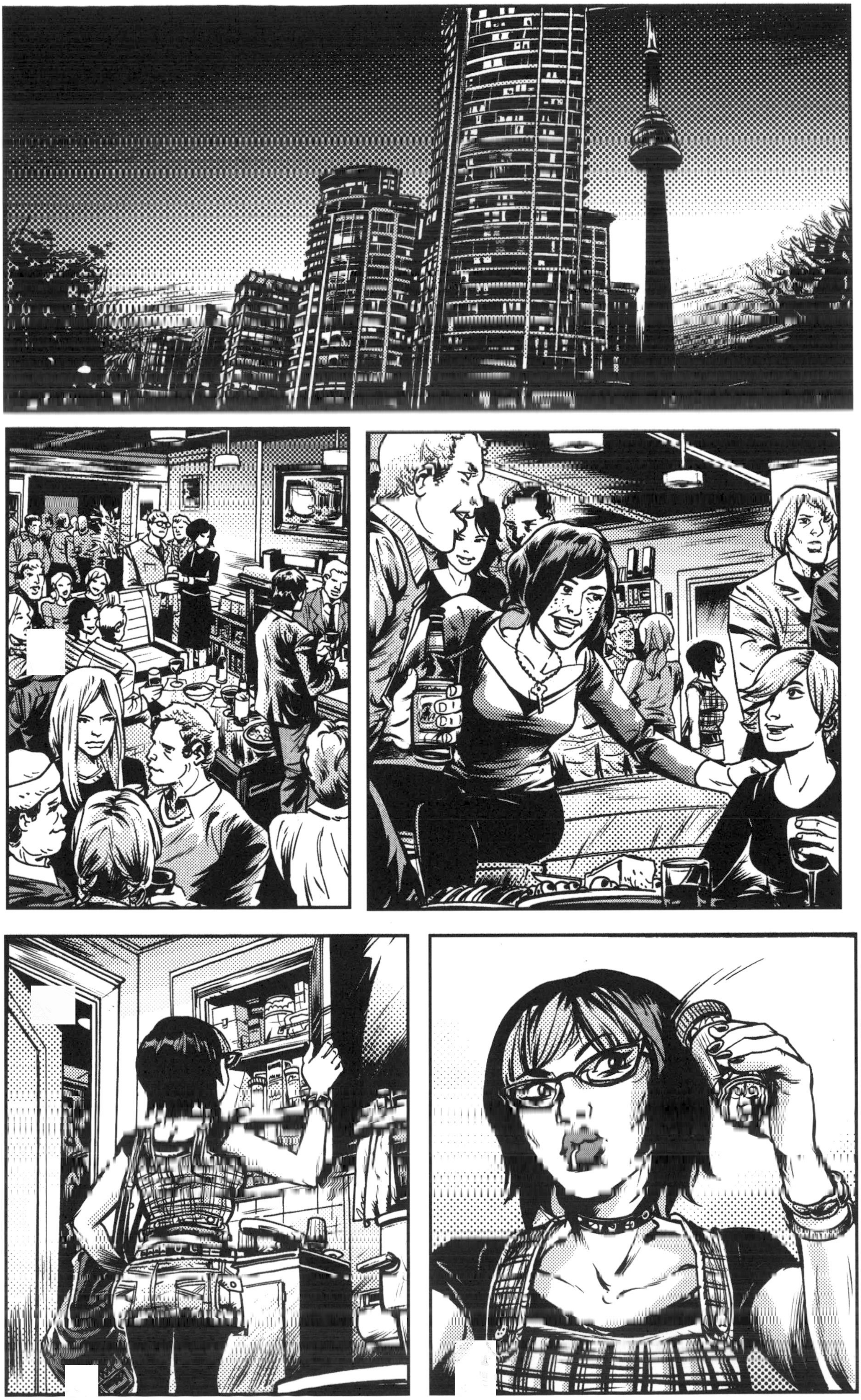

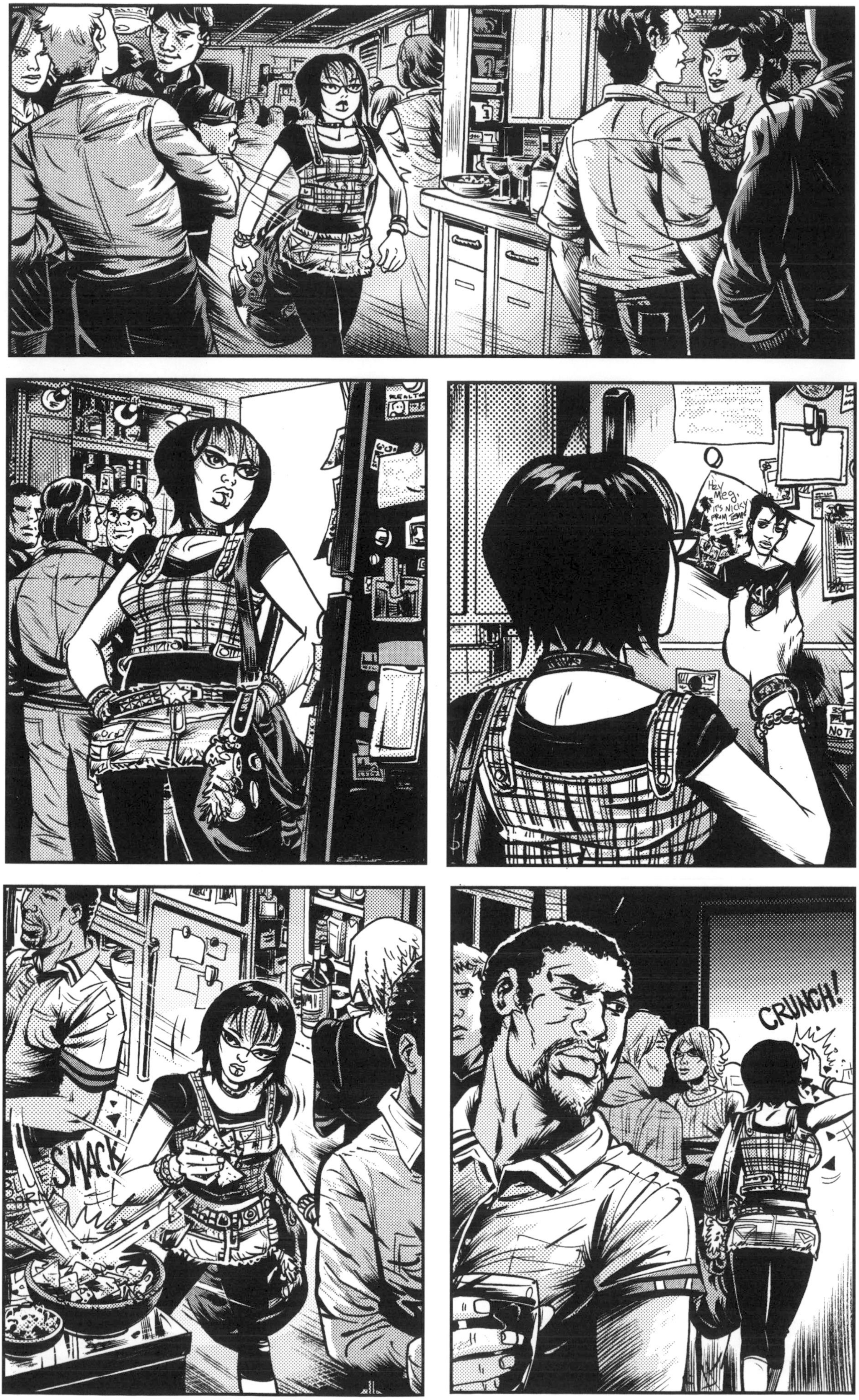
Hey Meg, IT'S NICKY FROM TEMP
SMACK
CRUNCH!

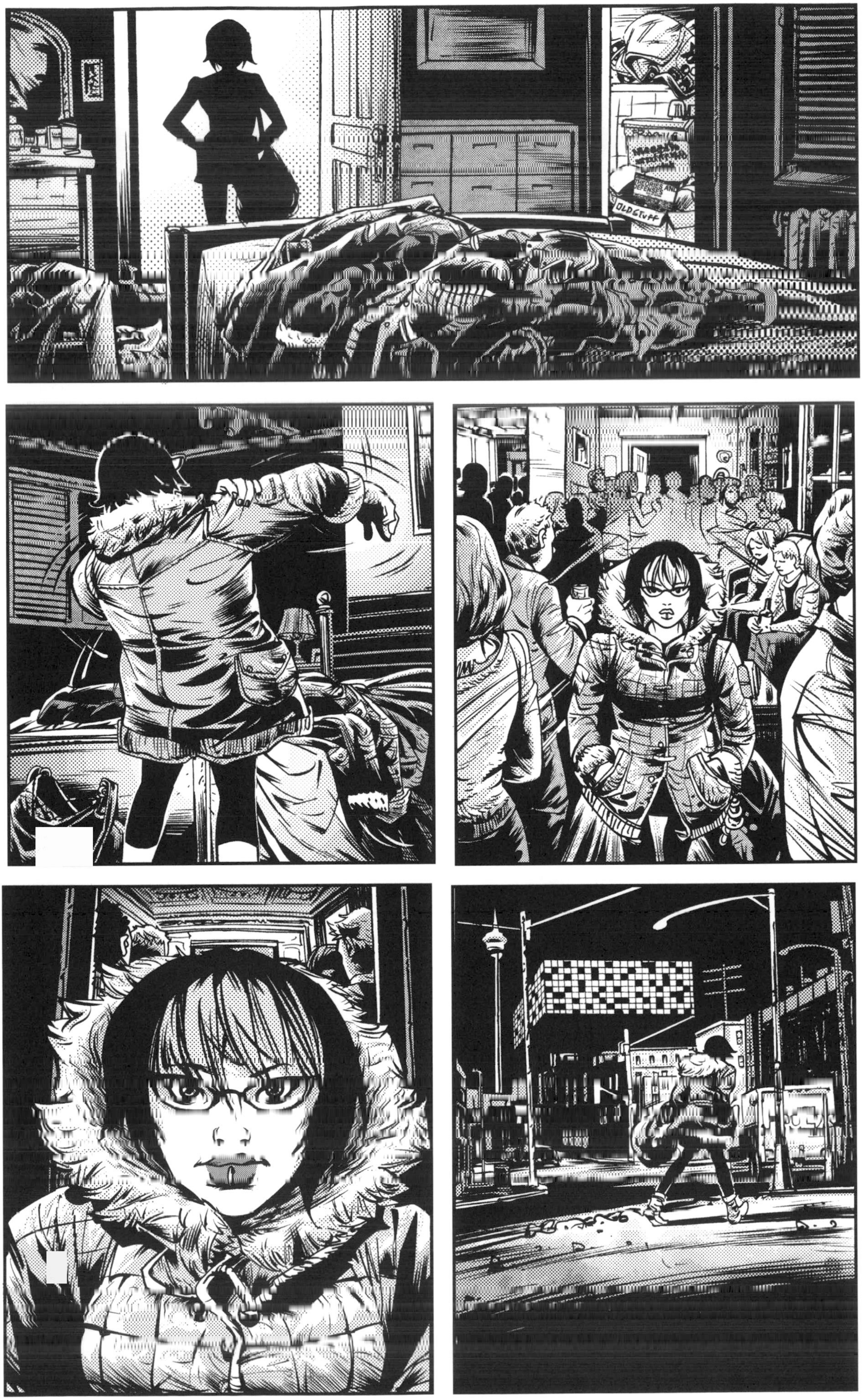
THEORIES AND DEFENSES
OLD STUFF

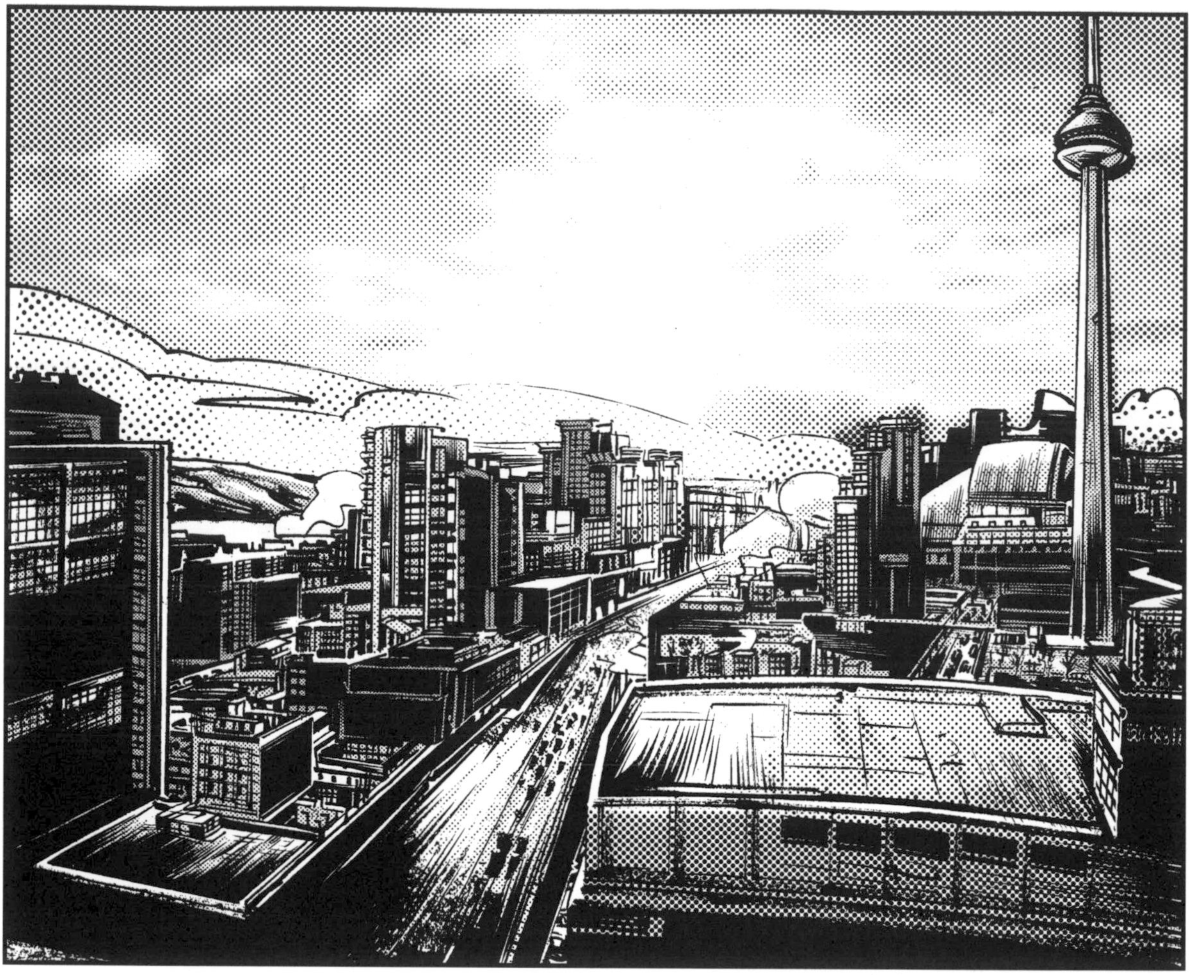

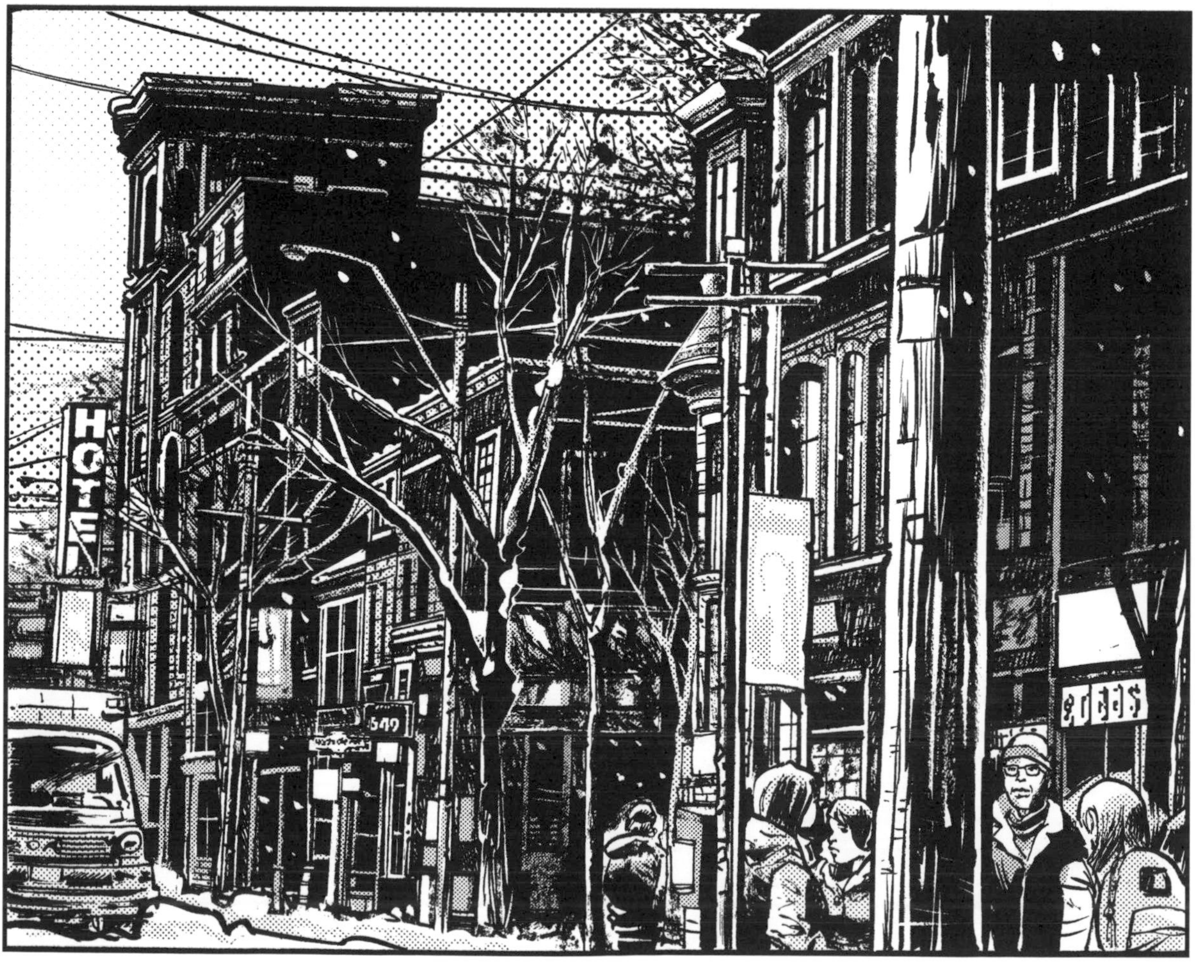
HOTE
549

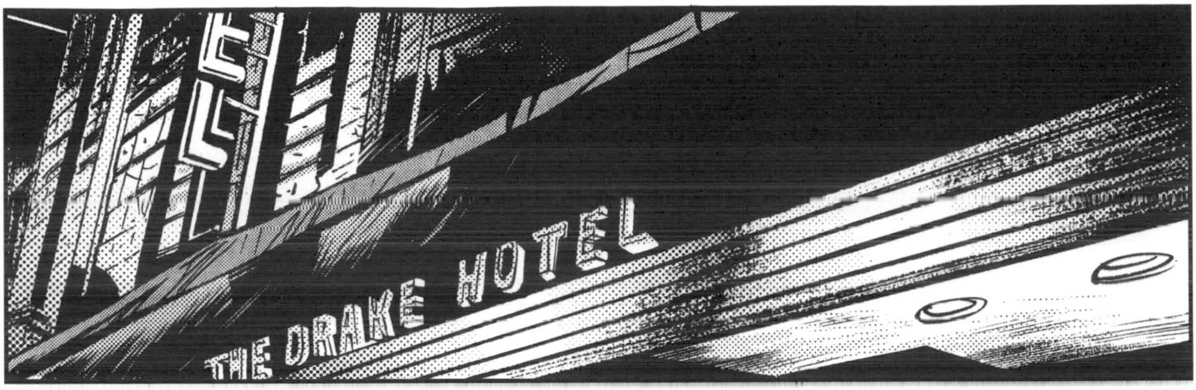
THE DRAKE HOTEL

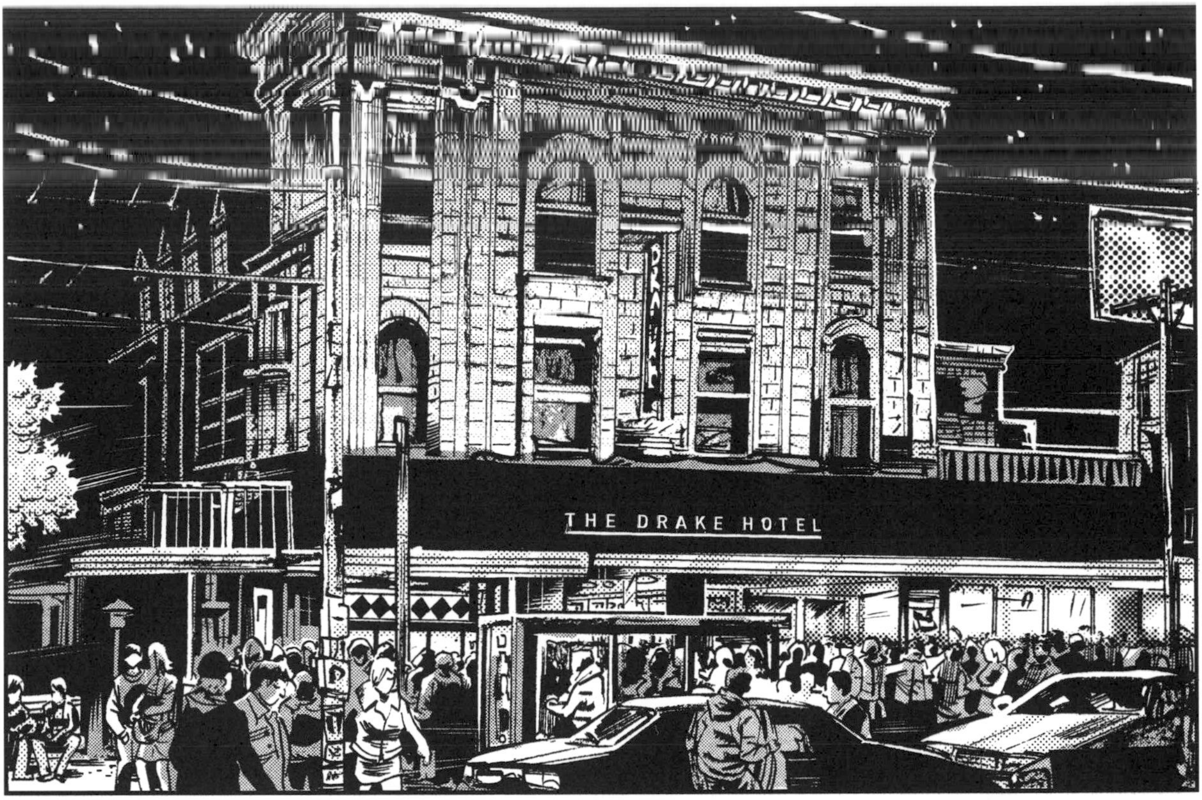
THE DRAKE HOTEL

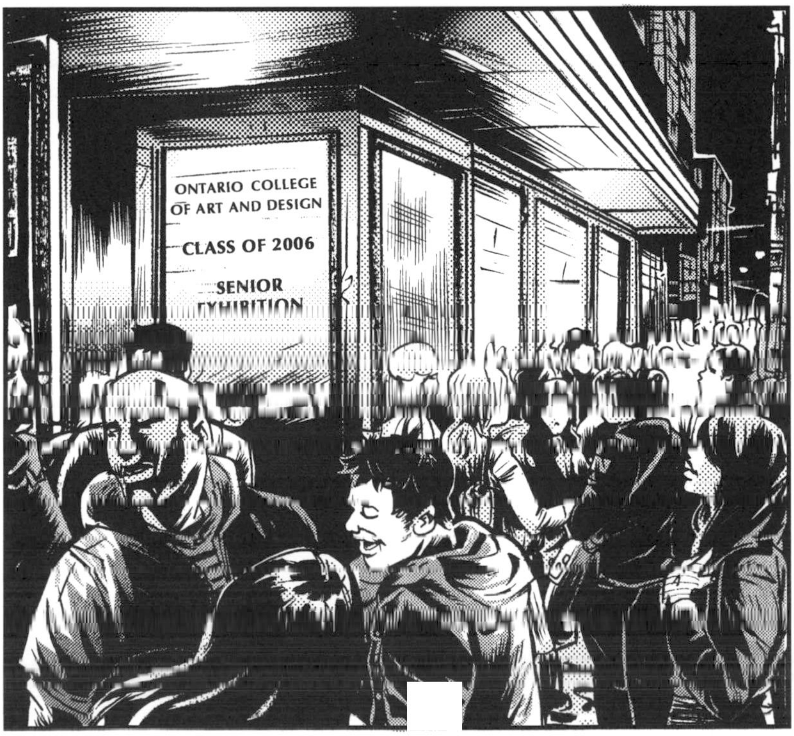
ONTARIO COLLEGE
OF ART AND DESIGN
CLASS OF 2006
SENIOR
EXHIBITION

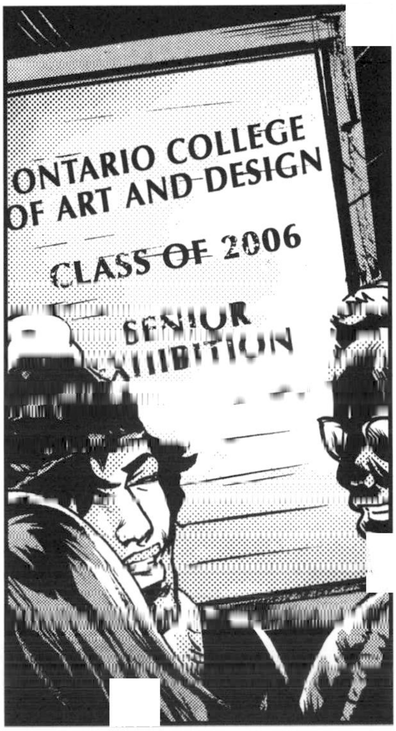
ONTARIO COLLEGE
OF ART AND DESIGN
CLASS OF 2006

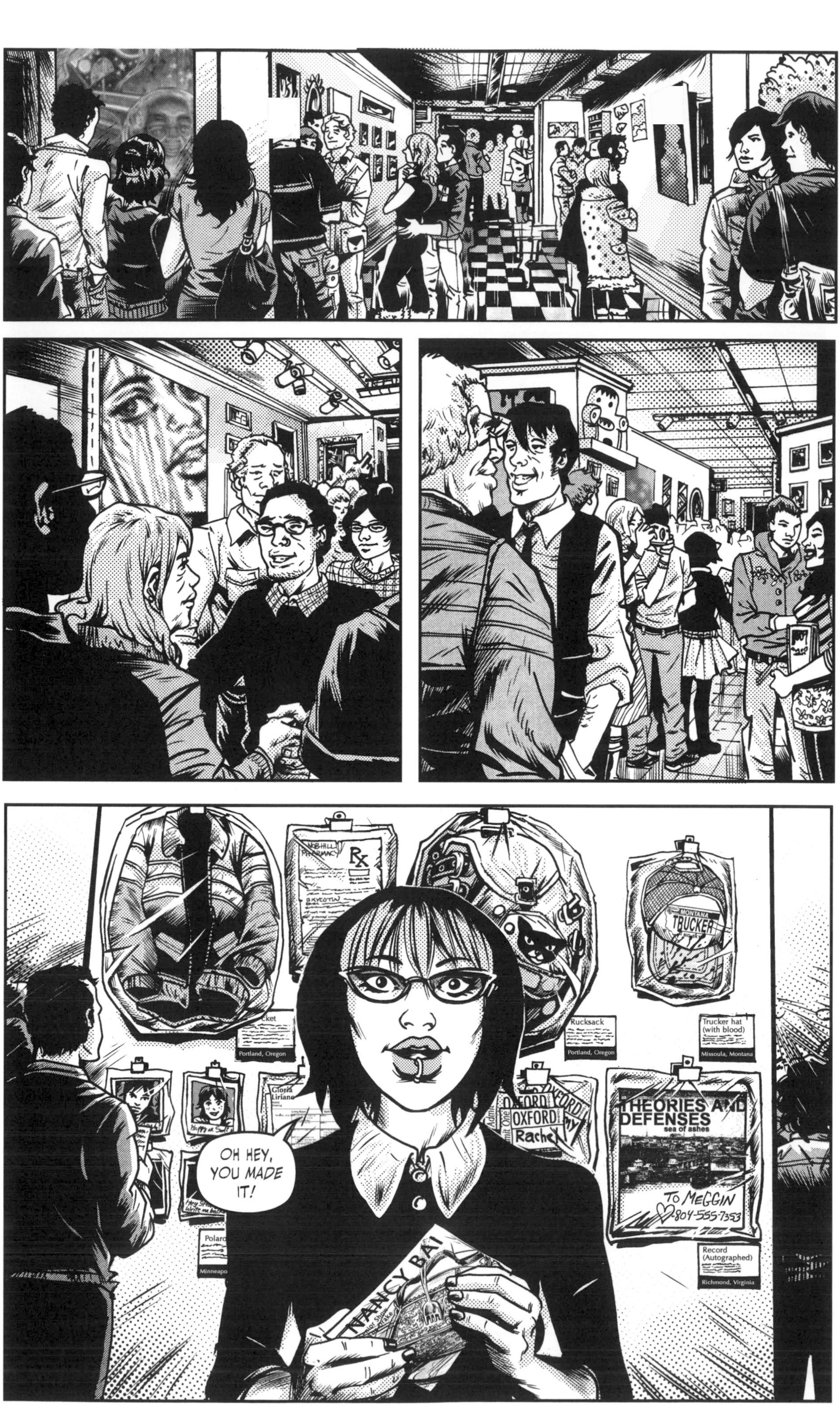
NOB HILL PHARMACY
RX
OXYCOTIN
MONTANA
TRUCKER
Portland, Oregon
Rucksack
Portland, Oregon
Trucker hat
(with blood)
Missoula, Montana
Gloria
Liriano
OXFORD
OXFORD
Rachel
OH HEY, YOU MADE IT!
THEORIES AND DEFENSES
sea of ashes
TO MEGGIN
804-555-7353
Record
(Autographed)
Richmond, Virginia
NANCY BAI

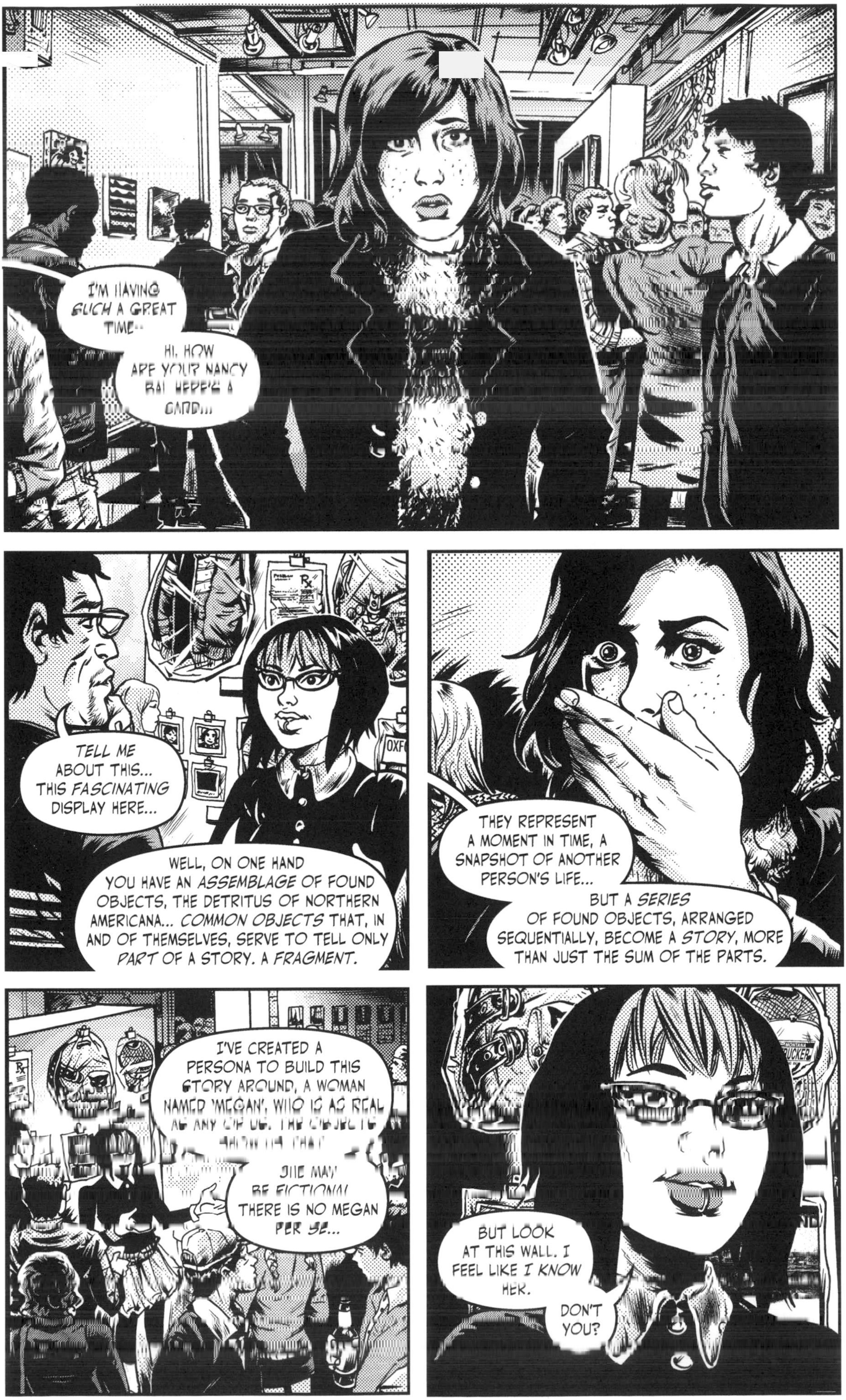
I'M HAVING SUCH A GREAT TIME...
HI, HOW ARE YOU? NANCY BA! HERE'S A CARD...
TELL ME ABOUT THIS... THIS *FASCINATING* DISPLAY HERE...
WELL, ON ONE HAND YOU HAVE AN *ASSEMBLAGE* OF FOUND OBJECTS, THE DETRITUS OF NORTHERN AMERICANA... *COMMON OBJECTS* THAT, IN AND OF THEMSELVES, SERVE TO TELL ONLY *PART* OF A STORY. A *FRAGMENT.*
THEY REPRESENT A MOMENT IN TIME, A SNAPSHOT OF ANOTHER PERSON'S LIFE...
BUT A *SERIES* OF FOUND OBJECTS, ARRANGED SEQUENTIALLY, BECOME A *STORY*, MORE THAN JUST THE SUM OF THE PARTS.
I'VE CREATED A PERSONA TO BUILD THIS STORY AROUND, A WOMAN NAMED 'MEGAN', WHO IS AS REAL AS ANY OF US. THE OBJECTS
SHE MAY BE FICTIONAL THERE IS NO MEGAN PER SE...
BUT LOOK AT THIS WALL. I FEEL LIKE I *KNOW* HER.
DON'T YOU?

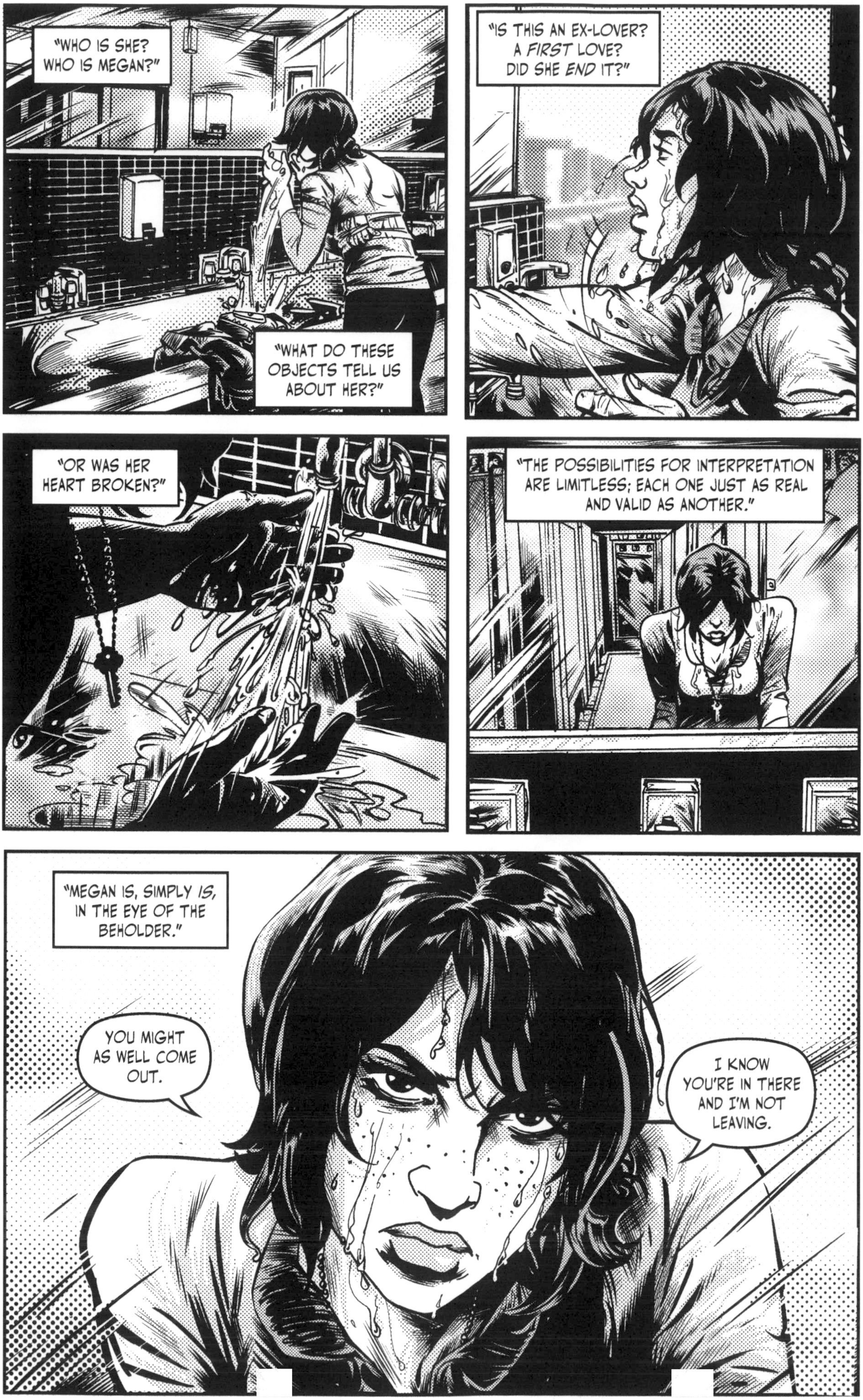
"WHO IS SHE? WHO IS MEGAN?"
"WHAT DO THESE OBJECTS TELL US ABOUT HER?"
"IS THIS AN EX-LOVER? A *FIRST* LOVE? DID SHE *END* IT?"
"OR WAS HER HEART BROKEN?"
"THE POSSIBILITIES FOR INTERPRETATION ARE LIMITLESS; EACH ONE JUST AS REAL AND VALID AS ANOTHER."
"MEGAN IS, SIMPLY *IS*, IN THE EYE OF THE BEHOLDER."
YOU MIGHT AS WELL COME OUT.
I KNOW YOU'RE IN THERE AND I'M NOT LEAVING.

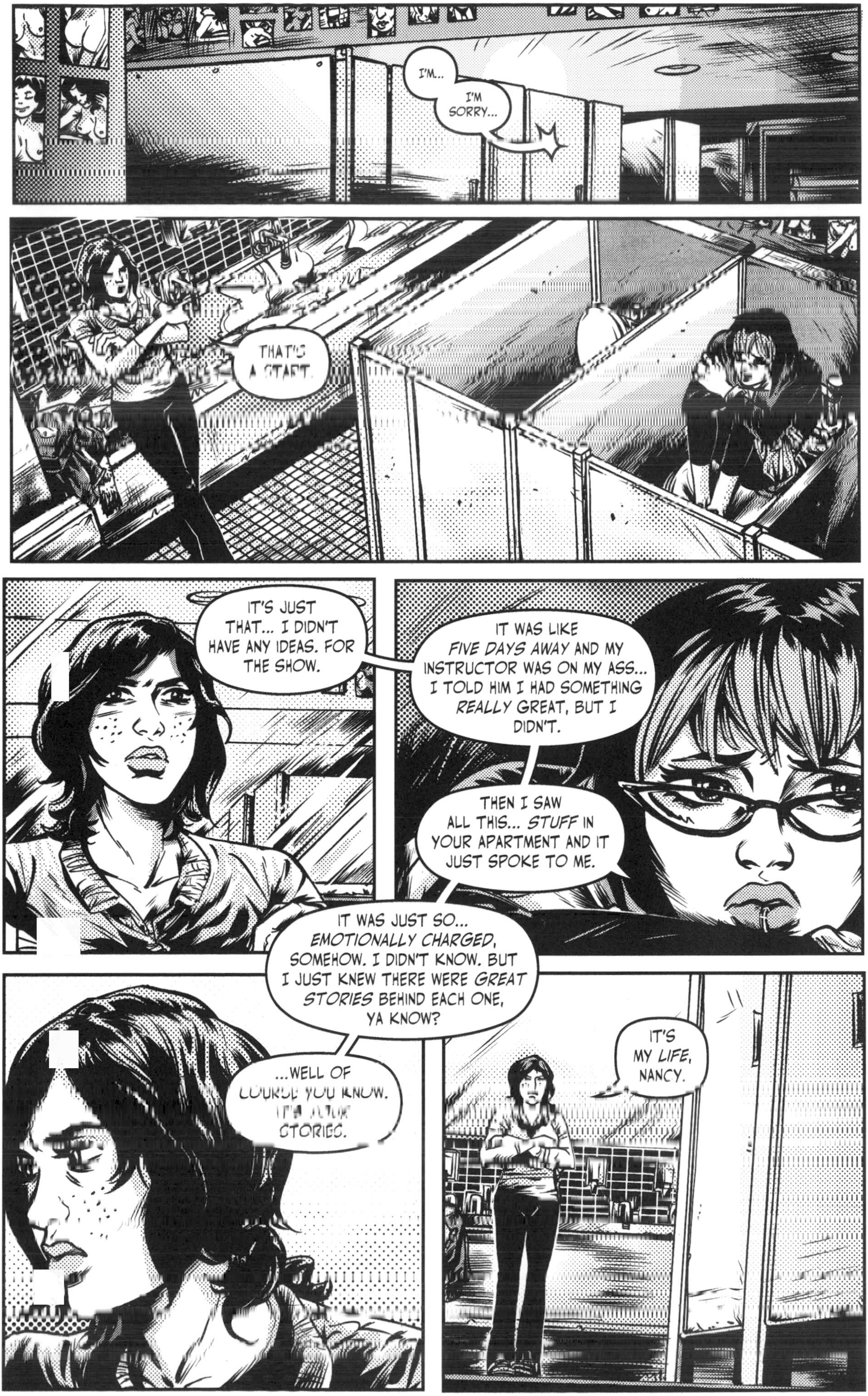
I'M...
I'M SORRY...
THAT'S A START.
IT'S JUST THAT... I DIDN'T HAVE ANY IDEAS. FOR THE SHOW.
IT WAS LIKE FIVE DAYS AWAY AND MY INSTRUCTOR WAS ON MY ASS... I TOLD HIM I HAD SOMETHING REALLY GREAT, BUT I DIDN'T.
THEN I SAW ALL THIS... STUFF IN YOUR APARTMENT AND IT JUST SPOKE TO ME.
IT WAS JUST SO... EMOTIONALLY CHARGED, SOMEHOW. I DIDN'T KNOW. BUT I JUST KNEW THERE WERE GREAT STORIES BEHIND EACH ONE, YA KNOW?
...WELL OF COURSE YOU KNOW.
STORIES.
IT'S MY LIFE, NANCY.

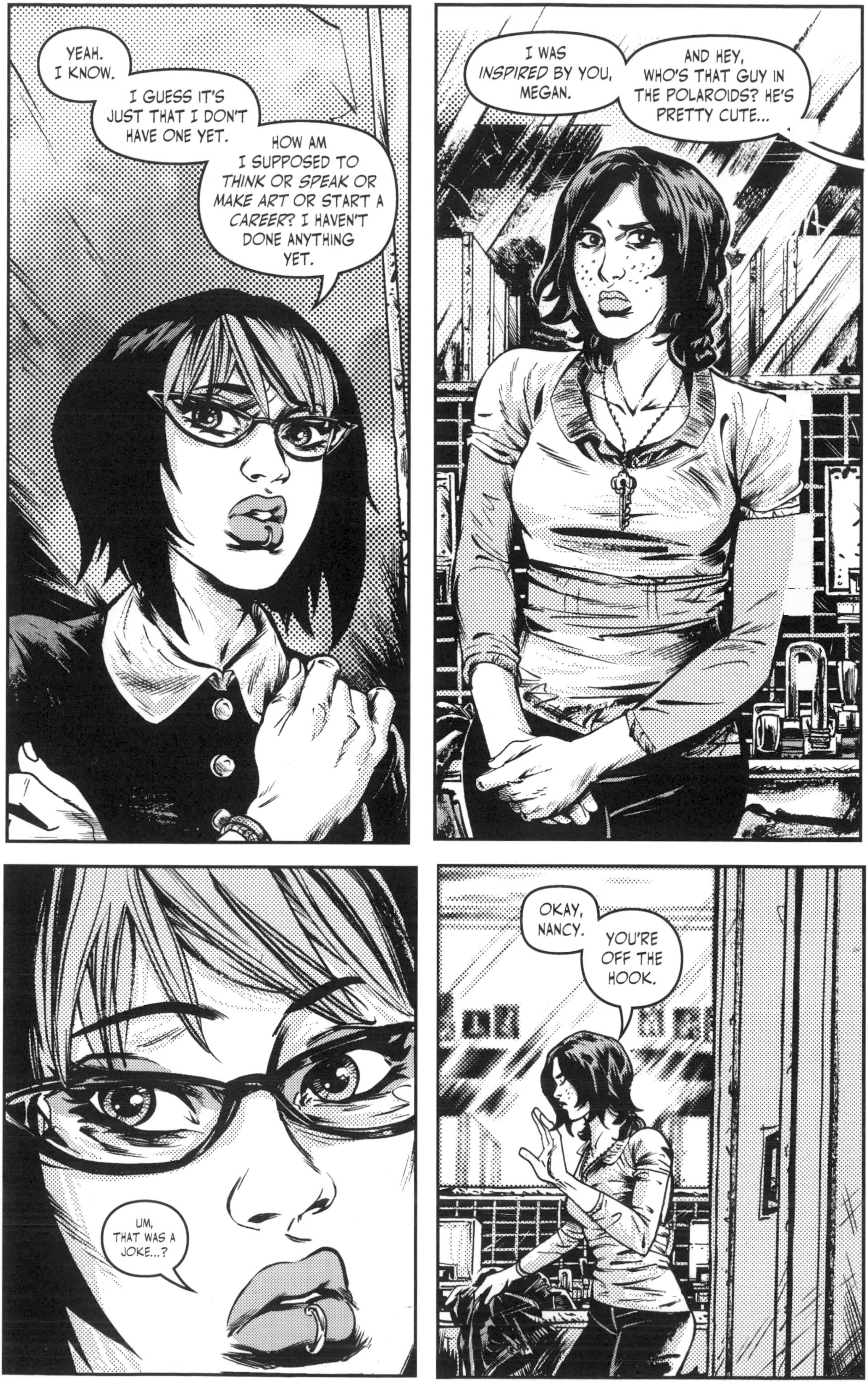
YEAH. I KNOW.
I GUESS IT'S JUST THAT I DON'T HAVE ONE YET.
HOW AM I SUPPOSED TO *THINK* OR *SPEAK* OR MAKE *ART* OR START A *CAREER*? I HAVEN'T DONE ANYTHING YET.
I WAS *INSPIRED* BY YOU, MEGAN.
AND HEY, WHO'S THAT GUY IN THE POLAROIDS? HE'S PRETTY CUTE...
UM, THAT WAS A JOKE...?
OKAY, NANCY.
YOU'RE OFF THE HOOK.

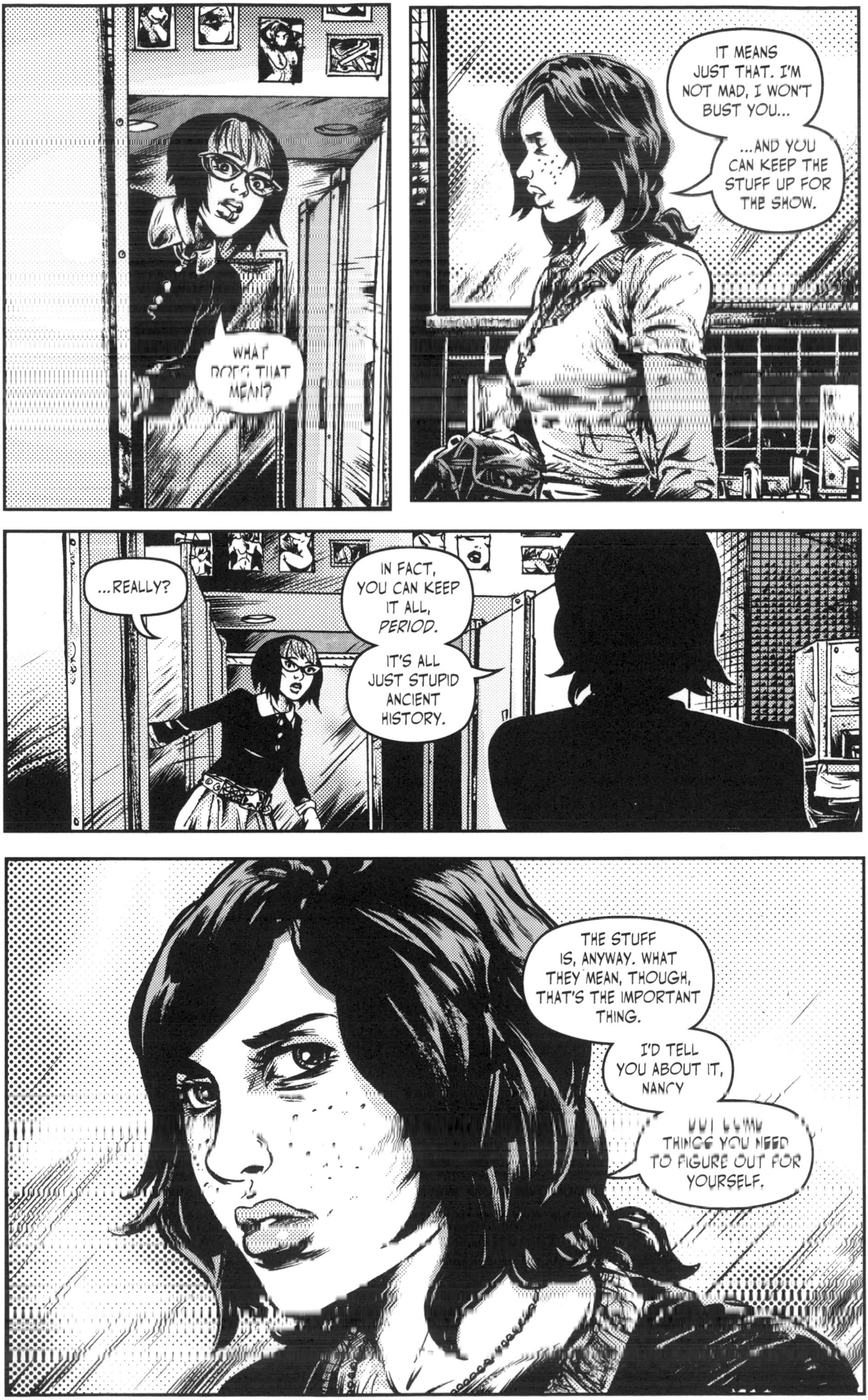
WHAT DOES THAT MEAN?
IT MEANS JUST THAT. I'M NOT MAD, I WON'T BUST YOU...
...AND YOU CAN KEEP THE STUFF UP FOR THE SHOW.
...REALLY?
IN FACT, YOU CAN KEEP IT ALL, *PERIOD.*
IT'S ALL JUST STUPID ANCIENT HISTORY.
THE STUFF IS, ANYWAY. WHAT THEY MEAN, THOUGH, THAT'S THE IMPORTANT THING.
I'D TELL YOU ABOUT IT, NANCY
THINGS YOU NEED TO FIGURE OUT FOR YOURSELF.

CHAPTER 12
"THE HOUSE THAT MEGAN BUILT"
Vormont, U.S.A.

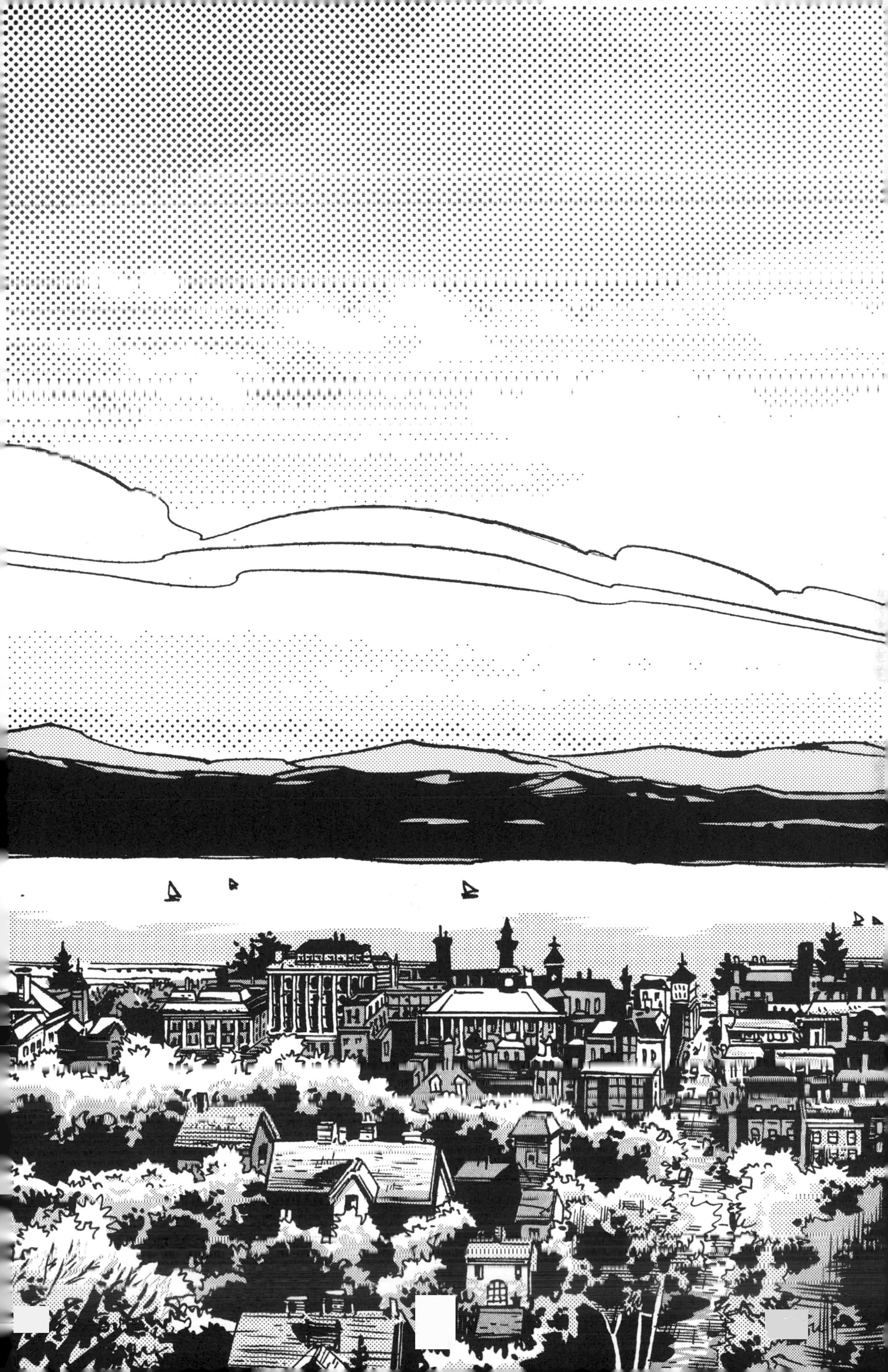

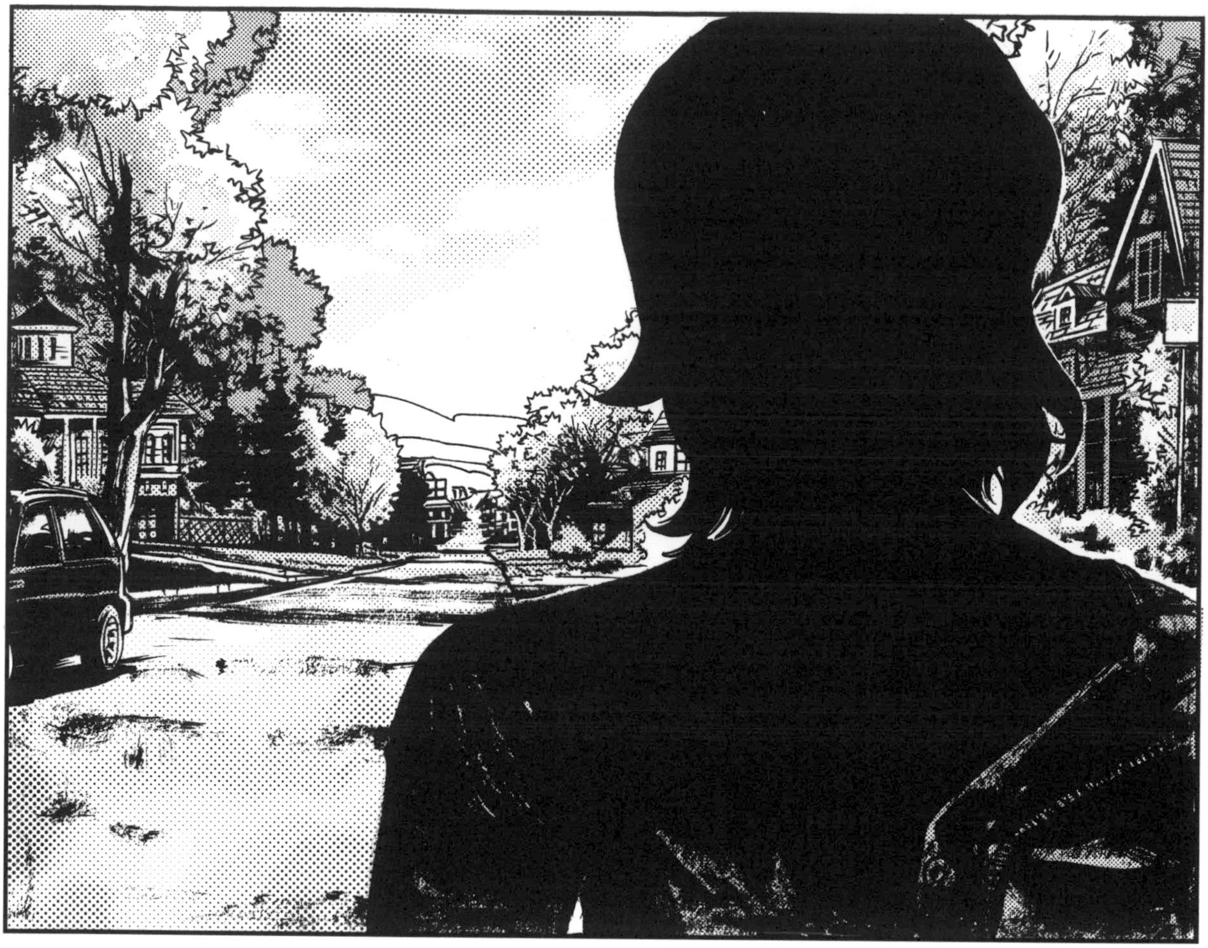

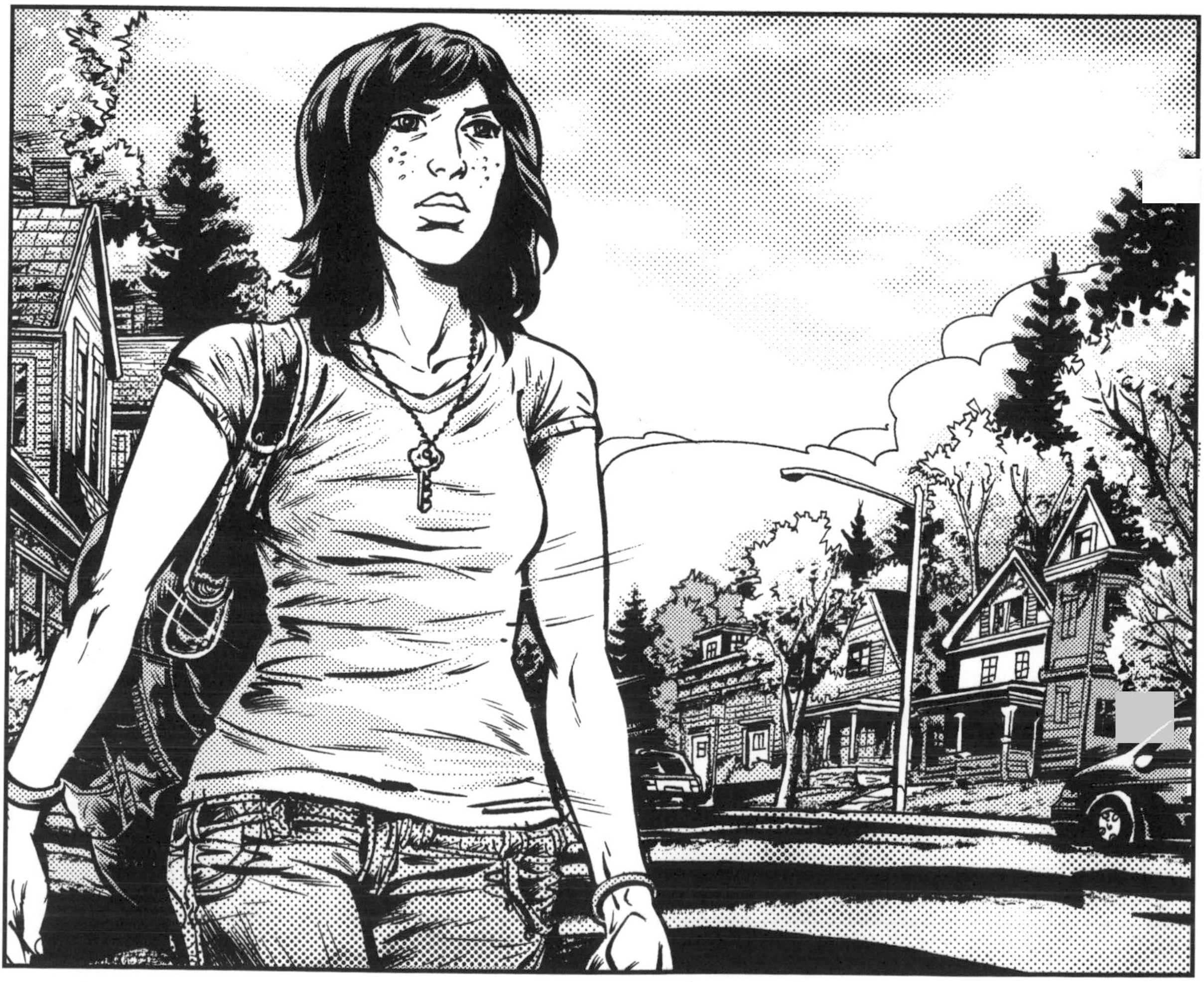

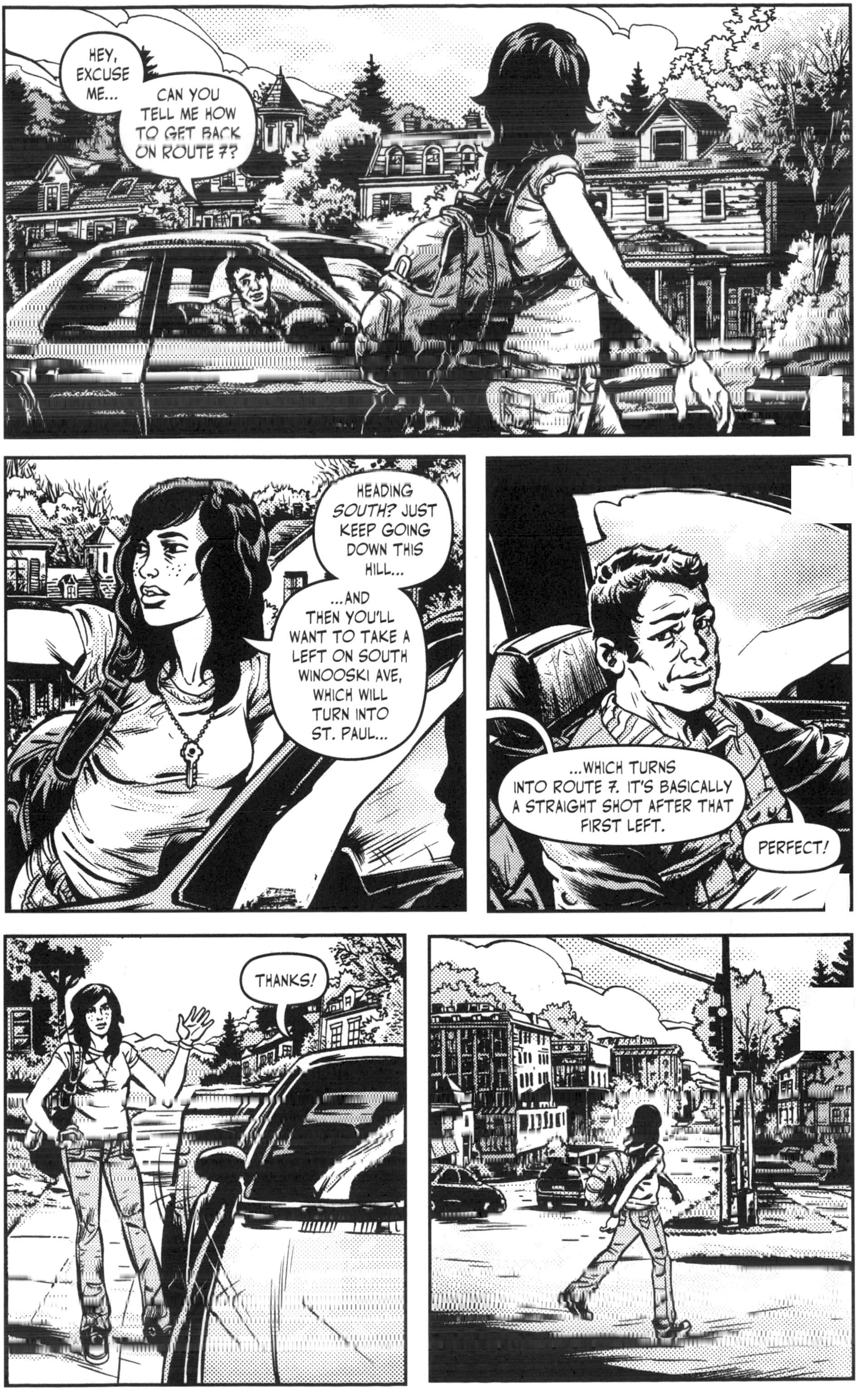
HEY, EXCUSE ME...
CAN YOU TELL ME HOW TO GET BACK ON ROUTE 7?
HEADING *SOUTH?* JUST KEEP GOING DOWN THIS HILL...
...AND THEN YOU'LL WANT TO TAKE A LEFT ON SOUTH WINOOSKI AVE, WHICH WILL TURN INTO ST. PAUL...
...WHICH TURNS INTO ROUTE 7. IT'S BASICALLY A STRAIGHT SHOT AFTER THAT FIRST LEFT.
PERFECT!
THANKS!

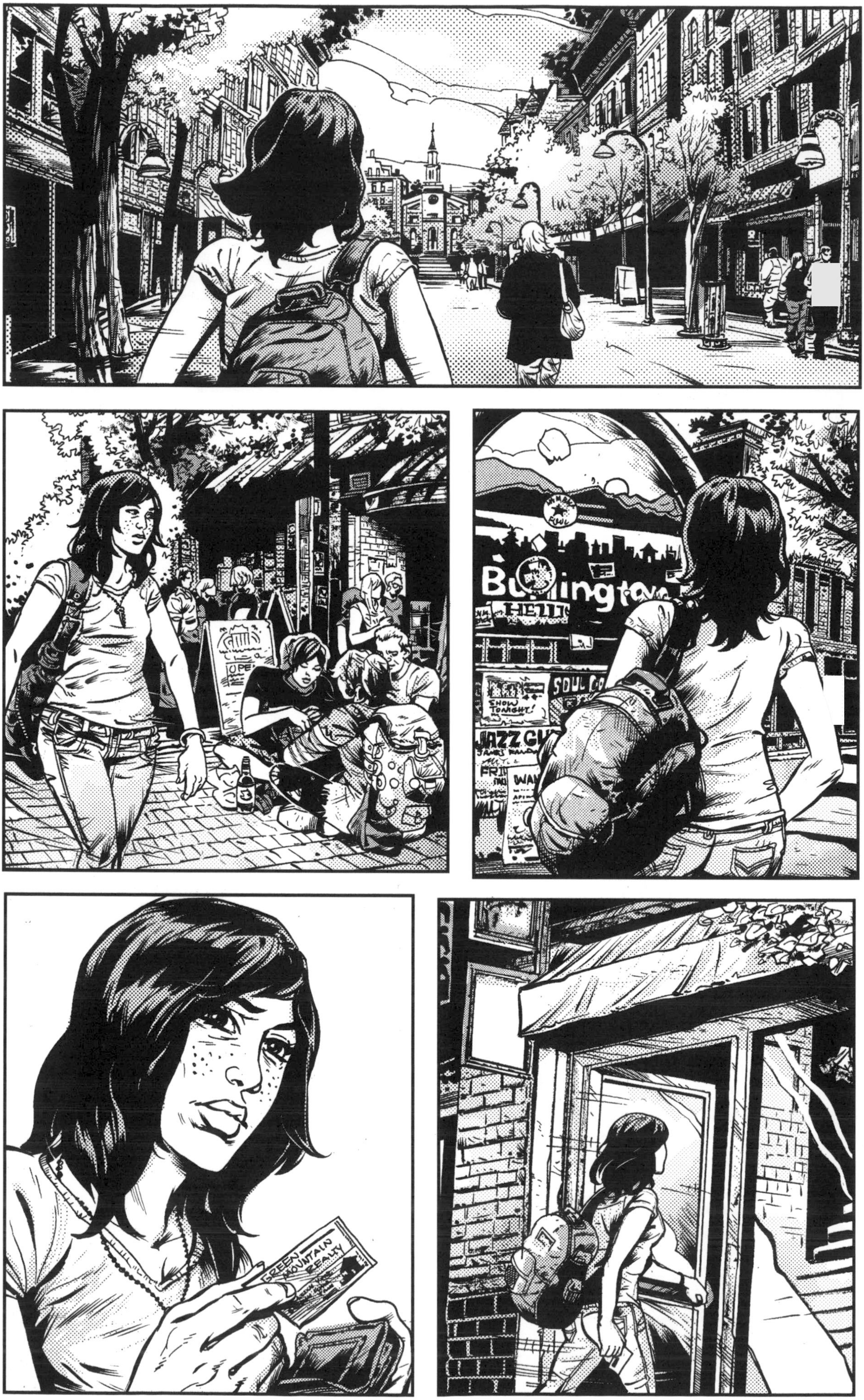
SHOW TONIGHT!
GREEN MOUNTAIN REALTY

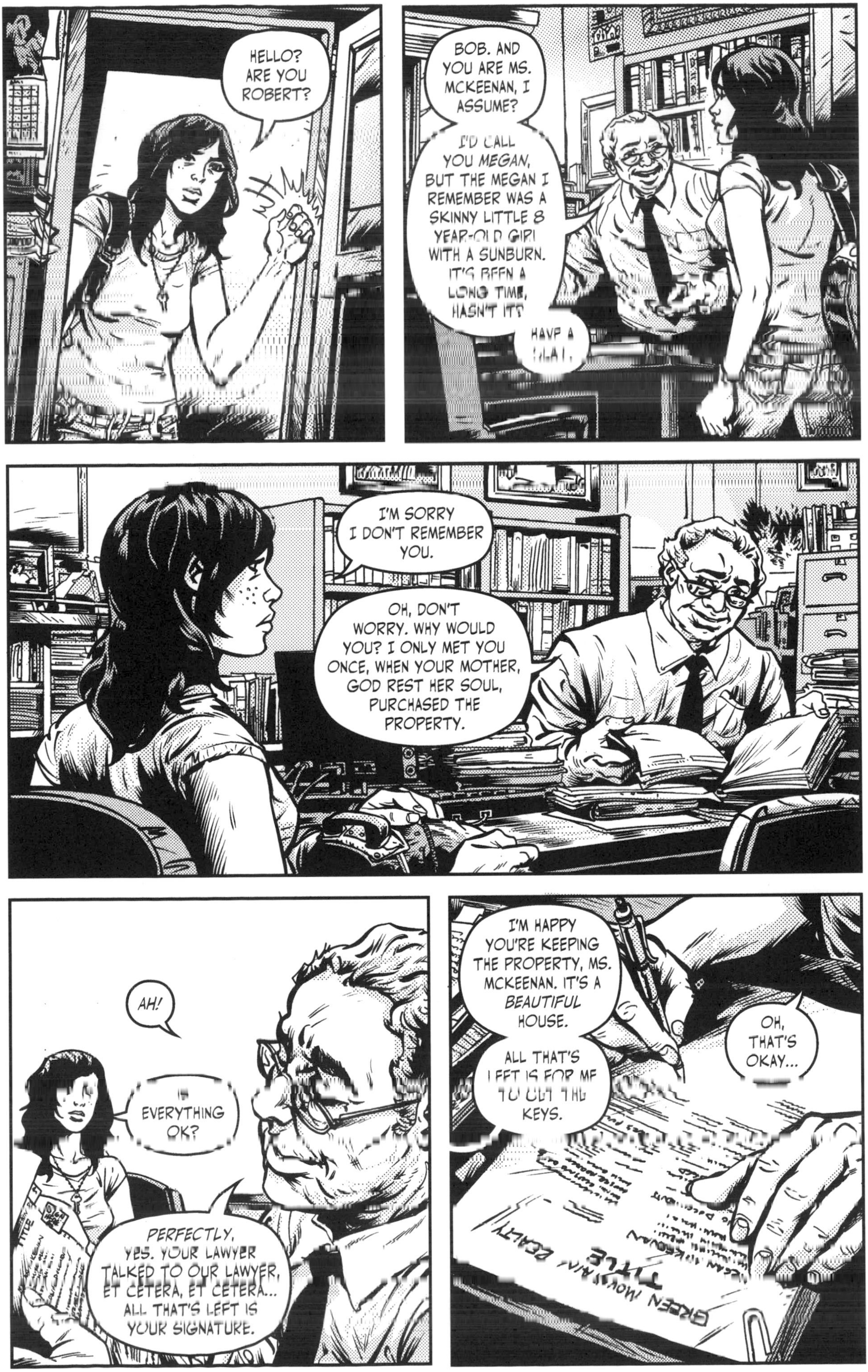
HELLO? ARE YOU ROBERT?
BOB. AND YOU ARE MS. MCKEENAN, I ASSUME?
I'D CALL YOU *MEGAN*, BUT THE MEGAN I REMEMBER WAS A SKINNY LITTLE 8 YEAR-OLD GIRL WITH A SUNBURN. IT'S BEEN A LONG TIME, HASN'T IT?
HAVE A SEAT.
I'M SORRY I DON'T REMEMBER YOU.
OH, DON'T WORRY. WHY WOULD YOU? I ONLY MET YOU ONCE, WHEN YOUR MOTHER, GOD REST HER SOUL, PURCHASED THE PROPERTY.
AH!
IS EVERYTHING OK?
PERFECTLY, YES. YOUR LAWYER TALKED TO OUR LAWYER, ET CETERA, ET CETERA... ALL THAT'S LEFT IS YOUR SIGNATURE.
I'M HAPPY YOU'RE KEEPING THE PROPERTY, MS. MCKEENAN. IT'S A *BEAUTIFUL* HOUSE.
ALL THAT'S LEFT IS FOR ME TO GET THE KEYS.
OH, THAT'S OKAY...
TITLE

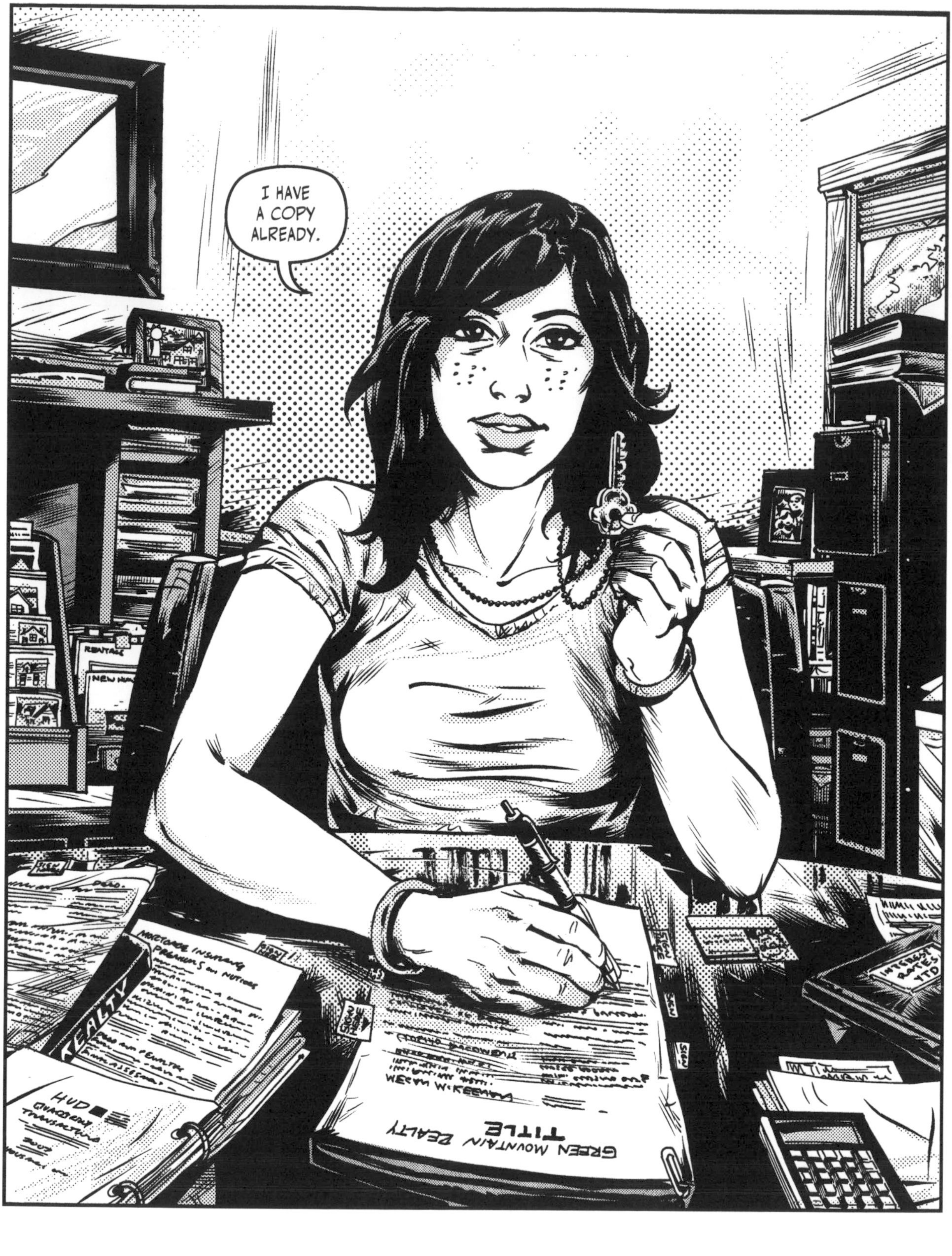
I HAVE A COPY ALREADY.
REALTY
GREEN MOUNTAIN REALTY
TITLE

LOCAL #12

"the house that Megan built"

STORY: BRIAN WOOD / ART: RYAN KELLY

LETTERED BY DOUGLAS E. SHERWOOD

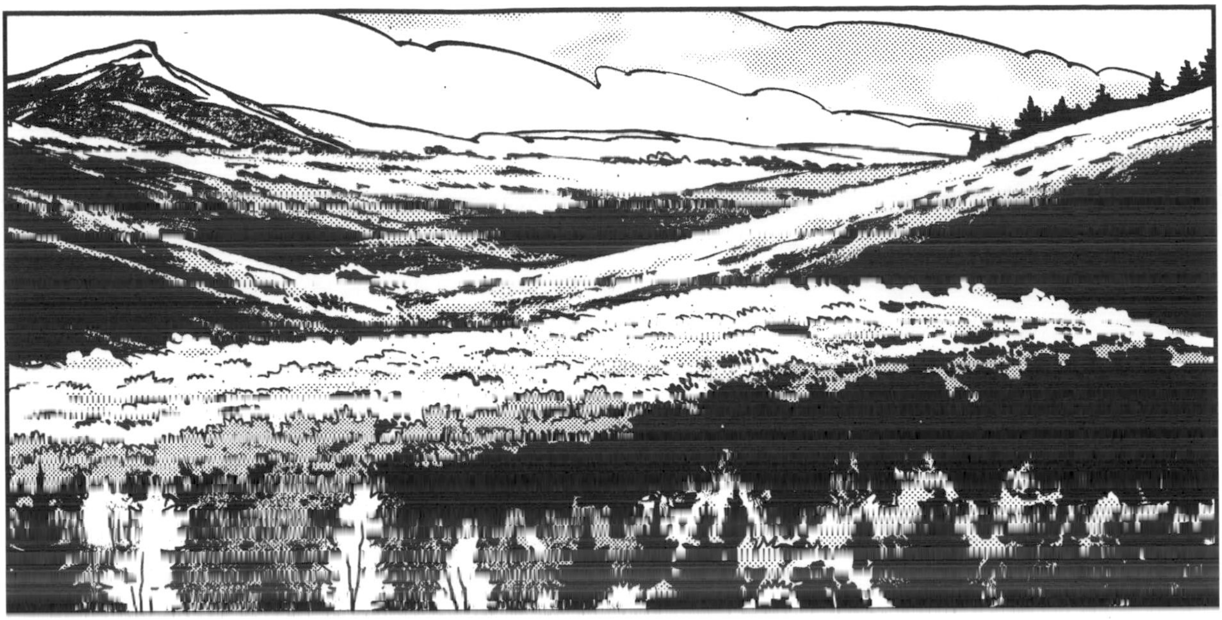
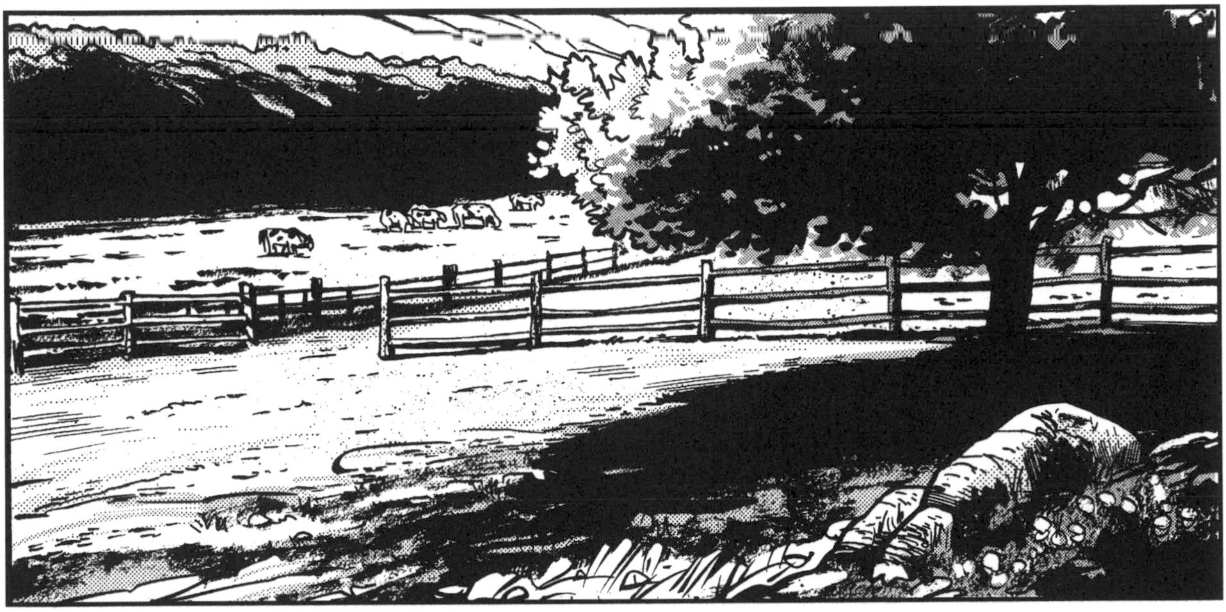
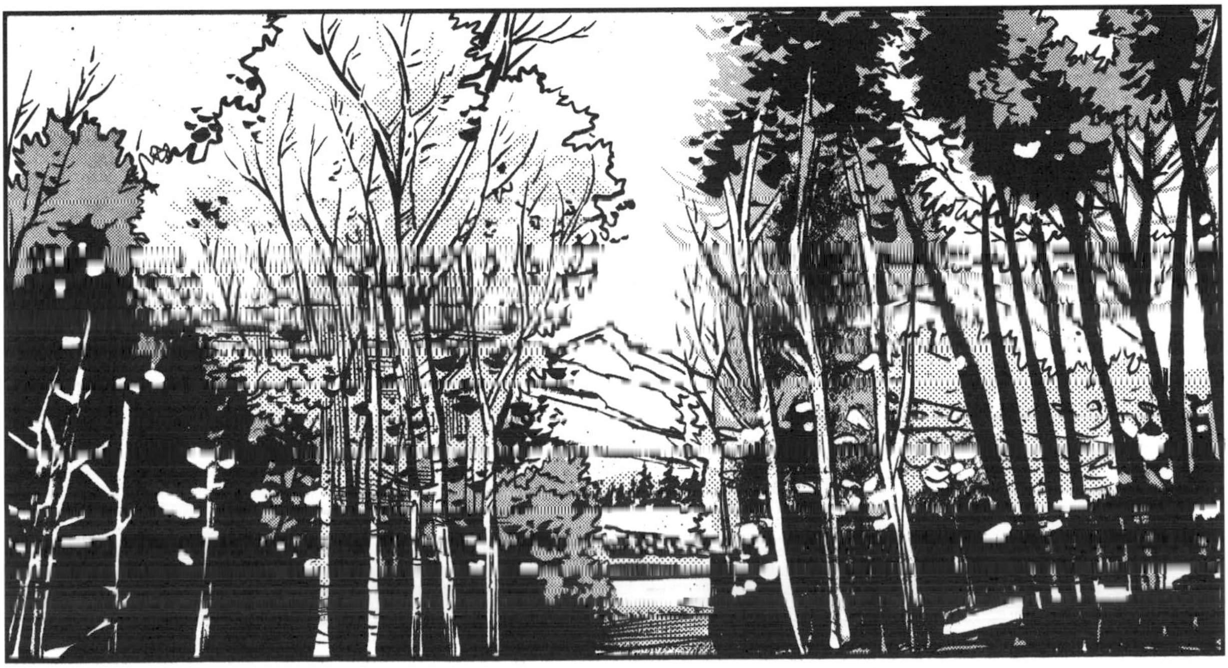

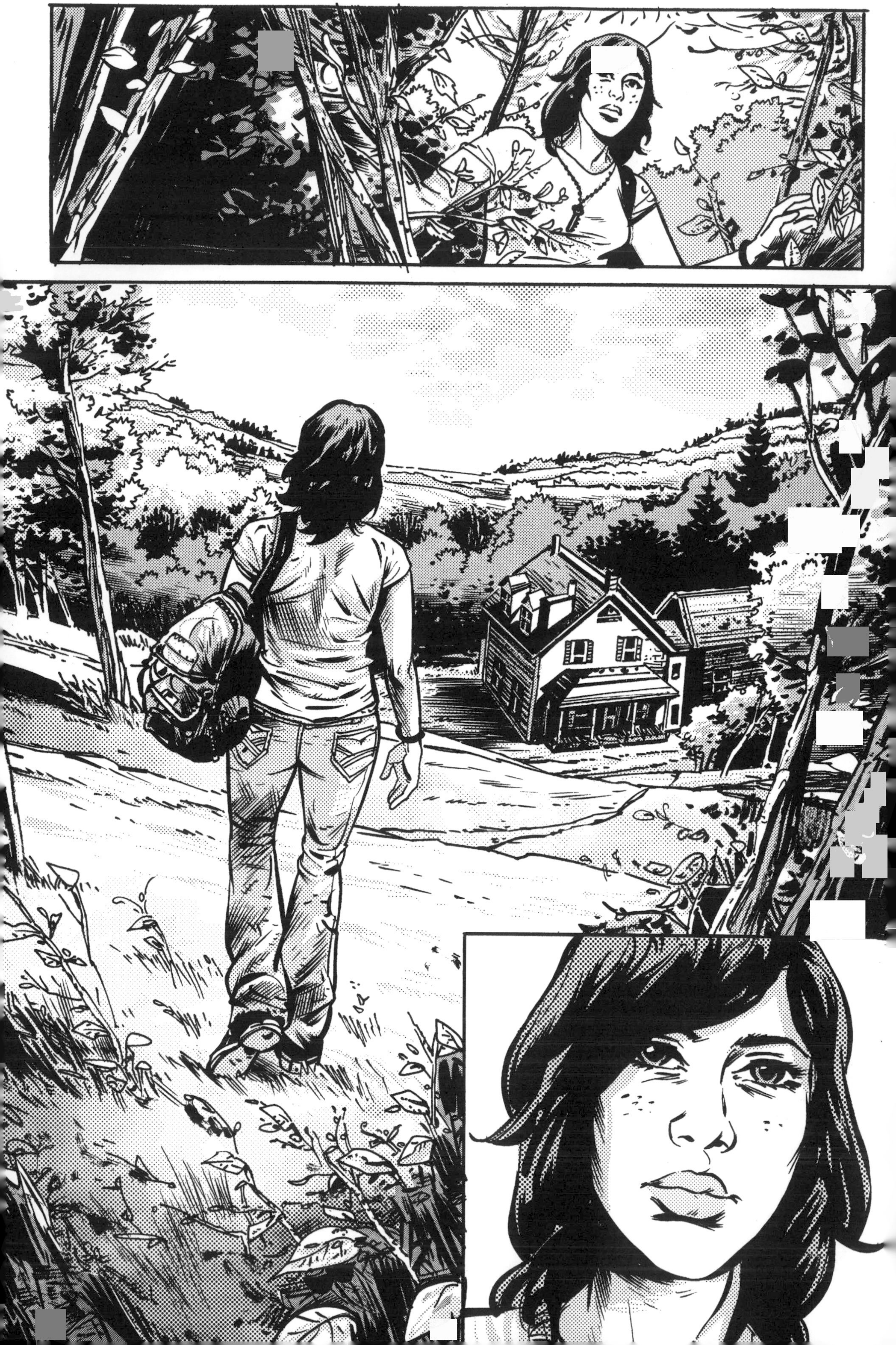

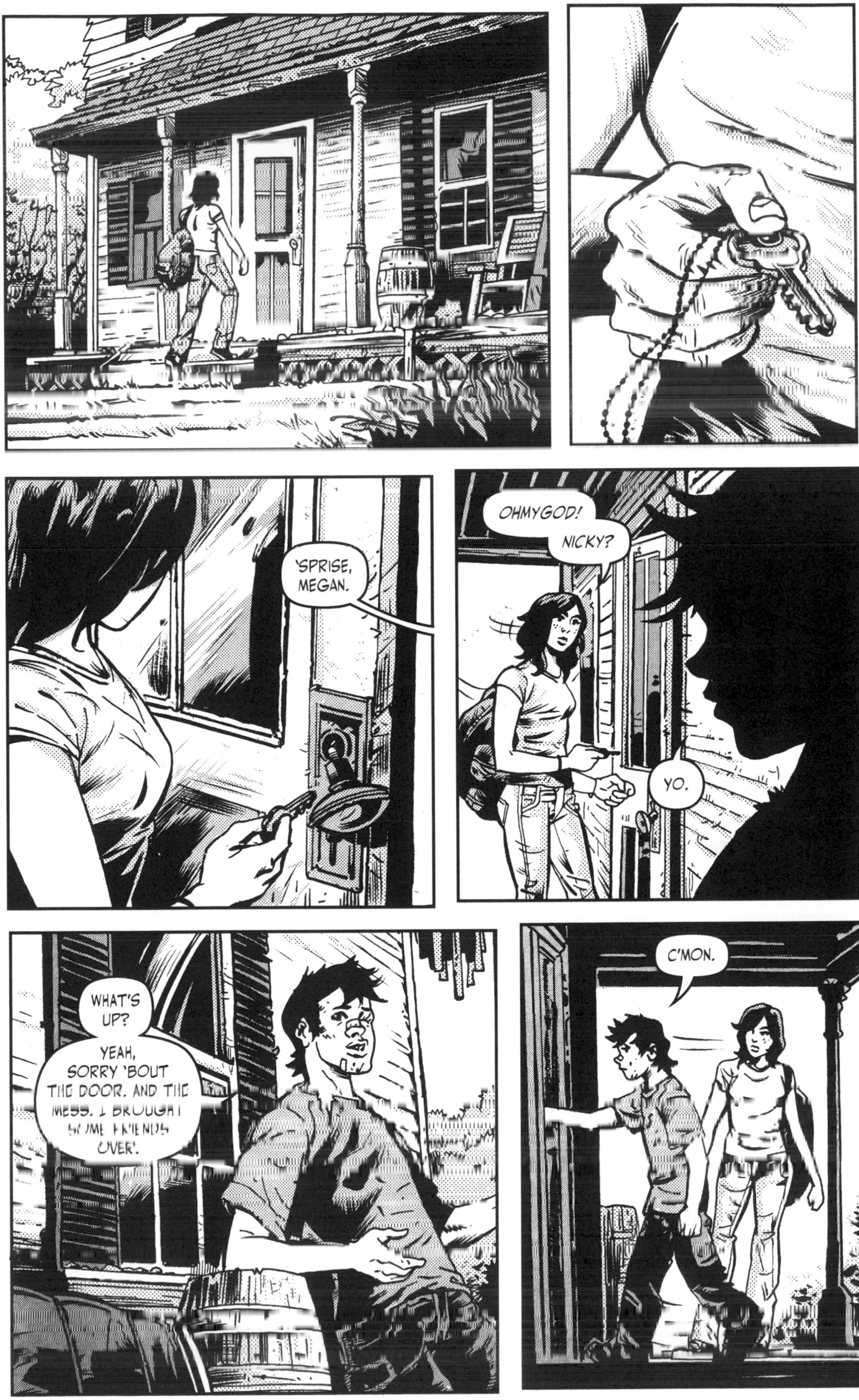
'SPRISE, MEGAN.
OHMYGOD!
NICKY?
YO.
WHAT'S UP?
YEAH, SORRY 'BOUT THE DOOR. AND THE MESS. I BROUGHT SOME FRIENDS OVER.
C'MON.

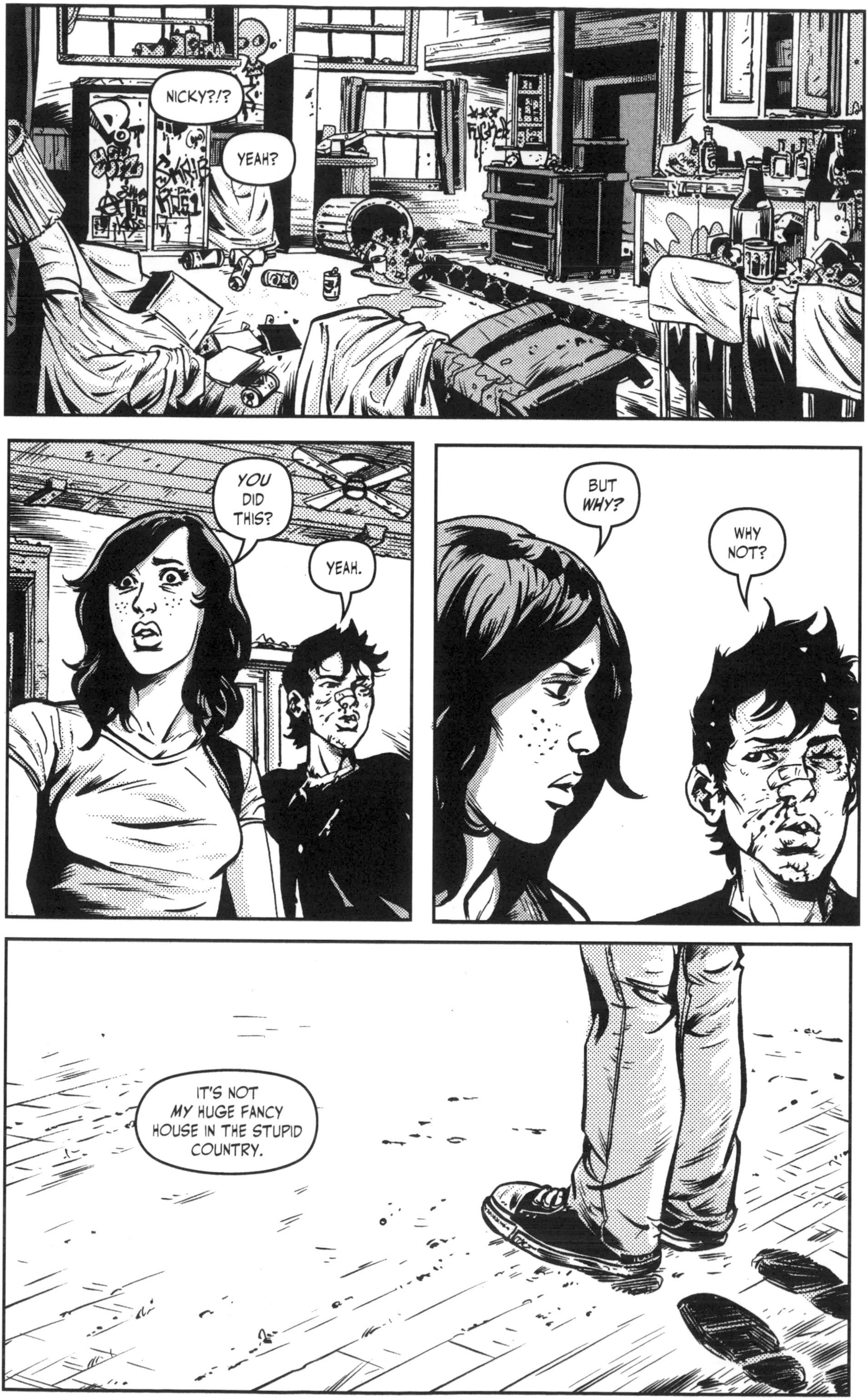
NICKY?!?
YEAH?
YOU DID THIS?
YEAH.
BUT WHY?
WHY NOT?
IT'S NOT MY HUGE FANCY HOUSE IN THE STUPID COUNTRY.

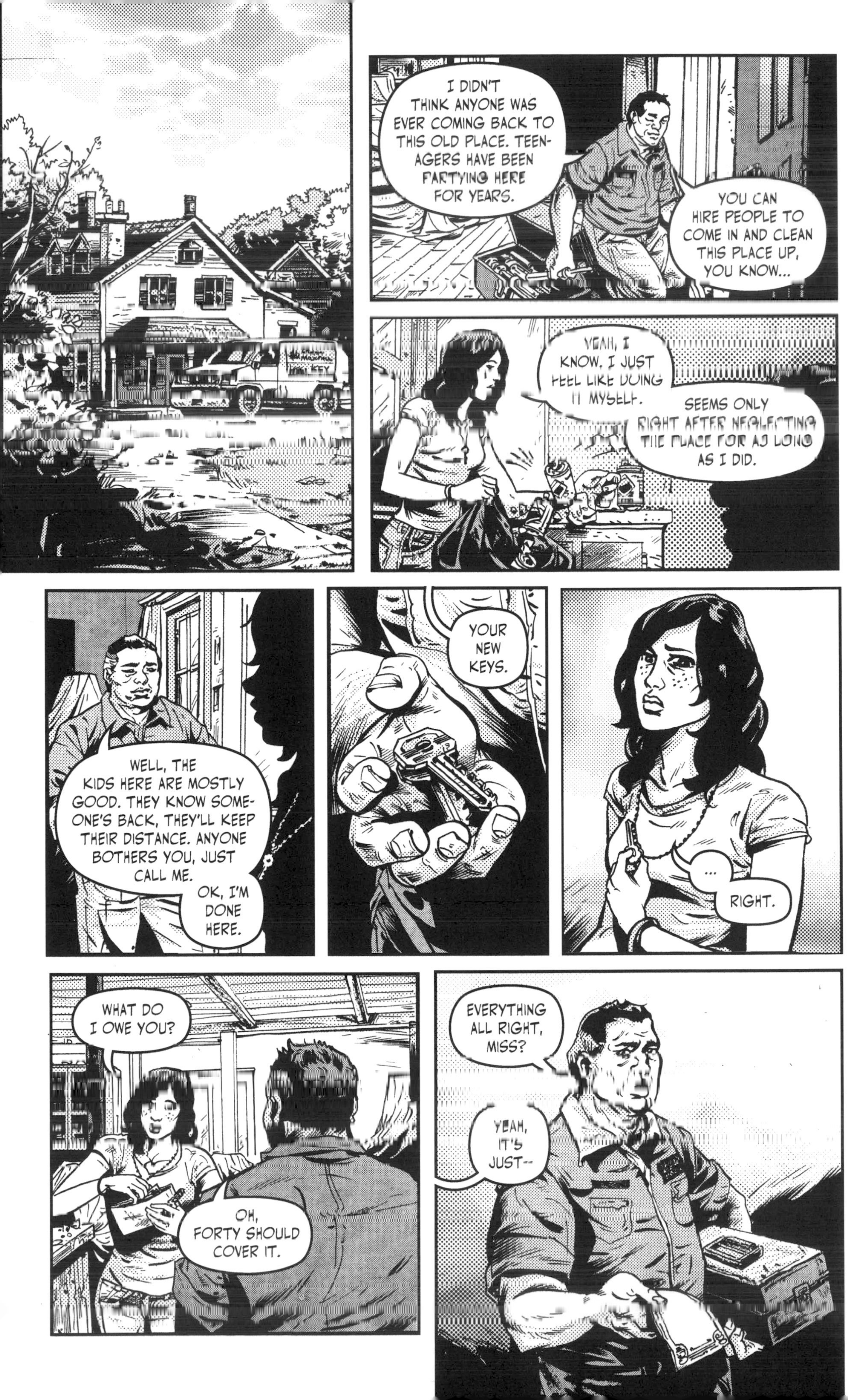
I DIDN'T THINK ANYONE WAS EVER COMING BACK TO THIS OLD PLACE. TEEN-AGERS HAVE BEEN PARTYING HERE FOR YEARS.
YOU CAN HIRE PEOPLE TO COME IN AND CLEAN THIS PLACE UP, YOU KNOW...
YEAH, I KNOW. I JUST FEEL LIKE DOING IT MYSELF.
SEEMS ONLY RIGHT AFTER NEGLECTING THE PLACE FOR AS LONG AS I DID.
WELL, THE KIDS HERE ARE MOSTLY GOOD. THEY KNOW SOME-ONE'S BACK, THEY'LL KEEP THEIR DISTANCE. ANYONE BOTHERS YOU, JUST CALL ME.
OK, I'M DONE HERE.
YOUR NEW KEYS.
...
RIGHT.
WHAT DO I OWE YOU?
OH, FORTY SHOULD COVER IT.
EVERYTHING ALL RIGHT, MISS?
YEAH, IT'S JUST--

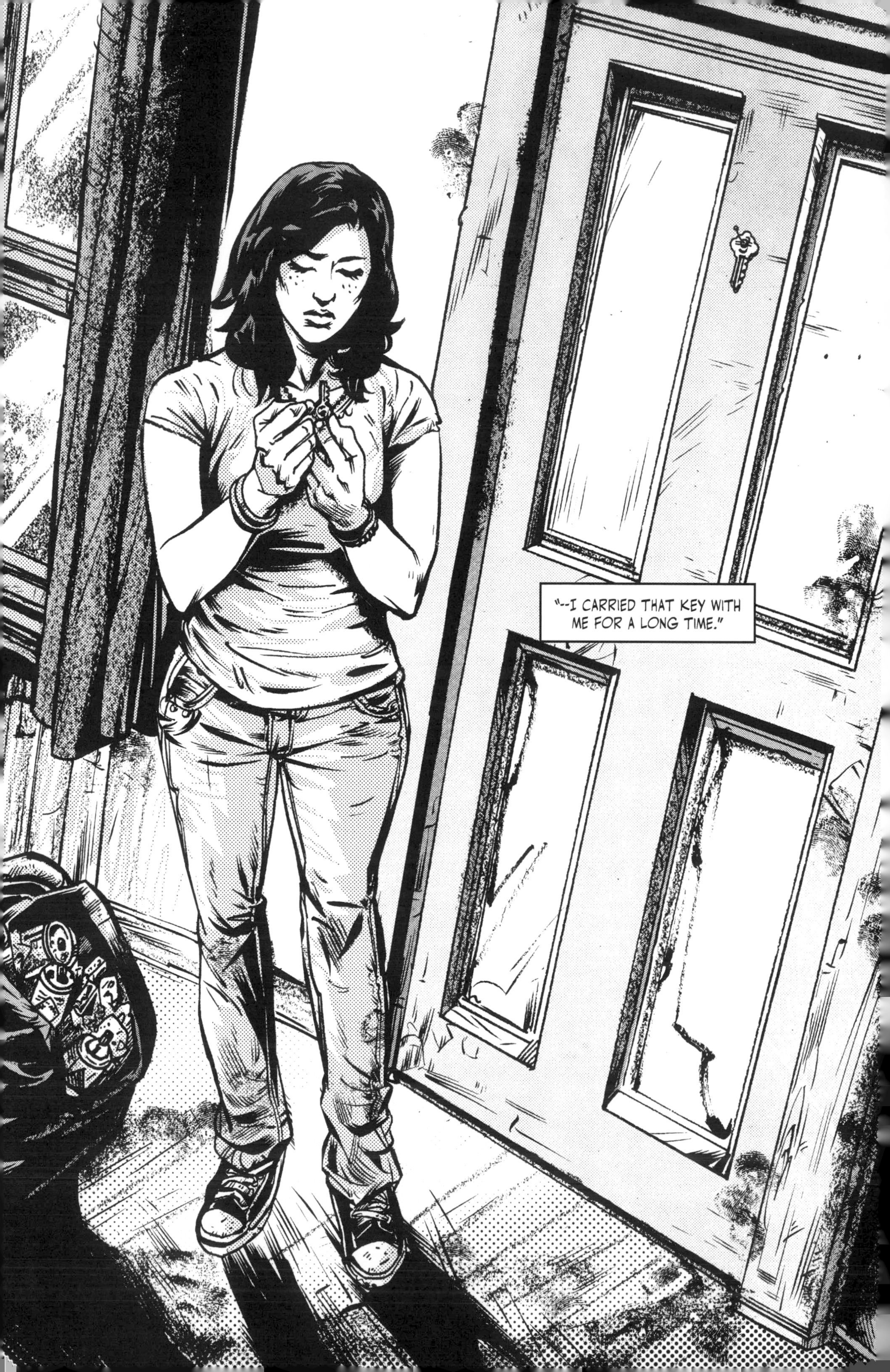
"--I CARRIED THAT KEY WITH ME FOR A LONG TIME."

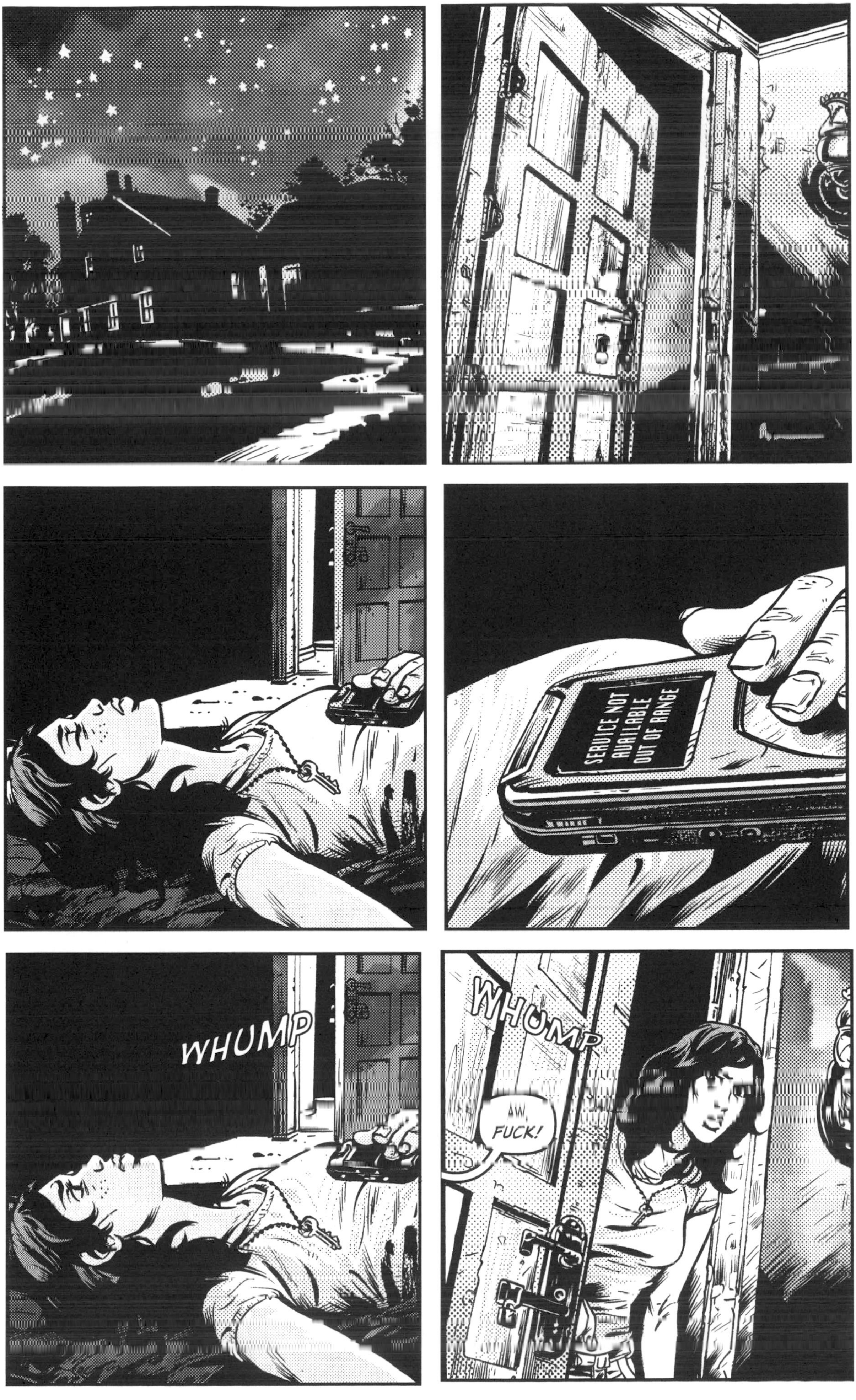
SERVICE NOT AVAILABLE OUT OF RANGE
WHUMP
WHUMP
AW, FUCK!

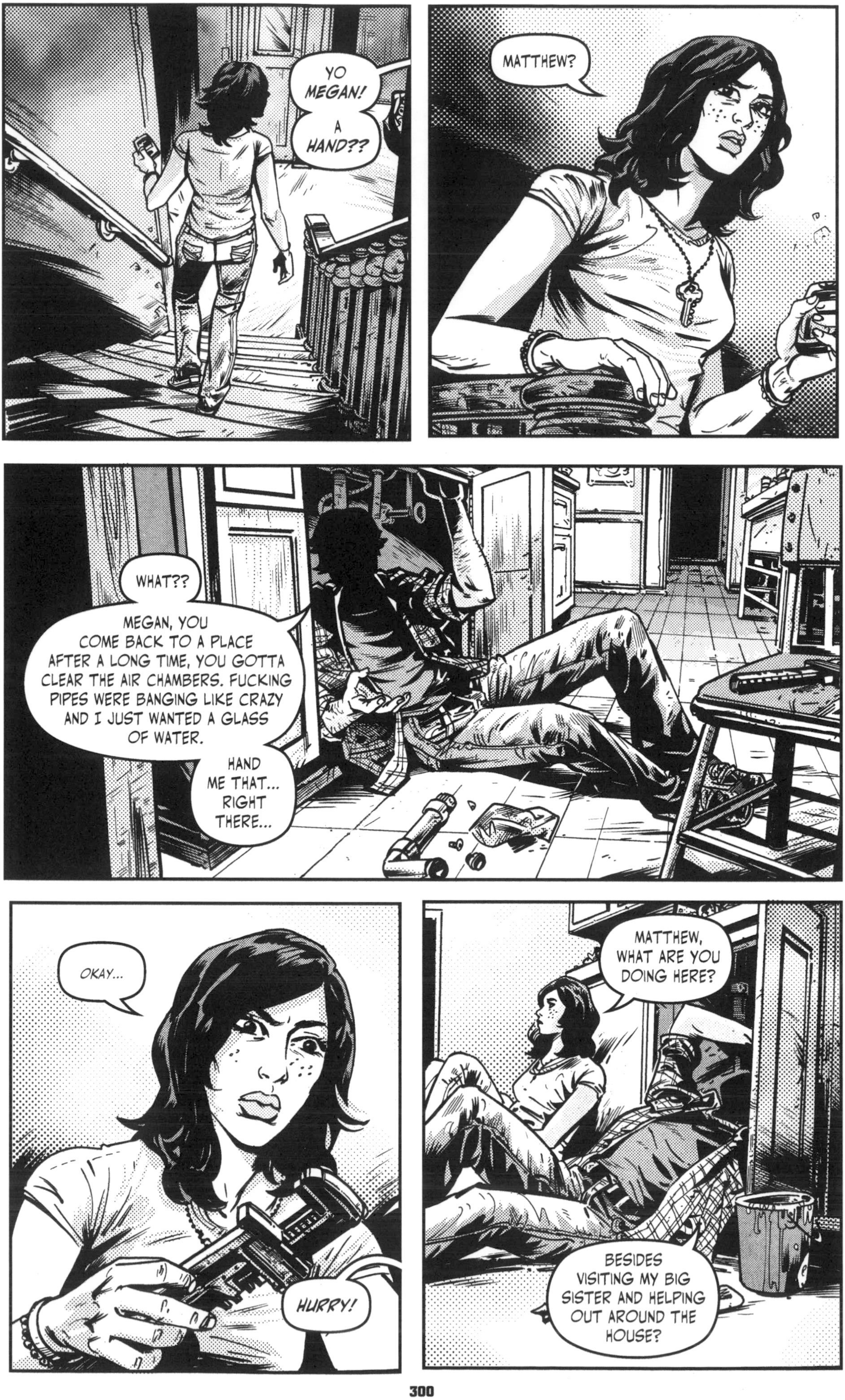
YO MEGAN!
A HAND??
MATTHEW?
WHAT??
MEGAN, YOU COME BACK TO A PLACE AFTER A LONG TIME, YOU GOTTA CLEAR THE AIR CHAMBERS. FUCKING PIPES WERE BANGING LIKE CRAZY AND I JUST WANTED A GLASS OF WATER.
HAND ME THAT... RIGHT THERE...
OKAY...
HURRY!
MATTHEW, WHAT ARE YOU DOING HERE?
BESIDES VISITING MY BIG SISTER AND HELPING OUT AROUND THE HOUSE?

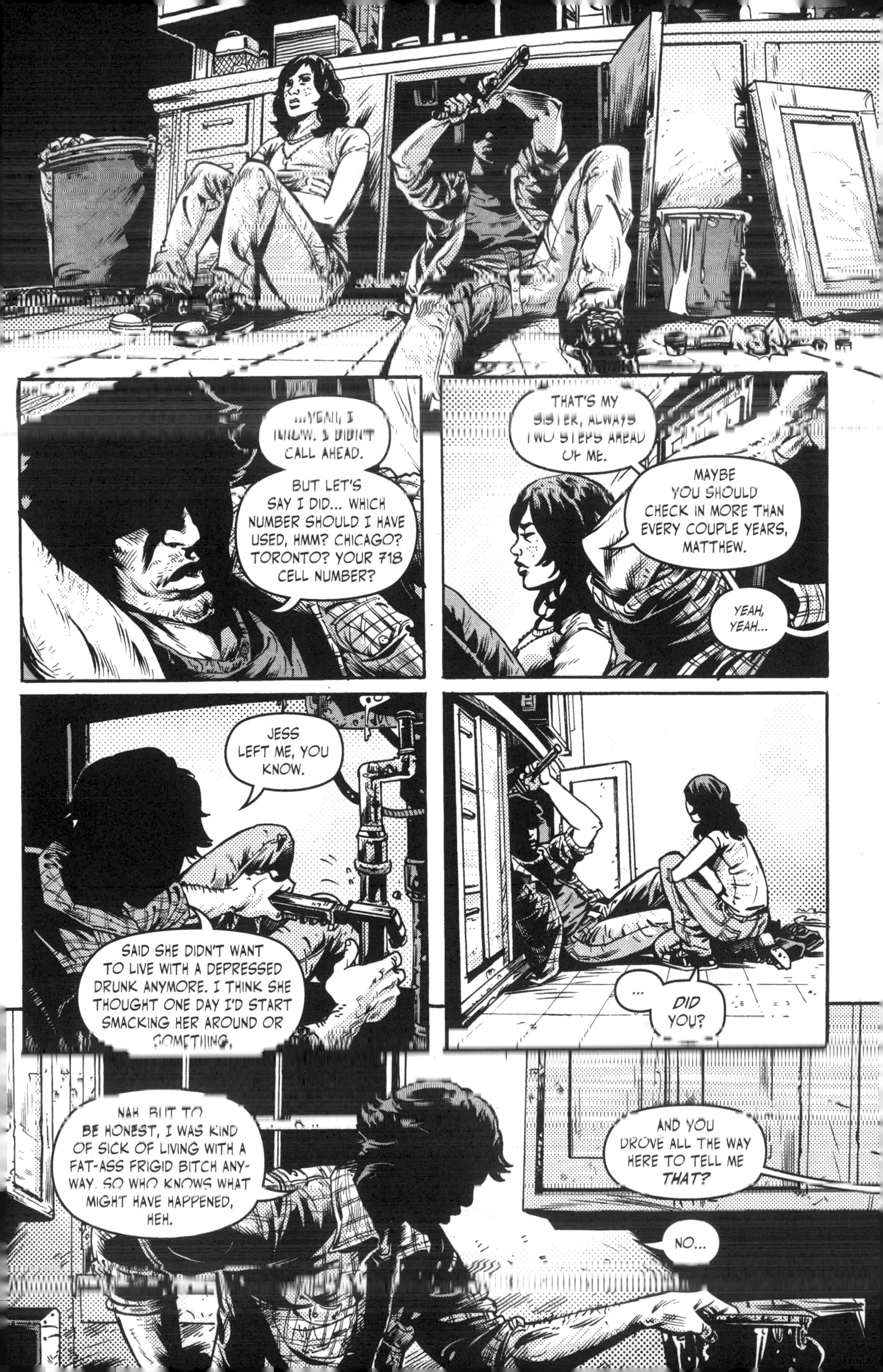
...YEAH, I KNOW. I DIDN'T CALL AHEAD.
BUT LET'S SAY I DID... WHICH NUMBER SHOULD I HAVE USED, HMM? CHICAGO? TORONTO? YOUR 718 CELL NUMBER?
THAT'S MY SISTER, ALWAYS TWO STEPS AHEAD OF ME.
MAYBE YOU SHOULD CHECK IN MORE THAN EVERY COUPLE YEARS, MATTHEW.
YEAH, YEAH...
JESS LEFT ME, YOU KNOW.
SAID SHE DIDN'T WANT TO LIVE WITH A DEPRESSED DRUNK ANYMORE. I THINK SHE THOUGHT ONE DAY I'D START SMACKING HER AROUND OR SOMETHING.
... DID YOU?
NAH. BUT TO BE HONEST, I WAS KIND OF SICK OF LIVING WITH A FAT-ASS FRIGID BITCH ANYWAY. SO WHO KNOWS WHAT MIGHT HAVE HAPPENED, HEH.
AND YOU DROVE ALL THE WAY HERE TO TELL ME THAT?
NO...

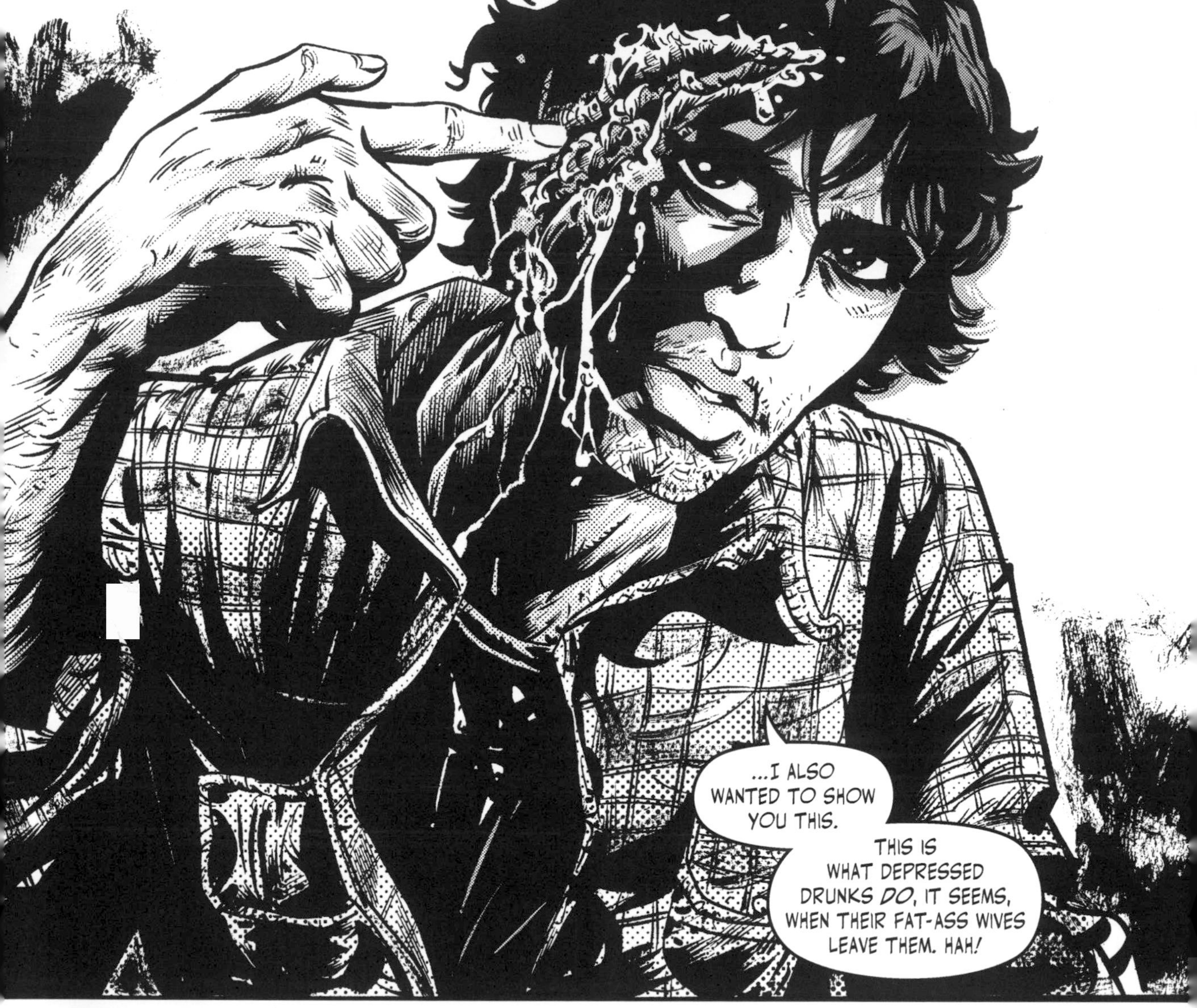
...I ALSO WANTED TO SHOW YOU THIS.
THIS IS WHAT DEPRESSED DRUNKS *DO*, IT SEEMS, WHEN THEIR FAT-ASS WIVES LEAVE THEM. HAH!

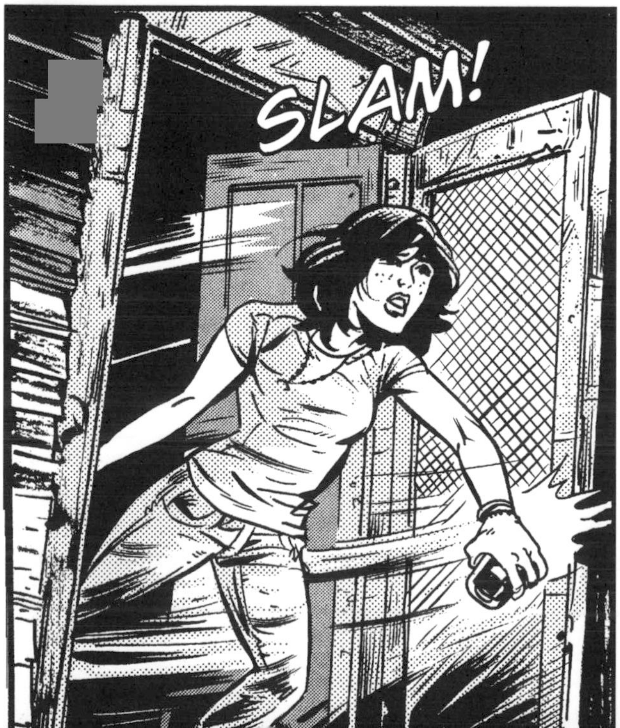
SLAM!

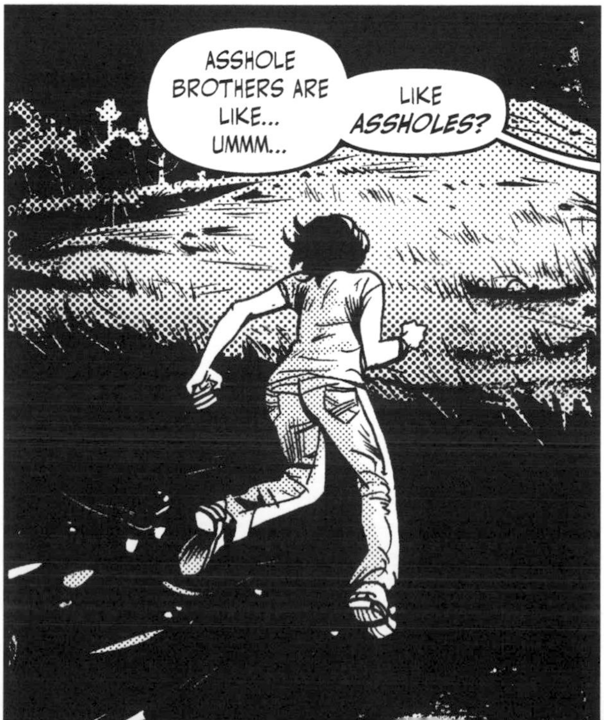
ASSHOLE BROTHERS ARE LIKE... UMMM...
LIKE *ASSHOLES?*

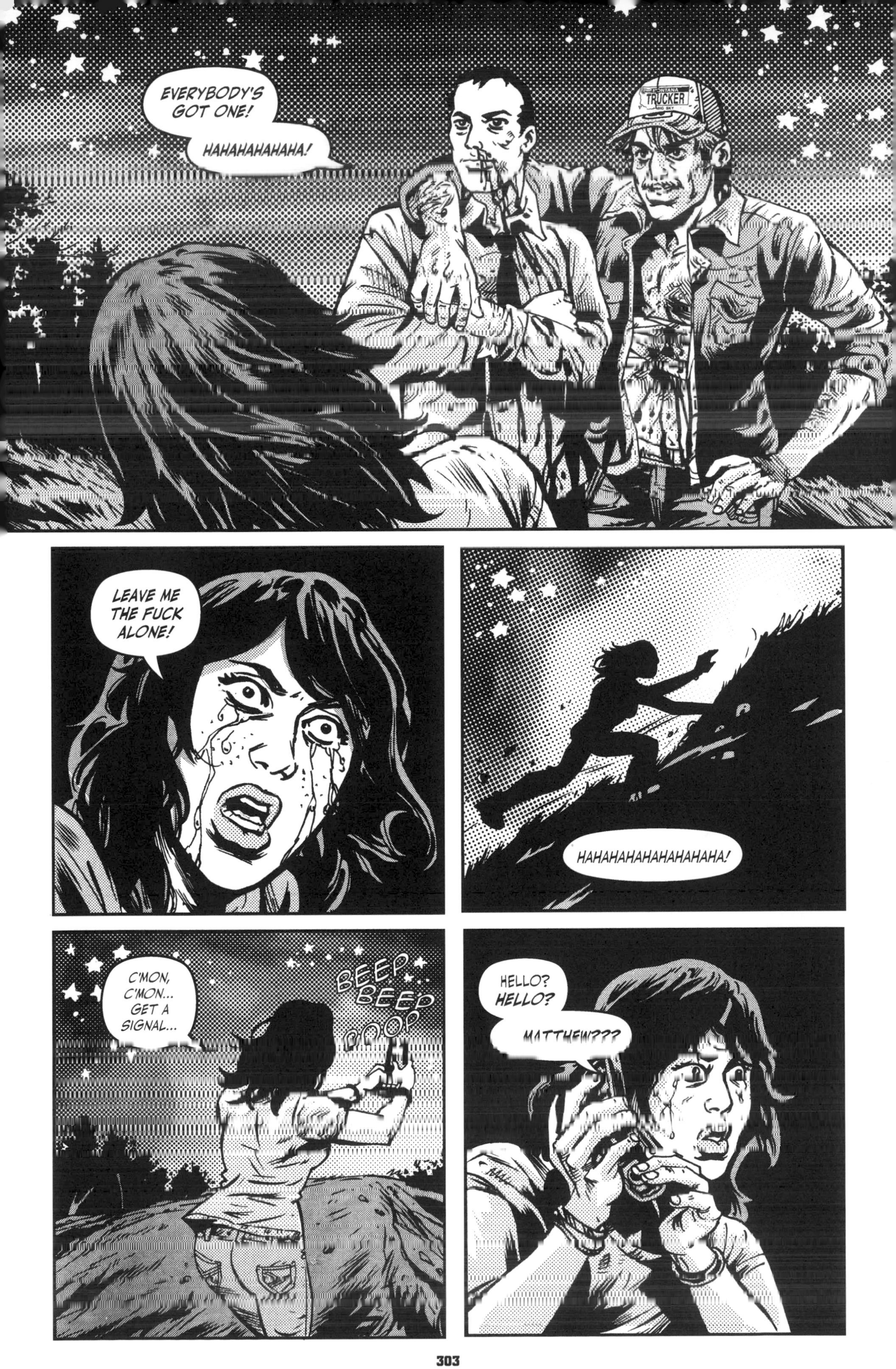
EVERYBODY'S GOT ONE!
HAHAHAHAHAHA!
TRUCKER
LEAVE ME THE FUCK ALONE!
HAHAHAHAHAHAHAHAHA!
C'MON, C'MON... GET A SIGNAL...
BEEP BEEP BOOP
HELLO? HELLO?
MATTHEW???

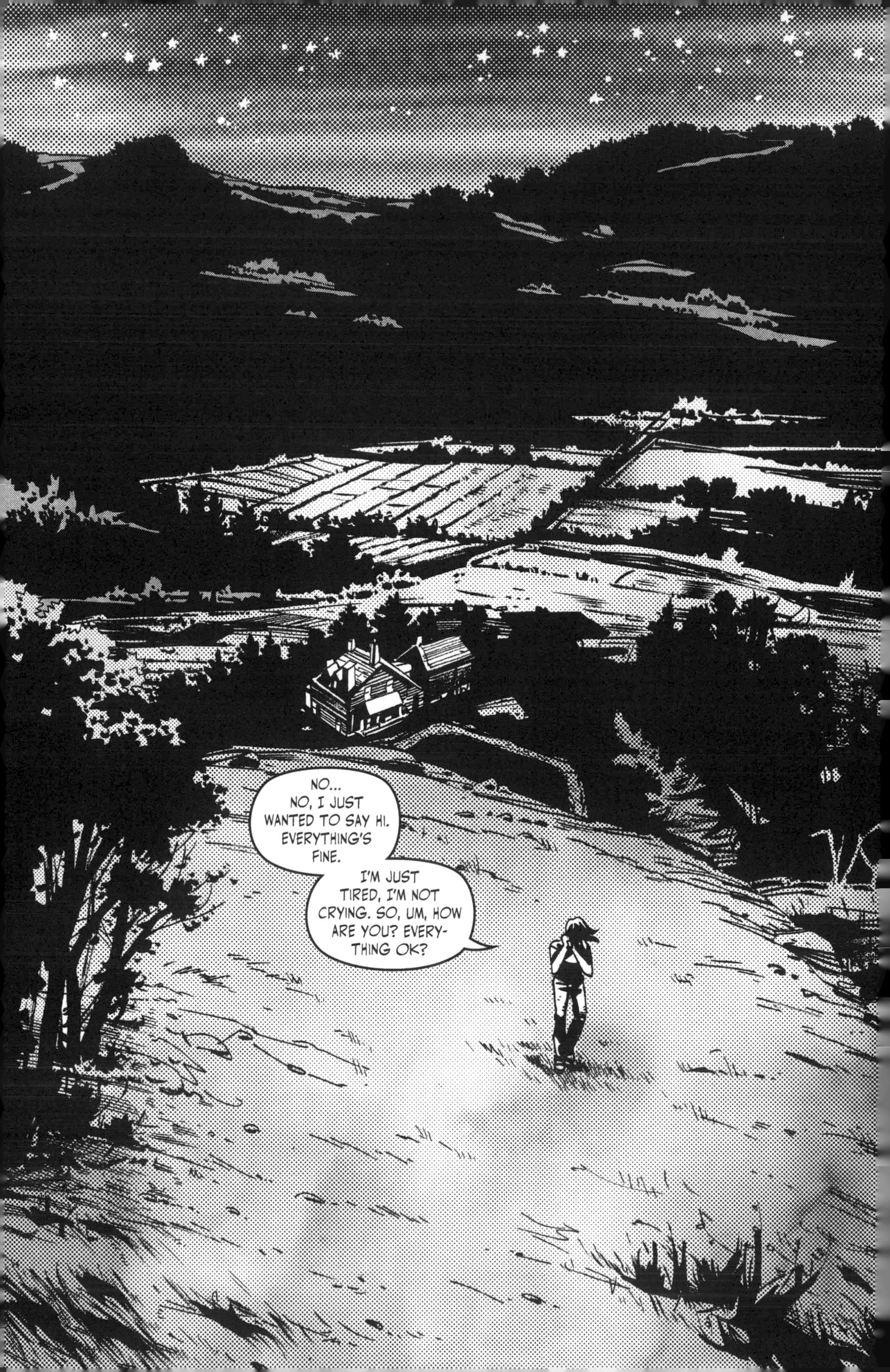
NO... NO, I JUST WANTED TO SAY HI. EVERYTHING'S FINE.
I'M JUST TIRED, I'M NOT CRYING. SO, UM, HOW ARE YOU? EVERY-THING OK?

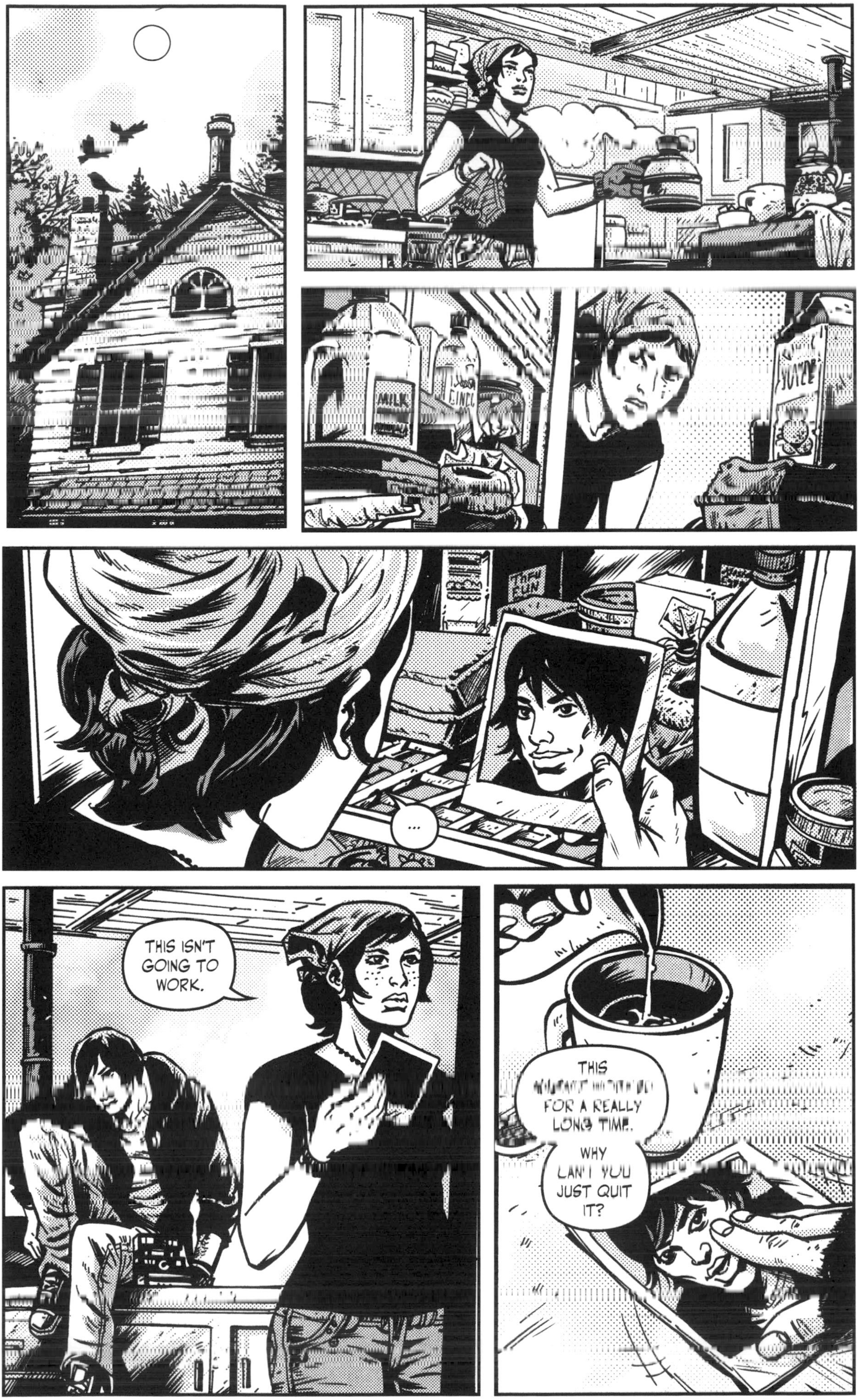
...
THIS ISN'T GOING TO WORK.
THIS
FOR A REALLY LONG TIME.
WHY CAN'T YOU JUST QUIT IT?

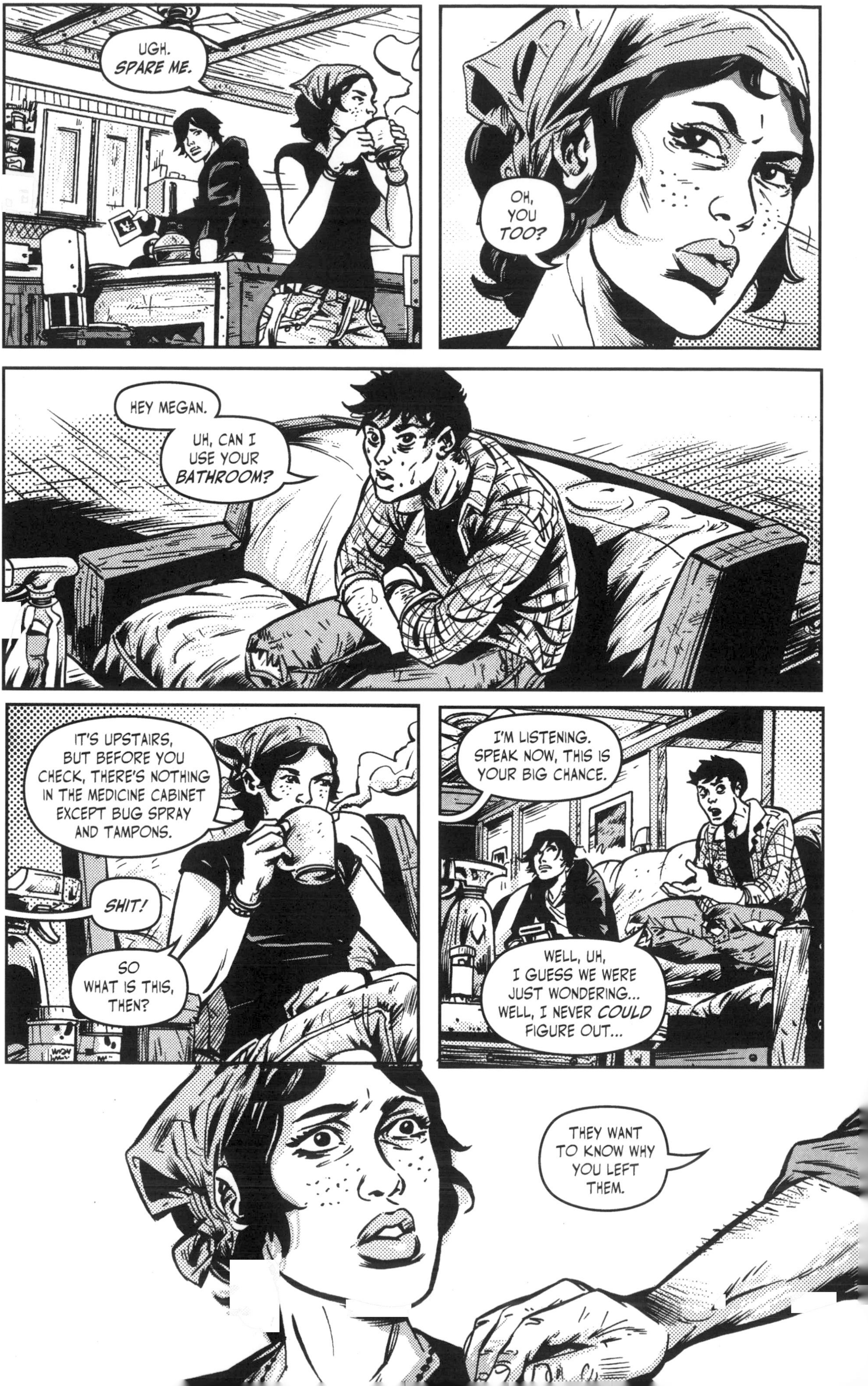

UGH. SPARE ME.
OH, YOU TOO?
HEY MEGAN.
UH, CAN I USE YOUR BATHROOM?
IT'S UPSTAIRS, BUT BEFORE YOU CHECK, THERE'S NOTHING IN THE MEDICINE CABINET EXCEPT BUG SPRAY AND TAMPONS.
SHIT!
SO WHAT IS THIS, THEN?
I'M LISTENING. SPEAK NOW, THIS IS YOUR BIG CHANCE.
WELL, UH, I GUESS WE WERE JUST WONDERING... WELL, I NEVER COULD FIGURE OUT...
THEY WANT TO KNOW WHY YOU LEFT THEM.

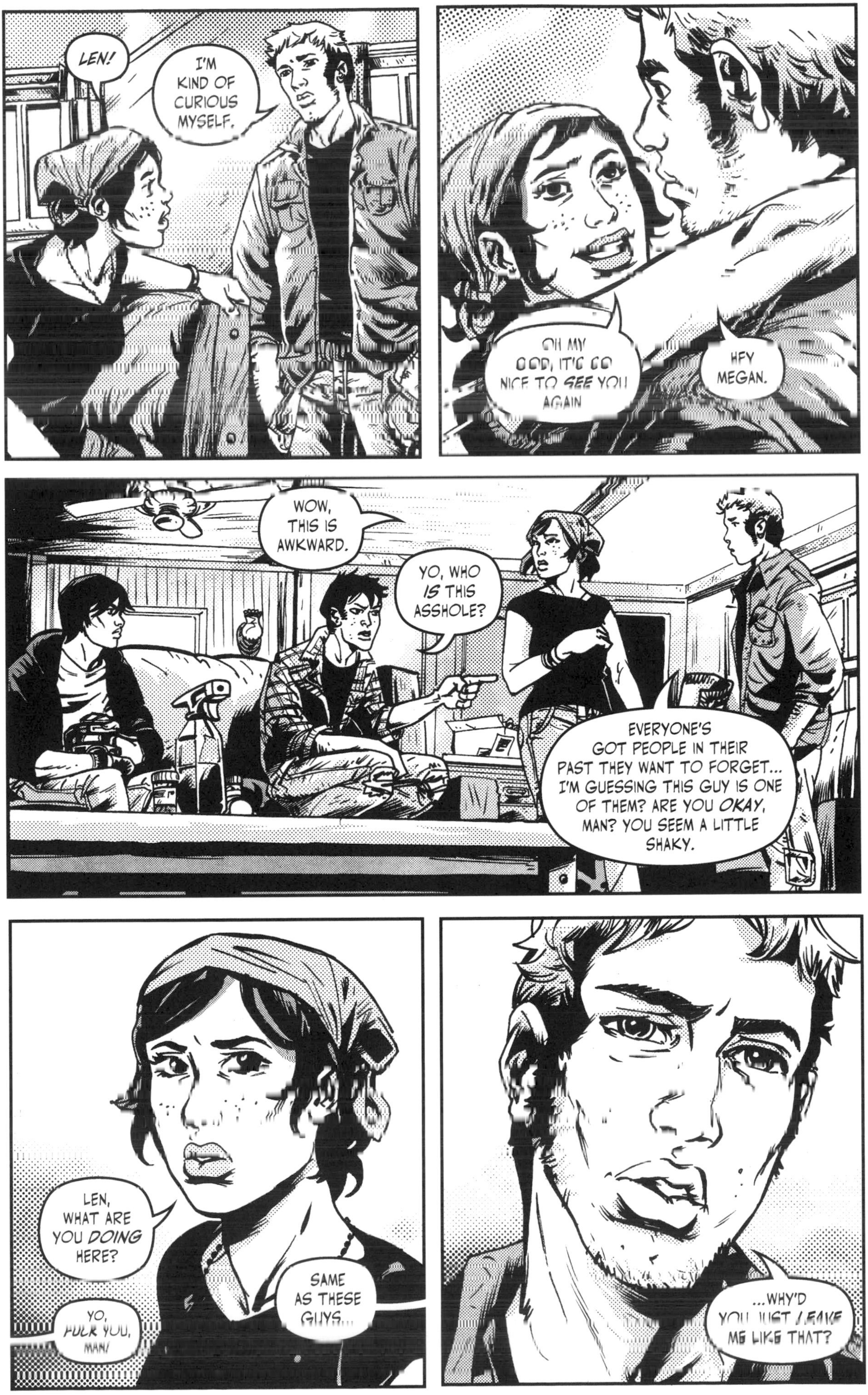
LEN!
I'M KIND OF CURIOUS MYSELF.
OH MY GOD, IT'S SO NICE TO SEE YOU AGAIN.
HEY MEGAN.
WOW, THIS IS AWKWARD.
YO, WHO IS THIS ASSHOLE?
EVERYONE'S GOT PEOPLE IN THEIR PAST THEY WANT TO FORGET... I'M GUESSING THIS GUY IS ONE OF THEM? ARE YOU OKAY, MAN? YOU SEEM A LITTLE SHAKY.
LEN, WHAT ARE YOU DOING HERE?
SAME AS THESE GUYS...
YO, FUCK YOU, MAN!
...WHY'D YOU JUST LEAVE ME LIKE THAT?

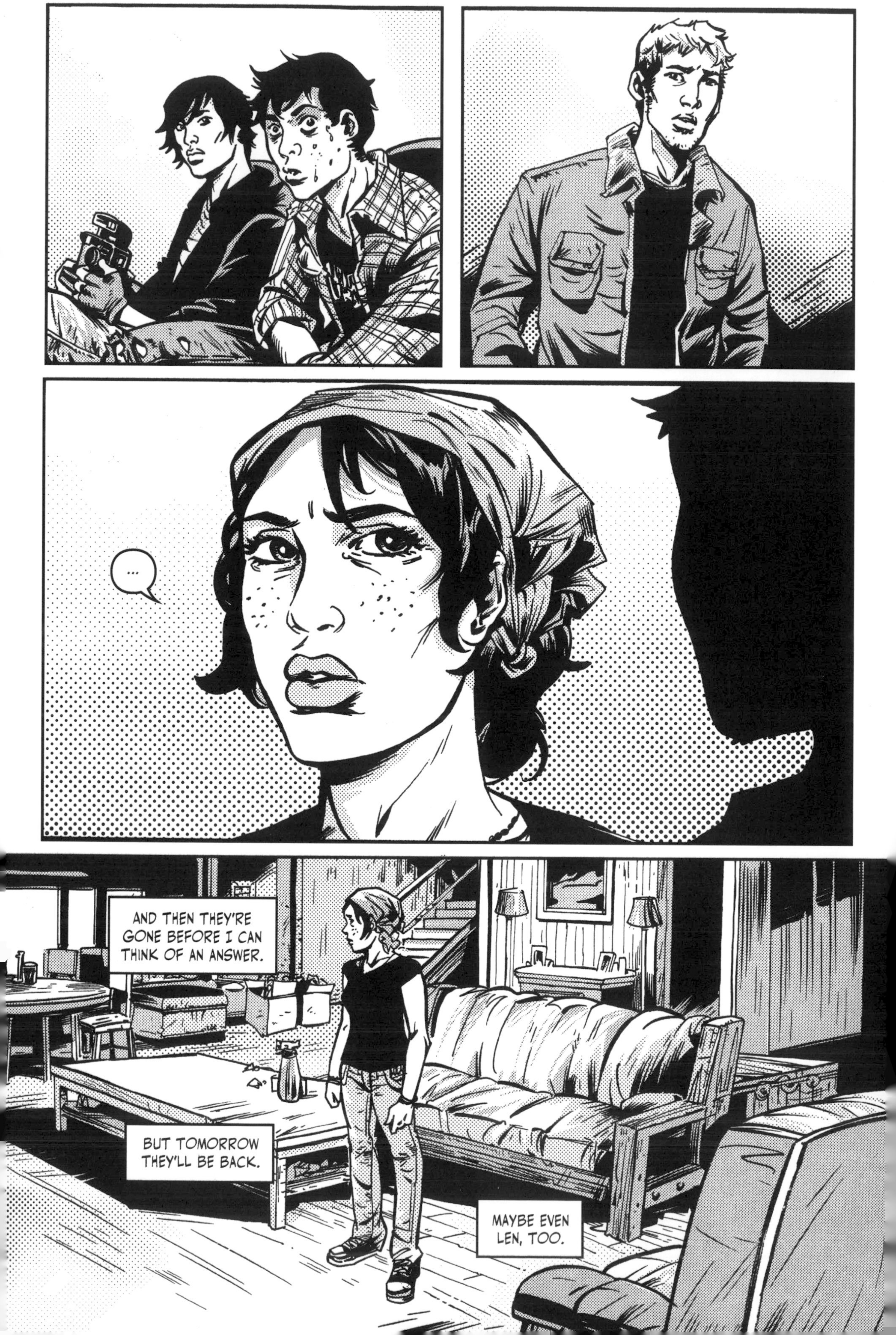
...
AND THEN THEY'RE GONE BEFORE I CAN THINK OF AN ANSWER.
BUT TOMORROW THEY'LL BE BACK.
MAYBE EVEN LEN, TOO.

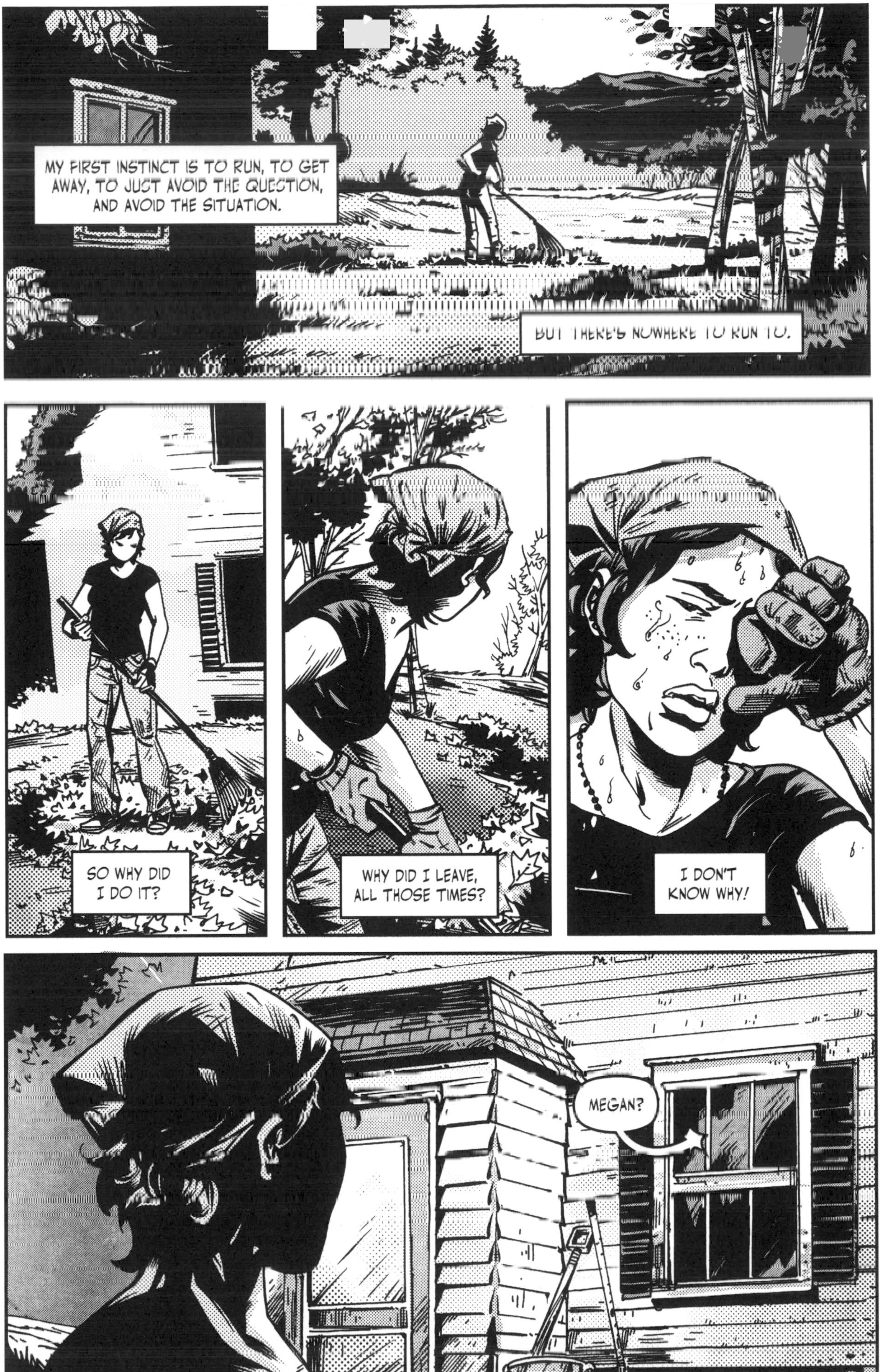
MY FIRST INSTINCT IS TO RUN, TO GET AWAY, TO JUST AVOID THE QUESTION, AND AVOID THE SITUATION.
BUT THERE'S NOWHERE TO RUN TO.
SO WHY DID I DO IT?
WHY DID I LEAVE, ALL THOSE TIMES?
I DON'T KNOW WHY!
MEGAN?

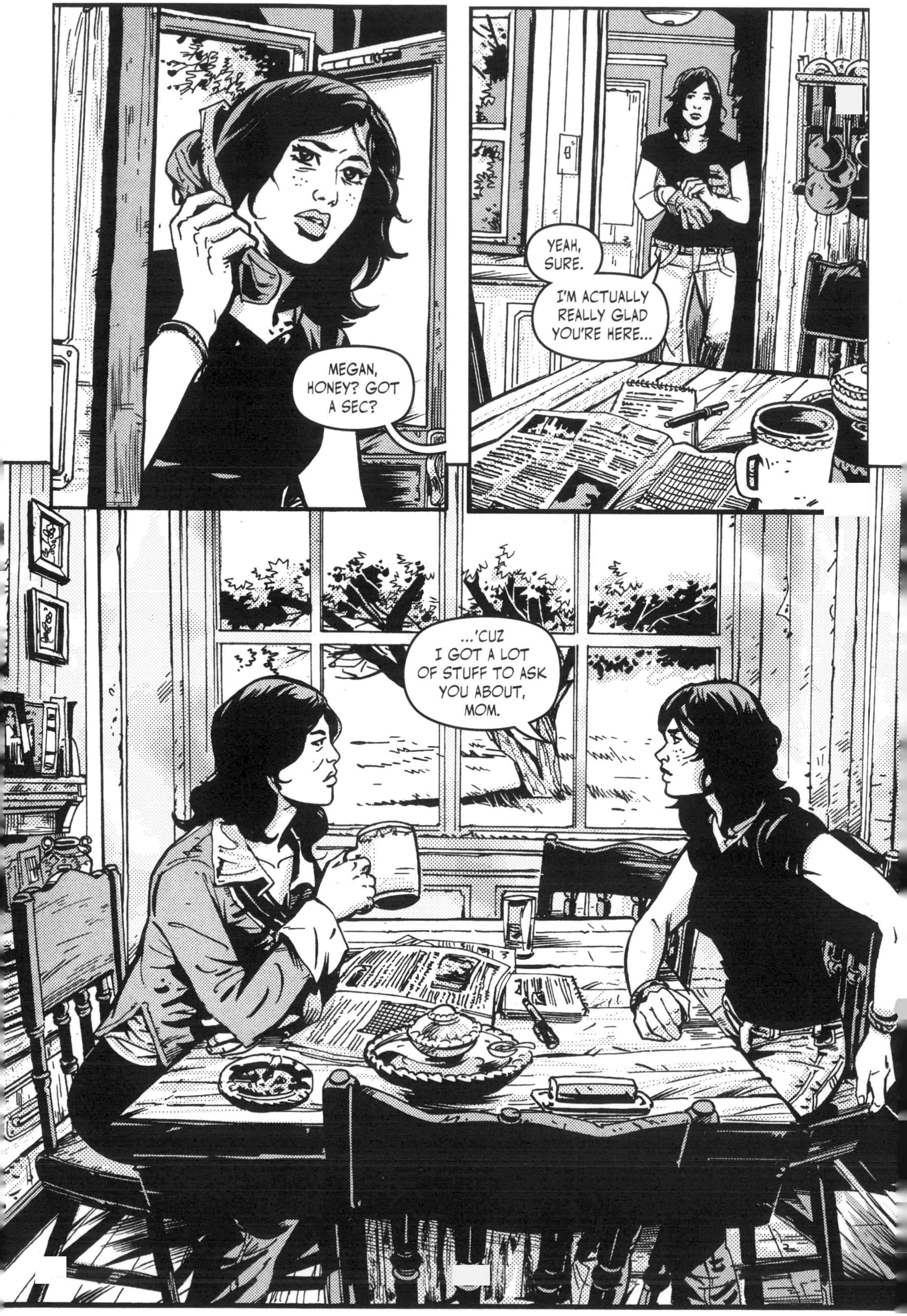
MEGAN, HONEY? GOT A SEC?
YEAH, SURE.
I'M ACTUALLY REALLY GLAD YOU'RE HERE...
...'CUZ I GOT A LOT OF STUFF TO ASK YOU ABOUT, MOM.

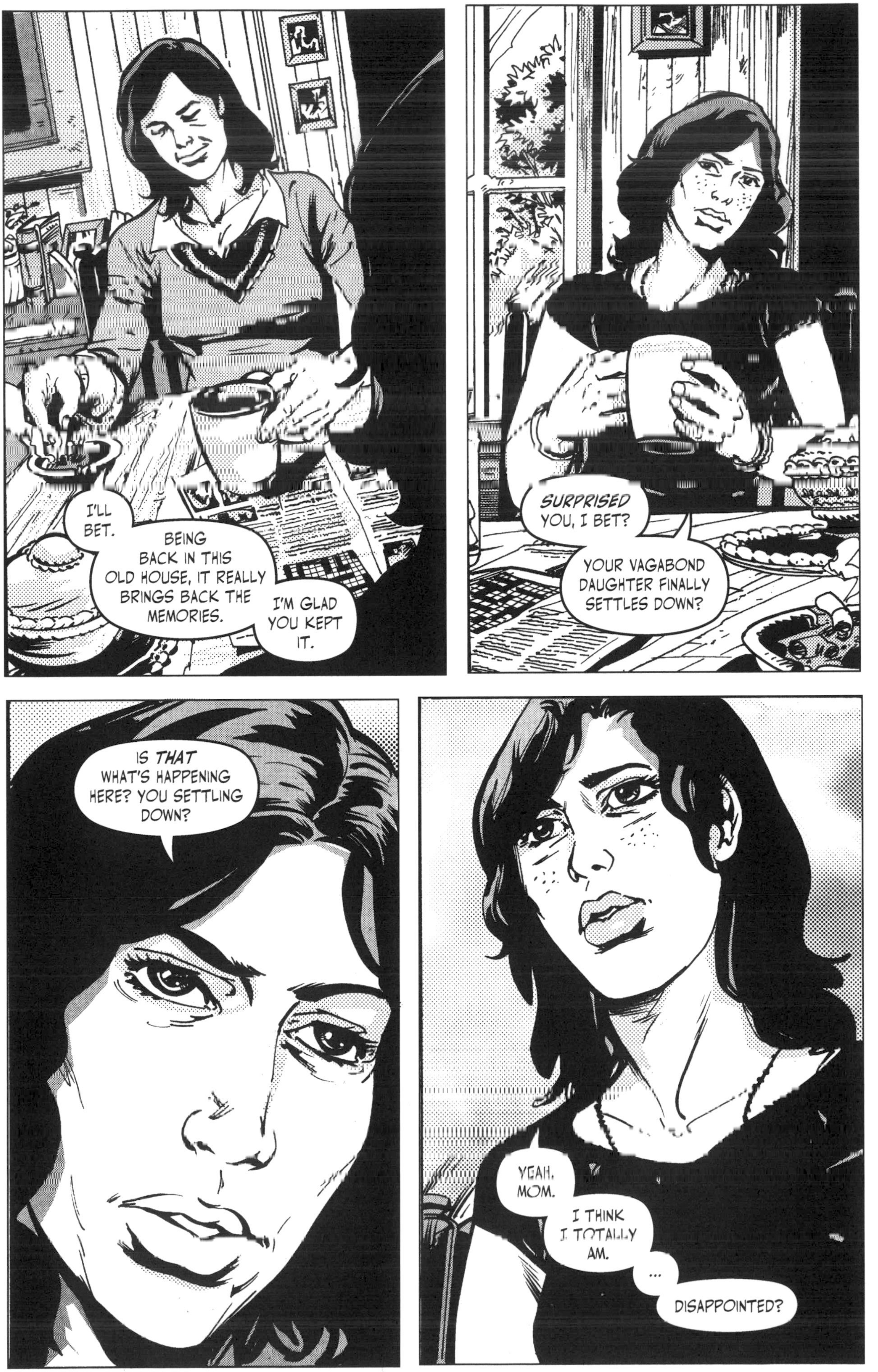
I'LL BET.
BEING BACK IN THIS OLD HOUSE, IT REALLY BRINGS BACK THE MEMORIES.
I'M GLAD YOU KEPT IT.
SURPRISED YOU, I BET?
YOUR VAGABOND DAUGHTER FINALLY SETTLES DOWN?
IS THAT WHAT'S HAPPENING HERE? YOU SETTLING DOWN?
YEAH, MOM.
I THINK I TOTALLY AM.
...
DISAPPOINTED?

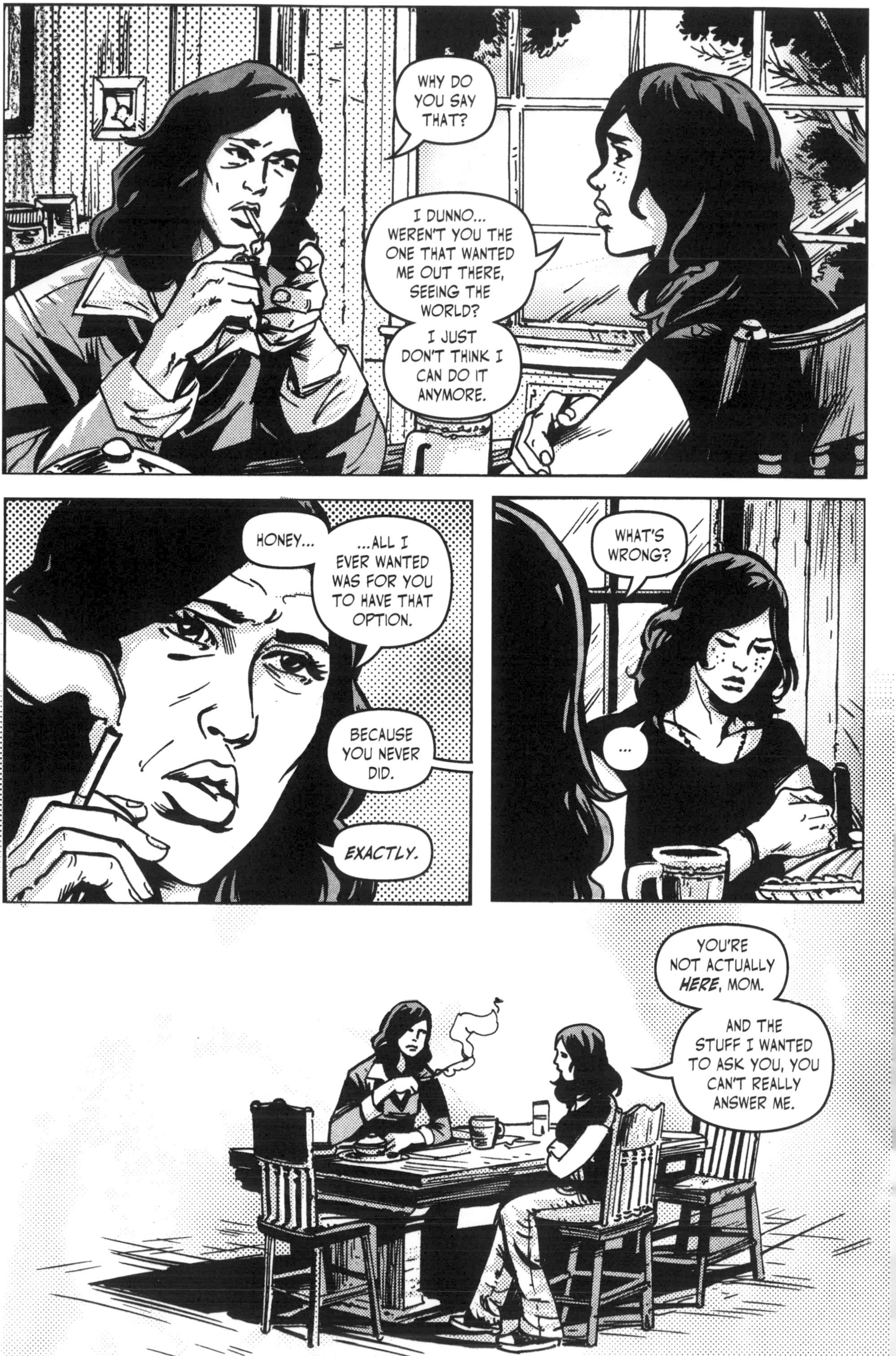
WHY DO YOU SAY THAT?
I DUNNO... WEREN'T YOU THE ONE THAT WANTED ME OUT THERE, SEEING THE WORLD?
I JUST DON'T THINK I CAN DO IT ANYMORE.
HONEY...
...ALL I EVER WANTED WAS FOR YOU TO HAVE THAT OPTION.
BECAUSE YOU NEVER DID.
EXACTLY.
WHAT'S WRONG?
...
YOU'RE NOT ACTUALLY HERE, MOM.
AND THE STUFF I WANTED TO ASK YOU, YOU CAN'T REALLY ANSWER ME.

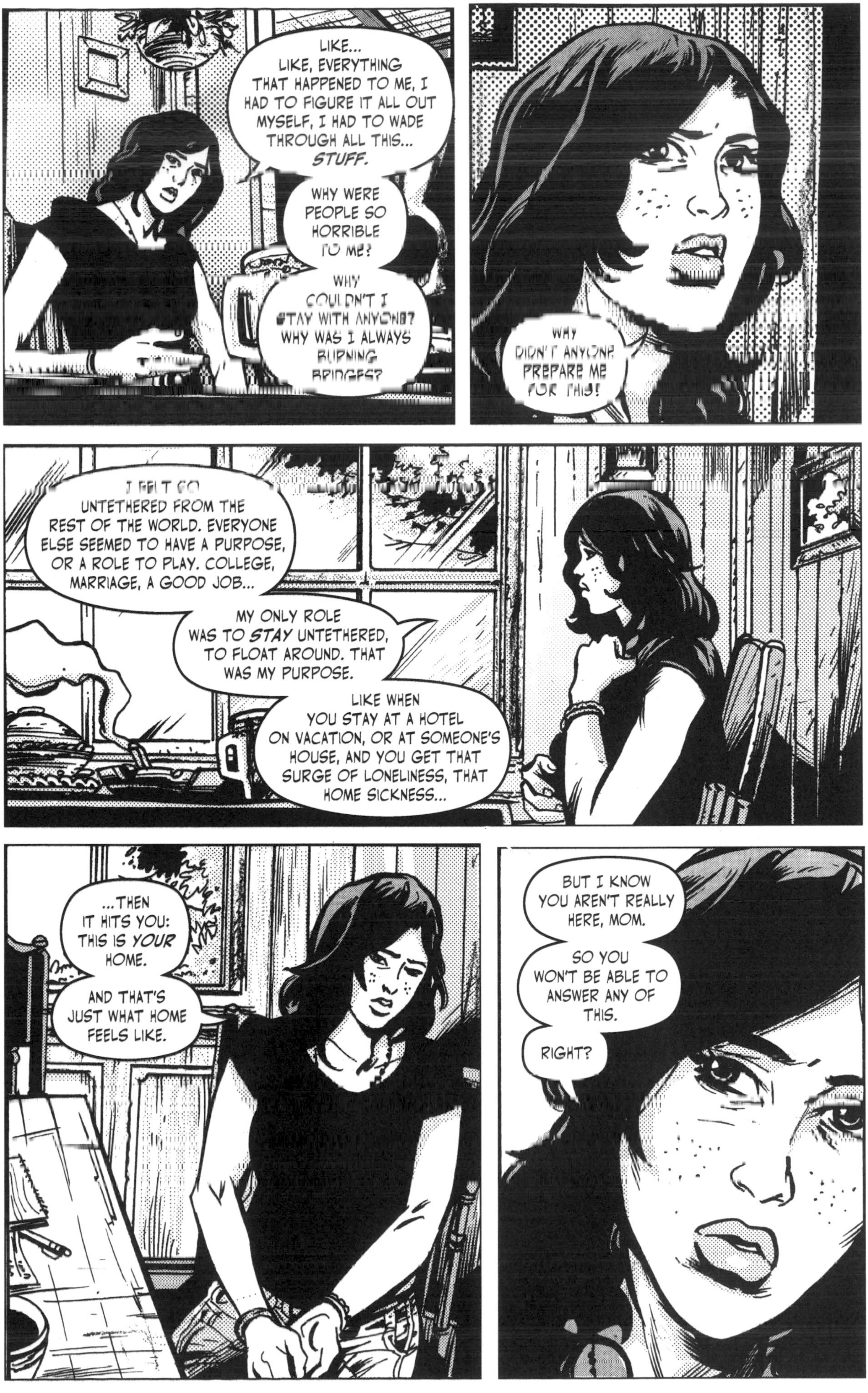
LIKE... LIKE, EVERYTHING THAT HAPPENED TO ME, I HAD TO FIGURE IT ALL OUT MYSELF, I HAD TO WADE THROUGH ALL THIS... *STUFF.*
WHY WERE PEOPLE SO HORRIBLE TO ME?
WHY COULDN'T I STAY WITH ANYONE? WHY WAS I ALWAYS BURNING BRIDGES?
WHY DIDN'T ANYONE PREPARE ME FOR THIS!
I FELT SO UNTETHERED FROM THE REST OF THE WORLD. EVERYONE ELSE SEEMED TO HAVE A PURPOSE, OR A ROLE TO PLAY. COLLEGE, MARRIAGE, A GOOD JOB...
MY ONLY ROLE WAS TO *STAY* UNTETHERED, TO FLOAT AROUND. THAT WAS MY PURPOSE.
LIKE WHEN YOU STAY AT A HOTEL ON VACATION, OR AT SOMEONE'S HOUSE, AND YOU GET THAT SURGE OF LONELINESS, THAT HOME SICKNESS...
...THEN IT HITS YOU: THIS IS *YOUR* HOME.
AND THAT'S JUST WHAT HOME FEELS LIKE.
BUT I KNOW YOU AREN'T REALLY HERE, MOM.
SO YOU WON'T BE ABLE TO ANSWER ANY OF THIS.
RIGHT?

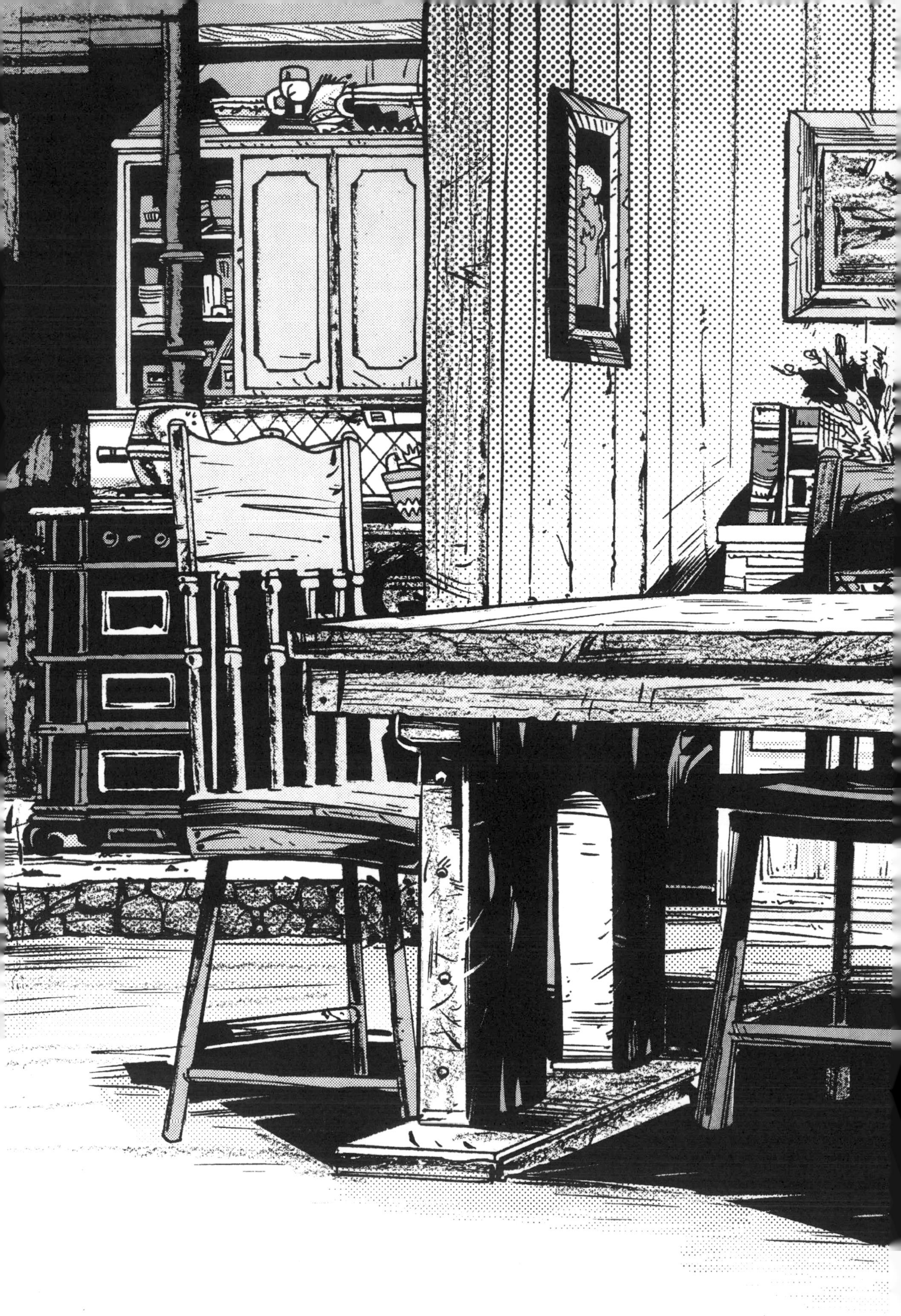

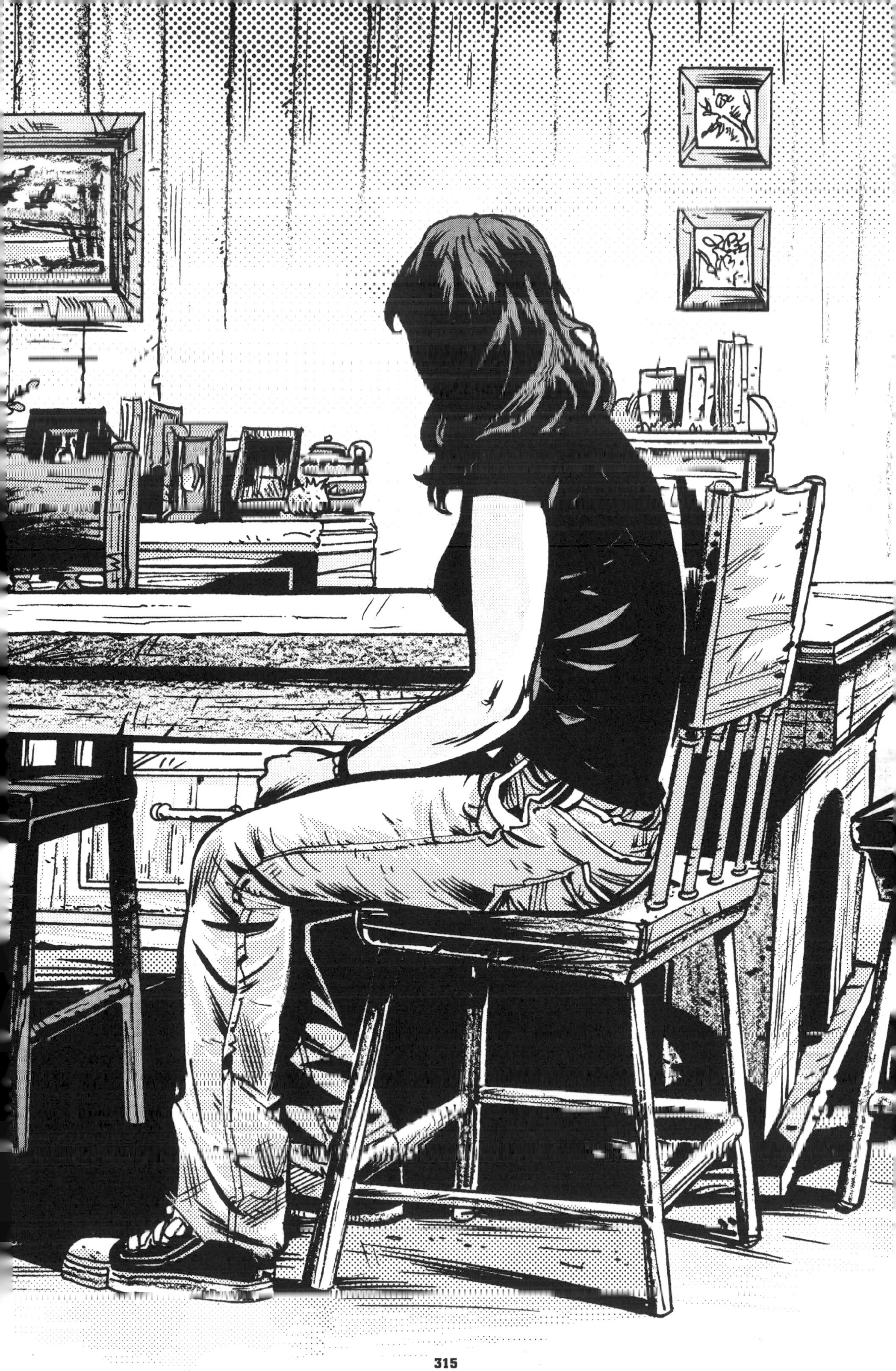

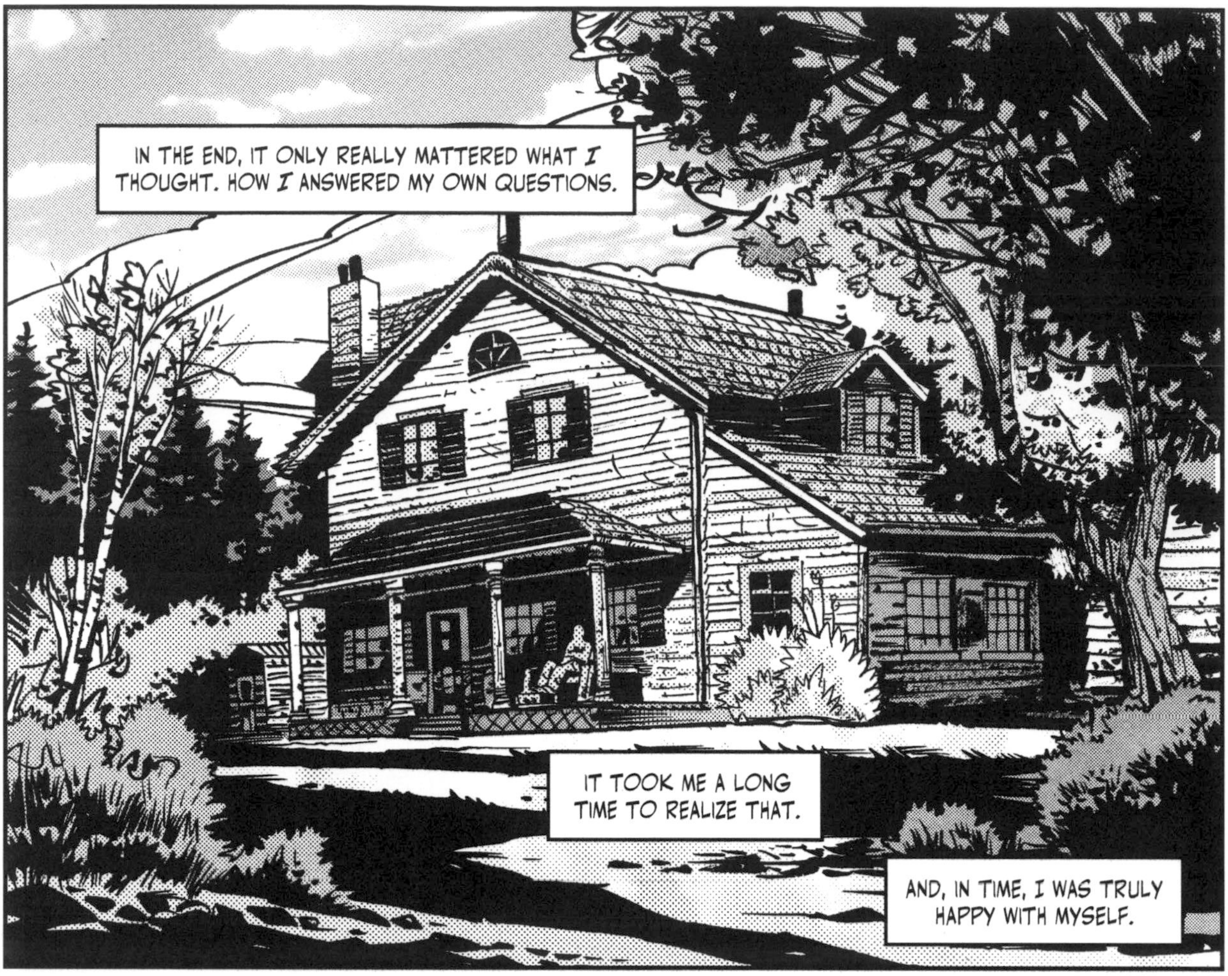
IN THE END, IT ONLY REALLY MATTERED WHAT *I* THOUGHT. HOW *I* ANSWERED MY OWN QUESTIONS.
IT TOOK ME A LONG TIME TO REALIZE THAT.
AND, IN TIME, I WAS TRULY HAPPY WITH MYSELF.

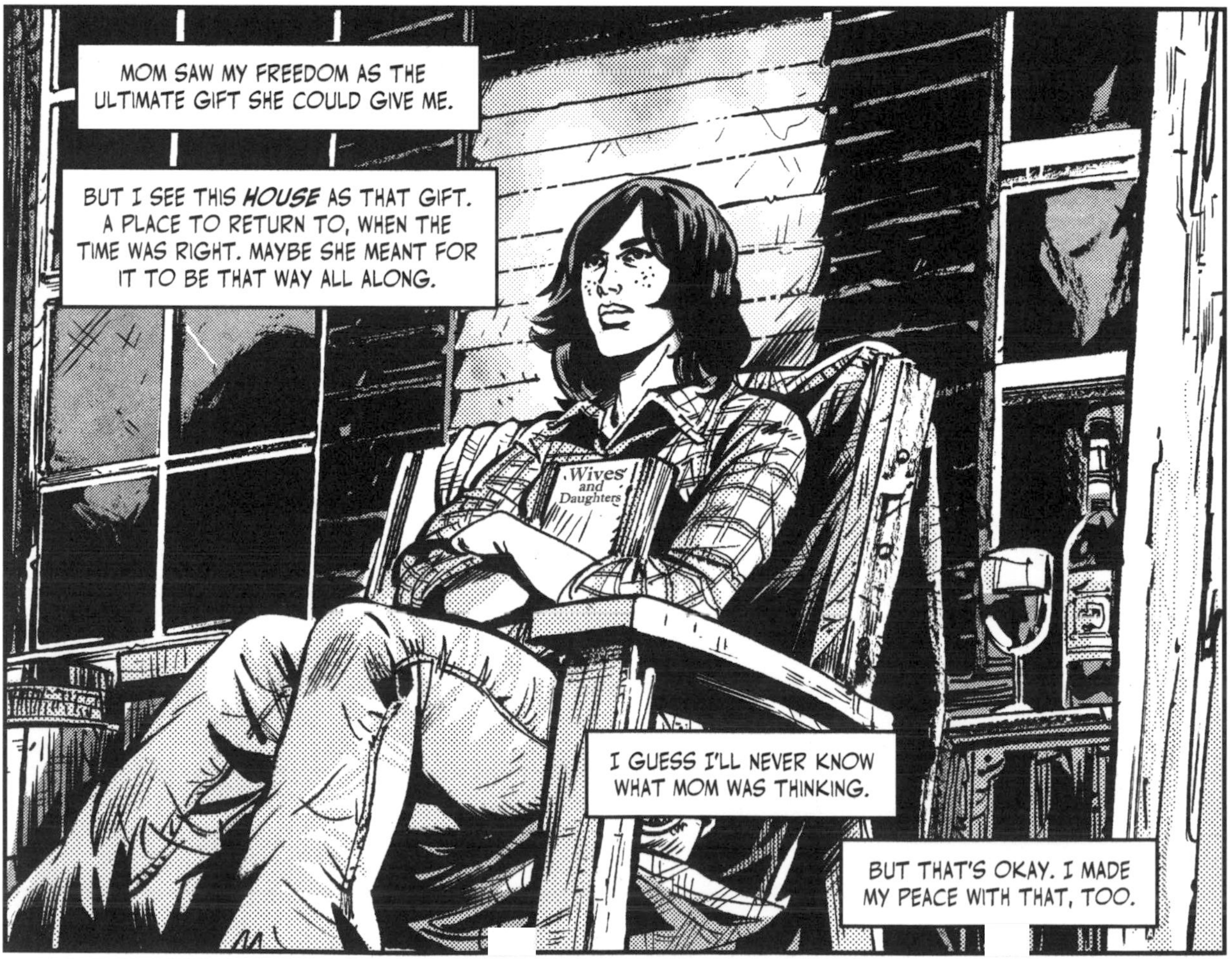
MOM SAW MY FREEDOM AS THE ULTIMATE GIFT SHE COULD GIVE ME.
BUT I SEE THIS ***HOUSE*** AS THAT GIFT. A PLACE TO RETURN TO, WHEN THE TIME WAS RIGHT. MAYBE SHE MEANT FOR IT TO BE THAT WAY ALL ALONG.
Wives and Daughters
I GUESS I'LL NEVER KNOW WHAT MOM WAS THINKING.
BUT THAT'S OKAY. I MADE MY PEACE WITH THAT, TOO.

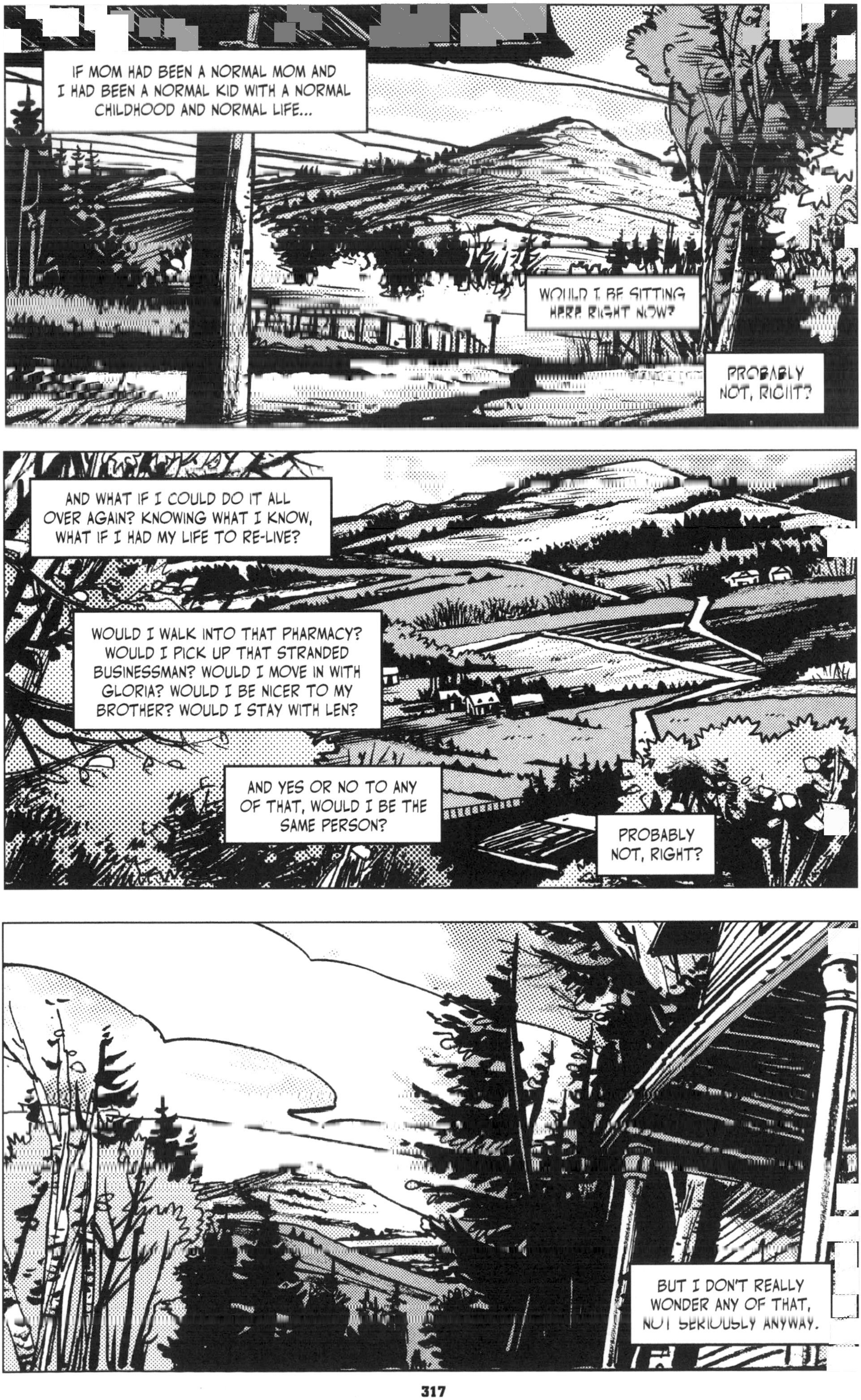
IF MOM HAD BEEN A NORMAL MOM AND I HAD BEEN A NORMAL KID WITH A NORMAL CHILDHOOD AND NORMAL LIFE...
WOULD I BE SITTING HERE RIGHT NOW?
PROBABLY NOT, RIGHT?
AND WHAT IF I COULD DO IT ALL OVER AGAIN? KNOWING WHAT I KNOW, WHAT IF I HAD MY LIFE TO RE-LIVE?
WOULD I WALK INTO THAT PHARMACY? WOULD I PICK UP THAT STRANDED BUSINESSMAN? WOULD I MOVE IN WITH GLORIA? WOULD I BE NICER TO MY BROTHER? WOULD I STAY WITH LEN?
AND YES OR NO TO ANY OF THAT, WOULD I BE THE SAME PERSON?
PROBABLY NOT, RIGHT?
BUT I DON'T REALLY WONDER ANY OF THAT, NOT SERIOUSLY ANYWAY.

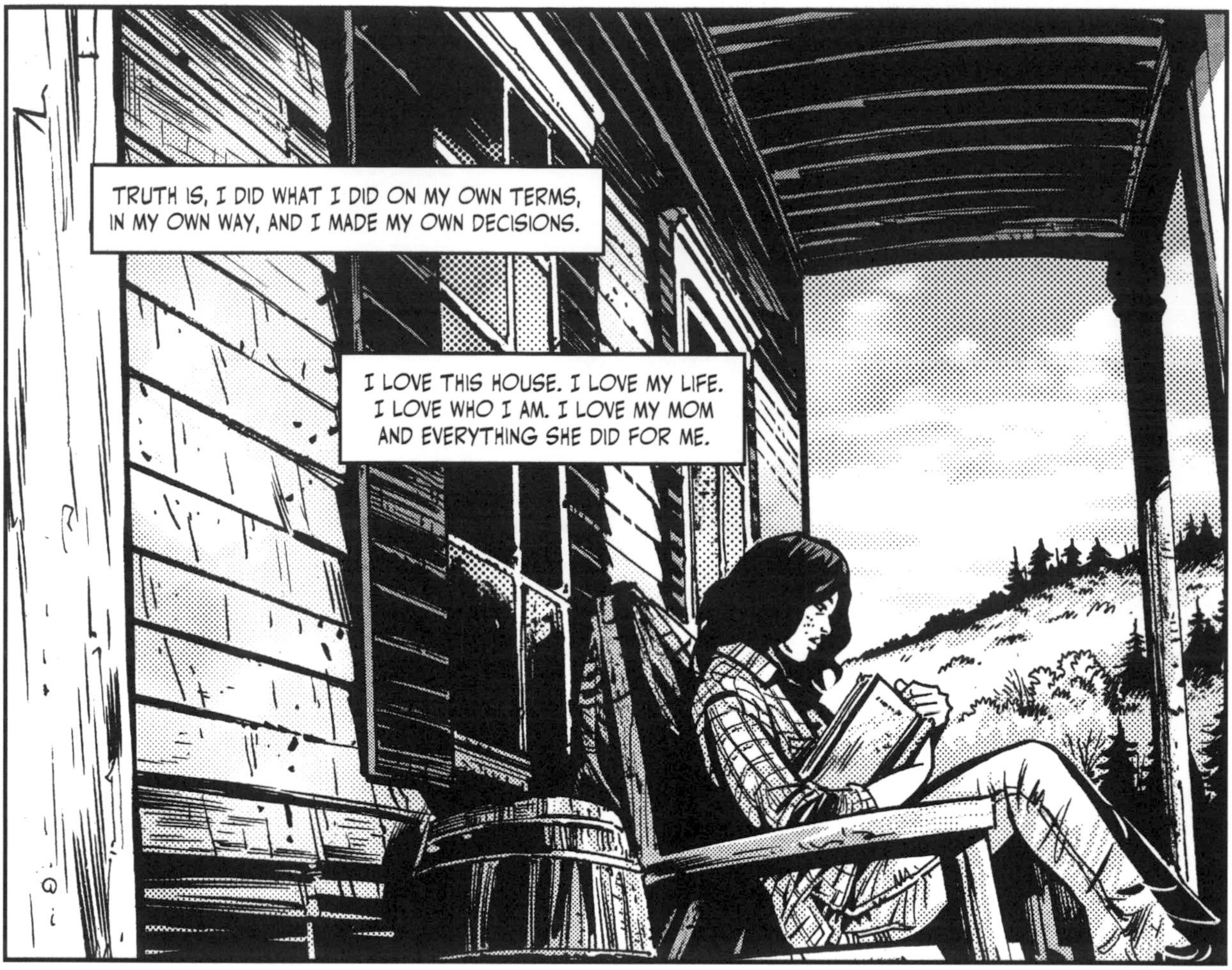
TRUTH IS, I DID WHAT I DID ON MY OWN TERMS, IN MY OWN WAY, AND I MADE MY OWN DECISIONS.
I LOVE THIS HOUSE. I LOVE MY LIFE. I LOVE WHO I AM. I LOVE MY MOM AND EVERYTHING SHE DID FOR ME.

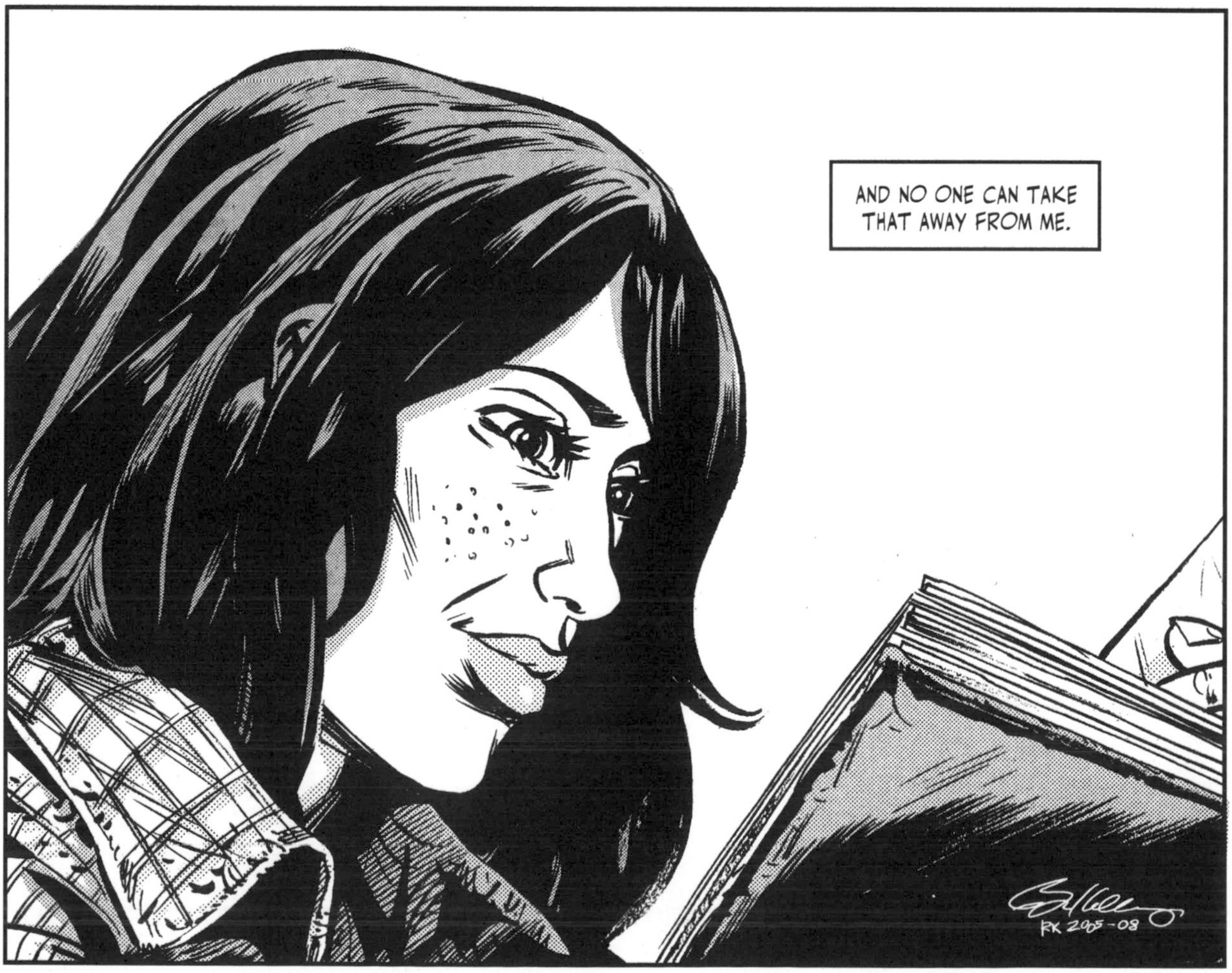
AND NO ONE CAN TAKE THAT AWAY FROM ME.
RK 2005-08

LOCAL™

THE ESSAYS / PRODUCTION NOTES & ART

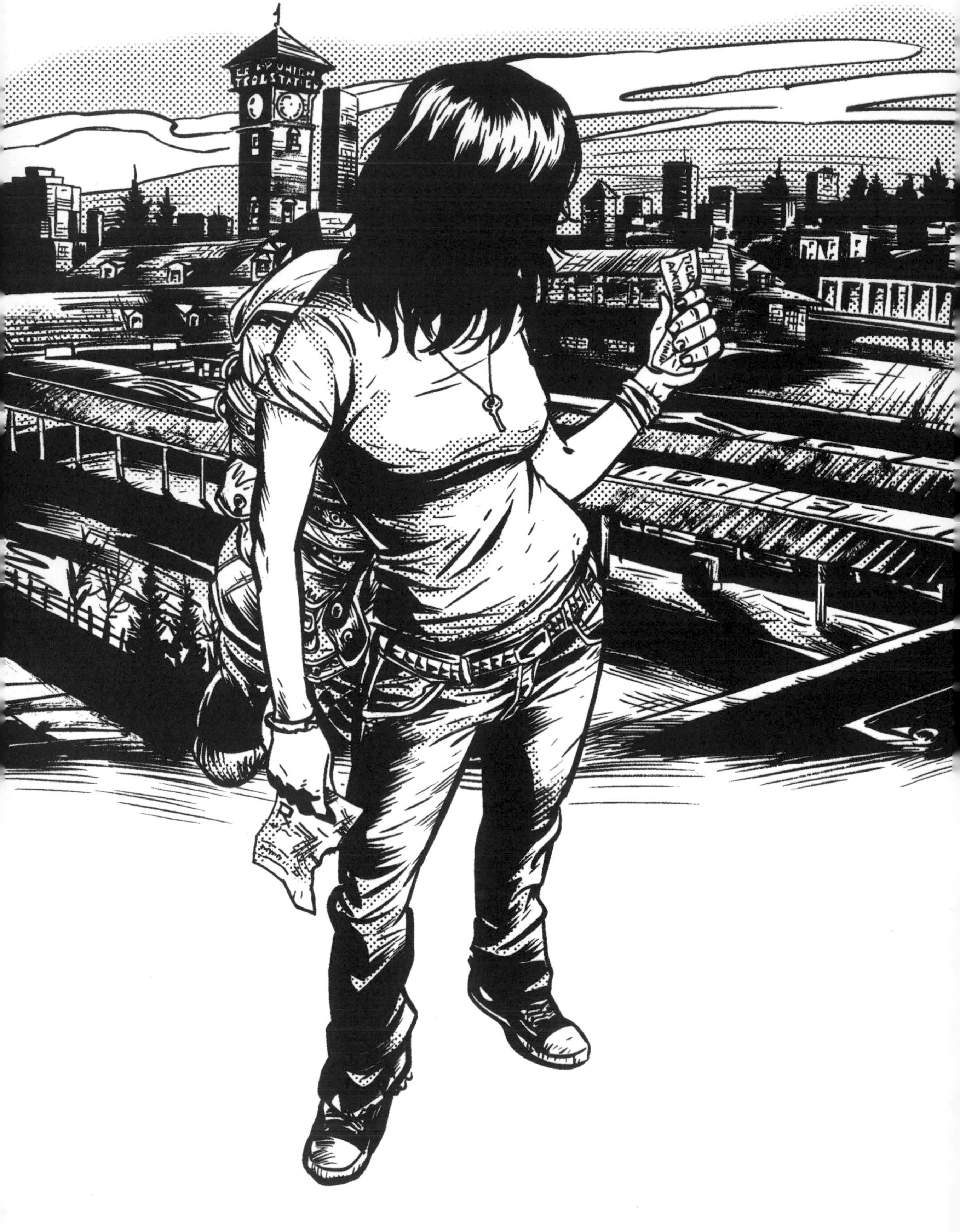

LOCAL #1 - TEN THOUSAND THOUGHTS PER SECOND

November, 2005

BRIAN WOOD:

What am I, some kind of idiot?

Last fall, as I handed off my files for *Demo#12* to letterer and production guy Ryan Yount, I vowed I would never again do a series like this, a monthly indie book. Too much work, too much stress. I was officially burned out. But not even a month later I was on the phone with Mr. Yount, telling him I had this idea for a new series, and was thinking of pitching it to Oni Press. He laughed, that sort of fake laugh people do when they think you are, in fact, some kind of idiot.

But I pitched it anyway. James Lucas Jones, Oni Editorial Chief, may have also thought me the idiot, but if he did, he didn't let on. And he accepted the project, offering me princely sums and creative freedoms. James and I actually spent most of this year artist hunting, but as anyone who works in American comics will tell you, finding an appropriate, available artist that can handle a monthly book is a pretty difficult task. I have a copy of Ryan's *Giant Robot Warriors* on my shelf, and it stared me in the face for six months before I finally focused on it, and said, hey, Ryan Kelly's art in this is killer! Lemme talk to this guy. The extremely accurate and truthful account of what happened next can be found below.

Local, simply put, is a series of short stories about people and the places they live in. I've been a little obsessed with the idea of locations and hometowns for a while now, even creating my own little t-shirt company* dedicated to it. Life operates very differently when you get out of major population centers, and some of the best films I've seen and books I've read take place in locations I would never have thought about otherwise.

The location can't be the story, though. Getting into the minute details of any specific place runs the risk of alienating anyone who doesn't live there. The *Local* stories will be universal, whether to live in Portland, the Pacific Northwest, America, or the rest of the world. But, for the locals, the stories will contain landmarks and references that'll be instantly recognizable.

Poor Megan McKeenan. Look for her to pop up in every issue of *Local*, sometimes as the lead, sometimes as just a background character. One of the "secrets" of this book (well, not so much a secret anymore), is that Ryan and I are setting the series off in 1994, progressing roughly a year per issue after that. You'll probably never be able to tell, except in details like clothing or car manufacturers and names of businesses that may now be changed or gone. I actually heard just recently that Nob Hill Pharmacy, seen in this issue, is out of business**. So as the years tick by, Megan'll grow a little older and wiser, and by the time you read *Local #12*, she'll have gone from the 17-year old you see on the previous page to a very well-travelled 30-year-old

*Northern Boy, which is no longer in operation.
**The Nob Hill Pharmacy has become a coffee shop, but the proprietors retained the original signage because of its legacy in the Portland area.

My soundtrack:
"Does Your Hometown Care?" - Superchunk
"Girl With X-Ray Eyes" - The Cassettes
"Fortress" - Pinback
"Up In The North" - Fiery Furnaces
"Bottle Up And Explode!" - Elliott Smith
"The Get Away" - Pretty Girls Make Graves

RYAN KELLY:

When Brian Wood, one of the finest writers in comics, contacted me in search for an artist to paint the ceiling of his new apartment, he caught me a little off guard. I was at home, twiddling my thumbs and waiting for my clothes to dry.

"Randy," he said.

"It's Ryan," I said, embarrassed.

"I need someone to paint the ceiling of my new apartment and decorate the vault with customary designs. For this, we will pay you three thousand large gold ducats. My son, you are dismissed."

"What about comic books?" I asked, "These things with words. And pictures. Words and pictures working together to tell a story. Folded together. And stapled."

"Well, I do have a new project, called *Local*." Brian said, "But I'm not sure it's your cup of tea. It's not a ceiling."

"Try me," I said.

"You sure you don't want the ceiling?"

"No way. Give me *Local*."

So, Brian Wood grabbed his pipe and told me about *Local*, "It's going to be big, bold and brassy. With Dancers. Maybe. First, You have to become the character. You have to move to Portland, get a messed-up boyfriend, and stake out a local pharmacy in the rain for a couple of hours a day."

Well, after I did that for 8 weeks, I needed to actually draw the book. I had a week or two to do that. Along the way, I had to teach myself a new invention called Adobe Photoshop. I had to push myself to learn all the digital stuff I ignored in art school to help see this book come to its fruition. I did the layouts and scanned them in. Then I made corrections on the digital file. I printed the layout design as a blue line on manually fed 11x17-inch Bristol paper. On top of the blue line, I did some necessary penciling and inked everything with a single sable hair round brush and a ton of correction tape. After that, I scanned the final pages and painted in zipatone patterns on a separate layer over the line art.

Laboring day in and day out, my hands soaked with ink before sunrise, Brian Wood comes by to evaluate my progress.

"When will it be ready?" insisted the writer stubbornly.

"When it is finished," I replied.

Well, here it is. It's finished. I think it looks decent. I hope you think so too.

And maybe some day I'll get to paint that ceiling.

Favorite part of *Local #1*:
The fact that the boyfriend isn't even worth having a name.

Less than favorite part of *Local #1*:
Not quite nailing down the look of the pharmacist character and settling on depicting our Secretary of State, which actually turned out really good. Nevermind.

The songs that are sewn into every line and stroke of *Local #1*
"Portland Oregon" - Loretta Lynn & Jack White
"Ramblin On My Mind" - Robert Johnson
"Set Out Running" - Neko Case and Her Boyfriends
"Let It Ride" - Ryan Adams and The Cardinals
"Where You Are" - Sleater Kinney
"Who Are You" - Tom Waits
"Keep On Running" - Cat Power
"Push" - The Cure
"Cool Your Boots" - Ride
"Girl From The North Country" - Bob Dylan and Johnny Cash

And my segue to Minneapolis:
"Portland" - The Replacements

★

LOCAL #2 - POLAROID BOYFRIEND

December, 2005

RYAN KELLY:

I absolutely never had any time to draw this issue. Every morning I got up and looked for time to draw Issue #2: Polaroid Boyfriend. Nope, none, nowhere. I was trying. But time was not there. Days turned weeks and turned into months. In fact, I seriously doubt that I actually drew this issue. I certainly don't recall one moment in time ever in my life that I was physically working on this artwork. Oh sure, you're holding this in your hands and you say, "Ryan Kelly, your name is on the cover." But I, and no one I am associated with, can ever recall me drawing any of this for one second. And although this is, and probably will continue to be called a Ryan Kelly effort, I have to officially declare it a hoax.

That said, I have to say, "What artist wouldn't want to illustrate a story that takes place in their hometown?" Especially a place I know like the back of my brittle, aging, ink-stained paws.

I do recall a significant amount of lobbying by me went into getting Minneapolis chosen as the destination spot for Issue #2 in the first place. Initially, I obtained the most prominent lobbyists and yes-men adept at the art of persuasion to form a united front in the goal at getting Minneapolis chosen. I hired other artists and tacticians to construct graphs, charts and maps to package Minneapolis as a gutsy yet whimsical locale that is unmatched in its festive yet down-home atmosphere. We mobilized a grassroots campaign that took to the streets with pamphlets and free samples of General Mills cereal, Malt-O-Meal, Post-It Notes, and those hilarious gigantic foam hands you see at sports events. We went door to door with posters featuring photos of Brian Wood and editor James Lucas Jones with the headline running "Sir, why haven't you chosen Minneapolis yet? The American people have a right to know." I spent upwards of $500,000 in television and radio ads. Getting Minneapolis chosen was no doubt going to be a public relations nightmare and my team needed to grease the palms of the fat cats in charge. Bribes were taken. Deals were brokered. Lives were ruined.

Then Brian Wood said, "Well, I don't have a place picked for issue #2. Minneapolis sounds like as good as any place. May as well."

Boy, I felt pretty silly.

And once again, I blew all my time on frivolous pursuits and had little time left to draw the book.

So I drew it. At least, you say I did. I do remember settling down and being more impressionistic with the inking and not relying so much on photo reference. I could be more impressionistic because no one could come to me and say, "Hey, you forgot to put in that tall shelf behind the counter of OarFolk/Treehouse records!"

I know I forgot it. I've lived here my whole life.

Favorite part of *Local* #2: The guy who drew this book accidentally drew the same pose on Megan in Page 19 panel 1, and page 24 panel 1. Wacky.

Less than favorite part of *Local* #2: My freaking schedule, because I still don't think I drew this.

Additional tones and effects provided by Kelly Brown and Marcus Smith.

Local #2: Polaroid Boyfriend, Minneapolis is read in the precise order of these tracks:
Page 1: "A New Career In A New Town" - David Bowie
Page 2-3: "Gentlemen Take Polaroids" - Japan
Page 4-6: "Dirty Mind" - Prince
Page 7-9: "Pictures Of You" - The Cure
Page 10: "Somebody's Watching Me" - Rockwell
Page 11: "Control" - Janet Jackson
Page 12: "Single Girl" - Lush
Page 13: "Obsession" - Siouxsie and the Banshees
Page 14: "Keith" - Discount
Page 15-16: "Could You Be The One?" - Husker Du
Page 17: "Contact" - The Police
Page 18: "No Ordinary Love" - Sade
Page 19: "One Way Or Another" - Blondie
Page 20: "The Movement of Fear" - Tones On Tail
Page 21: "Burning Photographs" - Ryan Adams
Page 22-25: "Words" - Low
Page 26: "Love Is The Law" - The Suburbs

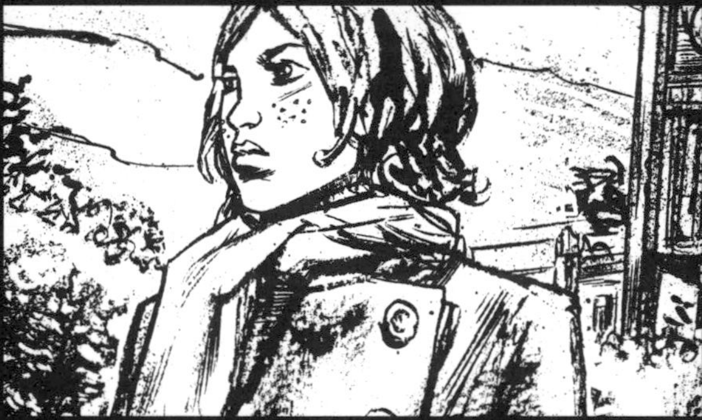

BRIAN WOOD:

Ryan kids, yes he does. He drew this issue, of that there is no doubt. He drew the FUCK out of this issue. Yeah, dude! I actually had to write a lot of this story "blind," since he'd be supplying his own reference. Parts of my script read like:

"Megan leaves her building and walks right (Ryan - or left?), to the corner (if one is nearby) and gets on the bus (or train or subway or into a cab?)..." and so on, since I don't know from Minneapolis and didn't have reference in front of me while I wrote. But he managed to filter all that out and adjust and make it work out right. And hey, Minneapolis locals - anything wrong with this issue? TALK TO RYAN!

(But I'll take the heat for the panel of Megan's underwear drawer. Yeah, that was all me. Sorry.)

As I was wrapping this up, I thought this story was particularly *Demo*, the largely silent scenes, the open ending, the conflict, the dysfunction. And why not? Megan's probably only 18 or 19, still figuring the world out, and clearly she has yet to learn that guys creeping through her apartment, no matter how smoldering their eyes may be, is not an acceptable sort of relationship to encourage. She'll learn. We all did. Eventually.

Silent scenes, while pretty easy to write, are tricky to draw, as it requires the artist to actually slow the reading time down, lest someone blow through the book in 30 seconds. I think Ryan did great, pacing the book just right, cramming it with detail, and building the tension.

That record shop: If you went to Minneapolis and looked for it, you'd find it as Treehouse Records. But this story takes place in 1995, back when it was still called Oarfolkjokeopus, a legendary record store dating back to the 70s.

My soundtrack:
"If You See Her, Say Hello" - Bob Dylan
"Bones Of Her Hands" - Archers of Loaf
"Things I Will Keep" - Guided By Voices
"Song Against Sex" - Neutral Milk Hotel
"Write You" - Snoozer
"I'm From Further North Than You" - The Wedding Present
"Ghosts" - The Jam

And if this issue were a movie, this is what would play over the final credits:
"I Don't Want To Get Over You" - The Magnetic Fields

★

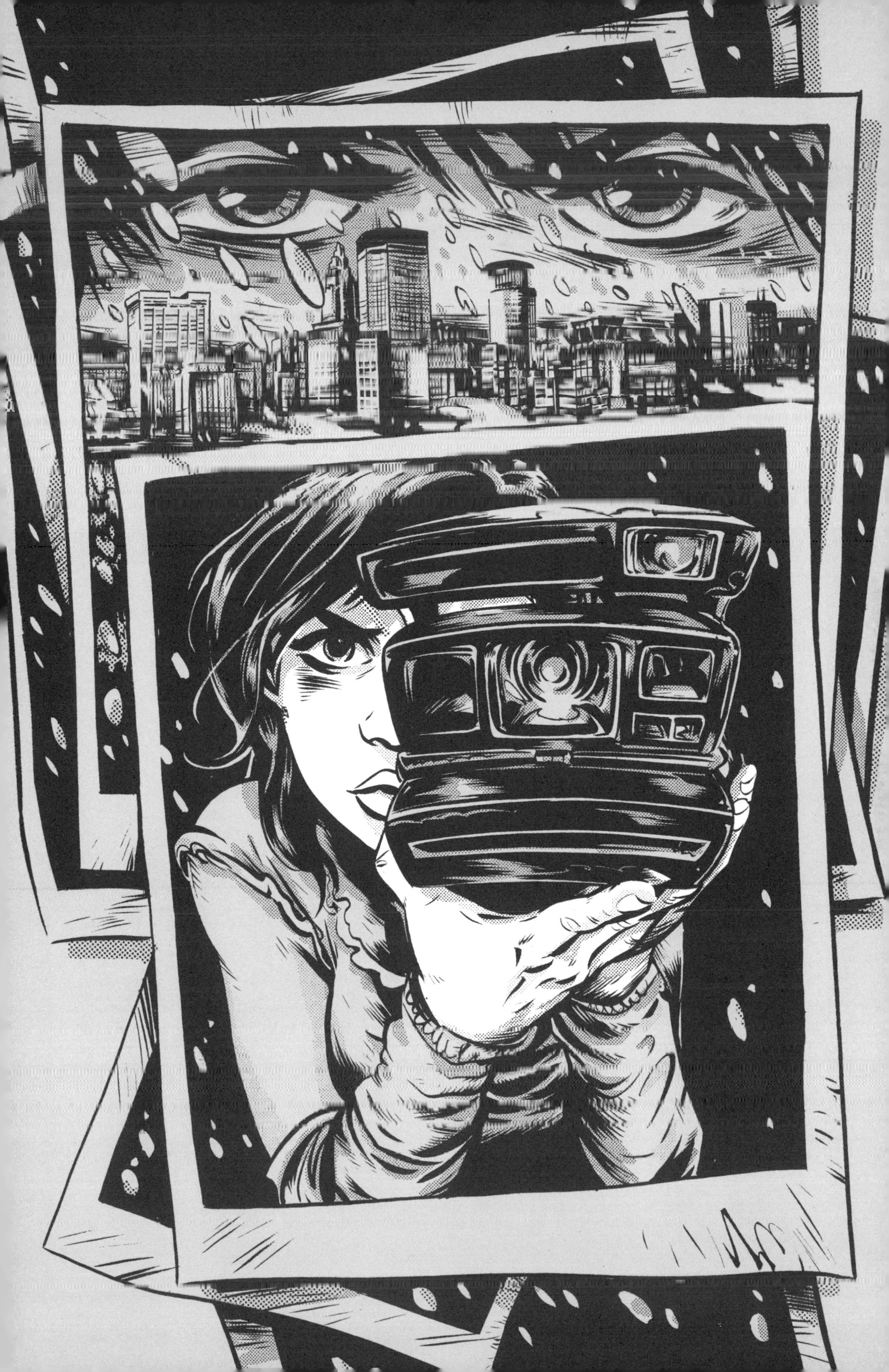

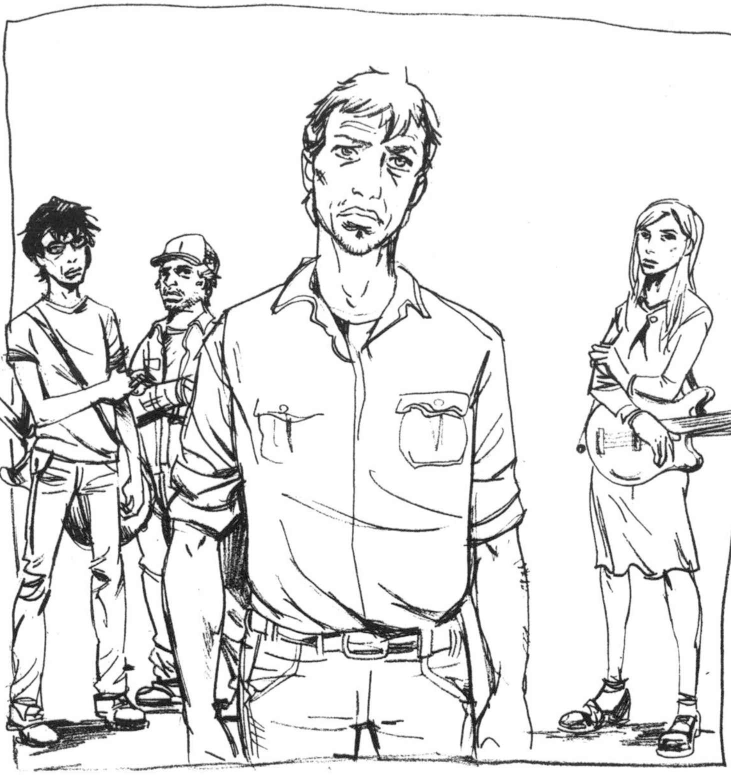

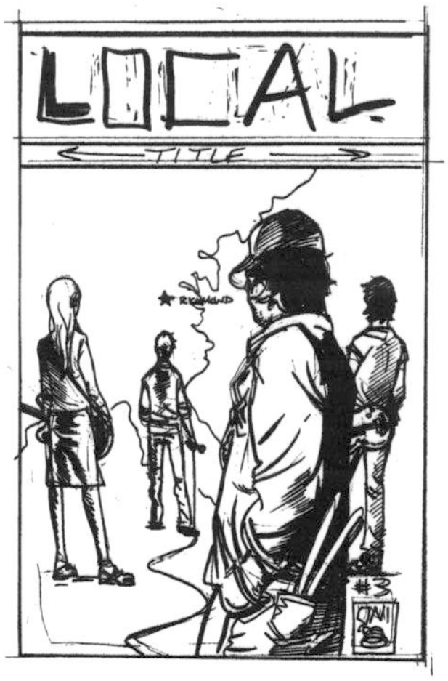
LOCAL
TITLE
#3

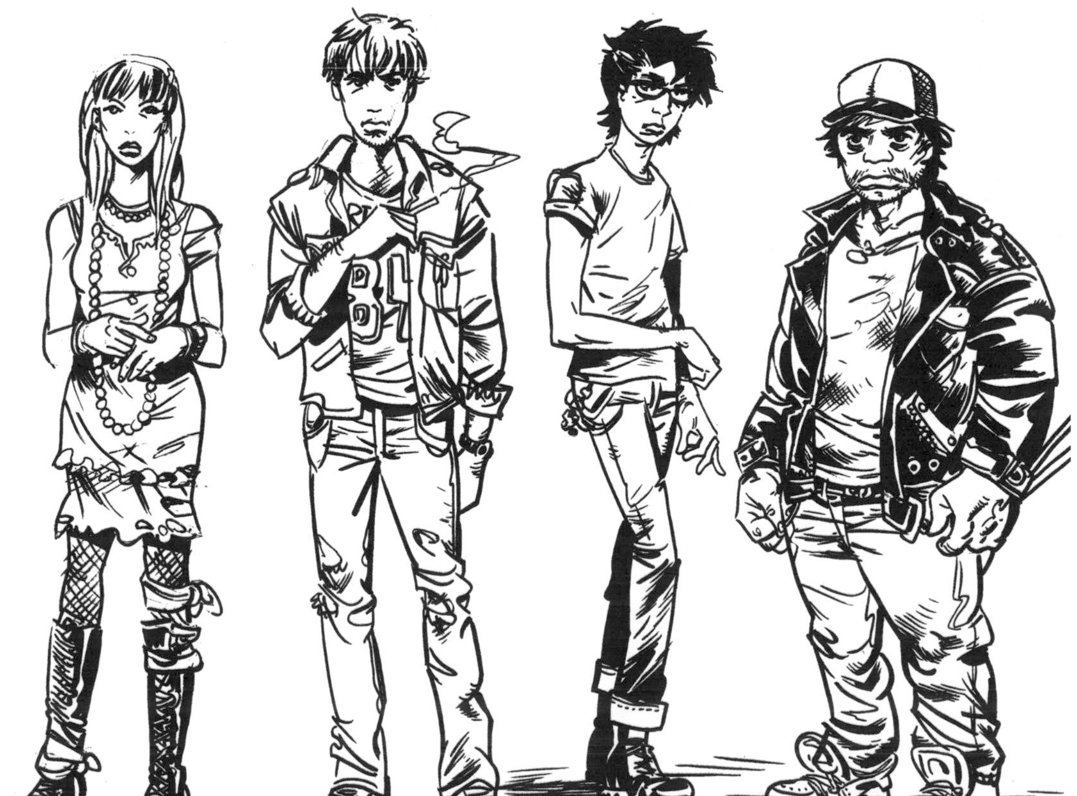

LOCAL #3 - THEORIES AND DEFENSES

January, 2006

RYAN KELLY:

Whatever you do, don't join a band.

But let's say, for argument's sake, that it is too late and you've already joined a band. Oh sure, you will be accepted by your peers and feel like you belong to something important. You are using your skills in a creative field with plenty of potential. You buy one of those Econoline vans that no normal human being would drive. You're going to exciting new destinations that you thought you'd never go before. Like Green Bay. You are making friends that share the same interests as you and pretending that their band just played a really tight set. You're up there on stage jumping around like a fool, sweating, screaming, flailing, and vomiting.

Finally, you get on the cover of *Maximum Rock'N'Roll*. Well, a week later, you leave a Chicken Soft Taco wrapper on somebody's distortion pedal and years of suppressed anger and resentment erupt in a monsoon of fury and unconquerable bitterness. A fight ensues. Words are exchanged. The band breaks up. And when the ash and dust settle, you must go on with your life somehow, bandless and a mere civilian.

The same band members who were there with you when you were on the floor of the van in freezing temperatures, lying in a pile of your own filth while using a Cheetos bag as a pillow and your knees pressed against a stack of Marshall amps praying for God's deliverance, will not even talk to you now as you pass them on the street.

THAT is Rock and Roll.

OK, I did it and I loved it. I admit it. If I had never joined a band I could never say I was gobbed on, harassed by skinheads, booed off stage, or visited Green Bay. Can any of you say that? You wish!

But seriously, out of all the *Local* issues, this was by far my favorite story. I've read many "life as a band" stories before and seen it in movies. This was different. It was about life AFTER the band, when all you're left with is four distinct human beings, alone, picking up the pieces of their life in a town that had moved on without them.

You'd think that Brian was in a band for 15 years. He took all the gloss and glamour off of being in a band. Too me, it seemed so real. We create an idealistic view of our favorite bands because we only really experience them through a screen of popular media. We forget that they are people who have broken hearts and pawn their records just like you and me.

On a technical note, I switched from rough paper to smooth paper for issue #5, that means bye-bye drybrush. If you don't like drybrush then you're no friend of mine, partner. I want my rough paper back, jack. That's a fact.

Arranged and composed by Ryan Kelly.

Other instruments played by Aaron Quist, Josh Lynch, and Kelly Brown.

Local 3: Theories and Defenses Track list
1. Frank: "Tour Spiel" - The Minutemen
2. Bridget: "But I'm Different Now" - The Jam
3. Kevin: "Cut Your Hair" - Pavement
4. Ross: "The Golden Age" - Cracker
5. Page 26, as the movie credits roll: "Left Of The Dial" - The Replacements

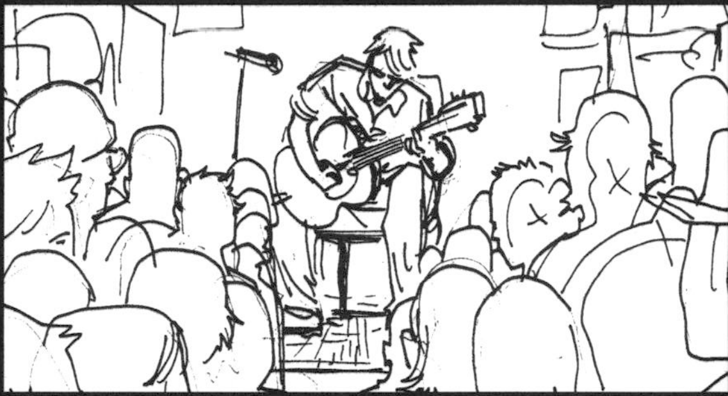

BRIAN WOOD:

I got a lot of "local" help this issue.

Sean Kennedy provided the bulk of the reference photos, as well as general Richmond knowledge. He proofread and fact-checked the script and was the official Richmond cheering section. Be sure to check out:

The Funwrecker Ball with Sean Kennedy
Richmond Indie Radio, WRIR-LP 97.3 FM
Thursdays, 9 to 11 PM Eastern
http://www.wrir.org/ (you can listen online)

Rawn Gandy was our second reference photographer, who, along with Velocity Comics owner Patrick Godfrey, responded to my frantic phone call one afternoon and trotted down the street to shoot the exterior and interior of Ipanema Cafe.

Literally, this comic could not have happened without their help. Same goes to everyone in all the *Local* towns that helps us out with info and photos.

Also, thanks to Katherine Keller for the Sequential Tart cover quote.

Writing this issue took forever. Like most of the *Local* stories, and a lot of the *Demo* ones, I start off with a basic idea, a general point I want to get across or a topic I want to talk about. That's the easy part. Next I actually have to craft the story around that basic idea, and sometimes that's really challenging.

I stumbled across a news story online about the real life Richmond band, Engine Down, who recently called it quits. Theories and Defenses are in no way supposed to be stand-ins for Engine Down, but that was where the basic notion for this story came from. Local band quits, returns home. Now, what's the STORY going to be?

I banged my skull against the desk for a couple weeks until I decided to cut this short story up into four even shorter stories, and deal with the band members separate from one another, four moments in time, four aspects of returning home. I figured I needed some sort of narrative structure to tie it together, though, and I've always like the interview as an interesting and natural way to get a lot of information to the reader, both in direct dialogue and as a voiceover. Once I had that worked out, the actual scripting of the story was really quick and easy.

Ryan Kelly deserves a lot of extra praise for taking a script that was pretty much just page after page of talking heads and making it all work the way he did.

I've never been in a band, but these ideas and situations you just read can be applied to any creative person, in any field. It totally translates.

My soundtrack:
"Second of February" - Engine Down
"Cover" - Engine Down
"The Skin Of My Yellow Country Teeth" - Clap Your Hands Say Yeah
"A Different City" - Modest Mouse
"Tell Me Lies" - Swingin' Utters
"Timorous Me" - Ted Leo
"Bells" - Rival Schools
"Did You Say You Were Grown?" - Corrina Repp

Ryan Kelly stole one of mine - "Cut Your Hair" - Pavement

Roll credits song - "King Of Carrot Flowers Part 1" - Neutral Milk Hotel

LOCAL #4 - TWO BROTHERS

February, 2006

BRIAN WOOD:

I don't have a lot to say about this issue. I like it, there are some moments of dialogue here and there that really stand out for me, make me proud. It's almost an entirely dialogue-driven story, and the process of writing it was very organic. I established the characters in my head at the outset and just let them go. Aside from the opening scene, I had little planned in advance. I knew this was going to be dark, very violent in parts, and as the solicitation copy warned, about "the ultimate in family breakdowns." I also knew poor Megan was going to suffer a trauma of some sort.

The characters wrote the story. Each line of text suggested the next, and I just kept going, waiting for the ending to come to me, and hoping it wasn't too much longer than 24 pages when it did. As it turns out, the ending was more gruesome and depressing that I would have expected. I mean, jesus christ. I was so wrapped up in the process and the ending felt natural as I was writing it, but after I hit 'save' and sat back and thought about it, I was a little surprised at myself.

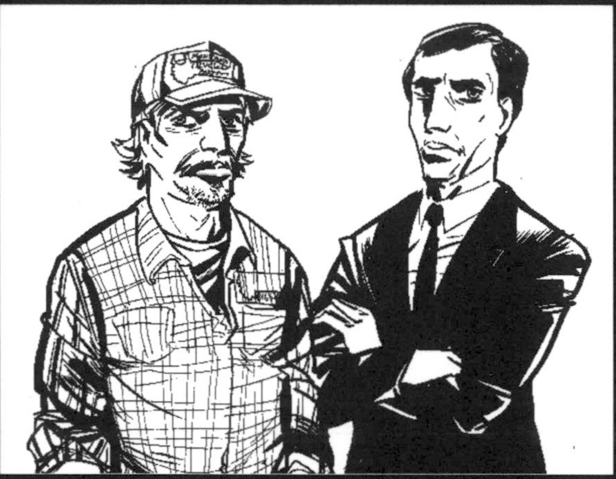

(Then, as I attached the final draft to an email to Ryan, I realized that I was sending him this heart-warmer on Christmas Eve, literally around 6pm my time. Whoops. So I added a disclaimer that maybe he'd want to wait until the 26th or so to read it. I had a mental vision of a shattered Ryan sitting in some dark corner of his house with a 12-pack of beer, wondering why, god, why does he have to draw this horrible fucking story, and elsewhere his son is crying for his papa to come join him to open presents, but Ryan can't hear him, deep in his dark place.)

I also feel a little bad to rep Missoula in such a way. I visited there a couple years ago, guests of the lovely Muse Comics & Games (www.musecomics.com) and it's truly a very pretty place. Muse owner Amanda supplied the reference photos for this issues, set at Dixie's Diner in East Missoula, and I remember asking her for a greasy spoon, a total dive, really seedy and out of the way, and understand, living in Brooklyn, I've seen some real cesspits. She kept recommending these diners that looked downright bucolic, nestled in trees and near babbling brooks. Eventually I settled on Dixie's, and Manda & Fam took a trip there to shoot photos. Dixie's actually isn't that bad, and it's a testament to Missoula that even the worst eatery is actually pretty nice.

Next issue, Megan's off and up in Halifax, staying out of the way. It'll be out 2 months after this one, as Ryan and I are taking one of our scheduled months off.

My soundtrack:
"Castanet" - Bluetip
"Misery Loves Company" - Mike Ness
"Highway Patrolman" - Bruce Springsteen
"September" - Ryan Adams & The Cardinals
"My Wave" - Soundgarden

Roll credits song - "Dying Days" - Screaming Trees

RYAN KELLY:

I just finished drawing *Local* #4 in my usual 27-hour drawing session I do towards the completion of every book. I'm physically exhausted writing this so it is a completely suitable state of mind for this story. Whereas the previous *Local* stories had some push and pull, reading this story was like having a steel pole pushed through my vertebrae, welded to the front grill of a train going full speed on a one-way track to hell from beginning to end.

And I blame Brian Wood for ruining my Christmas with a depressing story.

Just when I think I know what this series is all about, I'm thrown a curve ball and my secure notions are thrown off balance. From what I've seen so far, *Local* utilizes an element of life found in comics but not always obvious: Chance. Chance can be found in the script in the form of conflict or a jarring turn-of-events in the plot. But often it is very neat and it will have a happy ending. This has been a year of big-event surprises in comics. But, sometimes, what you have are ideas tailor-made for the comic book world and nothing that reflects the haphazardness of real life. But don't dismiss erased memories and multi-universes in *Local*. Who knows, anything could happen!

Life is messy, unpredictable, and emotionally draining. The difficulty is connected to your station in life, your personal experiences, but also your own perception of how hard your life is. You learn to adapt in your own way and whether you rise up to gain control, whatever that may mean, or shrink back in surrender is interrelated with your own persona. But there is that other element: chance, or (bad) luck as it is sometimes called. Some people haven't the stamina to deal with the cards they have been dealt in life.

I love that element of chance, or risk-taking, in comics. It's something that's hard to find in other mainstream media, hardwired with its consumer focus groups and legions of boards of directors and management. Somewhere, in some corner of life, someone is creating something new and amazing, and you might be lucky to experience it if you claw through the walls of popular media junk. One thing I really loved about Brian Wood's *Demo* is artist Becky Cloonan's change of styles in each individual issue. That presentation had me guessing, "What am I going to get this time?" with each trip to the comic book store. The little things makes life exciting and worth living. Yes, even a comic book store can be exciting!

Unfortunately, I may not have it in me to radically change my style with each issue. I did try to make this one more stark and direct with stronger black areas and less emphasis on the tones. But it seems Brian is using the series to offer something strangely new and unique with each episode. You write a story, finish it on page 24, wipe the slate clean, and do something completely different next time. That's how it's done. My favorite bands don't just stick to the same successful formula with each album, they use the success to grow and change.

That is why I don't pry Brian to find out what happens next in the series. I want to be kept in the dark. I want to be surprised. Like life, *Local* hinges on that element of chance that makes it worth enjoying, good or bad.

Local #4 soundtrack:
"Murder She Said (Miss Marple's Theme)" - Ron Goodwin
"War" - Tones On Tail
"The Good Son" - David Sylvian
"Banging The Door" - Public Image Limited
"Drop Dead/Celebration" - Siouxsie and the Banshees
"Murder" - New Order
"Public Pervert" - Interpol
"Money Greedy" - Tricky
"Plans" - Bloc Party
"The Good Son" - Nick Cave and the Bad Seeds

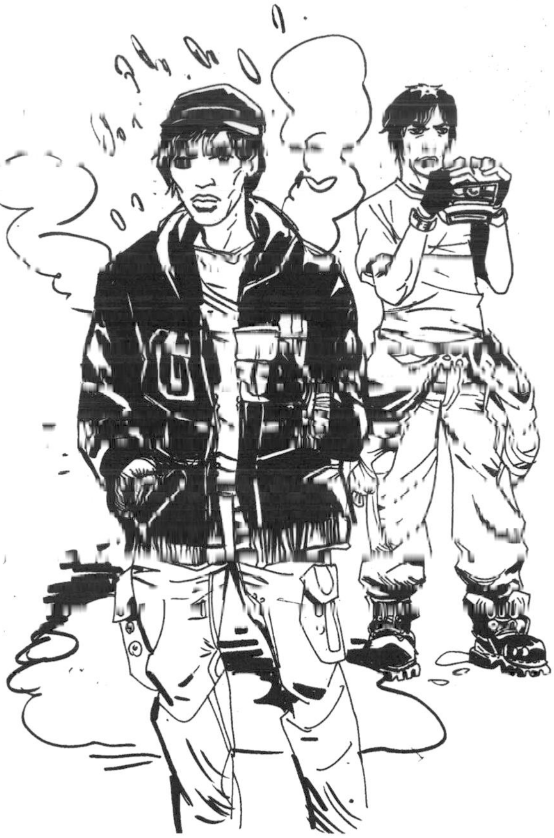

LOCAL™

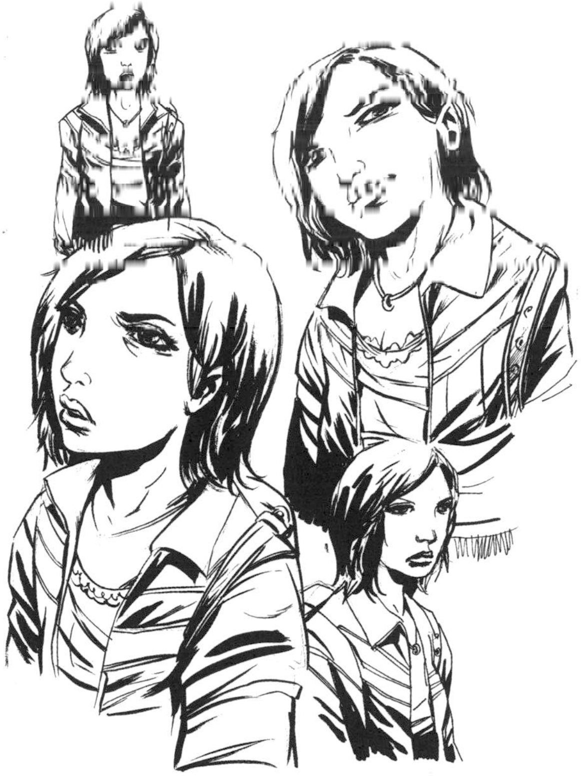

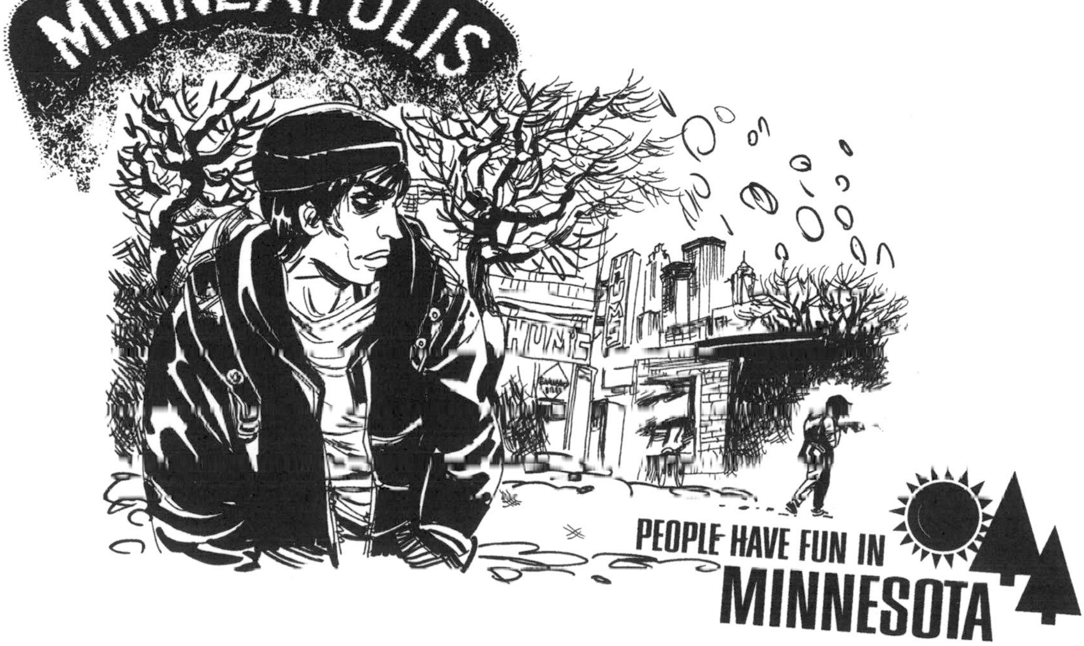
MINNEAPOLIS
PEOPLE HAVE FUN IN
MINNESOTA

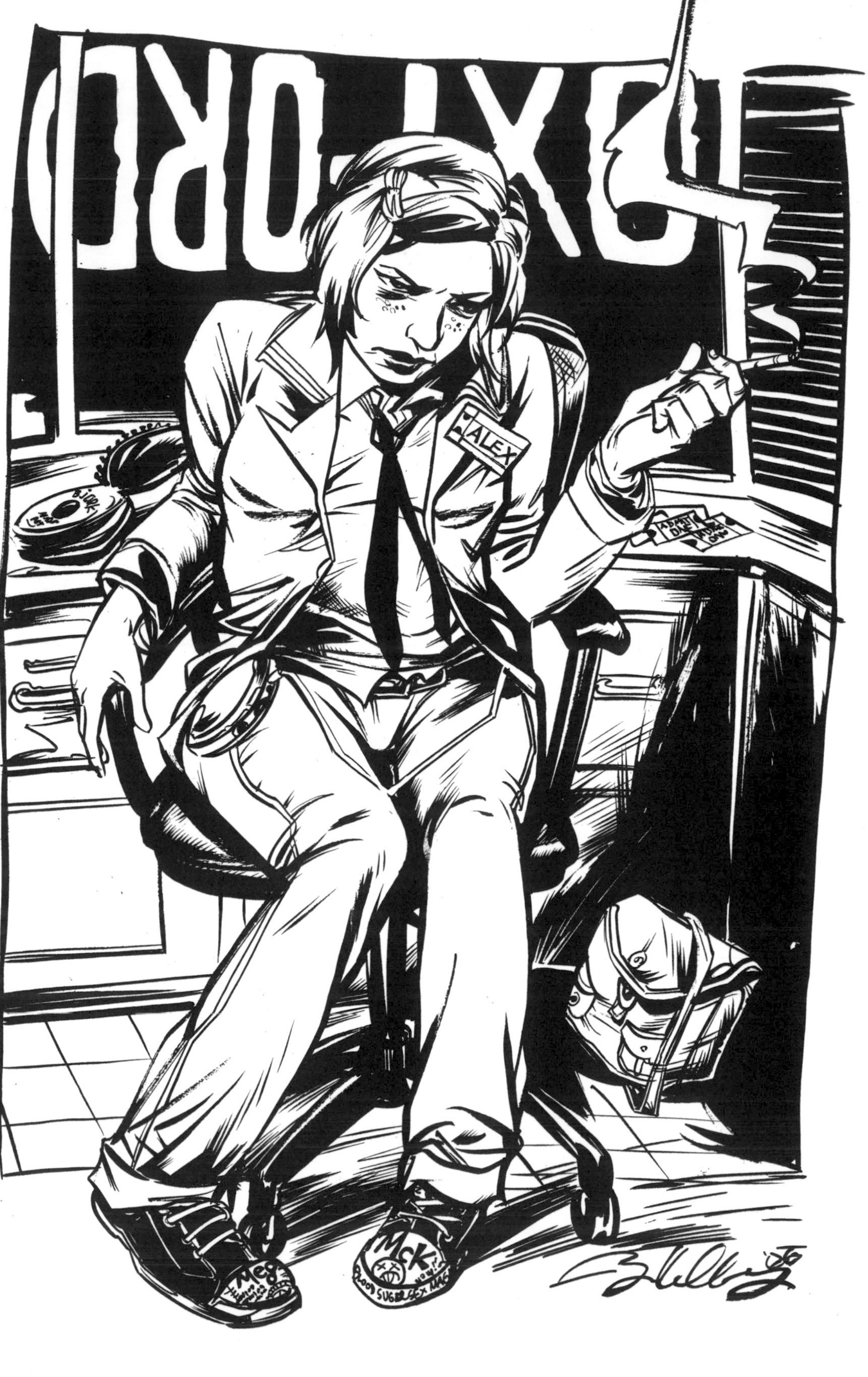
ALEX
Meg
McK

LOCAL #5 - THE LAST LONELY DAYS AT THE OXFORD THEATRE

April, 2006

RYAN KELLY:

Poor Megan. I find myself saying that after every book. No matter what happens in my life I know I can just redirect all my angst and sorrow onto Megan. If we all agree when Barbra Streisand sings, "People who need people are the luckiest people in the world," then Megan is in some deep trouble. She just can't get any breaks. But as sure as I know she wears Converse, I know she is a cool coper and will eventually work it out.

If you've ever wondered what a comic book that took 16 days to draw looks like, well, you're looking at it. Ok, it took a long time to do. But strip away the hours devoted to family time, other projects, and hours of paralyzing fear and you have 16 days. Typically, the first 12 pages take weeks of self-indulgent tinkering and caffeinated drinks. And then, the last 12 pages are produced in a 5-day blitzkrieg of drawing and more caffeine. Brian will possibly mention that he took a while to finish the script. If he doesn't, take out a black marker and cross out that last sentence.

Brian's subtlety was in top form in this story and I tried in earnest to capture it all in the characters' facial expressions, especially Megan's. Usually, my methodology follows something like this: I pencil out a face and it looks great. Then, I ink it and it looks like dook. Finally, I spend an inordinate amount of time nit picking at the face with white-out, correction tape, and numerous power tools. Often, I will redraw the face on a separate piece of paper, scan it, and patch it into the digital art file. Thus, I have an entire drawer of orphaned Megan faces on tiny paper oddments. Every time I open the drawer they are staring back at me, exhibiting every emotion imaginable and constantly reminding me of my shame and artistic shortcomings.

I was looking forward to drawing this issue. The great thing about this project is that I'm allowed some time to explore a place I've never been to. I've heard of Canada. I've seen it in pictures. But my only experience with the place was a juvenile high school excursion to Thunder Bay to take advantage of the legal drinking age of 19. Sad, I know. But all one is left with trips like that are memories of heavy metal bars and family restaurants with cheap French table wine. Nova Scotia can't be like that, is it?

I take music seriously, and *Local* gives me a chance to explore a region's musical history. I always feel a little narcissistic for putting in a soundtrack, but I seriously listen to these songs on a constant loop when I'm working on the book at hand. I also feel guilty for listing mostly defunct post-punk British bands for a comic book in a "This American Life" style. So, in a hierarchal order I look for local bands, then music that moves me emotionally, and finally, songs with similar lyrical themes. I look around. Wow! The singer for Metric sings with Broken Social Scene! Wolf Parade opens up for Arcade Fire! Neil Young was in Crosby, Stills, Nash, and Young! Canada is like one big Degrassi Junior High.

I've been teaching an inking class at the local art college and I've been thinking a lot more about inking on an academic and even a spiritual level. Good inking can elevate your drawing to a higher level and reshape the way people perceive your work and the story subject you are communicating. I ink almost exclusively with a sable brush. That includes profile lines, accent lines, spotting blacks, feathering, everything. I use the tabled Windsor & Newton series 7 (no.2). But I don't discriminate. I explore other natural hair brushes and other manufacturers. Even the synthetic brushes yield satisfactory results if they are taken care of. Ink with a reed, metal nibs, a sponge, a feather, a stick, or even your fingers. Don't hold back. Just do it.

Local #5 soundtrack:
"Helpless" - Neil Young
"Hold On, Hold On" - Neko Case
"Empty" - Metric
"7/4 (Shoreline)" - Broken Social Scene
"Kidnapped By Neptune" - Scout Niblett
"Human Behaviour" - Björk
"To The Shore" - Duran Duran
"Don't Get Me Wrong" - The Heavy Blinkers
"She's Lost Control" - Joy Division
"Shine a Light" - Wolf Parade
"Night Birds" - Ryan Adams
"Rebellion (Lies)" - The Arcade Fire

JAMES LUCAS JONES:

I know what you're thinking. Seriously. I do. You're thinking, "Where the heck is Brian Wood? His insightful little notes at the end of the issue are one of the things I look forward to every month!" Well, I know how you feel. Reading Brian and Ryan's final thoughts is usually my last task before we shuttle any issue of *Local* off to the printer. I sit down with the story pages and the back matter on the super-comfortable couch that resides in the front reception area of the Oni office and read.

By this time I've already read through the issue a dozen times or more, but it always seems different when followed by the Brian and Ryan's short personal accounts in the back. I find it not unlike a meal at my favorite restaurant (Mother's Bistro in downtown Portland). The food is always good, but it's made all the better by the owner/chef and her habit of walking the floor checking in with each table. Lisa loves talking with the patrons about the meal and the history of the old family recipes that were utilized when preparing it. It's that extra bit (paired with a cup of French press coffee) that pushes every dining experience there over the top.

The essays in the back of *Local* do the same thing. They give context to the creation without robbing the reader of their interpretation. For me, they also represent the exhale of relief I push out at the close of each vignette—a moment to reflect before we start the crazy race to the end of the next issue.

But alas, this month it wasn't meant to be.

You see, Brian went and got a corneal ulcer. And it did a **nasty** little number on his eyeball. Now, don't worry. He's going to make a full recovery and should be on well on his way to a perfect bill of health by the time you read this. The only real consequence of this ailment for you is that you get me rambling in the back of this issue of *Local* instead of Mr. Wood, and for that, I am truly sorry.

I've never actually been to Halifax but have a fondness for the place regardless. Two of my favorite people on earth live just outside of town in a pretty little farmhouse. Those two people are also responsible for the lettering on *Local*. Hope Larson and Bryan Lee O'Malley are not only an indie comic book power couple, but also bring sunshine to gray skies and laughter to children both short and tall. For their residency alone, Halifax is a great town. Once you factor in other considerations like Halifax's bustling music and arts scene, plus one of the best comic stores in North America in Calum Johnston's Strange Adventures and it's no wonder why this was one of the first burgs Brian and I talked about when he first pitched *Local*.

The story for this issue, however, was not as obvious a choice as the locale. The plot for this issue went through a bit of a metamorphosis during Brian's writing of it. A lot of that is just process. Brian's writing style is so organic, he really takes the opportunity to feel out the story beats as they come rather than force them into an artificial structure. Sometimes that leads the characters down paths not even their creators mapped out beforehand. For me, this is definitely one of those "sometimes." I didn't know how Megan would deal with the events of "Two Brothers" and I'm not sure Brian did either. He discovered it in the process though, and what he found were some fairly pronounced and fairly ugly scars.

Next month, Brian returns to the essay page as Megan turns up in Bri's current hometown of Brooklyn, and I move back to my spot on the sidelines. Get well soon, sir.

My soundtrack for this issue:
"John Wayne Gacy, Jr." - Sufjan Stevens
"Manic Depression" - Jimi Hendrix
"July, July" - The Decemberists
"Give Me Your Eyes" - The Cardigans
"Born Slippy" - Kupek

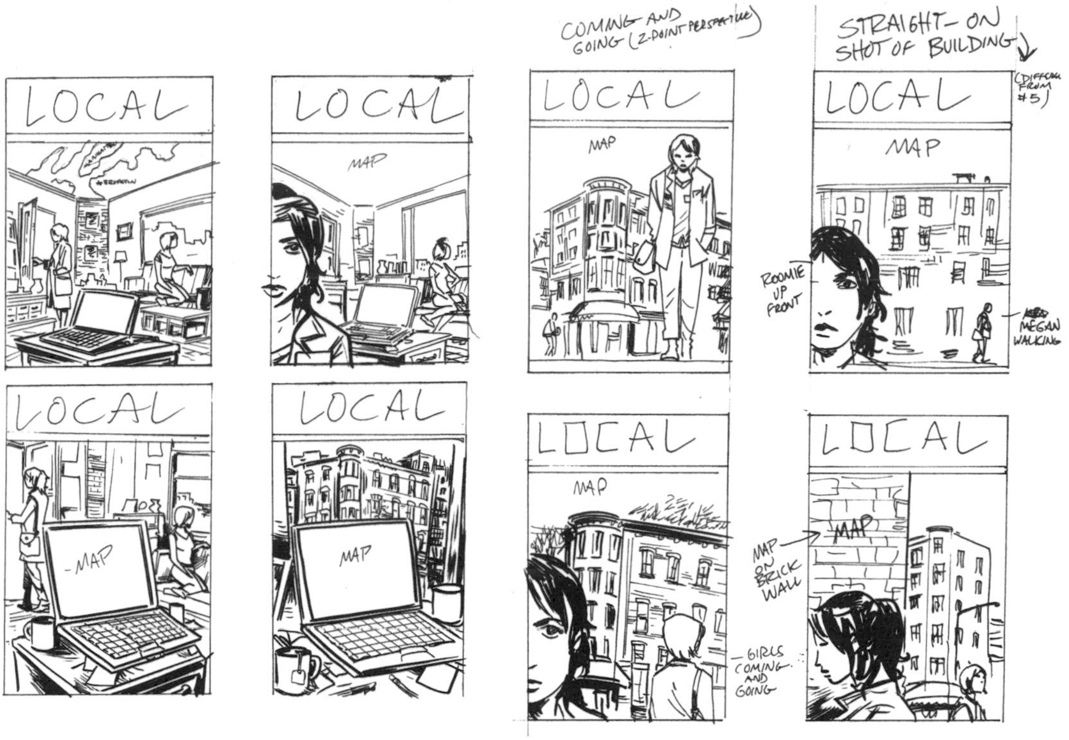
COMING AND GOING (2-POINT PERSPECTIVE)
STRAIGHT-ON SHOT OF BUILDING
(DIFFERENT FROM #5)
LOCAL
MAP
LOCAL
MAP
LOCAL
MAP
LOCAL
MAP
ROOMIE UP FRONT
MEGAN WALKING
LOCAL
MAP
LOCAL
MAP
LOCAL
MAP
GIRLS COMING AND GOING
LOCAL
MAP
MAP ON BRICK WALL

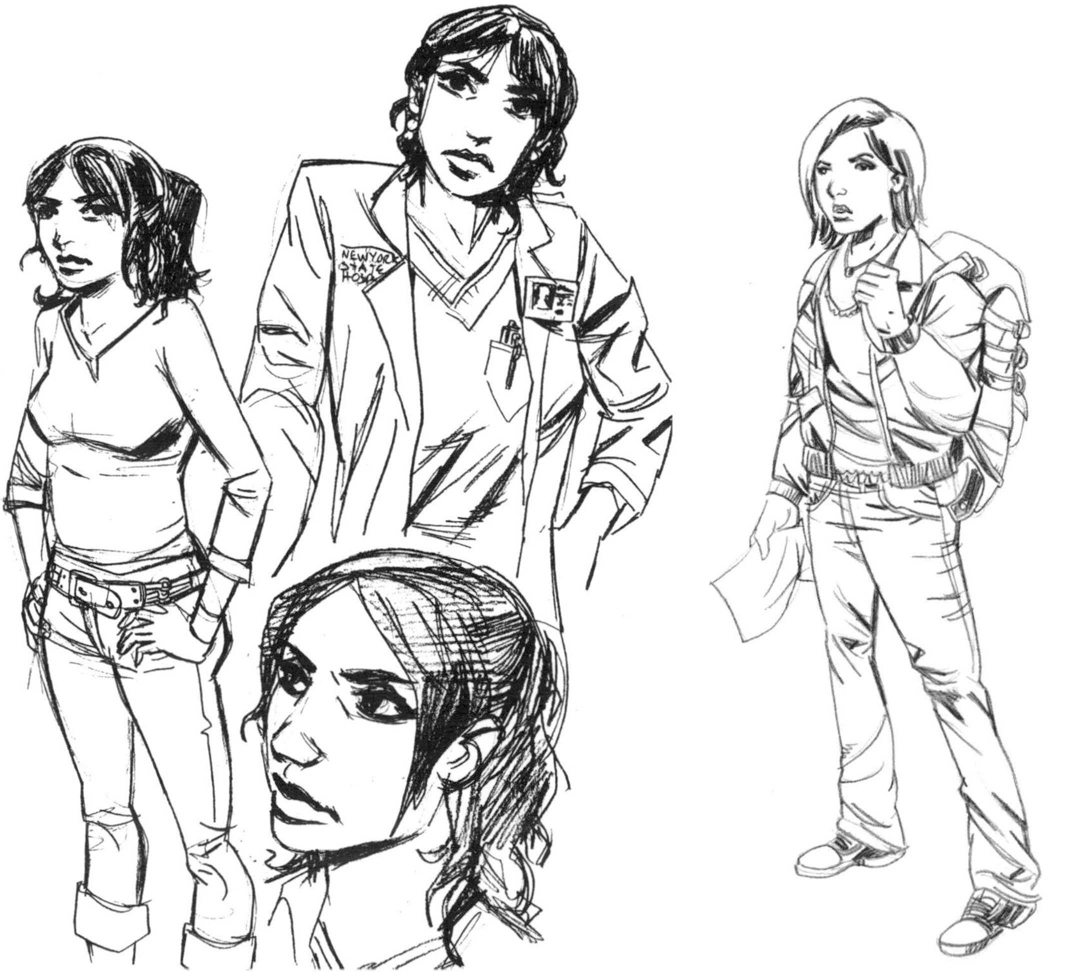

LOCAL #6 - MEGAN AND GLORIA, APARTMENT 5A

July, 2006

RYAN KELLY:

Ah, New York; I can smell it now. In fact, I smelled it this June when I visited old New Amsterdam to attend the Mocca 2006 convention at the Museum of Cartoon and Comic Art. That was a fine convention. Darn good people make some darn nice comic books.

But, more important than that, Brian played host to me at his place in Park Slope, Brooklyn. Thank you Brian and Meredith and their cats! Let me just use this essay to make one very important fact clear. What the people on the streets and the national media are telling you is true. There are lots of baby strollers in Park Slope. Everywhere. Committed mothers and fathers saunter up and down the streets with babies and toddlers in tow. They're smiling and waving to each other and sharing past accomplishments and future plans. Children are everywhere at all hours of the day, playing, socializing, and loitering. New York is just one big Neverland children's paradise! Hey, I want to live here! It looks like a great place to raise children. And by the time you read this, I will be pushing around two more strollers. Actually, it will be a double stroller, an SUV sized model suitable for ushering around twins. So, if the art starts sucking from here on out, don't blame me, I'm cleaning up puke! But it won't, because the best is yet to come.

Visually, I needed the art in this story to be a noticeable contrast from the doom and gloom depicted in the Nova Scotia issue. That started, foremost, with the cover in which (I think) it was Brian's idea to have the roommates' hands ghosted over the computer. But that decision arrived only after I'd kicked around several cover concepts. I intended the cover to represent everything glamorous about summers in New York. The afternoon sun illuminating the tops of the red and yellow flesh of the those old brownstone buildings, stoically lined up like loyal old friends as happy and hopeful people walk up and down its streets, lined with vibrant green trees and blushing cool blues from the pavement below. The kind of scene that makes you want to whistle a Paul Simon song to yourself. The New York I set out to depict is lively, fun, carefree, friendly, and optimistic. In other words, everything that isn't the hellish war-zone called New York depicted in the other book by Brian Wood. You know the one. In a cheeky way, I wanted the cover of *Local* #6 to be a cheery oasis from the ongoing struggle in the *DMZ*.

As a technical note, I received the #6 script in small increments so I never had any idea what the story was really about. I was almost worried until I did the last 5 pages and remembered how much I love doing this book. Finally, the best advice I can give this time around is that if you're a comic book artist and you pass a bar on the street that you have to depict it from various vantage points in an abundance of scenes: Go inside, sit down, order a tall one and draw like an idiot. You'll thank yourself in the morning.

Local #6 soundtrack:
"The Telephone Always Rings" - Fun Boy Three
"Mind" - Talking Heads
"Fake French" - Le Tigre
"Summertime" - Miles Davis (George Gershwin)
"New York, New York" - Grandmaster Flash and the Furious Five
"Citysong" - Luscious Jackson
"Spoon" - Cibo Matto
"Quitting Time" - The Roches
"Warrior" - Yeah Yeah Yeahs

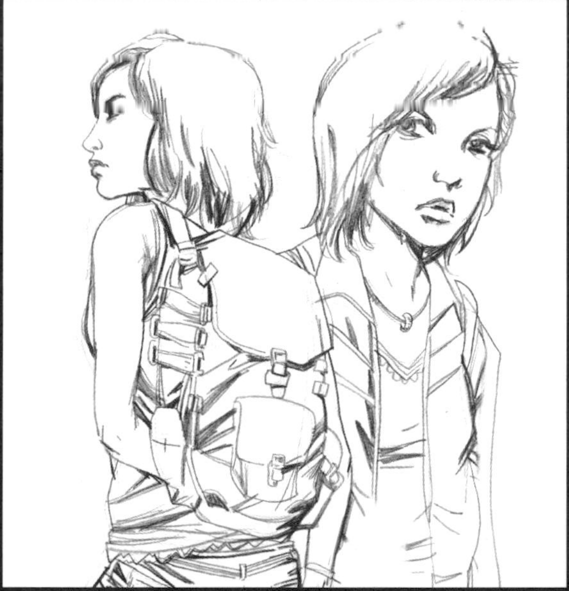

BRIAN WOOD:

Around the time I started writing this issue I spotted some old ex-roommates of mine at a convention. I lived with them very briefly back in 1998. Very briefly, meaning, I got out of there as soon as I could. They were filthy and creepy and incredibly dysfunctional. They didn't recognize me at the con, thank god, but I will never forget them. Last time I ever lived with roommates. Scarred for life.

But it did get me thinking about roommates. New York's such an expensive place, it's one of the few places in this country I suspect that you can be in your forties, holding down an excellent job - a career, even - and still find no shame in having to share your space with several strangers. I find that interesting. I find any instance of people striving for normalcy in abnormal situations fascinating, as anyone familiar with my work would know.

On to this story here. This is possibly one issue of *Local* that doesn't work so perfectly as a single-issue story, only because of the end bit. We've seen Megan struggle with personal relationships of all kinds for the last six months, and here's hoping she sticks to her words and makes this latest disaster her last. I'm not sure how much more of this she can take. Or you, or Ryan, or even me. Something's gotta give, and next issue we'll give Megan the month off, focusing instead on her cousin Nicky down in Tempe, AZ.

As Ryan said, I delivered this script in chunks, something I absolutely hate to do to an artist, but it has to happen sometimes. Sometimes it's a matter of timing (me being late) or a matter of logistics (me no write so good), or, in the case of *Local* #6, it's both. But I think in the end the staggered delivery saved the day, as I was able to see the first part of the book finished first, and it helped clarify a few things in time for me to wrap up the story. In my darkest hours, when I'm sitting in my little room trying to get these stories out, I realize just how fucking hard it is to write these... both *Local* and *Demo*. Is it the format, or the types of stories? Not sure, but it kills me every time. But I love both of the books dearly, so I must be a sucker for the punishment.

Park Slope: my home for the last few years, and probably the only place I would live in NYC. For the record, Megan and Gloria live on 8th Ave near 11th St, upstairs from that laundromat. I live about a block away from them. Music Matters, a great little shop. Dizzy's, great breakfast sandwiches. Two Little Red Hens, fantastic, if expensive baked goods and homemade lemonade. The F-train, the slowest, smelliest train in the system. Great Lakes, a great bar that wasn't so keen on me taking reference pictures for Ryan. So he had to imagine what the bathroom looked like, and anyone who's had a pee there will know that Ryan nailed it.

My soundtrack:
"You Said Something" - PJ Harvey
"Reena" - Sonic Youth
"Everyone Chooses Sides" - The Wrens
"Y Control" - Yeah Yeah Yeahs
"Letter From an Occupant" - The New Pornographers

Roll credits song - "The Littlest Bird" - The Be Good Tanya's

LOCAL™

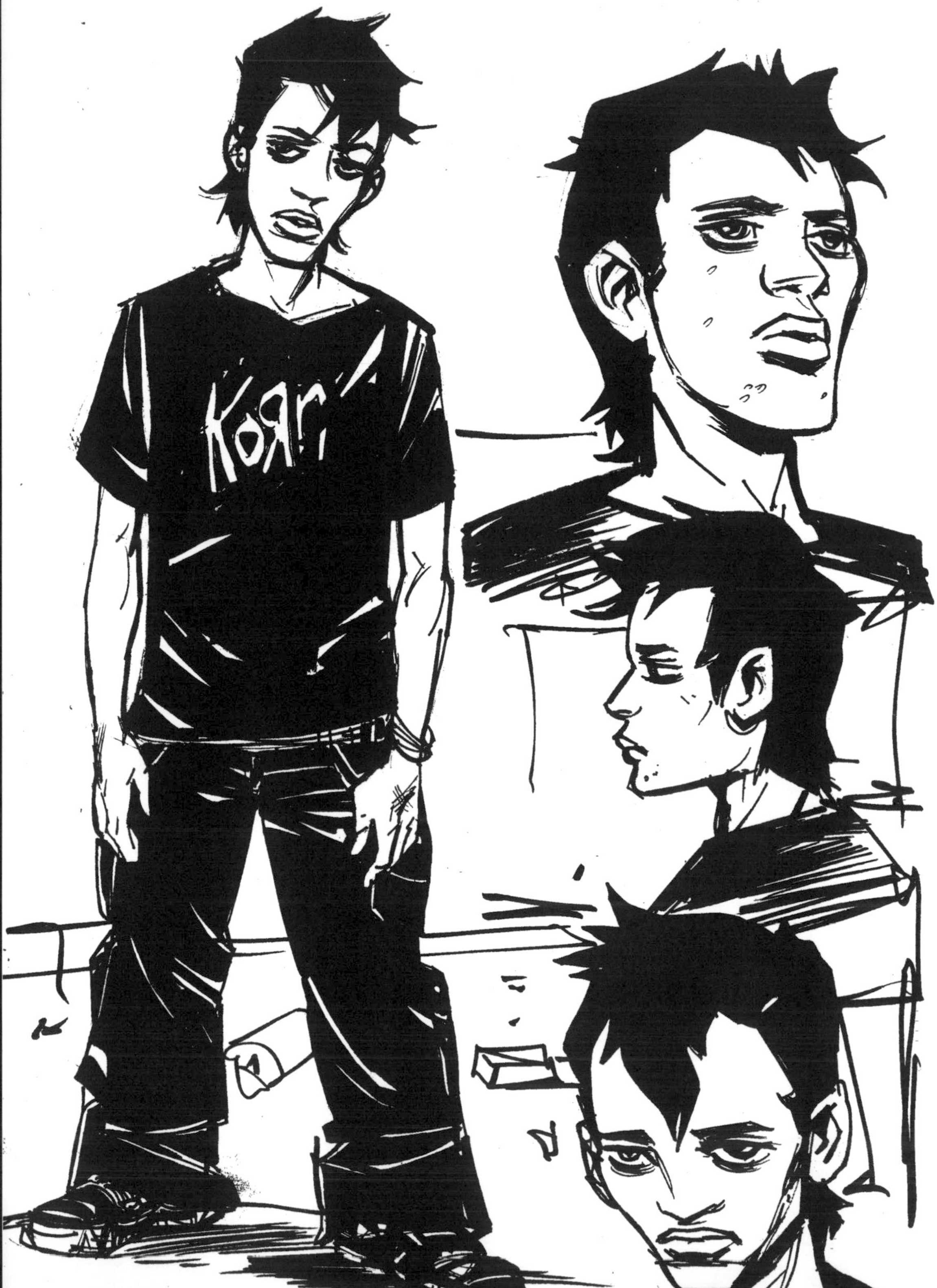
KoЯn

RYAN KELLY:

If you are reading this, then congratulations, you have successfully purchased this comic book! Please fill out the enclosed comment card and answer the following questions as to the satisfaction of your comic book.

Was the comic book satisfying? Did it meet your expectations? Was the comic book store where you purchased this product neat and clean? Did the restroom emit a foul odor? Was the comic store clerk friendly and accommodating? Was he neat and clean or did he emit a foul odor? Will you buy more comic books from this series?

Overall, I think this issue came out really well. So how does it happen? Let's break it all down piece by piece.

The Writer: If you were to slice up the content of a single book in edible pieces like a cut of beef, then the last 3 pages would be called Prime Wood. The final 8 pages of the last 5 issues still give me goose bumps. Every issue gives me everything I need, no more and no less. To get the story. For instance, I can decipher Nicky's life story and personal history from just a handful of well-crafted scenes in the space of 24 pages. There's no exposition laced dialogue, no flashbacks, and no hefty back story. I just get it. I also like the small visual details Brian uses often to stress a point like shots of the characters looking into mirrors reflecting on themselves. I love how he has the shot of the apartment door in #6 and then Megan breaks through it to get away. That is followed by, in this issue, the shot of the apartment door that Nicky then smashes to pieces. Brilliant.

The Artist: He's all right. Not great, not bad. He can hold a brush. He knows what a panel is. He's breathing at the moment. But let's be fair to him, I did notice that this was the best-looking issue yet. It has to be, right? Please? I noticed how it took him at least 3 issues to get Megan's look down and it took only 3 pages to get Nicky's look down.

The Letterers: I want you to know you're looking at the only book on the stands where the letterers are bigger stars than the primary creators. I occasionally teach an introductory comic art class. On the first day of class, I lay out virtually every comic book I own on the table and explain that these are what comic books look like and then offer the knowledge and skill that goes into making them. On the second day of class, I only lay out "Gray Horses" and "Scott Pilgrim," and then I say "Screw all that garbage I showed you yesterday. I was just kidding. This is how comics are really done." Thank you to Hope Larson and Bryan Lee O'Malley for the lettering and the Nova Scotia reference.

The Company: If you were to walk down a busy urban street at just the right time, you could grab hold of the nearest comic book creator by the shoulders, firmly, and shake them. Shake them really hard, repeatedly, until their nose starts to bleed and they begin to collapse and faint. After that, ask them, "How is it done? How do comic books happen?" What they'll say, in between the coughing up of blood and begging for an ambulance, is that good comic books happen when all the parties involved trust each other enormously and essentially say, "Hey, go do your thing." The publisher trusts the writer. The writer trusts the artist. The artist trusts the letterer. All this trusting circulates back and forth into one big, never ending, hot and steamy "Trust Orgy" where good books are birthed. The name, ladies and gentlemen, is Oni Press. Never forget.

Well, there it is.

I think this Local #7 would make for a great early 80s west coast punk album. When drawing it I had to get really mad, I mean, I had to get really youthful, piss and vinegar mad at the world. Well, more than usual. I had to remember what it was like to be 15 years old again. I believe that a person's personality fully develops by the age of 18. And this was Local's life story about how boredom can be established at a young age. Deep down, in a fatalistic way, I was hoping Nicky was going to make it in the end.

So, in closing, this issue is dedicated to the pricks and tough guys that slammed me against the lockers and ripped me everyday on the school bus. I hate you.

Art assistants: Richard Flood, Kyle Frink, and Tou Vue

Local #7 soundtrack:
"Short Side Of Nothing" - Los Lobos
"Who Didn't Kill Bambi?" - Dillinger Four
"My Name Is Mud" - Primus
"Mommy's Little Monster" - Social Distortion
"You Drive Me Nervous" - Alice Cooper
"Mommy Can I Go Out And Kill Tonight?" - Misfits
"World Up My Ass" - Circle Jerks
"Amoeba" - Adolescents
"Thirsty And Miserable" - Black Flag
"Blinded By The Lights" - The Streets
"Too Drunk To Fuck" - Dead Kennedys
"Baggy Trousers" - Madness
"Arizona Skies" - Los Lobos
"Listen" - Generation X
"Cut" - Minutemen
"Telling Them" - Social Distortion
"Fuck The System" - System Of Down

Song for the final credits of the film version:
"World Destruction" - Afrika Bambaataa w/John Lydon

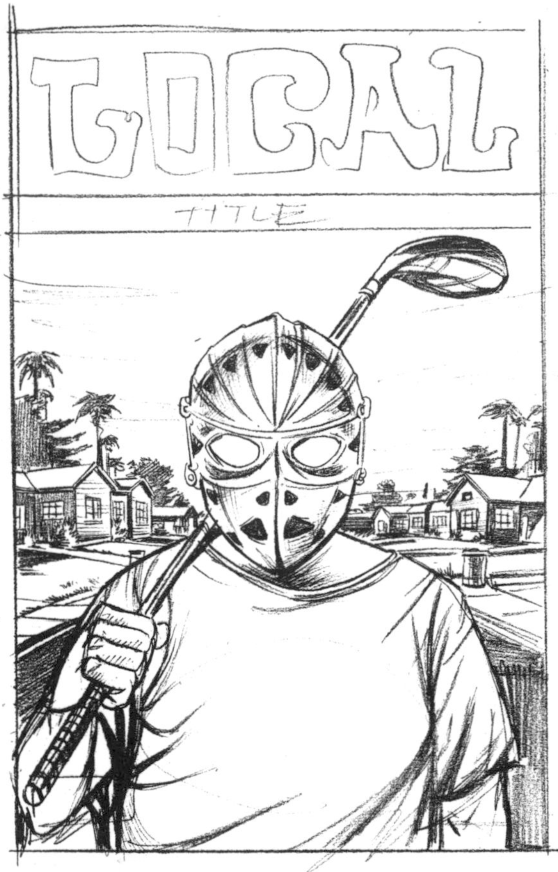
LOCAL
TITLE

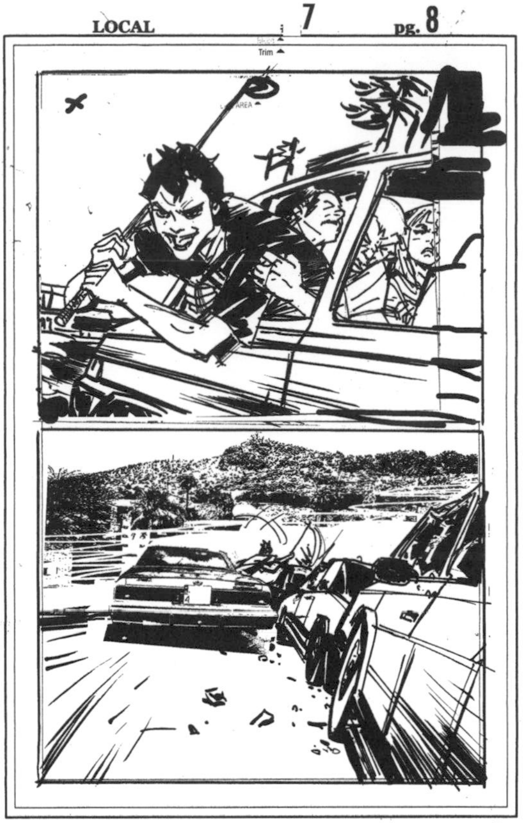
LOCAL
7
pg. 8
Trim

BRIAN WOOD:

In case anyone was paying attention, the title of this story changed just before publication. It was called "Smash The State!" but, as is common with my writing, things are adjusted on the fly, and Nicky went from an angry little armchair anarchist type to more of a run of the mill fucked-up kid, a hazardous youth, which is a phrase I heard on some Eminem song. Eminem is probably one of Nicky's favorites.

I spent a short amount of time a couple years ago in Tempe, a guest of Ash Ave Comics, and while they were perfectly amiable chaps (and chapettes), it was somewhat of a terrifying weekend. It was the weekend of the Fiesta Bowl, so the streets were full of rabid football fans, scary cops clearing the streets of homeless people and skateboarders, a military "air show" which consisted of helicopter overflights, and drunken college kids. All this in a climate and environment that's about as polar opposite as what I'm used to as you can get, and it felt like an oppressive police state. Now, I know I was there on an unusual weekend, and friends tell me of perfectly safe and beautiful parts of town, and I believe them. But if I was a kid like Nicky and I had a cop running me down because my skating might offend some face-painted out-of-town lunatic of a football fan, I would be seriously pissed off.

What would make it more tolerable is loud music, getting drunk, and postcards sent from a cool cousin who told me about all the great places I couldn't wait to visit myself. A cousin that, while older, seemed to think what I was all about was cool and would talk to me as an equal.

You just read the story, so you know what happens. This is another important chapter in the overall story of Megan, one that runs parallel to some of the previous chapters. She's swinging around now, realizing in both this issue and the last that she needs to make some changes, and as you can see in the preview on the very last page of this book, she's jumping back into a relationship with both feet. Here's hoping she doesn't repeat past mistakes.

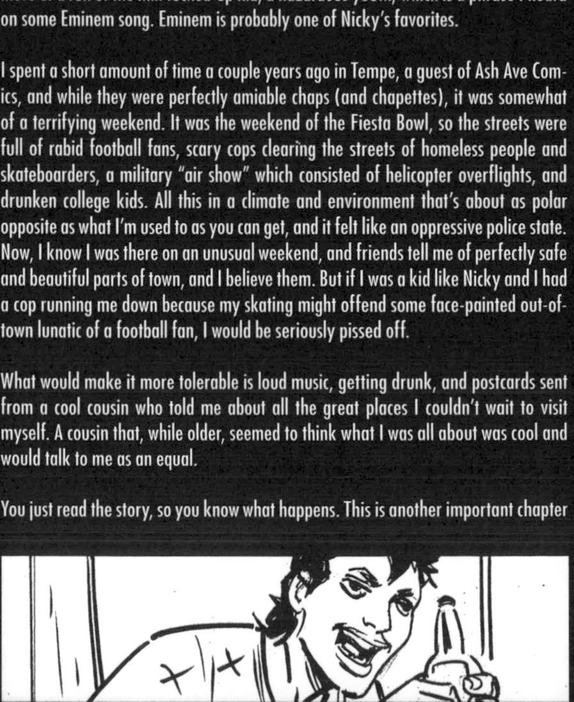

Huge thanks to everyone involved with this issue, especially Rob and Michelle for the pinups, and also Brian Scot Johnson and his wife Tatum for supplying the reference photos. Brian's a longtime friend of mine, and runs www.khepri.com as well as Khepri Comics, a new shop located in Tempe, at 1219 South McClintock (@ Apache). Stop by and say hello. He's something of a veteran of the Tempe comics scene.

Just above, Ryan really flatters the hell out of all of us. I agree with everything he says 100%, and am a little embarrassed he said it before I did. I'm blessed, and I always am, to work with such great people and they'll have my thanks to my dying day. I think this book is a special book, something that when it's all completed will end up being more than the sum of its parts. We're not just inventing a character and putting her through a few scenes and situations. We've really invented someone's life, here, and you're seeing the most exciting, most tumultuous part of it develop right in front of you. I hope that when all 12 issues are done, you'll feel like Megan is a friend... and if not a friend, a real person you knew once, awhile back and in that other place, like the ex you can't get out of your head.

Soundtrack:
"Radiohead" - Cage
"A Life Of Possibilities" - The Dismemberment Plan
"White America" - Enimem
"Lunchbox" - Marilyn Manson
"Bloodclot" - Rancid
"Right To Life" - Wartime
"Diamonds And Guns" - The Transplants

Roll credits - "The Last Good Time" - Chisel

LOCAL #8 - FOOD AS SUBSTITUTE

RYAN KELLY:

Like most artists (I assume), I'm unhappy with 90% of the work I do. After an art project (or comic book) comes to completion, I immediately divorce myself emotionally with it and I eagerly await the next thing. On occasion, the anticipation for that next thing turns on prematurely and spoils that current endeavor with boredom and a lack of inspiration. Luckily, that hasn't happened with *Local*. But working on *Local* is such a thrill ride for me that I can't push past issues behind me fast enough to get the next story. So, a few weeks after finishing this eighth issue, I have returned to write the essay, but I've emotionally moved on to *Local #9*.

Finally, after 8 issues, I'm very much becoming a part of Megan's life. I didn't feel like that before, but know I do. Like memories of a lifetime past, the older issues are experiences I want to forget so I can deeply focus on Megan's current problems and conflicts. And, I have a feeling that in the final 4 issues, the moments of Megan's past will return to the surface and it will be fascinating to see how she will come to terms with those things.

It took a few issues for Megan's look to truly materialize and grow, but she has come to be what she is and I accept that. Approximately one year is passing in between each issue, but I wasn't prepared to make Megan look "old" just yet. I knew there was going to be a time in her life when she looks very pretty, happy and optimistic and that issue #8 would be the height of that period. It was always important for me, artistically, not to draw the perfect pretty comic book girl. She has a big nose and freckles. She has once been compared to the actress Kristy McNichol and I've taken that very seriously, actually. She is about 26 years old now and looking for love and I figured that her... um, well, "hotness" level could be dialed up a little bit. But don't quote me on that. Megan's not my type. She's a little weird.

I am miles away from perfect. I'm becoming a better artist and by issue twelve my artistic powers will reach to such a level that I will be able to lift objects off the table with my mind. But for now, I occasionally draw Megan's face terribly and I must nit-pick at the most minute of details on the digital scan.

Here is a trick I learned from artists before me; I scan my final art page. Once in Photoshop, I immediately do a "Flip Canvas Horizontal" on the art. This action instantaneously exposes the inaccuracies and proportional blunders in your forms that weren't apparent in the original perception of your work. This new perspective provides me the ability to easily make the changes. Move an eyelash 10 pixels to the right. Move that nostril 5 pixels to the left. Sound like fun? Hey, this is Comics! Of course it's fun!

Look at the Megan face samples below. Examine the before and after. The improvement is larger-than-life. Could you accept that first version her face and honestly enjoy the book? The answer is no.

I've come to really enjoy drawing backgrounds. Sometimes, a photograph will work with my layout and I'll cut and paste it in the art, blue line it, and re-ink it my way. Chicago was great fun to draw. It was the first issue since the Minneapolis story that had places I was familiar with and that I was comfortable drawing. I've visited the Wicker Park area most every time I visit. I've been to that Davern Station. I like the Blue Line train. It's a big city with its own personality, but still very distinctly Midwestern. Going to Chicago to me is like coming to a final chapter in a book that includes Kansas City, Des Moines, Minneapolis/St.Paul, Milwaukee, Madison, and Detroit. It's all very cozy and familiar.

Brian put his unique spin on a rags to riches to rags love story. I cringe at the word "love story." But I think this love story was played out the way it really is in life: uncomfortable, unusual and uncertain. Brian depicted restaurant life like it is. I've worked as a waiter and I can say he illustrated that world with all the behind the scenes sexual tension and smoldering lust, smells and flavors to spicy perfection.

But sorry, no, I've never had a "quickie" in the storage room. Get your mind out of the gutter.

Entrée: Ryan Kelly in Drawn Butter
Hor D'ourves: Richard Flood and Kyle Frink with Sautéed Pears & Gorgonz

Soundtrack:
"Enjoy Yourself" - The Specials
"She Breathes Fire" - Blue Meanies
"Erotic City" - Prince
"Music is my Hot, Hot Sex" - CSS
"Good Sex Rumples The Clothing" - Adam Ant
"Stop! The Red Lights On" - Anita O'Day and Gene Krupa
"What I Like Most About You Is Your Girlfriend" - Special AKA
"(He Was) Really Saying Something" - Bananarama
"In The Morning" - Junior Boys
"Nice Guy Eddie" - Sleeper
"Tir Au Pigeons" - Prototypes
"Hands Off, She's Mine" - English Beat
"Let's Call It Off" - Peter Bjorn and John
"Winona" - Mathew Sweet
"Aphrodisiac" - Bow Wow Wow
"Meantime" - The Futureheads
"This Modern Love" - Bloc Party
"Explain It To Me" - Liz Phair
"Medium Blue" - Christopher Willits
"Tenderness" - General Public

MAP
MAP
MAP
WINDOW
NEIGHBORHOOD
MAP
WINDOW
CHICAGO
OUTSIDE
MAP

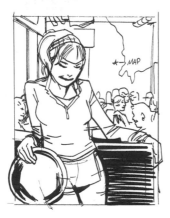

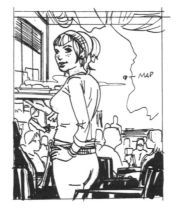

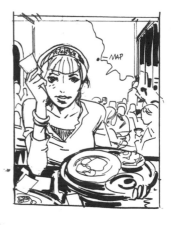

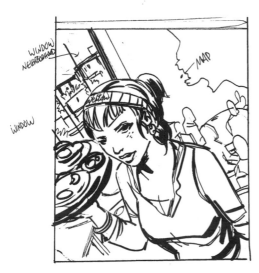

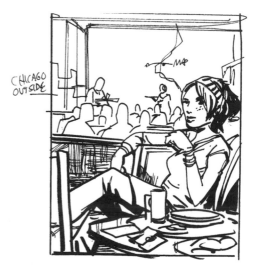

BRIAN WOOD:

Ryan flatters me. The closest I've come to restaurant life is watching marathons of *Gordon Ramsay's Kitchen Nightmares* on BBCA.

Ryan also calls this story a "love story," quotes intentional, and I would agree with that. Clearly, I have little interest in conventional love stories, the kind you see in romantic comedies. I don't think it works that way, and besides, all the ugly, awkward stuff is way more interesting.

We've seen Megan stumble her way along, not having much success in love, but there's a progression here, a narrative to it. In the life of this series – Megan's life - she gets burned, gets reckless, withdraws, gets lonely and more than a little desperate, opens up, screws up, learns a lesson... and now, has she finally figured it out? But, does anyone have it all figured out at age 26?

I was reflecting a bit on this series recently on my livejournal, about how as this book progresses it changes, specifically Megan's story, which was originally intended to just be a minor through-line, a simple narrative very secondary to what was the main point of this book: To tell single-issue, fully stand-alone stories. If you've been reading *Local* regularly, you know that Megan's story is becoming much more than that. The book's transcended the "done in one" format and is now an epic of Megan's life. I'm becoming much more aware of how *Local* will read as a single volume, and I think it will be more than the sum of its parts. *Demo*, the predecessor to *Local*, is advertised as a book of twelve short stories. *Local* is more like a novel in twelve parts.

Which makes me happy but also a little sad. I always felt the format I devised for *Demo* was a special one, the combination of the added extra material restricted just to the singles, the high production values, the increased story pagecount, and most importantly: the pure single issue story. I love it, and it's exciting to see other creators take it and adapt it in their own ways. I miss it, and like I said, it is what I intended *Local* to be like. But what *Local* is turning out to actually be I love just as much, and I wouldn't change a thing.

(and being able to think about and write these essays, analyzing and reflecting on the work as it goes... well, it helps me creatively and I hope you find it interesting as well.)

So where do we go from here? Next issue is Norman, OK, although if you look at the preview pages at the end of this issue, you'll see Chicago again. It's just a prologue scene before we switch to Norman. After that is Austin, TX, and another example of the shifting format with this book: Those two issues are both separate and a two-parter. You'll see how.

And finishing off the series is #11, set in Toronto and co-written by Ryan Kelly, and finally the finale, issue #12, set in and around Burlington, Vermont (my hometown), and since it is the final issue we'll be filling the book from cover to cover with story, all 32 pages, and leaving out the extras. That's 300 pages total of *Local* comics. Megan from age 18 to 30. About two years of work for me and Ryan.

Thanks to Jim Gary and Meredith Gary for supplying reference photos for this issue.

Soundtrack:
Roll credits - "Thinking About You" - Radiohead

RYAN KELLY:

Some comic creators never read reviews of their book. Some read reviews of their book and say that they don't read reviews of their book. And some read every single review and admit it. I'm in the latter group. So, I know that not every single issue of *Local* is for everyone.

And, some people have a favorite issue over others. That's what we're going to get with these deeply personal, self-contained single stories. It's always interesting to hear who loves which story and why.

For instance, the violent intensity of issue #4 may not have jived with every reader. But where would the series be without that story? Our overall tale would be pretty weak without that story coming into play and running its way through Megan's life. So, I hope now with the series beginning to wind down, readers will see that we're weaving an overall tapestry that will eventually be greater than its individual parts.

I don't think there is some great master plan here at the *Local* factory, other than trying to provide good stories. We finish an issue, knock down all the pieces and start over again. It's a hoot to work with a writer that is determined to challenge himself with each new thing and experiment. It's rubbed off on me and I hope to move my art in new directions in the final chapters of this series.

Like *Local* #4, "Wish You Were Here" is another story that needed to be told, a vital turning point, and an important passage in Megan's evolution. I couldn't approach this story like all the others, so I broke out the toolbox. *Local* is very brushy. Therefore, in Megan's flashbacks, I used anything but brush. I broke out the crowquills, the grease pencil, the graphite, and the acrylic paint. Heck, I used a stick somewhere in there.

I look forward to doing something completely new in *Local* #10, a track that focuses on Megan's brother. In many ways, it is the b-side to Megan's "Wish You Were Here" story.

Art assist:
Kip Knutson, Kyle Frink and Craig Johnson.

Songs in the fold of *Local* #9, "Wish You Were Here":
"Hammond Song" - The Colourfield
"New Slang" - The Shins
"Razor That Wins" - Haley Bonar
"There Is No There" - The Books
"[illegible]" - The Winter Blanket
"Country Mile" - Camera Obscura
"Return" - Siouxsie and the Banshees
"Songbird" - Willie Nelson

Song for the closing credits:
"Hammond Song" - The Roches

BRIAN WOOD:

If you were to have seen the process of creating this issue of *Local*, it would have a title like "how not to make a comic book."

It's no secret to any of you that the book hasn't maintained its monthly schedule since about issue #5. Ryan and I will both blame that on our new babies, and in the scramble to try to make up time, the "normal" way of creating comics goes out the window. In this case, I delivered script to poor Ryan in little dribs and drabs, 4 pages here, 6 more here... and in the middle of all of that I was drastically re-envisioning what I wanted this issue to be (heard me say that one before, right?). Anyway, we eventually got there, and I think it's a testament to how well he and I work together. I love this issue. I think it's a vital part of the Megan epic and communicates volumes not only about why she does what she does in this one story, but also in the previous eight.

Never thought I'd be doing flashbacks, but here we are. And look for more of the same in the next issue – Megan's brother Matthew deals with the death of their mother, but in a very different way.

(I also notice how certain things tend to mirror each other, with the books I write. First was the appearance of Park Slope's Methodist Hospital in *Local* #6 and *DMZ* #7, and now with this issue and *DMZ* #18-19, the 'two different takes on the same event' thing.)

Three issues left to go. We won't get back on a monthly schedule, by the way, but the series will finish and it'll be the best we could make it. Already I think this is my favorite of everything I've written, and after reading #12, you all will see it in a whole new way.

Thanks to:
Matt and Annette Price for the reference pics this issue. Matt owns the great (by all accounts – I've never been, sadly) shop SPEEDING BULLET COMICS.

Soundtrack:
Roll credits - "Rebel Girl" - Bikini Kill

★

LOCAL #9, NORMAL OK
#1
LOCAL
WHITE
WHITE
#2
LOCAL
#3
LOCAL

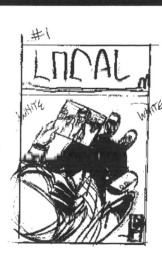

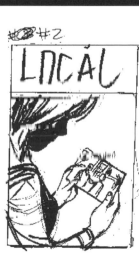

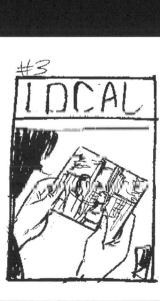

LOCAL™

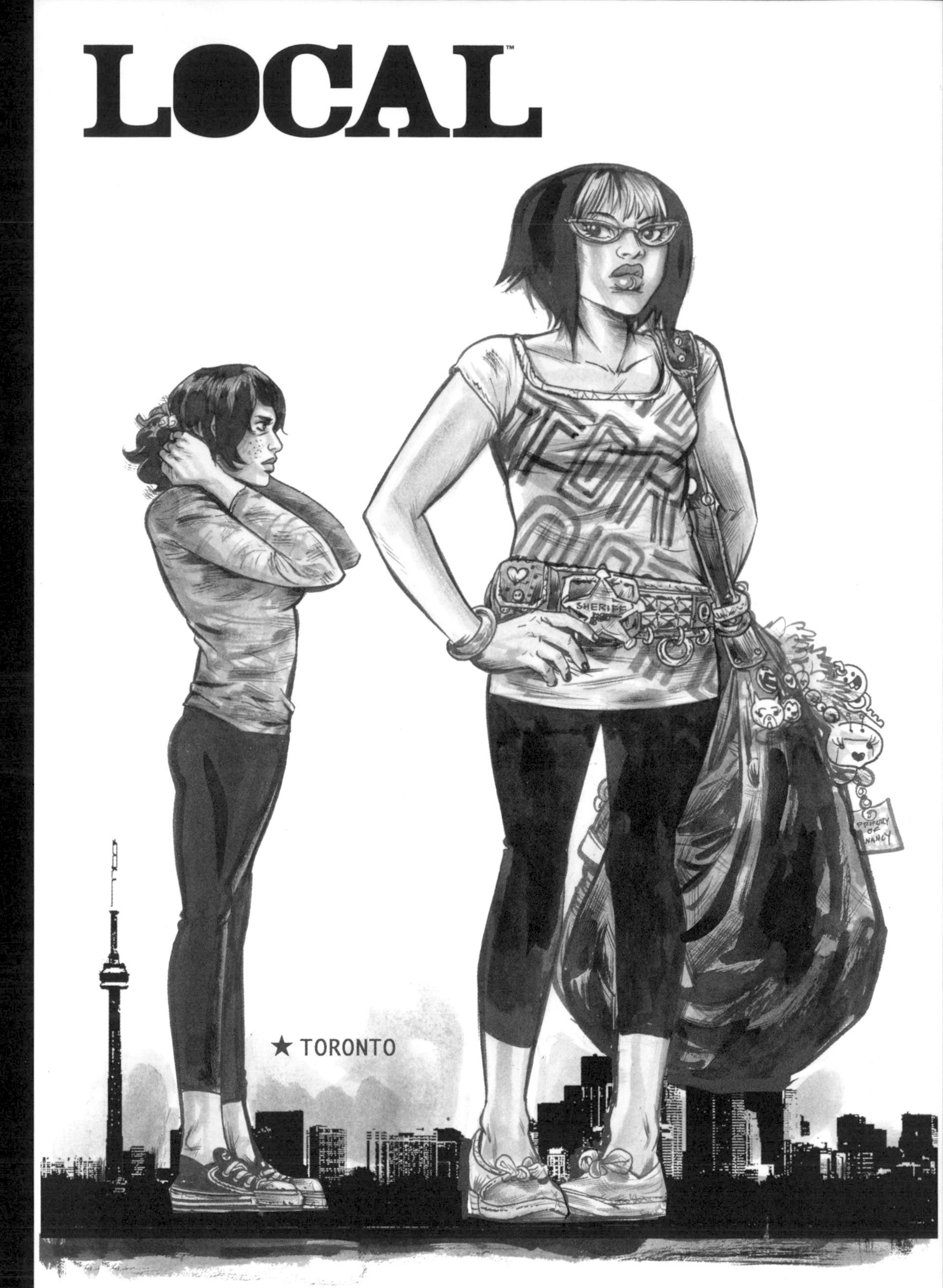
SHERIFF
★ TORONTO

LOCAL #10 - BAR CRAWL

AUGUST, 2007

RYAN KELLY:

Just how bad does this book treat you? You wait and wait and wait for this sad little rag to hit the stands while the Earth's tectonic plates, 60 miles thick, shift and slide at a rate of a centimeter a year. The orbital speed of the Earth averages about 67,000 miles per hour as it goes around a huge star every 365 days, yet, somehow at that time, on a tiny of speck of dust in the universe, an issue of *Local* is actually being completed. Anticipation fills your beaten and broken heart daily and the lonely longing for the next issue of *Local* reaches a crescendo of feverish intensity when it finally arrives. And then you read it and it's another depressing, down in the dirt, morbid tale of somebody's personal grief. Why do you do this to yourself?

As with every issue of *Local*, I shoot for a new way of approaching the visuals. For me, each new story is a completely different entity, a world away from the previous story, and I don't feel satisfied illustrating it the same way each time. I never have any set plans, but when it was time to do Matthew McKeenan's flashbacks, I settled on a look that was sharper, simpler and blacker. I'm getting a better grasp at black and white storytelling with every new project. When making black and white decisions with objects in a 2-dimensional plane, everything needs to be either pure black or white, no more and no less. Tones are irrelevant and the feathering and all the dynamics with it are just unnecessary. Whereas Megan's flashbacks are light, airy and sentimental, Matthew's are stark, dark and penetrating. I'm using *Local* to experiment and try different things as an artist. I hope it looks OK. I'm sure the next issue will have a significant look to it.

One of the major points that people neglect to mention when discussing Brian's work is his skill for writing on issues of family. Much attention gets placed on his grasp of large themes placed in the context of current sociopolitical events but not enough on the micro-level story-telling of family issues such as tradition, uncompromising love, growth, responsibility, and survival. Too many times, stories about family are Odd Couple dynamics with wacky, zany characters. But, obviously this comes from a deep, personal awareness of things and I'm sure all of us have points of sorrow as well as joy in our past. It's a point I wanted to make because Brian's *Demo* #4 was one of my all-time favorite books.

Well, as the world turns, like sands through the hourglass, so are the Days of our Lives. Just ponder that as you wait for *Local* #11 and it will all come quickly. Get ready, I'm "co writing" the next issue with Brian, so it will either be magnificently great or magnificently awful.

Art Assist by:
Craig Johnson, David Kaneen, Kip Knutson and Nicole Vanska

Local #10 "Bar Crawl" Soundtrack:
"Bar Lights" - Whiskeytown
"Return Of The Grievous Angel" - Gram Parsons
"Steal The Crumbs" - Uncle Tupelo
"Not Dark Yet" - Bob Dylan
"Wheels" - The Flying Burrito Brothers

Credits rolling song:
"Mother" - John Lennon

BRIAN WOOD:

This story depressed me, much more so than anything else I've written. And I'm not sure where it came from, some of the scenes, which I guess probably means it comes from my dark place in my own mind I've yet to recognize? Or I saw something like it on TV. Who knows.

I like to wait to write these essays until I read Ryan's, and find something in his to comment on. The topic of family - he flatters me. But those sorts of topics are what really inspire me. The nuts and bolts of how people work and interact with each other, flawed human beings coming to grip with their fuckups and problems and bad decisions. I was just talking about this on a panel discussion at the San Diego Comic Con - why do I gravitate towards writing these flawed characters? All my books are full of them, and maybe that's why I am not drawn to superheroes? The idea of a "heroic" status quo that those guys have to return to time and time again just feels boring to me. It feels like a cop out. It's not what I look for when I read fiction.

A lot of you out there, and you know who you are, have a big problem with this book and with Megan McKeenan specifically because she is "annoying." Presumably, and I've taken the time to ask a couple of you so this is accurate in part, because she is flawed, because she is young and whiny in the beginning, because she makes stupid decisions and acts "wrong." I can only think that these readers (and bloggers) find a degree of comfort in reading characters that act a certain way all the time and/or conform to a standard that they themselves are comfortable in reading. Which seems - IS - so contrary to how the world is as to baffle me. Young Megan (or Pella in *Supermarket* or Jennie in *Channel Zero* or several people in *Demo* or Matty in *DMZ*) are dumb and naive and screwed up because that's what young people in transition ARE, and sure, they can come off as hard to deal with. Show me someone who isn't.

So to all you people who (disturbingly) like to tell me how they would punch Megan in the face if they could, I hope you have an open enough mind to wait for the big picture, to see how she goes from her youth to adulthood and all that entails, much like, I'm assuming, you all did yourself.

ANYWAY, back to this issue (sorry, I've had this on my brain for most of a decade). This is a pretty rough story. It actually haunted me afterwards. I shut the Word document when I was done but couldn't get rid of the thought of it. Was it too much for the book? It feels "worse" to me than the #4 story, which was dark as well. But I don't second-guess myself so much when it comes to creative things, so I went with it. Contrast it with the previous issue, go back and read #9, see how they work together. I think for the collected edition of this book I'll combine the two somehow, a single story with two chapter breaks. One needs the other.

I hope Megan is feeling more real to you. She is to me.

Thanks to Karin Kross Levenstein and Co. for the reference photography!

Soundtrack:
"Distopian Dream Girl" - Built To Spill
"Good News" - Corrina Repp
"Wrong" - Archers of Loaf

Roll Credits:
"World Of Shit" - The Eels

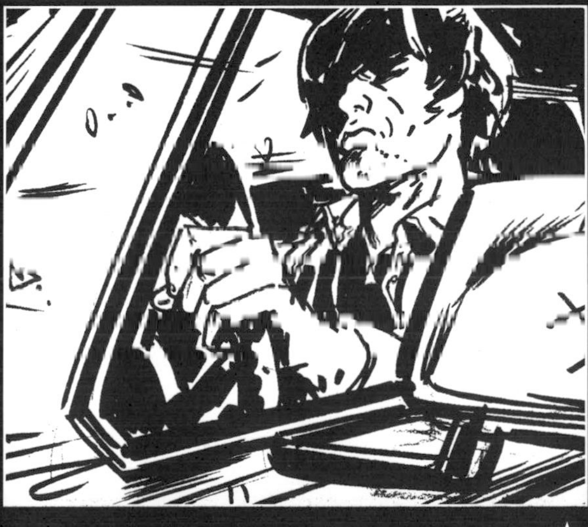

LOCAL #11 - THE YOUNGER GENERATION

MARCH, 2008

RYAN KELLY:

When it was time to decide what to do for this Toronto issue, Brian, the writer, came to me, Ryan Kelly, the non-writer. Brian had all the stories settled for the other books in the series but no great plan for this one. This issue was almost going to be a one-shot, a brief non sequitur in the ongoing life story of Megan. I pitched him one story idea that, now in hindsight, was awful. It just didn't jive with what Brian does well. So, we didn't have a clue for this issue. What to do?

Sometimes when you're stuck and you can't go forward, you have to go backward. So I went backward.

When we first began *Local*, Brian and Oni gave me a lot freedom with the art and the formal decisions involved in the interior look of the book. I knew what I had to do with the storytelling, and I had to remain true to the real-life locations. But after that, it was an open field for me to play in. So, as the series grew I had to fill Megan's little world with all of those small mundane details that add color and personality to our surroundings. I did it to make the backgrounds look interesting, but it turned into something else.

What I'm saying is I planted Easter Eggs. I drew The Nob Hill Pharmacy prescription form on her refrigerator in issue 2: Polaroid Boyfriend. I drew Richmond's Theories And Defenses record in *Local* #5: Nova Scotia. The Missoula Trucker cap (with blood) hangs in her apartment in *Local* #6: Park Slope, Brooklyn. Right behind Brian's back, I created a stupid little sub-plot. It was another minor story about Megan, quietly being told as the larger plot was unraveling. She was holding onto things. Even as Megan was moving from place to place, unable to settle into a life, she was keeping small pieces of her past. They were small tokens, but they represented major turning points in her life and she couldn't let go of them. Which, favorably for me, was a metaphor for what *Local* was all about anyway.
Oh my God, I had a story!

To quote the A-team, "I love it when a plan comes together."

Oh, never mind.

This is my last essay. I apologize if I am unable to pull my final thoughts together for a proper eulogy because as you read this, I am frantically drawing the final 32 pages for *Local* #12. Only when we have this entire series wrapped up, will I be able to look back on it with some sort of acceptance and pride. Like Megan's life, each story, or each piece, was a fragment. Only when we put all the pieces together, will they have the shine of grace and maturity. Through the duration of the series my life, and Brian's as well, have gone through major events. Our lives changed. We adjusted the book. We changed the meaning and the direction. It wasn't always going to be so much about Megan, and then it was. It was going to be a lot about location, then it wasn't. It was always changing.

Local is some of Brian Wood's best work. If you don't think so, you have to go backwards. Read them all together again. The next issue will kill you. I will produce better work after *Local*. I'd better! But I'll never work on anything again as important as *Local*. Hands down.

So long, Megan.

Art assistants:
Nicole Vanche, Seamus Burke, JP Pollard, Ryan Carr and Carol Gesbeck

Local #11 Soundtrack:
"Zerox" - Adam And The Ants
"Shoplifting" - The Slits
"Been Caught Stealing" - Jane's Addiction
"Hold Up" - Girl Talk

Roll credits:
"Staring Back" - Siouxsie and the Banshees

Special Note:
Thanks to Kayla Hillier and Eric Kim for the photos and the help on this issue, and a double thanks to Christopher Butcher for championing Toronto in the first place (sorry, Ann Arbor, you totally got bumped - blame Chris) and providing crucial intel and last minute corrections.

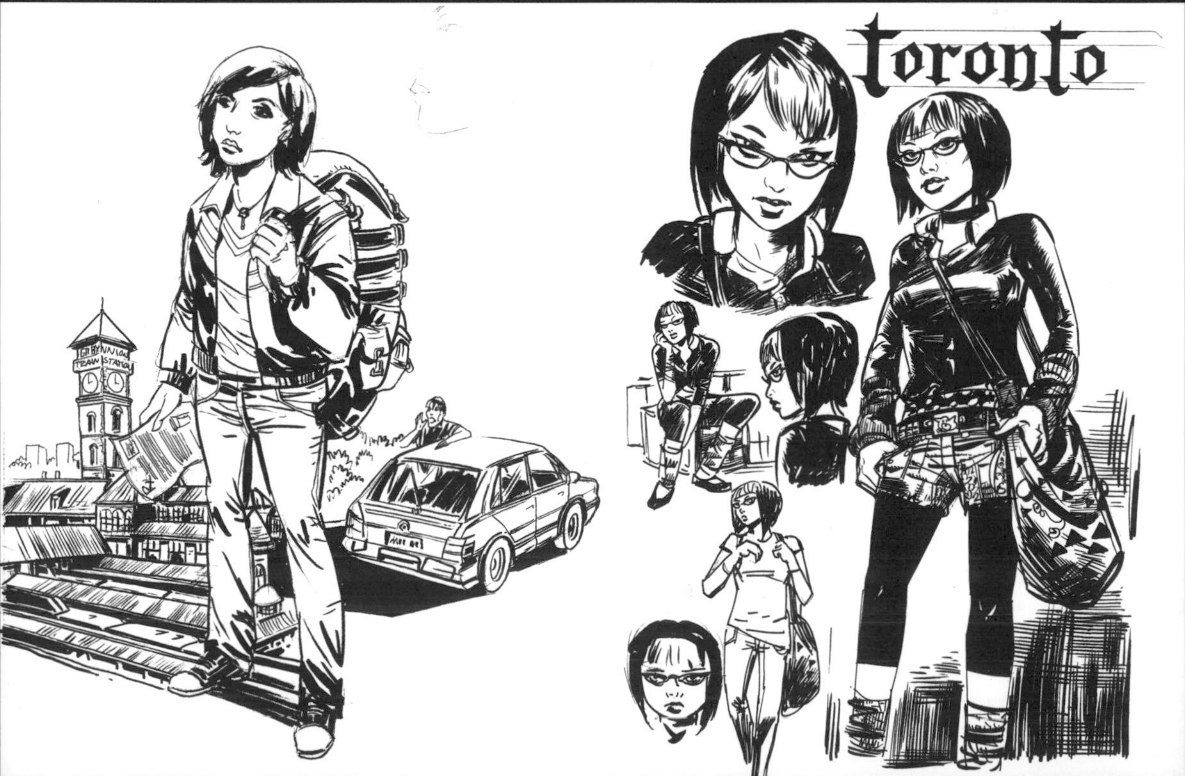
toronto

BRIAN WOOD:

This is the last essay of the series, as Ryan already said. #12 will be longer, taking up the entire 32 pages, so we're saying goodbye now.

We started *Local* in 2005 and when all is said and done, it'll have been a two and a half year process. Just to get it out of the way, yeah, it shouldn't have taken us two and a half years to complete a series meant to run just one year, but it did, and in some ways I think its a better book for it. Not that it makes it any less frustrating for you guys, or comic shop owners, or the crew at Oni Press, but the extra time gave me more of a chance to think about the series and grow along with it. I think where we're at now with Megan is not where we would be if it was October of 2006 and I was here writing the essay for *Local* #11.

Megan McKeenan: to love her or to hate her? I hear from people on both sides. Many women I know personally and who have contacted me via email tell me THEY are Megan, that they identify closely with her, having similar vagabond-esque experiences in their lives. Others loathe her for her imperfections. I've spoken on this before, I know, but I strongly feel it's her imperfections that round out her character and make her feel as real as she does to people.

I'm looking over the original series proposal document (which has a 2004 date on it, yikes!) and what strikes me is to what degree Megan takes a backseat in it. It leads with five or six paragraphs on the subject of what constitutes a "local" and how the series will be structured and formatted. She doesn't even have a name, here. Look at how I described her:

"I want her to be more universal, a person that more people can relate to. She is, in short, the vessel our readers will be using to access many of these stories."

Wow, that comes off pretty cold! But it underscores how important Megan became to me as time went on, that she changed from a nameless tour guide to, basically, the outright star of this series of initially unconnected stories.

And why it's as hard as it is for me to be writing the final scene of the last issue, saying goodbye to Megan. Hopefully not forever.

Ryan Kelly was amazing throughout this. I loved his work already, but what he's done on *Local* really broadened my appreciation and made, I believe, a hell of a lot of people sit up and take notice. He sweated and bled and cried and suffered through a lot in the last couple years, and the work never suffered. I owe him, hugely, for making this book what it is.

The guys at Oni Press - James and Joe and Randal and Douglas - were nothing but cool and accommodating and thoughtful and hardworking, far more than we deserved. I also owe them thanks.

Many thanks to Bryan Lee O'Malley and Hope Larson, for being early cheerleaders and grunt workers and pinup artists and reference collectors.

And a collective but still utterly sincere thanks to all my friends, to all the retailers, people in the press, people online, everyone who helped up with photos and signings and events and who sent me postcards and letters. One of the reasons I treasure this series as much as I do is for how interactive and collaborative it felt. So much of my career is spent alone in my office writing, this was a chance to reach out and work with a lot of people. Our interactions may have been brief, but they were crucial to the success of the book.

Soundtrack (roll credits):
"Does Your Hometown Care?" - Superchunk
(What else would it be?)

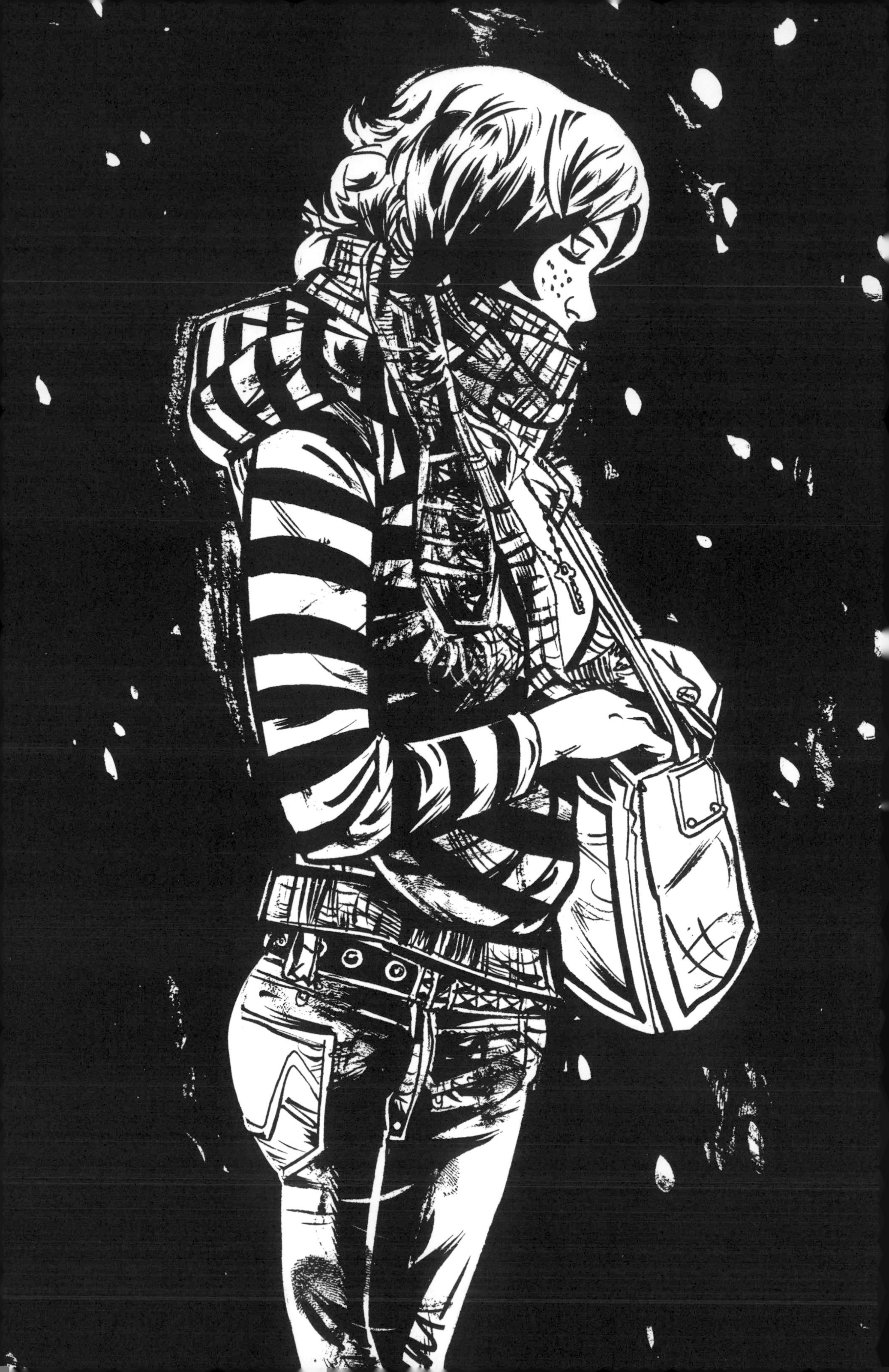

LOCAL ™

THE PIN UPS & COVERS

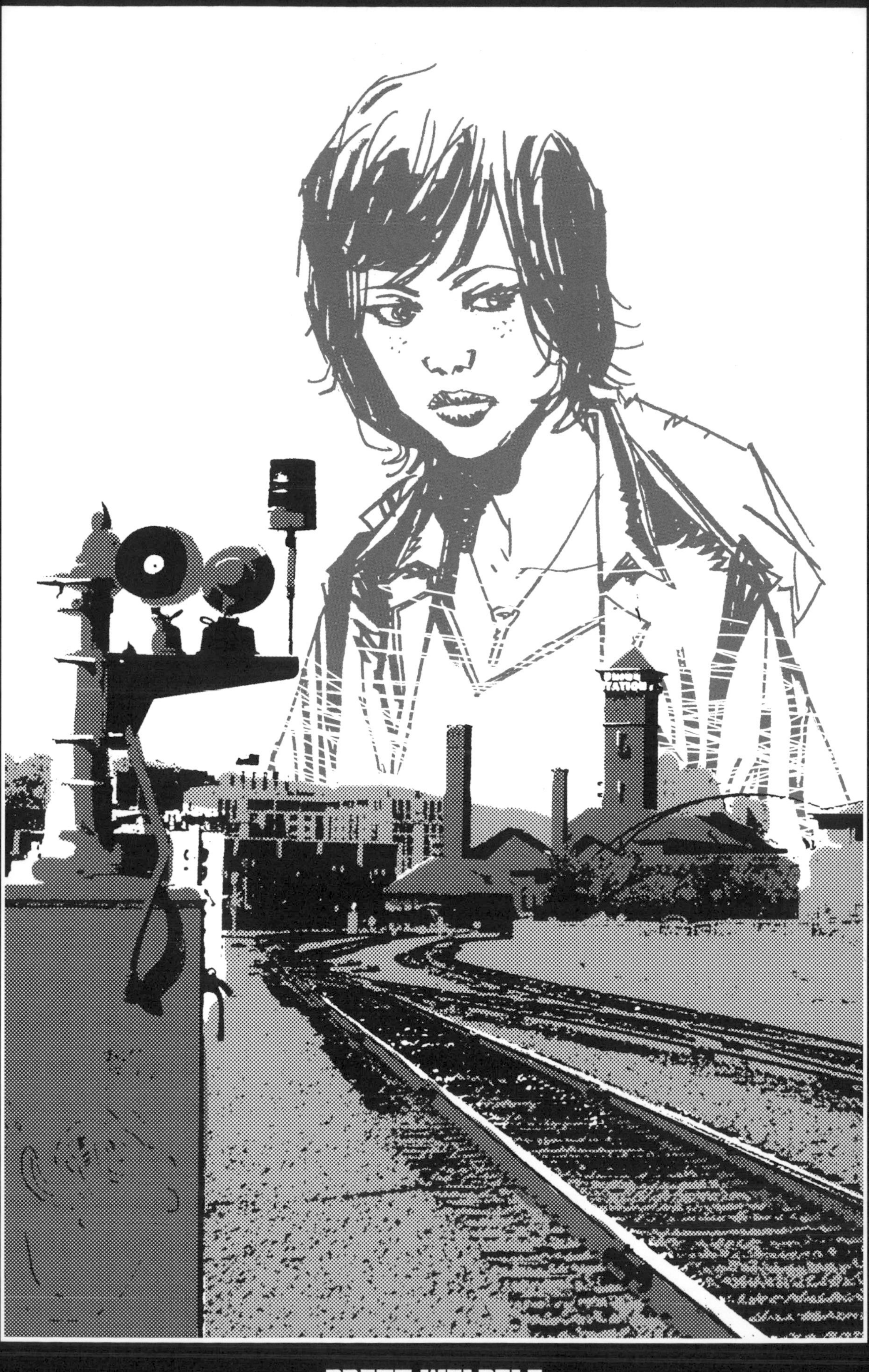

BRETT WELDELE

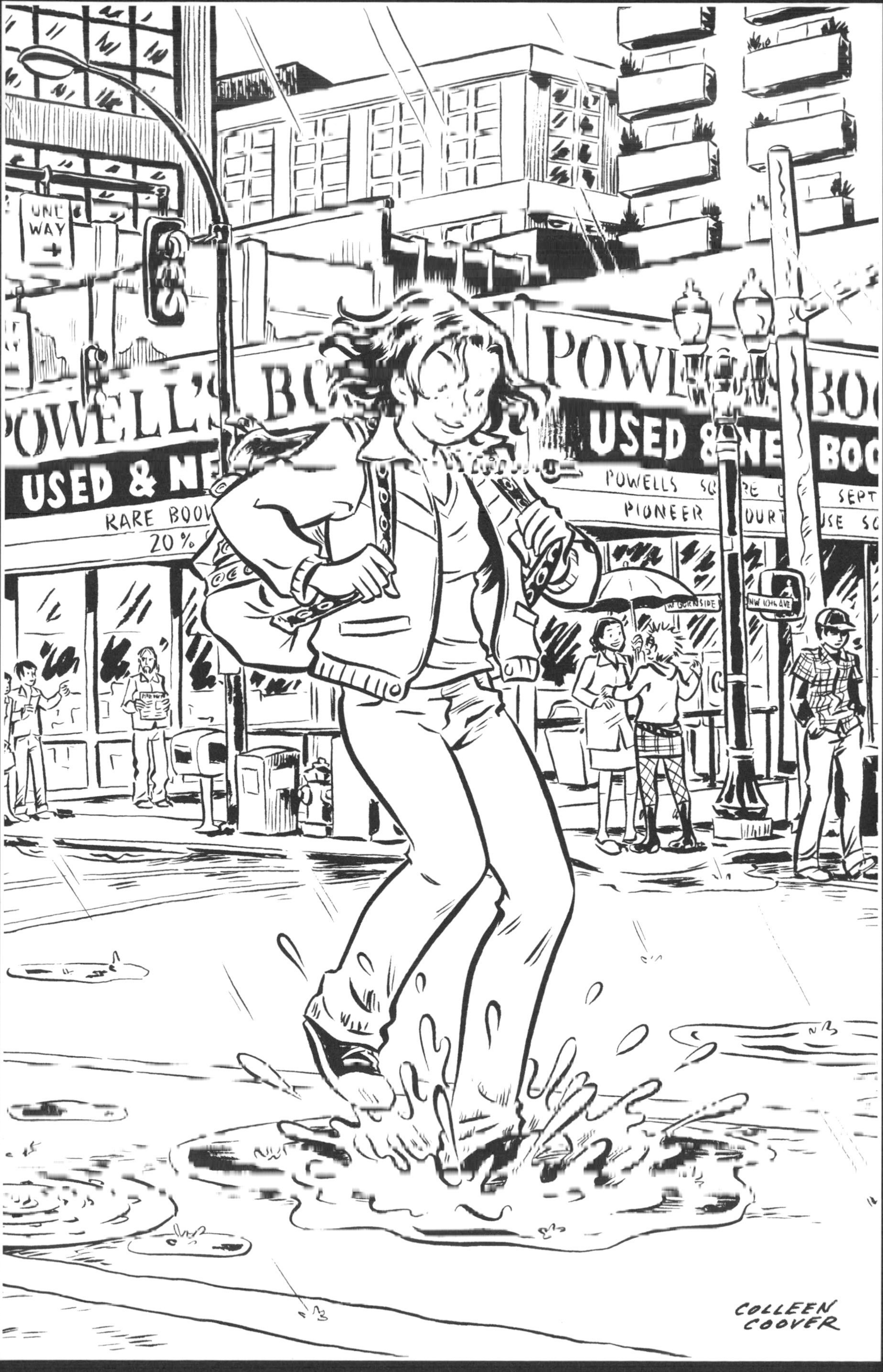
ONE WAY
POWELL'S BOOKS
USED & NEW
RARE BOOK
20%
POWELLS
PIONEER
SEPT
USED & NEW BOO
W BURNSIDE
NW 10th AVE
COLLEEN COOVER

COLLEEN COOVER

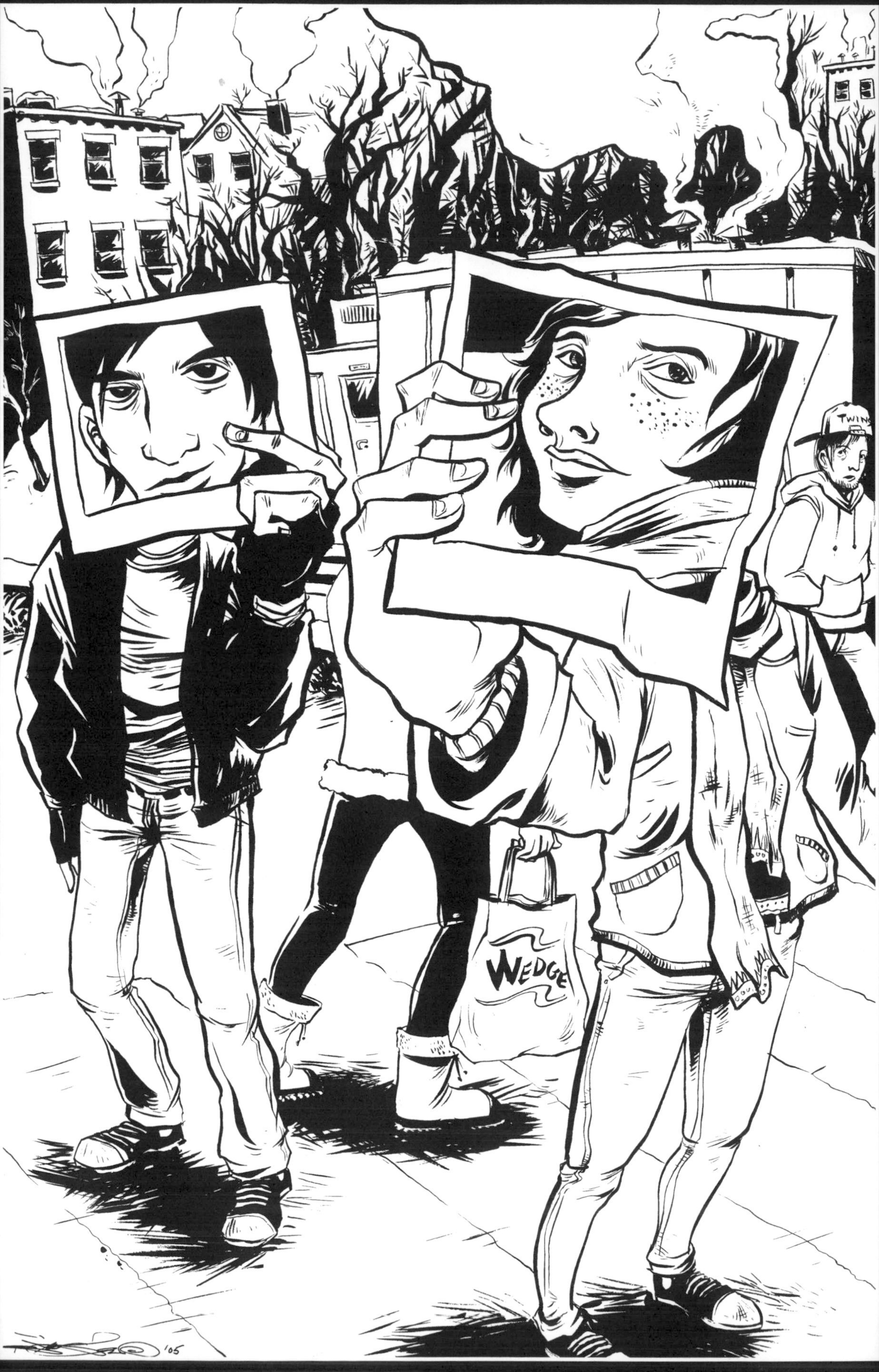
WEDGE

BRITTNEY SABO

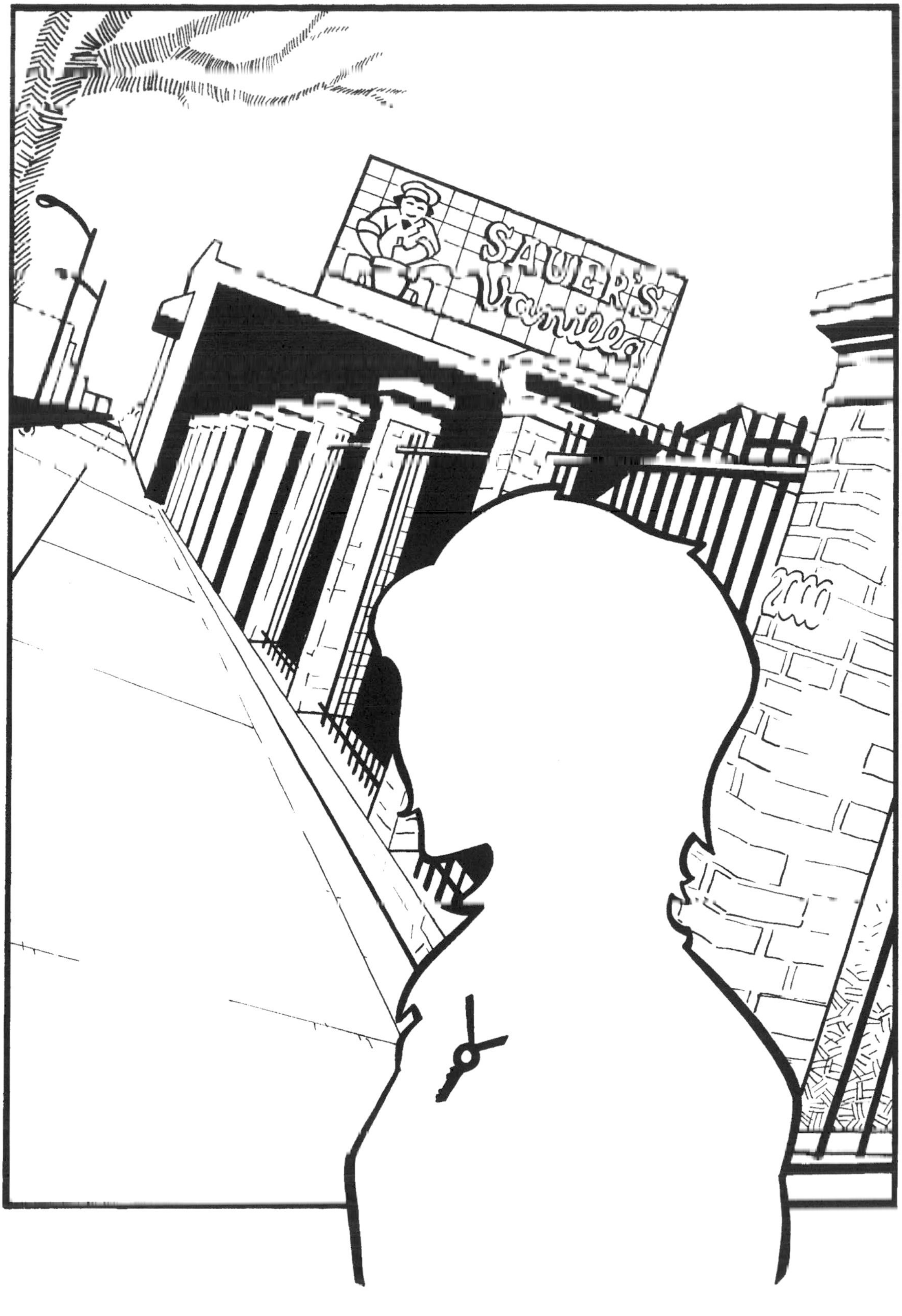
SAUER'S
Vanilla
2000

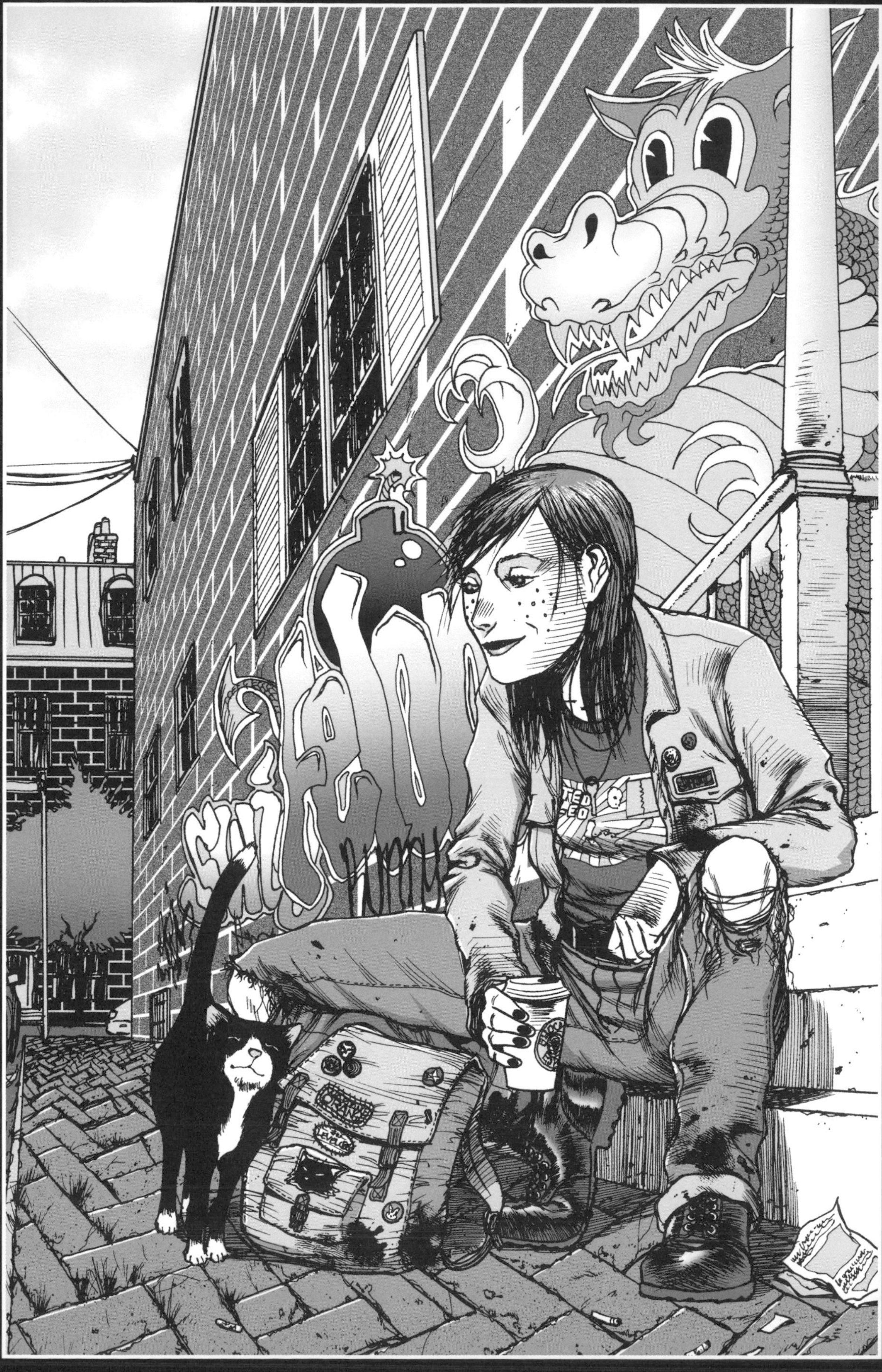

ROB G

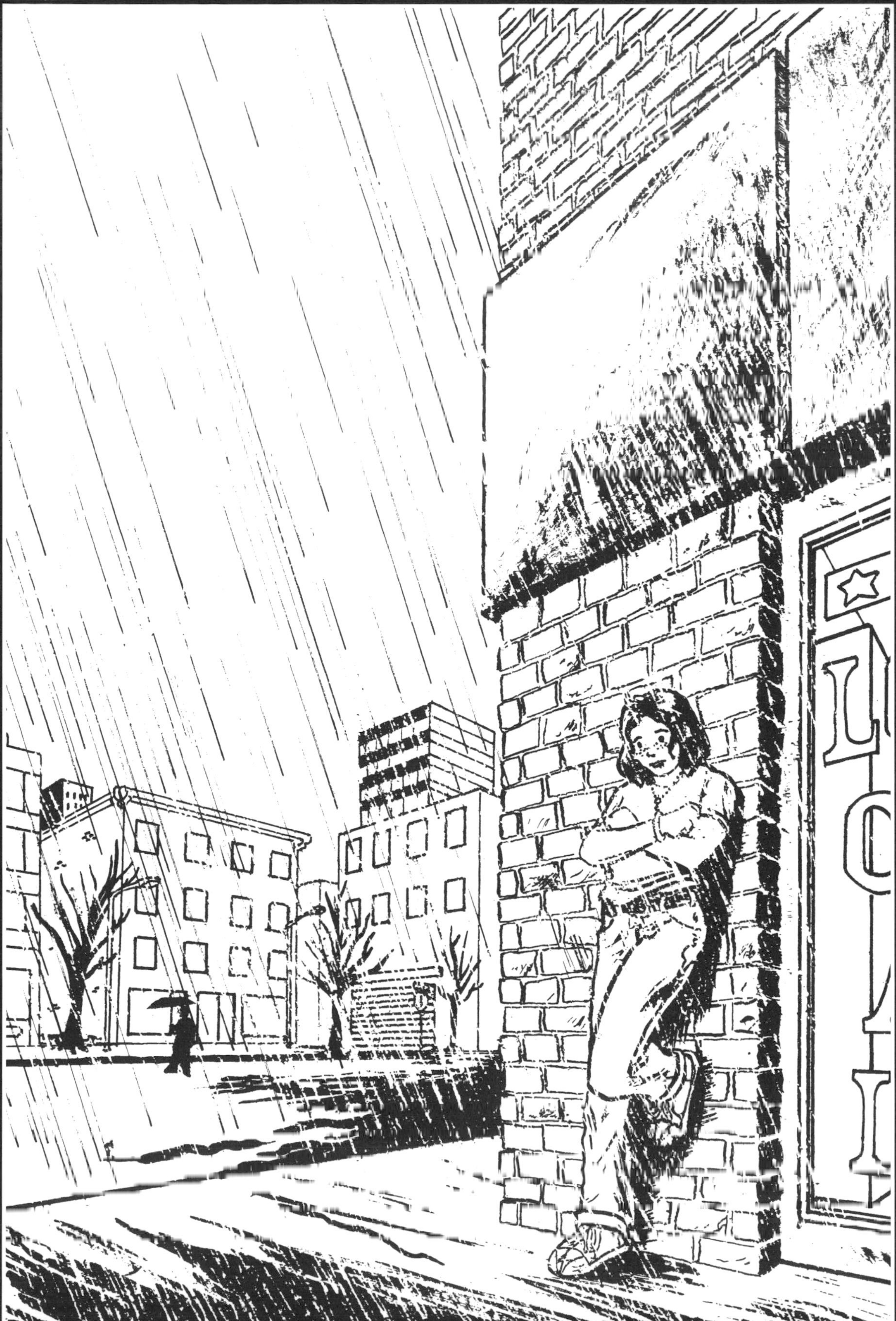

DENNIS CULVER

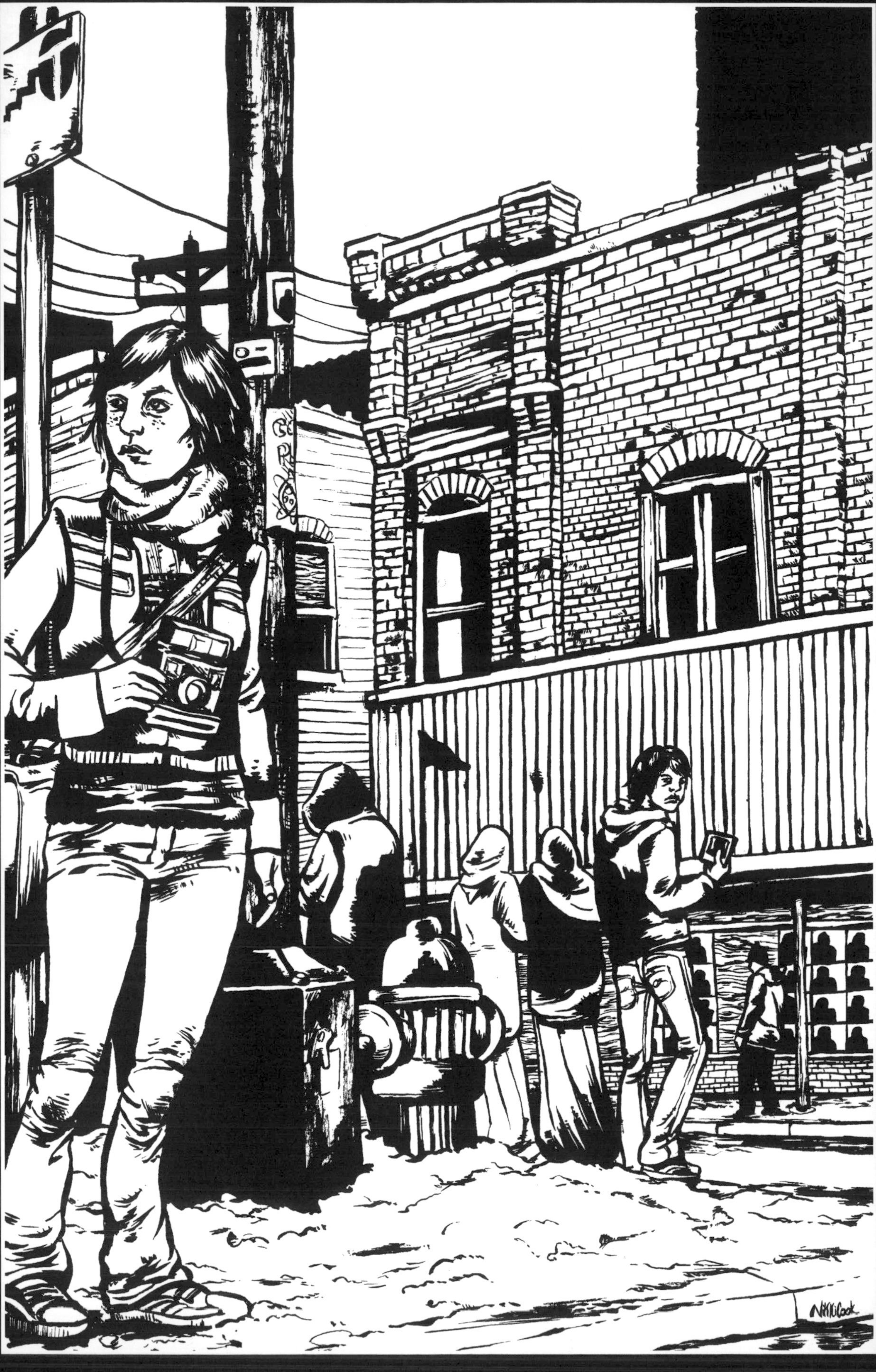
NikkiCook

NIKKI COOK

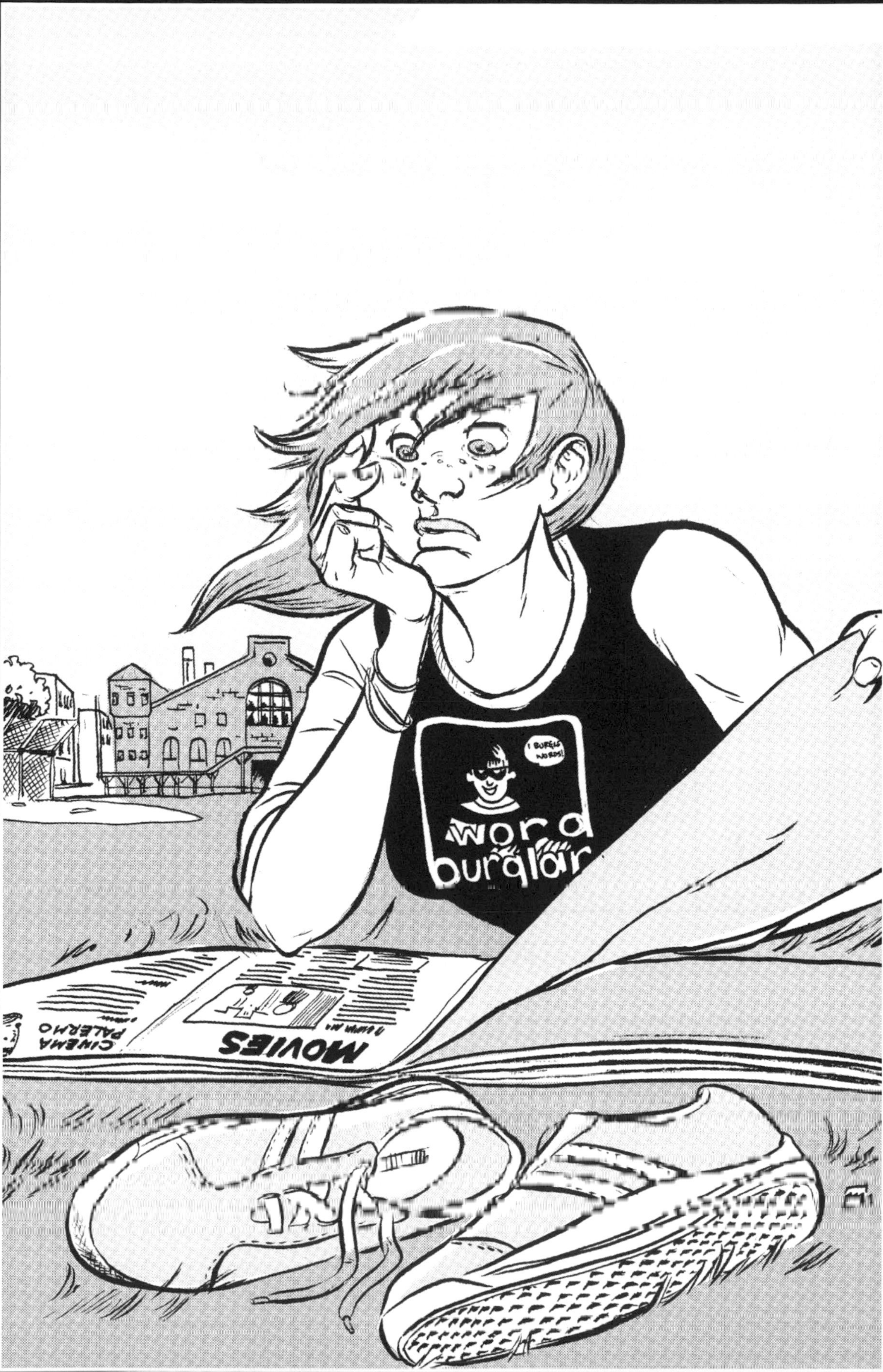
word burglar
MOVIES
CINEMA PALERMO

MIKE HOLMES

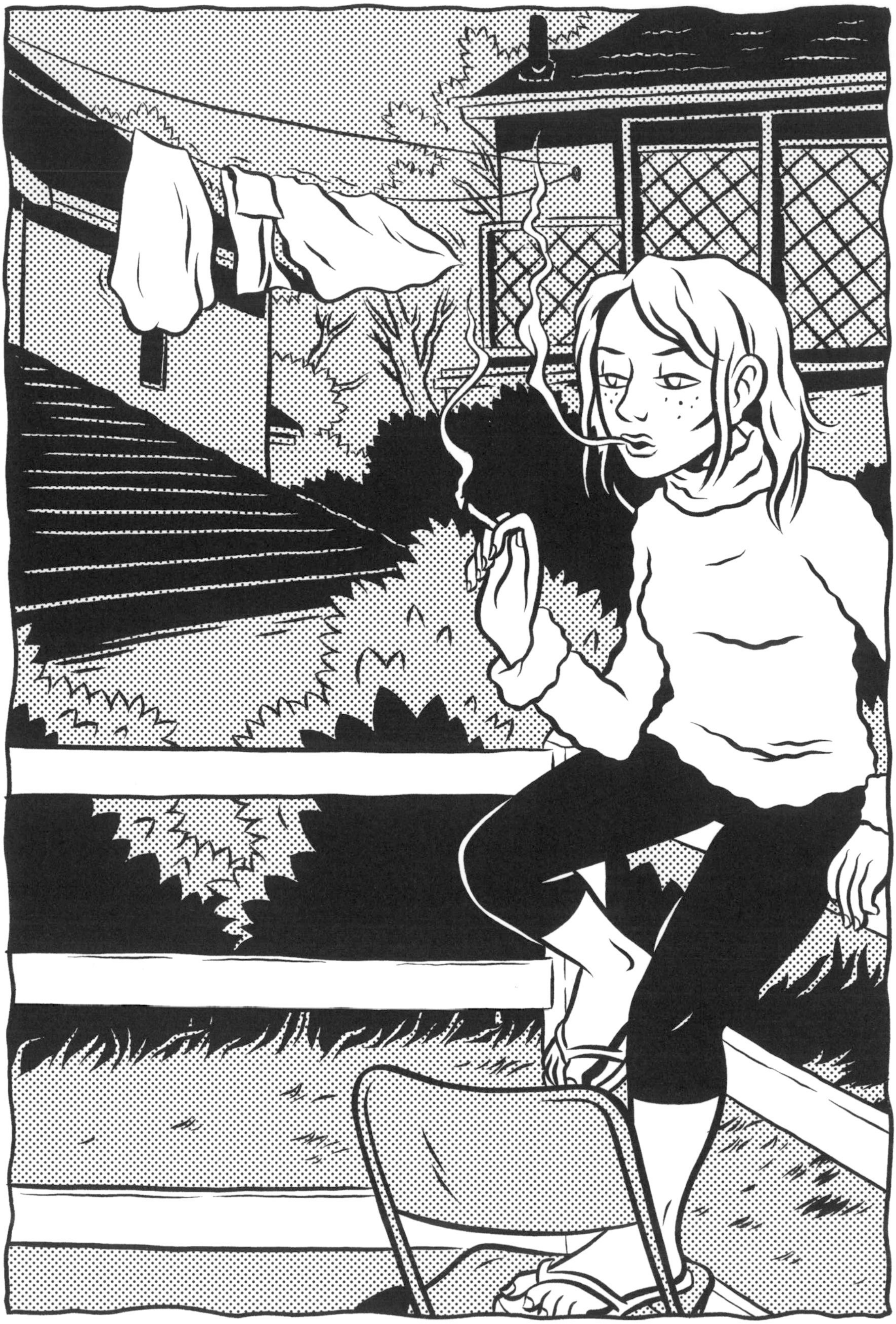

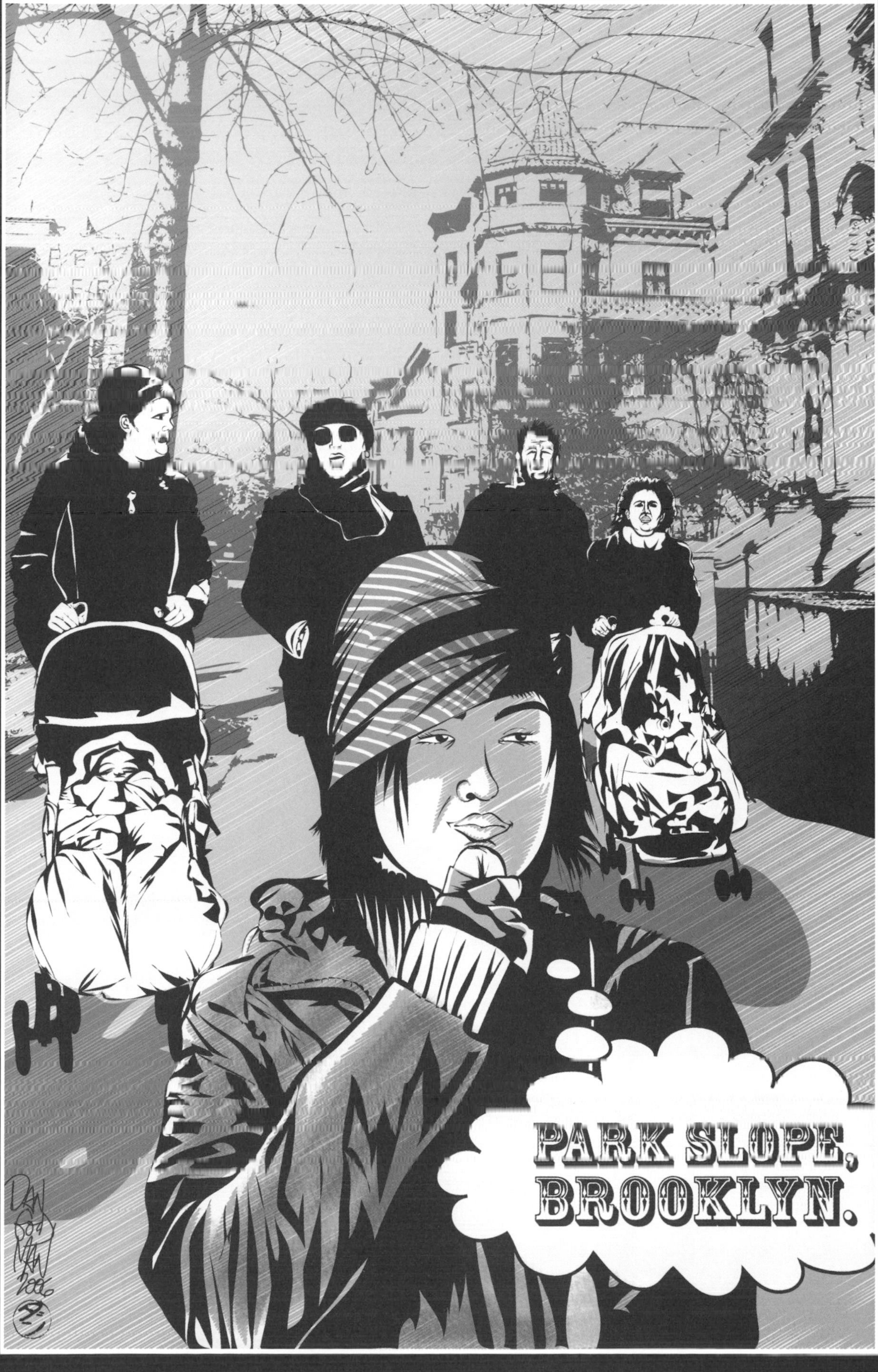
PARK SLOPE,
BROOKLYN.

DAN GOLDMAN

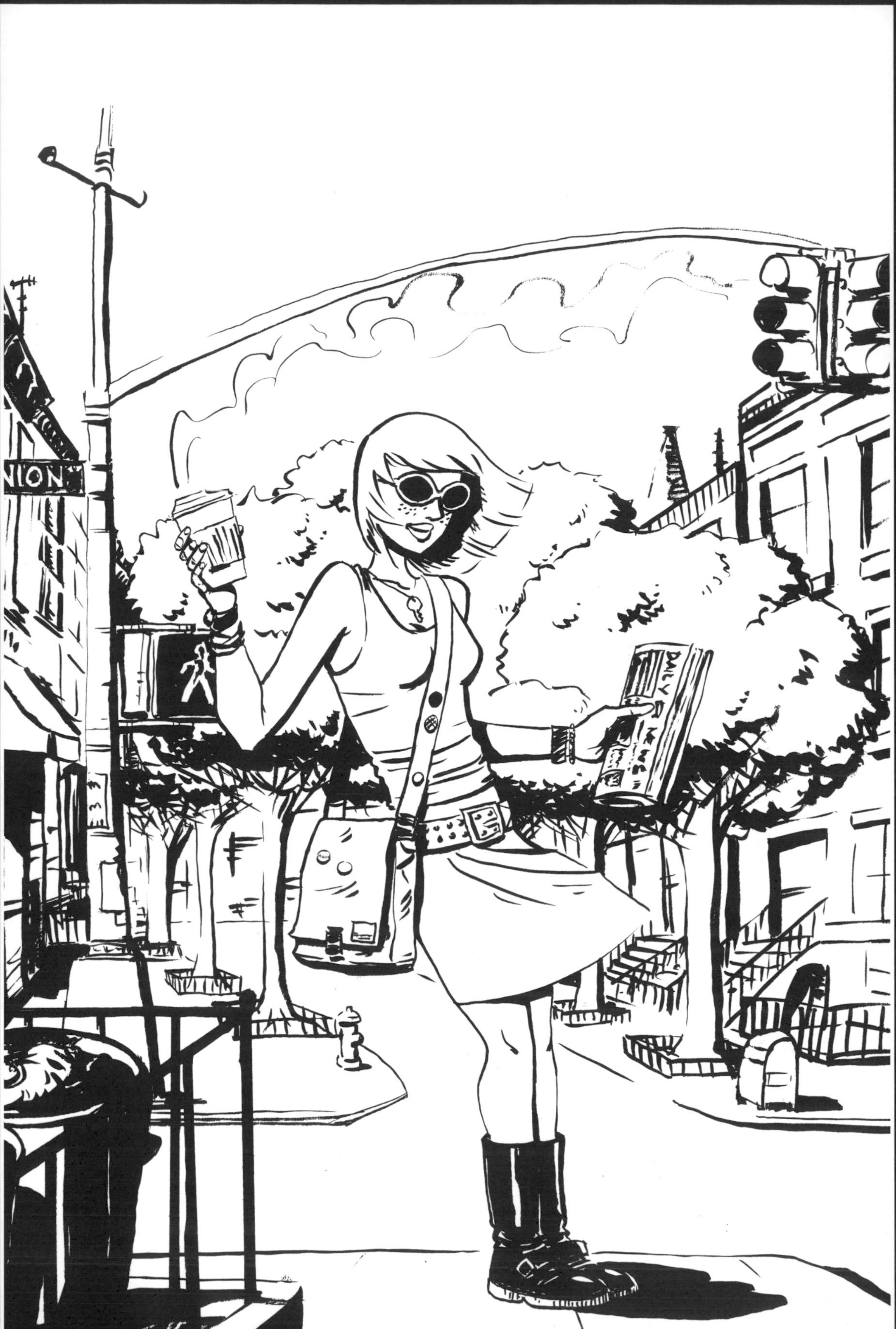
NION
DAILY

ALEX COX

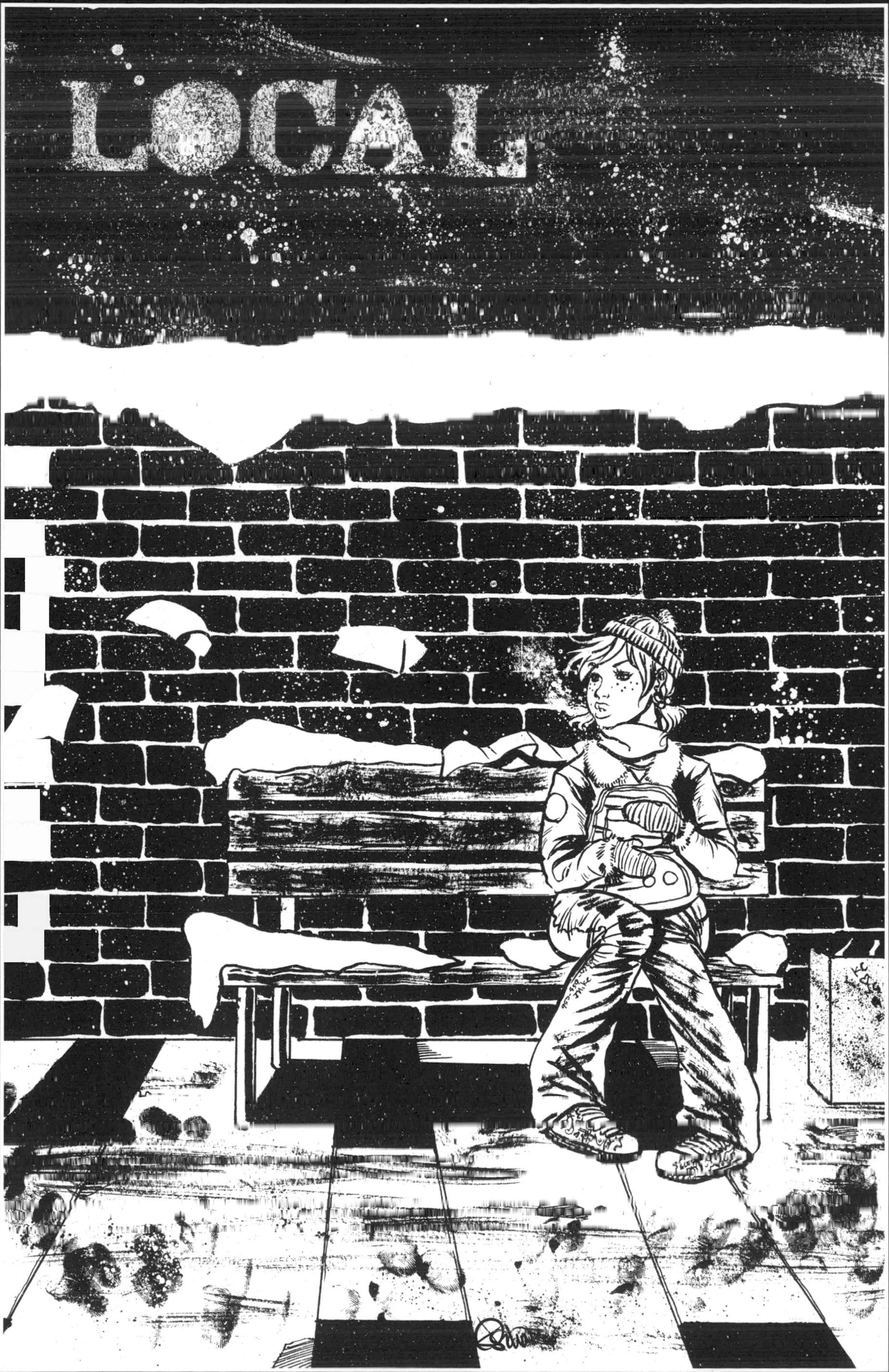
LOCAL

MICHELLE SILVA

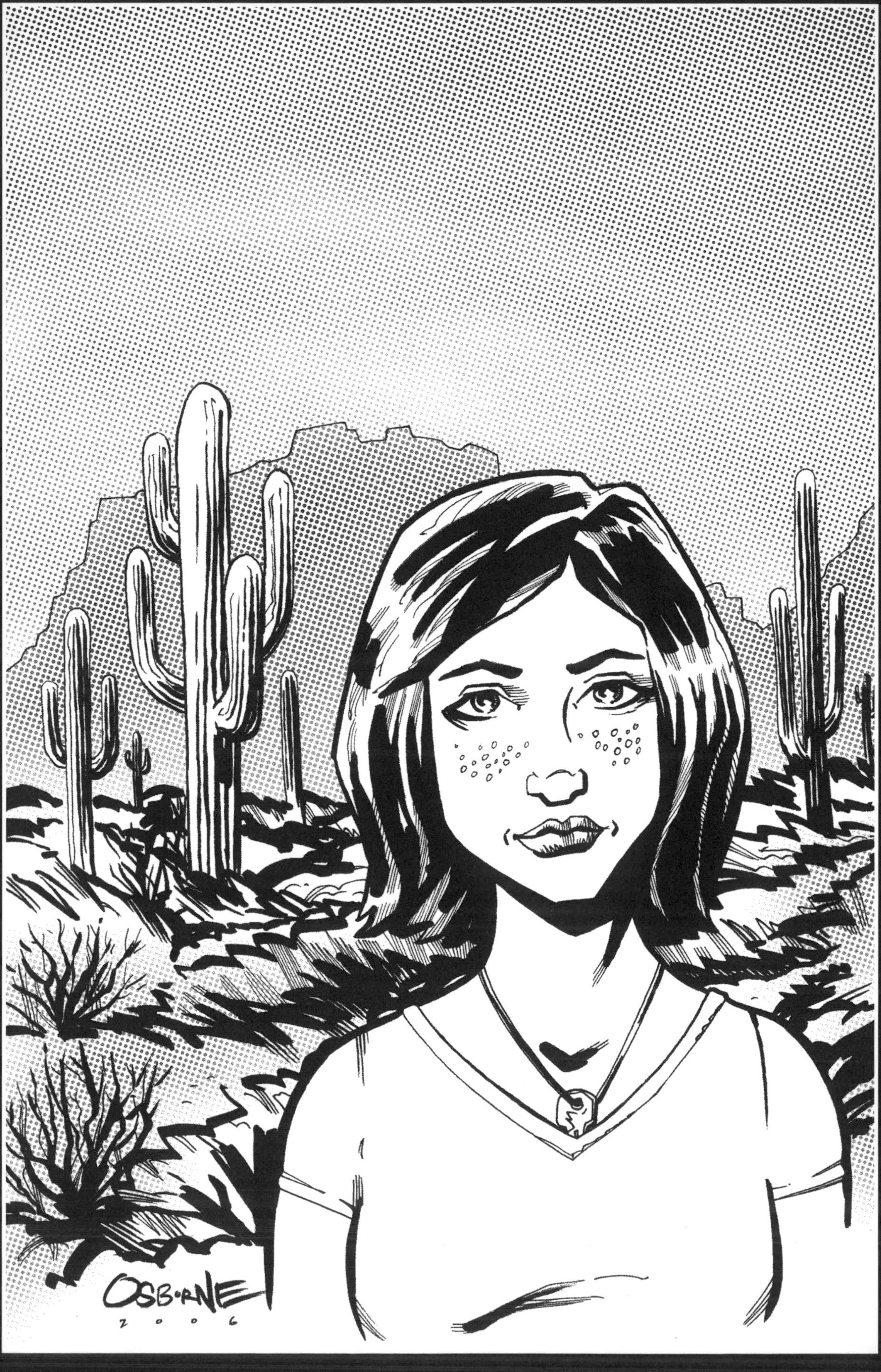
OSBORNE
2006

ROB OSBORNE

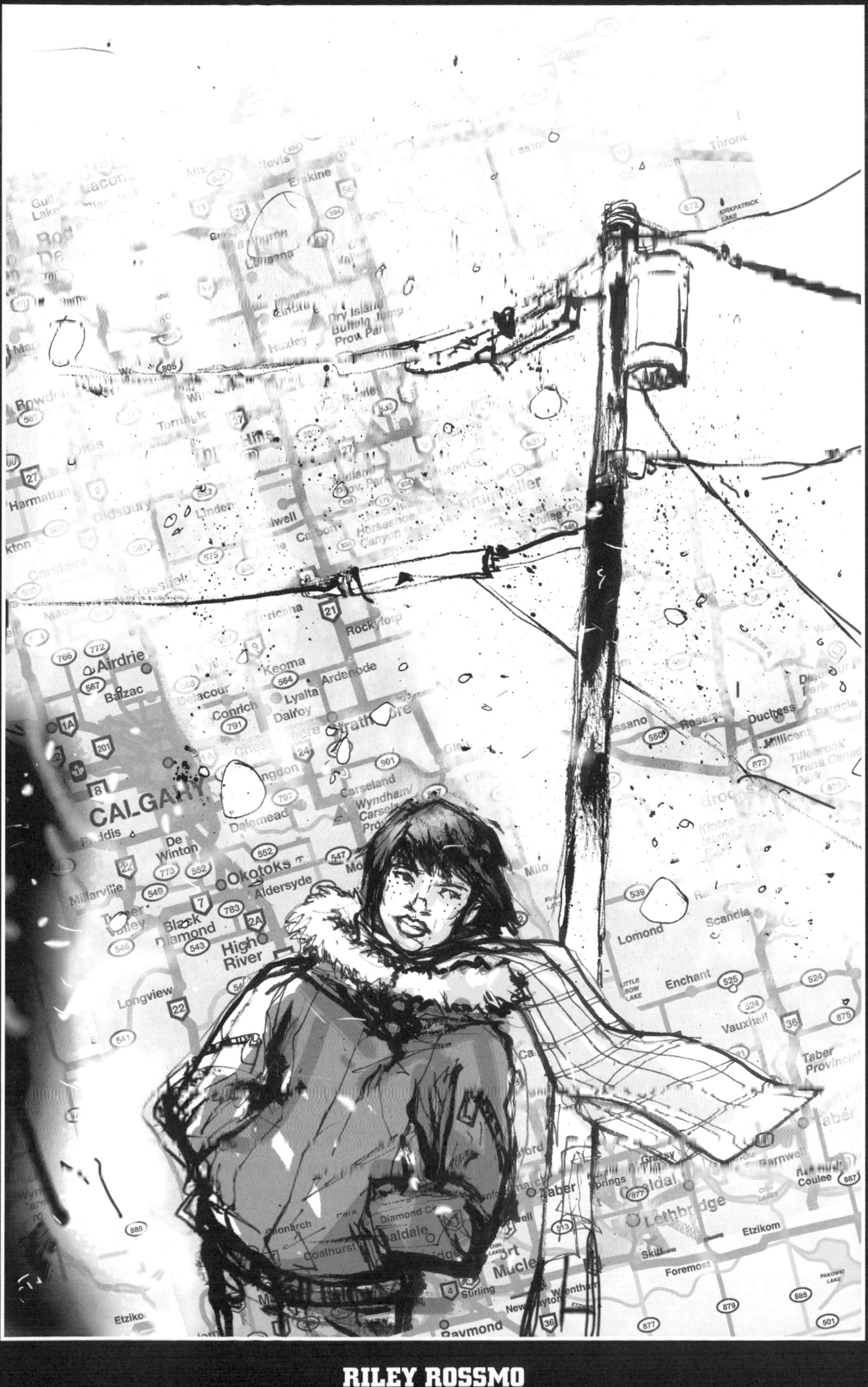

Throne
KIRKPATRICK LAKE
Nevis
Erskine
Alix
Gull Lake
Castor
Dry Island Buffalo Jump Prov. Park
Huxley
Bowden
Torrington
Three Hills
Drumheller
Harmattan
Didsbury
Linden
Swalwell
Carbon
Horseshoe Canyon
East Coulee
Carstairs
Crossfield
Irricana
Rockyford
Airdrie
Balzac
Keoma
Ardenode
Delacour
Lyalta
Conrich
Dalroy
CALGARY
Carseland
Wyndham/Carseland Prov. Park
Dalemead
De Winton
Okotoks
Aldersyde
Millarville
Black Diamond
High River
Longview
Duchess
Patricia
Millicent
Tillebrook Trans Canada Park
Milo
Lomond
Scandia
Enchant
LITTLE BOW LAKE
Vauxhall
Taber Provincial
Barnwell
Coulee
Taber
Coaldale
Lethbridge
Etzikom
Skiff
Foremost
PAKOWKI LAKE
Stirling
Raymond
Coalhurst
Diamond City
Etzikom

RILEY ROSSMO

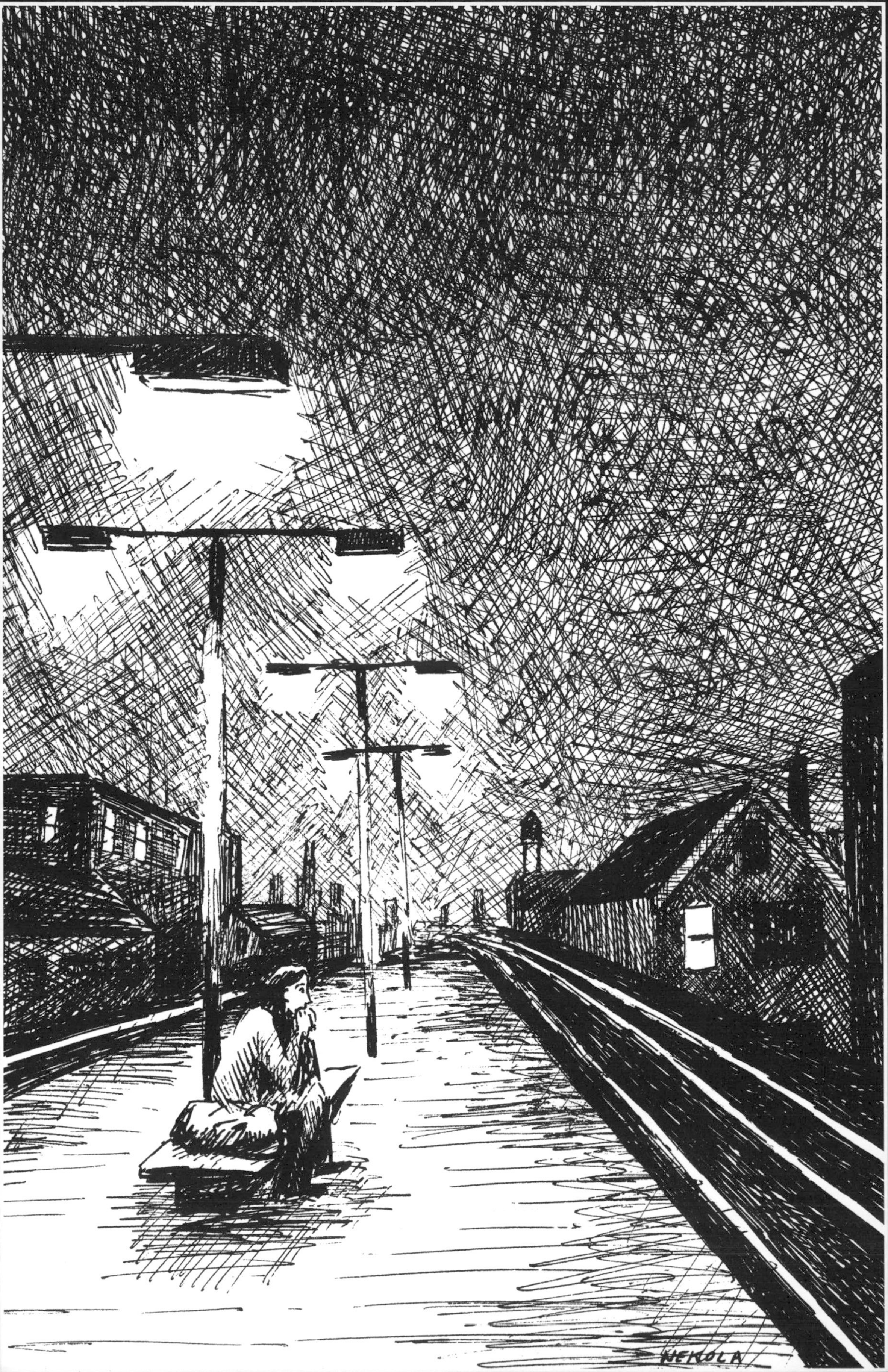
NEKOLA

PETER NEKOLA

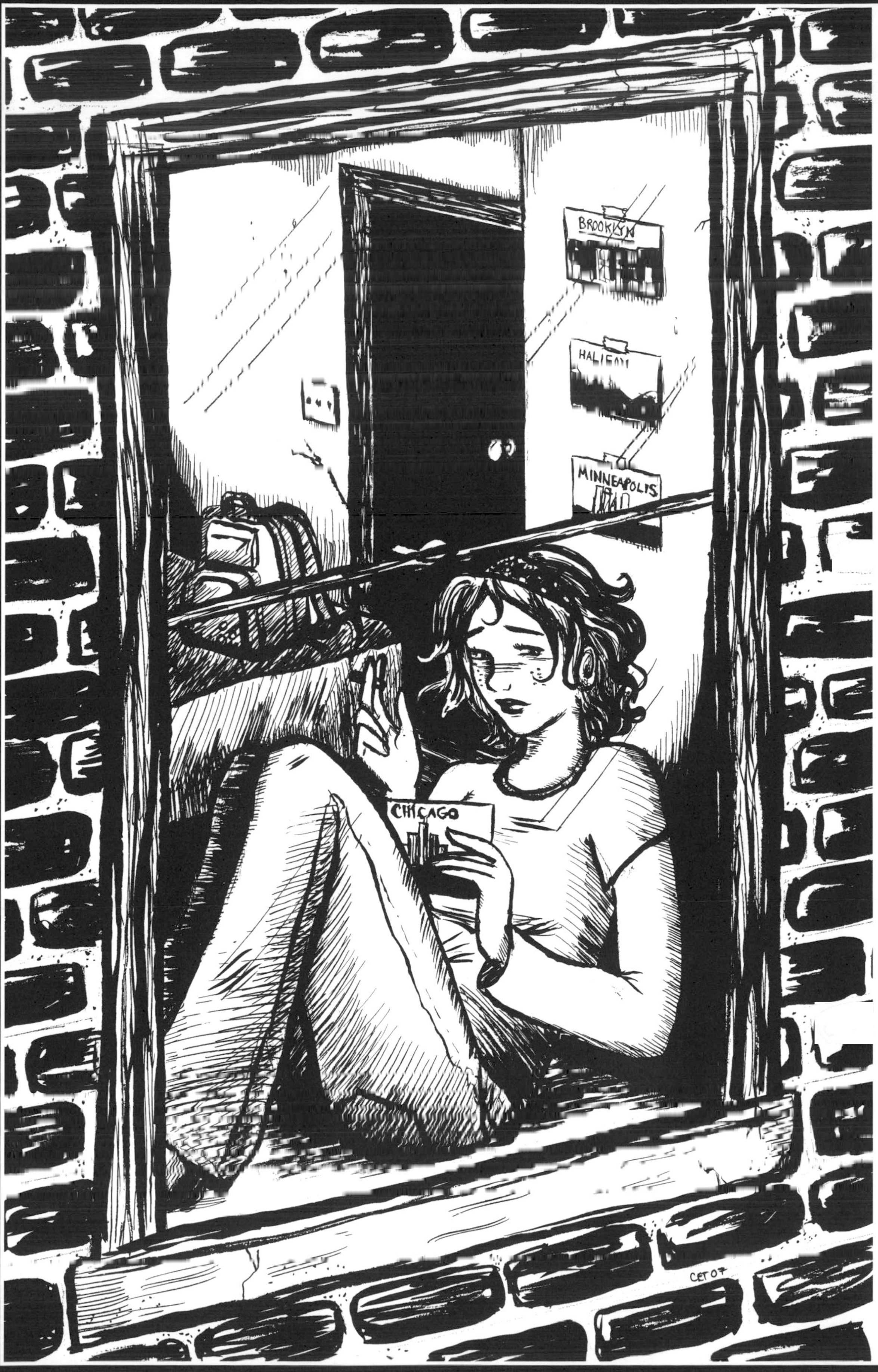
BROOKLYN
MINNEAPOLIS
CHICAGO
CET 07

COURTNEY THOMAS

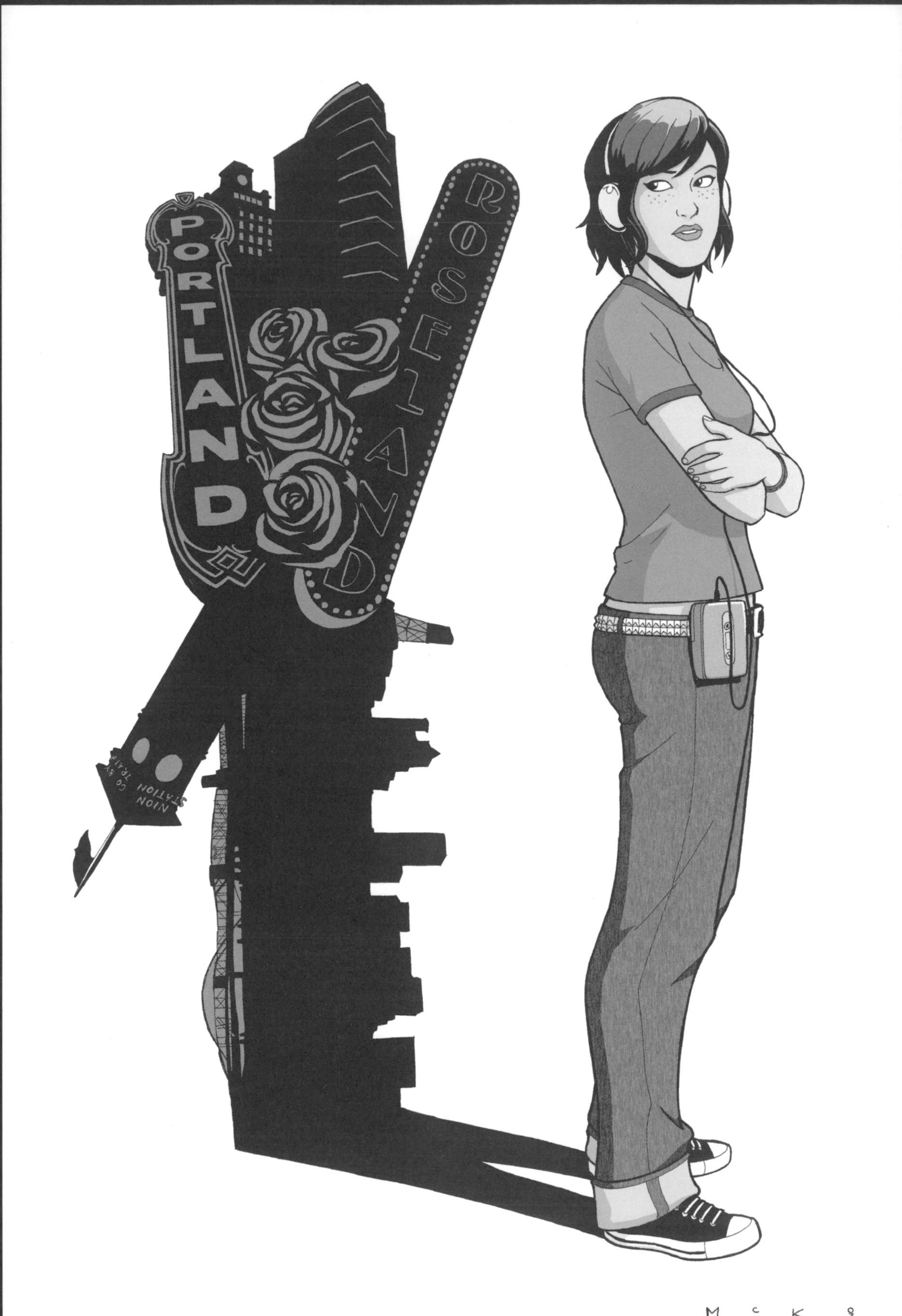
PORTLAND
ROSELAND

JAMIE McKELVIE

"The perfect three-minute single. You're going to want this one." - WARREN ELLIS

BRIAN WOOD / RYAN KELLY

LOCAL

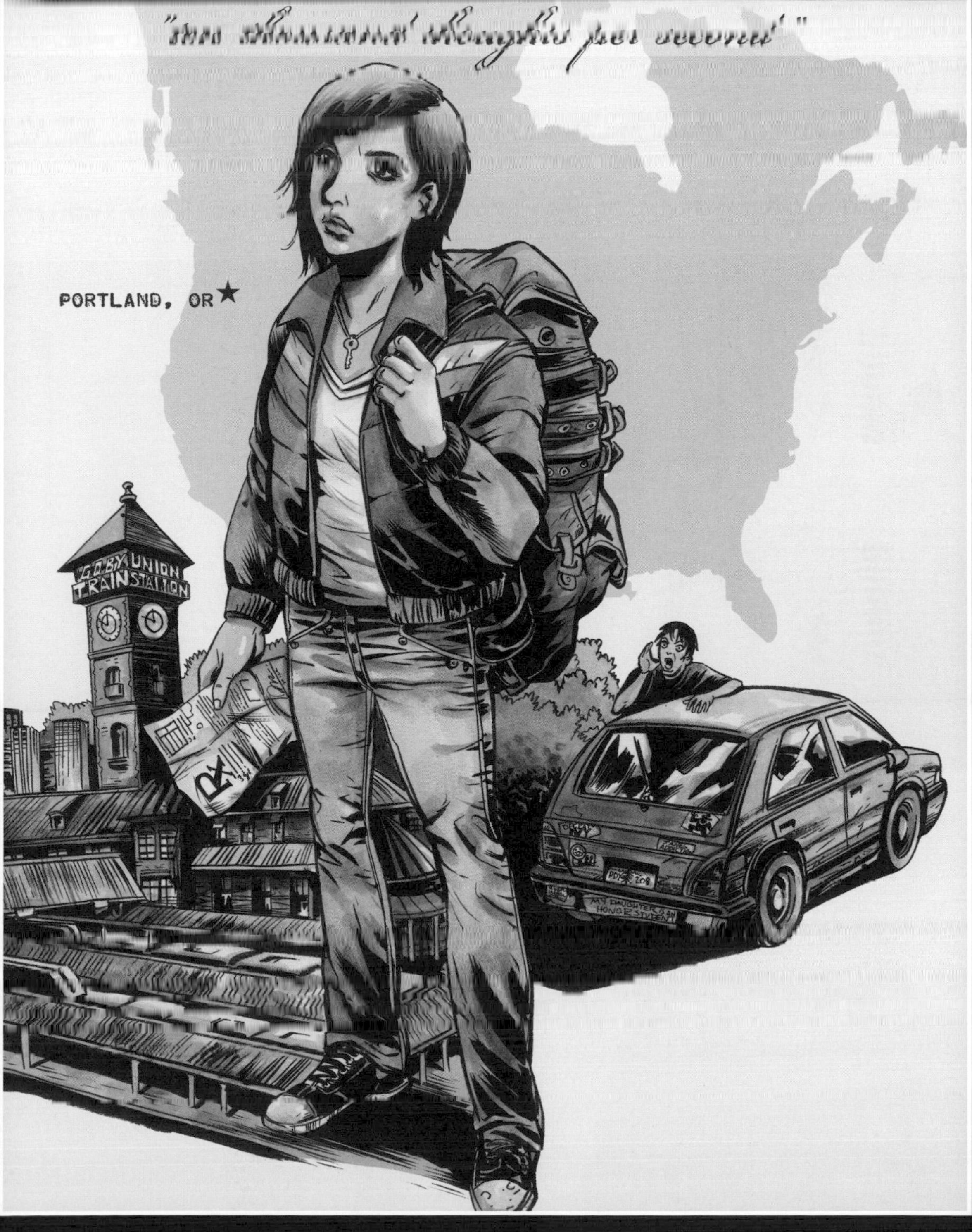
PORTLAND, OR
GO BY UNION
TRAIN STATION

ISSUE #1

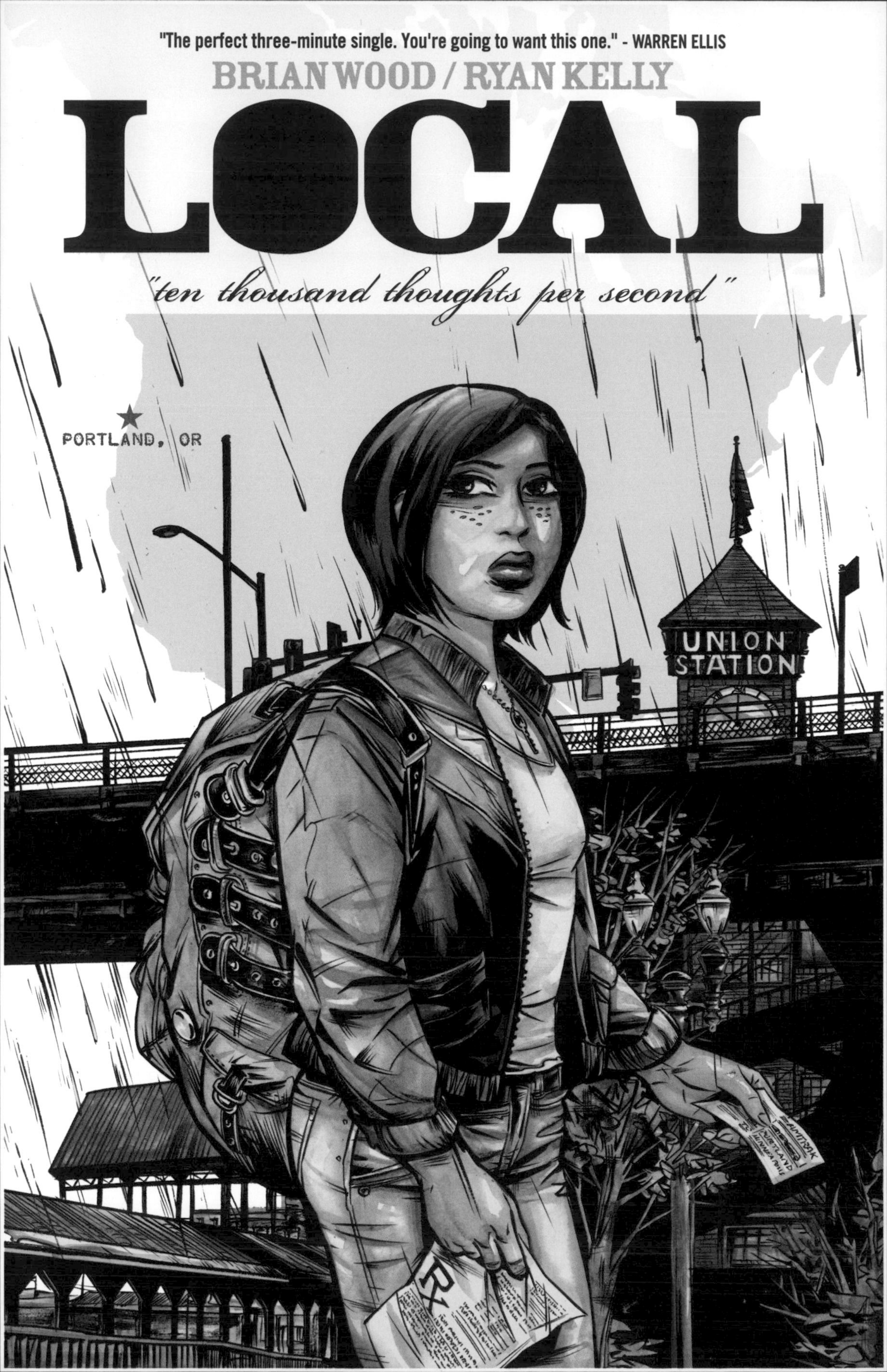
"The perfect three-minute single. You're going to want this one." - WARREN ELLIS
BRIAN WOOD / RYAN KELLY
LOCAL
"ten thousand thoughts per second"
PORTLAND, OR
UNION
STATION

ISSUE #1, SECOND PRINTING

"Some of the sharpest slices of life the medium has ever seen" - BRIAN K VAUGHAN

BRIAN WOOD / RYAN KELLY

LOCAL

"polaroid boyfriend"

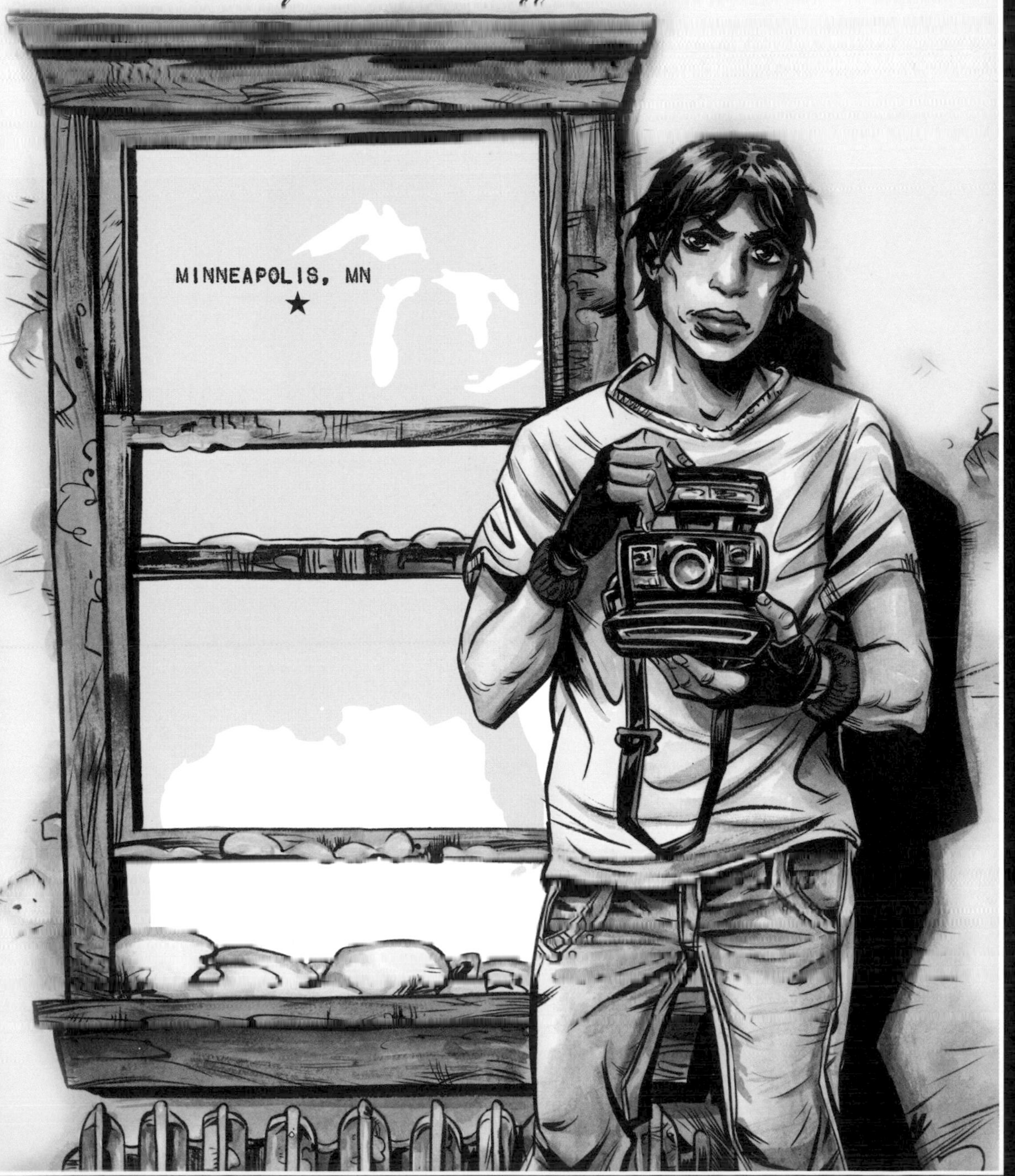
MINNEAPOLIS, MN

ISSUE #2

"the coolest short film never shown on the IFC or Sundance Channel." - SEQUENTIAL TART

BRIAN WOOD / RYAN KELLY

LOCAL

"theories and defenses"

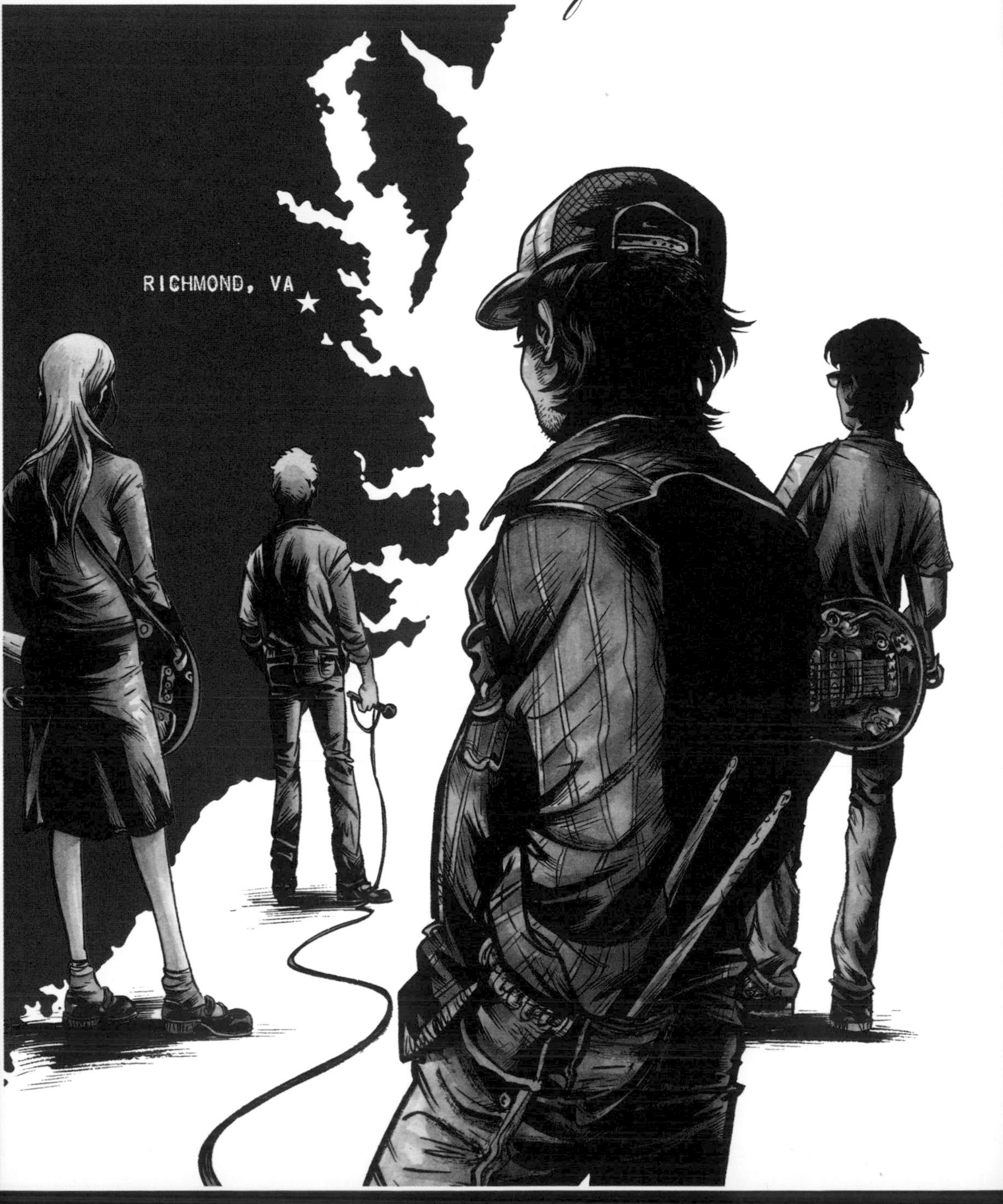
RICHMOND, VA

ISSUE #3

"At the forefront of the movement to revitalize the stand-alone issue in comics" - AICN

BRIAN WOOD / RYAN KELLY

LOCAL

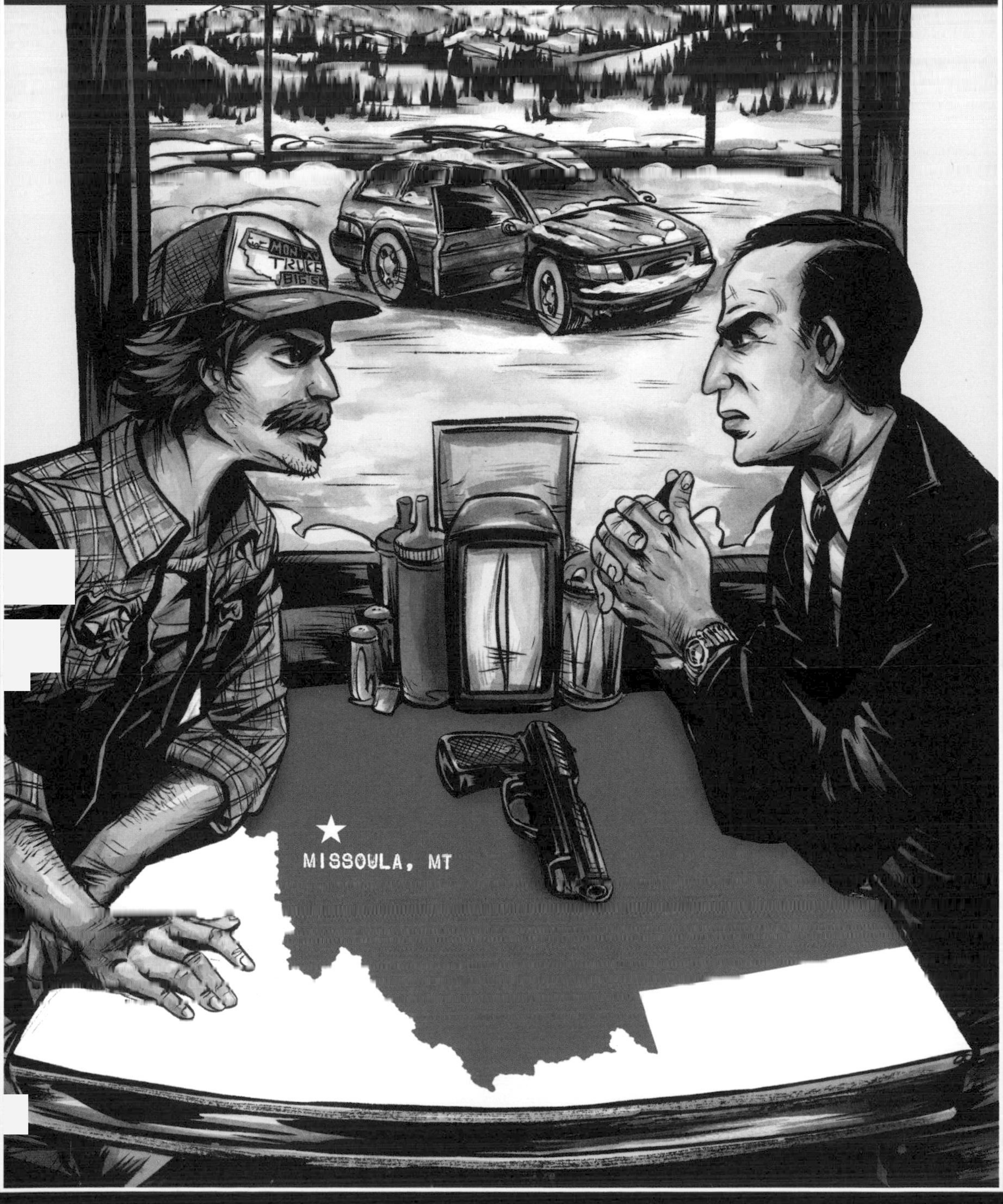
MONTANA
TRUCK
BIG SKY
MISSOULA, MT

ISSUE #4

"all the raw emotion and dusty Americana of a classic Bruce Springsteen album, with every issue a different cut" - CHRISTOPHER GOLDEN

BRIAN WOOD / RYAN KELLY

LOCAL

"the last lonely days at the oxford theatre"

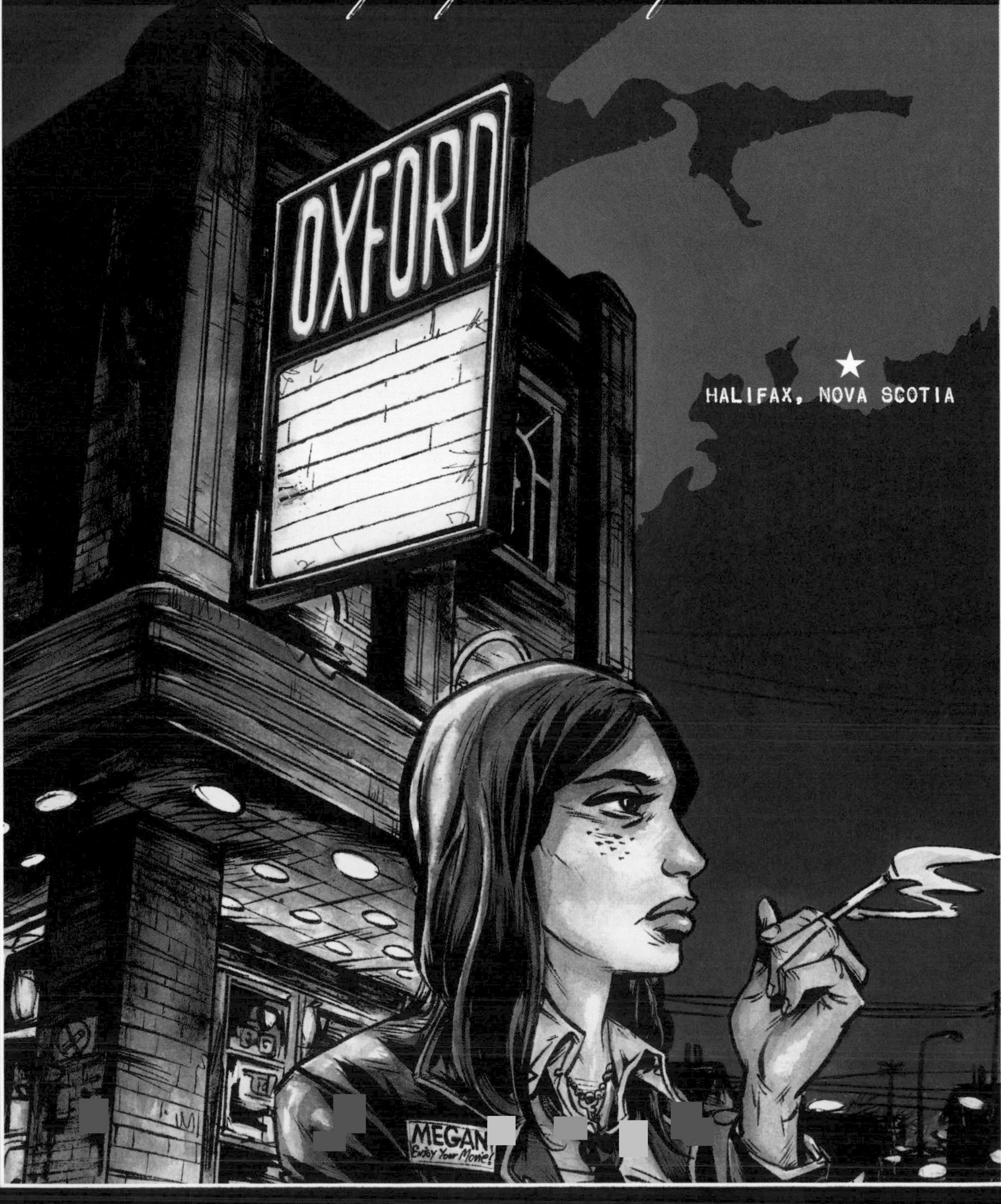
OXFORD
HALIFAX, NOVA SCOTIA
MEGAN
Enjoy Your Movie!

ISSUE #5

"...one of the best non cape-and-cowl stories I've read..." - BLAIR BUTLER

BRIAN WOOD / RYAN KELLY

LOCAL

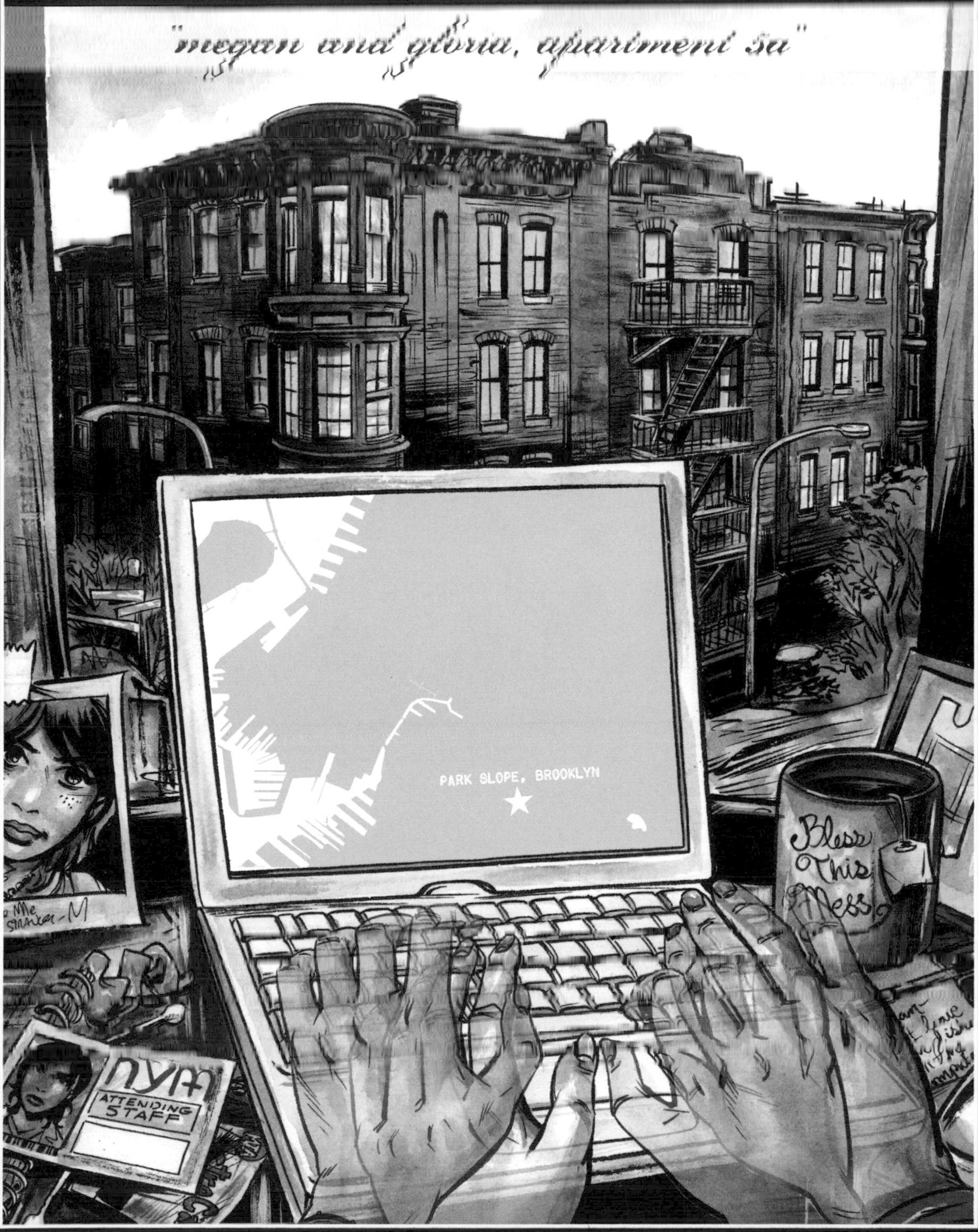

ISSUE #6

"...each page is a lush, inky image to be savored." - VARIETY

BRIAN WOOD / RYAN KELLY

LOCAL

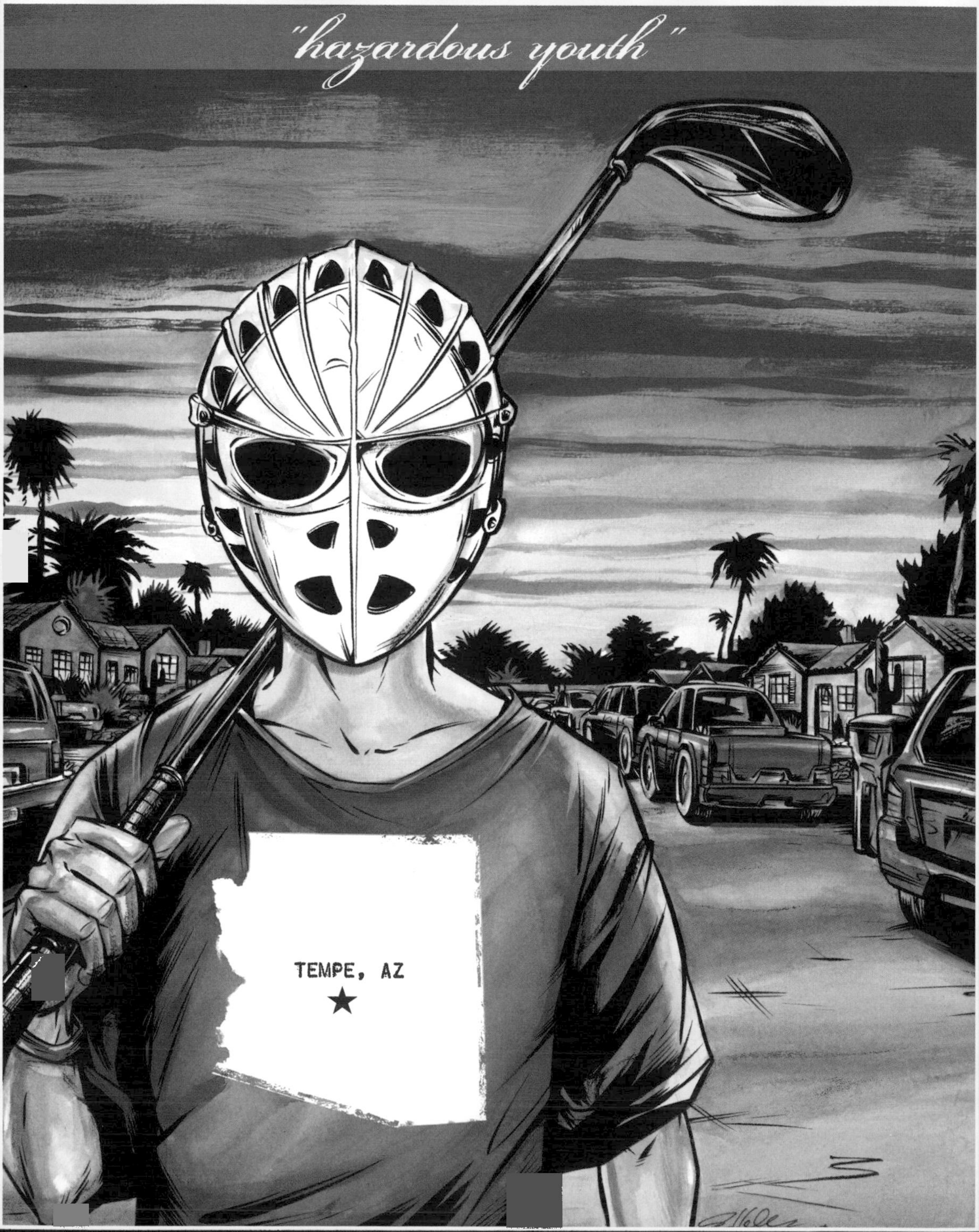
"hazardous youth"
TEMPE, AZ

ISSUE #7

"...strong, character-driven storytelling and [the] continued elevation of self-contained storytelling." - EYE ON COMICS (Best of 2006)

BRIAN WOOD / RYAN KELLY

LOCAL

"food as substitute"

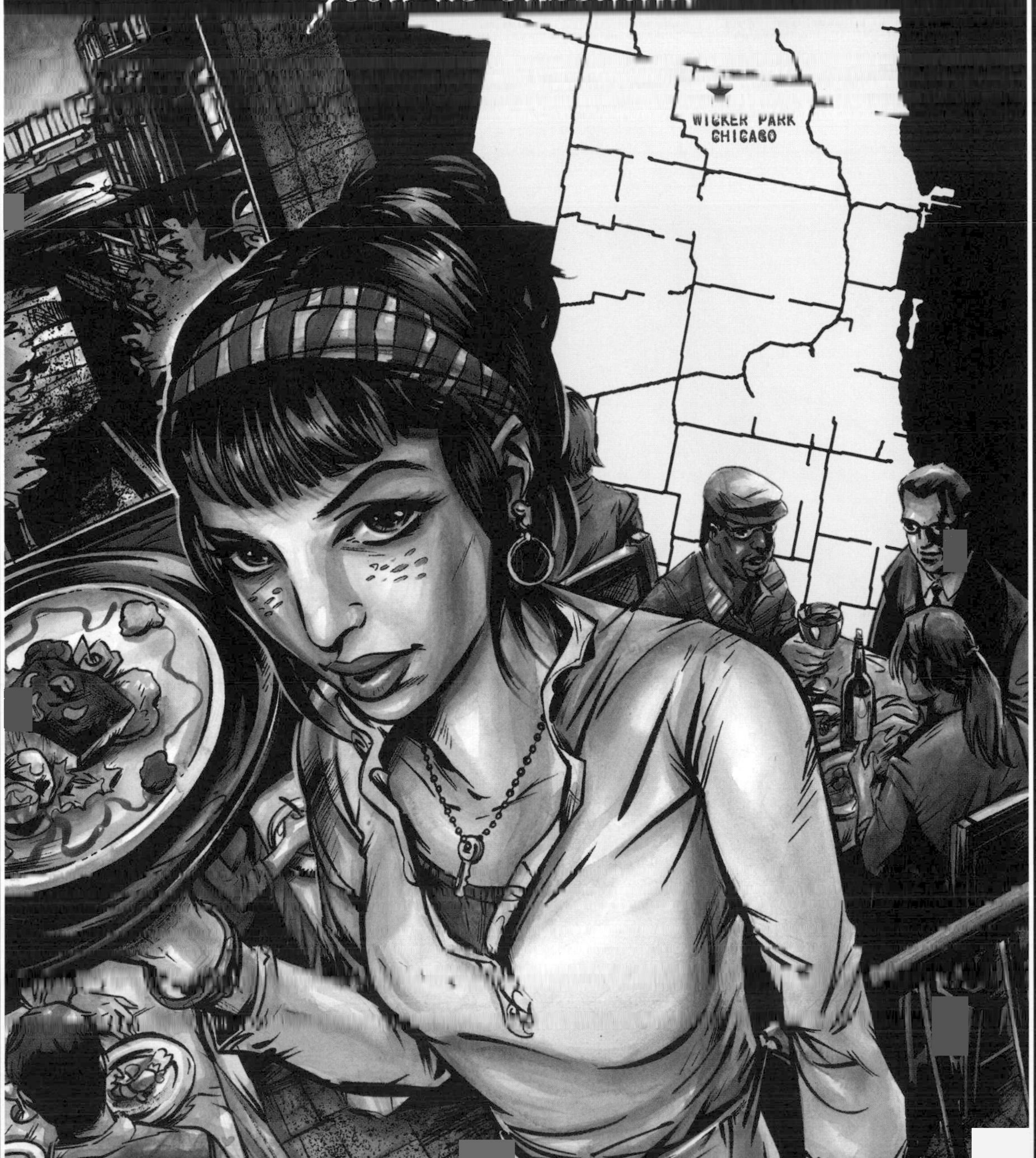

WICKER PARK
CHICAGO

ISSUE #8

"a vivid portrait of a single character... precise and evocative." - COMICS BLOC

BRIAN WOOD / RYAN KELLY

LOCAL

"wish you were here"

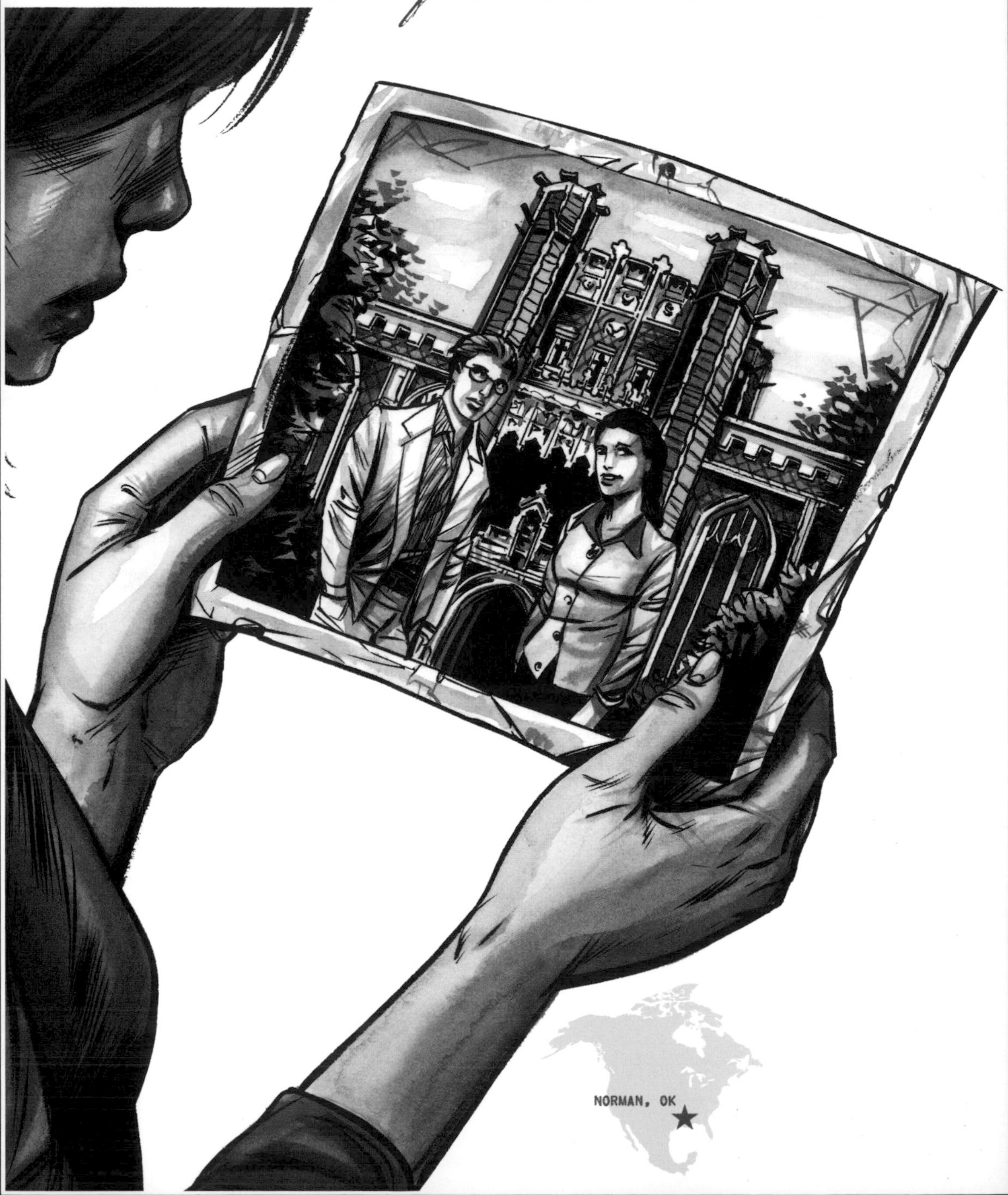
NORMAN, OK

ISSUE #9

"...one of the most rewarding reads in recent memory." - POP SYNDICATE

BRIAN WOOD / RYAN KELLY

LOCAL

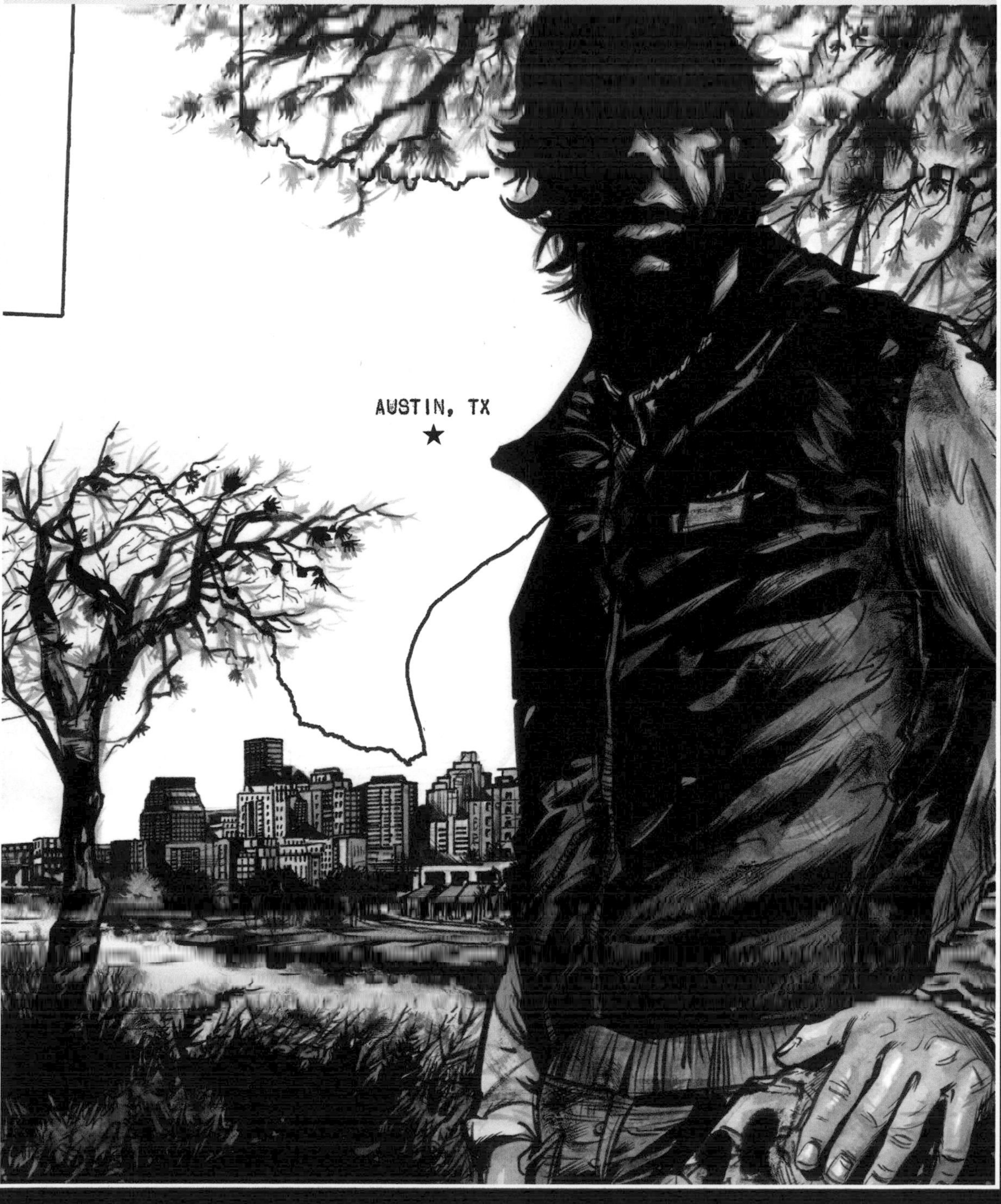
AUSTIN, TX

ISSUE #10

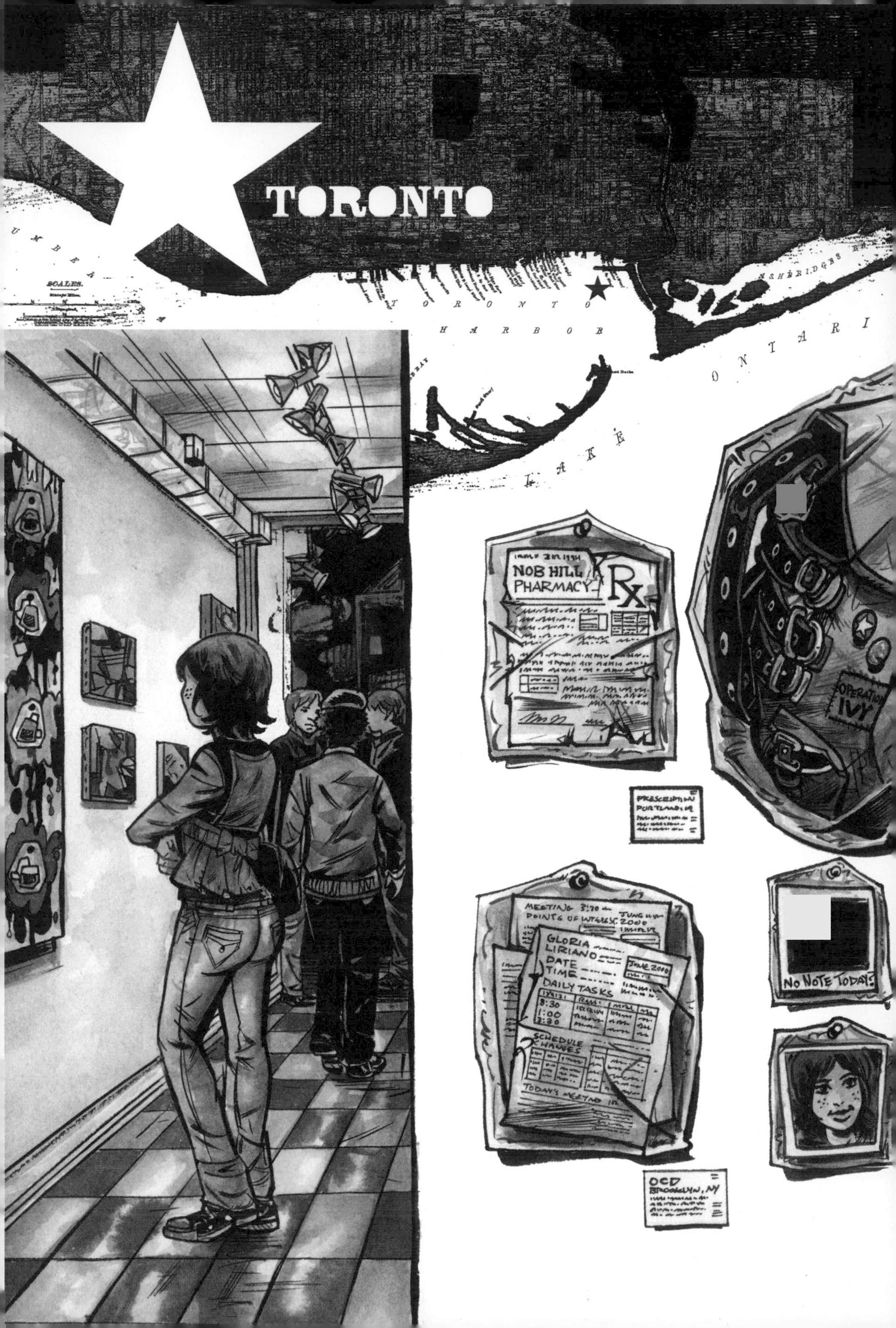
TORONTO
T O R O N T O
L A K E
O N T A R I
NOB HILL PHARMACY
Rx
PRESCRIPTION PORTLAND, OR
OPERATION IVY
MEETING 3:30
POINTS OF INTEREST
JUNE 2000
GLORIA LIRIANO
DATE
TIME
DAILY TASKS
SCHEDULE CHANGES
NO NOTE TODAY?
OCD BROOKLYN, NY

VOTED THE "BEST ONGOING INDIE COMIC OF 2007" BY G4 TV

BRIAN WOOD / RYAN KELLY

LOCAL

"the younger generation"

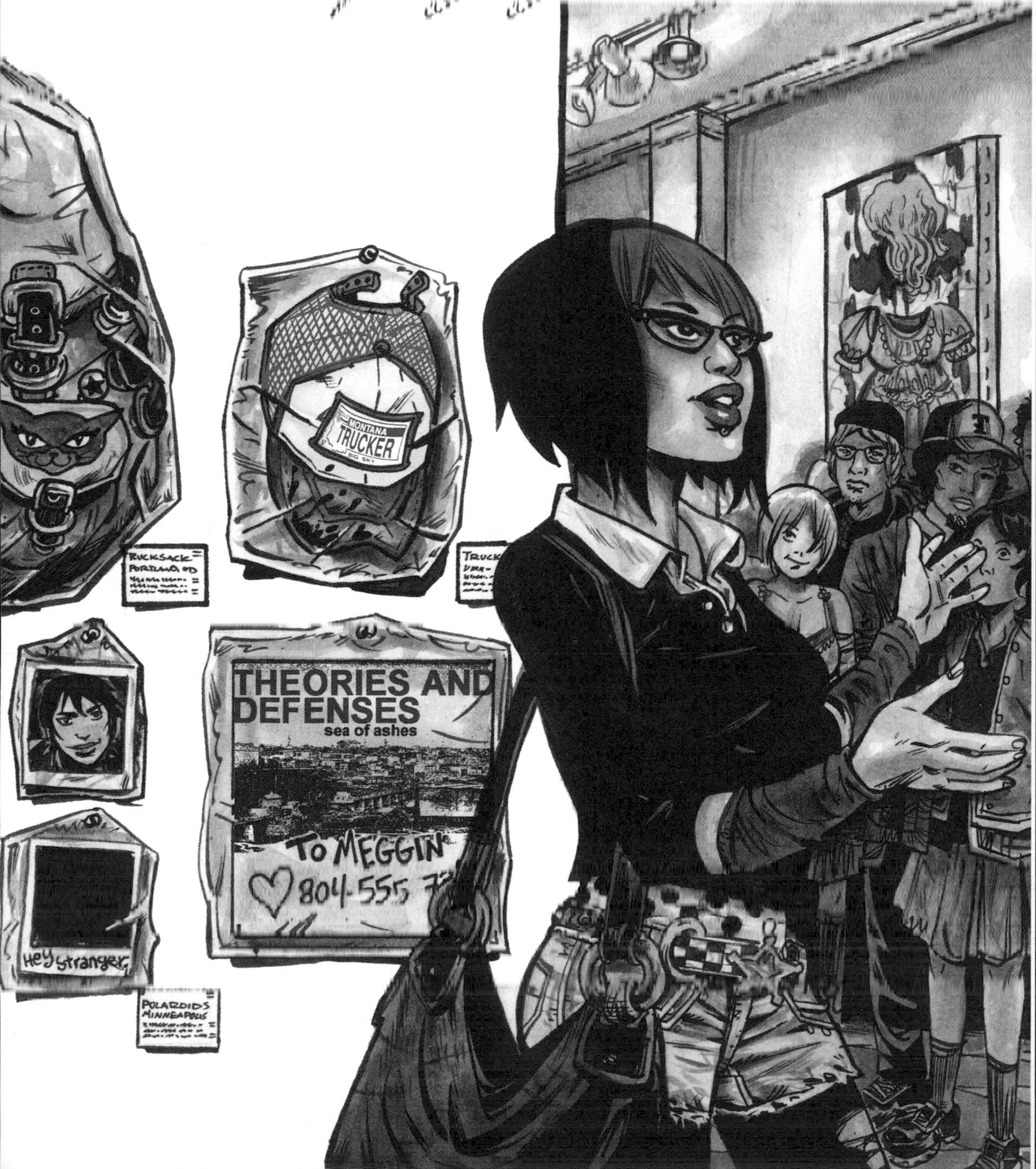

MONTANA
TRUCKER
BIG SKY
RUCKSACK
THEORIES AND DEFENSES
sea of ashes
TO MEGGIN
804-555
Hey stranger
POLAROIDS
MINNEAPOLIS

ISSUE #11

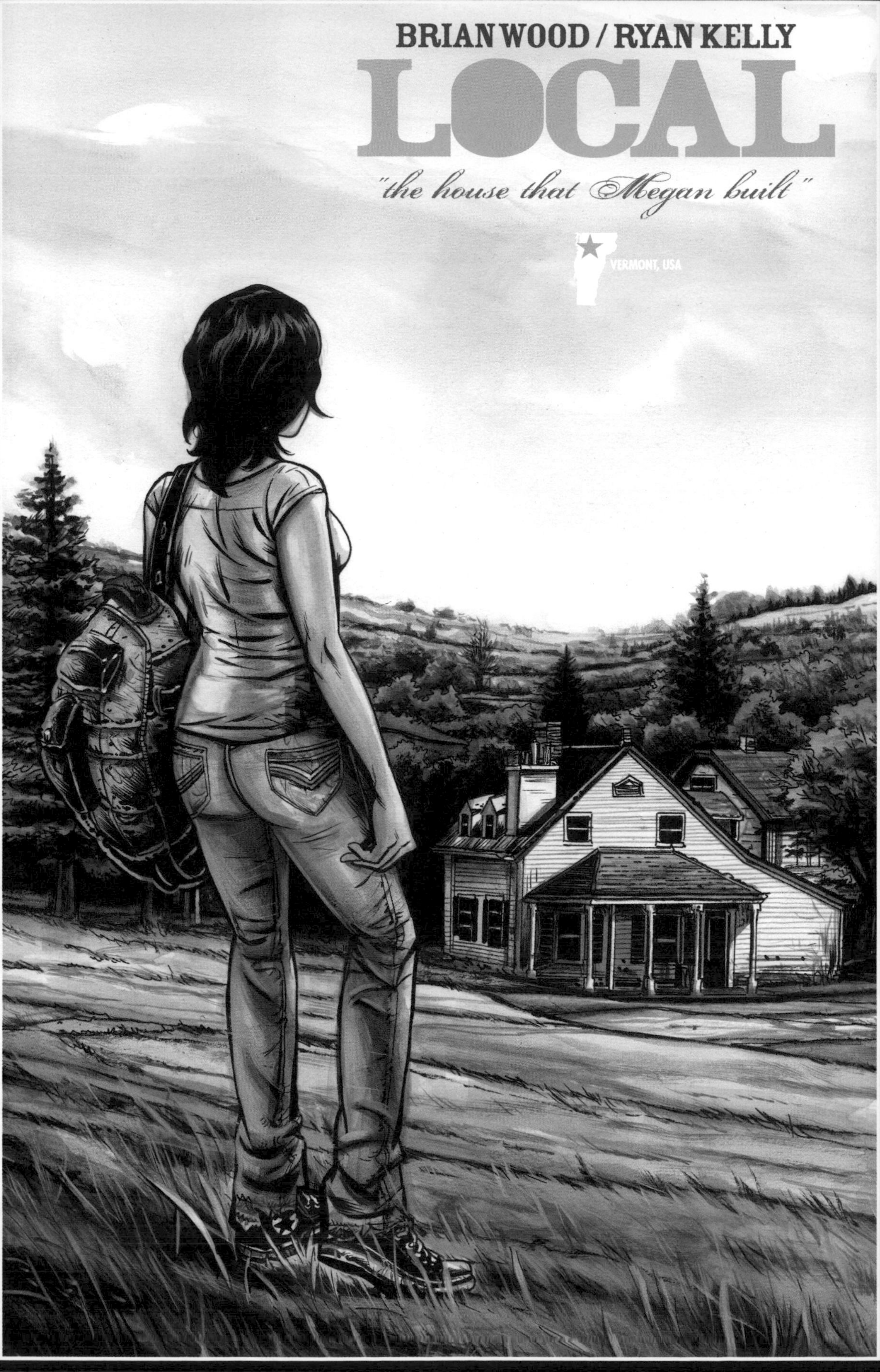
BRIAN WOOD / RYAN KELLY
LOCAL
"the house that Megan built"
VERMONT, USA

ISSUE #12

LOCAL™

THE CREATORS

BRIAN WOOD:

Brian Wood released his first series, *Channel Zero*, in 1997 to considerable critical acclaim and has continued to produce comics and graphic novels at a brisk pace ever since. Focusing almost entirely on creator-owned works, he's become one of the most important indie creators of the last decade. Standout works include his *The Couriers series*, *Supermarket*, *Demo*, *DMZ*, and *Northlanders*. He has earned multiple Eisner Award nominations and editions of his work have been published in close to a dozen foreign markets. *Local*, of which he is most proud, is a product of several years work, during which time he's moved back to Brooklyn, got married, and had a beautiful daughter.

Thanks to the following people for the help and support: Jim Gary, Meredith Gary, Bryan Lee O'Malley, Hope Larson, Sean Kennedy, Rawn Gandy, Patrick Godfrey, Katherine Keller, Blair Butler, Warren Ellis, Brian K Vaughan, Gail Simone, Manda Fisher, Alex Cox, Mary Gibbons, Brian Scot Johnson, Matt and Annette Price, Karin Kross Levenstein, Chris Butcher, Kayla Hillier, Eric Kim, and everyone at Oni Press, including James, Randy, Joe, and Douglas.

RYAN KELLY:

For the past eight years, Ryan Kelly has charted a path in the visual arts working as a comic book artist, illustrator, painter and art organizer at the Minneapolis College of Art and Design. His work has been recognized by American Illustration and The Society of Illustrators. Since turning his focus to comics, he has drawn the original graphic novels *Giant Robot Warriors* and *The New York Four* as well as the series *Lucifer*, *Books of Magic*, *American Virgin* and *The Vinyl Underground*. *Local* remains his proudest achievement as well as a record of personal growth and depth as a storyteller. Ryan lives in Minnesota with his high school sweetheart and sons Oliver, Jax and Harold.

Special thanks to: Kelly Brown, Aaron Quist, Josh Lynch, Marcus Smith, Tou Vue, Duane Nichols, Richard Flood, Kyle Fritik, Kip Knutsen, Craig Johnson, David Karrow, Nicole Vanche, Carol Gesbeck, JC Pollard, Ryan Carr and Seamus Burke.

OTHER BOOKS FROM ONI PRESS...

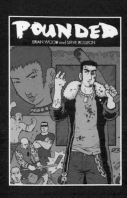

POUNDED™
By Brian Wood & Steve Rolston
104 pages, digest, black and white interiors
$8.95 •ISBN 978-1-929998-37-1

12 REASONS WHY I LOVE HER™
By Jamie S. Rich & Joëlle Jones
144 pages, 6x9 trade paperback, black and white interiors
$14.95 • ISBN 978-1-932664-51-5

BREAKFAST AFTER NOON™
By Andi Watson
208 pages, standard, black and white interiors
$19.95 •ISBN 978-1-929998-14-2

GRAY HORSES™
By Hope Larson
112 pages, digest, 2-color interiors
$14.95 •ISBN 978-1-932664-36-2

LOST AT SEA™
By Bryan Lee O'Malley
168 pages, digest, black and white interiors
$11.95 •ISBN 978-1-932664-16-4

MARIA'S WEDDING™
By Nunzio DeFilippis, Christina Weir & Jose Garibaldi
88 pages, digest, blak and white interiors
$10.95 •ISBN 978-1-929998-57-9

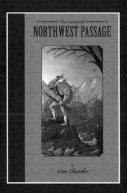

THE ANNOTATED NORTHWEST PASSAGE™
By Scott Chantler
272 pages, hardcover, black and white interiors
$19.95 • ISBN 978-1-932664-61-4

SCOTT PILGRIM™
VOLUME 1: SCOTT PILGRIM'S PRECIOUS LITTLE LIFE
By Bryan Lee O'Malley
168 pages, digest, black and white interiors
$11.95 • ISBN 978-1-932664-08-9

AVAILABLE AT FINER COMIC BOOK SHOPS AND BOOKSELLERS EVERYWHERE!

To find a comic book store near you visit http://comicshops.us.

For more information on these and other fine Oni Press titles, visit the our website at www.onipress.com.